# TRYING SOCIOLOGY

# TRYING SOCIOLOGY

*KURT H. WOLFF*
*Brandeis University*
*Waltham, Massachusetts*

*A Wiley-Interscience Publication*

JOHN WILEY & SONS, New York • London • Sydney • Toronto

**Library of Congress Cataloging in Publication Data:**

Wolff, Kurt H   1912-
  Trying sociology.
  "A Wiley-Interscience publication."
  Bibliography: p.
1. Sociology.  I. Title.

HM24.W65      301      74-13165
ISBN 0-471-95940-5

Printed in the United States of America

10 9 8 7 6 5 4 3 2 1

# ACKNOWLEDGMENTS

Help in writing the chapters of my book is acknowledged in the text. For assistance in their preparation my thanks go to the publisher: to Eric Valentine, Editor, Wiley-Interscience, to Valda Aldzeris, Editorial Supervisor, and especially to Aline Walton, my Manuscript Editor.

KURT H. WOLFF

# CONTENTS

# TRYING SOCIOLOGY

# INTRODUCTION

## *This Book from Its Title*

The first of the five meanings reflected in the title *Trying Sociology* is that this book represents my *attempt* (not yet, I hope, completed) to clarify what I could hold myself responsible for meaning by sociology today. I have tried to do so by moving in from various positions, suggested by the headings of the six parts under which I have presented my views.

A second meaning is *trying out* or trying on, tasting sociology, checking its fit. The result is more for the reader to assess than for me.

"Trying" also may be defined as *sitting in trial on* as well as *surrendering to* sociology. The two are intimately connected. To arrive at a true judgment the judge searches for the best possible understanding of the matter to be judged. It is this search that I call "surrendering to." (The idea of surrender has been my chief concern for many years. In this book, too, it is much more conspicuous than I expected it to be.) Some chapters, especially in Part IV, are explicitly critical of important features of contemporary sociology (sitting in trial); others, especially in Parts V and VI, are more nearly tries at sociology (surrendering to it).

But *trying* can be used in a fourth way, as an adjective. The discussions that follow, or some of them, may be trying: boring in their irrelevance, or irritating, or difficult. I hope that they will be no more boring and irrelevant than other efforts whose major virtue is to be intellectual (on this problem see Chapter 11). I also hope that whatever irritation they may produce will be overcome by recognizing their obstinacy—which should really not be irritating unless the obstinacy itself is considered boring, irrelevant, or serving a wrong cause. There are also likely to be passages, if not pages or even chapters, that are difficult because their writing was difficult, and no matter how hard I tried to make them easier, I must now throw myself on the reader's mercy in the hope that

Franz Rosenzweig's advice on how to read "philosophical books" [which I used to introduce the concept of central attitude (Chapter 26)] may without impropriety also recommend itself applicable to what follows.

Finally, a former student (Louise Hale—thank you!) reminded me of the chapter "The Try-Works" in *Moby-Dick*, in which *trying* signifies "melting, rendering," or "separating out impurities" (*The American Heritage Dictionary of the English Language*). Trying out blubber produces a smoke that "is horrible to inhale, and inhale it you must, and not only that, but you must live in it for the time." Such a stench, however, is not the note on which I have chosen to close this introduction, but on a wish for your courage and curiosity!

# I

## AMERICA
### *Pareto, Durkheim, and Simmel*

*In memory of Ludovico Limentani, John H. McGinnis,
and Walter T. Watson. For Henry Nash Smith*

After I had done this book (except for the epilogue) I reread the introductions to its parts. I stopped; for I heard a disapproving voice, outraged, bored, or both, asking, "Who cares?", for what I had written
might be of no interest to anybody but just possibly myself. But I wanted,
and I still want, to record publicly my gratitude and indebtedness to a
number of people who had helped me and thus contributed to my development. I have tried to resolve this dilemma by letting the more general
part of the present introduction stand and by distributing the more
personal remainder as footnotes under the first three chapters.

The world of sociology had been revealed to me by Karl Mannheim
at the University of Frankfurt in the first years of the thirties. Karl
Mannheim has influenced my thinking in many areas—not only in sociology. I became aware of this long after I had studied with him, even
after my introduction in 1939 to the United States and *its* sociology.
Nevertheless, sociology had been only one interest among others for me—
no doubt second to that of literature and art. I had begun, under Mannheim's guidance, to work on a dissertation on the intellectuals in my
hometown (Darmstadt). After the rise of Hitler I was forced to leave the
university and a few months later I left the country for Italy. My *tesi di
laurea* at the University of Florence (1935) was concerned with the sociology of knowledge, to which Mannheim had also introduced me. It was

a strange topic to deal with in Fascist Italy, and an unusual one to be supervised by a professor of philosophy; but Ludovico Limentani was most encouraging, generous, and tolerant. (He was dismissed from the university at which he had taught for decades, shortly after the outbreak of World War II, when Hitler became Mussolini's master. Only then did I realize that he was a Jew, such was my innocence.)

Compared with the lot of most refugee-immigrants, mine was easy. I arrived in the United States in April and in the fall I became a research assistant in sociology at Southern Methodist University. Particular tasks I might wish to undertake were suggested by two sponsors, the late John H. McGinnis, a wise and charming professor of English, and the late Walter T. Watson, a professor of sociology, who was unforgettably generous in his effort to introduce me to American sociology.

The three papers assembled in Part I—on Pareto, Durkheim and Simmel, and Simmel—have different origins and were written 27 years apart. In one respect at least they are alike: all three strive for interaction between the reader and the thinkers they describe. To anticipate (see especially Chapter 29), these papers sought to mediate "existential" knowledge by recognizing (the) sociologists (they deal with) as men and women, by introducing self into sociology and by trying to show that sociology is a human enterprise.

The theme of these first three chapters is discernible in many others, a good reason for beginning the book by exemplifying its continuity in the introduction of individual sociologists as human beings.

# 1

# VILFREDO PARETO. 1941

Herr, die Not ist gross!
Die ich rief, die Geister
Werd' ich nun nicht los.
  —Goethe, *Der Zauberlehrling*.

Pareto's life and writings form an indivisible whole. In this unity there
is an element of greatness—untouched by the clouds that have overcast
his memory. The Paretos were an old Genoese family ennobled by
Napoleon; his father, the Marquis Raffaele—engineer, Liberal, Mazzinist
—fled his homeland for political reasons, married a French woman, and
became a French citizen. Vilfredo Federico Damaso was born in Paris in

---

John H. McGinnis, founder and editor of the *Southwest Review*, published at
Southern Methodist, invited me to write an essay on Vilfredo Pareto. He held
out the promise of publication in his periodical and had the library secure the
relevant materials. Perhaps he assumed that, having obtained a doctorate in
sociology in Italy, I was a "natural." I forget whether I confessed to him that
I had never read Pareto (probably not, since I felt that I had to make a start
and must not spoil my chances); at any rate, I went to work on all of Pareto's
published writings and took the most copious notes. The resulting paper was
translated from my own comical struggle with a language not my own by Henry
Nash Smith, another benefactor, long since a distinguished professor of English
at Berkeley, who also helped me with several other ventures, both scholarly and
literary. The paper on Pareto was my first in the new environment, although it
appeared almost simultaneously with the report on the Jewish population of
Dallas (Chapter 7). It is also the first to deal with a particular sociologist. These
two "firsts" may justify its position in the book.

1848. Ten years later the family returned to Italy. Vilfredo studied engineering in Turin, and after four years as a railway engineer in Rome became general supervisor of the Italian iron mines. The family's tradition of liberal politics took hold of him, but under the protectionist program of Depretis he found no chance for his free-trade platform. Pareto, the industrialist and man of affairs, therefore retired from public life and from business to spend the next decade with his wife, the Princess Bakhunin (Michael Bakhunin's daughter), and his mother in a villa at Fiesole, trying in vain to obtain a chair in economics.

When in 1893 the Swiss economist Léon Walras nominated him as his successor at the University of Lausanne, Pareto, with some bitterness, left Italy, living at first in a cottage near the city that became the haven of Italian socialists, French clericals, and other dissidents. The Princess soon persuaded him to move into a sumptuous town house in which they entertained lavishly at balls and dinners and established a salon well known for its *esprit*. Suddenly the professor inexplicably withdrew to the Villa Angora at Céligny, where he became a mysterious figure even to his neighbors. In 1906 he gave up his chair at Lausanne and a year later inherited a fortune from an uncle.

At Céligny Pareto cherished his two dozen Angora cats whose pedigrees reached back to Saladin. He also cultivated orchids and fruit. On occasion he would take his candle and keys to the cellar to fetch a bottle of wine—French, German, Spanish, Hungarian, or Swiss—selected according to the taste of his guests. He drank little himself, and then only after some dialectic hesitation on the score of his weak heart. He habitually wore several cloaks, adding to or decreasing the number many times a day with every slight change of temperature. Only in his own two rooms (which were, with the cats' terrace, the warmest in the house) would he free himself from hat and wraps. Here, with interruptions only on the most strictly observed schedule for lunch, dinner, and exercise, he buried himself from seven in the morning to eleven at night among thousands of books. New books and magazines continued to pour into his studio (he had a weakness for Italian comic papers): books covered tables, chairs, and floors, and lined the walls up to the ceilings in double and triple rows. He wrote on small pieces of cellulose cut from large sheets specially ordered, one slip for each subject, attaching new pieces with glue as the treatment of the subject expanded, thus forming the paragraphs of his books—some one line in length, others ten pages. He read the dailies with great intensity and cut clippings endlessly, creating a vast record of contemporary political history. He slept, when he could conquer his insomnia, on an iron bed in a bare room—with Fanfinou d'Amour, his favorite cat, covering his feet. Madame Régis, his second wife, carrying her ring of keys, reigned efficiently over the household and protected the Maestro from petty annoyances. Her private domain was her boudoir, perfumed, cushioned, and mirrored. The remaining rooms of the house contained only commonplace furniture and trivial paintings of cats and veiled women.

Pareto had no taste for art; he hated music and noisy children. He knew no German and read English with difficulty but was at home in Latin and Greek. In his conversation he alternated between a Tuscan Italian and an argot-flavored French. According to Roberto Michels' daughter, he had "flaming, piercing eyes; pale, nervous, fine hands, with protruding blue veins; very long fingernails." There is a rather obviously posed photograph of him in his later years, sitting at a table looking with raised brows at a book, his beard long and white, his skull large and rounded. In another photograph, from a somewhat earlier period, he is standing in his garden, somber and serious, surprisingly suggestive of Dostoevsky. A scarf shows beneath his well-worn coat, which hangs open; he holds his cap in his hand; his eyes tell that he knows much—but not all. In a still earlier portrait his black eyes are direct and challenging, his black beard sharp-cut.

His reserve and his solitary habits had caused his first wife to leave him. He was better with animals than with men—markedly so as he grew older. He not only had his cats, but rabbits, squirrels, and a goat. As the years passed he saw almost no one not in his household, although he was proverbially witty, an excellent *causeur*, and generous with his guests. He could thunder, fear, and despise, but best of all he could hate. He hated the Italian government (but had cheerfully adapted himself to the Swiss); he hated the Italian people who, he thought, had conspired to bury him in silence; he hated the democrats ("those parvenus"), the Pan-Germanists, Hegel (whom he would serve up hilariously to his guests after dinner in French or Italian translations). He hated temperance agitators and humanitarians—the humanitarians more than all the rest—but beyond his likes and dislikes, his studio, books, and blue veins, he was in ghastly contrast to his milieu, a sort of feline, mischievous voice announcing the end of liberalism, democracy, plutocracy—even more, the end of two thousand years of European life.

The prolificness of his writing—nine or ten fat tomes, several more slender volumes, a pile of articles—and its repetitiousness reflect his eagerness to grasp "facts," write them down, paragraph them. He was free of the doubts and scruples that might have developed from a familiarity with sociology and psychology. He felt smug with his enormous store of information on contemporary and earlier politics, mathematics, and economics, supported by his vast erudition in Greek, Roman, Italian, and nineteenth-century European history.

His method for getting at "things" was to bring what was outside into his vaguely articulated system. "Things" were things if they fitted this system—books, people, anything, from Caesar or Bismarck to the swans of Lake Geneva, his Angoras, or Madame Régis' dogs. He was almost superstitiously intent on collecting all and losing nothing. (Was this the reason why he forbade the servants to destroy cobwebs or kill spiders in his villa?) As soon as his things were systematized, he labeled them; "words are only labels." In this sense he was an opportunist in quoting, selecting, translating. He had no inkling of the scope of language; he scoffed at etymology. He insisted on definitions because they seemed necessary in "logico-experimental science," but he failed to produce a single rule that could be applied consistently, even within the chapter that introduced it. He liked classifying, dividing, subdividing, sub-subdividing; his graphs indicate the successive points of which he stopped in his labyrinth of thought, and even though he emphasized definitions he insisted that only illustrations and examples could show all the ramifications of concepts. He heaped illustration on illustration, in his compilation of examples of the most variegated phenomena pertaining to the social sciences—examples which, for that matter, still have for readers today the stimulating, even revelatory, effect they had for him. This is true also of the many passages in which he digresses from his announced subject. Such detours could be taken as material for a significant study of how he managed to find his way through his notes, excerpts, and clippings and where he landed at the end of his minor excursions. The digressions, however, are only piquant and incidental aspects of a laborious journey for which he found a label only after his sixtieth year. Not until then did he become aware that he was trying to uncover "the structure of society."

This revelation followed the insight that he must embrace fields outside economics if he wanted to go on with his voyage of exploration; or, in his own terms, he discovered that not economics alone but a comprehensive sociological synthesis was required to explain society. He had begun as an economist, absorbed in an effort to work out mathematically the ideas represented by Walras' Lausanne school of free trade and free prices. He was especially interested in determining the curve of the distribution of incomes (which he found to be almost constant). He was a well-known investigator and an originator of important logical bases in this field. Up to the time of his treatise on general sociology his published works had included technical books on economics, an angry and biting polemic against "virtuism and immoral literature" (even this was filled with excerpts and footnotes and sallies against contemporary French bigotry), and *Les systèmes socialistes*, the first step into a vaster terrain of already vague and vanishing borders—a work in which by the analysis of parallel movements in the past he tried to find explanations of his own world and time and especially for socialism and Marxism. In *Les systèmes socialistes* his personal attitude—which earlier had appeared at most here and there in the footnotes of the economic studies or in the polemic of *Le mythe vertuïste*—is drawn for the first time into the body of a programmatic text. He is torn between demonstrating the unscientific character of humanitarianism, liberalism, and socialism and affirming their social weight, whether useful or malign (but principally malign). His conclusive "dialectic synthesis" (he would have detested the Hegelian term) is a rather heated insistence that his contemporaries (socialists, antisocialists, and merely apprehensive observers alike) should maintain greater detachment in dealing with the socialist movement. His book seems to suggest that socialism is no more than the form that the struggle for life had assumed in his and their time, that the elite are destined always to be pushed aside by other groups—this time the bourgeoisie by the socialists. The theory, of course, embodies no program, but merely a statement on withdrawal.

Pareto was too thoroughly a classicist and rationalist to entertain for a moment the thought that his time was no longer living on traditions but only picking over and loathing them; saddening, escaping, dying; he looked no further than at immediate antecedents, and in his own world saw Enlightenment, positivism, Marxism, socialism, democracy, humanitarianism, liberalism, and plutocracy. His familiarity with these phenomena enabled him to discover the "residues," the "derivations," the "elite" (as well as "class circulation" and the theory of the cyclical form of social change) and led him to use the concept of "nonlogical action" with its distinctions between logicality and "social utility" and between the ends of the individual and those of the "community." These concepts and his attempts to define them are the products of Pareto's experience which were autonomous enough to become part of the generally usable apparatus of sociology. So far, nevertheless, scholars have treated them only polemically or with respect to the history of sociology and economics or their logical structure; no comprehensive and systematic study has been made of them, but such an analysis would be necessary to remove from them the highly personal significance they had for Pareto himself. He was so much a rationalist that he overlooked his own irrational presuppositions and motives; he took his own ideas literally, as he took his goal of finding the structure of society; he lacked the historical and sociological perspective that might have revealed to him that his ideas were conditioned by his contemporary social surroundings and that his facts there-fore were somewhat less absolute than he thought.

Pareto was certainly no prophet, but with such a perspective he might also have seen that these same ideas were pregnant with indications concerning the future. What were these indications? The structure of society, to be sure, is Pareto's private affair, a mere frame of verbal reference with which his own laborious efforts were crowned; but his well-known complex made up of the notions of residues, derivations, the elite, non-logical action, and social utility has indeed more than personal significance. This complex has an energy related to its very formlessness; it has shown a tendency to engulf any system of ideas ready to receive it with-out being able to assimilate it. Again, the ideas of this complex have united with the similarly vague idea-systems, for example, of fascism, with a resultant increase of strength in both. In either event the concepts remain productive of *malaise* in a given society unless they are faced with resolution and rendered harmless by being clearly analyzed. Pareto's leading ideas passed beyond his own sphere of thought and experience and became themselves residues, prefixed selective schemes of action and reaction (including knowledge, feeling, belief, and judgment); further-more, just as Pareto, satisfied with having reached this stage in his search, failed to examine the elements and factors that had prefixed his own scheme of action and reaction, so has our time neglected to examine their provenience. In his distinction between residues and derivations—the verbal manifestations (or, in a less inclusive sense, rationalizations) of the residues—Pareto failed to ask whether the residues themselves might not be derivations of something else. He did not feel the existence of that something else, of the emptiness of his time—the emptiness that had called forth in him the response embodied in his system, which excites the irritated nerves of fascists and potential fascists to action and which has become crystallized in their ideologies. The slogans and maxims that vulgarize and exaggerate Pareto's thought are all too familiar: the injunc-tion, *vivere pericoloso*; the belief that logic has little or no relation to human behavior; the assertion that the skillful and strong, not the scien-tists, govern the masses and that their control is based on force and their ability to manipulate emotions with catchwords; the proposition that there is nothing good or bad except what is good or bad according to the dominant will of a given elite in a given society at a given time, which explains why the elites (originally called aristocracies by Pareto) cannot last but are continually being replaced by the newer and more capable.

The means by which Pareto arrived at this "sociology"—his historical sources, such as Machiavelli, Bentham, Spencer, Darwin, Comte, and how many others (often unacknowledged, often unperceived by the writer himself), and the methodological suggestions of biology, mathematics, mechanics, economics, and astronomy—certainly are of historical interest. A systematic, nonhistorical treatment of his concepts, however (as well as a psychoanalytical study of the man himself, which, so far as I know, is yet to come), should not only have considerable worth for sociology but might also eventually deprive Pareto's ideas of their essentially emotional nature. The fact that such a study has been begun seems to indicate our increasing resistance to the fascist appeal. The extent to which the results of a systematic analysis can find acceptance, and the reach within which its findings are able to spread and in turn become "residues," "be in the air," "be common sense," would be an even more reliable index of our detachment from *vivere pericoloso*, force, and power. Pareto's vogue in America in 1933–1935, as Eduard C. Lindeman has pointed out, had its root in the opportunity it offered certain groups to find a new mirror in which the monstrous spawn of our time—unemployment, waste, fascism, communism, nazism—could conveniently be reflected and contemplated. Like the earlier cult of Freud it satisfied those who longed for a justification of nonlogical behavior much more than it incited others to cope intellectually with the problems in question.

Pareto was moved by the same needs and fears as Nietzsche and Spengler, but the natures of the three men, their dimensions and functions, were widely diverse. Almost any man may become a fascinating image to someone he has enchanted, but Pareto will almost certainly prove to have a lasting attraction for fewer and less important disciples than Spengler, just as Spengler will prove less influential than Nietzsche. Nietzsche will be referred to as long as Europe lives (or European civilization survives transplanted in America). Spengler and Pareto will die with our present age, to be mummified in the archives of specialists, but Pareto will be exhausted even sooner than the profounder and freer Spengler. Nietzsche, the solitary seeker, Spengler, the growling prophet, Pareto, the peevish philosopher, but Nietzsche, the poetically pure type: there is something less formidable, even potentially comic, about the others—at least from a superficial point of view. They do not attain the stature of myths and symbols.

All three men have been mentioned as forerunners of present-day totalitarian movements; but whereas Nietzsche would have found the aggressive dogmas of nazism intolerable and Spengler uttered an ominous exhortation to the Nazis in *The Hour of Decision* in 1933 before lapsing into a silence unbroken at his death in 1936, Pareto's relation to Italian fascism is more complex. Pareto died shortly after the March on Rome, named by Mussolini as senator and Italy's delegate to the League of Nations, but his confusion and naïveté were so great that he not only felt uncomfortable at the practical uses the Fascists were making of his doctrines but even ventured to ask Mussolini (his former student at the University of Lausanne) to maintain freedom of opinion and liberty of university teaching. Pareto's treatise of general sociology had seemed to its author only a scientific (and perhaps therefore merely speculative or academic) "approximation to truth," as it seems to us primarily the record of his private and personal experiences or perhaps a symbol of Europe dying or being transformed. Pareto's alarm at the Fascists' program of acting on his "scientific" conclusions suggests how far from rigorous and definitive his own system seemed to him.

Here are some examples of Pareto's work which were destined to receive interpretations that would have made him uncomfortable:

> Let us imagine a country where the governing class, $A$, is inclining more and more in the direction of humanitarianism . . . and, while awaiting the advent of the "reign of reason," is becoming less and less capable of using force and is so shirking the main duty of a ruling class. Such a country is on its way to utter ruin. But lo, the subject class, $B$, revolts against the class $A$. In fighting $A$ it uses the humanitarian derivations so dear to the $A$'s, but underlying them are quite different sentiments, and they soon find expression in deeds. The $B$'s apply force on a far-reaching scale, and not only overthrow the $A$'s but kill large numbers of them—and, in so doing, to tell the truth, they are performing a useful public service, something like ridding the country of a baneful pest. . . .
>
> If one judges superficially, one may be tempted to dwell more especially on the slaughter and pillaging that attend a revolution, without thinking to ask whether such things may not be manifestations—as regrettable as one may wish—of sentiments, of social forces, that are very salutary. If one should say that, far from being reprehensible, the slaughter and robbery are signs that those who were called upon to commit them deserved power for the good of society, he would be stating a paradox, for there is no relationship of cause and effect, nor any close and indispensable correlation, between such outrages and social utility; but the paradox would still contain its modicum of truth, in that the slaughter and rapine are external symptoms indicating the advent of strong and courageous people to places formerly held by weaklings and cowards. In all that, we have been describing in the abstract many revolutions that have actually occurred in the concrete,

> from the revolution which gave imperial rule to Augustus
> down to the French Revolution of '89 (*The Mind and Society*,
> § 2191).

This is Pareto *in nuce*. The seemingly objective discourse is pervaded by his hatred of "humanitarianism." (Franz Borkenau has suggested that this hate was caused by Pareto's antagonism to his father, and a psychoanalytical study might bear out the interpretation). The last sentence brings the whole passage back into the grooves of historical discourse, but Pareto's preoccupation with the role of force leads him to oversimplify the definition of the "duty of a ruling class," and subsequently calls up his obsessive vision. He *sees* the ruin of a country (and illustrates it abundantly) but analyzes it no more clearly than does a street-gossiper or a run-of-the-mill journalist. The *A* and the *B* are actually symbols of the elite and the governed, but Pareto is convinced that the letters allow him to avoid the danger of words that provoke sentiments in addition to expressing facts. His wavering between unemotional description of the impending debacle and hatred of humanitarianism seems to be arrested in the midst of his description of slaughter and he withdraws into his scientific analysis of outrage and social utility. His analysis takes its departure from the weighing of weak and strong and the abandonment of the category of cause-and-effect in favor of correlation (interdependence)—all stimulating and useful to sociology if freed from the confused Paretan overtones.

There is no logical contradiction between the preceding passage and the following one, although the shift of accent is so obvious that we almost look for a non sequitur:

> . . . freedom to express one's thought, even counter to the
> opinion of the majority or of all, even when it offends the sen-
> timents of the few or of the many, even when it is generally
> reputed absurd or criminal, always proves favourable to the
> discovery of objective truth (accord of theory with fact). But
> that does not prove that such liberty is always favourable to
> good order in a society or to the advancement of political and
> economic prosperity and the like. It may or may not be,
> according to the case (*The Mind and Society*, § 568).

This leaves open the question of subordinating society as a whole to individual liberty or vice versa. In the fascist case Pareto—as adviser to his *Principe*, but an adviser much more afraid for himself than Machiavelli had been—asked Mussolini for liberty.

Indeed, Pareto seems to be moving in the procession of a tawdry European carnival, an uneasily honest, anxiously gay masque:

> . . . the distinction between the utility of experimental science and social utility is fundamental. I wrote about it at length in the *Sociologia*; here it was necessary to mention it only to avoid the danger, which has frequently occurred with other writings of mine, that where I report simple observations of facts there should be seen exhortations to operate in a certain sense. If the facts seem to me such as to warrant the conclusion that our bourgeoisie is moving rapidly toward its own ruin, I do not intend to pass any judgment on the "good" or the "bad" of such an event, just as I should not know how to pass judgment on the similar fact of the ruin of the feudal lords prepared by the Crusades; or how to exhort the bourgeoisie to choose another course, or how to preach in order to reform customs, tastes, prejudices; or, much less, how to pretend that I have in store some prescription or other to heal the disease from which the bourgeoisie is suffering. . . . On the contrary, I explicitly declare that such a remedy, supposed but not granted there be one, is entirely unknown to me (*La trasformazione della democrazia*, pp. 12–13).

He is sincere in stating that he knows no remedy but at the same time he is afraid to use the liberty of expression to say what he might have or might want to say; he fears possible misunderstanding and misuse of his ideas—the attitude of a nostalgic liberal, helpless, and menaced, mumbling *Laissez faire!* The passage quoted above is from Pareto's last book, published three years before his death and two before the March on Rome. Only a decade earlier, instead of trembling on the island where he had been marooned, he was asserting defiantly:

> . . . to dare question in our day the dogma that the sole purpose of society is the "good of the greatest number," and that it is the strict duty of every individual to sacrifice himself for the good of the lowly and the humble, would be to arouse if not universal at least fairly general indignation. But scientific problems are solved by facts, not by the holy horror of the few, the many, the all (*The Mind and Society*, § 379).

The "facts," then, were the waves of humanitarianism; in the end they were the bourgeoisie in dissolution. So emphatically did Pareto insist on both sets of phenomena as facts that he could not perceive their difference. Once his answer could have been scientific, the unveiling of the supposedly unscientific character of humanitarianism, merely a statement concerning ideologies; in his last years he had no answer, but half felt, half embodied the end of Europe, his eyes riveted in mischief and horror on the rout of the bourgeoisie.

In a footnote near the end of *The Mind and Society* something more general than Pareto's own concern is foretold:

> Some day, when our present plutocratic régime has been overthrown by the Anarchists, or the Syndicalists, or the militarists, or by any party, in fine, whatever its name, which will meet the cunning that is now triumphant with force, the world will perhaps remember words such as Sallust, *Bellum Catilinae*, XX, 8-10, puts into the mouth of Catiline: "So all influence, all power, all honour, all wealth is theirs [Of the powerful of his day, counterparts of the speculators of ours.] or of those on whom they choose to bestow them. To us they have left the dangers, the defeats, the exiles, the poverty. How long will you endure such things, O men of heart? Is it not better to die bravely than to lose a wretched and contemptible life in ignominy, after making sport for the insolence of others? Of course it is, by the faith of gods and men! Victory is within our grasp. Youth is our strength, courage our watchword. And they? They are weaklings and dotards, sapped by age and high living" (*The Mind and Society*, § 2577, Notes 2, 3).

Neither liberalism nor any other ideology can confer on a man the insight that makes him worthy of the name of prophet. Such seers grasp, embody, and forever challenge the limits of human greatness. Pareto lacked the vision. Nevertheless, he perceived the provisional character of the world of European liberalism and strove to transcend it, groping and stammering, as if to say that a prophet was needed but had not yet appeared. Max Weber, the great sociologist—who had no personal acquaintance with Pareto—uttered the same opinion quite explicitly in 1919, a year before his own death and a few years before that of the Italian. Weber referred to a prophet who might answer the question whom among the warring gods or what unknown god we should serve. He was roused by the godlessness of our time but he avoided the temptation to conjure deities from his science. Pareto, in spite of his logico-experimental emphasis, wanted his science to be all-embracing. Like Comte, whose metaphysical character he recognized, he wanted to settle the questions of the world. Both were enchained by a jealous and grudging positivism that kept them hemmed in by a naïve allegiance to the supposititious facts. Yet both, though in different ways and degrees, have helped sociology toward its contemporary role of world interpretation.

Pareto's intellect never attained equilibrium; it continued to waver between the thoughts and emotions of a scientist and a passionate citizen of a Europe in agony. Yet the man was a whole, a *signore*, a liberal lord. He was outdated—like feudalism and magnificence—but like them still latently alluring; he embodies an emotional lag full of tensions and potential conflicts.

---

Reprinted from *Southwest Review*, **26** (1941), 347–359, by permission of the publisher. The essay has been edited and partially revised by the author.

# 2

# THE CHALLENGE
# OF DURKHEIM
# AND SIMMEL. 1958

The publication of two books—a new Durkheim translation and a German collection of writings by Simmel [1]—is not by way of commemorating the one-hundredth anniversary of the birth of these authors, but we can hardly be prevented from trying to relate their works to such a commemoration. On this occasion may we not ask, again, who these men were, what they attempted to do, what they accomplished, and, also, who, in their eyes, we are and what *we* are trying to achieve?

We must remember, it seems to me, an avalanche of things about Durkheim and Simmel: possibly that they are our fathers and our tyrants and, aside from being sociologists, men and philosophers. I begin with the last element because they may just manage to lord it over us if we ignore

---

This chapter was written 18 years later as a contribution to the issue of *The American Journal of Sociology* dedicated to the commemoration of the hundredth anniversary of the birth of Durkheim and Simmel (1958). In the meantime I had translated some of Simmel's writings in sociology [*The Sociology of Georg Simmel* (Glencoe, Ill.: Free Press, 1950); *Conflict*, together with Reinhard Bendix's translation of *The Web of Group Affiliations, ibid.* (1955)] and was at work on commemorative volumes for both Simmel and Durkheim [*George Simmel, 1858–1918*, and *Emile Durkheim, 1858–1917* (Columbus: Ohio State University Press, 1959 and 1960)]. The chapter was suggested by the appearance of the first English translation of a work by Durkheim and of an anniversary volume for Simmel in German.

them as men and philosophers and tend to take them at their face value as sociologists.

In the first place they are philosophers by education and (Simmel more clearly than Durkheim) by profession; in their writings it is stated publicly, but this is only the most "sociological" sense of the predication. More relevant, their work in sociology is based on philosophical assumptions; it raises philosophical questions and has philosophical aims. The first two of these characteristics, of course, apply to all scientific, hence also to all sociological work; the last, a matter of intent, does not. Thus it may be well to remember all three. As to philosophical assumptions, it is enough to recall that Kant was a major influence on both Durkheim and Simmel, even though he did not furnish them with quite the same viatica. "Philosophical questions" refer to characteristically Kantian queries—ontological, moral, epistemological—concerning the nature of reality and of those parts of it (such as society, religion, the individual, history) that our authors singled out, and our relation to reality, particularly the relation of knowledge. Philosophical aims include the establishment of sociology as a science, demanded by the time—the same time—in which Durkheim and Simmel lived, even though they differed in their conceptions of, as well as in their involvement in, both the sociology to be founded and the time which argued such a goal. The goal, of course, they share with most of the earlier practitioners of our discipline, but it is no less philosophical or less worthy of reinspection for that.

# I

Durkheim's *Professional Ethics and Civic Morals* is the translation of *Leçons de sociologie: Physique des mœurs et du droit* (1950), "a course of lectures given by Durkheim between the years 1890 and 1900 at Bordeaux and repeated at the Sorbonne, first in 1904, then in 1912, and revised some years before his death" (Preface, p. ix). Although this information makes it fairly certain that the material precedes Durkheim's last major work, the *Elementary Forms*, it is not specific enough to locate it in the chronology of his three earlier important books, all of which appeared in the 1890s, although part of the manuscript (p. x) stems from 1898–1900; that is, it is later than the *Division of Labor, Rules,* and *Suicide.* Still, most of what this book tells us about the development of Durkheim's thought requires the assembling and sifting of internal evidence, a task I shall not broach.

The book consists of eighteen chapters, three on professional ethics, six on civic morals, one on murder, one on theft, three on property, and four on contract. Its concern, characteristic of Durkheim, is mixed: orderly exposition and plea—among other things, for professional groups and for accepting and acting on an evolutionary view of history or social change. We have problems, we are in trouble, Durkheim says. What are these problems; what must we do? Where do we come from, and might this tell us how we should move? "One of the gravest conflicts of our day" is between the "national ideal" and the "human ideal," between "patriotism and world patriotism" (p. 72). It could be solved if civic duties were to become "only a particular form of the general obligations of humanity," which would be in line with evolution (p. 74): "it is human aims that are destined to be supreme" (p. 73); societies could "have their pride, not in being the greatest or the wealthiest, but in being the most just, the best organized, and in possessing the best moral constitution" (p. 75). This, to Durkheim, appears more feasible than a world society, a solution of the problem only "in theory"; and a "confederation of European States" is dismissed as just another "individual State," not "humanity" (p. 74).

This series of arguments shows how Durkheim's academicism handicaps his practical concern: the consideration of a European union leading to world society is dropped because Europe is not the world. But his practical concern does not leave him alone: so long as there is no world society there can be no world morality, for "man is a moral being only because he lives within established societies" (p. 73), "civilized," quite generally, meaning "socialized" (p. 25). This blunt equation reflects Durkheim's "sociologism," a limitation often criticized—and once more in this book, in Georges Davy's interesting introduction (esp. p. xliii). Durkheim himself, however, has his doubts about the exalted place he has given society. He does not feel at ease with its large modern variety (cf. pp. 15–16, 60-61), and his doubts go back to his first book. Even there he tries to find grounds on which to applaud the development from "mechanical" to "organic" and to argue the moral nature of the division of labor but finds his optimism dampened by the realization of anomie and in need of a fresh impetus, provided by the vision of a society reorganized on the basis of professional groups.

The argument in favor of professional groups is restated in the first three chapters of this new book, but it appears in many other places in the book as well. It culminates in some practical proposals (pp. 37 ff.; see also 94–97) which are in keeping with Durkheim's evolutionary conception of social change. Social change itself—which must always be preceded by careful reflection (p. 90)—has brought us to the age of democracy, which he characterizes in this way: the democratic state is distinguished by "(1) a greater range of the government consciousness, and (2) closer com-

munications between this consciousness and the mass of individual con-
sciousnesses" (p. 88); democracy is

> the political system by which the society can achieve a con-
> sciousness of itself in its purest form. The more that delibera-
> tion and reflection and a critical spirit play a considerable part
> in the course of public affairs, the more democratic the nation.
> . . . [Democracy] is the form that societies are assuming to an
> increasing degree (p. 89).

Reflection, furthermore, increases readiness to change, whereas "sacredness," to use the term employed by Howard Becker in a similar proposition, makes change difficult (pp. 84, 87). Finally, democracy "is the political
system that conforms best to our present-day notion of the individual"
(p. 90), which is that of the "autonomous" individual who understands
"the necessities he has to bow to and accept[s] them with full knowledge
of the facts" (p. 91).

Durkheim believes that history tends toward such autonomy (pp. 56, 68,
112). His optimism is supported by his conception of the state. The state
is the "social brain" (p. 30) which "decides for" the society (p. 49) but
"does not execute anything"; its "principal function" is "to think" (p. 51).
It increases its functions and consciousness along with the development of
individualism (p. 57). This "in its essence individualist" view (p. 69) is to
overcome the "mystic" conception, according to which the state has aims
higher than the individuals' on whom at best it may shed some rays of its
glory (pp. 54, 64). Yet, if the state "is to be the liberator of the individual,
it has itself need of some counterbalance; it must be restrained by other
collective forces" (p. 63); that is, by professional groups.

This analysis, these assessments, Durkheim insists, are superior not only
to the Hegelian *mystique* (p. 64) but also to the views of classical economists and Socialists alike (pp. 10, 15, 29, 122, 216). Neither economists nor
Socialists, for instance, see the state for what it is, "the organ of moral
discipline" (p. 72); nor would a shift from private to collective ownership
of the means of production solve our basic problem, which is the infusion
of moral rule into economic life (p. 30). This is an instance of Durkheim's
conviction that the examination of our past shows us that things are as he
sees them. Nevertheless,

> the right to say that this or that form . . . must disappear
> requires more from us than merely showing that these forms
> conflict with an earlier principle. There still remains to dem-
> onstrate how they were able to establish themselves and under
> the influence of what causes, and to prove that these same

causes are no longer actually present and active. We cannot demand that existing practices be put down on the score of an a priori axiom (pp. 124–25).

Here we have Durkheim's conception of social change, including its far-reaching confusion. It commissions causal explanation to decide on how things are and hang together but smuggles the "ought" back into the facts by giving causal explanation a second task, that of serving as a recipe for practice. The classical case of this confusion is *Suicide,* which opens with rigorous causal analysis, then, in effect, abandons the law of one-cause-one-effect laid down in the *Rules,* and ends up in a vision, plausible and troubled, of the relations among types of social cohesion and types of suicide and in practical questions of policy. Durkheim confuses or mixes history with social change, interpretation with explanation (on this see Davy, toward the end of his introduction), practice with theory, ontology with methodology, plea with exposition. Once these dichotomies are espoused, once the two elements in each of them are separately torn out of reality, as they are by Durkheim's positivism and in his strenuous effort to establish a scientific sociology, their synthesis is impossible, its only deceiving hope being verbal legerdemain [2].

Durkheim was moved by two forever muddled inspirations—the improvement of our society and the development of an instrument carefully and passionately forged to be inadequate to the task. He was a man who eats his cake or his bread and is poor—reformer, historian, philosopher—or keeps it and starves—theorist, scientist, sociologist. In his search for what he could believe in as real he found himself incapable of accepting anything but society. He sanctified it as the source of all that he loved—religion, morality, knowledge; he sanctified it as the reality behind all these realities—and mustered all the more fervor dissecting it in his piacular rites of the scientist who longs for a lost sacred world.

Something of this sort may suggest Durkheim's philosophical aims. In less emphatic metaphors he wanted to design a society and wished his fellow men to accept it—a secular society, to be embraced with sacred passion. This is one of the numerous ties that connects him with his predecessor, Comte, and distinguishes him from his contemporary, Weber, who affirmed secularization as definitively as Durkheim did but who suffered from his clearer knowledge that one meaning of such affirmation is to accept "the fundamental fact" of being "destined to live in a godless and prophetless time."

Do we not recognize ourselves? Do we not have aims similar to Durkheim's and perhaps similarly confused? Is not Durkheim thus one of our fathers and must we not emancipate ourselves from him? And is this not

painful because we love him and, in outgrowing him, must go through
the pain that was his own? Is he, then, not one of us, a little older, to be
sure, since he helped to push us to where we are?

# II

With Simmel matters are quite different. We hardly know him yet. We
are just discovering, thanks to new translations, that there is more to him
than the invention of formal sociology, which the critical and enthusiastic
Albion W. Small presented to the readers of his *American Journal of
Sociology* in the 1890s and which has long since demonstrated its academic
respectability in one history of sociological thought after another. But, so
far, there are only a few of us for whom he is among the fathers. Emancipation is still far off because we have not even gone through domination
and love. Perhaps we can take another road, learning from the history of
our relations with Durkheim.

Simmel reminds us of things we tend to forget but would gain from
remembering. The central concern of Comte, Durkheim, Weber, and
many other nineteenth- and twentieth-century sociologists and philosophers was the time in which they lived, particularly as the promises of
liberalism and the Enlightenment were being broken, ever more incontrovertibly, before their eyes. Unlike theirs, Simmel's concerns included only
that over his historical period. It was not primary. A remarkable sociologist, he was, much more clearly and purely than Comte or Weber or any
of those referred to (or than many professional philosophers), a philosopher, a man who "wonders"—who also wonders about received notions,
of which, since he was an unusually alert, perceptive, sensitive person, he
had a wealth at his disposal.

He was far less deeply time-bound than Durkheim, although, of course,
his time influenced him. Thus, for instance, he thought that people who
were on their way to self-realization and abhorred the detours that led
them outside themselves hated "culture" (p. 90): here a nineteenth-century
bourgeois notion of "culture" is slipping in. He thought that it was the
nature of the inner life to seek artistic expression in self-contained forms
which contrast with its dynamic and perhaps torn character (p. 99): this
is directed against expressionism—he thought that it was the essence of
art to present the human body in a way that shows it controlled and unified by mind or soul (p. 132); this would disqualify much twentieth-
century art. He thought that it was inherent in the sociology of the meal
for the dinner table not to exhibit "the broken, differentiated, modern

colors but the broad, glossy ones which relate to wholly primary sensitivities: white and silver" (p. 248). Simmel occasionally mistook matters of his time as timeless, but such confusion detracts less from his achievement than it reminds one of a distracted professor's pet notions or absentmindedness.

To go beyond characterizing Simmel as a wonderer whose locale rather infrequently intrudes, it is convenient to indicate the content of the twenty-eight pieces brought together in *Brücke und Tür*. In time they range from 1896 to 1918, the year of his death. In content they are placed under six headings: "Life and Philosophy," "History and Culture," "Religion," "Aesthetics and Art," "Historical Figures," and "Society." Only three of them, or less than one-sixth—"The Field of Sociology," "The Metropolis and Mental Life," and "The Individual and Freedom," all under "Society"—are available in English [3]. Of the title essay, Michael Landmann, the editor, writes:

> As one of the most beautiful examples of Simmel's way of letting himself be inspired by the nearest things [around him] and wresting their ultimate meaning from them, . . . ["Bridge and Door"] is placed at the beginning. The human capacity of "connecting" which it isolates and elucidates is so characteristic of Simmel himself that . . . its title . . . seemed suitable as that of the whole collection [p. 271].

Man, in the title essay, is presented as connecting and separating, building bridges and making doors, which can be opened and closed. Does the doorlessness of contemporary American living rooms symbolize or promote the disappearance of both privacy (separation) and—since doors can also be opened, whereas no-doors cannot—freedom? It is a Simmelian kind of question, although American homes were not among his "nearest things." Yet many items might and did become the occasion for his thought, which skipped time and place and could descend on any of them:

> While the world surely determines what the content of our cognition shall be, but only because cognition determined beforehand what can be world to us, so fate surely determines the life of the individual, but only because the individual chose, by a certain affinity with them, those events on which it can bestow the meaning whereby they become his "destiny" ["The Problem of Destiny" (1913), p. 13].

For human life has a double aspect, causality and meaning, and, without both of them, "destiny" cannot emerge. Animals follow only causality, gods, only meaning; man alone must live with both. It is this same distinction between causality and meaning (see also pp. 51, 76, 86) that, in a sociological frame of reference, we know from Max Weber's definition of sociology (causal explanation and understanding) and whose inadequate appreciation I urged as characteristic of Durkheim.

It plays a central role in Simmel's mature view of history. His paper "On the Nature of Historical Understanding" (1918), relevant to an illumination of theories of understanding, including historicism, of the nature of the Thou, the mind-body problem, and the concept of secularization, in effect distinguishes between intrinsic and extrinsic understanding [4] ("We should never understand the What of things from their historical development if we did not somehow understand this What itself" [p. 77]). This dichotomy is related to the one just referred to (causality versus meaning), as well as to its variant, the objective versus the historical (psychological, meaningful):

> Psychological development is controlled and made understandable by objective development, and objective by psychological. This signifies that both of these are only sides, methodologically made independent, of a unity, of the historically understood event. . . . For life can be understood only by life. To this purpose, life lays itself apart in strata, each of which mediates the understanding of the others, and which, in their mutual interdependence, announce its unity [p. 83]

This passage, written in Simmel's last period, that of the philosophy of life, contains, in addition to the theme of the supremacy of life, two others: what may be called the "autonomization of parts of a whole" and the "understandability of a whole only through its parts." These three themes are connected.

> The Marxian scheme of economic development, according to which in every historical epoch the economic forces engender a form of production which is adequate to them, in which, however, they grow to magnitudes no longer manageable within that form but bursting it and creating a new one for themselves—this scheme is valid far beyond the economic sphere. . . . Creative life continuously engenders something which itself no longer is life, something life somehow runs up against, something which opposes it with a claim of its own, and which cannot express itself except in forms which are and mean something in their own right and independently of it ["Transformations of Cultural Forms" (1916), pp. 98–99].

> That the part of a whole becomes an independent whole,
> growing out of and claiming its own right over against it;
> this, perhaps, is altogether the most basic tragedy of the spirit
> —a tragedy which in the modern era has reached its fullest
> development and has taken over the direction of the cultural
> process ["Philosophy of the Landscape" (1913), p. 143].

It is noteworthy and characteristic of Simmel that, despite its strong tie
to Hegel-Feuerbach-Marx's "alienation," Simmel does not apply his idea
of the autonomization of a part to an interpretation of his time, as Durkheim did with the concept of anomie, which is no more closely or distantly related to alienation. Rather, less time-bound philosopher that he
was, he chooses that conceptual aspect of "alienation" which he could best
put to epistemological purposes, the illumination of the process of understanding. Hence the connection with the second theme, the understandability of a whole only through its parts: "Perhaps the nature of our
activity to us is a mysterious unity which, like so many other unities, we
can grasp only by splitting it up" ("On the Metaphysics of Death" [1910],
p. 32). Or in respect to the problem of understanding a philosopher and
his work:

> When we infer an innermost personality from . . . [its] achieve-
> ment, and again understand the achievement through the
> personality, this [procedure] may well be circular. But it is
> one of those circles which are unavoidable for our thinking;
> it . . . merely [corresponds to] the complete unity of the
> phenomenon which expresses itself in the fact that each of the
> elements into which we split it up becomes understandable
> only through the other ["On the History of Philosophy" (1904),
> p. 41] [5].

This suggests the last of the themes that I wish to call attention to in
this wholly fragmentary sample, designed only to lead the reader to Simmel's work itself. It is that of relatively autonomous and irreducible attitudes toward the world, or the theme of "worlds," connecting Simmel with
Husserl and later developments in phenomenology, especially in the work
of Alfred Schutz [6].

> The great categories of our inner life—Is and Ought, possi-
> bility and necessity, wish and fear—form a series through
> which pass the objective contents of consciousness, the logi-
> cally fixable conceptual meanings of things. These categories
> may be compared to the various states which one and the
> same chemical substance can adopt, or to the multiplicity of

musical instruments on which one and the same melody, but every time in a particular tone color, can be played. Perhaps it is only different accompanying feelings which show us the same objective content now as being, now as non-being, now as an Ought, now as hoped for—or more correctly: these feelings *mean* that the content now is one and now the other. According to its over-all posture, our soul responds to the same content or perception with completely different attitudes, thus giving us completely different meanings of it ["Contributions to the Epistemology of Religion" (1902), p. 106].

In and of themselves, religion and art have nothing to do with one another . . . because each of them by itself alone expresses, in its particular language, the whole of existence. One can conceive of the world religiously or artistically, practically or scientifically: it is the same contents which each time, under a different category, form a cosmos of a consistent and incommensurable character. Our soul, however, with its short-lived impulses and its limited ability, is incapable of developing any of these worlds as wholly as it ideally demands. Each of them remains dependent on the haphazard stimuli which permit now this, now that, portion of it to grow up in us. But it is precisely the fact that these world images lack the self-sufficient rounding out called for by their objective content which creates the deepest vitalities and psychic patterns, because it urges each of these images to take from the others impulses, contents, and challenges which, were it completely developed, it would find in its own inner structure ["Christianity and Religion" (1907), p. 140].

# III

If Durkheim's philosophical aim is to infuse morality into the society of his time, thus being predominantly practical and historical, Simmel's is to understand the world and, above all, is theoretical and ahistorical. If it is true that we feel closer to Durkheim because our aims resemble his more than they do Simmel's, it is also true, I think, that in a sense we need Simmel more urgently than Durkheim. Being deeper-seeing and more self-conscious, he has, on a systematic, theoretical, ahistorical view, more for us to tackle. Our indebtedness, as sociologists, to Durkheim has been driven home to us with poignancy and conviction, notably by Talcott Parsons and Robert K. Merton, and some of Simmel's achievements in sociology have recently begun to be rediscovered, appreciated, and made use of in various fields, especially in the study of small groups and the phenomena of secrecy and secret societies. But I have tried to comment on Durkheim and Simmel less as sociologists than as men. I have endeavored to show some of their philosophical concerns as the concerns of men who lived in a given time and place and who, as men, also to an extent transcended them.

Together they challenge us to do right by them and to do better. More specifically, we may want to identify Durkheim's confusions and avoid them by being as fully aware as we can of their seriousness and pregnancy and we may wish to pay more attention than Simmel did to the relation between a theoretical and a historical preoccupation. Both, though in different ways, also invite us to reconsider our own and sociology's philosophical premises. Of course, we can learn from them many more things in respect to which we want to do them justice or surpass them. Unfortunately or fortunately, even the narrow, selective focus of the present allusive observations may serve to remind us that there is no textbook that teaches us how to approach them or go beyond them—how, if you will, to commemorate them. They are a challenge to us, too, as men, to the best in us, and on *this* ground, as sociologists.

### NOTES

1. Emile Durkheim, *Professional Ethics and Civic Morals*, translated by Cornelia Brookfield, preface by H. N. Kubali, introduction by Georges Davy. ("International Library of Sociology and Social Reconstruction.") London: Routledge & Kegan Paul, 1957. Georg Simmel, *Brücke und Tür: Essays des Philosophen zur Geschichte, Religion, Kunst und Gesellschaft,* in collaboration with Margarete Susman, edited by Michael Landmann, with an introduction by Michael Landmann, and a bibliographical appendix. Stuttgart: Koehler, 1957.

2. Another element in Durkheim's makeup as a sociologist is his conservatism, shown in the present work in some of the conceptions mentioned as well as in his poor grasp of power and stratification and his respect for the status quo (cf. Lewis A. Coser "Durkheim's Conservatism and Its Implications for His Sociological Theory," in Kurt H. Wolff, Ed., *Emile Durkheim, 1858–1917: A Collection of Essays, with Translations and a Bibliography.* Columbus: Ohio University Press, 1960, pp. 211–233). I must also abstain from talking about what are, from a theoretical and sociological standpoint, the most challenging chapters of the present book, those on property and, above all, on contract, the latter fully justifying Parsons' praise of Durkheim's treatment of the subject (cf. *The Structure of Social Action* [1937] [Glencoe, Ill.: Free Press, 1949]).

3. See *The Sociology of Georg Simmel*, translated, edited, and with an introduction by Kurt H. Wolff (Glencoe, Ill.: Free Press, 1950), pp. 3–35, 409–424,

and 58–84; the last of these is a later and much longer version than the essay reprinted in *Brücke und Tür*.

4. Except for terminology, this is similar to Karl Mannheim's "The Ideological and the Sociological Interpretation of Intellectual Phenomena" (1926) [translated (1963) by Kurt H. Wolff, in Wolff, Ed., *From Karl Mannheim*, New York: Oxford University Press, 1971, pp. 116–131], although to my knowledge Mannheim does not refer to Simmel in his discussions of problems of interpretation or understanding.

5. See also pp. 102–103 and 149 and the cases collected in Donald N. Levine, "The Structure of Simmel's Social Thought," and Rudolph H. Weingartner, "Form and Content in Simmel's Philosophy of Life," in Kurt H. Wolff, Ed., *Georg Simmel, 1858–1918: A Collection of Essays, with Translations and a Bibliography* (Columbus: Ohio State University Press, 1959), pp. 9–32 and 33–60.

6. Weingartner, *ibid.*

---

Reprinted from *The American Journal of Sociology*, **63** (1958), 590–596, published by the University of Chicago, by permission of the publisher. The essay has been edited and partially revised by the author.

# 3

# GEORG SIMMEL. 1968

Georg (Friedrich Eduard) Simmel was born in Berlin on March 1, 1858, of Jewish parents, both of whom had early converted—his father to Catholicism, his mother to Protestantism. He was baptized a Protestant but left the church during World War I, without, however, embracing Judaism. After graduating from the gymnasium he studied at the University of Berlin, beginning with history under Theodor Mommsen, moving to psychology, especially *Völkerpsychologie* (Moritz Lazarus), then to ethnology (Adolf Bastian), and at last to philosophy (Eduard Zeller, Friedrich Harms); he minored in Italian, specializing in Petrarch. Among his other more or less important teachers were the linguist Heymann Steinthal, the historians Gustav Droysen, Heinrich von Sybel, and Heinrich von Treitschke, and the art historian Herman Grimm, none of whom, however, had the influence to shape him as did Wilhelm Dilthey, Edmund Husserl, and Henri Bergson, let alone what might be called his coordinates: above all Kant and Goethe, but also Nietzsche, Spinoza, and Meister Eckhart.

As his dissertation he submitted a paper on "Psychological-Ethnographic Studies on the Beginnings of Music" (cf. Etzkorn, 1964); it was rejected; he obtained his doctorate instead (in 1881) with an essay for which he had received an academic prize two years before, *Description and Assessment of Kant's Various Views of the Nature of Matter.* On the basis of a second essay (again on Kant) and a "test" lecture, "On the Theory of the Associa-

This chapter is an article, commissioned for the *International Encyclopedia of the Social Sciences*, which was rejected but appeared later in *Praxis* (Zagreb) in 1968, the year of the fiftieth anniversary of Simmel's death. I have not changed the format characteristic of an encyclopedia entry.

tion of Ideas"—the written work and the lecture being required to secure the *venia legendi*—he was appointed *Privatdozent* in 1885 at the University of Berlin, a post he held for the unusually long period of 15 years, after which he was promoted to *ausserordentlicher Professor*. In 1914, almost as long again, he became an *Ordinarius* at the University of Strasbourg, four years before he died (September 26, 1918).

His career thus was exceptionally slow, despite his fame as a brilliant lecturer who had large student registrations and many more "unregistered" listeners and as an extraordinary, as well as extraordinarily prolific, writer (his bibliography contains some 30 books and 250 articles), despite the efforts of such men as Max Weber to have him appointed a full professor at other universities, notably Heidelberg, and despite the numerous, even formal academic testimonials. The reasons are not wholly clear, but anti-Semitism and in some places his reputation as a predominantly critical and relativistic spirit played a part. At least Simmel himself thought so. Writing to Max Weber (on March 18, 1908), he rejected this reputation as wholly unwarranted and mistaken:

> In certain circles the idea exists that I am an exclusively critical, even destructive spirit, and that my lectures lead one only to negation. Perhaps I don't have to tell you that this is a nasty untruth. My lectures, as, for many years, all my work, tend exclusively toward the positive, toward the demonstration of a deeper insight into world and spirit, with complete renunciation of polemics and criticism in regard to divergent conditions and theories. Whoever understands my lectures and books at all, *cannot* understand them in any other way (Wolff, 1950, p. XIX; Gassen and Landmann, 1958, pp. 127–128).

Although he was not a political man, he spoke and wrote in an extremely nationalistic manner during the first years of World War I, even though he was shocked and hurt by the chauvinism of Henri Bergson, a philosopher who had impressed him deeply and whom he had introduced in Germany; yet a year before he died he listed the Thirty Years' War and the régime of William II as the two catastrophes of German history.

Margarete Susman (1959), who, with Gertrud Kantorowicz (1923), has drawn the most sensitive portrait of Georg Simmel as the unique phenomenon he represents, accounts for his continuous exploration of so many perhaps seemingly heterogeneous areas by his "certainty of finding himself in an inexhaustible world that is unattainable to the thinker" (Susman 1959, p. 18); like the wanderer, discovering ever new sights, unable to rest, he knows that his wandering has no end. Among the areas in which Simmel stayed longest to "dig" (Simmel, 1911, Introduction),

thus finding or erecting landmarks in his wandering, and among the minor
things that he observed and by which he was led on are ethics (1892–1893),
history (1892, 1916a, 1918c), sociology (1890, 1900, 1908, 1917), religion
(1960b), philosophy (1910), art 1916b, 1922), culture (1911–1912, 1918a),
philosophers (1904, 1906a, 1907), Goethe (1913), the handle, bridge and
door, the human face, the actor, the picture frame, the adventure, the
ruin, the Alps, fashion, coquetry (the essays on these topics are collected
in *Philosophical Culture* [1911], the posthumous *Philosophy of Art* [1922],
or *Bridge and Door* [1957]). *View of Life* (1918b), which became his last
book, written in clear knowledge of his impending death (from cancer of
the liver), might be called the book of his relative arrival. Its last chapter
is entitled "The Individual Law."

"Before he died," his widow wrote ten years later (Gertrud Simmel,
1928, p. 221),

> Georg Simmel said emphatically and on more than one
> occasion that he died at the right time, that he had done his
> essential work, that he could merely have applied his way of
> looking at things farther and farther and to ever new objects
> —to something really new it would not have come any more.
> And yet one felt something like a reservation in these utter-
> ances, and in fact he once spoke of it by adding, "Unless I
> had another twenty years of full strength ahead of me, some-
> thing which in my age is not at all my lot." His reservation
> presumably concerned studies which would have been in the
> pursuit of the line traced by his last book, *View of Life*—in the
> pursuance of this line, or perhaps in a new turn.

It is possible to show that the relativism attendant on such a life voyage
has never been overcome by the voyager (e. g., Maurice Mandelbaum
[1938, pp. 101–119] in regard to Simmel's historical relativism; but if *The
Problems of the Philosophy of History* (1892) is read along with others of
Simmel's writings on our relation to history—notably *The Problem of
Historical Time* (1916a) and *On the Nature of Historical Understanding*
(1918c)—it may become apparent that Simmel's own preoccupation was
not so much the overcoming of relativism as the grasp of history as a
world of its own, a world in the phenomenological sense of the term (particularly as in Schutz 1945; cf. Weingartner, 1959, esp. p. 60, n. 84, and,
on Simmel and Husserl, Weingartner, 1962, pp. 23–28), and that he was
concerned with the presentation of the study of history as a particular
relation to the world of history, and similarly for others of his worlds,
among them art, religion, money, and sociology. It is true, however, that
in his effort to articulate worlds he was less attentive to the ways in which

these worlds are interrelated, other than as objects of the individual's "attitudes," which, in turn, are emergents of life, for human life itself is more than life, creating as it does objective structures or, most briefly put, culture.

It is also possible to argue, as, among others, Paul Honigsheim (1953) has done, that there are three phases in Simmel's voyaging. There is the early phase of evolutionism and positivism, followed by the middle period, influenced by Kant but also by Schopenhauer and Nietzsche, with epistemological idealism as its general philosophical basis, with its distinction between historical and natural laws, its rejection of all determinisms, and its attention to sociology, conceived as a non-natural-scientific discipline that deals with individuals in interaction and with the results of such interaction (e.g., social processes and institutions), and analyzes, as general sociology, "the whole genetic process of the development of human culture" in relation to society; as philosophical sociology, the relation between sociology and metaphysics; as formal sociology, social relations as such, for example, of the stranger (Simmel, 1950, pp. 402–408) or of the third party (Simmel, 1950, pp. 145–169); then there is the last period, with its explication of a thread present from the beginning, preoccupation with the nature of human life.

Such an approach concentrates more on product than on process, more on result than on travail, more on the done than on the doing, more on destinations than on wandering, more on "more than life" than on life. Closer to Simmel himself are efforts that try to grasp him as a living phenomenon, as do those (in addition to Susman's and Kantorowicz') of Emil Utitz (1920), Max Frischeisen-Köhler (1920), and Michael Landmann (1957). There is a third way, which is to catch the product in the process, the result that emerges in the travail, the done that is thrust out by the doing, the destinations that guide the wandering, the life that is ripening into the more than life. This is to reconstruct Simmel's philosophy in his philosophizing, as Weingartner (1962) does: "From the beginning to the very end of his career, Simmel's major interest was the examination and analysis of culture products," whether "money, the work of Michelangelo [in Simmel, 1911], the phenomenon of secrecy [in Simmel, 1908], the discipline of history, the philosophy of Kant, or philosophy itself considered as a product of human experience" (Weingartner, 1962, p. 11), although Weingartner focuses on two cultural products only, historiography and philosophy.

As consciousness of a legitimate place of relevance, the grasp of the social is an element of all of Simmel's worlds, including, for example, that of religion, in which, to be sure, it is more manifest than in some others, such as philosophy or art. Thus the "transposition into the religious key" is most palpable, Simmel thinks, in man's relation to nature, to fate, and to other men. In regard to the latter, religion "appears as the absolute, unified form of feelings and impulses which in beginnings and, as it were, tentatively, are developed already in social life insofar as it is oriented religiously in mood or function" (Simmel, 1906b, 2nd ed., 1912, p. 24). Simmel takes this occasion (as he takes others) to introduce sociology; that is, the study of human interaction and sociation. Sociology thus conceived sees that religion is a force of social sanction and cohesion, that the individual's attitudes of dependency toward the godhead and toward society are analogous, both being characterized by a mixture of freedom and unfreedom, that religious duties accrue to the individual as a member of a group, that roots of religion lie in the relations among individuals (Simmel reminds us that we speak of faith not only in God but also in man and men), and that the idea of the unity of life, comprehended in the concept of God, mirrors or sublimates that of the group. The character of Simmel's position here stands out more clearly if it is compared with Durkheim's, who is concerned far less with the phenomenology of the religious world and far more with the social genesis and function of religion as an institution.

Indeed, a long, important road led Simmel to, and through, the world of sociology. Looking back at his itinerary we can see that he approached it with his early "Psychological-Ethnographic Studies on the Beginnings of Music" (1882), properly entered it with a monograph on social differentiation (1890), reached a highpoint with the *Philosophy of Money* (1900) (and a bifurcation with the world of history in the chapter on historical laws in the second edition [1905] of *The Problems of the Philosophy of History* [1892]), gathered his views in *Sociology* (1908), a collection of previously published essays, and nine years later, in the *Fundamental Problems of Sociology* (1917), told a wider public where he had arrived. This mentions only the most important way stations, which, nevertheless, span 35 years, from a year after he began publishing to a year before he died.

*On Social Differentiation* (1890) shows the influence, above all, of Marx, Tönnies, and Dilthey—with Dilthey also remaining perhaps the most direct influence in Simmel's subsequent work in sociology. The book is arranged in six chapters: on the epistemology of social science, on collective responsibility (which contains the first important record of Simmel's thought on the individual, on which theme see Lipman, 1959), on the extension of the group and the development of individuality, on the social level, on the crossing of social circles, and on differentiation and the principle of saving energy. Even some of these titles suggest Simmel's initial evolutionism, which was gradually to be shed, and most of the

rest of the book was to be taken up in *Sociology*, Chapters 3 and 5, in
expanded form, as Chapters 10 and 6, respectively (the latter, "The
Crossing of Social Circles," translated as "The Web of Group Affiliations" in Simmel 1955). Here Simmel is already concerned with determining the subject matter of social science or sociology as "society"; but

> one must not begin with the concept of society the nature of
> which would yield the relations and mutual effects of its
> components. On the contrary, the latter must be ascertained,
> and "society" is only the name for the sum of these mutual
> effects, applicable only in the degree in which they are ascer-
> tained. It therefore is not an evenly fixed but gradual concept,
> of which also more or less is applicable, according to the larger
> number and the intimacy of the mutual effects that obtain
> among the given persons (Simmel, 1890, p. 14).

The *Philosophy of Money* (1900) is not, as the title might suggest, a
book on economics but above all three other things. It is a study in substantive sociology, namely, of the modern market society, to that extent
resembling *Das Kapital*. It is also a diagnosis of its time (still in significant
respects the time six or seven decades later). Thus it shares with Max
Weber's *The Protestant Ethic and the Spirit of Capitalism*, published
only a few years later, a common historical-diagnostic concern as well as
important theoretical elements (on the great similarities of Simmel's and
Weber's theoretical approaches, see Tenbruck 1958, 1959). The diagnostic
character of the book is particularly apparent in the last chapter, "The
Style of Life." Finally, it is a study in the social phenomenology of money
(paralleling the genetically related study of the metropolis, a phenomenon
akin to it [Simmel, 1903]). The nature of this aspect may be suggested by
such chapter glosses as "Money as a substantiation of a general form of
existence according to which things find their meaning in each other, in
their reciprocity"; "Original requiredness of valuable money. Development of ideas of equivalence beyond this stage and toward the purely
symbolic character of money"; or "Historical development of money from
substance to function; sociological conditions of this development. The
reciprocal social effects and their crystallization into special structures;
the common relation of buyers and sellers to the social unit as the presupposition of monetary relations." The phenomenon of money as the
starting point of so searching, imaginative, and widely knowledgeable a
mind as Simmel's leads him to embark on the presentation of a vast and
rich panorama, the three major aspects of which by no means exhaust it,
for the book contains many other finds regarding social change, types of

society, the means-end scheme, "ideal-types," the study that was later to be called the sociology of knowledge, and that which, later still, was to become the sociology of development, and many more topics and areas. But it remains largely to be exploited.

*Sociology* is Simmel's most explicit and most comprehensive description of his sociological approach to the world. Characteristically, it is presented in the form of essays or, as the subtitle of the book says, "studies on the forms of sociation." They start out with Simmel's last of several formulations of "the problem of sociology," containing the *Exkurs* on "How is Society Possible?" This first chapter is followed by chapters on, (II), the quantitative determination of the group (which has had much influence on "small group" studies); (III), super- and subordination; (IV), conflict (the principal basis of Coser, 1956); (V), the secret and the secret society; (VI), the crossing of social circles; (VII), the poor; (VIII), the self-preservation of the social group; (IX), space and the spatial orders of society; and (X), the extension of the group and the development of individuality. In the short preface to this work Simmel points out that sociological investigation can employ no formula to be found in any of the existing disciplines; that, consequently, the location of sociology "within the system of the sciences, the discussion of its methods and potential fertilities, is a new task in itself which requires its solution not in a preface but as the first part [Chapter 1] of the very investigation," and that the present work tries to give "the fluctuating concept of sociology an unambiguous content, dominated by one, methodologically certain, problem-idea." Simmel, therefore, requests the reader "to hold on, uninterruptedly, to this one method of asking questions, as it is developed in the first chapter (since otherwise these pages might impress him as an accumulation of unrelated facts and reflections)" (quoted in Wolff, 1950, p. XXV).

This one method of asking questions is the focus on the forms of sociation, or societal forms, rather than on content or matter. In the beginning of an autobiography that remained a fragment Simmel wrote on this method

> I started out with studies in epistemology and in Kant; hand in hand with them went historical and social-scientific studies. The first result of this was the fundamental motif (carried through in *The Problems of the Philosophy of History*) that "history" means the structuring, according to the apriorities of the science-creating spirit, of happening in its immediacy, such as can only be experienced, just as "nature" means the structuring, by the categories of reason, of matter given to our

> senses. This separation of form and content in the conception
> of history, which originated for me in a purely epistemological
> frame of reference, subsequently developed for me into a
> methodological principle within a special discipline: I gained
> a new conception of sociology by distinguishing the forms of
> sociation from the contents, that is, drives, purposes, objective
> elements, which become social only when taken up by inter-
> actions between individuals; in my book [*Sociology*], therefore,
> I undertook the analysis of these kinds of interaction as the
> subject matter of a pure sociology. This sociological signifi-
> cance of the concept of interaction, however, gradually grew
> for me into a wholly comprehensive metaphysical principle
> (Simmel, n. d., p. 9).

Although the literature on Simmel's form and content is considerable
(cf. Wolff, 1950, p. L, n. 57), it is for the most part concerned with clarifying the meaning of these concepts, particularly in regard to their relevance for sociology. Their pervasiveness in Simmel's thought as indicative
of his mode of relating to the world or as giving unity if not system to his
work has only recently begun to be appreciated, notably by Weingartner
(1962) but also by Tenbruck (1958, 1959), Levine (1959), and a few others.
Form-content has also been related to the post-Simmelian structure-
function (Wolff, 1950, pp. XXXVI, LI, n. 60; Tenbruck, 1959, pp. 77–78);
and form, to Max Weber's ideal-type (Tenbruck, 1958, pp. 604–609).

"The theory of sociation, abstracted from all the social sciences which
are determined by a special content of societal life" (Simmel, 1959, p. 333),
is the legitimating basis of sociology. Like all sciences, sociology, too, is
bordered by two philosophical inquiries, the epistemology and the metaphysics of the discipline. The former deals with its fundamental concepts
and other presuppositions; the latter, with ontological inquiries into the
subject matter it treats empirically—such as Simmel's own into that of
sociology: "How is Society possible?"

In the first chapter, "The Field of Sociology," of his last programmatic
statement on sociology, the *Fundamental Problems of Sociology* of 1917
(Simmel, 1950, pp. 1–84), he somewhat modifies this classification by
speaking of three kinds of sociology: general, pure, or formal, and philosophical. General sociology is "the sociological study of historical life,"
the study "of the whole of historical life insofar as it is formed societally"
(Simmel, 1950, pp. 16, 22); pure, or formal, sociology is "the study of
societal forms," that is. what he had called sociology pure and simple; and
philosophical sociology is "the study of the epistemological and metaphysical aspects of society," which emerges "as the epistemology of the

special social sciences, as the analysis and systematization of the bases of their forms and norms" (Simmel 1950, p. 24). The following are examples of these three sociologies: "The Social and the Individual Level (an example of general sociology)," "Sociability (an example of pure, or formal, sociology)," and "Individual and Society in Eighteenth- and Nineteenth-century Views of Life (an example of philosophical sociology)." Neither the definitions of the three sociologies nor their exemplifications are wholly clear or consistent, but among the important hints they contain are, in regard to general sociology, the idea of looking at history sociologically, the idea of sociology as a perspective, or approach or method; in regard to formal sociology, its fundamental conception mentioned before; in regard to philosophical sociology, attention to the empirically intimate connection between sociology—and all science—and philosophy, as well as their analytical distinction; in regard, finally, to the examples, their substantive wealth which illustrates the capacity of the human mind, emphasized by Simmel himself, to erect "solid structures, while their foundations are still insecure" (Simmel, 1950, p. 18).

Yet, "Again and again the question arises for me," Margarete Susman wrote almost 40 years after Simmel's death,

> why he, one of the most famous philosophers of his time, has remained without proper succession . . . But then I tell myself that about two years before his death, he himself gave me an answer to this question, an answer that later he placed as motto at the head of his posthumous diary: "I know that I shall die without spiritual heirs (and this is good). My estate is like one in ready money, which is distributed among many heirs, and each of them invests his share in some livelihood that corresponds to his nature but whose provenience from that estate is unrecognizable" (Susman, 1957, p. 278).

In sociology Simmel's prediction has on the whole been correct, although less so in the United States than elsewhere, including Germany, where the single most famous work that bears his mark is Leopold von Wiese's. In the United States he was well known as a sociologist during his lifetime and a few years beyond, mainly through the efforts of Albion W. Small, who in the years before and after the turn of the century translated several of his essays in sociology in *The American Journal of Sociology*, and of Robert E. Park, who in his and Ernest W. Burgess's influential *Introduction to the Science of Sociology* (1921) drew on him heavily and praised him explicitly; then his fame declined and his name was largely forgotten, although subterraneously, as he predicted, work in such areas as social processes and social types "cashed in" on him. He came to new life with translations in the fifties and, contrary to his prediction, has been acknowledged and recognized as relevant mainly, but not exclusively, in studies of small groups and of conflict, as witnessed by original research that draws on him, in new translations and in reprints of those existing.

It is possible that the reason why Simmel has had less influence on the development of the social sciences than Durkheim or Weber, for example, is that his conception of sociology was historically premature, that is, ahead not only of his own time but also of the time half a century later. The image of society drawn by Durkheim and Weber, and further developed by Talcott Parsons, as of a very structured social system may be more in line than Simmel's with the advanced stage of industrial society that we know today. Simmel's looser conception may correspond instead to an even later industrial stage characterized by, among other things, a far greater role played by automation and free time and a far slighter role played by work and labor. This would correspond to the nature of the worries formulated by these three sociologists: Durkheim's by anomie, Weber's by the cost of rationalization, bureaucratization, the "disenchantment of the world," and Simmel's by the "socialization of the spirit," against which he insisted on its autonomy: unlike Durkheim's and Weber's worries, which come out of their time and are responses to it, Simmel's is one we shall yet have to face even in a "postindustrial" society. Among the many expressions of his insistence on the autonomy of the spirit may also be his conception of society: it is characteristic that he did not formally distinguish it from "group" (he left its boundaries undefined) and that he wavered between including and excluding the interacting individuals (cf. Wolff, 1950, pp. XXXVI–XXXVII). His indecision on such questions not only calls for—understandable—criticism but may also suggest that the vagueness of the boundaries of society around and within the individual is an intuition of a future form of society that is yet fully to develop.

## BIBLIOGRAPHY

Gassen, Kurt (1958) (Georg Simmel-Bibliographie," pp. 309–365 in Gassen and Landman, 1958. (Contains books, papers, translations, courses and seminars by Simmel; literature on Simmel, the latter reprinted in Wolff, 1959a, pp. 357–375.)

Wolff, Kurt H. (1959b), "Bibliography of Simmel's Books in German and His Writings Which Are Available in English," pp. 377–382 in Wolff, 1959a.

## References to Simmel's Writings

n. d.  *Anfang einer unvollendeten Selbstdarstellung*, pp. 9–10 in Gassen and Landmann, 1958.

1882  "Psychologische und ethnologische Studien über Musik," *Zeitschrift für Völkerpsychologie und Sprachwissenschaft*, 13:261–305.

1890  *Über soziale Differenzierung. Soziologische und psychologische Untersuchungen* (Leipzig: Duncker & Humblot).

1892  *Die Probleme der Geschichtsphilosophie. Eine erkenntnistheoretische Studie* (Leipzig: Duncker & Humblot).

1892–93  *Einleitung in die Moralwissenschaft. Eine Kritik der ethischen Grundbegriffe*. 2 vols. (Berlin: Hertz).

1900  *Philosophie des Geldes*, (Leipzig: Duncker & Humblot).

1903  "Die Grossstädte und das Geistesleben," pp. 185–206 in *Die Grossstadt* [Dresden: v. Zahn & Jaensch (Jahrbuch der Gehe-Stiftung zu Dresden, Band IX)]. (Translated by H. H. Gerth and C. Wright Mills as "The Metropolis and Mental Life" in Simmel, 1950, pp. 409–424).

1904  *Kant. 16 Vorlesungen - gehalten an der Berliner Universität* (Leipzig: Duncker & Humblot).

1906a  *Kant und Goethe* [Berlin: Bard, Marquardt (Die Kultur, 10)].

1906b  *Die Religion* [Frankfurt a. Main: Literarische Anstalt Rütten und Loening (Die Gesellschaft, 2)]. (Translated as *Sociology of Religion* by Curt Rosenthal, introduction by Feliks Gross. New York: Philosophical Library, 1959).

1907  *Schopenhauer und Nietzsche. Ein Vortragszyklus* (Leipzig: Duncker & Humblot).

1908  *Soziologie. Untersuchungen über die Formen der Vergesellschaftung.* (Leipzig: Duncker & Humblot). (For content see text above. Translations of Chapter I in Wolff, 1959a, of II, III, V, and of parts of VII, VIII, IX in Simmel, 1950, of IV, V in Simmel, 1955; for translations of earlier and shorter drafts of some of these and other portions see Wolff, 1950, pp. LXI–LXIII.)

1910  *Hauptprobleme der Philosophie* [Leipzig: Göschen (Sammlung Göschen, 500)].

1911  *Philosophische Kultur. Gesammelte Essais.* (Leipzig: W. Klinkhardt). (Contains essays on the adventure [translated in Wolff, 1959a]; Fashion [translated, not literally, in *International Quarterly*, 10 (1905)]; The Relative and the Absolute in the Problem of the Sexes; Coquetry; The Handle [translated in Wolff, 1959a]; The Ruin [ditto]; The Alps; Michelangelo; Rodin; The Personality of God; The Problem of the Religious Situation; The Idea and the Tragedy of Culture [1911–12]; feminine culture.)

1911–1912  "Der Begriff und die Tragödie der Kultur," *Logos*, 2:1–25.

1913  *Goethe* (Leipzig: Klinkhardt & Biermann).

1916a  *Das Problem der historischen Zeit.* [Berlin: Reuther & Reichard (Philosophische Vorträge. Veröffentlicht von der Kant-Gesellschaft, 12)].

1916b  *Rembrandt. Ein kunstphilosophischer Versuch* (Leipzig: Kurt Wolff).

1917   *Grundfragen der Soziologie (Individuum und Gesellschaft).* [Berlin und Leipzig: Göschen (Sammlung Göschen, 101)]. (Translated by Kurt H. Wolff in Simmel, 1950, pp. 1–84.)

1918a   *Der Konflikt der modernen Kultur. Ein Vortrag* (München und Leipzig: Duncker & Humblot).

1918b   *Lebensanschauung. Vier metaphysische Kapitel* (München und Leipzig: Duncker & Humblot).

1918c   *Vom Wesen des historischen Verstehens* [Berlin: Mittler (Geschichtliche Abende im Zentralinstitut für Erziehung und Unterricht)].

1922   *Zur Philosophie der Kunst. Philosophische und kunstphilosophische Aufsätze.* Edited by Gertrud Simmel (Potsdam: Kipenheuer). (Contains essays on Böcklin's landscapes; Rome; Stefan George; The Picture Frame; Lionardo da Vinci's *Last Supper*; Florence; Venice; Stefan George's *Der siebente Ring*; L'art pour l'art; Caricature; The Problem of the Portrait; On a Relation Between the Theory of Selection and Epistemology; Bergson; "Become What You Are"; Historical Time [1916a]; Frankfurt University.)

1923   *Fragmente und Aufsätze aus dem Nachlass und Veröffentlichungen der letzten Jahre.* Edited by Gertrud Kantorowicz (München: Dei Masken). (Contains excerpts from Simmel's diary; A Fragment on Love; Essays on the Platonic and Modern Eros; On Historical Formation; On Lawfulness in the Work of Art; On the Philosophy of the Actor; On the Problem of Naturalism.)

1950   *The Sociology of Georg Simmel* (Translated, edited, and with an introduction by Kurt H. Wolff. Glencoe, Illinois: Free Press).

1955   *Conflict* (translated by Kurt H. Wolff); *The Web of Group Affiliations* (translated by Reinhard Bendix); foreword by Everett Cherrington Hughes (Glencoe, Illinois: Free Press).

1957   *Brücke und Tür. Essays des Philosophen zur Geschichte, Religion, Kunst und Gesellschaft.* Edited, together with Margarete Susman, by Michael Landmann (Stuttgart: K. F. Kœhler). (Contains essays on Bridge and Door; The Problem of Fate; Love; Death; History of Philosophy; Historical Time [1916a]; Historical Understanding [1918c]; The Nature of Culture; The Future of Culture; Change of Cultural Forms; Epistemology of Religion; Fundamental Religious Thoughts and Modern Science; The Salvation of the Soul; Christianity and Art; The Landscape; The Face [translated in Wolff, 1959a]; Germanic and Classic-Romanesque Style; The Actor; Nietzsche and Kant; Goethe and Youth; Sociological Æsthetics; The Field of Sociology [from 1917, Chapter I]; The Metropolis and Mental Life [1903]; the Sociology of the Meal; Individualism; The Individual and Freedom; also Aphorisms.)

1959   *The Problem of Sociology.* (Translation of 1908, Chapter I, by Kurt H. Wolff, pp. 310–336 in Wolff, 1959a).

### Other References

Coser, Lewis A. (1956). *The Functions of Social Conflict* (Glencoe, Illinois: Free Press).

Etzkorn, K. Peter (1964), "Georg Simmel and the Sociology of Music," *Social Forces*, 43:101–107.

Frischeisen-Köhler, Max (1920) "Georg Simmel," *Kant-Studien*, 24:1–51.

Gassen, Kurt, and Michael Landmann (Eds.) (1958), *Buch des Dankes an Georg Simmel: Briefe, Erinnerungen, Bibliographie* (Berlin: Duncker & Humblot).

Honigsheim, Paul (1953), "Simmel, Georg," pp. 270–272 in *Handwörterbuch der Sozialwissenschaften*, 4. Lieferung, I, 3. [Stuttgart: Gustav Fischer; Tübingen: J. C. B. Mohr (Paul Siebeck); Göttingen: Vandenhoeck & Ruprecht].

Kantorowicz, Gertrud (1923), "Vorwort," pp. V–X in Simmel, 1923.

Landmann, Michael (1957), "Einleitung," pp. V–XXIII in Simmel, 1957.

Levine, Donald N. (1959), "The Structure of Simmel's Social Thought," pp. 9–32 in Wolff, 1959a.

Lipman, Matthew (1959), "Some Aspects of Simmel's Conception of the Individual," pp. 119–138 in Wolff, 1959a.

Mandelbaum, Maurice (1938), *The Problem of Historical Knowledge: An Answer to Relativism* (New York: Liveright).

Schutz, Alfred (1945), "On Multiple Realities," *Philosophy and Phenomenological Research, 5* (June): 533–576. (Reprinted on pages 207–259 in *Collected Papers. I. The Problem of Social Reality*. Edited and introduced by Maurice Natanson. The Hague: Martinus Nijhoff, 1962.)

Simmel Gertrud (1928), "Aus Georg Simmels nachgelassener Mappe 'Metaphysik,' " pp. 221–226 in *Aus unbekannten Schriften. Festgabe für Martin Buber zum 50. Geburtstag* (Berlin: Lambert Schneider).

Susman, Margarete (1957), "Erinnerungen an Georg Simmel," pp. 278–291 in Gassen and Landmann, 1958.

Susman, Margarete (1959), *Die geistige Gestalt Georg Simmels* [Tübingen: J. C. B. Mohr (Paul Siebeck) (Schriftenreihe wissenschaftlicher Abhandlungen des Leo Bæck Institute of Jews from Germany, 3)].

Tenbruck, Friedrich H. (1958) "Georg Simmel (1858–1918)," *Kölner Zeitschrift für Soziologie und Sozialpsychologie*, 10:587–614.

Tenbruck, Friedrich H. (1959), "Formal Sociology," pp. 61–99 in Wolff, 1959a.

Utitz, Emil (1920), "Simmel und die Philosophie der Kunst," *Zeitschrift für Aesthetik und allgemeine Kunstwissenschaft*, 14:1–41.

Weingartner, Rudolph H. (1959), "Form and Content in Simmel's Philosophy of Life," pp. 33–60 in Wolff, 1959a.

Weingartner, Rudolph H. (1962), *Experience and Culture: The Philosophy of Georg Simmel* (Middletown, Connecticut: Wesleyan University Press).

Wolff, Kurt H. (1959a), *Georg Simmel, 1858–1918: A Collection of Essays, with Translations and a Bibliography* (Columbus: Ohio State University Press). (Contains preface, Kantorowicz, 1923; Levine, 1959; Weingartner, 1959; Tenbruck, 1959; Hugh Dalziel Duncan, "Simmel's Image of Society"; Lipman, 1959; E. V. Walter, "Simmel's Sociology of Power"; Paul Honigsheim, "The Time and Thought of the Young Simmel," and "A Note on Simmel's Anthropological Interests"; Heinz Maus, "Simmel in German Sociology"; Masamichi Shimmei, "Georg Simmel's Influence on Japanese Thought"; Howard Becker, "On Simmel's *Philosophy of Money;*" Arthur Salz, "A

Note from a Student of Simmel's"; translations: "The Adventure," "The Ruin," "The Handle" [all from Simmel, 1911]; "The Æsthetic Significance of the Face" [from Simmel, 1957]; "On the Nature of Philosophy" [Simmel, 1910, Chapter I]; "The Problem of Sociology" and "How Is Society Possible?" [Simmel, 1908, Chapter I]; bibliographies [cf. above].)

---

Reprinted from *Praxis* (1968), 3–4: 404–414, by permission of the publisher. The essay has been edited and partially revised by the author.

# II

## THREE OVERVIEWS AND
## A SURVEY
### *Supplemented by Recollection*

*In memory of my brother, his wife, and their son*
*Hanns, Lulu, and Uli*

At first reading perhaps some of the papers in Part II will seem uncon-
nected. A relation may be apparent between the first two, Chapters 4 and
5, on social control and social change, but if the title of this part suggests
that, in addition to their customary or indeed topical affinity, they are
"overviews" (of the pertinent literature), a connection between them and
the third paper, Chapter 6, "An Elementary Syllabus in the Sociology of
the Jews," may also emerge. All three, predominantly didactic, attempt
to introduce the student to the subject matter with which they deal.
Chapter 6 is related to the remaining two: all three treat of the Jews.
Chapter 7, "Traditionalists and Assimilationists: A Sample Study of the
Jewish Population in Dallas, Texas," is a traditional population survey.
With it and the preceding chapter—both sober exercises—I contrast a
quite different essay on the Jews, " 'Exercise in Commemoration' " (Chapter 8). The topic is one with the two chapters it follows, but it is neither
a summary of literature nor a survey but a much more unconditional effort
to comprehend the Nazi holocaust. It is a reminder—a *recordatio*—to the
sociologist, as well as to myself, to those who listened to the original
delivery, and to its readers in published form. It is less sociology than raw
material for it—some of it tragically so.

On rereading this introduction to Part II (what you have just read and what is to follow), I did not react as I did to Part I. It is slightly less autobiographical, and we are beginning to get into the work, which is the main concern; that is to say, we are moving from the empirical, idiosyncratic self (which I also am) to the self as defined by its product— the self that is related to what I came much later to refer to as the transcendental subject.

The limits of Chapter 4, "Social Control," written for Joseph S. Roucek's *Contemporary Sociology* (1958), are defined in the initial paragraph. I have become far more aware now than I was then how restrictive these limits are, how it might well be argued that the really illuminating statements on social control are found not so much under its literal heading as in the literature on politics, economics, or psychoanalysis. Although I thought so then, if less decisively, I found myself incompetent to do justice to this larger and more difficult task and instead tried to present and assess, not without misgivings over what I found (alleviated by a shade of malicious triumph), the efforts that had been made under the title social control itself. This paper bears witness, especially in its first section, to perhaps an all too earnest diligence, but it does take sides and ends critically, in which it resembles the papers reprinted as Part IV, "Sociology." [I note here, that I wrote a much shorter article on social control, which, although similarly limited to explicit literature, is not restricted to the period covered in the larger one reprinted (1) as Chapter 4].

Chapter 5, "Some Considerations Preliminary to the Study of Social Change," was written in 1963 as a lecture I gave in several European countries under a Fulbright grant (University of Rome). It is only in part a survey of the relevant literature; indeed, far more outspoken than the paper on social control, its main thrust is its preoccupation with our time and with a conception not of the study of social change alone but of sociology as a whole. This preoccupation generally pervades most of my papers from the 1960s on (and some even before, for example, Chapter 9; it should be remembered that in this volume the chapters are not arranged in strict chronological order). The last two footnotes in Chapter 5 make reference to essays in which I discussed more fully some problems only alluded to here [two kinds of knowledge and truth and their relation (see Chapters 29 and 15) and theory and practice, especially in respect to differences between sociology and historiography (Chapter 17)]. To explain the "we" I use, "not as a *pluralis maestatis* but as the subject of a collective enterprise," I anticipate a relation between writer and reader that is more clearly discernible in subsequent writings and practiced most explicitly in Chapter 30 ("Ernst Grünwald and the Sociology of Knowledge: A Collective Venture in Interpretation"). Further-more, the paper shows me, equipped with American acquisitions, return-ing to my European background; I re-embrace my European origin, as I do again in most of the papers written since the early sixties. In this together, perhaps, they constitute a variant of the "commemoration" of Chapter 8. Finally there is the first anticipation (in the sequence of this volume) of an idea essential to "surrender." This is the definition of the truth criterion of "existential knowledge" as "agreement with the result of the most rigorously imaginable intrasubjective examination of the student's most important *experiences*"—the knowledge and truth attained in surrender.

The genesis of Chapter 6, "An Elementary Syllabus in the Sociology of the Jews," is indicated in its title note. It represents the most didactic paper I have ever written—even more apparent than "Social Control" and far more than the essay on social change. Although many of its references might well be updated (it also precedes the independence of Israel and India), the three aspects on which it focuses—numbers, the question of race, and antisemitism—still strike me as essential to a soci-ological study of the Jews. The "Elementary Syllabus" still appears useful to me, especially if some of the suggestions contained in the notes are followed, not only as an introduction to the topic but also as an opportunity to add to one's knowledge in an orderly fashion, which I find as relevant now as I did then. In addition to some of its references (or at least their dates), however, I also consider the optimistic tone of the last section, "A Possible Policy Regarding Antisemitism," obsolete, that is, historically inadequate. It relies on increased understanding (presum-ably by education and group work) and on "the elimination" of eco-nomic, technological, and moral causes of frustration by participation in democracy. It should be remembered (as indicated in the title note) that it was written during World War II, and the optimism, which now might strike some readers as frivolous or even stupid, exhibits the hope, far more than I was aware of at the time, that the defeat of nazism and fascism would result in the spread of democracy. Still, the statistics pre-sented are as correct and as worth knowing or tracing today as they were then, nor have other points been invalidated by what has happened since the article was written.

Chapter 7, "Traditionalists and Assimilationists: A Sample Study of the Jewish Population in Dallas, Texas," goes back again to my begin-nings at Southern Methodist. For some time Walter T. Watson had been interested in minorities, especially those in Dallas. He suggested that I do a study of the Jews for possible publication in *Studies in Sociology*, a journal he had started to promote research—above all by his students—

that perpetuated the tradition of the Chicago School, in which he himself
had been formed. His influence is conspicuous also in the finished product. I remember his suggesting that I start out with a portrait of the
"typical," that is, the statistically average, Dallas Jew, which would
alleviate the monotony of the subsequent statistics. Nevertheless, he, and
I wholeheartedly with him, considered the statistical data the sine qua
non of the enterprise (they may have some use now, more than thirty
years later, as historical source material). At the time, a novice to American sociology, I was eager to get the figures I needed, but I experienced
some of the difficulties in collecting statistics on Jews, referred to in the
"Syllabus" (especially at the end of n. 2) and I more nearly guessed at a
total Jewish population in Dallas of 9000. Only on rereading Chapters
6 and 7 did I realize that in Chapter 6 I had flatly indicated the (1937)
figure as 10,400 (Table 4). Despite the dry, unexciting nature of the
work, I was implored by one or two "assimilationists," among them,
probably, the woman quoted in the study, not to undertake it, which
circumstance contributed to the formulation of the first of the "elements
characterizing the group to which this informant [for, of course, she was
one, even if against her will] belongs"—the "fear of drawing too much
attention to the Jews." (I remember I entertained the idea of writing a
paper on the inescapability of sociology.) I did the survey three or four
years before I wrote the "Syllabus," a few months after the outbreak of
World War II; fear and uncertainty concerning the fate of the Jews were
felt everywhere by the persons I interviewed, although almost certainly
none of them, and surely not I, could imagine the enormities to come.
We all lived in a dream, even though we sometimes had nightmares.

The nightmares, or nightmare, are what Chapter 8, " 'Exercise in Commemoration,' " tries to exorcise. A few months after I joined Brandeis
University (1959), a number of students asked me to speak at chapel
(April 25, 1960) on the accasion of the anniversary of the Warsaw ghetto
uprising. On such an occasion, however, I wanted to speak out about
what I knew, not about something I had not experienced myself. Thus
the speech did not follow the assigned topic: it is an outcry that does not
ask how it might be classified by type of communication, let alone discipline. It is both too personal and too universal for that, and meets the
occasion, I think, only to the extent that it is precisely so.

1.  In Julius Gould and William L. Kalb, Eds., *A Dictionary of the Social Sciences*
(New York: Free Press [for UNESCO], 1964). I have also written articles of
this kind: "Cultural Lag" and "Definition of the Situation," *ibid.*; "Cultural
Lag," "Definition der Situation," "Soziale Kontrolle (Social Control)," and "Wis-

senssoziologie, II. Vereinigte Staaten," in Wilhelm Bernsdorf et al., Eds., *Wörterbuch der Soziologie*, 2nd rev. ed. (Stuttgart: Enke, 1969), and articles on American contributors to the sociology of knowledge (Bernard Barber, Howard Becker, Arthur Child, Gerard DeGré, Frank E. Hartung, Virgil G. Hinshaw, Thelma Z. Lavine, Robert K. Merton, C. Wright Mills, Talcott Parsons, Pitirim A. Sorokin, Louis Wirth, Edgar Zilsel) in Wilhelm Bernsdorf, Ed., *Internationales Soziologenlexikon* (Stuttgart: Enke, 1959). (See also Chapter 31.)

# 4

# SOCIAL CONTROL. 1958

This chapter is concerned with explicit concepts of social control used or developed in the United States since 1945. It does not consider post-war studies of what on some grounds may be argued to be the workings of social controls, especially in contemporary American society [1], and it does not discuss trends in postwar sociology that could profitably be analyzed with reference to concepts of social control contained in or exemplified by them [2].

## TRADITIONAL USES OF SOCIAL CONTROL

A third type of literature—studies of rather miscellaneous matters designated as social controls—is as voluminous as the application of the term has been prolific and variegated ever since Edward Alsworth Ross introduced it in the 1890's [3]. Although likewise tangential to this chapter, it serves to highlight its focus and is therefore quickly surveyed.

The sixty-odd years during which the concept of social control has been in use show, almost of necessity, some modifications and shifts in accent; yet the bulk of the literature even in the last decade can hardly be argued to transcend Ross or other founders of American sociology, notably Cooley and Sumner, either in removing ambiguities inherent in the early treatments or in proposing new concepts. To suggest its nature and scope and to show its traditional character it is briefly indicated as it appears in sociological journals, in introductory, and in social-control textbooks.

*Periodical Literature.* Aside from a few general considerations of social control problems [4], the concept of social control or rough equivalents have been applied to many different subject matters which are no more related to one another than are any portions of the field of sociology. Among them (in alphabetical order) are communication [5], community [6], drug addiction [7], economy (including industry and labor) [8], fashion [9], humor [10], law [11], mental illness [12], military life [13], nonliterate peoples [14], philanthropy [15], political apathy [16], race relations [17], religion [18], small colleges [19], social types [20], and war, particularly World War II [21].

*Introductory Sociology Textbooks.* Some of the postwar introductory textbooks which contain no, or only incidental, treatment of social control are (in chronological order) those by Hiller, Sorokin, Bennett-Tumin, Davis, Ogburn-Nimkoff, McCormick, Lundberg-Schrag-Larsen, Biesanz, Cuber, and Green [22]. Among recent readers in introductory or general sociology which do fall in this category are those by Wilson-Kolb, O'Brien-Schrag-Martin, Schuler-Gibson-Fiero-Brookover, Freedman-Hawley-Landecker-Miner, and Davis-Bredemeier-Levy [23].

The authors of these works apparently find it possible to present an overview of sociology—its principles, social science, social life, society, social relations, or, in the case of Davis-Bredemeier-Levy, American society—without or only casually using the concept of social control. Instead they operate with such ideas as norms (Hiller, Davis, and Cuber), normative integration (Freedman et al.), integration (Sorokin), social order and sanctions (Bennett-Tumin) or order in society (Green), and social organization (McCormick); they treat social control in a discussion of group life and man's adjustment to culture (Ogburn-Nimkoff), deviant behavior (Lundberg et al.), or roles, social relations, culture, political organization, and types of society (Wilson-Kolb); and in the predominantly descriptive (Schuler et al., Davis et al.) or methodologically oriented (O'Brien et al.) readers in this group a focus on social control or on any of its alternatives or substitutes is either highly selective or altogether absent.

On the other hand, the concept is given conspicuous treatment in introductory and similar textbooks (again in chronological order) by Lee, MacIver-Page, Roucek-Warren, Bogardus, Biesanz, Hertzler, Broom-Selznick, Burma-DePoister, Queen-Chambers-Winston, Rose, Sutherland-Woodward-Maxwell, and Koenig-Hopper-Gross [24]. Everett C. Hughes (in Lee) discusses it under the heads of formal, informal, and institutional controls, social sanctions, institutional policy, and propaganda in which the "fundamental concepts" are those of folkways, mores, and public opinion; Hughes is thus continuing the Park-Burgess tradition [25]. MacIver-Page analyze codes and sanctions: loyalty, authority, leadership, ritual and ceremony, coercion and organized force, and utopian communities as experiments in social control. Roucek-Warren distinguish between informal and formal, primary and secondary groups, regulative and suggestive and external and internalized social controls, and comment on institutions, public opinion, and social movements. Bogardus' chapter contains a treatment of "control by art." Hertzler deals with unconscious and conscious, group, situational, noninstitutionalized, and institutionalized, negative and positive, exploitative, regulatory, and reorganizational controls and with force, dominance and submission, power, and authority. Queen et al., operating with a continuum from total social control to unlimited choice, discuss social controls in American society (family, education, religion, and other institutions and processes) and their internalization. Rose considers customs (common values and meanings), parental and other transmission of culture, rewards and punishments, positive formal social controls (e.g., income and power), law and penal sanctions, deliberate and nondeliberate informal sanctions (public esteem, gossip, ostracism, public opinion, and exclamations and gestures).

In succinct definitions MacIver-Page (p. 137) understand by "social control" "the way in which the entire social order coheres and maintains itself—how it operates as a whole, as a changing equilibrium"; Roucek-Warren (pp. 163, 263) describe it as "all processes by which society and its component groups influence the behavior of individual members toward conformity"; Biesanz (p. 64), "the means by which society establishes and maintains order"; Hertzler (p. 306), "the way social power and social influence *function* to regulate, direct, adjust, and organize the social conduct of individuals and groups"; Queen et al. (p. 28), "the regulation of the behavior of an individual by a group"; Rose (p. 58), "the ways in which people, as members of a society, influence one another" and (p. 567) "any means, or the sum total of means, by which a group influences or directs its individual members"; and Sutherland et al. (p. 369) identify a "form of social control" as "any social attitude, custom, or institution which modifies behavior in the direction of group unity" [26].

*Social-Control Textbooks.*   It took almost a quarter of a century after Ross for another textbook on social control to appear (Frederick E. Lumley, *Means of Social Control*, 1925). Three more were published in the 1930s (Jerome Dowd, *Control in Human Societies*, 1936; L. L. Bernard, *Social Control in Its Sociological Aspects*, 1939; and Landis, *Social Control: Social Organization and Disorganization in Process*, 1939), and one each in the forties (Roucek) and fifties to date (La Piere); the present decade also saw the revision of Landis and Roucek (both in 1956.) Post-

World-War-II textbook literature thus consists of four books—the two Roucek editions, the Landis revision, and LaPiere.

Roucek's original work [27], written by 27 contributors, has 30 chapters in five parts: Foundations, Institutions, Means and Techniques, Social Control and Public Opinion, and Contemporary Problems of Social Control. Despite minor changes and a strong topical orientation, the 1956 edition has not caught up with Stalin's death, altogether contains little on the Soviet Union, and shows only slight revisions in the treatment of the atomic bomb.

Landis's first edition was analyzed by Gurvitch in his critical survey of the field up to 1945 [28]. Although much more revised than Roucek's book, the basic outlook remains the same: a social-problems approach, if somewhat intensified, and the diagnosis that no substitute for the primary group has been found. The reiterated belief "that social control is the major problem of our time" (p. v) and the topical interest which this text shares with others, nonetheless have failed to result in the discussion of such topics as automation, the atom bomb, totalitarianism, or genocide.

Richard T. LaPiere, *A Theory of Social Control* (New York: McGraw-Hill, 1954), introduces a concept that would account for behavior that cannot be understood by reference to socialization or the actor's situation. This "third dimension of behavior" (pp. 64–65), social control, operates "on the basis of the individual's desire for social status, induces him to conform to group standards of conduct whatever his personal inclinations or situational temptations" (p. 325). Regard for status is universal. Its locus is the primary group, even when the larger group is a *Gesellschaft* ( pp. 19–24) [29], for the "status [-granting] group" exercises the more control over an individual member, all other factors remaining equal, the smaller it is, the longer it lasts, and the more often the members associate with one another (pp. 101–106). "Status groups cannot be defined in categorical terms" (p. 106), but some groupings—population categories, aggregations, assemblages, publics, institutional organizations—may safely be excluded. Despite their modern great variety, they fall into the few categories of work, community, recreational, and peer groups, and the many different methods by which their members try "to bring a deviant member into conformity to the group norms" are based on "a few universal principles or more properly, techniques" (p. 220), namely physical, economic, psychological, and ideological. A conceptual supplement to social control is countercontrol, which "results from the efforts, continually being made but rarely successful, of an individual to gain ascendancy over the other members of the group," or of a group or organization over another (p. 325). It would have helped if "control" and "countercontrol" had been compared with Ross's distinction between social and individual ascendancy (for Ross social control, it may be recalled, was one of two subdivisions of the former) and with various definitions of social control, among them several quoted in this chapter, which resemble the concept of countercontrol. The means of gaining individual ascendancy are force or intimidation, inducement, seduction, or trickery (classed together as autocratic control), and conviction, persuasion, and conversion (democratic control); conquest, that is, organizational ascendancy, may similarly be military, economic, or cultural. (In these discussions of countercontrol "counter" is usually dropped.) The final chapter, "Social Crisis, Demoralization, and Control," is written on the recognition that a "theory of social control would be incomplete without at least some acknowledgment of the fact that upon occasion the complex system of social control operating in any society may be disrupted and, indeed, temporarily suspended" (p. 523).

*A Comment on the Intellectual Status of Social Control.* This rapid survey suggests that like many other sociological concepts social control has neither a standardized area of application [30] nor a standardized referent. This range of its extension reflects decisions on, or between, dichotomies (such as intentional or conscious versus spontaneous or unconscious or personal versus impersonal, commented on by Gurvitch in respect to the pre-1945 literature [31]), as well as a variety of approaches, notably that which sees social control as a problem of social integration (positive: order, normative order, cohesion, etc.) as against one of constraint (negative: control of deviance) [32]. The confusions and uncertainties can be found in Ross's original treatment [33] which, along with their persistence, suggests the unexamined influence of extratheoretical factors on the field. Among these there may be the attractiveness of the word "control" against the feeling that it jars, at least semantically, with the tradition and profession of democracy; the faith in the automaticity of the order of our society against fears lest it be not secure but in need of controls to be enacted; the survival of trust in a *laissez-faire* harmony against temptation by planning, organizing, manipulating. At any rate, the largely nontheoretical, nontechnical nature of the concept may be related to the absence of social control from two more theoretical and technical types of sociological presentation: histories of social thought, social philosophy, and sociology itself [34] (except for occasional treatment in reference to particular thinkers), including the UNESCO survey of postwar American sociology [35] and two recent and important assessments of the social and behavioral sciences [36], and the annual reports of the American Sociological Society on "Current Sociological Research."

## NEWER APPROACHES TO SOCIAL CONTROL

The work presented in this section differs from the writings surveyed so far in that it is less tied to tradition, whether Ross's or Cooley's or one that is more diffuse. It consists of studies (in chronological order) by Gurvitch, Homans, Parsons, Skinner, Nadel, and Nett.

*Gurvitch* [37]. Gurvitch claims that a viable theory of social control must rid itself of the restrictions imposed on it by nineteenth-century sociology; that is, it must realize that social control is universal, not a matter of evolution or progress, that it advocates neither order nor progress, neither society nor the individual, and that kinds of social control are cultural phenomena, chief among which are religion (and magic), morality, law, art, knowledge, and education, that must be distinguished from agencies, which are social phenomena, namely social bonds (forms of sociability), groups, and inclusive societies. Social control is

> the whole of cultural patterns, social symbols, collective spiritual meanings, values, ideas and ideals, as well as acts and processes directly connected with them, whereby inclusive society, every particular group, and every participating individual member overcome tensions and conflicts within themselves through temporary equilibria and take steps for new creative efforts (p. 291; original in italics).

Gurvitch anticipates the objection that thus defined the study of social control is identical with the sociology of culture; he counters it by arguing that although the subject matters of the two disciplines are indeed the same, their approaches differ. Social control focuses on the interrelations of kinds, forms, and agencies of social control, whereas the sociology of culture ("sociology of human spirit") explores the "functional relationship of the ideational elements with the social conjunctures" (pp. 292–293) [38]. The forms of social control, then, are depth-levels or strata within each kind, namely, routine forms (cultural usages, patterns, rules, symbols, often organized, that is, standardized and stereotyped, hence exercising constraint and losing touch with the more spontaneous forms); the more spontaneous control through values, ideas, ideals; and "the even more spontaneous social control through direct collective experiences, aspirations, and creations, including revolts and revolutions" (p. 294; original in italics). Finally, "means" (or techniques or instruments) are numerous, variable, and not typically associated with kinds, forms, or agencies.

Gurvitch's conceptual scheme gains in clarity by acquaintance with some of his other work in sociology [39]. Whether for lack of such acquaintance or because the tradition out of which Gurvitch's sociology develops is French rather than American [40] or because of weaknesses intrinsic to his conception of social control, it has not, as far as could be ascertained, been analyzed in the American literature in the field [41]. As the theoretically most relevant reason for this failure it could be argued that Gurvitch has actually laid out a scheme for the sociology of culture, if not for general sociology, and has merely called it one for social control; there is good evidence that he has done so. If so, it may suggest that social control was considered an acceptable or necessary topic in a survey of twentieth-century sociology as it was undertaken in 1945; and the observations reported at the end of the preceding section may indicate that such a view has since changed. Aside from these extrinsic comments, an intrinsic analysis of Gurvitch's conception of social control might well show that his "social control" has no part in his "sociology of culture."

*Homans* [42]. The task Homans has set for himself in *The Human Group* is the development of a theory of small groups. He proceeds by collating observations made by "a few able students of social behavior" (p. 442) [43] and deriving from them systems of interrelated, generalizing, analytical hypotheses. One of these systems emerges on such questions as "What makes custom customary?" (p. 311), "Why does structure persist?" (p. 282), "How and why do the members of a group comply with the group norms or obey the orders of the group leader" (p. 281)? The answer is what Homans proposes to mean by social control.

> 1.  Control is the process by which, if a man departs from his existing degree of obedience to a norm, his behavior is brought back toward that degree, or would be brought back if he did depart. The remaining statements hold for both actual and virtual departures.
>
> 2.  There is nothing new about control, no separate element that we have not already found coming into social organization (p. 301).

In other words, social control and social organization are not different subject matters; rather, the former is an aspect that emerges if the latter is approached with the above questions.

> 3.  The separate controls [that is, the relations between a man's disobedience to a norm and the various consequences

of that disobedience (p. 295)] are nothing more than the old relations of mutual dependence [among norms, activities, sentiments, and interaction (p. 288)] taken differentially.

4. Control as a whole is effective insofar as an individual's departure from an existing degree of obedience to a norm activates not one but many separate controls (p. 301). The effects are, so to speak, out of proportion to the cause. A departure from the existing level of activity may have consequences for a man's materials gains . . . for his interaction with others, and for his social rank, because his activity is related to all of these things and not one only (p. 449).

5. That is, any departure activates the system of relations so as to reduce future departures.

6. Punishment does not necessarily produce control [but may vindicate the violated norm and bring the group to the point where the offense occurred; cf. pp. 308–311]. The state of a social system in which control is effective [in which, e.g., punishment produces control] we shall call a state of equilibrium of a system (p. 301). [That is, a state in which] not all conceivable states of the system can be actual states (p. 312).

The control inherent in the external system—the state of the elements of group behavior (sentiment, activity, interaction) and of their interrelations considered from the standpoint of the group's survival in its environment (cf. p. 90)—is based on individual self-interest and is thus automatic (p. 286); but there is also control based on sentiment; and control constituted by "the mutual dependence between social rank and performance in a certain activity" (p. 288). Control may be described "in the language of reward and punishment" or of "distribution of goods," tangible and intangible (cf. p. 294). Further, there is the distinction between formal or external control, by which Homans seems to refer to control exercised by agencies other than the actor, and informal or internal control, which appears to denote internalized controls (cf. p. 284). This distinction is related to similar dichotomies found in social-control literature, including "law" versus "mos." Authority in Homans' scheme is limited to a relation between group leader and member, namely the member's acceptance of an order given by the leader (p. 418).

Homan's theory of social control is systematic not only in the sense of being developed in an orderly procession of self-conscious methodological steps but also in the very different sense of undertaking the construction of a social system from its elements, their interrelations, and, to some extent, the interaction between the system and its environment. In Homans' own view the greatest weakness of his theory in general is that it has not yet reached the stage at which values can be assigned to its variables (cf. pp. 444 ff). Yet in respect to social control, and perhaps other concepts as well, a conceptual analysis may be necessary before such a quantifying phase can be aimed at, for it could be that social control is not a necessary element in Homans' conceptual scheme. If this should turn out to be the case, social control would have to be reformulated as such an element or it would have to be shown why it should stay what it wholly or in part seems to be at the present stage of development, namely, more an adjunct pragmatically justified on methodological and substantive grounds than an element arrived at by logical or empirical explication of the other elements of the system. Such an analysis might be made by logical and methodological investigations and by inquiry into the sociological and historical nature of Homans' undertaking.

*Parsons* [44].   Parsons' major treatment of social control is found in *The Social System*. The concept complements that of deviance. From the standpoint of the actor deviance is behavior in violation of a norm; social control, the actor's (and his interactor's) motivation to counteract such behavior. From the standpoint of the interactive system deviance is disequilibrating behavior and social control the complex of forces resulting in re-equilibration. Ego (an actor in an interactive system) is motivated to deviant behavior when alter (with whom ego interacts) frustrates ego's expectation of him. This results in various solutions constituting either re-equilibration by a change in the system, restoration of its former state, or compromise. Compromise refers to an ambivalence in ego's attitudes (need-disposition), affects (cathexis), or value orientation. It has a negative (alienative) and a positive (conformative) component. The domination of the latter results in compulsive conformity; inversely, in compulsive alienation. Deviant orientation must also be differentiated in regard to activity (the actor's taking more initiative than he is expected to) and passivity (taking less). A third differentiation is between ego's orientation toward alter as a person (social object) and his orientation toward the normative pattern. These three differentiations result in an eightfold typology of deviant behavior (*ibid.*, p. 259, Table 4). The discussion of their social structure follows the analysis of deviance from the standpoint of the foci of strain inhering in the normative patterns of the social system, from the angle of the sanctions connected with it, and from that of role conflict in relation to deviance (a disturbance in the order of allocations of ego's roles resulting from ego's deviant motivation or from conflicting role expectations in the social system itself).

Social control, with its preventive and re-equilibrating aspects, begins in socialization and displays its "most fundamental mechanisms . . . in the normal processes of interaction" (p. 301) and "in the institutional integration of motivation and the reciprocal reinforcement of the attitudes and actions of the different individual actors involved in an institutionalized social structure" (p. 302). Only the breakdown of ordinary social controls calls for more specialized and elaborate mechanisms, among which Parsons discusses two, ritual and secondary institutions. Ritual, conspicuous in the fields of religion and magic, health and bereavement, is characterized by permissiveness, the opportunity to "act out" tensions accompanying strains, and by support, which emphasizes the concern of the group with the situation. The "American youth culture," Parsons' example of a secondary institution, also exhibits permissiveness, functions as a safety valve, shows its own integration with major institutional structures (especially through formal education), and is self-liquidating (youths becoming adults). Secondary institutions raise the question of the functional significance to society of certain instances of malintegration which produce such phenomena as religious toleration, limitations on formal controls and status rankings, tact, anonymity, and the segregation of activities and population elements. They gain this functional significance from two processes that are at work in them: "insulation" and "isolation." The former localizes potentially conflicting elements; the latter forestalls the structuring, the spread of which insulation would check—reaction to illness roughly illustrates the first, reaction to criminality, the second. The analysis of illness, particularly the physician's role, applies to that of the mechanisms of social control in general. They exhibit support (by which some characteristics of deviance can be reconnected with institutionalized values), permissiveness (e.g., encouraging confession, channeling the expression of grievances, guaranteeing anonymity), and the refusal to reciprocate deviant expectations [45].

It can hardly be doubted that Parsons' treatment of social control is the most comprehensive and systematic (in both senses of the term used in the comment on Homans) that has been achieved so far. Despite its importance, however, it raises serious problems, only one complex of which can be mentioned here. It may be introduced by pointing to the unclarity of the relationship between two types of social control, the first inherent in the social system, the other (social controls) appearing when the first breaks down. Inasmuch as the first develops in the process of socialization, its failure must result from socialization that is inadequate, especially in respect to its forestalling or preventive features. The implication seems to be that adequate socialization would obviate the need for social controls. On this view Parsons appears to postulate, by implication, an adjustive individual [46] or to have a concept dominated by the image of this type of individual at the neglect of society [47] and culture (which, along with personality, are the three "systems" he has set himself the task of connecting in a unified theory). To say this may be to specify Clark's contention that his theory is psychological rather than sociological [48], for which comment it is further relevant to note that neither power nor force (coercion) figures in Parsons' treatment of social control: power is not mentioned at all; force is mentioned twice, once emphatically as a psychological concept (pp. 277–278), again in discussing the treatment of the criminal, clearly as a matter that has no corresponding element in his conceptual scheme (p. 312). Coser [49] has called attention to the relative absence of a third pre-eminently sociological concept, that is, conflict, from Parsons' work as a whole; he characterizes this work as "an extended commentary on the Hobbesian question: How is social order possible?" [50]. Conflict tends to be replaced by such psychologically oriented terms as tension, "strain, sickness [51], and the increasing importance of the therapeutic paradigm in the Parsonian treatment of social control itself has been noted. It could be that Parsons exhibits a tendency, characteristic of recent Western, particularly American, culture generally, namely, to find the examination of the individual more acceptable than that of society. Among many manifestations of this tendency is the widespread interest in psychology, especially psychoanalysis, as against the insulated status (to borrow one of Parsons' terms) of the sociology of knowledge with its analysis of society [52].

*Skinner* [53]. Skinner's discussion of control is part of his attempt at outlining a "science of human behavior." It is developed in two stages. The first, an analysis of controlling agencies (government and law, religion, psychotherapy, economic control, and education), is introduced by a short chapter on group control and leads to the second, the crux of the matter, the control of human behavior on the whole. Much more explicitly than the three authors previously discussed in this section, Skinner conceives of his undertaking in its relevance to our time (cf., especially, Chapter I, "Can Science Help?") [54] and thus is pushed beyond analysis into advocacy and faced with such problems as the possibility of scientific value judgments (pp. 428–430), of a scientific ethic (pp. 328–329), of a scientific answer to the questions what culture should be "designed" (pp. 426–428) and who should control (pp. 445–446). His answer to these questions is in terms of survival, an evolutionary practice only recently and, in an important sense, misleadingly formulated as a value (p. 433). If this is accepted—whereby Skinner himself insists on the difficulties of assessing the survival value of cultural practices (pp. 434–436)—the question "Who should control?" becomes "Who *will* control in the group that does survive?" (p. 446), and the answer to it is the probability that "the most reliable estimates [made by a science of behavior] of the survival value of cultural practices" furnish the basis for the most effective control. This does not mean, however, that scientists will be the controllers; only that science can "supply a description of the kind of process of which it itself is an example" (*ibid.*).

> If a science of behavior can discover those conditions of life which make for the ultimate strength of men, it may provide a set of "moral values" which, because they are independent of the history and culture of any group, may be generally accepted (p. 445).

We thus envisage "a possible safeguard against despotism" (p. 443), for instead of condemning a government that slaughters or enslaves a captured population as wrong or contrary to the dignity of man (thus acting on notions not "independent of the history and culture of any group") it is possible to condemn it as eventually weakening the government itself and reducing the effectiveness of the enslaved (pp. 444–445). Yet, again, science is not justified in setting up a group or state over the individual, or vice versa, for these are "segments in a continuous series of events," and scientific interpretation "must eventually apply" "to the whole series" (p. 449).

Only a commitment to ignore the valuational character of such a position and not to examine its consequences permits one to call it, as Skinner does, the result of scientific analysis and to anticipate its distastefulness "to most of those who have been strongly affected by democratic philosophies" (*ibid.*). This anticipation is one of the consequences of the position that Skinner has selected for emphasis on no plausible theoretical grounds but on the basis on which his whole book is built, namely, relevance to our time (including people, among them those commented on). Yet this time disappears before an evolutionary and allegedly scientific "ultimate" ("survival value," p. 449; "strength of man," p. 445), and science becomes formalistic, loses its subject matter, and turns into scientism.

*Nadel* [55]. As the title of Nadel's paper indicates, its major emphasis is the distinction between social control and self-regulation. This distinction is suggested by the fact that a society may keep its orderliness and culture even though such specific controls as legal sanctions, procedures of enforcement, and formalized apportionments of rewards and punishments are weakened. It is thus seen to be, in some measure, self-sustaining. Indeed, if it were not, it would need controls in an infinite regression—controls of legal sanctions, controls of these controls, etc. [56]. Instead there are true elements of self-regulation, namely, the conditions under which traditional behavior (in Max Weber's meaning) is desirable, good, and a safe and known routine. We do find that in primitive societies the most important behaviors have the weakest specific controls: those that occupy a focal position in an "instrumental nexus" and are stated to be most important by the actors (who attach value to them) [57]. "Instrumentality" in respect to an action refers to the appropriateness of a means to an end, and an appropriate means not only tends to become routinized but, in primitive more than in other societies, is sanctified as well. Because socially approved behavior thus is at once instrumental and valuable, deviation from it provokes penalization (demonstrable failure and irreparable guilt over the violation of the internalized norm) rather than punishment (following a redeemable sin). Instrumentality and value (value referring to classes of ideologically founded objects held to be intrinsically worthwhile) tend to differentiate with the separation of social roles, the specialization of offices and tasks, and, indirectly, the size of the group—that, is, with increasing civilization.

Every act that follows a prescribed norm demonstrates the norm's validity as much as explicit assertion or teaching does [58]. This "circularity" parallels the feedback in physical systems: output, that is, conduct in accordance with a norm, is partly returned as input, or "information sustaining further action of that character" (p. 273) [59]. On the other hand, unorthodox conduct which fails to carry its own penalty also weakens the underlying values. This possibility makes any social system vulnerable and, if actualized, results in its breakdown or refashioning. Nadel mentions only one way in which such actualization may occur:

> when rulers, judges, legislators or, for that matter, teachers
> and moralists apply or preach a doctrine in which they them-
> selves do not believe . . . [thus standing] outside the value
> system they wish to maintain (*ibid.*).

This situation raises the question of controls of the controls—the answer is self-interest and political expediency.

> And here, if you like, we touch upon social controls in purest
> form, exercised from outside and unobscured as well as un-
> aided by any self-regulation (*ibid.*).

Nadel thus distinguishes, in effect, between Parsons' social control and social controls, and his functional approach makes the connection between the two clearer than Parsons' more psychological orientation. Yet it is precisely in regard to the latter that Nadel's theory falls short. It would be greatly strengthened by the incorporation of a typology of "orientations to social controls," as developed by Merton and used in Gerth and Mills's treatment of the problem (cf. n. 26). Nadel's analysis has the great merit of exhibiting the advantages of a functional approach and thus, beyond the observation just made, inviting comparison with other approaches, thereby helping to codify social-control theory and make it more tenable.

*Nett* [60]. Nett begins his paper with a critical historical survey of social control in American sociology. The earliest writers, especially Sumner and Cooley—involuntarily—established society as something with which the individual can conform. Park and Burgess made social control into a science of strategy, but in leaving much of the discussion of the rational to political scientists they set a precedent for subsequent scant attention to its rational and strategic aspects, which neglect may perhaps be explained by the fact that "the level of human behavior at which rationality occurs is less easily stereotyped than are the levels of human behavior which are irrationally determined" (p. 43). Following Lumley, Landis, and Bernard, "unified theories" of social control have receded behind examinations of specific aspects treated under such headings as "structure and function," "collective behavior," "role and status"—all of them underlining "conformity tendencies of man" (p. 40) [61].

On the whole, social control has been seen characteristically as the manner in which society "orders, conditions, and controls its membership" (p. 41), but it may equally well be formulated as the task of regulating a society "to tap, organize, and adapt its creative strength" (*ibid.*) [62]. The first view stresses conformity as a product of social organization; the second, deviance as engendering "continuous social organization" (*ibid.*):

> instead of asking how society orders and controls the individual, students of social control might ask how society takes its organization and momentum from its behaving individuals (p. 43).

Evidence in favor of this view lies in the observation that conformers, rather than deviators, "bring society to ruin" (p. 42). In the first place, it takes masses of the former to support the latter before any revolutionary ideas can become effective; and indeed there is

> an assumption among political realists that most demagogues simply play the known areas of conformity and do not reckon truly with social deviators at all (*ibid.*).

In the second place, historical experience shows that society loses its vitality in periods of domination by conformers, yet there is frequent hostility

toward innovators. The reason is their refusal to choose among the prescribed alternatives of action (whereas the violation of an accepted alternative merely demonstrates its excellence [cf. n. 58]). The more accepted
alternatives there are, the less dangerous the deviator. An ideal democratic
society would not keep him in a marginal position, would thus substitute
a "smooth change continuum" (p. 43) for radical change, and would gain
a maximum chance of survival. (Compare this assessment of a projected
type of society with Skinner's.)

Nett's analysis is distinguished by bringing at least some elements of a
sociological perspective to bear on the American treatment of social control, hence arguing an alternative approach on the strength of its empirical plausibility. His comments on rationality, however, need expansion
and clarification, including the analysis of the relevance of rationality
(against commonsense, perhaps) in American history and culture in light
of which the sociological treatment of social control seems to be viewed.
A similar and related explication appears to be called for in respect to his
hypothetical democratic society and its maximum survival chance.

THE INTELLECTUAL STATUS OF SOCIAL CONTROL: TEMPORARILY CONCLUDED.
If it is significant to locate the literature surveyed in the first part of this
chapter in the tradition launched by Ross, it may be no less significant to
call the newer writings discussed essentially traditional as well, although
in line with several and later traditions. Gurvitch aside, chief among
them, appearing as more or less important elements in these writings, are
(in chronological order) a Pareto-influenced, sober attempt to build a
theory (Homans), an effort toward interdisciplinary integration (Parsons),
scientism (Skinner), a Weberian and cultural-anthropological functional
analysis (Nadel), and dissatisfaction with the limitations imposed by a
traditional view (Nett), but the latter may well be grounded as an accepted
alternative. To point out such traditional elements is not to ignore or
slight the importance of the intrinsic development of a science. It calls
attention to the fact that the writings surveyed (like many others) show
no trace of asking whether the social sciences are sciences for which intrinsic development has the same meaning it has for physics or whether, on
the contrary, they are mixed concerns for which such a development, and
its being taken for granted, also depend on the existence of an orderly
society (rather than a panicky, resigned one [63])—and, if the latter,
whether we live in such a society. The traditions named as elements in
these writings can themselves in part be understood as reactions to disor-
der. Thus it may be argued that the current fascination with interdisciplinary studies is a variant of scientism, itself an anxious embrace (rather
than a scientific analysis) of secularization and its concomitants and con-

sequences. Homans' and Nadel's treatment of social control is more generally traditional than indicated above simply by virtue of not raising the question whether the concept is as purely theoretical, sociologically and historically as neutral, as they assume in employing it. The textbooks referred to under "Traditional Uses of Social Control" fall short in their treatment of totalitarianism, death and slave camps, the administered nature of life in the West, atomic energy, automation, and other novelties of our time which may be seen to have changed and to be further changing individual, society, freedom, choice, and privacy alternatives and other fundamental phenomena and their meanings, all of which are in need of sociological analysis. The works discussed under "Newer Approaches to Social Control" appear to exemplify, rather than confront, this need. If it were to be confronted, the concept of social control would probably be transformed beyond recognition, and the recent uses surveyed here would reveal their historical nature with incomparably greater clarity than this cursory analysis has been able to achieve [64].

## BIBLIOGRAPHY

DeGrazia Sebastian (1948), *The Political Community: A Study of Anomie* (Chicago: University of Chicago Press). A conception of social control (without using the term) from the standpoint of "ruler" (in a broad sense of the word) and belief systems as ordering society and with special emphasis on simple and acute anomie.

Friedrich, Carl J., Ed. (1954), *Totalitarianism* (Cambridge: Harvard University Press). A collection of conference papers designed to illuminate the nature and various aspects of totalitarianism.

Gurvitch, Georges (1945), "Social Control," in Georges Gurvitch and Wilbert E. Moore, Eds., *Twentieth Century Sociology* (New York: Philosophical Library), pp. 267–296. A survey of major American concepts of social control, from Ross to Landis, and a presentation of Gurvitch's own.

Hollingshead, A. B. (1941), "The Concept of Social Control," *American Sociological Review*, **6**, 217–224. A history of the concept, with attention to precursors of Ross and to its dual source (Ross and Cooley) in American sociology and a statement of Hollingshead's own position.

Homans, George C. (1950), *The Human Group* (New York: Harcourt, Brace), especially Chapter 11, "Social Control," pp. 281–312. A clear and important analysis of the emergence of the concept of social control in the process of developing a theory of small groups.

LaPiere, Richard T. (1954), *A Theory of Social Control* (New York: McGraw-Hill). An attempt to formulate a theory of social control on the basis of the key concepts of desire for status, status groups, and countercontrol; also useful as a textbook.

LEMERT, EDWIN M. (1942), "The Folkways and Social Control," *American Sociological Review, 7,* 391–399. A critique of Hollingshead's paper and a counterproposal of a concept of social control which stresses process and group structure.

MILLS, C. WRIGHT (1948), *The New Men of Power: America's Labor Leaders* (New York: Harcourt, Brace, 1948); *White Collar: The American Middle Class* (New York: Oxford University Press, 1951); *The Power Elite (ibid.,* 1956). These studies of three important strata of American society contain much enlightening material on the structure of contemporary organization and stratification, hence on social control.

NADEL, S. F. (1953), "Social Control and Self-Regulation," *Social Forces,* **31,** 265–273. A theoretical functional analysis of society as a self-regulating mechanism.

NETT, ROGER (1953), "Conformity-Deviation and the Social Control Concept," *Ethics,* **64,** 38–45. Proposes a concept of "social control" oriented toward creativity rather than order and conformity.

PARSONS, TALCOTT (1951), *The Social System* (Glencoe, Ill.: Free Press), especially Chapter 7, "Deviant Behavior and the Mechanisms of Social Control," pp. 249–325. Based on Parsons' comprehensive theory of social systems, this is the most systematic attempt at a theory of social control.

ROUCEK, JOSEPH S. et al. (1956), *Social Control,* 2nd ed. (New York: Van Nostrand). A useful textbook that introduces the reader to a wide variety of areas in contemporary life studied from the standpoint of social control.

SKINNER, B. F. (1953), *Science and Human Behavior* (New York: Macmillan, 1953), especially Chapter 29, "The Problem of Control," pp. 437–449. An application of Skinner's view of science to the problems of controlling society, present and future.

SPEIER, HANS (1938), "The Social Determination of Ideas," *Social Research,* **5,** 182–205, and Talcott Parsons (1938), "The Role of Ideas in Social Action," *American Sociological Review* 3, 652–664. Two supplementary essays, suited to show the connection between theoretical concerns with social control and certain trends in the sociology of knowledge.

WHYTE, WILLIAM H., JR. (1956), *The Organization Man* (New York: Simon and Shuster). In an analysis resembling Mills's this perceptive study of the various facets of the "organization man" offers much for the development of a historically more realistic conception and theory of social control.

## NOTES

1. The reader is invited to consult a number of chapters in this book [*Contemporary Sociology*] for their relevance to the understanding of social control, notably those on political sociology, the sociology of bureaucracy and professions, the sociology of economic organization, public opinion and propaganda, and military and industrial sociology.

2. Particularly in three otherwise rather disparate areas of study: group dynamics, totalitarianism, and certain emphases on the sociology of knowledge. On the first see the chapters on sociometry and role theory and sociodrama; on totalitarianism note, most recently, Carl J. Friedrich and Zbigniew K. Brezinski, *Totalitarian Dictatorship and Autocracy* (Cambrige: Harvard University Press, 1956), and on the "sociology of knowledge," see the relevant chapter in this book.

3. In a series of 20 articles published in *The American Journal of Sociology*, Vols. I (1895–1896) to III, V and VI (1900–1901), and worked into his famous text, *Social Control: A Survey of the Foundations of Order* (New York: Macmillan, 1901). For predecessors of Ross and the dual source of social control in American sociology (Ross and Cooley) see A. B. Hollingshead, "The Concept of Social Control," *American Socciological Review*, **6**, (1941), 217–224.

4. Emory S. Bogardus, "Methods of Influencing People," *Sociology and Social Research*, **31** (1947), 458–465 (which lists eight, from publicizing to educating); Frank T. Carlton, "Free Enterprise and Social Control," *ibid.*, **33** (1949), 348–354 (need for steering between totalitarianism and anarchy); John W. Morgan, "Notes on Common Values and Social Control," *Social Forces*, **27** (1949), 418–421 (the problem of common values in a heterogeneous society); Lee M. Brooks, "Fifty Years' Quest for Social Control," *ibid.*, **29** (1950), 18 (glimpses of "social control"; need for more social control at this perilous time).

5. Warren Breed, "Social Control in the Newsroom: A Functional Analysis," *Social Forces*, **33** (1955), 326–335 (predominance of publisher's policy over other forces).

6. Floyd Hunter, *Community Power Structure: A Study of Decision Makers* (Chapel Hill: University of North Carolina Press, 1953). This study of a "Regional City" (population, 500,000) analyzes its power structure by focusing on individual power holders or decision makers. Although not a periodical article, it is cited here as one of the few recent studies that apply a control concept to the analysis of a community and as having the same tenuous relation to a theory of social control as the magazine articles cited in this paragraph. The subtitle of this book suggests the conceptual affinity of "social control" to still another area of substantive and theoretical efforts (cf. ns. 1 and 2), namely decision making. This area connects most directly with those of bureaucracy, group dynamics, and leadership (cf. references in ns. 1 and 2) but also with recent developments in operations research, communications, and information theory. As a broad introduction to its theoretical and empirical significance, see Herbert A. Simon, *Administrative Behavior* (New York: Macmillan, 1945 and later).

7. Howard S. Becker, "Marihuana Use and Social Control," *Social Problems*, **3** (1955), 35–44 (marihuana use in relation to the controls of the general and the marihuana users' societies).

8. Clyde William Phelps, "The Social Control of Consumer Credit Costs: A Case Study," *Social Forces*, **29** (1951), 433–442; Melville Dalton, "Industrial Controls and Personal Relations," *ibid.*, **33** (1955), 244–249 ("industrial sociol-

ogy"); Louis Kriesberg, "Occupational Controls Among Steel Distributors," *American Journal of Sociology*, **61** (1955), 203–212 (differential ocupational norms held by distributors participating and not participating in a steel gray market).

9. Nancy K. Jack and Betty Schiffer, "The Limits of Fashion Control," *American Sociological Review*, **13** (1948), 730–738 (dress lengths as prescribed by fashion magazines and followed by "women-on-the-street").

10. Richard M. Stephenson, "Conflict and Control Functions of Humor," *American Journal of Sociology*, **56** (1951), 569–574 (the function of jokes to minimize conflict, especially stratificational).

11. Edwin M. Lemert, "The Grand Jury as an Agency of Social Control," *American Sociological Review*, **10** (1945), 751–758 (power and objectives, means, and forms of grand jury control compared with county-government agencies, preceded by a brief critique of the state of the theory of social control at the time); Robert C. Sorensen, "The Influence of Public Opinion Polls on the Legislator," *Sociology and Social Research*, **34** (1950), 323–328 (power and impotence of the influence and the possibility of strengthening it).

12. Edwin M. Lemert, "Legal Commitment and Social Control," *Sociology and Social Research*, **30** (1946), 370–379.

13. Edward C. McDonagh, "Military Social Controls," *Sociology and Social Research*, **29** (1945), 197–205; Morroe Berger, "Law and Custom in the Army," *Social Forces*, **25** (1946), 82–87 (dual source of authority in the army; official decree and tradition; similarities with Catholic Church). (See also references in n. 21.)

14. James G. March, "Group Autonomy and Internal Group Control," *Social Forces*, **33** (1955), 322–326 (analysis of 15 nonliterate cultures regarding the relation between the autonomy of the group and its control over its members); Walter B. Miller, "Two Concepts of Authority," *American Anthropologist*, **57** (1955), 271–289 (European versus Algonkian "authority"; warning against the cross-cultural use of the concept of vertical or hierarchical authority; a codification of this paper with Bierstedt's important clarification of authority would be illuminating: Robert Bierstedt, "The Concept of Authority," in Morroe Berger, Theodore Abel, Charles H. Page, Eds., *Freedom and Control in Modern Society*, New York: Van Nostrand, 1954, pp. 67–81).

15. Aileen D. Ross, "The Social Control of Philanthropy," *American Journal of Sociology*, **58** (1953), 451–460 (effect of different pressures on philanthropic giving).

16. Morris Rosenberg, "Some Determinants of Political Apathy," *Public Opinion Quarterly*, **18** (1955), 349–366 (political activity as threatening, futile, and lacking significance for the individual).

17. Leo Kuper, "The Control of Social Change: A South African Experiment," *Social Forces*, **33** (1954), 19–29 (Apartheid); Frank F. Lee, "Social Controls in the Race Relations Pattern of a Small New England Town," *ibid.*, 36–40.

18. M. F. Nimkoff and A. L. Woods, "Effect of Majority Patterns on the Reli-

gious Behavior of Minority Groups," *Sociology and Social Research,* **30** (1946), 282–289 [adjustment of Catholic minority to a culture dominated by the Protestant majority; operating within the concepts of majority and minority, this paper might profitably be analyzed in the light of the arguments developed in Robert Bierstedt, "The Sociology of Majorities," *American Sociological Review,* **13** (1948), 700–710]; Chester L. Hunt, "Religious Ideology as a Means of Social Control," *Sociology and Social Research,* **33** (1949), 180–187 (the Protestant Church in Nazi Germany, with special attention to the importance of its theology).

19. Philip M. Smith, "Control of Behavior in the Small College," *Sociology and Social Research,* **31** (1946), 132–137 (programs and practices relating to smoking and dancing in various small colleges).

20. Orrin E. Klapp, "Heroes, Villains and Fools, as Agents of Social Control," *American Sociological Review,* **19** (1954), 56–62 (a functional analysis).

21. Thomas D. Eliot, "A Criminological Approach to the Social Control of International Aggressions," *American Journal of Sociology,* **58** (1953), 513–518 (the argument of modern criminology for the control of war by a community of nations); Edgar C. McVoy, "Wartime Controls in a Democratic Society," *American Sociological Review,* **11** (1946), 85–89 (apportionment of labor in the United States during World War II); Emory S. Bogardus, "Price Control and Social Control," *Sociology and Social Research,* **31** (1947), 297–305 (see also his "Rationing and Social Control," *ibid.,* **27** (1943), 472–479); Bruno Bettelheim and Morris Janowitz, "Ethnic Tolerance: A Function of Social and Personal Control," *American Journal of Sociology,* **55,** 137–145 [veterans' feelings of deprivation, ethnic hostility, and social mobility and community tolerance of minorities; anticipating the authors' *The Dynamics of Prejudice: A Psychological Study of Veterans* (New York: Harper, 1950)].

22. E. T. Hiller, *Social Relations and Structures: A Study in Principles of Sociology* (New York: Harper, 1947); Pitirim A. Sorokin, *Society, Culture, and Personality: Their Structure and Dynamics* (New York: Harper, 1947); John H. Bennett and Melvin M. Tumin, *Social Life: Structure and Function* (New York: Knopf, 1948); Kingsley Davis, *Human Society* (New York: Macmillan, 1949); William F. Ogburn and Meyer F. Nimkoff, *Sociology,* 2nd ed. (Boston: Houghton Mifflin, 1950); Thomas Carson McCormick, *Sociology: An Introduction to the Study of Social Relations* (New York: Ronald, 1950); George A. Lundberg, Clarence C. Schrag, and Otto N. Larsen, *Sociology* (New York: Harper, 1954); John F. Cuber, *Sociology: A Synopsis of Principles,* 3rd ed. (New York: Appleton-Century-Crofts, 1955); Arnold W. Green, *Sociology: An Analysis of Life in Modern Society,* 2nd ed. (New York: McGraw-Hill, 1956).

23. Logan Wilson and William L. Kolb, *Sociological Analysis: An Introductory Text and Case Book* (New York: Harcourt, Brace, 1949); Robert W. O'Brien, Clarence C. Schrag, and Walter T. Martin, *Readings in General Sociology* (Boston: Houghton Mifflin, 1951); Edgar A. Schuler, Duane L. Gibson, Maude L. Fiero, and Wilbur B. Brookover, *Outside Readings in Sociology* (New York: Crowell, 1952); Ronald Freedman, Amos H. Hawley, Werner S.

Landecker, Gerhard E. Lenski, and Horace M. Miner, *Principles of Sociology: A Text with Readings,* rev. ed. (New York: Holt, 1956); Kingsley Davis, Harry C. Bredemeier, and Marion J. Levy, Jr., *Modern American Society: Readings in the Problems of Order and Change* (New York: Farrar and Rinehart, 1945).

24.   Alfred McClung Lee, Ed., *New Outline of the Principles of Sociology* (New York: Barnes and Noble, 1946), Chapter 29, "Social Control," by Everett Cherrington Hughes; R. M. MacIver and Charles H. Page, *Society: An Introductory Analysis* (New York: Rinehart, 1949), Chapter 7, "The Mores and Social Control"; Joseph S. Roucek and Roland L. Warren, *Sociology: An Introduction* (Ames, Iowa: Littlefield, Adams, 1951), Chapter 19, "Social Control"; Emory S. Bogardus, *Sociology,* 4th ed. (New York: Macmillan, 1954), Chapter 13, "Group Controls"; John and Mavis Biesanz and others, *Modern Society: An Introduction to Social Science* (New York: Prentice-Hall, 1954), Chapter 25, "Social Control Through Government" (also in connection with the discussions of the functions of culture and social change); Joyce O. Hertzler, *Society in Action: A Study of Basic Social Processes* (New York: Dryden, 1954), Chapter 19, "Social Order and Social Control"; Leonard Broom and Philip Selznick, *Sociology: A Text with Adapted Readings* (Evanston, Ill.: Row, Peterson, 1955), Adaptation 1, "Group Behavior and Social Control," by Ronald Lippitt (also in connection with the discussion of sentiments and the structure of group, association, and family); John H. Burman and W. Marshon DePoister, *Workbook in Introductory Sociology* (New York: Prentice-Hall, 1955); Chapter 8, "Social Control"; Stuart A. Queen, William W. Chambers, and Charles N. Winston, *The American Social System: Social Control, Personal Choice, and Public Decision* (Boston: Houghton Mifflin, 1956), *passim;* Arnold M. Rose, *Sociology: The Study of Human Relations* (New York: Knopf, 1956), Chapter 3, "Social Control"; Robert L. Sutherland, Julian L. Woodward, and Milton A. Maxwell, *Introductory Sociology,* 5th ed. (Philadelphia: Lippincott, 1956), Chapter 28, "Social Reorganization and Social Control" (also in connection with the discussion of government); Samuel Koenig, Rex D. Hopper, and Feliks Gross, *Sociology: A Book of Readings* (New York: Prentice-Hall, 1953), Chapter 21, "Social Control" [H. C. Brearley, "Nature of Social Control," *Sociology and Social Research,* 2 (1943); Harold D. Lasswell, "The Garrison State," *American Journal of Sociology,* 46 (1941); and Simon Marcson, "Control of Ethnic Conflict," *Social Forces,* 24 (1945)].

25.   According to whom social control pervades legislation, which is based on public opinion, which is based on mores, which are based on human nature. Compare Robert E. Park and Ernest W. Burgess, *Introduction to the Science of Sociology* (Chicago: University of Chicago Press, 1921), Chapter 12, especially p. 786.

26.   "Social control' 'is hardly, if at all, discussed in textbooks on social psychology (although Ross conceived it as a subdivision of that field). It is all the more interesting to note its central place in Hans Gerth and C. Wright Mills, *Character and Social Structure: The Psychology of Social Institutions* (New York: Harcourt, Brace, 1953), a book that tries to "restore the balance" between

the more customary focus in social psychology on "the psychological nature of social interaction" and "the psychological nature of the major social institutions that constitute the historically significant forms of such interaction" (p. vii). Among the implementations of this objective is the discussion in two important chapters (8 and 9) of institutional orders and social controls under the heads of political order, nation and state, democracies and dictatorships, economic institutions, types of capitalism, the military order, and types of army (Chapter 8), and of religious institutions, characteristics of world religions, the kinship order, the educational sphere, types of social control, and orientation to social controls (Chapter 9). In regard to types of social control, the authors, acknowledging their indebtedness to Karl Mannheim and Max Weber (p. 256, n. 24), take up custom, fashion, conventions, law, rational uniformity (exemplified by agents in a free economic market), ethical rules, and institutional controls. Under orientation to social controls they follow Robert K. Merton's fourfold typology [developed in "Discrimination and the American Creed," in R. N. MacIver, Ed., *Discrimination and National Welfare* (New York: Institute for Religious and Social Studies, 1948), pp. 99–126] of verbal and behavioral affirmation, expediency and fear of sanctions, verbal affirmation with behavioral deviation, and verbal and behavioral deviation.

27.   Joseph S. Roucek and associates, *Social Control* (New York: Van Nostrand, 1947). The second edition, 1956, is likewise written by 27 contributors, of whom two are replacements.

28.   Paul H. Landis, *Social Control: Social Organization and Disorganization in Process* (Philadelphia: Lippincott, 1939), pp. 283–284; Georges Gurvitch, "Social Control," in Gurvitch and Wilbert E. Moore, Eds., *Twentieth Century Sociology* (New York: Philosophical Library, 1945), pp. 267–269.

29.   This section, "Rediscovery of the Primary Group," may be collated profitably with "Primary Group Relationships in Modern Society" by Harry C. Harnsworth [*Sociology and Social Research,* **31** (1947), 291–296] to stimulate possible inquiry into the relation between theoretical concern with primary groups, on the one hand [cf. especially Edward A. Shils, "The Study of the Primary Group," in Daniel Lerner and Harold D. Lasswell, Eds., *The Policy Sciences* (Stanford: Stanford University Press, 1951, pp. 44–69)], and inclination toward the primary group as an attitude found in American sociology, on the other [cf., for example, C. Wright Mills, "The Professional Ideology of Social Pathologists," *American Journal of Sociology,* **49** (1943), 165–180; Roscoe C. Hinkle, Jr., and Gisela J. Hinkle, *The Development of Modern Sociology: Its Nature and Growth in the United States*, Garden City, N.Y.: Doubleday, 1954, 3–4].

30.   See especially the periodical literature mentioned above; also the use of the term control in titles like *Controls from Within: Techniques for the Treatment of the Aggressive Child* by Fritz Redl and David Wineman (Glencoe, Ill.: Free Press, 1952).

31.   Gurvitch, *op cit.,* pp. 267–285, *passim.* For an older but still useful survey and critique of different conceptions of social control see Earl Edward Eubank,

*The Concepts of Sociology* (Boston: Heath, 1932), Chapter 11, "Concepts Pertaining to Societary Control," especially pp. 215–220.

32.  Here the cited literature on introductory and social-control texts is perhaps more instructive than that found in the magazines. For an analysis of social controls treated in some 70 introductory, social-problems, and family textbooks see A. H. Hobbs, *The Claims of Sociology: A Critique of Textbooks* (Harrisburg, Pa.: Stackpole, 1951), pp. 125–135. See also Gurvitch, *loc. cit.*, Eubank, *loc. cit.*, Hollingshead, *loc. cit.* (n. 3), and Edwin M. Lemert, "The Folkways and Social Control," *American Sociological Review,* 7 (1942), 394–399.

33.  See Gurvitch, *op. cit.*, pp. 271–273, and some of the sources cited in the preceding note.

34.  Also in Florian Znaniecki's profound *Cultural Sciences: Their Origin and Development* (Urbana: University of Illinois Press, 1952), although the whole approach of this analysis centers on the idea of order in its several distinct meanings. The nontreatment in some of the texts and readers cited in ns. 22 and 23 may also reflect the nontheoretical, nontechnical nature of social control.

35.  Hans L. Zetterberg, Ed., *Sociology in the United States: A Trend Report* (Paris: UNESCO, 1956).

36.  Leonard D. White, Ed., *The State of the Social Sciences* (Chicago: University of Chicago Press, 1956), and Roy K. Grinker, Ed., with the assistance of Helen MacGill Hughes, *Toward a Unified Theory of Human Behavior* (New York: Basic Books, 1956).

37.  Gurvitch, *loc. cit.*

38.  This not altogether satisfactory attempt at distinguishing between the sociology of the human spirit and the study of social control can probably be disregarded as far as Gurvich is concerned, inasmuch as he himself disposes of it as purely terminological in at least two places, where he says that the sociology of human spirit is what American sociologists call social control: *La Vocation actuelle de la sociologie: vers une sociologie différentielle* (Paris: Presses Universitaires de France, 1950), pp. 339, 411.

39.  Little of it available in English. On the sociology of human spirit, see, however, Georges Gurvitch, *Sociology of Law* (New York: Philosophical Library, 1942), pp. 42 ff.; on microsociology (the study of forms of sociability), "Microsociology and Sociometry," in Georges Gurvitch, Ed., *Sociometry in France and the United States* (New York: Beacon House, 1950), pp. 1–31. Gurvitch's main work in sociology is *Vocation actuelle* cited in the preceding note, especially Part I (pp. 1–348); for a brief exposition see my review in *American Sociological Review,* 16 (1951), 119–121. See also René Toulement, *Sociologie et Pluralisme dialectique: introduction a l'œuvre de Georges Gurvitch* (Louvain: Editions Nauwelaerts; Paris: Beatrice-Nauwelaerts, 1955), an analysis of all Gurvitch's work to date [briefly reviewed by me in *American Journal of Sociology,* 62 (1957), 430].

40.  This may be relevant despite the fact, noted by Hollingshead (*op. cit.*, 217), that social control is a Comtean notion: it was developed in America.

41. Among the postwar textbooks on social control, Landis and Roucek cite it; the works discussed in the remainder of this chapter do not.

42. George C. Homans, *The Human Group* (New York: Harcourt, Brace, 1950), especially Chapter 11, "Social Control," pp. 281–312. Two circumstances have left their characteristic imprint on this work: L. J. Henderson's influence on Homans' conception of science and scientific method (cf. Robert K. Merton, "Introduction" to *The Human Group,* p. xix, and Homans' "Preface," p. xxv) and Homans' own long-standing study of Pareto [cf. Homans and Charles P. Curtis, Jr., *An Introduction to Pareto: His Sociology* (New York: Knopf, 1934)].

43. Reported chiefly in the Hawthorne studies (E. Mayo, T. N. Whitehead, F. J. Roethlisberger, and W. J. Dickson) in *Street Corner Society* (William F. Whyte) and in work on the Tikopia (Raymond Firth).

44. Talcott Parsons, *The Social System* (Glencoe, Ill.: Free Press, 1951), especially Chapter 7, "Deviant Behavior and the Mechanisms of Social Control," pp. 249–325.

45. The therapeutic situation has already been introduced (*ibid.,* p. 301) and is further developed as a paradigm in an appendix to the chapter, pp. 321–325, which adds the manipulation of reward to permissiveness, support, and the denial of reciprocity as the control functions of therapy. These functions are identical to the phases through which task-oriented groups studied by Robert F. Bales tend to go [Talcott Parsons and Robert F. Bales, *Family, Socialization and Interaction Process* (Glencoe, Ill.: Free Press, 1955, pp. 38–41)]. For additional developments beyond *The Social System* (largely a further elaboration of the therapeutic paradigm), see Parsons and Bales, *ibid.,* pp. 36, 58, 156. For earlier phases of Parsons' theory of social control, cf. *The Structure of Social Action* (New York: McGraw-Hill, 1937), especially on Durkheim's theory of social control (pp. 376–408, 435–441, and 463–465); "Propaganda and Social Control" (1942) in *Essays in Sociological Theory* (Glencoe, Ill.: Free Press, 1954), Chapter 13 (rev. ed., Chapter 8); and with Edward A. Shils and the assistance of James Olds, "Values, Motives, and Systems of Action," in Parsons and Shils, Eds., *Toward a General Theory of Action* (Cambridge: Harvard University Press, 1951), pp. 227–230 (almost contemporaneous with *The Social System* but much less worked out, given the context of the book in which these pages appear). Elaboration and new application of Parsons' social-system theory later than Parsons and Bales, *loc. cit.,* contains nothing on social control: Parsons' contributions to Grinker, *op. cit.* (n. 36), and Parsons and Neil J. Smelser, *Economy and Society: A Study in the Integration of Economic and Social Theory* (Glencoe, Ill.: Free Press, 1956).

46. This, perhaps needless to say, has nothing to do with Parsons' recent insistence on the interpretation and interdependence of social and personality systems and their resulting in uneven degrees of internalization in the participants in an interactive system and in uneven degrees of internalization of the roles in the same individuals; cf. Parsons in Grinker, *op. cit.,* p. 331.

47. Which for Parsons is an empirically self-subsistent (*The Social System,* p.

19) or the most inclusive type of social system (Grinker, *op. cit.*, p. 327). The latter term resembles Gurvitch's (cf. mention above) but Parsons' and Gurvitch's "conceptual histories," hence the meanings of this term, are quite different.

48. S. D. Clark, review of *The Social System, American Journal of Sociology,* **58** (1952), 103–104. "This is perhaps most evident in his [Parsons'] chapter on deviant behavior . . ." (103b). I cannot agree with several of Clark's other contentions regarding Parsons' book.

49. Lewis A. Coser, *The Functions of Social Conflict* (Glencoe, Ill.: Free Press, 1956), especially pp. 21–23, 34, 161, and n. 6.

50. *Ibid.*, p. 21.

51. *Ibid.*, p. 22.

52. Among the writers on social control treated in this chapter Gerth and Mills (n. 26) contrast most with Parsons. Their outlook is predominantly Weberian, whereas Parsons, though "one of the foremost Weberian scholars in this country and . . . deeply influenced by Weber's thought," seems in his peripheral interest in social change and conflict "more directly related to the Durkheimian quest for social cohesion . . ." (Coser, *op. cit.*, p. 21).

53. B. F. Skinner, *Science and Human Behavior* (New York: Macmillan, 1953), especially Chapter 29, "The Problem of Control," pp. 437–449.

54. In this respect, though hardly in any other, his resemblance is greater to Mannheim than to Gurvitch, Homans, and Parsons. See Karl Mannheim's discussion of social control in *Man and Society in an Age of Reconstruction,* translated by Edward Shils (New York: Harcourt, Brace, 1941), Part V, pp. 265–366; also *Freedom, Power, and Democratic Planning,* Ernest K. Bramsted and H. H. Gerth, Eds. (New York: Oxford University Press, 1950), *passim.*

55. S. F. Nadel, "Social Control and Self-Regulation," *Social Forces,* **31** (1953), 265–273.

56. See Homans' questions, "What makes custom customary, why does structure persist?" In his answers, however, Homans does not distinguish between Nadel's self-regulation and social control, which for Homans is the same as social organization (roughly corresponding to Nadel's self-regulation), differently looked at. See comments on Homans.

57. This distinction between *zweckrational and wertrational* [Max Weber; see Nadel, *The Foundations of Social Anthropology* (Glencoe, Ill.: Free Press, 1951, p. 31)] pervades Parsons' analysis of action and has entered, as an ingredient transformed, his scheme of "pattern variables" [cf. Parsons, Shils, Olds, *op. cit.* (n. 45), p. 48, and Chapter 1; Parsons, *The Social System, loc. cit.*, Chapter II, especially pp. 58–67].

58. See Ronald Freedman et al., *Principles of Sociology: A Text with Readings,* revised edition (New York: Holt, 1956), p. 187: ". . . strong normative integration exerts pressure toward its own maintenance. A high degree of normative integration generates intense indignation as a typical reaction to nonconformist behavior. In turn, the occurrence of this response has a restraining effect on potential nonconformists and thus tends to preserve a high level of normative

integration." Nadel does not explicitly analyze this "cohesive function" of the breach of norms, which had been developed earlier by Durkheim and Simmel. See also Coser, *op. cit.*, Propositions 1, 2, 8, 9, 13, and 16, and Nett (n. 60).

59. Among the authors discussed in this chapter only Parsons operates with input-output concepts, although, unlike Nadel, not in conjunction with the concept of social control. See Parsons and Bales, *op. cit.*, pp. 174–178 and Smelser, *op. cit.*, p. 296, 307, and *passim*.

60. Roger Nett, "Conformity-Deviation and the Social Control Concept." *Ethics,* **64** (1953), 38–45.

61. As examples, Nett cites Herbert Blumer in Alfred McClung Lee, *op. cit.* (n. 24), Richard T. LaPiere, *Collective Behavior,* Robert K. Merton, *Social Theory and Social Structure,* Ralph Linton, *The Study of Man,* and George Peter Murdock, *Social Structure.*

62. A similar line is taken by Melvin M. Tumin in respect to creativity in his "Obstacles to Creativity," *Etc.,* **11** (1954), 261–271, and to stratification, in "Some Principles of Stratification: A Critical Analysis," *American Sociological Review,* **18** (1953), 387–394.

63. A society characterized by acute anomie [Sebastian DeGrazia, *The Political Community: A Study of Anomie* (Chicago: University of Chicago Press, 1948)], by disequilibrium [Godfrey and Monica Wilson, *The Analysis of Social Change* (Cambridge: University Press, 1945)] and by apathy, passivity, and conformity. A symptom of these features is the moral dilemma of the "organization man," keenly analyzed (along with a criticism of Erich Fromm's *The Sane Society*) by William H. Whyte, Jr., in *The Organization Man* (New York: Simon and Schuster, 1956), especially pp. 357–362.

64. A fuller but still far from satisfactory critique of sociology in relation to our time may be found in Kurt H. Wolff, "Before and After Sociology," *Transactions of the Third World Congress of Sociology* (1956), **7**, 151–160 [Chapter 15 of this book].

---

An abridged version of this chapter appeared in Joseph S. Roucek, Ed., *Contemporary Sociology* (New York: Philosophical Library, 1958). Reprinted by permission of the publisher. The essay has been edited and partially revised by the author.

# 5

## SOME CONSIDERATIONS PRELIMINARY TO THE STUDY OF SOCIAL CHANGE. 1963

I shall try to show how I think about social change. I begin with our place in history, as best I can, for I think about social change (and about many other topics in sociology) with this question in mind. An important way of determining where we are is a consideration of the premise of "one world," whose meanings, especially when taken together, are quite new in the history of mankind. I want to mention three of these meanings.

The first is the technical possibility of world destruction. There are no longer any far corners of the earth, except in the sense that, if the possibility became fact, the devastation might be slower in some areas than in others. One reaction to this is global claustrophobia and the attendant effort to escape into what we call "space" (as if, indeed on earth no space existed). Another reaction is intellectual and moral, rather than fearsome.

The second meaning embraces totalitarianism and the degree of its success in changing people's minds and their ideas about the changeability of people's minds. This success is unthinkable without modern technology, communications in particular.

The third meaning is the enormous acceleration witnessed in recent decades of two simultaneous and worldwide processes: the political decline of the West and its cultural vindication. The first refers to such phenomena as the challenge to Western hegemony, the recession of colonialism, and the attendant spread of nations, with concomitant industrial-

74

ization and militarization in non-Western countries, the redistribution of power and competition for it by the two nations in which it has been concentrated, the United States and the Soviet Union. The second, which may also be called Westernization, refers to the spread of Western technology and other cultural traits, including nationalization itself, whose adoption brings the first process about.

The first meaning of "one world," the likelihood of our own destruction, clearly has the greatest urgency: whatever we may mean by social change, the nuclear bomb will surely be included—whether as an example, a result, or a cause. Thus it could be argued that at this time in our history the foremost task of the *student* of social change (rather than of the more immediate changer) is a reconsideration of the literature relevant to social change in order to become above all more intelligent about the nature of the potential dangers inherent in it and the ways of averting them. Whether one should *be* a student or should participate more directly in change by promoting, preventing, or protesting is not the subject of this chapter.

The literature on social change is both voluminous and confusing, but even an attempt at ordering it facilitates its survey and assessment. It is then possible to see that some of its contributors are interested in social change chiefly as *a pattern of world or Western history*, that others conceive of its study primarily as a search for *causative factors*, and that a third group considers social change as *process*.

In trying to show these things I need hardly point out that what I say here about particular thinkers is limited by the purpose of arriving at a surer grasp of some of the problems associated with the notion of social change. My remarks are exceedingly brief, for I can attempt no more than an approximate location of the thinkers to be mentioned in relation to the three concepts of social change I have indicated. Later we shall try to draw some conclusions.

First, then, *social change understood as the pattern of history*. Herbert Spencer [1], the evolutionist, thought of mankind as evolving through two major phases, the military and the industrial. Auguste Comte [2], to whom we owe the terms "positivism," "social physics," and "sociology," instead posited three stages and held that this insight entailed on him and his contemporaries and subsequent generations the promotion of the third. the scientific stage. Hegel [3] interpreted the history of mankind as the process by which reason comes into its own. Marx [4] secularized this view, substituting for reason the class struggle for the means of production and by equipping man with this realization of the meaning of history making him the master of history rather than its victim or the victim of Hegel's "cunning of reason." Durkheim [5], like Spencer and a number of other thinkers, was a historical dichotomist who argued that societies pass through two "types," the mechanical and the organic. Max Weber [6] interpreted the course of Western history as one of increasing rationalization. In an elaboration of this view Karl Mannheim [7] observed that the increase in "functional rationality," characteristic of the modern age, has not been accompanied by an increase in "substantive rationality." Pitirim Sorokin [8] argued for fluctuations between three "supersystems" rather than for development and locates us in the last phase of the second recurrence of the Sensate supersystem, a phase that will soon be replaced by a return to another among the three, the Idealistic. Among other thinkers who hold a dichotomous view of human or Western decelopment, in addition to Spencer (from military to industrial), Durkheim (from mechanical to organic), and Weber (from traditional to rational), I mention Henry Maine [9] (from status to contract), Ferdinand Tönnies [10] (from *Gemeinschaft* to *Gesellschaft*), Howard Becker [11] (from sacred to secular), and Robert Redfield [12] (from folk to urban).

If we ask what kinds of statement these thinkers make, we find that most of them, most of the time, claim that they are descriptive statements of fact, the result of investigation (we shall ask the same question also of the thinkers in the other two categories). Furthermore, the writers in this first group, among whom Marx is the most notable exception, are little interested in recommendations derived from the facts they claim to have discovered. Nevertheless, contrary to this more or less explicit position, most of them do draw practical consequences from their concepts. Spencer, despite his insistence on the inevitability of evolution and his espousal of *laissez-faire*, which he thought followed from it, fought in the very name of *laissez-faire* the expansion of government and the rise of social services. Hegel glorified the Prussian state, in which he found reason embodied. We have already seen the relation between theory and practice in Comte, whose insight into the three stages entailed for him the active promotion of the third. As for Durkheim, although he welcomed the complex division of labor characteristic of organic society, he was also deeply worried by its concomitant anomie. As for Weber, although he was incapable of repudiating the contemporary phase of rationalization and bureaucratization, he feared both the sterilization of life lived too exclusively according to the principle of efficiency and the false prophet that might appear in reaction to it. He shuddered before the alternatives that he believed his historical analysis showed—namely, between "specialists without spirit or vision and voluptuaries without heart." As for Mannheim, his search for substantive rationality may be said to have found its answer in social planning. Among the more recent writers I have mentioned Mannheim probably comes closest to abandoning the separation of practice from theory more or less pointedly asserted by most of his contemporaries, immediate predecessors, and a few of the older writers.

Second, now, *the study of social change understood as the identification of causative factors.* Some of the writers in the first group also emphasize, explicitly or implicitly, the factors that bring about social change. Thus for Marx the cause lies in the relations of production, for Durkheim, in the increasing density of population, which in turn increases and enriches social interaction. Weber, in a "life-long dialogue with the ghost of Karl Marx," stressed the causative role of ideas (without, of course, denying those of other factors).

Other writers are predominantly rather than secondarily or incidentally concerned with causative factors. Vilfredo Pareto [13] accounted for his limited concept of social change (the circulation of the elites) by referring to the struggle for political power brought about by the alternating victories of the chief means employed (force and ruse); their use, in turn, is the special tendency of two social-psychological types of men. William Fielding Ogburn [14] and several students influenced by him stressed the developments of technology as the prime force influencing social change. Fred Cottrell [15], in a related concept, calls attention to the energy available to a given society as significant to the nature of that society and its actual and potential changes.

The practical consequences these men have drawn from their concepts of social change decrease in the order in which they have been presented, except for Cottrell. In regard to the first three—Marx, Durkheim, and Weber—these consequences have already been mentioned. Pareto's view of sociology (not only of the "circulation of the elites") also found expression in his antiliberalism and antihumanitarianism. Ogburn seems to have drawn nothing from his theoretical insights related to his attitudes or actions. On the other hand, the connection between Cottrell's understanding of social change and his interest in establishing the conditions of peace is clear: peace costs less energy than war [16]. It should be added that Ogburn is only one of perhaps the majority of contemporary sociologists and other social scientists, especially American, who follow Max Weber's elliptic, misconceived, and misunderstood recommendation that the roles of scientist and citizen be split [17] and who consequently separate whatever practical concerns they may have from their scientific work. On the whole, though, relatively few students of social change make this separation except for our third group, authors who conceive of social change as process. This may mean that social change is an area in which the separation is more difficult than in many others; it may also mean that it makes the study of social change more difficult than that of phenomena that are more static or in which we are less involved.

Finally, *social change understood as process*. This concept shares with the first—social change as the pattern of history—an interest in pattern; unlike the first, however, it is not concerned with the pattern of *history* but with the pattern to be discovered ideally in every case of social change: the concept is systematic and ahistorical, and it shares this ahistoricity with the second concept—the study of social change understood as the search for causative factors—particularly with those of its representatives who focus on power (Pareto) and technology (Ogburn) as causative of social change. Unlike this second conception, however, it is generally less interested in cause. For Robert M. MacIver [18] social change is one in the mode of adjustment among the three orders that compose a historical unit (the cultural, utilitarian, and material orders). Similarly, for Godfrey and Monica Wilson [19] social change is the increase or decrease in the scale of a given society (i.e., the number of people in relation and the intensity of these relations—a concept that suggests Durkheim's physical and moral density, or population density and intensity and complexity of interaction, especially the division of labor). For Talcott Parsons [20] social change is one *of* social systems (as against change *in* the system), and Parsons explicitly denies the possibility of generalizing about the source of social change.

In these three concepts a historical concern is not absent. It finds expression in MacIver's and Parsons' illustrations and in the Wilsons' dichotomous view of history (from primitive to civilized). This concern, however, is largely missing in numerous contemporary studies of social changes summarized by Otis Dudley Duncan [21] and classified by frames of reference (equilibrium, growth, evolution, process, social causation, and planning) and kinds of quantitative patterns (temporal, time series, population changes, cross-sectional and longitudinal analyses, rates, and models). In many of these studies the emphasis on identifying the process (the regularities, the mechanisms) of social change is so central that the question of the meaning of social change itself, that is, the subject matter of the monograph and of the research discussed, tends to get lost.

So far we have observed, roughly, what certain thinkers mean by social change. Although we have not asked what *we* might mean, we could not even recognize it when others were talking about it if we did not have at least an implicit notion. (I use "we" not as a *pluralis maiestatis* but as the subject of a collective enterprise, of something we are trying to get at together.)

Where does our implicit notion about social change come from? I think it comes from the fact that we live continuously with past and future, that we live in history, of which we have an idea, no matter how nebulous, including historical periods that we somehow find significantly divided from one another, and an idea about dividing lines that we single out as significant. We posit these periods and dividing lines, for which the best reason is that we cannot help it, although this is most rare: usually we follow the periodization made by others, which, in turn, is commonly fifthhand. In either case, the rare and the usual, the dividing is a *practical* affair—and I use the term in the same sense in which I used it in regard to the concerns of the thinkers whom I have mentioned: the word "concern" itself, in fact, refers to a practical, not a theoretical phenomenon.

This consideration leads to another, namely, the difference between the study of social change and the study of history and their relation. I should think that the person who calls himself a student of *social change* is aiming at what we ordinarily mean by scientific knowledge [22], but it is useful to characterize it with other adjectives: pragmatic, hypothetical, stipulative, propositional, external, objective, and theoretical. The knowledge he seeks is *pragmatically* true in relation to the *hypotheses stipulated*; its truth is predicated on *propositions* that concern a world *external* to the student whose *objective* characteristics are to be ascertained in these propositions, which are organized as a *theory*. In an ideal-typical, more than empirical contrast the student of *history* [23] may be said to aim at what I prefer to call existential knowledge; this knowledge is experiential, relatively ultimate, relatively absolute, subjective, practical. For its truth criterion is agreement with the result of the most rigorously imaginable intrasubjective examination of the student's most important *experiences*. Thus, whenever obtained, it is relatively *ultimate* or *absolute*—that is, in relation to new examinations; each examination, however, involves the whole person, and the knowledge resulting from it may be called *subjective* and *practical* because the search for it is motivated by the quest for optimal conduct or action.

We must qualify this distinction at once. It is far more pervasive than the distinction between the student of social change and the student of history, for it applies to two types of knower who exist within each of us and are separately institutionalized only most approximately or typically, as well as precariously, in the scientist, and the philosopher and student of humanities. The second qualification is that the distinction between scientific and practical knowledge is ideal-typical in at least three respects.

First, and most obvious, not all extant theories and studies of social change exhibit the aim of scientific knowledge and not all extant historiographic work exhibits the aim of practical knowledge. I have insisted all along on the practical concerns of the thinkers on social change mentioned, particularly of those who understand social change precisely as the pattern of history.

Second, the distinction between scientific and practical knowledge itself is not only systematic but historical; that is, not only do two types of inquiry exist, theoretical and practical or scientific and existential, regardless of any particular time, but the very meaning of the distinction itself depends on history. The answer to the question *what* study should be conceived of as theoretical or practical is the answer to a quest for practical knowledge.

Finally, and perhaps most importantly, the two types of knowledge are not mutually exclusive; on the contrary, they are supplementary. This is so particularly in the sense that practical knowledge is as dependent on scientific knowledge as philosophy is on science, for practical knowledge *is* not knowledge if it contradicts the scientific. Furthermore, the latter is among the sources of the former, for practical knowledge interprets scientific knowledge in its relevance to its own quest for optimal conduct or action.

When we ask ourselves as students of social change what it is we are aiming for, our answers are likely to vary and they may well include the three that we have found in our look at the extant literature; that is, some of us may want to trace the pattern of history, others to isolate causative factors or to understand social change as process. If we continue in our desire to realize what we are doing, thus asking ourselves *why* it is that we want to find the pattern of history, to isolate causative factors, or understand social change as process, it might be at this point or perhaps only at a later point in our continuing inquiry that we will recognize our answers as practical—in other words, as responding to our desire to know what to do. In temporal, dynamic, or diachronic terms, this question may resolve itself into a threefold scheme: Where do we come from? Where are we? What, therefore, must we do? We may find that the crucial combination is that of the second and third and that the first—Where have we come from?—must be answered to complete the other two.

In this quest for practical knowledge we assume that knowing where we are can tell us what we must do. This means that we assume the Is is capable of disclosing the Ought. Such an assumption contravenes longstanding scientific belief, which separates Is and Ought, which seeks to demonstrate that no Is entails any Ought, which holds that any claim of an Ought following on an Is has the authority only of tradition or taste but not of scientific knowledge or even logical argument. It is true that in this view of science any Ought that is embraced by taste, religion, or culture is also an end for which the means can be found or at least sought scientifically. For the person who holds such a view—for the traditional scientist—Oughts or ends are scientific theoretical phenomena, not practical existential phenomena that would commit him to a certain course of action: they simply *are*. On the other hand, for the seeker of practical knowledge, the Is—and there is no reason why he should not carry on his investigation with the curiosity traditionally associated with scientific search—can indeed disclose the Ought, for he lives in the world of exploration in which all men share and from which neither the most awful horrors of history nor the most haunting scientific findings and technological inventions can eject us.

These considerations of some of the consequences of the differences and connections between theoretical and practical knowledge are meant to be both systematic and historical. In other words, they claim to be valid scientifically and relevant practically; they claim to exemplify the connection between Is and Ought with which they deal. The historical moment, as it were, selects from the *Is* what it needs to act on, what *ought* to be done, without, of course, claiming or deluding itself that it thereby exhausts either knowledge or action.

In the sociological literature on social change with which I am familiar there is a lack of definitions of the topic that would permit us to identify their referents with any degree of clarity. To be sure, most definitions are somewhat less vague than the one that states, "Social change means simply the process of becoming different in any sense." I have not been able to devise one that could approach the requirements without specifying two variables, namely, the social unit and the time span with which the change is to be associated. In regard to the first, however, not even Parsons' elaborate discussion goes beyond predicating change of a social system, according to which the birth of a baby is as much an example as a revolution, the difference lying merely in the system—a family and a society. In regard to the second variable, the period, Parsons says no more than that we must specify the time before the change occurs so that we can trace it more clearly; but this means that just as we have the freedom (or license) to take either a family or a society as our unit so we may "choose," as the misleading term goes, either five minutes or the years since the end of World War II or Christ or Adam. I suspect that the reason for the characteristic absence of these specifications of place and time from the discussion of social change is their root in a view according to which place and time are in some sense *significant*. "Significance," however, is fundamentally a practical criterion and thus inadmissible or unacceptable to the traditional social scientist. Yet in rejecting such a criterion the traditional social scientist in fact denies his own historicity, his continuity and our continuity with past and future. This means that he is irrelevant—which, in turn, would be irrelevant were it not that the irrelevance of the kind of person who in all other respects is best suited to tell us about social change is dangerous and thus highly relevant at this time in our history.

## NOTES

1. Herbert Spencer, *The Principles of Sociology* (1879–1882), Vol. II, Book II, Sections 212–217, 223, 270–271, reprinted in Talcott Parsons, Edward Shils, Kaspar D. Naegele, and Jesse R. Pitts, Eds., *Theories of Society: Foundations of Modern Sociological Theory* (New York: Free Press, 1961), Vol. I, pp. 139–143 (henceforth: "PSNP").

2. Auguste Comte, *The Positive Philosophy* (1830–1842), translated and condensed by Harriet Martineau (New York: Calvin Blanchard, 1858, Chapter I, pp. 25–30; Book VI, Chapter VI, pp. 522–540, the latter reprinted in PSNP, II, pp. 1332–1342).

3. Georg Wilhelm Friedrich Hegel, "Philosophical History," from *Philosophy of History* (1820s), Introduction, reprinted in part in *Introduction to Contemporary Civilization in the West*, 2nd. ed. (New York: Columbia University Press, 1954), Vol. II, pp. 64–87, or (only partly overlapping) in Patrick Gardiner, Ed., *Theories of History* (Glencoe, Ill.: Free Press, 1959), pp. 60–73.

4. Karl Marx, *Selected Writings in Sociology and Social Philosophy*, T. B. Bottmore and Maximilien Rubel, Eds. (London: Watts, 1956), Part One, I, "The Materialist Conception of History," pp. 51–56 (selections from various of Marx's writings); *A Contribution to the Critique of Political Economy* (1859) (Chicago: Charles H. Kerr, 1904), pp. 9–15; "Material Life and Ideology" [selections from Marx and Friedrich Engels, *The German Ideology* (1846)], reprinted in Arthur Naftalin, Benjamin N. Nelson, Mulford Q. Sibley, Donald C. Calhoun, and Andreas G. Papandreou, Eds., *Personality, Work, Community: An Introduction to Social Science* (Chicago: Lippincott, 1953), Book I, pp. 98–104; Marx and Engels, *Manifesto of the Communist Party* (1848).

5. Emile Durkheim, *The Division of Labor in Society* (1893), translated by George Simpson (Glencoe, Ill.: Free Press, 1947), pp. 256–282.

6. Max Weber, *The Protestant Ethic and the Spirit of Capitalism* (1904–1905), translated by Talcott Parsons (1930) (New York: Charles Scribner's Sons, 1958), Chapter V, "Asceticism and the Spirit of Capitalism," pp. 155–183, 258–284.

7. Karl Mannheim, *Man and Society in an Age of Reconstruction*, translated by Edward Shils (New York: Harcourt, Brace, 1940), Introduction, "The Significance of the Age of Reconstruction," pp. 3–35; *Freedom, Power and Democratic Planning*, Ernest K. Bramsted and H. H. Gerth, Eds. (New York: Oxford University Press, 1950), Part I, "Diagnosis of the Situation," pp. 3–37.

8. Pitirim A. Sorokin, *Social and Cultural Dynamics: A Study of Change in Major Systems of Art, Truth, Ethics, Law and Social Relationships* (1937–1941),

one-volume edition (Boston: Porter Sargent, 1957), pp. 630–663; *Society, Culture, and Personality: Their Structure and Dynamics—A System of General Sociology* (New York: Harper, 1947), Chapters 45–46, pp. 675–706.

9.   Henry Sumner Maine, *Ancient Law: Its Connection with the Early History of Society and Its Relation to Modern Ideas* (1861).

10.   Ferdinand Tönnies, *Community and Association (Gemeinschaft und Gesellschaft)* (1887), translated and supplemented by Charles P. Loomis (London: Routledge & Kegan Paul, 1955).

11.   Howard Becker, "Current Sacred-Secular Theory and Its Development," in Howard Becker and Alvin Boskoff, Eds., *Modern Sociological Theory in Continuity and Change* (New York: Dryden, 1957), Chapter 6, pp. 133–185.

12.   Robert Redfield, *The Primitive World and Its Transformations* (Ithaca: Cornell University Press, 1953); Chapter II, "Later Histories of the Folk Societies," pp. 26–53, "The Natural History of the Folk Society," *Social Forces,* **31** (1953), pp. 224–228.

13.   Vilfredo Pareto, *The Mind and Society* (1916), 4 vols., translated and edited by Arthur Livingston (New York: Harcourt, Brace, 1935), Sections 2026–2059, 2233–2236; reprinted in PSNP, I, pp. 551–558.

14.   William Fielding Ogburn, *Social Change* (New York: Huebsch, 1922), "The Hypothesis of Cultural Lag," pp. 200–212, reprinted in PSNP, II, pp. 1270–1273.

15.   Fred Cottrell, *Energy and Society: The Relation between Energy, Social Change, and Economic Development* (New York: McGraw-Hill, 1955).

16.   Fred Cottrell, *Men Cry Peace* (Amsterdam: North-Holland, 1954).

17.   Max Weber, "Politics as a Vocation" (1918), in *From Max Weber: Essays in Sociology,* translated, edited, and with an introduction by H. H. Gerth and C. Wright Mills (New York: Oxford University Press, 1946).

18.   Robert M. MacIver, "Social Causation and Change," in Georges Gurvitch and Wilbert E. Moore, Eds., *Twentieth Century Sociology* (New York: Philosophical Library, 1945), pp. 121–138, reprinted from MacIver, *Social Causation* (Boston: Ginn, 1942), pp. 300–308, 320–321, 332–334, 382–393; "The Historical Pattern of Social Change," *Journal of Social Philosophy,* **2** (1936), pp. 35–54, reprinted in *Harvard Tercentenary Publications: Authority and the Individual* (Cambridge, Mass.: Harvard University Press, 1937) pp. 126–153.

19.   Godfrey and Monica Wilson, *The Analysis of Social Change Based on Observations in Central Africa* (Cambridge, England: University Press, 1945).

20.   Talcott Parsons, *The Social System,* Chapter XI, "The Processes of Change of Social Systems" (Glencoe, Ill.: Free Press, 1951), pp. 480–535.

21.   Otis Dudley Duncan, *The Study of Social Change* [draft for review only; prepared as a working paper for Discussions of Social Statistics and Social Trends sponsored by the Social Science Research Council, New York (hectographed)], May 1958.

22.   The following discussion of scientific and existential knowledge goes beyond that in "Scientific *vs.* Existential Truth," pp. 579–580, in my "The Sociol-

ogy of Knowledge and Sociological Theory," in Llewellyn Gross, Ed., *Symposium on Sociological Theory* (Evanston, Ill.: Row, Peterson, 1959), pp. 567–602 [Chapter 29 of this book].

23.   See also my "Sociology and History; Theory and Practice," *American Journal of Sociology,* **65** (July 1959), pp. 32–38 [Chapter 17 of this book].

---

This chapter has not been published previously in English.

# 6

# AN ELEMENTARY
# SYLLABUS IN
# THE SOCIOLOGY
# OF THE JEWS. 1946

The following pages constitute a syllabus [1] to be used in connection with whatever college course the instructor who contemplates its adoption may deem appropriate. Courses in race relations, social disorganization, minorities, or, if the syllabus is treated more briefly, in introductory sociology suggest themselves most readily. The document may be utilized as a lecture and study outline for two or three class meetings or as a text core, in combination with the literature indicated or with other literature, for perhaps several weeks. Suggestions for using it in the latter capacity, or in a capacity somewhere between the two, are provided in the notes, which for this reason are somewhat lengthy.

The syllabus is called elementary because it is clearly partial in the selection of its topics, because it is far from covering all facts about statistics of Jews and about the question of the Jewish "race," and because it does not try to arrive at an even relatively final conclusion regarding the nature of antisemitism. Rather, with reference to numbers, it provides those figures that I believe most important for an orientation regarding the distribution of the Jews in the world and, in particular, in the United States; with reference to the Jews as a "race" it presents those scientific findings that I believe can clarify this emotionally and politically charged question most economically; and with reference to antisemitism it assembles those hypotheses that in my opinion best lend themselves to attempts at understanding the nature of this puzzling phenomenon.

The same pedagogical reasons that determined the treatment of the three topics—statistics, "race," antisemitism—decided their selection, rather than that of others. My experience has led me to believe that it is these three, more than other questions, that need clarification most urgently and from which others may in turn receive a clearer perspective. Again it should be noted that the suggestions, bibliographical and other, contained in the notes, will make it relatively easy for the instructor to discuss additional problems or particular aspects not dealt with in the syllabus but in which teacher or student is especially interested.

Insofar as I have striven to be objective, the syllabus may be called a scientific document; insofar as the topics are sociological or represent sociological reactions to nonsociological errors, the title "sociology of the Jews," in spite of the elementary and selective character of the treatment, may be justifiable.

I do not believe that education alone, however broadly applied, can eliminate antisemitism but I think that education can play an important role in this task. More specifically, I do not believe that a study of the present document will remove the causes of antisemitism as they may be operative in the student of the syllabus, but I think that reading it may reinforce an objective attitude that the reader may already have or that in some cases it may even arouse.

## SOME STATISTICS OF JEWS IN THE
## CONTEMPORARY WORLD [2]

*World Distribution of Jews* (see Table 1): *Nazism and World War II and Jewish Population.*    Between 1933 and 1943 more than three million Jews emigrated or were deported from their respective countries of residence in Europe—almost one-third of all European Jews, or close to 18 percent of all Jews in the world. If one adds the Jews who migrated within their respective countries of residence, the figure is estimated to amount to 5,261,000, or more than 55 percent of all European Jews, and close to one-third of the total Jewish population of the world [3]. Up to 1941 the emigrated or deported Jews included three-fourths of the Jews in Germany and Austria, and 10 to 40 percent of the Jews in Italy, Poland, Czechoslovakia, Rumania, France, and Belgium. Of this total number approximately 800,000 Polish, Rumanian, and German Jews fled or were deported to Soviet Russia and about 700,000 were admitted in other countries all

*Table 1.  Jews in the World*

| Continent and Country | General Population | Jewish Population | Percent Jewish to General Population[1] |
|---|---|---|---|
| | (in thousands) | | |
| Americas | 274,200[2] | 5,500[3] | 2.0 |
| North America and and West Indies | 153,600[2] | 5,000[3] | 3.3 |
| Continental United States | 133,200[2] | 4,800[3,4] | 3.6 |
| South and Central America | 120,600[2] | 500[3] | 0.4 |
| Argentina[5] | 13,500[2] | 350[3] | 2.6 |
| Brazil[5] | 42,500[2] | 111[3] | 0.3 |
| Europe | 530,000[2] | 9,500[6] | 1.8 |
| Africa | 150,000[7] | 600[3] | 0.4 |
| Asia | 1,100,000[7] | 800[3] | 0.1 |
| Palestine | 1,500[2] | 425[3] | 28.3 |
| Australasia | 10,000[2] | 25[3] | 0.3 |
| Total | 2,171,000[2] | 16,700[8] | 0.8 |

[1] Computed from preceding columns.

[2] "World Population in Transition," *Annals of the American Academy of Political and Social Science* (January 1945), 237.

[3] *American Jewish Year Book*, Vol. 46, 1944–1945 (Philadelphia: Jewish Publication Society, 1944).

[4] 1943 estimate: 5,199,200; *ibid.*, p. 491, note.

[5] South and Central American countries other than Argentina and Brazil have less than 50,000 Jews each.

[6] Arieh Tartakower and Kurt R. Grossman, *The Jewish Refugee* (New York: Institute of Jewish Affairs of the American Jewish Congress and World Jewish Congress, 1944), p. 337.

[7] Lester E. Klimm, Otis P. Starkey, and Norman F. Hall, *Introductory Economic Geography* (New York: Harcourt, Brace and Co., 1940), Statistical Appendix, Table I.

[8] Arieh Tartakower, "The Jewish Refugees," *Jewish Social Studies*, 4 (October 1942), 313.

over the world, including European countries, where many refugees stayed in expectation of their overseas visas and where many were caught after the outbreak of World War II [4]. Between 1933 and 1943, among the various countries of immigration, the United States received the largest number, 190,000, or 23.5 percent of the total. Next ranks Palestine with 120,000, or 14.8 percent. The Western Hemisphere outside the United States received about 136,000 (17 percent); Europe, about 283,000 (35 percent); China, 25,000; Australia, 9000; South Africa, 8000 [5]. Almost 80,000, or half the Jewish refugees admitted to the United States between 1933 and 1941, came from Germany [6].

Most of these figures, and likewise some of those contained in Table 1, will be obsolete once we can more definitely ascertain how many millions of Jews have lost their lives in Nazi-dominated Europe by starvation, extermination, and the hazards of migration. As of late 1945 a well-documented estimate is 5,978,000—almost 72 percent of all European [7] or 35 percent of all Jews in the world.

*Some Figures Pertaining to the Distribution of Jews in the United States.* The total Jewish population of the nine states shown in Table 2— 3,758,950—represents 78.79 percent of the Jewish population of the United States (4,770,647), whereas the total general population of these nine states—44,639,216 (1940)—represents only 33.90 percent of the 1940 total general population of the United States (131,669,275).

The concentration of the Jewish population appears even more conspicuous if it is shown that the number of Jews residing in the five states with the largest Jewish communities (New York, Pennsylvania, Illinois, New Jersey, and Massachusetts)—3,559,189—represents 74.61 percent of all Jews in the United States, whereas the general (1940) population of these five states—39,753,449—makes up only 30.19 percent of the total;

*Table 2.  States Having Three Percent or More Jewish Population (1937)*[1]

|  | Jewish Population | |
| --- | --- | --- |
| State | Number | Percent of General Population |
| New York | 2,206,328 | 16.70 |
| New Jersey | 267,970 | 6.50 |
| Massachusetts | 262,945 | 6.07 |
| Connecticut | 93,080 | 5.54 |
| Illinois | 387,330 | 4.96 |
| Pennsylvania | 434,616 | 4.43 |
| Maryland | 76,124 | 4.31 |
| North Dakota | 2,744 | 4.21 |
| Rhode Island | 27,813 | 4.02 |

[1] Source same as for Note 3, Table 1. The percentages of the Jewish population are based on the total population for 1937, estimated by the U.S. Bureau of the Census.

hence the Jewish population is concentrated approximately two-and-a-half times as strongly as the general population [8].

Table 3 shows that the percentage of Jews in the general population decreases with decreasing community size, being more than 100 times as high in the cities of 100,000 population and over as in rural unincorporated areas.

The Jewish population is even more highly concentrated in terms of its larger communities than in terms of its distribution by states. In 1937 there were 967 Jewish communities in the United States. Of these 47 had 10,000 or more Jews; the total population of these 47 communities—3,937,525—represented 82.54 percent of all Jews in the United States. Four Jewish communities (New York, 2,035,000; Chicago, 363,000; Philadelphia, 293,000; Boston, 118,000) had 100,000 or more population each and totaled 2,809,000 or 58.88 percent of all Jews in the United States, whereas the general population of these four communities—13,553,913—represented only 10.29 percent of the total general population.

*Distribution of Jews in Our Own State.*   How are the Jews distributed in our own state? Texas, in 1937 [9], had a population of 6,172,000, of which 49,196 or 0.8 percent, were Jews. According to the latest figures available (see Table 4), seven communities, representing 20.65 percent (1,324,418) of the total 1940 population of Texas (6,414,824), had (in 1937) 1000 or more Jews each, or a total of 37,600, representing 76.43 per cent of all Jews in Texas.

*Jewish Immigration to the United States.*   Three periods may be distinguished. From 1492 to 1815 approximately 15,000 mainly Sephardic (Spanish) Jews arrived. From 1815 to 1881 approximately 200,000 Jews, mainly German and Central Europeans, settled in this country—thirteen times as

*Table 3.   Percentage of Jews in Urban Places and in Rural Territory (1937)*[1]

| Type of Community and Area | Percent Jewish to general population |
|---|---|
| Population 100,000 and over | 10.94 |
| 25,000–100,000 | 2.77 |
| 10,000– 25,000 | 1.22 |
| 5,000– 10,000 | 0.75 |
| 2,500– 5,000 | 0.63 |
| Rural Incorporated | 0.38 |
| Rural Unincorporated | 0.10 |

[1] Source same as for Note 3, Table 1.

*Table 4.   Texas Communities Having 1000 or More Jewish Population*

| | | Jewish Population[2] | |
| Community | General Population[1] | Number | Percent of general population |
|---|---|---|---|
| Dallas | 294,734 | 10,400[3] | 3.6 |
| San Antonio | 253,854 | 6,900[3] | 2.7 |
| Houston | 384,514 | 10,000[4] | 2.6 |
| El Paso | 96,810 | 2,250[3] | 2.3 |
| Waco | 55,982 | 1,150[3] | 2.1 |
| Galveston | 60,862 | 1,200[3] | 2.0 |
| Fort Worth | 177,662 | 1,500[5] | 0.8 |

[1] *16th Census of the United States, 1940.*
[2] Source same as for Note 3, Table 1.
[3] 1937.
[4] Local estimate, 1941.
[5] Local estimate, 1943.

many in these 65 years as in the preceding 325 years. From 1881 to 1940 approximately 3,500,000 Jews mainly Russian and other Eastern Europeans, found their home here—sixteen times as many in these 60 years as in the preceding 390 years or 233 times as many as in the first 325 years of American history [10]. Although the average number of immigrants per decade for these last 60 years thus amounted to almost 585,000, it should be remembered that during the last decade (1933–1943) this number represented fewer than one-third of the average, namely, 190,000 in spite of the especially acute need for emigration from Europe. The paradox can be explained by the fact that since the Immigration Acts of 1921 and 1924 the United States has allotted only limited quotas of immigrants to each country of emigration [11].

## THE QUESTION OF THE JEWISH "RACE" [12]

The five (and other) subsubtypes of the Mediterranean subdivision (Figure 1, upper right corner) made up the population of ancient Palestine. As early as 50,000 B.C., according to recently found skeletons, individual differences made it untenable to speak of a Jewish subrace. Nevertheless, anthropometric measurements of contemporaneous Jews and surrounding populations in many parts of the world compel one to speak of a certain degree of ethnic identifiability of scattered Jewish groups, which seems to be irreconcilable with the above but which can be explained by

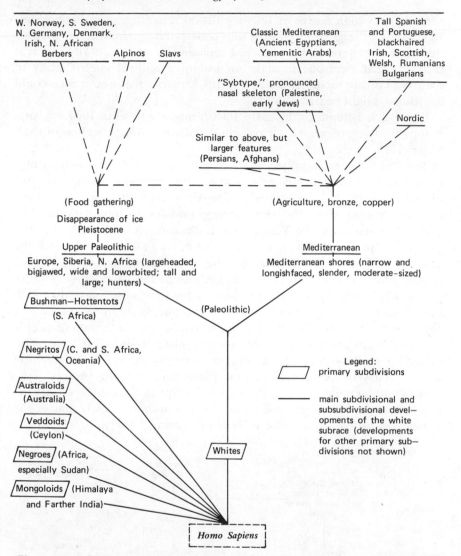

*Figure 1. Primary subdivisions of man (Homo Sapiens) and main subdivisional developments of whites. (Adapted from Carleton Stevens Coon, "Have the Jews a Racial Identity?" in Isacque Graeber and Steuart Henderson Britt, Eds., Jews in a Gentile World (New York: Macmillan, 1942), pp. 20–37.*

the relatively high degree of Jewish cultural separateness and endogamy. In contrast, other Mediterraneans who penetrated northward, for instance, the Etruscans, were wholly absorbed biologically *and* culturally; yet it is probable that were one to make an intensive anthropometric study in Etruria (Tuscany) today individuals with Etruscan features, if such could be defined, might be traceable [13].

Figure 2, a synopsis of the main Jewish migrations since 1000 B.C., provides a bird's-eye view of their present-day distribution as well as of their history [14].

The Yiddish-speaking ("Jewish," i.e., stationary medieval German plus elements of surrounding languages and some Hebrew) Ashkenazim (see Figure 2) are more differentiated among themselves than the Sephardim, but are less so than the surrounding non-Jewish populations. The Sephardim are more like Yemenitic, Mesopotamian, and other Oriental Jews than Spaniards. During the course of history all strains of which the Jews are composed have re-emerged, the most outstanding being Nordic, Alpine, and Eastern Mediterranean. Because of the "accidents" (anthropologically speaking) of their migrations, Jews are much more like Italians, French, and Spanish than like Germans and Slavs. In conclusion, the Jews are not a "race" like the Nordic or Alpine, but a "group of people as united biologically as is the average intermarrying social or geographical unit [e.g., Bavarians, Ukrainians, Swabians] living in relative isolation over a relatively long period of time found among white peoples" [15].

It should be pointed out that, racist literature to the contrary, "Aryan" is a language (not a race) and its origin is as unknown as is that of the prehistoric peoples who spoke it. It is the assumed parent-tongue of the

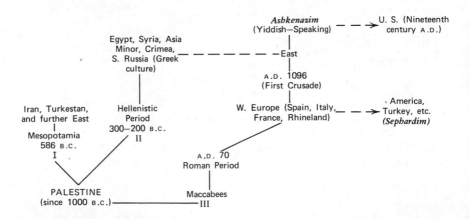

*Figure 2. The three great emigrations from Palestine and further main migrations of the Jews. (Source: Same as for Figure 1.)*

Indo-European languages. Thus the Yiddish language is as Aryan as German, English, or Kurdish and hosts of other languages, dead and living.

### *ANTISEMITISM* [16]

A. Some important features of the religio-cultural heritage of the Jews.

1. God, originally probably local, became the "Lord of Hosts," the commander of his soldiers, the Jews.
2. The interpreters of God's will were the Levites, priests who developed the Torah, an elaborate body of laws that undifferentiatedly embodies divine right (*fas*) and "everyday" right (*jus*).
3. The Prophets devaluated the sacrificial elements of the Jewish religion and further elevated the Torah. "Israel (the Jews) and the Law (the Torah) are one."
4. The universality of God, who availed himself of Assyria-Babylonia or other peoples to punish the Jews for not having adhered strictly to the Torah, is a culture trait that prevented the Jews from becoming merely a religious sect and made them a nation—a people without territory and subsequently without a common tongue (Hebrew becoming for the great majority only a ritual language, if used at all).

B. Characteristics of the Jews explained by their cultural heritage (see above) and their post-Biblical history [17].

1. Intellectualism, that is, respect for learning based on high regard for the Torah and its study and on the need to reconcile local conditions with Torah teachings; hence the legalistic and casuistic character of learning. (Legal heritage elaborated and incorporated in Talmud—literally, "study," "instruction," "doctrine"; nonlegal tradition, for example, interpretations of scriptural passages, legends, historical notes, epigrams, theological discussions, integrated in the Midrashim—literally, "investigation," "interpretation.")
2. Business sense, developed because Jews were for long periods and in many places barred from agriculture and therefore compelled to live in urban communities [18]. Trade and, particularly, peddling, pawnbroking, and moneylending were prohibited (only later stigmatized) to non-Jews.
3. Hypersensitivity, more intense than among other minorities, resulted from a long tradition of being torn betwen pride and humiliation—pride in representing monotheism (whose extreme formulation is the idea of the "chosen people"), humiliation because they were prevented from instituting a national state of their own.

These three characteristics appear to be more nearly objective than

many others frequently attributed to the Jews; that is, they are less created by a hostile attitude toward the Jews, less biased, and less merely
stereotypes. For other characteristics, see below.

C. Some important characteristics of contemporary Western society, especially the United States.

1. Urbanization; industrialization; importance of occupation (job); breakdown of *Gemeinschaft,* i.e., importance of secondary contacts and com-
plication of the social and economic order; nationalism; social disorganization and susceptibility to psychosis and faddism (e.g., Father Divine, Ku
Klux Klan).

2. United States

   a. Mores of white, Protestant, Anglo-Saxon rather than indiscriminate
   equality.

   b. The broad base of low-economic, low-status jobs within the occupational pyramid is the seat of potential frustration; outlets for this
   frustration disappeared with the passing of the Frontier and with the
   decline of large-scale immigration (no new immigrants for earlier immigrants to look down on; cf. Upton Sinclair, *The Jungle*).

D. Jews in contemporary United States.

1. Fallacy that Jews control basic industries; true that Jews are overrepresented in some parts of New York City and in some occupations (motion pictures, department stores, clothing), less so in some others (theater,
press, law, medicine).

2. Occupations in which Jews are overrepresented are themselves conspicuous; that is, they provide social and economic prestige; also, they are
developed in the urbanized, non-*Gemeinschaft* sphere in which there is
less discrimination against the Jews; the Jews' greater skills in these
occupations; possibly latent rural (and *Gemeinschaft*)-urban (secondary-
contact society) tension channeled into and exploited by anti-semitism.

E. Sociology and psychology of modern antisemitism [19].

*Note.* The term "antisemitism" was first used in 1879 by the German
Wilhelm Marr.

1. Antisemitism as a social-psychological phenomenon can perhaps be
best conceived of as passing through one or both of the following cycles:

   Cycle 1. (a) Mos of antisemitism, (b) stereotype of Jew, (c) intensification of stereotyped Jewish traits, (d) intensification of hostility, (e) mos
   of antisemitism; cycle repeats.

   Cycle 2. (a) Social disorganization, (b) insecurity, (c) frustration, (d) explosion of ingroup-outgroup tension, (e) hostile racial attitude, (f) stereotype of Jew, (g) intensification of stereotyped Jewish traits, (h) intensification of hostility, (i) social disorganization; cycle repeats.

2. Jews as scapegoats for frustration.

a. Jews are different from non-Jews: Jewish religion only non-Christian religion among Christians; no intermarriage; dietary habits; circumcision (perhaps attenuated castration increasing Jew's inferiority feeling and at the same time increasing non-Jew's fear of Jew); physiognomy.

b. Jews are like non-Jews: same God; same holy book (Old Testament); "family quarrel"; Jews are cultural and biological equals of non-Jews, hence conflict is more emotional than in case of white-black, white-yellow relations which on the whole can be better understood in terms of mere social distance.

c. Face-to-face ubiquity: Jews everywhere present; antisemitism everywhere readily understood (not a "domestic" affair).

d. Traditional scapegoat: ready availability of familiar channel of frustration (mos).

e. Characteristics of Jews transformed into hostile stereotypes:

Close attachment of Jews to Jewish culture becomes lack of attachment to adopted country (especially true in strongly nationalistic environments).

Bargaining ingenuity becomes "sharpness," "skinflintery," "smartness," "diabolical cleverness."

Jewish solidarity becomes "clannishness," "double morality," "Jewish world conspiracy" (*The Protocols of the Elders of Zion*).

Economic success makes all Jews moneybags.

Conspicuousness in certain occupations, especially in public entertainment, makes all Jews "show-offs," "loud," "egotistical."

Past migratory experience and adaptability of Jewish culture everywhere make Jews "cosmopolitan," "radical," but also "international plutocrats" and "capitalists."

f. Christ: killed by Jews, as many Christian children are taught in their religious-school textbooks [20]; at the same time Christ is a Jew who must be loved; frustration resulting from this ambivalence readily diverted toward Jews (cf. Samuel, *op. cit.*, in Note 19).

g. Economic myths: "the guileless Gentile" (who had no part in the formation of capitalism); the "myth of Solomon" (whose wealth proves the existence of a Jewish business empire in Biblical times); the "myth of Shylock" (the Jew as the bloodsucker); the "international financier" (the Jew controls the finances of the world); mainly initiated by Werner Sombart and all untenable before even a slight knowledge of economics and history.

These and other points are elements in a vicious circle; that is, they provoke the Jews to become, in self-defense and insecurity, more like the hated stereotypes, thus increasing the hostility. Psychologically, anti-semitism works via the mechanisms of displacement (Jew, instead of true object of antagonism, is the target), of projection (Jew is accused of one's own motives), and of rationalization (Jews are inferior, anti-Christ, Bolsheviks, and so on).

h. Jews as scapegoats in outstanding crises of modern history: 1096 A.D., first Crusade (large-scale emigration of Jews to the East began; see Figure 2); 1241, Mongolian invasion of Europe up to Silesia; 1348–1350, Black Death; 1575, depression; 1618–1648, Thirty Years' War; 1873, depression, followed by the formation of antisemitic parties, by anti-semitic massacres and legislation in Russia, and by large-scale emigration of Russian Jews to the United States.

F. A possible policy regarding antisemitism. Long-range and widespread sociological and psychological understanding by Jews and non-Jews alike of antisemitism and the problems involved in it may eventually attenuate ingroup-outgroup tension [21]. Such understanding will be possible only if efforts toward it are linked up with the elimination of the more tangible causes of frustration (economic and technological) and of the moral causes of frustration (especially the obstructions to participation or adequate participation in democracy).

---

### NOTES

1.   This syllabus originated from notes for two lectures I gave on the sociology of the Jews and antisemitism in Dr. Walter T. Watson's course on race relations at Southern Methodist University, June 1943. It has since been tried out on several occasions and has been revised in the light of the experiences gathered. I am indebted to Dr. Carleton S. Coon, Department of Anthropology, Harvard University, for a critical reading of a former draft and for several important suggestions, to Mr. Leo Shapiro, Director of the Department of Inter-cultural Relations of the Anti-Defamation League of B'nai B'rith, Chicago, for

a close reading of this paper, for numerous criticisms and suggestions, and for valuable bibliographical references, and to Dr. David Lefkowitz, Rabbi, Temple Emanu-El, Dallas, Texas, for bibliographical references.

2. The instructor may want to point out some of the difficulties inherent in a census of Jews. For a brief elementary statement see *American Jewish Year Book*, Vol. 46, 1944–1945 (Philadelphia: Jewish Publication Society, 1944), p. 491; for a more comprehensive treatment see Sophia M. Robison, "Methods of Gathering Data on the Jewish Population," in Sophia M. Robison, Ed., *Jewish Population Studies* (New York: Conference on Jewish Relation, 1943), pp. 1–9; for a critical analysis of statistical compilations of Jewish populations see Jacob Lestchinsky, "Anent Statistics in the *American Jewish Year Book*," *Journal of Jewish Bibliography*, 3 (January–April 1942), 15–18.

3. Arieh Tartakower and Kurt R. Grossman, *The Jewish Refugee* (New York: Institute of Jewish Affairs of the American Jewish Congress and World Jewish Congress, 1944), p. 336, Table I.

4. Arieh Tartakower, "The Jewish Refugees," *Jewish Social Studies*, 4 (October 1942), 314 ff.

5. Tartakower and Grossman, *op. cit.*, p. 343, Table III.

6. Tartakower, *op. cit.*, 316, Table III, and 321, Table VII.

7. Jacob Lestchinsky, *Balance Sheet of Extermination* (New York: Office of Jewish Information, "Jewish Affairs," Vol. I, No. 1, February 1, 1946), p. 10.

8. Here the instructor may point out the greater urbanization of the Jewish than of the general population by giving figures, or having his students compute figures, that will show the relative percentages of the Jewish and general populations residing in the largest cities of the nine states listed in Table 2, of the five states with the largest Jewish populations or of Jewish and general populations residing in urban places (of 2500 population and over) throughout the nation or in selected regions or states. These computations would make the significance of Table 3 more explicit. All of them (or others that may readily suggest themselves to teacher or student) can be made easily from the latest edition of the *American Jewish Year Book* [in the 1944–1945 edition (1944) from Tables V and VI] and from the latest census.

9. Because this syllabus was first used in Texas, that state was most interesting. The instructor will want to choose the state in which his or her school is located. This may be done with the help of the sources mentioned in n. 8.

10. Here the instructor can discuss the uneven immigration of Jews to the United States and other nineteenth-century events. A useful elementary text is Lee J. Levinger, *A History of the Jews in the United States* (Cincinnati: Department of Synagogue and School Extension of the Union of American Hebrew Congregations, 2nd. ed., 1935), pp. 12–16; see also Oscar I. Janowsky, Ed., *The American Jew, A Composite Portrait* (New York: Harper and Brothers, 1942), pp. 5 ff.

11. If needed, a brief explanation of the quota regulations and their political

background could be supplied here by the instructor. Any general encyclopedia article is sufficient for the purpose. Some instructors may find it appropriate to call attention to some recent, though unsuccessful, attempts at admitting refugees outside the quotas.

12. In this section an attempt is made on the basis of the latest scientific evidence available at the time of writing to dispose of the question of the Jewish "race" according to its biological meaning. Some considerations of race as a *sociological* concept (a "race-conscious group" or something similar) are discussed and more can be inferred by instructor and students from the statements made.

13. I owe this suggestion to a personal communication (August 7, 1945) from Dr. Carleton S. Coon. In the same communication Dr. Coon writes: "One thing that impressed me very much in the Middle East during my [recent] service overseas was the greatly improved physique of the Jews of Central European stock born in Palestine. They are large, heavy boned, big chested, muscular, erect; fine physical specimens, with none of the narrow-chested, stooped appearance of some of their parents. Life out of doors, as farmers and ranchers, seems to have done them a lot of good, with better food and more sunlight." The instructor may want to make some statement on the influence of diet and environment on physique, as measurably demonstrated in Franz Boas's well-known *Abstract of the Report on Changes in Bodily Form of Descendants of Immigrants* (The Immigration Commission, Washington, U.S. Government Printing Office, 1911). For classroom purposes this paper is available in abstracted form in A. L. Kroeber and T. T. Waterman, *Source Book in Anthropology* (New York: Harcourt, Brace, 1931), and in Franz Boas, *Race, Language and Culture* (New York: Macmillan, 1940). The instructor may also engage in a briefer and more general discussion of the influence of environment on variability for which the brief and elementary but illuminating treatment in William F. Ogburn and Meyer N. Nimkoff, *Sociology* (Boston: Houghton Mifflin, 1940), pp. 82–94, may provide a point of departure.

14. Here the instructor may apply a general race-relations theory to the Jews and, in particular, their history; for example, Jewish history might be considered in the light of Park's ideas about race relations and their poles, isolation and assimilation [cf. Robert E. Park, "Racial Assimilation in Secondary Groups with Particular Reference to the Negro," *American Journal of Sociology*, 19 (March 1914), 606–623], somewhat as follows: a first phase, from about 1000 B.C. to the early Hellenistic period, is characterized by isolation (Palestinian state) and later by increasing contacts that led to a second phase of voluntary isolation (the beginnings of the ghetto in which to hide from religious conversion in the later Hellenistic state), followed by compulsory isolation (throughout the Middle Ages); the third phase, emancipation, is one of assimilation, which in turn was replaced by (Nazi) isolation and extermination and by partly voluntary, partly compulsory isolation (Zionism). The instructor may examine the applicability to Jewish history, or to certain phases of it, and to certain aspects of Jewish-Gentile relations of Emory S. Bogardus' race-relations cycle ["A Race-

Relations Cycle," *American Journal of Sociology*, **35** (January 1930), 612–617]. Other investigations will suggest themselves.

15. Carleton S. Coon, "Have the Jews a Racial Identity," in Isacque Graeber and Steuart Henderson Britt, Eds., *Jews in a Gentile World* (New York, Macmillan, 1942), p. 35. For another physical anthropologist's concise and readable analysis of the racial position of the Jews see William Howells, *Mankind So Far* (Garden City, N. Y.: Doubleday, 1944), pp. 241–243.

16. This part is based largely on Graeber and Britt, *loc. cit.* For reasons of space it is presented in outline form. Notes provide bibliographical references for classroom discussion, reports, term papers, and further general study.

17. History of the ghetto and Jewish settlement patterns and personality types, especially in Chicago. Louis Wirth, *The Ghetto* (Chicago: University of Chicago Press, 1928).

18. For more general information see relevant articles in *Universal Jewish Encyclopedia, The Jewish Encyclopedia, Encyclopedia of the Social Sciences,* and others; Salo W. Baron, *Social and Religious History of the Jews* (New York: Columbia University Press, 1937), 3 vols., and *The Jewish Community* (Philadelphia: Jewish Publication Society, 1942), 3 vols.; Cecil Roth, *The Jewish Contribution to Civilization* (Cincinnati: Union of American Hebrew Congregations, 1940); Uriah Z. Engelman, *The Rise of the Jew in the Western World* (New York: Behrman's, 1944) (largely demographic); *American Jewish Year Book, loc. cit.;* and Arthur Ruppin, *The Jews in the Modern World* (London: Macmillan, 1934). For the history of the Jews in America, Levinger, *loc. cit.;* Peter Wiernik, *History of the Jews in America* (New York: Bloch, 1930); *Americans, All: A Short History of American Jews* (Chicago: Anti-Defamation League, n.d.); and Anita L. Lebeson, *Jewish Pioneers in America, 1492–1848* (New York: Brentano's, 1931). For economic and occupational aspects of Jewish life in the United States, Editors of Fortune, *Jews in America* (New York: Random House, 1936); Jacob Lestchinsky, "The Position of the Jews in the Economic Life of America," in Graeber and Britt, *op. cit.,* pp. 402–416; Nathan Reich, "Economic Trends," in Janowsky, *op. cit.,* pp. 161–182 (see also pp. 294–295 for a bibliography on the occupational distribution of Jews); several articles in *Jewish Social Studies,* Vol. I, 1939 ff.; Gabriel Davidson, *Our Jewish Farmers and the Story of the Jewish Agricultural Society* (New York: Fischer, 1943) (Jewish farmers and the Jewish farm movement in the United States, a little-known aspect of Jewish life); Sophia M. Robison, *loc. cit.* (socioeconomic and demographic studies of Jewish communities in Trenton, Passaic, Buffalo, New London, Norwich, Detroit, Pittsburgh, Chicago, Minneapolis, and San Francisco). The last-named book not only contains information on economics and occupations but also throws light on Jewish community life in the cities discussed. More comprehensive Jewish community studies are Leonard Bloom, "The Jews of Buna," in Graeber and Britt, *op. cit.,* pp. 180–199 (medium-sized metropolitan center of American industrial Midwest); Samuel Koenig, "The Socioeconomic Structure of an American Jewish Community," *ibid.,* pp. 200–242 (Stamford, Connecticut); Jessie Bernard, "Biculturality: A Study in Social

Schizophrenia," *ibid.,* pp. 264–293 ("Milltown, Winnemac," stimulating social-psychological theory); Uriah Z. Engelman, "Medurbia," *Contemporary Jewish Record,* **4** (August and October 1941), 339–348, 511–521 (statistical-average Jewish community in the United States); David G. Mandelbaum, "A Study of the Jews of Urbana," *Jewish Social Service Quarterly,* **12** (December 1935), 223–232; Bessie Bloom Wessel, *An Ethnic Survey of Woonsocket, Rhode Island* (Chicago: University of Chicago Press, 1931); Hartford Communal Study Committee, *Hartford Jewish Communal Study 1937–1938,* Hartford, 1938; Joseph M. Papo, "The Jewish Community of Duluth," *Jewish Social Service Quarterly,* **18** (December 1941), 219–231; Harold Orlansky, "The Jews of Yankee City," *Commentary,* **1** (January 1946), 77–85; Kurt H. Wolff, "Traditionalists and Assimilationists: A Sample Study of the Jewish Population in Dallas, Texas," *Studies in Sociology* (Southern Methodist University), **4** (Summer 1940), 20–25 (predominantly statistical; see Chapter 8); David G. Mandelbaum, "The Jewish Way of Life in Cochin," *Jewish Social Studies,* **1** (October 1939), 423–460 (history and social life of contemporary Cochin in Southwestern British India, an old, largely isolated Jewish community); M. J. Karpf, *Jewish Community Organization in the United States* (New York: Bloch, 1938); Abraham G. Duker, "Structure of the Jewish Community," in Janowsky, *op. cit.,* pp. 134–160. The two last-named items deal largely with Jewish organizations. Jewish organizations: *American Jewish Year Book, loc. cit.;* with special reference to refugees, Tartakower and Grossman, *op. cit., passim* and Chapters 13 and 14; on Zionism, *American Jewish Year Book, loc. cit.;* Sulamith Schwartz, "Zionism in American Jewish Life," in Janowsky, *op. cit.,* pp. 231–250; for classics in Zionist literature consult the encyclopedias listed above; Americanization of refugees from Nazism: Gerhart Saenger, *Today's Refugees, Tomorrow's Citizens* (New York: Harper, 1941) (much concrete but scarce statistical material); intermarriage, Milton L. Barron, "The Incidence of Jewish Intermarriage in Europe and America," *American Sociological Review,* **11** (February 1946), 6–13 (contains many bibliographical references).

19.   Graeber and Britt, *loc. cit.* (perhaps the best single book on antisemitism and other problems of the Jews from a social-scientific and sociological viewpoint); especially recommended are Talcott Parsons, "The Sociology of Modern Anti-Semitism," pp. 101–122; J. F. Brown, "The Origin of the Anti-Semitic Attitude," pp. 124–148; Miriam Beard, "Anti-Semitism—Product of Economic Myths," pp. 362–401; J. O. Hertzler, "The Sociology of Anti-Semitism through History," pp. 62–100 (rich in illustration but less important as theory); Anonymous, "An Analysis of Jewish Culture," pp. 243–263 (characteristics of Jewish and non-Jewish, especially American, cultures). The most useful books on antisemitism are probably Hugo Valentin, *Antisemitism, Historically and Critically Examined* (New York: Viking, 1936), and Lee J. Levinger, *Anti-Semitism, Yesterday and Tomorrow* (New York: Macmillan, 1936) (good short bibliography). Best in its "historical and regional studies" is Koppel S. Pinson, Ed., *Essays on Antisemitism* (New York: Conference on Jewish Relations, 1942). Among the various pertinent articles in the *Encyclopaedia of the Social Sciences* those on antisemitism by Benjamin Ginzburg and on race conflict by Hans

Kohn are especially worthy of study. Valuable insights are found in Milton Steinberg, *A Partisan Guide to the Jewish Problem* (Indianapolis: Bobbs-Merrill, 1945), pp. 44–112; helpful data on specifics: Sigmund Livingston, *Must Men Hate?* (New York: Harper, 1944); see also *Questions and Answers Concerning the Jew* (Chicago: Anti-Defamation League, 1942) and *Answers for Americans: "They Say the Jews. . . ."* (Los Angeles: University Religious Conference, n.d.). Among the many historical studies, in addition to Pinson, *loc. cit.,* may be mentioned James Parkes, *The Conflict of the Church and the Synagogue: A Study in the Origin of Anti-Semitism* (London, 1934) and Joshua Trachtenberg, *The Devil and the Jews; The Medieval Conception of the Jew and Its Relation to Modern Antisemitism* (New Haven: Yale University Press, 1943). A useful introduction to the sociological view of antisemitism is M. Ginsberg, "Anti-Semitism," *Sociological Review* (British), **35** (January-April 1943), 1–11. More factual and with reference to the United States are Alexander Lesser, "Anti-Semitism in the United States," *Journal of Negro Education,* **10** (July 1941), 545–556 (especially contemporary antisemitism), and Max Meenes, "American Jews and Anti-Semitism," *ibid.,* 557–566 (valuable for its summary of numerous sociological and psychological surveys and tests). For antisemitism as an instrument of fascist power, David W. Petegorsky, "The Strategy of Hatred," *Antioch Review,* **1** (September 1941), 376–388. Antisemitism from the standpoint of social psychology, viewed as a psychosis: Read Bain, "Sociopathy of Anti-Semitism," *Sociometry,* **6** (November 1943), 460–464. More specifically, but probably more debatably, antisemitism as unconscious hatred of Christ and Christianity: Sigmund Freud, *Moses and Monotheism* (New York: Knopf, 1939) (historically, hence fundamentally, unconvincing), and Maurice Samuel, *The Great Hatred* (New York: Knopf, 1941), more plausible if only because it lacks Freud's historical commitments. For a study of American antisemitic organizations in the thirties: Donald S. Strong, *Organized Anti-Semitism in America* (Washington: American Council on Public Affairs, 1941). Literature on Nazi atrocities and Jewish life in Nazi-dominated Europe is numerous. On the latter topic there are several valuably objective papers in *Jewish Social Studies;* on the former, mention may be made of *The Black Book of Poland,* issued by the Polish Ministry of Information (New York: Putnam, 1942), of Leib Spiesman, "In the Warsaw Ghetto," *Contemporary Jewish Record,* **4** (August 1941), 357–366, and of S. Moldawer, "The Road to Lublin," *ibid.,* **3** (March-April 1940), 119–133.

20. The later edition of the widely used Baltimore catechism [Rev. Francis J. Connell, *Father Connell's, The New Baltimore Catechism No. 3* (New York: Benzinger, 1943)] contains no statement to the effect that the Jews killed Christ—a fact contrary to the belief popular among non-Catholics.

21. *The Journal of Social Issues,* Vol. I, Nos. 1 and 2, deal in nontechnical language with racial and religious prejudice in everyday living and contain many valuable cases and policy suggestions regarding majority-minority relations, including the Jewish minority. For forecasts of the fate of Jews see Jacob Lestchinsky, "The Post-War Outlook for Jewry in Europe," *Menorah Journal,*

30 (Winter 1942), 13–37 (mainly economic); Salo W. Baron, "Reflections on the Future of the Jews in Europe," *Contemporary Jewish Record*, 3 (July–August 1940), 355–369 (postwar plans); Morris R. Cohen, "Jewish Studies of Peace and Post-War Problems," *ibid.*, 4 (April 1941), 110–125 (problems needing study and planning); *Jewish Post-War Problems, A Study Course*, prepared by the Research Institute on Peace and Post-War Planning of The American Jewish Committee (eight pamphlets, 1942–1943: I, "Why Study Post-War Problems"; II, "The Two World Wars—A Comparison and Contrast"; III, "How the Jewish Communities Prepared for Peace During the First World War"; IV, "Europe between the Two World Wars"; V, "The Position of the Jews in the Post-War World"; VI, "Palestine in the New World"; VII, "Relief, Reconstruction and Migration"; and VIII, "Jewish Survival in the Democracy of the Future"). For Jewish life in a democracy, see H. M. Kallen, "National Solidarity and the Jewish Minority," *Annals of the American Academy of Political and Social Science*, 223 (September 1942), 17–28 (democracy seen as an orchestra, minorities it instruments); for contributions of numerous minorities, including the Jewish, to American culture see Francis J. Brown and Joseph Slabey Roucek, Eds., *One America* (New York: Prentice-Hall, 1945) (subtitle, "The History, Contributions, and Present Problems of Our Racial and National Minorities"). The instructor may want to call the attention of students who desire to follow Jewish current events to *Commentary* (monthly; formerly *Contemporary Jewish Record*).

---

Reprinted from *Social Forces*, 24 (1946), 451–461, by permission of the publisher. The essay has been edited and partially revised by the author.

# 7

# TRADITIONALISTS
# AND ASSIMILATIONISTS
## A Sample Study of the
## Jewish Population
## in Dallas, Texas. 1940

The typical Dallas Jew is a 33-year-old male, born in Dallas or elsewhere in Texas. He is a high school graduate and has been employed for ten years as a salesman in a downtown ready-to-wear store. He married at 26, already well established in the firm for which he now works (he had held two other positions, the first at the age of 17 and while in school sold newspapers). He has two children, a boy of five and a one-year-old girl, and lives in South Dallas. He has occupied his present home for six years but is considering the possibility of moving to the northern part of the city and eventually building a small house for himself and his family. He speaks English exclusively but may understand Yiddish. He belongs to the Reformed synagogue and will send his children to its Hebrew School as soon as they reach the required age. He is a Mason, a more or less active member of one or more Jewish organizations, and will later join the P.T.A. He contributes annually to the Jewish Federation and the Community Chest.

His wife, a native of Dallas, has lived most of her life in her present neighborhood and, like her husband, is inclined to move toward a more modern part of town. She is 29, a high-school graduate, now a housewife and mother, but before marriage was employed as a stenographer. She belongs to the women's auxiliary of the Reformed synagogue and to the Hadassah. She is a member of a bridge circle and plays at least once a week.

Both her own and her husband's parents were born in Russia but came to this country 35 years ago. They speak English fluently, though with an accent, for they spoke Yiddish in the old country and later in America when their children were too young to understand. Now they speak it only occasionally when they converse with elderly people like themselves.

They do not long for the old country, although they, as well as their children, are concerned over the fate of the Jews in Europe, the parents more religiously and emotionally, the younger generation more politically and rationally. The same viewpoints apply to their love for America. The family as a whole is happy to be here in the "best country on earth," the parents because they appreciate the conditions under which they now live in comparison to the hardships of their life in Russia, the children because they cherish the advantages of democracy over totalitarianism.

These exact types, of course, cannot be found in life, but their characteristics are derived from the statistical averages treated in the following pages.


## POPULATION CHARACTERISTICS [1]


*Size of Population.* No one knows how many Jews live in Dallas, but guesses center around 8000 to 10,000. Assuming that the average Jewish household contains 3.75 persons—this figure is derived from a sample of 200 families—the 1767 known Jewish families in the city account for some 6636 individual Jews. Allowing an additional third for families not identified with Jewish organizations or not otherwise covered by the master list compiled for this study, the total Jewish population of Dallas may be as high as 9000, or almost three percent of the total population (preliminary 1940 census figure, 320,726) of the city. This percentage is lower than the percentage of Jews in the United States as a whole (approximately 3.5) and is far below the figure for many northern and eastern centers of similar size.

*Age and Sex Distribution.* Table 1 shows the age and sex distribution of the 737 individuals constituting the sample used. The average ages are (in years) male, 32.99, female, 35.1, total, 34.06. Males constitute 48.98 and females 51.02 percent of the sample. If we compare the age distribution given with that of Dallas as a whole, it appears that in all age groups up to

*Table 1. Age and Sex of 200 Jewish Families (737 Individuals) in Dallas*

| Age in Years | Male | Female | Total |
|---|---|---|---|
| 0– 4 | 20 | 17 | 37 |
| 5– 9 | 23 | 21 | 44 |
| 10–14 | 31 | 27 | 58 |
| 15–19 | 31 | 32 | 63 |
| 20–24 | 33 | 33 | 66 |
| 25–29 | 30 | 40 | 70 |
| 30–34 | 34 | 24 | 58 |
| 35–39 | 25 | 30 | 55 |
| 40–44 | 29 | 41 | 70 |
| 45–49 | 34 | 20 | 54 |
| 50–54 | 23 | 24 | 47 |
| 55–59 | 16 | 17 | 33 |
| 60–64 | 12 | 18 | 30 |
| 65–69 | 9 | 15 | 24 |
| 70–74 | 8 | 6 | 14 |
| 75–79 | 2 | 7 | 9 |
| 80–84 | 1 | 1 | 2 |
| 85–89 | 0 | 2 | 2 |
| 90–94 | 0 | 1 | 1 |
| Total | 361 | 376 | 737 |

34 the percentages are higher for the total population. In the older groups (above 35) percentages for the Jews are higher. This means that the sample population is older than the total population (see Table 2).

## Family and Marriage

SIZE OF FAMILY AND HOUSEHOLD. First we compare the "small" family of parents and children exclusively; average size, 3.34 members. Then the "large" family in which there are additional relatives; average size, 3.69. Next is the "household," in which additional persons (boarders and roomers but excluding servants) live in the same habitation; average size, 3.75. The average size is slightly smaller than that of the general population of Dallas, which is 3.8.

NUMBER OF CHILDREN. The average number of children residing with family heads is 1.52. The average number of children alive, whether residing with parents or not, is 2.11. Children living and deceased average 2.22.

Table 2.  *Percentages of Dallas and Jewish Popu-*
*lation in Specified Age Groups*

| Age in Years | Total Population | Jewish Population |
|---|---|---|
| 0– 4 | 8 | 5 |
| 5–14 | 16 | 13 |
| 15–24 | 19 | 18 |
| 25–34 | 22 | 17 |
| 35–44 | 16 | 17 |
| 45–64 | 15 | 21 |
| 65 and over | 4 | 9 |
| Total | 100 | 100 |

Table 3.  *Types of Family with Specified Numbers of Members*

| Number of Members | Small Families | Large Families | Households |
|---|---|---|---|
| 1 | 11 | 8 | 8 |
| 2 | 44 | 33 | 32 |
| 3 | 56 | 50 | 49 |
| 4 | 59 | 58 | 55 |
| 5 | 23 | 33 | 36 |
| 6 | 3 | 12 | 13 |
| 7 | 3 | 4 | 4 |
| 8 | 1 | 2 | 3 |
| Total | 200 | 200 | 200 |

MARRIAGE AND OTHER DATA.  Among 186 marriages for which there are
data 174 are between Jews; twelve (6.5 percent) are mixed marriages
(Jewish man and non-Jewish woman, 9; non-Jewish man and Jewish
woman, 3). It is probable that the total number of mixed marriages is
underestimated, since persons involved in such unions are often not
identified with the Jewish community and are most likely to have been
omitted from the master list. In all there are ten cases of previous marriages. The age range of husbands at time of marriage is 15–20 to 45–50
years; the average is 26.35 years. Wives vary from 15–20 to 35–40 years;
the average is 22.05 years. The age range of the wives at the time of birth
of the first child is 17–36 years; the average is 24.64 years. The average
time elapsing between first and second births is 4.34 years (number of
cases, 71), that between second and third births, 4.92 (cases, 26). Extreme
differences in age between husband and wife are those in which the
husband is five years younger and 18 years older. In the average case he is
4.6 years older. Among the 200 families 35 (17.5 percent) are broken

(3 heads are widowers, 25 are widows, 7 are single men and women). The average number of years of marriage in the 165 cases of unbroken families is 21.93. The duration of these marriages, and those already terminated by death, is summarized in Table 4.

*Residential Distribution.* The Jews studied are widely scattered over the city, although their distribution according to census tracts is not proportionate. A classification of the 60 tracts (58, plus Highland Park and University Park) by number of Jews in each shows that seven tracts have no Jewish population, 18 tracts have a population of 0–4 families, 19 of 5–20 families, seven of 21–49 families, four of 50–99, three of 100–149, one of 150–249 (227), and one of 250–350 (338). If the percentages of Jews to total white population are calculated for individual tracts, we find that seven tracts contain no Jewish population, 19 have 0.1–0.4 percent, 16 have 0.5–1.4, eight have 1.5–4.9, five have 5.0–9.9, two have 10.0–14.9, one has 15.0–19.9 (16.8), and one has 50.0–55.0 (54.0) percent. For one tract no percentage is available because a total population figure is lacking.

*Nativity.* In the sample 72.76 percent are American-born (72.35, males, 73.16, females) and 27.24 percent are foreign-born. Among the 201 foreign born 89 are natives of Russia, 36 of Poland, 30 of Germany, and 14 of Lithuania. Twelve additional countries claim less than ten representatives each. The average age of 199 foreign-born on arrival in United States was 19.48 years (see Table 5).

Interesting variations in nativity are observed when the several generations are compared. Although 72.76 percent of the total sample are American-born, only 57.03 percent of the present generation (i.e., family heads) and 12.27 percent of the past generation (parents of heads and wives) were born in America. In contrast to these figures 92 percent of the children of the present heads and wives are American-born.

Table 4. Duration of 193 Marriages

| Length in Years | Number of Couples |
|---|---|
| 0– 9 | 43 |
| 10–19 | 51 |
| 20–29 | 51 |
| 30–39 | 29 |
| 40–49 | 11 |
| 50–59 | 7 |
| 60–69 | 1 |

*Table 5.   Age of 199 Foreign-Born at Time of Immigration
into the United States*

| Age in Years | Male | Female | Total |
|:---:|:---:|:---:|:---:|
| 0– 9 | 20 | 28 | 48 |
| 10–19 | 36 | 30 | 66 |
| 20–29 | 26 | 26 | 52 |
| 30–39 | 11 | 11 | 22 |
| 40–49 | 0 | 4 | 4 |
| 50–59 | 3 | 3 | 6 |
| 60–69 | 1 | 0 | 1 |
| Total | 97 | 102 | 199 |

*Citizenship.*   In the sample 92.09 percent are American citizens (93.82, males, 90.45, females), 79.41 percent are American-born, and 20.59 percent, naturalized.

*Language.*   English is spoken exclusively in 132 families (66.32 percent). In 46 families (23.12 percent) English plus the language of the original country is spoken (in 44, English and Yiddish), and in 21 families (10.56 percent) a foreign language is used exclusively (in 14, Yiddish, in 5, German).

*Occupational Distribution.*   Excluding housewives (27.95 percent), students (21.44 percent), and those under school age (5.56 percent), 45.05 percent of the population studied are, or have been, gainfully occupied. In this group (present or past) only thirteen of 254 males and four of 78 females are unemployed. Table 6 indicates that Dallas Jews are, above everything else, traders. A further inspection of this table shows that four out of five are engaged in trade, clerical occupations, or the learned professions.

Collating the data with special reference to present employment, we find 22 of the 200 (large) families with no male member now gainfully employed, 137 with no female member gainfully employed, but only eight families with none of either sex gainfully employed. Conversely, there are 128 families with one male, 52 with one female, 40 with two males, and nine with two females gainfully employed. At the extreme one family boasts six employed members. The average number of gainfully employed male members per family is 1.20, for female, 0.38, and for the family as a unit, 1.58.

The age at which the first paid full-time work was done regularly for at least one month ranges from 6 to 27 years for males and 10 to 55 years for females; the average is 16.91 years for males, 19.19 for females, and

Table 6.   Occupations of 254 Males and 78 Females by Percentages

| Occupation | Male | Female | Total |
|---|---|---|---|
| Retired | 5.91 | 1.28 | 4.82 |
| Professional Service | 11.02 | 11.54 | 11.14 |
| Trade | 53.54 | 35.90 | 49.40 |
| Manufacturing and Mechanical | 12.61 | 5.13 | 10.84 |
| Clerical | 12.21 | 42.31 | 19.28 |
| Transportation and Communication | 1.57 | 0 | 1.20 |
| Domestic and Personal Service | 1.57 | 1.28 | 1.51 |
| Not Specified | 1.57 | 2.56 | 1.81 |
| Total | 100.00 | 100.00 | 100.00 |

17.89 for the total group. The length of time employed in the same position ranges from a few days to 45 years; the average for males is 9.99 years, for females, 5.64, and for the total, 8.97.

*Mobility.*

LENGTH OF RESIDENCE IN THE UNITED STATES, IN TEXAS, AND IN DALLAS.   The average length of residence (see Table 7) of foreign-born in the United States is 30.40 years, in Texas, 23.69 years, and in Dallas, 20.91 years. Among the American-born 66.62 percent were born in Texas, 56.11 percent in Dallas, and 33.38 percent elsewhere in the United States.

Table 7.   Duration of Residence of 195 Foreign-Born Jews in United States, Texas, and Dallas, by Percentages

| Years of Residence | United States | Texas | Dallas |
|---|---|---|---|
| 0– 4 | 100.00 | 100.00 | 100.00 |
| 5– 9 | 88.21 | 82.05 | 79.07 |
| 10–14 | 87.70 | 78.46 | 74.96 |
| 15–19 | 84.11 | 69.23 | 65.73 |
| 20–24 | 77.95 | 62.05 | 55.99 |
| 25–29 | 74.36 | 53.84 | 46.25 |
| 30–34 | 53.85 | 32.30 | 25.74 |
| 35–39 | 33.34 | 20.51 | 16.51 |
| 40–44 | 24.62 | 14.87 | 9.84 |
| 45–49 | 17.44 | 9.23 | 5.22 |
| 50 and over | 13.33 | 7.18 | 3.69 |

LENGTH OF RESIDENCE IN PRESENT HOME. Residence in the present home is as long as 50 years (one case). Two-thirds have lived in their homes fewer than 10 years, and one-third more than 10 years. The average length is 8.27 years. Only 6.71 percent of all persons older than 10 years were born in the homes in which they were living.

*Education.* Table 8 shows the scholastic distribution of 158 students at the time the survey was made.

Excluding the 158 students in school at present, we find that 34.7 percent of the American-born not now in school have had college educations, 56.8 percent only high school, and 8.5 percent only grade school. Breaking these figures down according to sex, we see that 38.7 percent of the American-born males and 31.2 percent of the females have had college educations, 51.6 percent of the American-born males and 61.4 percent of the females have had high-school educations, and 9.7 percent of the males and 7.4 percent of the females have attended grade school only.

*Table 8. Scholastic Distribution of 158 Students*

| Types of School | Male | Female | Total |
| --- | --- | --- | --- |
| Private | 1 | 3 | 4 |
| Kindergarten | 1 | 4 | 5 |
| Grade School | 39 | 28 | 67 |
| High School | 25 | 25 | 50 |
| College | 16 | 16 | 32 |
| Total | 82 | 76 | 158 |

Table 9 summarizes the educational backgrounds of both American and foreign-born Jews in the group studied.

*Social Affiliation*

RELIGIOUS (CONGREGATIONAL) AFFILIATION. Among the 365 heads and wives 120 (32.88 percent) are not affiliated with a synagogue (congregation), 245 (67.12 percent) are (but 30 more membership listings resulted from affiliations with more than one congregation). Forty-five of the 245 who are affiliated belong to Congregation A, 14 to B, 14 to E—all religiously orthodox groups and all composed largely of members of Eastern European origin. Ninety-nine are members of Congregation C, a large conservative synagogue between the orthodox and the reformed type, 103 of D, a reformed church. The latter represent the most Americanized and tolerant sector of the Dallas Jewish population.

*Table 9.  Educational Distribution of 508 Jews in Dallas*[1]

| Type of School | American-Born | | Foreign-Born | | Total | |
|---|---|---|---|---|---|---|
| | No. | % | No. | % | No. | % |
| Grade School | 28 | 8.5 | 52 | 29.3 | 80 | 15.7 |
| High School | 188 | 56.8 | 48 | 27.2 | 236 | 36.5 |
| Private Religious Education | 0 | 0 | 56 | 31.7 | 56 | 11.0 |
| College | 115 | 34.7 | 21 | 11.8 | 136 | 26.8 |
| Total | 331 | 100.0 | 177 | 100.0 | 508 | 100.0 |

[1] Excluding students and those under school age.

OTHER AFFILIATIONS.  Among the 692 individuals more than five years old 248 (35.84 percent) are members of various kinds of Jewish organization. In addition, 50 (27.62 percent) of the 181 female heads and heads' wives belong to the Hadassah, a Zionist women's organization. Among those more than ten years old 120 (18.52 percent) are members of various school organizations (Jewish and non-Jewish), including the P.T.A., school clubs for children, Dads' clubs, fraternities, and sororities. Among the 172 male heads 53 (30.82 percent) are members of a Masonic organization. Fifteen heads and wives (4.11 percent) belong to non-Jewish social clubs, 14 (3.84 percent) to non-Jewish cultural clubs, which include literary and musical societies and similar organizations. Seventy heads and wives (19.15 percent) are not affiliated with any kind of organization, religious or otherwise.

## TRADITIONALISM AND ASSIMILATIONISM

In seeking to interpret Jewish life in Dallas our main thesis is that the Jewish population is divided into two groups. One may be called traditionalist, the other assimilatory.

For the *traditionalist group* religious and ritual prescriptions dominate every aspect of life. This group therefore lives near the synagogue and, consequently, close together. In former times they were evidently much more numerous. This is indicated both by census tract data and by the fact that many Jewish families, once in South Dallas (the most densely populated Jewish part of town), have moved, and are moving, to parts of the city more distant from the center of worship. Moving away not only means going to live in a non-Jewish environment but, if services are to be attended, also involves the necessity of violating the (Talmudic) prohibition against riding on the Sabbath. A trend toward more fashionable residential sections and, particularly, the FHA building program, have appealed to many Jews more strongly than has their concern with strict religious observance.

The traditionalist group, however, are characterized as Jewish not only by their religious performance but also by their attitude toward the world in general, that is, by a definitely Jewish culture. For them the only important viewpoint is the Jewish viewpoint. Furthermore, the circumference of interest is limited to personal, family, and local neighborhood matters. This limitation of intellectual horizon does not necessarily mean a limitation of the emotional horizon. On the contrary, detachment from strict religious observance seems to carry with it a reduction of general emotional faculty. This hypothesis may be illustrated by differences in concern for the "Jewish fate" of today. This concern—particularly for the suffering of Jews in Europe—is general among all Jewish groups, but three different attitudes toward it—"idyllic," "praying," "assimilatory"—may be distinguished. Those who have adopted the idyllic attitude complain about the terrible fate of European Jews and especially about the destiny of refugees. Simultaneously they boast acquaintance with everyone in their respective neighborhoods ("Well, many have moved away or have passed on"), including, of course, the rabbi and the principal of the Hebrew school ("I should say I know him!"). Concern for the Jewish fate is merged with and softened by the familiar environments of everyday life. Nevertheless, deep anxiety is a vivid element in this idyl. The praying attitude is characterized by a persistent and helpless worry about the sufferings of the Jews; it finds its expression in prayer—alone, in the family, or in the synagogue. Finally, those who represent the assimilatory attitude do as much as or probably more than the others to relieve the suffering of Jews. The main difference lies in a much more practical, less emotional, approach. The idyllic and the praying attitudes are found in the traditional group, whereas the attitude of the assimilatory group has in general a strongly constructive-defensive political color.

In the assimilatory group social control exercised by religious traditions has considerably weakened. New controls of a non-Jewish nature—common to our time in general, to American civilization, and to local fashions—have been and are being substituted. Wider housing trends which persuade many Jews to move from traditional residential sections near the synagogues to neighborhoods that are indifferent to Jewish viewpoints have already been cited. Reactions to this study reveal further characteristics of this group. A well-to-do woman, member of the reformed synagogue (Congregation D) and living in a neighborhood far from South Dallas, showed the most typical reaction: the study implied an unjustifiable distinction between Jews and non-Jews. The argumentation of this woman, though drastic and personal, seemed representative of a larger group.

> Many Gentiles think there are snakes in Jewish homes. They should come and see them, and see that they are just like any other homes. At a tea party in a Jewish house I overheard (purposely) the talk of two Gentile women. "Isn't it nice here?" one said. "Oh, I simply think it's gorgeous!" said the other. And I bet she didn't find any snakes! On another occasion, a Gentile woman working in the Community Chest told me she believed all Jews were rich because she had never seen a Jewish name in the Chest's charity list. I asked her, "Don't you know that we Jews give twice: once to the Chest and once to the Jewish Federation that cares for the Jewish indigent?" She was quite astonished to hear that we don't have religious prejudices and that we give to everybody, and she concluded that they, the Gentiles, were more prejudiced than we!

The elements characterizing the group to which this informant belongs are (1) fear of drawing too much attention to the Jews, (2) belief that there exists suspicion or/and ignorance about the Jews on the part of non-Jews, (3) belief in substituting understanding for this mistrust by casual and planned mutual acquaintance, (4) conviction of their own—Jewish—generosity and tolerance superior to those of non-Jews. All these elements seem to be rationalizations (individual or group) of an attempt to orient and guide the Jewish group in these agitated times.

As noted, the bulk of Eastern European immigrants is traditionalist, a classification much less common among the (less numerous) Western and Central European migrants found in Dallas. The reason for remaining traditional is that the circumference of cultural (occupational and social) interaction has remained unbroken by group self-sufficiency and a pervading religious control. The reason for becoming assimilated is the influence of the American (non-Jewish) environment—language, housing conditions, new technical commodities, new types of leisure (movies, cars, dances, and drugstores)—all introduced mainly by the younger generation, born or educated in America. Once these devices have weakened Jewish group self-sufficiency and religious control they appeal strongly by offering new possibilities for living and thereby result in Americanization.

The two extreme sociological situations represented by the Jews in Dallas (and presumably elsewhere) are the *state within the state* (traditionalists) and the total *absorption by the environment*, or Americanization (assimilatory group). Religious indifference or the adoption of a non-Jewish faith may characterize the latter. These two extremes are categories of a purity that is usually reserved to theory. In practice they are intermingled with each other and with other elements. Actually the Dallas Jewish population seems to be in transition toward more general and more thorough Americanization. When and where this process will stop and where it will lead depends largely on the general developments of our time.

### NOTE

Data for this study were derived from a sample of 200 families (every tenth name on a master list of about 2000 Dallas Jews). Deductions for duplications and other errors reduced the family count to 1767. The sample therefore represents 11.62 percent of this total.

---

Reprinted from *Studies in Sociology* (Southern Methodist University), 4 (1940), 20–25, by permission of the publisher. The essay has been edited and partially revised by the author.

# 8

# "EXERCISE IN COMMEMORATION." 1961

To be silent about what we cannot grasp is the only adequate mode of being: the only adequate mode of being when confronted with what we cannot grasp is *not* to be silent about it.

Between these two contradictory truths lies our dilemma, for we can neither be silent nor speak; we must speak but we cannot speak. "We," now, are those who in our own lives or in the lives of others with whom we have talked remember what we are called on to be silent about and what with equal claim we are called on to speak about so that we and others with whom we are silent or speak may hear—hear the silence or the words. The solution of the dilemma lies in the metamorphosis of one into the other, of silence into words, so that the words surpass even the silence in eloquence. This solution is the poet's.

To *talk* about it testifies to the presence of a mind that is incapable of achieving the metamorphosis of silence into words it knows it is called on to do. Such a report on the mind's impotence to transform wordlessness into words testifies to the mind's power as insight into its weakness and strength to face it; such a report thus makes the nature of the mind more visible, more palpable. To do this, to make the mind more visible, is at this moment emerging as of the Jewish essence, and as we say so or are told so we show or are shown that we have begun to commemorate, to bring back to mind, to receive back into our hearts, to begin our *recordatio* of what "Jew" means, hence of what the hunting down of the Jews by the Nazis means.

Our commemoration of the fate of the Jews under nazism proves that we have not forgotten this fate, not forgotten ourselves, and that those

115

of us who have not forgotten it want the younger ones among us who
have not experienced it to have it in their minds so that it may become
more ineluctably part of them, because this serves their identification.
Indeed, there is only a remote limit—it is almost no limit—to the distinctness with which we can bring something back to mind, with which
we can make it part of ourselves, so that—and only then have we reached
that limit—we are changed, we are new men who have heeded the imperative *memento*, have experienced *recordatio*.

This is what a poem can do. On one occasion of such metamorphosis—
the commemoration of a torso of Apollo—the German poet Rainer
Maria Rilke, inviting us to take part in the poem, was able to remind us
that this "torso is aglow," for

> *Otherwise this stone would stand struck down, struck small,*
> *under the shoulders' transparent fall*
> *and would not glisten like the fur of beasts of prey,*
>
> *and would not break apart its earthbound hive,*
> *a star arising: for there is no ray*
> *that does not find you. You must change your life* [1].

I have no poem for *our* occasion, but I hope, though with great diffidence, to make the nature of the mind more palpable. I must write prose,
but I shall try to make it evocative. I will submit a few fragments from the
illimitable material that bears on the fate of the Jews under nazism and
about which we must be silent if we would discipline ourselves toward
that receptivity to the word that may, one day, enable us to speak.

The fate of the Jews under nazism is many things. It is the history of
the Jews in Germany of which we must remind ourselves for some of the
light it would throw on their years under nazism; hence we must recall
the history of Germany and of the Germans themselves, and from it we
must go on to grasp what we can responsibly mean by "Jewish" and by
"German" in order to understand nazism and its version of Jewishness,
its treatment of the Jews, and the Jews' reaction to it. We must go further,
beyond Germans and Jews, into the fate of Western man and must move
toward ourselves, beyond nationality and religion, as Western men and
simply as men, today, in this world. Beyond all these matters of history
and identification we must allow ourselves to be led into their hearts, into
right and wrong, right suffering and wrong suffering, fulfillment and
misery—into *meaning*.

To say this can serve only to help us realize what we *cannot* do in this
hour, for to do it all would require much study, much information, much

pondering of information, much discussion, dialogue, and action. It *would* be a way of commemorating, but it would take a lifetime, more than an individual's. Of such exploring and meditating that it would take I have done only a tiny little, but I want you to come with me; let us engage in it together, in a brief exercise in commemoration.

QUESTION.   You mean to say the dead lay many weeks outside?

MISS LICHTHEIM.   Yes, they were lying there with nothing on. Often I would pass the crematory because at night we had to fetch those kettles with soup. Every day there was another shift. We passed the crematories and we saw mounds of dead, it was unbelievable—dead with whom the crematories could not keep up. There were mountains of dead, and from the air came all the sickness. . . .

QUESTION.   Who freed you?

MISS LICHTHEIM.   The English. In April, when we didn't expect it at all. We didn't expect any liberty. We absolutely did not know that liberation was so near. And it comes to us. We didn't have any contact with anybody. All at once we saw the SS men and the SS women carrying white bands on their arms.

QUESTION.   What did that mean?

MISS LICHTHEIM.   Armbands? That meant—they surrendered [2].

This from Bergen-Belsen is no more than an infinitesimal facet of a common story. Nor, obviously, could the man who, in his book *I Did Not Interview the Dead,* recorded these stories from labor camps and concentration camps interview even one of the millions who had been murdered or left to die.

A short passage from a conversation held a few years later, in 1950 or 1951, among Germans in Germany—and a large number of similar conversations are on record—goes as follows:

OTTO.   Yes, can't one say that in Western Europe in general there exists some hatred of the Jew? For I can still remember that Italy, too, was about to shove off the Jews, by and by—but not just in the fashion National Socialism did.

DISCUSSION LEADER.   Wasn't Italy under the influence of the Germans?

OTTO.   No, before, too.

DISCUSSION LEADER.   No, not before.

THOMAS.   No, no—France just the same. There is a hatred of the Jews there, just as in Germany.

DISCUSSION LEADER.   Yes, today.

THOMAS.   Chiefly by the capitalists, by the big ones, see.

DISCUSSION LEADER.   Something has remained there of the after-effect of German propaganda; for before the war, there wasn't.

THOMAS.   I believe there was. The Jew was just as hated in France; I experienced it, I heard it.

DISCUSSION LEADER.   Mr. Thomas says that the Jews were hated in other countries of Europe just as much as in Germany, and he thinks of France, too. That's what you said, wasn't it?

THOMAS.   Yes.

ETTINGER.   Yes, chiefly in France, too, the Jew is hated as he says, because of capital. The Jew usually had larger capital, and after all it is perhaps business competition or somehow. . . . The hate, it comes [ . . . ] Not race, as it was understood in Germany. A parasite it is who, perhaps in France among capitalists, is somehow understood as competition, or somehow.

DISCUSSION LEADER.   How come you mean as parasite in Germany?

ETTINGER.   Well, that's what was preached: the Jew is a parasite [3].

Many Germans did not know what went on, others did, and most, probably, stood in between. Here is part of a tortured, near-insane outburst of one of them:

> This flood from above, that's secured 100 per cent, it is overcoming us, and we, with it as Germans, are coming along into the Great Flood. But out of itself, through the inner revolutions that arise there, there is fight against fight, there is fratricide, let's say, the remnant are all socialists. We are building a new State. That's the socialist State, and he who once more sins against this State ends up on the tree of life, that's the gallows. That's what we build there, and there he'll be hanged [4].

This is a last but futile clutching before the Great Flood, above which stands the gallows as the tree of life. Death by violence is the only meaning left, and among the many slain there also is the Christian *arbor felix*, the trunk of the crucifix, whose wood came from paradise.

Except for heightening illustrations, I expected such things when I returned to Germany nineteen years after 1933, the year I left it; but to have my expectations confirmed made me heavy-hearted and so I still am. I saw people and ruins and landscapes, people I had known 30 years before, ruined people, abandoned ruins, and ruins with people in them though also people and things that had not changed, that could not be ruined. What did all that I saw refer to, what did it mean?

I remember the day I arrived, a beautiful Sunday in summer. People were out, walking with pride and dignity, and I suffered from their importance and felt good about their dignity; but what of the world in which I saw myself and these people walking? I remember that the question hit me most poignantly when I sat down in a garden café, tired, though I had not walked long: the people were marionettes, the café, the houses, and the streets, a stage, but I knew neither the play nor my own role or whether I was spectator or director. At any rate, I did not act. I had been in such a play before. I did not feel rejected by the company. I was no longer with it either. It was the past remembered, but there was no straight line connecting it with the present. The past was shoved aside, and I did not know the route I must follow to return to it to see how it still related to me. There was the unsubduable violence of the past, and much of this past had been wiped out, though the ruins remained over heaps of the dead and offered shelter to the living who could find no other.

There were other features of the past in the many tales I was told, mostly by friends I had known before that past, experiences they and others had had during the years until 1948, all of which were incredible to them even then. They did not understand how they had survived and could never have relived a recurrence of the extremes they somehow, through myriad accidents, had overcome. Of course, many had not, but how did those of us who are still here?

I very much wish you had forgotten that I have been talking as much, or more, about Germans as about Jews; that you were not asking yourselves whether I was talking about Jews or, in case I wasn't, why not? And when I say that I was talking about people, about mankind today, of which we are all a part, I do not mean to blur the differences between good and evil, innocence and guilt. Rather I am trying to make this Jewish commemoration a human commemoration. Nor do I mean to deny the differences between Jews and Germans; but the one most relevant here seems to be this: that some Germans play Jewish suffering against the German, whereas some Jews consider the German suffering *along with* the Jewish. For these people survival has engendered a greater generosity and a heightened consciousness of the gravity of the hour, when, as once again Rilke put it,

> *Whoever is now dying anywhere in the world,*
> *for no reason dying in the world,*
> *is looking at me* [5].

And now, my last document: a poem by Karl Wolfskehl, a German and a Jew. It is *Job-Samson,* one of the four parts of his book, *Job, Or the Four Mirrors.* Wolfskehl here sees Job as Samson, the blind singer, and his poem ends in an apocalypse not unlike that emerging from the raving speech of that unnamed German from which I quoted earlier.

### JOB-SAMSON

They had him brought out of his dungeon,
To sip his suffering, a heady drink.
They mocked him: he was allowed to sing again,
As up in the mountains, where spring hurls its song
Across the valleys, lusty in wild-sobbing pain:
"Strike up! Here, grab your kinnor, sing, we're listening!"

But he, unchained, stands heavy on the boards,
Feeling the sea's flood rushing towards him,
Who stood alone on the flat, shelly strand,
Twisted, alone, in the penitent's hair shirt.
They scream "Hold on to the pillar!" Red shame
Overcomes him, the blind one, for obeying them.
He gnaws his lip, his temples throb
Before the yelling hall, he dumbly gasps, neck bent
Under his heavy head of curls, as if he were asleep,
Nothing behind his eyelids. Knee knocks against knee.
"Do your duty, hand!" he breaks out, in a cramped sob,
He feels as if a leech were sucking out of him
The last drop of still-quivering life.
"Hey, why doesn't he sing?
Why doesn't he rave? Smash his mug!"
There, this noise around him, he groans, as if he forced
Into his breath all creatures' misery
Over the gloomy claim of our flesh.
There his mouth is foaming like breakers' roll,
His ache is like the hiss of world-fire going out,
There he lifts himself up, head and shoulders
Pushing near the high hall's ceiling,
There his mouth wells, darkly,
There he knows judgment, order, hour,
There he roars long and long, there he sings and calls:

"Who rammed me, fir of the dunes,
Into trickle under receding waves?

Must I hold up the quicksand, stem it
That it bunch up against the water's whirling rush,
Must I claw, must my groaning root hold it,
I, last stock on the edge of the sea?
Can I stand firm against the breakers,
Am I no longer their son?
Do waves break more than land?
Is my stubbornness
Not a crime?
I am set against God's verdict:
'It's over! There is no holding it! Smite, hammer!'
Why can I not be deaf to all this roar and wail?
Help? Whom? Whom no help befits?
That is why the world has tied and lashed me,
That is why I must hold out
In wind and cloudburst,
That is why God's fist
Has knocked me about, why I am plucked and ripped,
Why I am parched, have had to endure
The lack of flowers and fruits,
That is why my branches are twisted and matted,
Why a worm is locked in my sap,
Why my boughs are bare.
My claws, why don't you let go?
Why do you sink your hold into the rotten womb?
May it wither before tomorrow!
Why are you roaring behind your screen of wind, you lions of the flood?
Push in! Come over! I leave you to your course,
No fir is in your way,
I, the keeper, myself open your path:
Come!
God's lust and ruin are gone!"

The blood song becomes dusk. The vault cracks.
One death thrusts all life into night [6].

I have given you only some fragments that may seem disconnected, that were pushed out like splinters in a wound, of one source, the fate of the Jews under the Nazis. You have to put them together into a pattern. Now you are exposed to them, to these splinters, to these stabs: suffer them to become stronger. Or, instead of splinters or stabs, think of them as thorns and make them into a crown—not for wearing in hypocrisy or self-pity, the false pride of tragic feeling, but for changing them into flower and fruit. We don't know what the flower and fruit will be. It matters little, as long as they grow and you grow with them and know it. *"Out of this nettle, danger, . . . pluck this flower!"*

## NOTES

1.  *Archaischer Torso Apollos.*

2.  David P. Boder, *I Did Not Interview The Dead* (Urbana: University of Illinois Press, 1949), p. 160.

3.  Kurt H. Wolff, *German Attempts at Picturing Germany: Texts* ("Studies in German-American Postwar Problems, No. 3") [Columbus: Ohio State University, Department of Sociology and Anthropology, August 1955 (mimeographed)], p. 91.

4.  Kurt H. Wolff, "On Germany and Ourselves," *Southwest Review,* **41** (Winter 1956), 61–62 [Chapter 9]; translated from (another conversation among those drawn on in the previous quotation) Friedrich Pollock, Ed., *Gruppenexperiment* ("Frankfurter Beiträge zur Soziologie, Band 2"), (Frankfurt a.M.: Europäische Verlagsanstalt, 1955), pp. 349–350.

5.  *Schwere Stunde.*

6.  *Der zweite Spiegel: Hiob Simson. Hiob oder die vier Spiegel* (Hamburg: Claasen, 1950), pp. 12–14. The present translation is published with the kind permission of Dr. Margot Ruben, Karl Worlskehl's literary executor and trustee.

---

Reprinted from *Jewish Quarterly,* 8 (1961), 14–17, by permission of the publisher. The essay has been edited and partially revised by the author.

# III

# GERMANY,
## the United States
## and the Intellectual

*In memory of Hans Weil and C. Wright Mills; for Saul
Bellow, John W. Bennett, Stephen Gilman, Ellen B. Hill,
Everett Cherrington Hughes, Rudolph Kieve, Roy Harvey
Pearce, and Melvin Tumin*

In Part III I have assembled three papers: Chapter 9, "On Germany and
Ourselves" (1956), Chapter 10, "A Memorandum on the United States of
America" (1960), and Chapter 11, "The Intellectual: Between Culture
and Politics" (1971).

Chapter 9 goes back to my first visit to Germany after emigrating, at
which time I worked on German matters at the Frankfurt Institute of
Social Research (1952 and 1953). This paper was occasioned by an invitation from the German Department at Ohio State to speak at the annual
initiation of members into their honorary society (1954). It was received
with warm hostility, which, I remember, shocked my friend Guenther
Roth who had helped me considerably in its preparation. He had only
recently come from Germany and took it for granted that Americans,
even American scholars and their students who specialized in the German
language and German literature, would not be so nationalistic—and
some among them were sympathetically inclined toward nazism—that
their response would be defensive rather than critical.

Chapter 9 comes closest to (although it is by no means identical with)

the preceding chapter in tone and topic. Similarities emerge most clearly
in a comparison of the roles played in the two essays by the speech of
the "elderly, apoplectic worker," the end of which I quote in the " 'Exercise in Commemoration," and which I relate to the poem by Karl
Wolfskehl. In Chapter 9 I connect it with certain aspects of the
"German mentality," especially in the postwar period, which I have
tried to grasp. There is a similarity to Chapter 8 as well that relates
both essays to sociology: neither is an exercise in sociology but both contain its raw materials. By contrast Chapter 9 "On Germany and Ourselves"
comes closer to providing sociological propositions that can be tested
directly rather than mediately. Both Chapters 8 and 9 make similar
recommendations that foreshadow the idea of "surrender" (thus the
phrase in the paper on Germany: "to test what is offered—what is said,
for example—against the least doubtful truth one has managed to hold
on to").

Chapter 10, "A Memorandum on the United States of America," bears
no relation to Chapter 9. By now what I meant in the first paragraph of
the introduction to this book by "moving in from various positions," has
probably become quite clear. If it has not, a comparison of the essays on
Germany and America ought to make it so, even though the differences
do not exhaust the meaning of "variousness." In the present case "various
positions" means that I wrote the essay on Germany as a participant, if
only by recollection, in a culture to which I was native, whereas in the
essay on America I was trying to understand a culture to which I had
only recently been introduced. Of course, in both papers, as well as in the
" 'Exercise,' " I am also trying to alert my readers (in this sense all three
are rhetorical) and to point out what is to be done or avoided (in this
sense they are practical if one of the predicates of existential truth [Chapter
5] is recalled). These rhetorical and practical characteristics are also
shared by many other chapters, notably Chapter 11 on the intellectual,
and are made thematic in Chapter 14.

The "Memorandum" is indeed an attempt to understand America. My
first in this direction goes back to the early forties, only a few years after
I arrived—a foolhardy undertaking by one even more ignorant than the
author of the version printed here. I don't remember how many rewrit-
ings there were between the first and the final, but the decisive revision
was done in the midfifties, when with two friends, both Americans—the
anthropologist, John W. Bennett and the literary historian, Roy Harvey
Pearce—I worked seriously for a year or two at a reader on American
culture for which we collected much material to test and document the
outline submitted in the second part of the "Memorandum," "The
Dialectic of America." I was also motivated by courses I had taken at

Harvard with Oscar Handlin, Louis Hartz, the late Perry Miller, and Arthur Schlesinger, Jr. (1955–1956). One reason at least for giving up our project—despite the interest it had roused among the scholars just mentioned—was that all three of us who had been together at Ohio State had left that university at the same time (1959). I did not insist on continuing the work, not only because of the difficulties attendant on our geographical separation but also because I no longer felt so close to the subject. In fact, when much later I reread it for inclusion in this volume, I was surprised with what spontaneity I had identified with America: now I had to change the writer's *persona*; for instance, the first sentence had read:

> The course of American history has given rise to a number of ideas that have shaped our orientation, our reality— whether we take them for granted or espouse, reject, even abhor, or question or examine them.

It became

> The course of American history has given rise to a number of ideas that have shaped American reality—whether they are taken for granted or espoused, rejected, even abhorred, or questioned or examined.

Simultaneously I changed from "we" to "Americans," from participant to observer, from one pleading for a cause that is also his own to one no less passionately but far more distantly involved in a diagnosis not of his own national group but of contemporary man in general. I imagine that during the years between the last version of the "Memorandum" (1960) and the one offered here I have become sufficiently sure of myself as an uprooted person (driven out of his native land, then out of an adopted country in which he had been happy as a young man) to be far more at home in the United States—so much so that I can now see her problems as world problems and speak spontaneously not as a fellow citizen but as a fellow human being for whom there are no particular "we's" or "our's."

This change and its interpretation may become more plausible if the "Memorandum" is compared with the other two chapters that deal with particular nations. The one on Germany (Chapter 9) employs "they," whereas the voice of the " 'Exercise in Commemoration' " (Chapter 8) is that of "the only we"—mankind's.

There is another change in attitude toward the United States which I have *not* made in editing the "Memorandum." Basically it is no different from the failure to reduce the optimism of "An Elementary Syllabus

in the Sociology of the Jews" on which I commented in the introduction
to Part II. This is its "liberalism." It is not that I still hold such optimism
but that I do not wish to interfere with the historicity, the autobiographical character of the papers assembled here. Indeed, the reason I made the
change from "we" to "Americans" is that in this case my own feelings
must prevail over considerations of historicity (at least beyond those
pointed out), in particular because the "Memorandum" is the only contribution to this book that has not appeared in print before. In commenting on the optimism of the "Syllabus," I pointed to its having been
written during World War II, with its anti-Nazi faith in democracy. But
this obviously is not the date of the latest version of the "Memorandum,"
and my liberalism, my belief in legal procedure, education, rational persuasion, has evidently outlasted the war enthusiasm for democracy, as
well as the postwar period. In general, I have in recent years moved some
distance from such (unqualified) liberalism, toward radicalism, which,
to be sure, is vague, but not much vaguer than I am myself about the
matter. On one of its aspects, however, I can be more precise: I have
anchored (at least so far) my radicalism in the idea of "surrender," by
which I mean to "go to the roots." This is not radicalism in the usual
political sense, and indeed one of the problems I am trying to resolve is
precisely that of the relation between human or philosophical and political radicalism. Some of my few attempts at confronting this problem are
contained in this book—in the chapter on the intellectual, which follows
the "Memorandum," and in Chapter 25, "This Is the Time for Radical
Anthropology," in which I try to have humanly and politically radical
anthropologists "meet."

Despite all these qualifications, I still think that aspects of the "Memorandum" raise it beyond the status of the merely historical.

Chapter 11, "The Intellectual: Between Culture and Politics," combines two papers, one by this title (which I wrote in 1969) and "The
Enemy Within: Anti-Intellectualism" (published six years earlier). Its
central question is: What can I responsibly mean by "an intellectual" at
this time in our history? "Our" does not present the problem it did in
the "Memorandum." Even though most of the specific references are to
the United States, here I am one-of-us-in-the-same-boat, or at least one
of us—anywhere—who want to be (or for that matter do not want to be)
"intellectuals." Some passages, especially those on anti-intellectualism, are
polemical; they debunk sloppiness or hypocrisy. This tone, the emergence
of which probably follows my preoccupation with surrender (which is not
a substitute for calling things by their right names), is perhaps most specifically adopted in remarks about certain colleagues in institutions of
higher learning (colleagues typified or not personally known to me),

above all fellow social scientists who accommodate themselves to the inanities and comforts of holding a job, sometimes one that has power and glamor. It is also directed against detractors of Herbert Marcuse, detractors whose major ammunition is more ideological fanaticism than analysis.

Toward the end of my comment on the "Memorandum," I brought up the relation between human and political radicalism. The essay now under discussion also addresses itself to this problem, for the relation between culture and politics is a variant of it, and some passages are explicitly concerned with the two kinds or aspects of radicalism. Chapter 11 also reflects some ideas about surrender: the "advocacy of the maximum suspension of received notions" and of the social scientist's taking "as little for granted as he can manage" and the claim that the historical period we have reached is one in which "we have nothing to begin with but ourselves."

No matter how many pages follow in this book (including Chapter 25 on radical anthropology), I have not yet passed the stage attained here in my efforts toward resolving the problem of radicalism.

# 9

# ON GERMANY
# AND OURSELVES. 1956

I begin with two indisputable facts: Nazi extremism, an unsolved, hence most unpopular, problem, and the hope of the postwar "German miracle." Taken together, as they must be, they should be reason enough for serious preoccupation with the "German phenomenon." [1]. How account for the coexistent extremes of sensitivity, depth, organizational skill, and bestiality that must somehow be connected? We must also determine how such an inquiry would relate to Western, especially American, political concerns, some of them decisively responsible for the German comeback. Might this inquiry jeopardize our alliance? I hope that it will help to call into question the blind or irrational components and will strengthen our self-awareness and whatever rational basis our alliance has.

The ramifications of the question, "What is German?" suggest its gigantic dimensions and thus the likelihood of fragmentary answers. The approach I take is an attempt to identify the German image of Germany by identifying German ethnocentrism. German ethnocentrism is naïve, like that of nonliterate tribes who call themselves "people" as if there were no others. It is infused with belief and idea, typical of some religious groups who feel they alone have the truth, and it is political and economic, which are also attributes of imperialism. It is not adequately characterized as any or all of these. *Am deutschen Wesen soll die Welt genesen*, the notion that something is wrong with the world which the German will set straight, is not only naïve, missionary, or imperialistic but a childishly megalomaniac perversion of all three.

Terms like childish, megalomaniac, and perversion suggest a psychological or psychoanalytical approach that evokes other features of the

128

German mind characteristic of the adult—infantile, admirable, or dangerous, as the case may be. There is his extraordinary preoccupation with himself, with what, really, *is* German. There is the relation to German history as an oracle and object of longing. There is the unusual significance of landscapes, cultures, and types of man that function as counterimages. There is the proverbial attention to detail. There is the peculiarly German authoritarianism portrayed in the disillusioning image of the *Radfahrer*, the bicyclist—at once bowing and kicking. There are the incredibly violent escapes from the confines suggested by these images and what they stand for—whether in the poetry of Hölderlin, the plays of Kleist and Büchner, or Hitler's logorrhea and inhumanity.

These characteristics may be documented by illustrations. "The Frenchman," writes a contemporary student of popular nineteenth-century German fiction [2], "lives with his history, it is part of him: he does not need to contemplate it all the time. For the German . . . the question of 'what is German' never dies out." In this same literature the resolution of plots is often provided by the discovery of an event that took place at some extraordinary period of the national past, preferably the Thirty Years' War. The historical novel gives meaning to the present by surrogate rather than by the discovery of historical development: the past is better; it is an oracle that foretells the present; it is a womblike refuge and treasure cove. Contrast Wagner's "present"-ation of the Nibelungs with the silk and plush of his villa or see how in plays gray-bearded men break down to confess at their mother's breast. Or think of German Romanticism, the literary movement with its bards and *Minnesänger*, and the German youth movement with its glorification of the medieval knight and, indiscriminately, the mercenary. Consider also the periodic "purifications" of the German language. These are other examples of the preoccupation with what is German and of the freezing of both preoccupation and its object into magical stances.

The past is the other self but it is also the real self: a different formulation is historicism, which tells how it really was, as Leopold von Ranke put it; and for Wilhelm Dilthey there is no human nature other than history. The relation to the temporal other is paralleled by that to the geographic other, landscapes and peoples. Here the dialectic is between the Dionysian German and the Apollonian "sunny South," Italy, the Latin genius, and Nietzsche not only coined the terms but, like other Germans— Goethe and Thomas Mann—lived them. Goethe's "Mignons Lied" is not only a song of longing and fulfillment but also of escape and the realization of its impossibility. Goethe solved the tension by formulating it. He shows how the transcendence of the problem can be achieved through life and art, but no modern German has even envisaged its political or social transcendence. The tie with *Natur* also oscillates between sentimentality and extraordinary penetration. It runs through the burgher's raid on the woods on the family's Sunday excursion for berries and flowers—the shy violet, the hidden wild rose, the Blue Flower—and spiritual recreation in communion with nature. Fairytale figures—witches, sorcerers, the fairies themselves—live in nature, usually in the dark forest, but so also do some types of man. There are the noble robbers who played such an important part in the *Sturm und Drang* literature and in Schiller (by whom they were mobilized *in tyrannos*) and whose gruesome variants—who to a certain extent are merely deprived of earlier masks— are the Nazi functionaries.

Among the more real people the gypsies and the Jews are most important. In the traditional imagery the gypsies are envied for their freedom and mobility and dark secrets—witness the gypsy songs and *Zigeunertänze* and look at the whole German complex of "Bohemia," with its music, and you are led (notably through Spengler) on to the gateways of all-swallowing Asia. The gypsies flee into the dark woods, whence they emerge, fascinating and oracular but threatening, because there is no participation with them, only nostalgic longing ("Lustig ist das Zigeuner-leben . . . Lustig ist's im grünen Wald"—Jolly is gypsy life, it's jolly in the green wood). The Jews' forest is the ghetto, labyrinthine like the woods of fairy tale and ritual hike; their deals are obscure. The Jew is the stranger par excellence, as the philosopher Georg Simmel said. This is one of the points from which develops the apologia for the nihilistic ravages of the German fear-contempt, love-hate, elimination of the Jew.

From here we can also move to the passion for other executions: the rigidly scheduled one of detail and those involved in the intrinsically valuable bureaucratic orderliness and the infinitely satisfying and infinitely frustrating cleanliness of the housewife. The infantile fixation of passion, the compulsive mission: the witch on the broomstick is one of its absurd and horrible images, only the *Hausfrau* has no Blocksberg to ride to for the *Walpurgisnacht* but is forever doomed to travel the corners of her *Wohnung* with, if possible, its staunch heirlooms, at least solid pieces. The dust-devouring maenad and the rule-slinking ogre have neat appearances but conceal beneath them and beneath their knowledge the unsolved problem of relations to other men, which can typically be handled only as relations to figures of greater or less power, towering or negligible, perhaps eliminable. The middle range lies between arrogance and servility —arrogance perverted, perhaps, from the pride in one's "calling" (Luther); servility, betraying the humility outside it.

This is the horrible caricature of an orderly society, of a social order in which love and spirit would flourish in a rational structure. Although the nightmarish farce slumbers in any human group, in the German it tosses more wildly and wakes up more furiously and frequently in more places, instigated and at the same time petrified by the ultimate refuge of irrationality, the state. This state is epitomized most poignantly by Prussia and perverted in nazism. It was a German (Simmel, again, following Kant) who asked: "How is society possible?" This also is a profound question: the dignity that comes from unconditional asking has its soft underbelly, the mud of shamelessness and raving, the mud at the bottom of every genuine philosopher. Inversely, the compulsive execution of detail has its spiritual counterpart: the *Andacht zum Kleinen* (Jakob Grimm), the loving attention to detail, which elicits the meaning of the macrocosm (the spirit of a poet, of a man, an attitude, an epoch, a culture) from the microcosm (a short passage, a plot, an image, verse structure, syntactic peculiarity), as shown by some great nineteenth-century German philologists and, in our own time, by such men as Leo Spitzer, Erich Auerbach, or Ernst Robert Curtius. The question is what the bottomlessness can avail itself of, can seize on: compulsion or devotion, fanaticism or free choice, hate or love. Both, indeed, in the German, can take away one's breath.

The German is deep, and here the word does mean bottomless, without foundation, groundless. It involves a whirl of emotion without rational base, a momentary halt, and, as if there were direction and development to the sequence of such temporal states of hand-to-mouth life, its reification, formulation, and presentation. It comes, for example, as pure passion in *Tristan,* which entails the love-death as, in a catastrophic variant, does the union of *Volk* and *Führer.* "The German is an expert in taking furtive paths to chaos," Nietzsche wrote,

> and as everything loves its simile, so the German loves the clouds and all that is unclear, formative, crepuscular, damp, and shrouded: he feels uncertainty, inarticulateness, shiftingness, and growth of every kind as "deep." The German himself *is* not; he *becomes,* "develops." "Development," therefore, is the really German find in the great domain of philosophical formulae—a dominating concept which, in league with German beer and German music, is at work to Germanize all of Europe. Foreigners stand in astonishment and fascination before the riddles that the contradictory nature at the bottom of the German soul poses to them (which Hegel has brought into a system and Richard Wagner finally even set to music). . . . The German *drags* at his soul: he drags at everything he experiences. He digests his events badly; he never gets "done" with them; German depth often is only heavy, halting "diges-

tion." And as all habitually sick people, all dyspeptics, have a leaning toward comfort, so the German loves "openness" and "honesty": how *comfortable* it is to be open and honest! It is today perhaps the most dangerous and successful disguise the German is good at, this confiding, obliging, card-showing nature of German honesty: it is his proper Mephistophelian art; he will "go far" with it! As the German lets himself go, he gazes with faithful, blue, empty German eyes—and at once, the rest of the world mistakes him for his dressing gown.

The fascination with everything cloudy, shifty, inarticulate, groundless —but, for this very reason, the longing for form and base; intimate knowledge of dark woods and subterranean treasures (German forestry and mining) but also, as Arthur Salz has pointed out, of the sun's work (the equally old cultivation of wine); heaviness and clumsiness against grace from a diet steeped in olive oil; escape from sickness and death into the overstuffed chair; the blue-eyed vindication of one's malaise on the other who threatens one because he is not so sick or who arouses contempt because he is equally sick or sicker: these are some aspects of the circle Nietzsche tried to break out of, and tried successfully, by writing with extraordinary penetration and passion and by ending his life with ten years of madness. The former, the extraordinary achievement, is a positive German way, insanity (or suicide), a negative one, and sometimes, as in Nietzsche's case, the two are combined. "Two of the greatest physicians of our national disease," Wilhelm Kütemeyer (a German doctor) wrote recently,

> who were exploited for the glorification of our illness, namely, Hölderlin and Nietzsche, became the victims of their profession, paying for their insight into the sickness of the collectivity with their own, going insane. But they actually were physicians, not, it should be noted, exponents of the collective sickness. . . . There are sick people whose sickness consists in their taking, without knowing it, the guilt of the "healthy" upon themselves; there even are the guilty whose guilt is a manifestation of what the "innocent," in their cowardice, veil.

If the speechless shiver is all that the recognition of the tragic character of a Hölderlin or a Nietzsche results in, tragedy is compounded. The acceptance of such Goethean dicta as "the shudder is mankind's best part" and "feeling is all" can be tragic in a quite unintended sense if it brings with it the speechless tolerance of crime and the speechless penetration of crime rather than its unshivering rejection which in a cramped distortion of tragedy would be resented as a shallowly "enlightened" attitude offensive to a perverted sense of depth. It would be only a step removed from Himmler, who said:

> Whether other peoples live well or kick off from hunger interests me only insofar as we need them as slaves for our culture; otherwise it does not interest me. Whether in building a tank ditch 10,000 Russian women collapse from exhaustion or not interests me only insofar as the tank ditch gets done for Germany. We shall never be crude and heartless where it isn't necessary; that's clear. We Germans who alone in the world have a decent attitude toward the animal will have a decent attitude toward these human animals too, after all; but it is a crime against our own blood to worry about them and to bring them ideals so that our sons and grandsons only have it even harder with them.

Goethe offers the unique spectacle of Nietzsche's or Hölderlin's extraordinary achievements without their victimization. If in this respect he is un-German, he is German in what made it possible for him to avoid their fate: his willingness to stay within the social circle, even though not the narrowest, the family, but the next, the court and small town. Not that Nietzsche was political—he calls himself "the last anti-political German," the "good European"—but at least he rebelled against his society and time, whereas Goethe drew sustenance from them. When the Bourbons were being overthrown, he thought the news his Eckermann referred to concerned a scientific debate, which gained the more significance for him because it took place despite the political turmoil. This unconcern with politics has often been felt by Germans. Thus Theodor Mommsen in his testament stated:

> A political position and political influence I have never had and never aimed at; but . . . I wanted to be a citizen [*Bürger*]. This is not possible in our nation, in which the individual, even the best, does not get beyond service in the organization [*Dienst im Gliede*] and political fetishism. This inner discord with the people to which I belong has definitely determined me, as far as this was at all possible, not . . . to appear before the German public for which I have no respect.

Goethe, the "Olympian": the designation is only a heightened form of *Meister* (Mommsen was one of many) which, unlike *maître* or *maestro*, sets the person so addressed above mortals. The German "nobility of the spirit" *is* nobility, comparable to nobility of lineage or merit, but it is a noblesse that obliges no more than they do, while it seduces its possessor to arrogance and its beholder to servility. The alliance between spirit and democracy certainly is difficult and their relation complex and more often than not negative, but in German thought and conduct the spiritual and the social are less clearly separated than elsewhere, for the order of rank is far more than a matter of social arrangement, namely, a hierarchy inseparably spiritual *and* social, with voids between the steps. In contrast to America, for instance, where occupational status

> is to a relatively high degree segregated from the individual's "private life," . . . in Germany this seems to be considerably less the case; his [the German's] specific formal status, as it were, follows him everywhere he goes. In social life generally he is less significant as a person, as John Smith, than he is as the incumbent of a formal status, as an official, an officer, physician, a professor, or a worker [3].

The German "nobility of the spirit" approaches hero worship, with all the characteristics of hero and worshiper, and the Olympian aloofness and its milder form, the notorious infatuation with titles, is one of the aspects of the unsatisfactory, unsettled German social order. The challenge of a social order neither infuses the German quest for reality nor is a result of it; at the same time this absence accounts for the radicalness, the unhampered, "ground"-less nature of this quest and is one of the forces that permit or produce the otherwise totally dissimilar varieties of radicalness, bottomlessness, and baselessness of a Beethoven and a Hitler—whereas when such a strong tradition of social order is present it contributes to the shallowness of dictators such as Mussolini. In the greatest, most typical, and seminal expression of this German quest for reality, Goethe's *Faust*, no social order emerges; what social elements play a part are secondary or tertiary to the concern with the nature and destiny of the individual, on the one hand, and with the cosmos on the other.

Altogether, neither drama (least of all comedy) nor social philosophy is an outstanding German achievement. Characteristically, the dramatic tension unloads on philosophical ideas rather than on politics or persons (compare Goethe with Shakespeare). The exceptions prove the rule. Either, like some plays by Hauptmann and Wedekind, they are less radical and more directly traceable to the conditions of the time (and for this reason more dated) than is true of less socially focused works or, like Büchner's *Wozzeck* (1835) or the late Wolfgang Borchert's *Draussen vor der Tür* (1946), they are outcries, rebellious, passionate, ecstatic, apocalyptic but not political, not politically sophisticated. The great exception in social philosophy, Marx and his unvulgar followers, remained condemned to the ivory tower, whence mediation either failed or compromised, for politically Marxism has been weaker in Germany than in most other European countries. Not only have its political parties had less able leadership than elsewhere but the largest among them collapsed before nationalism in World War I. The failure to transcend certain German features, among them servility, and the lack of social conscience and consciousness parallel the prostration of so many intellectuals before nazism. Nationalism and national socialism (the semantical monstrosity is a symptom of intellectual and moral obtuseness) were more real than the ideas that had been espoused in easier periods.

Some of these characteristics of the German view of the world and of the German attitude toward the world also appear if we approach from a more strictly sociological perspective and concentrate on the burgher, the petty bourgeois, the *Spiessbürger*. We met him on his Sunday excursion; he lurked in the reference to Goethe's court and small town; we saw Nietzsche lash out against his leaning toward comfort. His world, Hoyt suggests, is concentric circles of family, neighborhood, community, region, Germany, perhaps Germans abroad. *Heimat*, one of the famous German words for which there is no equivalent, designates them all—which of them depends on the speaker's situation and intent. *Heimweh* (homesickness) may be the longing and suffering for any of them: the individual's for his family or the whole family's for their community or region. *Heimat* unifies the concentric circles and *Heimweh* is a powerful tie and image that contains the individual German or his more immediate circles within the larger ones. There is nothing specifically German in the pain and nostalgia of suddenly remembering a street turn, the cry of a bird, the sun on a roof, but *Heimat* and *Heimweh*, in their encompassing and differentiated referents and in the sly hypocrisy and violence hidden in the shiftiness of these referents, seem peculiarly so. Note what Thomas Mann's awe and irony did with them:

> . . . "our" Milky Way . . . The word "our" gives the immenseness to which it refers a certain intimacy; it enlarges, in almost comical fashion, the concept of home [*Heimatlichen*] toward a sense-benumbing expanse whose modestly but securely installed citizens we must feel ourselves to be.

The Milky Way, our comical fatherland: set this beside what a popular writer said some 70 years ago for many more than would dream in this way of our Galaxy. This writer is incomparably inferior to Mann but tremendously effective in his imagery, which has probably entered into the dreams of the great majority of German boys for the last two or three generations. At a high point in an adventure story in far-away Arabia his hero interrupts himself to ponder:

> If only one could travel with the sun! Could only follow it far, far on to the West where its rays still shine fully and warmly upon the *Heimat*! Here, on this solitary hill, *Heimweh* stretched its hand out to me, *Heimweh* which in foreign lands no man can escape in whose breast beats a feeling heart. *"Ubi bene, ibi patria"* is a saying the cold indifference of which finds its confirmation only in the lives of soulless [*gemüts-armer*], homeless men. The impression of youth can never wholly be wiped out, and memory can sleep, to be sure, but not die. It awakens when we expect it the very least, and brings that longing over us from whose pain the soul [*Gemüt*] can fall very seriously sick.

This from Karl May, another subject of Hoyt's sensitive analyses. Some biographical facts are relevant. As a young man May's petty thieveries were followed by jailings, which apparently led him to interpret his failure as the sign of a higher fate that guided his life. In realizing such an image in his books and his life, in "living his dream," he became a symbol of the "eternal German." Witness Heinz Stolte's appraisal of his stature, which appeared during the Nazi period:

> Out of the coming together of mystical and heroic entities [such as are found in Karl May], there forms the oldest task of our culture which awaits solution: the *"Heiland"* [savior] question, the union of the Germanic with the Christian into the form of the heroic legend peculiar to [that coming together]. Herein Karl May, be the strange and far ever so alive in him, is eternal-German.

Despite the recognition of the juvenile and lower-class character of Karl May's numerous works, the man and the symbol are accepted into the glorious gallery of Germans in which he occupies the place of the *Heimatsucher* who eternally explores what "German" means. Even the brilliant Marxist Ernst Bloch applauded (in 1929) the "genuine longing for the far-away" as the truth in the cheating of a "nostalgic Spiessbürger, who himself was a boy [and] broke through the foul air of his time"; and Bloch does not want the Nazis to claim Karl May. Yet there are certain parallels between him and Hitler. Both had frustrated childhoods which led to megalomania. Both rebelled against their failure to be accepted into *Heimat* circles. In Karl May rebellion led to the creation of a sentimental, hypocritical, moralizing concept of Germany and to his acceptance by that Germany, but in Hitler, it led to a magical-orgastic German deed. The differences go back to historical bases, but the likenesses to the German mentality, although other mentalities would have rejected either figure as a crackpot, disposing of the one as insignificant, fighting the other as dangerous.

Breaking out of the circles, or their expansion, is exceptional; the rule is to stay within them. Their center is *Gemütlichkeit*, coziness, comfort, security, unawareness of possible exposure to the chaos that waits outside for all members of the family as they are gathered around the table under the lamp that illuminates their lives: the other circles and the world at large, circled and uncircled, lie in unknown and irrelevant darkness. *Gemütlichkeit*, however, has vast variations, which are also reflected in the literature. There is its approval and portrayal, in much dialect and regional writing (for instance, Hebel, Niebergall, Gottfried Keller) and elsewhere. It may also supply the basis for a potentially universal view of man-in-his-habitat, as in Walter Benjamin's *Berliner Kindheit* (1950). Finally, it has appeared in its radical instability in Kafka's *Metamorphosis*, in which a member of the family is catapulted out of the family circle and thus out of all mankind and, unimaginably but transparently, wakes up an insect. (It may be significant that both Benjamin and Kafka, among the greatest transformers of *Gemütlichkeit*, were Jews.) In less extreme, more ordinary form, however, *Gemütlichkeit* makes units not only of family members but also of those of wider circles. Its fusing and developmental character is perhaps most conspicuous as local and regional patriotism, particularism. This made national unification an extraordinarily difficult task, achieved only with such regional concessions as ambassadors and postal systems and with Bismarck's violence—but sentimentality and cruelty are of one piece.

Yet *Gemütlichkeit* in its humdrum or gruesome forms has a counterpart, important but hard to grasp, and the term that stands for it is certainly untranslatable: *Innigkeit*, literally "inny-ness" (sometimes "inwardness," sometimes "intimacy" will do); it is said of relations both between persons and between persons and things, such as landscapes, nature, works of art. If inwardness is deprived of its direction and is restricted to the pure "in," another instance of radicalness becomes visible, the radicalness, the purity from all externals, that an *innige* relationship can have. If it is added that *innig* and *Innigkeit* are shy words—in the way we sometimes are shy or reluctant to use words like lovely or holy—there also emerges something of the characteristically German reverence for this radicalness, for an emotional radicalness that parallels the devotion of unconditional asking and the *Andacht zum Kleinen*. At the same time, the social weakness of an *innige* relation becomes apparent: in its rejection of compromise, it cannot extend beyond the smallest group, cannot be the basis of a social order but, if socially regulated at all, only of an esoteric elite. Its better-known social perversion is the contempt of the masses (*Masse* tends to be a derogatory term), of the "common man."

Here, then, is a list of particulars, which cannot be exhaustive but is striking enough to call for a key that would make sense of it. This key, as in other ways of life, is the way of life itself. Its identity can be approached by such questions as what is considered given, what is considered the nature of reality, hence what is considered man's relation to that reality—what is the immovable point whence everything moves; what is the absolute? These questions are already answers, formulations of non-verbalizable experiences, infused with meaning for the purpose of understanding and comparing them with those we are familiar with. My own purpose can at best be a proposal of how German intellectual history might be written. The aim underlying such a proposal is a better understanding of Germany and ourselves, hence of the world, the situation for action, today. Within these limits it is enough to quote from the beginning of Luther's *Treatise on Christian Liberty* for the key sought: "A Christian man is a free lord over all things and subject to nobody. A Christian man is a duty-bound servant to all things and subject to everybody." Spiritual freedom, material bondage, the tragic paradox, and the vision of a redeeming dialectic which makes the closed circle of liberty and servitude something that can be borne are contained in this clash of two fundamental propositions. Spiritual beatitude or grace is the absolute quest; everything else is irrelevant unless as a means to it. Where do I turn to search for beatitude? German history shows several avenues, successive and coexistent: from the Bible through Nature, History, Art, the State, to Race. They are not to be acted on; the attitude toward them is not pragmatic, as is characteristic of America: they are roads to heaven, "paths of life," findings, fates. The experience of grace, which gives meaning to one's life and the world, is the basis of the irreducible attitude of the experiencer, of his age and his people. It is verbalized and rationalized in his world view which tends to have the spite characteristic of absolute knowledge. Its pure expressions reach from Luther's relatively harmless "And if the world were full of devils!" to Hitler's insane spitting at humanity.

This German paradox, this explosive dualism, its highest flights, its most hellish descents, this groundlessness carries the German way of life, which has often been betrayed and strayed from, but nevertheless is one of man's genuine ways of life, of living in the world, of making sense of life by creating it. The question is not how to destroy or change it—really a wanton question—but how to make it more livable and more livable with. To show the magnitude of this problem it is necessary to realize what has happened to it, as it has to other ways of life, under modern conditions, so that some of what nowadays appears to be German actually is Western mass society, which stands under the impact of the material fact of One World but which has not faced it.

The reaction to this situation is revealed in German speech, speech being, in an important and specific sense, man's least controllable medium. What Karl Kraus, easily the most penetrating analyst of the modern German language, calls word imperialism and verbal expansionism, what Heinz Paechter discusses as characteristics of Nazi German, is more realistically seen as the same phenomenon that, with certain variations, can also be found in contemporary American and other Western languages. The transformation of human beings into expendable goods, including waste matter, is only in part conditioned by syntactical and grammatical peculiarities, as in the military *Mann,* instead of the plural *Männer,* men, and *Einheit* has its equivalent in "unit." Surely, there are Nazi intensifications of linguistic trends, but they are totalitarian-German, not simply German: for instance, *Einheiten verheizen,* to burn up units like fuel; *restlos zerstören,* to destroy without remnant (which probably derives from the commercial *restlos ausverkauft,* sold without remnant); and *Endlösung* (final solution), that is, the extermination of the Jews, who are *vergast* (burned in gas chambers), disposed of like garbage. One function of the dehumanization and technologization of language is to disinfect horror, as well as to veil it, but since this function is known to both speakers and listeners it also is a threat. "Final solution," for instance, both disguises and suggests the concrete horror of the *KZ,* the concentration camps, and the letters *KZ* themselves were the ciphers of fear. Knowledge of them was sufficient to frighten people but insufficient to make them see their agonizing reality. An American relation is brain washing.

To feel like a pawn, a cog, even a member of an audience watching the stage on which it does not act (and could not if it would) is indeed not specifically German, but the spread of the compensation of this feeling of powerlessness by an attitude in which men appear as objects and numbers and are treated accordingly may well be. If so, one reason might lie in the absence of such restraints to this compensation as in America, for instance, have traditionally been constituted by decency and common sense. In addition, peculiarities of the last twenty-five German years explain some of it: first the Nazi domination, then that by the Allies, and finally, after democratic institutions had been established, the problem of the West-East division and the threat of a new war. As members of Nazi and military organizations, people had learned *reibungslos zu funktionieren* (to function frictionlessly, smoothly; in both languages, the metaphor is modeled after the motion of machine parts). This, with its older basis of the rigid and hierarchical German scheme of social positions, appears in the phrase "I as," the identification of subject with role, its replacement by the role: there is no "I," but "I as" a farmer, a worker, an official. "I only did my duty as an officer," explained a man who during the Nazi period had denounced a policeman and thus sent him to a concentration camp; or "Ich habe meinen Sohn als Hauptfeldwebel verloren" (I lost my son as a first sergeant, that is, when he was one). Relations between people, even between father and son, themselves had become fuel burned by the fatherland.

Guilt, being a threat, cannot be faced. One mechanism of avoiding it is to substitute past acts for living people, to refer to inmates of concentration camps, for instance, as classes of crimes. Another is delegation of responsibility: to the bad Nazi (from oneself, the good) to the big shots (from oneself, an ordinary party member), to Hitler's entourage or to the Führer himself, who has become an important scapegoat. These delegations of responsibility may be associated with all kinds of attitudes toward nazism, from denial to proud confession of having been a National Socialist. (Not that scapegoats do not abound outside Germany.) A third mechanism is the morality of the balance sheet: if Coventry or Rotterdam is mentioned, Dresden is entered; if the treatment of the Jews, that of German POWs by the Allies: the grasshopper jumps from one side of the ledger to the other, and it is the jump that counts, not the comparability of credit and debit, nor even, sometimes, their existence. All of this is known in this country, best, probably, from political argument. Rarer, but even more violent and revealing, is the removal of threat by ecstasy— familiar to us, if from no other source, from occasional occurrences at religious revival meetings. It recalls prophetic and apocalyptic utterances, as well as some of Hitler's speeches, and also has its forerunners in German writing in the *Sturm und Drang* period and some of the plays by Kleist (*Penthesilea*) and Büchner. Thus (combined with stereotype: "the Freemasons"), in *Wozzeck*:

WOZZECK.   It goes behind me, beneath me. (*Stamps on the ground.*) Hollow. do you hear? Everything hollow down there. The Freemasons.

ANDRES.   I am afraid.

WOZZECK.   It's so curiously quiet. One wants to hold one's breath. Andres.

ANDRES.   Yes?

WOZZECK.   Say something. (*Stares.*) Andres. How bright. A fire runs around the sky, and a din, downward, like trombones. How it comes up! Away! Don't look behind you. (*Tears him into the bushes.*)

ANDRES (*after a pause*). Wozzeck, you still hear it?

WOZZECK.   Quiet, all quiet, as if the world were dead.

ANDRES.   You hear? They are drumming inside. We must away.

Observation of ecstasy in apocalyptic and prophetic literature and in *Wozzeck*, as compared with its occurrence in Hitler's speeches, once more raises the question of what the groundlessness can avail itself of: here, in particular, of a good cause or a bad cause. In contemporary spoken, sometimes even printed, German the cause, put curtly, often is Nothing. The function of ecstasy is escape, removal of threat, even though the materials with which it works are bound to be historical fragments, some very old, Christian, even pagan, some very recent—for instance, Marxist or Nazi. Read this speech, which was made by an elderly, apoplectic worker, who suddenly rose to deliver it during a discussion (in 1950 or 1951) in which he had been silent all the time, but realize that the oration was spoken and sometimes screamed with overweening emphasis, often with apparent incoherence, and with a passion verging on trance (it should be listened to), and, of course, it also loses much of its impact in translation.

> At that time, Mr. Gromyko, the deputy foreign minister, said in Russia: "The American lost the war politically and economically in occupying Europe." We always talk only of one problem: What is there? What is here? About the major causes, we haven't talked at all yet, and some people don't know at all what's up in the world. True socialism is what's up here! And its name is communism! Lenin said: "What is communism, and what is socialism in the embellished turn of Germanism, that's the wellbeing of the international proletariat." And in this sense, you here ask any nation. When today I come out of myself, this must be made part of the record what I say here, not that a ridiculous lie is placed over it. [The discussion was tape-recorded.] In this sense, the one above, who rules over everything, with the golden ball, he rolled it the wrong way, in the roulette! And I am telling you today: The majority of human beings do not know at all what is up, namely socialism! And the proletariat on the inside of the whole world wakes up one day and knocks the beast of prey down to the ground, that is Capital. They will knock the

power from under this egoistic beast of prey in clanking together the guns under themselves. . . . Now we will show you
what the game is here. You have calefactioned our International with the young as with the old Jews [4]. This ceases.
That one belongs to Palestine. Before the international one,
where he belongs.

. . . Stalin is a Bolshevik! A robber-murderer! He will be
eaten by his own people once it only starts, you understand?
Once the people only wakes up. The peoples among themselves, the nations will come to an accord with each other
and will say: So, our socialistic effort will wake up interna-
tionally and exterminate this pest which today has placed
us on the lowest rung! Why, for that we have hands and
hammer, sickle, as the others said. If it doesn't go then, and if
that doesn't go, we still have axes, what is? And if we get one,
then we shall squeeze him where he belongs. Then with this
hand we shall squeeze his throat apart, that he is thrown down
the abyss!

. . . Look: Why the American cries today! No man on earth
cries today as a nation. That's the American, because he says:
This flood from above, that's secured one hundred per cent,
it is overcoming us, and we, with it as Germans, are coming
along into the Great Flood. But out of itself, through the
inner revolutions that arise there, there is fight against fight,
there is fratricide, let's say, the remnant are all socialists. We
are building us a new state. That's the socialist state, and he
who once more sins against this state ends up on the tree of
life, that's the gallows. That's what we build there, and there
he'll be hanged! [5].

This is not simply a socialist, communist, anti-Stalinist, anti-American,
anti-Semitic tirade. It is a rejection of all order, with "socialism" clutched,
frantically and in vain, before the Great Flood, above which, in the horrible identification of life with death, only the gallows stands, imaginally
and substantively the "tree of life"—the Christian-mystical *arbor felix*,
the trunk of the crucifix, whose wood stems from paradise (Peter von
Haselberg). The passage is the conflagration of a man who does not
know what he is saying.

But nobody does; we are all human. In our society, whether German
or American, it is not the individual who speaks, but the society, the mass
society, even though qualified by cultural variations. We best meet this
misery if paranoia, ecstasy from anxiety, becomes catharsis and makes us
listen to our own words, carefully.

It is easier than this, but still extraordinarily difficult, to follow the injunction that we should "read our texts." I have tried to with reference to some German and American words, although the reading was cursory and purposive. But aside from any significance it may have in illuminating the contemporary mind, it may also show the dialectic of changing moods and the relevance of different moods for the same topic, such as criticism and charity, because *siamo tutti Cristiani*—we're all Christians (including the Jews, even the heathens)—which means that we are all weak *and* strong, ill *and* healthy, humble *and* proud, stooges *and* remakers of our society; that is, we can be strong, healthy, proud remakers if we know and face weakness, sickness, humility, and impotence.

What the Germans have gone through in the last twenty-five years is as extreme as ecstasy, as strong a transformer of judgment into charity. A Gothic cathedral above the razed old part of the city, tall and sitting in colossally arrogant judgment. On entering it, one discovers it is a shell with nothing in it, grass growing on the earth inside it, the sunshine passing through the holes in the walls undisturbed and indifferent. Many Nazis, half-Nazis, anti-Nazis do not understand how they survived, can do nothing with the accidental nature of their existence, could not go through a recurrence of the extremities which, by chance, did not kill but only maimed them.

*This must not be.* No matter how caused, no matter who is hit by it, whether anti-Nazis or Nazis, Jews or anti-Semites, anti-Communists or Communists—mankind must not suffer this again, in either sense of the word.

What, then, is a realistic attitude toward Germany? I want to point up some of my remarks by emphasizing the temptations to adopt a false, unrealistic attitude or to side with one or the other of the various types of person who have difficulty in attaining a realistic attitude: the remote scientist; the Nazi victim; the Nazi apologist; and the man who is so impressed by the crisis of our time that he cannot keep his attention long enough on a detail like Germany to analyze it. The temptations are the relief of detachment, the seduction of the righteousness which comes from denouncing the Nazis, the feeling that one is fair if he points to their merits and dissolves their evils in mankind's evils, and the reward derived from a conviction of political or economic realism in which Germany is transformed into an element in a global view.

There are temptations also that may dominate our behavior toward individual Germans. In the first years after the war an American in Germany was exposed to the temptation of absolving Germans and thus of betraying the millions who had been killed by the Nazis, of commiserating with his German acquaintances over the destruction of their country, and of exploiting his wealth and power as a representative of a conquering country. These temptations, I believe, still exist, but they are far less obvious. To comment only on the first, the most important—the temptation to forget all about it: in the meantime, and in connection with the developments referred to as the "German miracle"—not originally a German term—the moral problems associated with nazism have become even more repressed, the need for absolution is more readily denied, and American are less likely candidates for the high priesthood. In 1949 Everett Cherrington Hughes, who described the temptations of an American in Germany, which I have summarized, wrote that "contact with Germans is, like contact with mentally sick persons, a confrontation of one's self and one's own soundness." Not many can formulate so sensitive and humble a thought, but I suspect that the number of Americans who would do so today is even smaller than it was then, for by now we have become political allies and we have widely succumbed, in Germany and in America, to what at this time, I think, is the greatest temptation of all: to forget the past and thus, in effect, to deny it; but whether Americans or Germans, we cannot do so.

I want to point out that I have not said or implied anything about how, if at all, the features I have discussed characterize any individual German with whom we might personally come in contact. This would have required a different essay. I am trying to find answers to this question chiefly by listening to what individual Germans say, directly and indirectly. In such an enterprise of listening it is difficult to ascertain meanings, in part because people generally play roles appropriate to the situations they find themselves in, in part because people do not fully say or know what they mean in any society, and perhaps even less so in ours than elsewhere. If society by definition in some sense puts a mask on its members, in ours the mask has thickened and sometimes it is hard to find out whether anything is wriggling beneath it or whether the whole person has changed into a deceivingly transparent but actually opaque figure.

The only approach I know that promises some success in overcoming these difficulties is the one I have tried to follow here; that is, to test what is offered—what is said, for example—against the least doubtful truth one has managed to hold on to. If one proceeds in this fashion, he participates in a competition for truth. The result at any one time is preliminary but it salvages hope.

### NOTES

1. For the knowledge and support given me over many years my gratitude goes to Hans Weil; for suggestions on contemporary spoken German, to

Guenther Roth.

2.  Nelly Schargo Hoyt, in Rhoda Metraux and Nelly Schargo Hoyt, *German National Character: A Study of German Self-Images* [New York: American Museum of Natural History (multigraphed), 1953].

3.  Talcott Parsons, "Democracy and Social Structure in Pre-Nazi Germany" (1942), in *Essays in Sociological Theory*, rev. ed. (Glencoe, Ill.: Free Press, 1954), p. 112.

4.  "Ihr habt unsere Internationale mit den jungen wie mit den alten Juden verkalfakert." The last word is incorrect and improperly and elliptically used. *Kalfaktern* means "To meddle"; literally, to "make warm"; a *Kalfaktor* is a flatterer (one who blows hot air into one's ear), but it is more likely that there is a confusion with *kalfatern*, to calk: "You have stopped up our International with the Jews."

---

Reprinted from *Southwest Review*, **41** (1956), 50–63, by permission of the publisher. The essay has been edited and partially revised by the author.

# 10

# A MEMORANDUM ON
# THE UNITED STATES
# OF AMERICA. 1960

## TOWARD AN AMERICAN IDEA

The course of American history has given rise to a number of ideas that have shaped American reality—whether they are taken for granted or espoused, rejected, even abhorred, questioned, or examined: the idea of natural rights as formulated in the Declaration of Independence, the idea of individualism, as designated by a traveling visitor, the idea of stewardship, expressed and reinterpreted variously from Cotton Mather to the National Association of Manufacturers, or the idea of the individual's stake in society.

Such ideas may be counted among the elements, forces, or sources of American culture. Is there any one of them—a complex of several perhaps—that can be interpreted as *the* American idea? If it could be found, it might serve to interpret Americans both to themselves and to others. Such an interpretation appears to be important, as much at home as abroad. Americans might learn better who they are and therefore who they must be at this time in world history, thus being able to talk with others with more intelligence and dignity—even finding them, and vice versa, more interesting.

The ideas that characterize American reality are vague and emotionally charged. Thus the idea of democracy or capitalism cannot be clearly delimited: it holds in the face of other ideas and practices that are inconsistent with it. Neither "Give me your tired, your poor" nor Jim Crow is valid or real without qualification if only because the two contradict each other; still, both are real within the American sphere and history. And so with other ideas and the individuals such as Washington, Lincoln, and Lee who stand for them.

On this view American sociology [Part IV, esp. Chapter 12] (which is one of the most smoothly flowing, though comparatively little advertised American exports) appears as an unwitting and partly compulsive exercise in fixing the whole of reality. It has identified this reality, first, with "social life," and then with the social life as it is engaged in by men whose stature has a limited range, with no impressive smallness and greatness at the two extremes. A sociological view of human affairs is not confined to sociology itself. Thus the tension between citizen and artist, described, for instance, in Willa Cather's *The Sculptor's Funeral*, as the conflict between small-towners and the individual who does not comply with their folkways, is presented in an essentially sociological formulation, unlike the treatment given this theme by another American writer, Henry James, who, however, reveals the still comparatively sociological coloration of his view when juxtaposed with a third, though not an American, recent explorer of the theme, Thomas Mann. More generally and more crucially, the nature and power of the sociological attitude (not to be confused with C. Wright Mills' "sociological imagination," which, on the contrary, is a partial reaction to it) are manifest in the elevation to a quite, but nebulously, honorific entity of one of the vastly popular American social modes and models—human relations. The way in which this notion has been nursed in the social sciences, mental health, medicine, social work, and general parlance, resembles the care applied to the preparation of food, including its attendant folklore. Because human relations, however, is consumed without being edible, it tends, as so much else, to have no taste at all or to leave a bad one. Both human relations and cooking have been mechanized in perhaps intimately related ways.

Can we go beneath sociology and say something about the American reality in the light of which its formulation by sociology makes sense? The attempt to answer this question forces us to recognize *two* American realities—one, to stay with our small example in which belong Cather's treatment of citizen versus artist and the whole sociological attitude, the other, an outlook with which Henry James and many other phenomena in American cultural life must be classified. For the time being we shall examine the first kind of reality—what might becalled the official or conscious one—and only in the second part of this essay the second, the relation of the first to it, and then, necessarily, a third.

The official or conscious American reality is rational in the pragmatic sense of this word. It is not, for instance, romantic, which more nearly characterizes the German. Such a fundamental difference only confuses the issue unless we realize that the contrast refers to basic attitudes or ends, not to ways of acting on such attitudes, to subject matters toward which they are taken, or to means. Hitler does not become rational by virtue of his eminently rational organization nor does George H. Mead's interest in esthetics make him a romanticist. The contrast becomes quite clear when rationalists argue in defense of rationalism against romanticism: the more infallible their logic, the more apparent it becomes that their image of man falls short of some of man's possibilities. According to the dignity of the defender, the process is tragicomical or moving. Thus John Dewey's late "Anti-Naturalism in Extremis," logically perfect and humanly one-sided, moves one in its loyalty to the American reality— also perhaps because its brilliance derives from so passionate a desire for illumination as to transcend rationalism.

Other elements in American culture seem to be vehicles of this rational attitude. Some of them, such as the idea of stewardship, antecede its beginnings and were taken over and formed by it. Still others, such as that of functioning, or the whole phenomenon of functioning, were concurrent with its growth. This phenomenon itself has developed only with industrialization and may appear as a perversion or uncannily literal application of rationalism, more particularly of the rationalism of that *homo faber* for whom not only machines but also men can be made. Man can and must be made, namely, into a being that functions in a multitude of fellow beings as smoothly as the parts of a machine and as the machines in a powerhouse. The notion of functioning, grown supreme, has tended to become autonomous, conjuring up the specter of an inner totalitarianism and lending weight to pessimistic diagnoses suggested by labels such as Sorokin's "Sensate culture" and T. S. Eliot's "neutral society."

Certain comparisons between men and machines show how both are *made.* Thus compare the administration of psychological tests to determine the successful functioning of an individual and the testing of materials in laboratories, or the junkyards in which worn-out machinery is stacked and the social vacuum reserved for old people: both machines and men are discarded because neither grows old but wears down; neither dies but gives out; neither is even born but produced (this, to be sure, is only one angle from which to consider prenatal care, the spacing of children and other techniques of planned parenthood). Both scrap and the aged are collected and reused, when inanimate or animate materials are scarce, for example, in wartime.

There is a deep connection between the idea of functioning and the high place that money has attained in American culture. Functioning denotes movement but not the purpose of the movement; money is moved with the purpose of making goods available to the mover; its cultural significance depends on its use and on the attitudes with which it is employed. In its fusion with money functioning appears as the culminating product of American business enterprise. This product has changed the ideas that went into the formation of its rationale or theology; it has grossly diluted the idea of the sanctity of work, brutalized and stereotyped the doctrine of property as divinely sanctioned, profaned and caricatured the belief in the few saved and elect and in their stewardship, and has come close to monopolizing, for success in business, the philosophy of self-reliance—blurring all of them and making them less binding, subordinate to functioning itself. Thus functioning approaches the status of something in its own right, and a statement of its purposes is hard to distinguish from sheer defensiveness.

Money and functioning are one another's aims: man functions in order to make money, and he makes money the better to function. For this reason, added to the "Protestant ethic" or grown out of it, making money has become an end in itself, with the Joneses often serving as a goad (first equal, then excel them). Hence the conspicuous consumption, the ostentatious leisure, and, from the standpoint of the wondering, that is, malfunctioning, bystander, the vicariousness of life.

Not only from his point of view, however. When Americans broach the subject, they often seem to find themselves tired by the discomfort of a puzzle that appears to be unsolvable. Reactions to such bewilderment and its discomfort range from the most unreflective, habitual, automatically anticipatory avoiding to the most conscious, and they vary as well in many respects other than degree of consciousness. Among them are the vices just mentioned that were identified by Veblen; infatuation with sports; submission to the prophylactic of television; fascination with the beatific and the beaten, with drinking, dope, sex, love, *Existenz*. Drinking, for instance, appears to serve not only the obliteration of vicariousness but also the breakdown of conventions that facilitate functioning and are provoked by it. The extent to which drinking is used to dissolve a general conventionalism or shyness, to communicate free of functioning for other purposes or other moods appears to be characteristically American.

The official, conscious American reality, which includes sociology, human relations, rationalism, functioning, money making, and vicariousness, has still other and quite different aspects, alluded to as common sense, decency, and optimism. Functioning, to paraphrase Whitman, is not monstrous because of a corresponding largeness and generosity.

Common sense (among other things) is the sense common to members of a group who feel they understand one another and belong together.

Although in American society members of different groups realize that the term does not characterize their relations, actual or potential, adequately, most believe most of the time that there is a less specific but more profound common sense that ties them to all other Americans and of which, if the situation arises, they make use to rally together. In American culture common sense thus does not refer only to a sociological datum but to an emotional charge of great social and political power; it is a characteristic of the culture as well as an instrument for changing it when employed for the purpose. Its emotional charge is associated with its peculiarly abstract cognitive character: common sense is so deeply taken for granted that even an attempt at defining it would make many indignant or uneasy. True, the impossibility of analyzing fundamental characteristics is only another way of talking about their basic nature, and the religious or sacred character commonly attached to such characteristics is indeed not lacking in the idea of common sense. Yet this idea connotes the vicariousness darkly felt as a common lot. It may be that, as a general denominator of communication, common sense has lost in strength to the extent that functioning has gained in it.

If common sense is the accepted standard of understanding, decency is that of action; it is the corresponding moral category. The history of American ideas on ethics is outstanding for two features. One is the often noted naïveté with which at the time of the drafting of the Constitution well-articulated and complex moral thoughts were taken over and developed with an extraordinarily serious will to act on them. The other is the lack of a historically focused philosophy (such as Marxism) that would record socially relevant moral problems and be informed or inspired by them; for instance, so comprehensive a movement as transcendentalism is noteworthy for the absence of such a focus, even though the railroads ran close by Emerson's study in Concord. Historically, the approach to social and moral problems has been practical (e.g., the Muckrakers) and decency is indeed more a practical than a theoretical category. By and large, it is what it is right to do by the standard of common sense; and particular groups, especially power and pressure groups, aware of this relationship, have manipulated both concepts to suit their particular (i.e., not common) purposes. Nevertheless, many people are sensitive to such manipulations, for decency has preserved some of its moral persuasiveness.

The main component in the development of decency, common sense, and, most evidently, optimism appears to have been the overwhelmingly formative experience of the frontier. Whitman expressed its greatness and saw inseparably linked with it a challenge to man's adequacy—most succinctly, perhaps, in the quotation paraphrased earlier.

The largeness of nature or the nation were monstrous without a corresponding largeness and generosity of the spirit of the citizen. The pride of the United States leaves the wealth and finesse of the cities and all returns of commerce and agriculture and all the magnitude of geography or shows of exterior victory to enjoy the breed of full-sized men or one full-sized man unconquerable and simple.

We have moved far away from such cognizance as Whitman took of America, from the image of man he launched as an American possibility and a marvelous contribution to mankind.

Surely the consicousness of being able to move and expand has as much as any other been an American trait. Its origin lies in the concurrence, unique in the modern period, of a society, beginning and developing in an immense and ever more fully explored terrain. The continued awareness of this opportunity has resulted in an undaunted and exuberant optimism and in smugness as well—it has also resulted in such seemingly unrelated behaviors and attitudes as the bodily movements characteristic of some fundamentalist creeds and the jitterbug and in the tendency to be on the move if not to flee.

The optimism of the ever receding frontier seems to go deeper than all that industrialization, mechanization, and commercialization have done to it; it seems more ineradicable than the ruthlessness, exploitation, selfishness for one's own and one's own time, empty movement around money and power, which worldwide industrialization has imposed on it. The very things toward which it is easy to be critical or ambivalent— common sense, decency, and optimism—are those that have attenuated, even prevented, the festering of prejudices, anxieties, confusions, and defeatism which nazism, but not it alone, has seized on, institutionalized, and glorified. Yet however demoniacal fascism is, its mere absence or a mere negative attitude toward it does not constitute an idea. Where *is* the American idea?

The trends of industrialization and urbanization and the spread of science and scientific technology must not be confused with secularization. By secularization I mean the deepening and spreading conviction and attendant action that everything is open to examination and analysis and an examining, analytic attitude is the proper one to hold. Rather than this attitude, however, many aspects and products of the trends just mentioned have provoked fear, anxiety, panic, despair, apathy, or meaninglessness and vicariousness—in fact, totalitarianism—though nazism and communism in wholly different ways are, in part, a catastrophically inadequate response to these trends and to our dismal reactions to them. No matter how muddled, piecemeal, and almost somnambulistic, the American response has been far superior, thanks to the traditions of common sense, decency, and optimism. Can we not become more aware of these traditions, examine them, analyze them, act on them with greater knowledge of the world in which we live, determine the necessary changes, and circumspectly but steadfastly go about making them?

Once the question is posed in this way, the answer is positive. The answer is that we can make the idea of common sense, decency, and optimism strong and palpable enough for it to have universal appeal. For this to occur we must go the limit, as best we know at any one time, of practical analysis, that is, of an analysis that aims at finding out what we must do.

Thanks to the upheavals of this century, which have exceeded those of the past in spread and intensity and have been brought home by mass communication as well as transportation to more people than ever before, we know better and more surely what is bad, hence even some of what is good, for most people, whatever their differences. Thus we have learned that thermonuclear war is bad and that peace, even if only enforced by the threat of such war, is far less bad. We have also learned that we Westerners have made an inconspicuous beginning in putting the bee of democracy into the world's bonnet—to use a slight expression for this tremendous event—and that *therefore* we cannot and must not force it on anybody. We may be on the verge, too, of learning that man cannot live long without an awareness, and the response to it, that he is not only scientific and rational but also emotional and arational, that is, one who from time to time or place to place must be able to experience the unexpected, and that one of the crucial questions is how man can be free to be radical, to go to the roots and live by the roots of his idiosyncratic individuality in a peaceful, democratic world without blowing it up. Because man's world today is, in a sense wholly new in his history, one world, this question can be answered only by a clearer and more continuous awareness of the differences and relations between the individual's public and private sphere, an awareness that inevitably imposes limitations on those who would change the world on the basis of unanalyzed tradition or private revelation, just as much as it challenges habit.

The United States can be one of the major exemplifiers of the new world if it strengthens its ideas of common sense, decency, and optimism by the more thoroughgoing and intelligent implementation of democracy as the organization of the world. This proposition has strong and numerous implications in regard to changes that must be brought about in the United States itself. Perhaps the most relevant candidates for change are ones agreed on but without agreement on their nature or the means of bringing them about. Examples are the Negro and economic monopolism. In part, both involve unresolved competition for power. In both a change is made difficult by the fact that the majority believes that only minorities are involved—only every seventh or tenth American is a negro and only lately have larger numbers of customers and workers become aware of the effects of monopoly. A much more consistently analytical treatment of the implications of democracy for white-black relations within the school curriculum, from the grades up, and the introduction into the curriculum of economic and political analysis (rather than ideology) may contribute toward a more intelligent outlook on the part of more people, hence to greater readiness to sounder change. Consequently all educational efforts in this direction, in schools of all descriptions, as well as in adult education, need furthering and multiplying, and attempts at greater fixation of social stereotypes must be combatted. Yet the extraordinary momentum of power, which persuasion has little chance to touch, makes of scientific discussion and education a wholly inadequate lever of social change. Therefore other democratic means, including lobbying, petitioning, and legislation, must be employed. Sometimes, however, not even these means are effective, and we may have to face the question of violence. Of course, we must never forget that the further we move from persuasion and the closer to manipulation and force, the more we risk the democracy, secularization, common sense, decency, and optimism we wish to strengthen. It is the burden of the conscience of the individual or group and of the interpretation of these forces to know where, and where not, temporarily to give in because further fight would endanger these forces themselves.

The Negro and the monopolies also stand for the failure to integrate, despite the need for it engendered by industrialization, urbanization, secularization, worldwide communication, and the numerous and heterogeneous American cultures. We must remember that functioning or the vicariousness of life is less if at all characteristic of an Appalachian village, a Pennsylvania-Dutch, Mormon, or New-Mexican Spanish community, Little Tokyo, the Ghetto, or the culture of another minority, but more nearly of all individuals, whatever their origin, who have been drawn into the orbit of mass culture. The Negro is to a large extent the product of the culture of a horizontally segregated group, comparable to that of other cultural minorities, whereas the wealthy or monopolistic, which emerged from a period of comparative economic and social equality, is vertically segregated. What have the Joads and the Rockefellers in common, although both, in a rather distinct sense, are typical of the same process and system?

This question—what is shared culturally by the millionaire and the gasoline gypsie or shanty towner—is a reformulation of the inquiry into common features of American culture or into the American idea. Historically, America has been a country of independence, in which self-respecting, free, and equal citizens have built a new society. Now, however, self-respect, freedom, and, in particular, equality have to a large extent become slogans. Yet the institutions founded during the period of missionary enthusiasm—the state, its form of government, and body of laws—are still with us and all Americans share in them. The unique significance in American culture of at least two historical documents, the Constitution and the Bill of Rights, has often been commented on; they are not only manifestos of a revolutionary departure but by now are also hopeful, though perhaps not fully realized, signs that a new cultural integration may be possible. Are not common sense, decency, and optimism the philosophical nuclei of these documents?

They, and thus their nuclear ideas, have an aura of sacredness that analysis does not question. "Sacred" refers to what an individual, despite the most scrupulous analysis of which he is capable, cannot help but believe.

In all societies, thus also in the American, the most firmly institutionalized area of the sacred is, by definition, religion. As in many other places, in the United States as well, religion, systematized in theology and socially organized in accord with this systematization, has yielded to a more this-worldly institution; churches have tended to become more like business enterprises that stress not so much a concern for the soul and the rewards and punishments of afterlife as an interest in education, recreation, living together, and other moral, social, and economic matters. If religion is defined as the experience of the holy, it is obvious that in our mass society it cannot (any more than other social institutions—family, school, recreation, or occupation) maintain its institutionalization unchanged under the impact of the agencies of mass culture. The experience of the holy—whether defined as sacred as above or in any other way—is intimate, communicable to, and sharable by at most a few persons, and the traditional groups that once served this purpose and into which the individual was born—above all, the family—have increasingly changed their functions and have been replaced by other associations, with more of which the average individual has come to have less intimate affiliations. At the same time, the media of mass culture have not made the holy the basis of their message and therefore have not helped the increasingly detached individual to find in it a foundation on which to form friendships, even though urbanized society is essentially suited to the formation of such voluntary ties.

In comparison with the tradition of the United States, in those of Europe and Latin-America heroism, tragedy, and enchantment have been more generously added to religion as formative experiences and elaborations of the holy. We should realize, however, that the effort to arrive at an American idea, to come to terms with secularization and the sacred, to support and spread democracy, and to deepen mass culture offers us incomparable opportunities not only for work but also for heroism, enchantment, and tragedy simply if we have the faith that would inspire the acquisition of relevant scientific knowledge in common sense, decency, and optimism. These can indeed become enchanting ideas, and men can become heroes fighting for them; their names and images which are legion have been expressed by widely divergent American speakers and writers; for instance, Faulkner, Hemingway, Farrell, Bellow, Kazin, Cummings, Henry Miller. As Italy, according to Henry James, is "a land in which a love of the beautiful might be comforted by endless knowledge," so in America the belief in common sense, decency, and therefore optimism might thus be comforted, never endangered, but only transformed.

Perhaps the American culture is indeed a not yet integrated conglomeration of many cultures and will come into its own only in one world in which all of us must give up some element of our subcultures so that all may find life meaningful in a world that will create a culture of its own. Perhaps American culture, the American idea, has been impossible in man's history, but it is possible now.

## THE DIALECTIC OF AMERICA

"Possible" means formulable and enactable in one process, by virtue of the historical moment at which we have arrived. This moment is characterized by the simultaneity of the potential existence and the potentially quick destruction of man's one world, hence by the necessity of transforming this world from one of anxiety into one of hope. To this transformation Americans have much that entails their own transformation to contribute. The comments on the search for an American idea were intended as an introduction to what follows, which is an attempt at articulating this contribution and transformation.

The first part of this essay dealt with the official or conscious American reality and anticipated attention to a second and third and to the relation of the three. We must now try to make good this anticipation.

The first may be conceived of as the American thesis; the second, the antithesis; and the third, the synthesis. We said of the thesis that it is rational in the pragmatic sense of the word; that is, it is rational, in respect to the choice of means suited to achieve the ends sought, but the ends themselves are more nearly understood as self-evident. It is therefore no contradiction to say, and it is borne out by a reinspection of the ideas contained in the official concept, that the thesis, most briefly put, approaches subjective, irrational Lockean liberalism. We may also say that I am now trying to revise American liberalism.

We must consider three dimensions of our traditional liberalism: its intellectual dominance, its relation to the distribution of political power, and the historical development of liberal ideology toward an increasingly dominating and unexamined creed as well as the power distribution in the increasing monopoly of large organizations (government, business, and labor) and of the relation between them.

One of the major concerns of the American thesis is the development of a society whose members should also make this concern their own. They enter the society because they want to, by voluntary contract. They are encouraged to compete with one another for excellence in citizenship. The most conspicuous symbol of excellence is material success; the most conspicuous symbol of success is wealth. Except for compliance with these arrangements, they are free, that is, on their own; but the historically relevant way in which matters other than the development of the society itself have been served has once more been social, voluntary organizations. The enthusiasm and optimism that have accompanied the dominant preoccupation with bringing about a new and improving an established society have socialized many other concerns. These, by definition, have been secondary, whereas in older societies, with a more significant stratification and more options of outlook, they have been considered primary and of the individual rather than of the society. We have had no lasting alternative to liberalism, the thesis, and this is its second major characteristic. Even serious attempts have not been able to compete, and more often they have been variants or interpretations rather than essentially different possibilities.

The thesis, the universal outlook, does not include interests that, because they are human, have been primary for individual Americans but have remained theirs alone, even though people have been able, to a comparatively extraordinary degree, to act on their freedom in joining others of similar preoccupations. In doing so they have also, perhaps unwittingly, altered the thesis: they have established what might be called subsocieties, as other people earlier established American society. They were taught no other way to satisfy their social, political, and economic needs such as attempting to revise American society itself by initiating the tradition of a loyal-opposition party. When such unofficial concerns could not be met in this manner, loneliness, another feature of the Protestant element in the origins of America, later in league with a less religious or nonreligious loneliness, hit the individual American who has been less prepared to come to terms with it than have members of other societies, brought up as they were to consider their affairs essentially their own and only almost accidentally—as bliss or fate, not as the norm— social or even socializable.

Some of these matters, of which we know because they have found individual expression, deal with evil, suffering, sin, redemption, salvation, guilt, brutality, love, sex, tragedy, joy and pleasure, nature, and, most significantly, the past. Individuals have, of course (as the preceding paragraph implied), suffered or enjoyed, thought about, and been puzzled by these phenomena and have illuminated them (and, in the process, themselves and their society), but they do not belong in the liberal image of man, either as his concerns or, indirectly, his attributes. Liberal man's relation to them is pragmatic, and if the pragmatic attitude cannot control them they embarrass him or may even control him. Evil must be fought, suffering, reduced; sin, redemption, salvation, and the worries invested in them must be used for socially more constructive ends; actions leading to guilt must be avoided and the causes of brutality, recognized and removed; love, generally, must be cultivated; specifically, it must be marshaled as the basis of new social units; sex, actually, is one of those things, and education will eventually take care of it, too; tragedy is bad, and we must use all our forces to prevent it from recurring; joy is nobler than pleasure, but both are good, and social inventions help us find and increase them; nature must be conquered and used materially or aesthetically, and history is perhaps with us, but the past is past and what counts is the future.

Individuals have been relatively free to hold and express other views, to have other images of man, but neither general climate nor major institutions have sustained them. An examination of non-thesis expressions in literature, philosophy, and theology, as against the more numerous documentations of the thesis, will teach us more about each of the two, about their histories and their interrelations, and about the histories of their interrelations. These examinations will probably not invalidate the proposition that America has, in Louis Hartz's words, so successfully "solved the philosophical question" that it has mistaken itself for its thesis and has seen to it that its images abroad have followed this confusion, often in vulgarized and distorted forms.

Yet the optimism inherent in the thesis has also fired the imagination of Americans and of others all over the world. Focusing on particular aspects of man, notably freedom, hope, and youth, it has at times attained a poetic power, as in Walt Whitman's exuberance, in a nationally exuberant period, or in Thomas Wolfe's, in the anything but nationally exuberant 1930s. Such poetic power has transformed its omissions into things overcome or at least left behind. Today, however, no such poetic power seems attainable; rather it seems that the thesis will no longer do and that the time calls less for poetry born out of enthusiasm than for reconsideration, "remembrance," and the changes attendant on it.

"Antithesis" is a misnomer, for it is a residual category, referring to all that is not thesis. To recall a suggestion made before, American history is not characterized by any concerted effort to combat the thesis or to compete with it; the thesis has no alternative, but this time in world history makes it necessary to reinterpret America because the imagination, which has been exposed to war, the bomb, genocide, slave labor camps, clamors for a revision of the thesis. Not only this contemporary imagination, however, but imagination it its unpragmatic, searching, impatient nature, may well be the element common to all of the heterogeneous non-thesis concerns, many of which have been mentioned in this essay. To imagine, meditate, feel is antithetical to the performance, control, conquest, and domination that are inherent in the thesis; it is a threat, comparable to the threat of femininity to masculinity. Indeed, there are relations in need of investigation between the thesis and the "American male," between thesis and "antithesis," and between men and women.

The thesis also stands for America, the "antithesis" for Europe. This connection is shown by periods of Americanism or nativism, of the denial of Europe, that have coincided with phases of a heightened hostility toward the imagination and its representative human types—writers, artists, and intellectuals. The nineteenth century offers the most obvious examples; in our century relations have become complicated by shifts in Europe and its image—the betrayal of Western tradition by totalitarianism, specifically German, the decline of England, the British Empire, and France, Russia's shifting position between Europe and Asia, and by new, more intimate contacts with non-European parts of the world, most significantly Japan, so that one disturbing circumstance today is the dissolution of Europe as the mother toward whom ambivalence is an available and acceptable attitude.

The last two allusions, to sex roles and to Europe, suggest more psychological references of the incompleteness of the thesis and at the same time additional reasons for lumping non-thesis elements together as "antithesis." The argument may be strengthened by a caricature. A successful radio manufacturer is beset by two worries. One is that a competitor is threatening to make his plant obsolete. If this were his only problem, he could get over it by liquidating his firm and joining the competitor's, but he has another: the meaninglessness of the whole situation. No matter how vaguely, he begins to question the good of his making radios, the good of his joining the competition. What sense does his life make if, in the middle of a successful career, such radical questions are posed? He may even perceive a relation between his two worries—perhaps not beyond a dim feeling of discontent that something is wrong with his life. He may realize that his success is not enough to satisfy his goals and that he has never been clear about them. He had assumed implicitly that they would be served by the arrangements he now finds wanting—perhaps he even feels that his economic crisis is a message to tell him so.

He may then start thinking about his goals. He remembers things he was attracted by, but had forgotten, buried as fanciful, impractical, and unserious, such as ideals of relations with other men, poetry, philosophy, a beautiful house, or still others that he finds more difficult to formulate; but whatever they are, he has not done right by them, as he now sees as they come back to him. Perhaps he suspects that he is not alone in these thoughts, that his customers, or former customers, know them too—and that if they do not they will or, in some sense, should.

It is possible that he will take a big step from these reflections toward others on the nature of the society in which they occur. What is more, he may feel that whatever channels of communication this society has should be used to encourage its members to take their submerged feelings more seriously and to recognize that what he and they have consciously lived for has turned out to be no more than a means to an end which they have never considered as something that one might try to clear up. If they were to try, life would be more meaningful, more like what he now realizes he wanted it to be, and so would the lives of the others, including the radio users. Such a change would also make it impossible for technological and economic shifts, which now threaten him with bankruptcy, to raise radical questions. They would remain technical matters.

Until he came up against this crisis, the man was conscious of the standards, aims, and uses of knowledge that ordered his life but that, like his life itself, he now finds faulty. The contents of his consciousness, he learns, were not adequate. His culture, his tradition, all that he received and used to organize his life and to reject what else offered itself and now raises its claims, strike him as fragmentary, incomplete, and insufficient. only half the story.

Despite this caricature of a type (or perhaps it isn't really a caricature), some people may be able to find a comparable illustration, perhaps in their own lives.

In America in this interpretation the thesis is being recognized, or beginning to be recognized, as "only half the story": we want to acknowledge what has not been acknowledged as legitimate to have its claim at least in the imagination. Because of its tolerance, liberalism has allowed the contents of this imagination to interact, to some extent, with the thesis, and this, indeed, is one source of its historical modifications. If a particular group of individuals wanted to, it could withdraw from official America into a "subsociety," held together by a common desire. America itself has had periods of withdrawal: early in the nineteenth century, happy as well as smug for having established itself, and late in the nineteenth century, passively, having reached the frontier, about to be seeded with claustrophobia, frantically moving about (the automobile), dreaming of space (science fiction), and nativism, working toward the exclusion of immigrants, potential messengers of the "antithesis," betraying both the truth and the romanticism of the melting pot. Again, like some individual Americans, America has also fought against palpable reminders of the antithetical, such as the Indians, by repudiating these utterly unliberal, incomprehensible creatures, and by trying to contain the Negroes—these nightmarish candidates for affirmation—first in slavery, then in segregation.

Argument itself against, or even about, the thesis would have required its espousal of the contents of the imagination that were kept out.


There are at least two flaws in the parallel between the crisis of the individual, extravagantly typified in our businessman, and the crisis of America, both deriving from the obvious fact that the country is not one man but millions. The first is that in American society the distribution of thesis and antithesis is much more complex than in the individual; the other, that America's recognition of its crisis is even less clear than our businessman's.

Part of the liberal ideology is the denial of social classes and large numbers of Americans believe themselves to be "common middle-class" people. The thesis appears to be esposed more flatly by the successful and hoping-to-be-successful self-identified middle class than above or below it and probably by more upward- than downward-moving individuals. People lower on the vertical scale appear to be more traditionalistic than liberal (yeoman, peasant, artisan, farmer, and small-town businessman) or more pragmatically political (some labor groups); people higher on the scale likewise seem to be more traditionalistic (first families, aristocrats, and would-be aristocrats) or more egotistical or cynical (*nouveaux riches*, social climbers, and exemplifiers of Algerism, although all of them, especially the last two, also evince historically developed forms of liberalism).

These sociological suggestions provide a further label for the thesis: "mainstream." Marx's proposition that the "ruling ideas" are the ideas of the "ruling class" may be in general need of analysis. In respect to America it might be asked whether they have not been more nearly those of the middle class. Intellectual dominance and political power have, on balance, coincided less than in European countries. The concept of "ruling class" itself, and not only because of the American no-class ideology, is not so clear-cut. On the other hand, the modern development toward an administrative consciousness—as a development of the thesis it has probably begun sooner and been carried further in America than in other industrialized societies generally—raises the question whether there is any longer such a thing as a mainstream. Indeed, if it is true that liberalism has tended to become ritualistic as power has become lodged in large-scale organization, we should expect the mainstream to become a tyrannical monopoly.

Such an image reflects a catastrophic view of our time, alien to the liberal view and victimized by its own vision, giving in to the crisis, and forfeiting analysis and action attendant on it. A hope of transcending the crisis may lie in the synthesis between the rationality of liberalism and the sensitivity of the imagination to tragedy (e.g., to Hiroshima and Nagasaki), between the American thesis and antithesis.

The bomb, in fact, more than anything else, may have forced guilt, which had been a content only of the American imagination, on the consciousness of some Americans and on the subconscious of more. For them, at least, guilt can no longer be understood and disposed of as the consequence of actions to be avoided but is recognized, perhaps, as something that is always a threatening attribute of man, including American man. In contrast to guilt, shame has long been admitted as a legitimate, even praiseworthy emotion, which properly appears on the recognition of an error committed and entails the resolve of future improvement that will make up for the error, if it does not cancel it. This may account for the approval of confessions of mistakes by high-placed politicians, confessions that in other societies, on closer terms with guilt, might not be permitted or, if made, might end the politician's career.

As with guilt, Americans appear to be more familiar with despair. Both are reactions to something that was done or that happened in the past but cannot be undone. Hence their relation to the past, so inconspicuous in the future-oriented consciousness, may be changing, becoming unexpectedly important. Innocence is shaky or gone; its unexamined assertion is less and less possible and when insisted on nevertheless less and less creditable. The question is whether the frenzy of such insistence can be transcended toward maturity or whether it becomes ever more uncontrollably compulsive, to the demise of America.

The second flaw in the parallel between the individual and the United States—his comparatively greater clarity about his crisis than America's about its own—disappears, by definition, if "America" recognizes its crisis. Whether the interpretation outlined here serves to approach such recognition depends on its persuasiveness, that is, on the degree of coincidence between what it submits as true and what those to whom it is submitted feel to be true.

For the moment, the synthesis of thesis and antithesis·must be expounded, but in the end, the only hope for this memorandum lies in its dialogue with those who read it.

If thesis and antithesis are taken as sketched here, the synthesis is their recognition; thus their change by the act of recognition is to become conscious of them, to confront and come to terms with them, to confront oneself. So to become conscious also means to become conscious of the connection between this consciousness and the historical moment in which it emerges, whereby three characteristics of this moment seem most relevant. First, movement, withdrawal, and violence, the mechanisms by which the confrontation of thesis-antithesis-synthesis and of the historical moment itself might seem avoidable or at least postponable, as it was possible in the past, are hardly viable any longer. In particular, the United States can no longer go it alone or exterminate its enemies, not only because its military power is no longer, and can no longer be, unquestionably superior to all others, but also because the outlines, if not the nature, of friend and enemy have become blurred. This is so because of a second characteristic: among industrialized societies the historically relevant cultural, political, economic base unit is no longer, as in the modern period just passed, the nation but, in some respects, the West, in others industrialized society itself, and in still others the earth. The concentration of power, wealth, information and knowledge, and the administered nature of the individual's life are not national but Western, or as wide as industrialization or as the earth. The United States finds itself in the company of nations, all of which are disfigured by these phenomena as if by masks. Behind the mask each nation has its own history, of which it is still more aware than America is of hers because of the domestic universality of the thesis and its unquestioned assumption that the people of all other nations are also striving after life, liberty, and the pursuit of happiness. The

Americans thus are poorly equipped either to wear their masks or to take them off and show their faces. Even in this crisis they can marshal only their own thesis which—to say it once more—suggests no recognition of evil, suffering, guilt, brutality, tragedy, or history, despite totalitarian exterminations and their being alone in having used the bomb.

Much must be said about other countries, but in embarking on the transcendence of the historical moment we must note, most urgently, a third characteristic. This is that large areas of the sea on which the American vessel must move and which it cannot escape, yet on which it cannot move unless it can identify itself, are totalitarian and that home waters are no longer liberal but "administered." Knowledge of its own ship, self-knowledge, and remembrance are contained in the first step toward the formulation of a nonadministered, nontotalitarian, free society. In America it is the crucible of liberalism that must yield America's contribution to a free society by overcoming her own crisis, potentially the world crisis, by enriching her consciousness with her imagination and offering the synthesis to the world and history.

---

This chapter has not been published previously.

# 11

# THE INTELLECTUAL: BETWEEN CULTURE AND POLITICS. 1971, 1963

*For Herbert Marcuse*

To think about intellectuals without at the same time considering the world we live in strikes me as preposterous. The intellectual as a topic is historical. There is no sense in discussing it independently of the world. In fact, I must start with this world to find out where, if anywhere, intellectuals are; I must constitute both, intellectuals *and* world, if I am to have any hope of attaining either.

So to argue is to be much starker than I found being on either of two previous occasions on which I turned to the topic—much starker because the situation has become starker. Recalling those occasions will help the argument.

# I

Ten years ago I wrote a review of *The Academic Mind,* a book on *Social Scientists in a Time of Crisis,* the McCarthy period, by Paul F. Lazarsfeld and Wagner Thielens, Jr. [1], which is a report on the interviews held in

1955 with some 2400 professors of the social sciences in 165 colleges of various types concerning their experiences during "the difficult years." Constructed as central among the characteristics of the professors were the indices of their apprehension (made up of worry and caution) and permissiveness. The apprehension index was derived from the respondent's answers to such questions as whether he wondered if his politics affected his job security, whether he toned down recent writing to avoid controversy or worried about student misinterpretation causing trouble. The permissiveness index was derived from indicators of a permissive orientation (e.g., would not fire a teacher who admittedly is a communist) and of a conservative orientation (e.g., considers a radical teacher a luxury for a college); it ranged from clearly permissive to clearly conservative.

The authors found that permissiveness correlated with the Democratic vote, approval of classroom discussion, high importance given to students' education as contributors to the improvement of society, opposition to teacher oaths, and interest in civil liberties. They found that the more permissive a teacher, the more apprehensive he was and the more he thought that his own academic freedom had been threatened, that he had been reported to higher authorities, and had felt pressure to conform politically. They found that the better a college (as measured by several criteria), the clearer its administration's stand and the higher the proportion of respondents who expected administrative support if accused of leftist leanings. They found patterns of worry and caution to have been reflected in colleagues' behavior, in the respondent's own behavior in the classroom, and in impaired relations with students.

In responding to the book, I recalled Max Weber's lecture on "Science as a Vocation" (1918). I pointed out that the widespread concurrence with Weber's view by American social scientists largely ignored the historical circumstance in which this view had been set forth. Weber's pleas remained impotent. Not much more than a decade later the world witnessed the enthronement, by due process, of the *Führer*, whose destructiveness Weber had not foreseen [2], even though he had a distinct sense of the tragic.

Many social scientists, I suggested, are impatient with terms like tragic— if only because they have no operational definition for it. "The difficult years" could have given them one if they had inquired into their own experiences and found that "tragic" had one of two quite different meanings: either the professors' fight for their right to say, in and out of the classroom, what to their best knowledge and conviction was the case or the conscious acceptance of having lost all interest in this right. I quoted Lionel Trilling [3]:

> I am not asking for heroism. . . . I am only wondering why
> there is no record of some sense of outrage. . . . At no point
> do any of the responses suggest that the pressure in this in-
> stance had been exerted upon a very special group, upon
> scholars, upon men of the mind. Indeed, nothing is more
> striking than the teachers' inability to think of themselves as
> special in any way—as special because they are superior, as
> special because they have a certain relation to ideas, as special
> because they are committed to certain ideas. . . . no respon-
> dent feels that in his person Mind itself has been belittled and
> mocked.

This fear of identification as intellectuals had been noted before, I
recalled, by Melvin Seeman in "The Intellectuals and the Language of
Minorities" [4], a study of professors at a large state university. Seeman
had not asked whether there might be a difference between intellectuals
and professors, and Lazarsfeld and Thielens had not called professors
intellectuals. Trilling apparently had thought they were and had found
them wanting. He had supposed that it was Lazarsfeld-Thielens' desire
for objectivity that had prevented them from expressing their own outrage. I disagreed, insisting that their fear of value judgments had prevented them from being objective and bore witness to

> their alienation from history, from a common tradition, from
> a common world, and from a common sense of what it is to
> be a man in history, in tradition, in the world.

# II

My conception of the intellectual and the world did at that time little
more than stress certain elements of the liberal conception: vigilance
against threats to academic freedom and the complaint that intimidation
had been successful and vigilance and academic freedom weakened. There
was no analysis of the world in which this had been made possible, no
hint even at the relevance of such an analysis. This conception was not
idiosyncratic, but not the less shortsighted for it. Its strongest component,
because it was the least history-bound if history-bound at all, was the
moral plea directed at fellow intellectuals to recall their own, our own
experiences, to take them, thus us, more seriously than we had been
"trained" to do and to act and live accordingly.

# III

Two or three years later I wrote an essay on anti-intellectualism, "the enemy within" [5]. It belongs here.

In the early fifties, a journal of the social sciences devoted an entire issue to anti-intellectualism. This phenomenon, the editor wrote in his introduction,

> can be described as a fairly broad attitude . . . a negative attitude or prejudice against those who believe that society continually changes, and who favor using scientific and democratic methods to guide and control the changes. . . . Our contributors do not all have the same view of anti-intellectualism, but all of them deplore it to a greater or lesser extent. . . . My own favorite suggestion sounds very conservative: re-emphasis on the fundamental American principles of freedom, and tolerance of dissent. . . . Parents can aid school and community agencies in showing how originality and independence of thought and expression are largely responsible for that which is best in our nation today!

He thus ended with an exclamation point, though not without adding a footnote:

> A parallel is furnished in studies of the best way to answer prejudicial remarks, which showed that an appeal to American principles was most effective.

Anti-intellectualism, a deplorable negative attitude or prejudice, calls for some response, be it ever so humble (my own favorite) and old-fashioned (very conservative), but let us not forget that our attic harbors some downright revolutionary knicknacks—namely, the fundamental American principles of freedom and tolerance of dissent. Parents in particular should remember this, because if they do they can help school and community agencies to show how nice, if not wonderful, originality and independence of thought and expression really are—and this does deserve an exclamation point, for has not an appeal to American principles proved the best and most effective answer to prejudicial remarks, a parallel to anti-intellectualism and, of course, equally deplorable? Studies in this area of our national life, an area as delicate as it is important, appear to tease a tentatively affirmative answer from the data, no matter how difficult it may be to compensate for their slipperiness by neat design and statistical elegance.

My animus is quite impersonal, nor is it in the least directed against the publication in which this sample of editorial merchandise appeared. Examples can be found everywhere, in our newspapers, their editorials, news items, feature stories, and ads, vitiating our newsreels, and at their hottest or coldest in the commercials. Nor, surely, are they altogether absent from our learned or literary periodicals, as my sample suggests. This sample, of course, is especially useful or, to adopt blander language, "not random," for being taken from the introduction to a symposium on anti-intellectualism itself and it suggests that the writer exhibits what he means to analyze. He exhibits one kind of anti-intellectualism, its most pernicious kind, just because it is so customarily engaged in and so little examined: the merchandization of our culture.

# 1

"Our" is more than American, for the merchandization of culture is indeed not limited to the United States, although different here from what it is elsewhere. The expression "our culture" suggests that the phenomenon is not anything perpetrated by a small malicious band or cultural elite on the rest of us but is in ourselves or, again to use blander language, has been internalized by members of society. This language, which I have euphemistically called blander and of which I have given several examples, both quoting and parodying—is at once the most inconspicuous and the most reliable clue to "merchandization." This term refers to a view of culture as a vast inventory of values that can be bought, sold, advertised, and manipulated and to the cultured man or valuable member of society as duty-bound so to view and treat it. Did not the editor write that

> anti-intellectualism can be described as a . . . negative attitude
> or prejudice against those who believe that society continually
> changes, and who favor using scientific and democratic methods
> to guide and control the change?

Not "anti-intellectualism is," but "can be described as," that is, looked at, displayed, arranged, namely, as a "negative attitude or prejudice"—as if the two were the same. From there he issues a whole string of shoddy merchandise: first intellectuals, a package labeled "those who believe that society continually changes," which tells us far less about its contents than the label on a can of orange juice; then in an abrupt change, he insists that the very same package also contains those "who favor using scientific and democratic methods"—as if they were identical or even always compatible, rather than in an often problematical relation—"to guide and control the change." The editor wants to sell an idea. Some of us may buy it, though others will not. Contrary to the saying, however, ideas are *not* salable.

We see that language itself is afflicted with merchandization and it is the deadliest carrier of the disease. Most of us, most of the time, are only its victims, but we may count on the vigor and continued growth of the plague if only we place our trust in the communications industry, inside and outside the schools. Indeed, communications is being widely researched and even more widely put to practice, but some of us, subversives and deplorably wanting in confidence, cannot manage to forget that it is not the same as language. It follows the means-end scheme, as language does not. It instructs, informs, commands, forbids, warns, insinuates, cajoles, and takes on innumerable other roles, addressing itself to categories of men, men taking on roles, not to people, not to unmistakable individuals. It aims at, aims to, uses means—anything but *is*, no more than the categories *are* which it addresses. When we react to communications, we are not ourselves either. When I speak, on the other hand, I am; I become as I speak; indeed, I reveal myself to others as I speak.

What does it mean to say that this merchandization of our culture, which I have merely illustrated at its core, in language, is a form of anti-intellectualism? Anti-intellectualism, in a broad understanding of the term, refers to two things: hostility or related feelings toward ideas and other intellectual matters and hostility and the like toward kinds of people who in some fashion stand for such matters—intellectuals. Although the two are related, they must also be distinguished. So far I have mentioned only the first and have given examples not so much of hostility toward ideas as of disrespect and uneasiness toward language and so toward culture more generally. But it is men who speak and men who have culture, and disrespect and uneasiness in regard to language and culture are therefore disrespect for human activities and characteristics and uneasiness in relation to them. These human activities and characteristics are, of course, not those of intellectuals alone nor of people other than those who show disrespect and betray uneasiness, for they, too, are human; they too speak and have culture. Thus they are disrespectful and uneasy about their own activities and characteristics and the essential features of both themselves and other men. This suggests that the anti-intellectualism I have referred to as the merchandization of our culture develops psychologically (though in a typical rather than an empirical sense) from the fear or distrust of people, of oneself and others.

Ideas are indeed powerful—wonderful and fearful—recalling, in this power, the age-old ambivalence of the sacred, of the holy and cursed, blessed and damned. Why then should there not be a tendency to attenuate man's encounters with the sacred, whether its forms be God or gods, saints or angels, Satan or devils, or ideas, religious or not? Thus, for instance, in most or all societies special times are set aside for men to approach the sacred, and the approach is further attenuated by that psychological crutch of prescription which is known as ritual. In quite a different, much milder example often what we call relaxation serves to justify our turning away from preoccupation with ideas, from thinking. Hence the surrounding of the sacred with ritual and, in more secularized periods, the intermittent turning away from intellectual matters are both understandable phenomena and by no means exclusive of our time or place. By contrast, the fear of persons, actual people, Unamuno's "men of flesh and bone," the fear that I suggested at the bottom of the merchandization of our culture, *is* a historical, and a recent, phenomenon, and it is a problem for us to understand.

It was caught early by Dostoyevsky. " 'I must make a confession to you,' " says Ivan to his younger brother Alyosha in *The Brothers Karamazov*;

> I never could understand how one can love one's neighbours.
> In my view, it is one's neighbours that one can't possibly love,
> but only perhaps these who live far away. . . . To love a man,
> it's necessary that he should be hidden, for as soon as he shows
> his face, love is gone. [And a bit later in the same conversa-
> tion:] Theoretically it is still possible to love one's neighbours,
> and sometimess even from a distance, but at close quarters
> almost never.

The fear of persons is involved in a gerat many more things than in the anti-intellectualism under discussion: in all kinds of psychological defenses, in racial and other prejudices, in dogmatism, bigotry, intolerance, fanaticism, in much compulsive behavior, aggressiveness, hate, contempt, infatuation, in hysteria and many other mental disturbances, in more localized fears, such as men's of women or women's of men, adults' of children or teen-agers, in wars, and, most awful of all, in the consideration and use of thermonuclear weapons. We all know some of these fears—though fears being what they are we probably prefer to know them in others rather than in ourselves. Assume them indeed so widespread that there is some justification in calling our time, as Auden has, the age of anxiety, and we see that the anti-intellectualism that draws on such fears is located in an extraordinarily vast landscape that I cannot possibly trace, let alone attempt to show in its evolution, for this would require a broad study of the total recent history of man.

Instead, we must be content to take this scene, this characterization or at least this characteristic, of our time as unproblematic, hoping that it may throw light on the anti-intellectualism I have recalled, the one that is in all of us.

# 2

I suggest that if this anti-intellectualism is a manifestation of the fear of human beings anti-intellectualism in the second sense of the term, that directed against intellectuals, is a manifestation of the first. Just as focused fear is more tolerable than diffused anxiety and just as scapegoats are easier to handle than reality, so it is a relief to discharge our intellectual discontent on to those who would remind us of it, compared with our having to live with this reminder, and with no end of it in sight. This discontent is a historical phenomenon; it is neither the ahistorical disquietude over injustice and evil, error, constraint, and ugliness nor the discontent Freud claimed to be intrinsic to civilization—although Freud's writing about it when he did *is*, of course, a historical fact symptomatic of our age and related to the discontent referred to, perhaps even an expression of it. *Our* discontent, both the anti-intellectualism in us and that directed against intellectuals, has to do with our attitudes toward tradition.

By traditions I mean group habits—habits of doing, feeling, conceptualizing, judging, and so on; when we use tradition in the singular in such expressions as "the American tradition," "the Western tradition," "the Judeo-Christian tradition," the group, Americans or Westerners, is very large, often the largest the speaker can think of as having a common tradition. In a strict sense there are as many traditions as there are groups, though much of what we say on this will depend on what we mean by group. At any rate, traditions are often in conflict with one another and perhaps more often felt to be in conflict by people to whom one or the other is important. Much of the so-called conflict between science and religion, for instance, can be understood as conflict between traditions. On the other hand, pluralism refers to the coexistence of traditions without conflict.

The question is, which circumstances favor the perception of coexisting traditions as conflicting, as against the perception of them as unproblematic or acceptable? It seems that when the tradition of the group a person identifies with is felt to be threatened by another tradition, in other words, when one's own tradition has become problematic, the two traditions are perceived as conflicting and pluralism becomes a difficult or impossible arrangement. This is to say that the likelihood of conflict increases as the tradition weakens, provided it does not weaken to the point of being given up. If I were a deeply religious man, science would not threaten me, either because I honored its right, which I consider unquestionable, or, in a very different sense, because I completely dis-regarded or despised science; but if I came to have doubts about my religion, yet wanted to hold on to it, I might defend it violently against what I then perceived as the threatening claims of science—provided I did not abandon it and move, as it were, over into the scientific camp, looking back in glee at the superstitions I had left behind me. In this case conflict has disappeared with the disappearance of one of the parties to it.

Obviously, not all conflict is over traditions or intellectual matters. What is important here about this seemingly trivial reminder is that much anti-intellectualism, or hostility toward intellectuals, is not either, hence is called by the wrong name. A common phenomenon is the attack against intellectuals because, as Lewis Coser observes in *The Functions of Social Conflict*, they transform "conflicts of interests into conflicts of ideas." "It is precisely this function of the intellectuals," Coser continues, that, for instance,

> has earned them the enmity of those theoreticians of the American labor movement who are concerned with confining conflicts to immediate issues rather than extending them into political and ideological spheres.

The antagonism concerns the misplacement of ideas, their false insertion, not the ideas themselves. Anti-intellectualism here, as it often does, means hostility to misplacers, abusers, and squanderers of intellectual issues. It does so, for instance, in Julien Benda's "treason of the intellectuals"—their treason consists in their taking part in political and social affairs, which Benda thinks they should not—or in Bertrand Russell's warning to those who would call him an intellectual, for to him this is "a person who pretends to have more intellect than he has" [6], that is, a braggart or charlatan, who also is a misuser of things intellectual. So, indeed, it does in much of the talk about "eggheads," "double domes," "professors who have never met a pay roll," and the like, talk that betrays hostility and contempt for ideas that are irrelevant, ridiculous, phony, or high-falutin in relation to the *real* conflict, which is over political, social, or economic, not intellectual, matters.

Any example of our second form of anti-intellectualism, that directed against intellectuals, must be examined to determine whether it is gen-uinely that or rather the antagonism toward those who threaten certain nonintellectual interests or who symbolize the threat. If we remember what I suggest about the conflict between traditions, we will realize that genuine antagonism toward intellectuals is of two kinds: either toward those who stand for a threatening tradition, existing or emerging, or toward those who stand for the threat to tradition as such, either toward the enemy—such as the scientist perceived as the enemy by the person of weakened religious beliefs—or toward the stranger.

## 3

What, then, do we mean by intellectuals? Edward Shils suggests that they have their own traditions, of which that

> of awesome respect and of serious striving for contact with the sacred is perhaps the first, the most comprehensive and the most important of all [7].

If we recall the relation between ideas and the sacred, we find that Shils's definition may be understood as restating, in more comprehensive, history-conscious language, the popular definition of the intellectual as the man who is concerned with ideas. I would go a step further and submit a most *un*popular—and, inevitably, an ostensive—definition; that is a person who is devoted to the spirit.

It becomes immediately clear that such persons should not be expected to be identical to people in certain occupations, such as scholars, artists, philosophers, authors, some editors, and some journalists, who, in Seymour Martin Lipset's analysis of American intellectuals, are their hard core, because they create culture, although in his discussion Lipset also includes those who distribute culture, that is, performers in the various arts, most teachers, most reporters [8]. Only one of the five commentators on this analysis, Karl Deutsch, raises a question about this identification, commenting on

> the difficulty of defining intellectuals in terms of a social function, rather than in terms of an inner attitude. One might consider an intellectual a person who takes a wide range of abstract symbols and ideas seriously, and who does so in relation to a wide range of topics outside his immediate field of professional specialization [9].

In comparison with Shils's definition and my own, Deutsch's strikes me as more modest and also as hardly distinguishable from that of an educated man. Of course—though Deutsch fails to mention this—if we did not identify intellectuals with social categories, we could not make the studies that Lipset made: we would have no available statistics. Yet we could make a study like Melvin Seeman's, previously referred to, for the number of intellectuals Seeman interviewed—the assistant professors in the humanities and social sciences in one university—was only forty. Seeman, too, preferred the use of categories to define and search for referents—which latter procedure might have had the advantage of yielding an even smaller, hence more manageable, number of interviewees. I suggest that at least one of the components in the attractiveness of such procedures is the predilection for making products that are considered scientific compared with the satisfaction of studying people or of finding out what is going on in our society—and that this component is another expression of what I consider the basis of our first form of anti-intellectualism, which is in all of us: the fear of persons, of "men of flesh and bone." The two studies mentioned are useful and interesting, but not in regard to the topic they claim to deal with—intellectuals—because they do not deal with that topic. They more nearly exhibit a conception of it.

Deutsch's proposed definition of the intellectual is more nearly, I ventured, that of an educated man. In the more recent period of our history Schopenhauer was probably one of the first writers to distinguish the two, and both from the specialist. The latter may

> be likened to a man who lives in his own house and never leaves it. There he is perfectly familiar with everything, . . . but outside it, all is strange and unknown.

By contrast, for the educated man

> it is absolutely necessary . . . [to] be many-sided and take large views; and . . . an extensive acquaintance with history is needful.

Finally, the intellectual, that is, the person devoted to the spirit, is Schopenhauer's philosopher, of whom he says:

> He, however, who wishes to be a philosopher, must gather into his head the remotest ends of human knowledge: for where else could they ever come together? [And he adds:] It is precisely minds of the first order that will never be specialists. For their very nature is to make the whole of existence their problem; and this is a subject upon which they will every one of them in some form provide mankind with a new revelation [10].

The specialist or expert, Ortega y Gasset's learned ignoramus [11], strictly speaking, is noncommittal in regard to tradition—he neither promotes nor fights it—and therefore there is no such thing as antiexpertism or hostility to specialists. When there *seems* to be a case of it, examination will show that the antagonism is directed toward the expert who is perceived as not remaining one, as illegitimately leaving his special field; for instance, toward Einstein, not the physicist but the social, moral, political commentator. It is directed, again, not toward a man's expertise but toward his activities, character, or personality, which, however, must be distinguished from it, as they often are—remember Robert Oppenheimer. Probably many if not most of these cases—and instances of red-baiting and egghead persecutions abound—are genuine anti-intellectualism—that is, expressions of hostility toward conflicting traditions, existing or arising.

# 4

Another form of anti-intellectualism will emerge from a brief consideration of two American comments on the Dreyfus affair.

> "Les intellectuels!" What prouder club-name could there be than this one, used ironically by the party of "red blood," the party of every stupid prejudice and passion, during the anti-Dreyfus craze, to satirize the men in France who still retained some critical sense and judgment!

William James, who said this, was proud to apply the designation to himself and the group he identified with, for he honored the critical sense and judgment to which the adversaries of those possessing them were blinded. Compare James's remark with Russell Kirk's:

> Les intellectuels was the term of contempt employed by the factions of the Right, during the Dreyfus controversy, to describe the café-revolutionaries, the men who had broken with tradition, the enemies of patriotism, order, and the wisdom of the ages. It implied an opposition between the life of the mind and the life of society—or, at least, an inimicality between "advanced social thinkers" and [the transition is breathtaking and disarming] the possessors of property and power.

Dreyfus was a military officer rather than an intellectual, but both James and Kirk, though almost fifty years apart and at opposite poles, are agitated by the anti-intellectual aspects of the affair. Both take it as an occasion to vindicate traditions—James that of men of critical sense and judgment, Kirk that of some variety of conservatism—and to fight other traditions: James the one of red blood and stupid prejudice and passion, Kirk that of rootlessness. Kirk's enmity is a mixture of the antagonism toward the person who threatens tradition as such, the stranger, a form of anti-intellectualism we anticipated, and another form, antagonism toward the bloodless or lifeless intellectual, which we indulge whenever we use "academic" or "academicism" in a pejorative sense. Nietzsche, of course, was full of this anti-academicism; much earlier the satirist and aphorist Georg Christoph Lichtenberg castigated the wordmongers, for which Kierkegaard thanked him:

> Thanks, Lichtenberg, thanks!, for having said that there is nothing so feeble as the conversation of learned literary men who have never thought for themselves but know a thousand historical-literary facts. Like Leporello [he adds] they keep a list, but the point is what they lack; while Don Juan seduces girls and enjoys himself—Leporello notes down the time, the place and a description of the girl.

This form of anti-intellectualism, antiacademicism, is also of two kinds. One is contempt for pretense, fuzzimindedness, or fakery; it plays a conspicuous role in Bertrand Russell's definition of the intellectual, quoted earlier, as the "person who pretends to have more intellect than he has," and finds expression in many derogatory terms, ranging from pompous ass, stuffed shirt, intellectual, thinker, and high-brow, in the derogatory sense of these words, to the professor who has never met a payroll, the egghead and double dome, the crackpot, charlatan, and the nut, with its numerous equivalents. However different from one another, none of the persons so designated is to be taken seriously inasmuch as he presents the less as the more, the obscure as clear, the spurious as genuine. Thus he strikes the person who calls him by these terms as disrespectful of what matters to that person and often as disrespectful of what he considers most important in the tradition of his group. The second form of antiacademicism, which is also reflected in the passage from Kierkegaard and in many other places, notably in "philosophies of life" and existentialist writing but also in the Nazi literature of "blood and soil," is hostility toward the man who presents ideas that he has not tested in experience, in his own life. Sometimes such a man is unfavorably compared with people who are thought to be closer to life—for instance, the peasants in many nineteenth-century Russian writers, most conspicuously Tolstoy. This form, too, as the examples suggest, has its range from the most admirable to the most obnoxious, depending on the admixture of nonintellectual elements —that is, the manifestations of political, demagogical, prejudicial, and destructive interests, which in the Nazi case all but overpower antiacademicism itself.

Antiacademicism is a strong ingredient of the culture of the United States. It is essential to the whole tradition of pragmatism, by which I mean far more than the philosophical school, namely, a basic characteristic of our outlook: the emphasis on practice and on improving practice, with an essentially practical if not utilitarian attitude toward tradition. Thus "almost all the great truths relating to society," writes Merle Curti in *American Paradox*, are (as Wendell Phillips said in his Phi Beta Kappa address at Harvard in 1881) ". . . . not the result of scholarly meditation, but have been first heard in the solemn protests of maryred patriots and the loud cries of crushed and starving labor." Much better known is Emerson, in *his* Phi Beta Kappa address, also at Harvard, more than forty years earlier (1837): "The so-called 'practical men,'" Emerson said,

> sneer at speculative men, as if, because they speculate or *see*, they could do nothing. . . . [Yet this is not so:] Action is with the scholar subordinate, but it is essential. Without it he is not yet man. Without it thought can never ripen into truth. . . . Inaction is cowardice, but there can be no scholar without the heroic mind. . . . Only so much do I know, as I have lived. Instantly we know whose words are loaded with life, and whose not.

Although Emerson called him the scholar, he is identical with the man devoted to the spirit. In a statement that is wholly compatible with Shils's view of the intellectual, Emerson calls the scholar

> the delegated intellect. In the right state he is *Man Thinking*. In the degenerate state, when the victim of society, he tends to become a mere thinker, or still worse, the parrot of other men's thinking.

His duties are

> such as become Man Thinking. They may all be comprised in self-trust. The office of the scholar is to cheer, to raise, and to guide men by showing them facts amidst appearances.

His everyday, minimal obligation is to search honestly and patiently for what is the case, since he knows that without honesty and patience his self-trust will not bless him with being "Man Thinking."

Neither Emerson's American scholar nor William James's college-bred (1908), who comes up to the best claim we can make for the higher education, namely, to enable us to know a good man when we see him, is an academician nor is he an expert or specialist. A century and a quarter ago, when Emerson delivered his address, and seventy years later, when James gave his on the college-bred, the American practice, with its pragmatism, optimism, and liberalism, had not yet been tested by world wars, the Great Depression, totalitarianism, Hiroshima, and Nagasaki, the rise of African and Asian nations, and automation, to mention only some of what has happened to this and other nations during the last few decades. It is so extraordinary an onslaught of novelties, one of them threatening the end of mankind, another the end of the West, a third the end of the white man's era, that it would be amazing if the meanings of intellectualism and anti-intellectualism had not changed as well. I have in fact remarked on one of the changes: the emergence of anti-intellectualism within ourselves, the first kind that I commented on. Why, indeed, should we not be afraid of individual human beings if recent years have produced such fearsome men as Stalin and Hitler and a harassing number of smaller destroyers? People often ask, most recently during the Eichmann trial, whether we would have been different if we had been where they were, and if we had been their victims would we have been nobler than many of their victims?

## 5

How did some students of man, professors of the social sciences, stand up to a minor monster, though the biggest in recent American history—the late Senator McCarthy? In *The Academic Mind*, Paul Lazarsfeld's and Wagner Thielens' study of more than 2000 such professors, the question is so operationalized into indices and subquestions and the professors' answers are therefore so submerged in their specificity to questionnaire items that instead of being answered we are bored and instead of bread we receive, not stones, but the cotton imitation we have long since become accustomed to accept as the real thing—another case of injury unsuffered [12], to borrow Harold Rosenberg's shattering description of the tone of some other recent sociological studies. This one is a fine example of academicism—quite a response to the McCarthys!—and its title, *The Academic Mind*, stares us in the face as a pun, referring not only to that mind investigated but also that mind laboring.

More than forty years ago, in his lecture on "Science as a Vocation," which he addressed to university students shortly after Germany's defeat, Max Weber sketched a picture of the college professor—distinct, noble, and moving. His mission, Weber urged, is to purvey knowledge and to teach students to think and not to indulge in value judgments, least of all by letting "facts speak for themselves." The many American adherents of this picture probably ignore the historical circumstances of its emergence. One of them was the chauvinism that had invaded many classrooms during the second *Reich*. Although it had just been overthrown, Weber's plea for objectivity on the lectern was still pointed at that misplaced patriotism. Another, more immediate circumstance was the reaction to the defeat in the form of a longing for leadership and personality. Against this longing Weber summoned all the passionate severity at his command to urge scholars and scientists, and the future scholars and scientists he was addressing, not to be tempted into playing the role of "prophet and leader. This plea could not turn German history, which had led to the enthronement of a prophet whose monstrosity Weber, with all his sense of the tragic, could not have foreseen.

A revision of Weber's picture of the professor might include his *right and duty* to transmit knowledge—that is, whatever to the best of his own knowledge and conviction is in fact the case—his *right and duty* to teach students to think—that is, to develop their knowledge and clarify their convictions so that they might learn even better the inexhaustible meaning of the phrase "to the best of their own knowledge and conviction." This meaning is always relative, but it can be clarified to the point at which, at a given time, it is relatively absolute. An example is the right and duty to tell the truth publicly as best we know it if we would be true to our profession as teachers, scientists, or scholars.

These rights and these duties entail sensitivity to threats and the announcement of such threats; cowardice, indifference, adjustment are acts of treason here. As far as *The Academic Mind* is concerned, the general impression I gained of American professors of the social sciences was more miserable and shameful than not. I have already quoted from Lionel Trilling's review of the book, with which I concurred and still do. Here, as in so many other places, academicism is the anti-intellectualism in ourselves that rises from our fear of human beings: we are back in the wild, enormous landscape in which we with our anti-intellectualism are located—in which, to quote Rosenberg again, "everyone has won a fairy tale luxury and lost himself."

To make this landscape commensurate with us, to make it fit human dimensions, instead of merely glancing at it and panicking, is the problem into which our ramble in that small part of it, anti-intellectualism, has led us. It gives us a task, both urgent and promising, in an unforeseeable future, and this in two very different, though intimately connected ways: sociological and human. Sociologically, the task is the clarification of what can from now on be accepted as public and what as technical issues. In public issues all citizens, and foremost men devoted to the spirit, must participate lest the expert not remain what he must, namely, an invaluable servant, and instead become his own demonic caricature, an impossible master [13]. The expert cannot be allowed, for instance, to decide whether nuclear tests should be resumed, and he should thank those individuals who have proclaimed it, keep on proclaiming it, and have acted on their proclamations, for no matter what the outcome they have infused some clarity into our landscape.

Humanly—and the example just recalled of the protests shows the connection with the sociological aspect—let us recall Emerson's definition of the scholar as "Man Thinking" who, when the victim of society, degenerates; or Poe's "The Man That Was Used Up"; or Melville's Confidence Man, whom he contrasted, not only with Ahab, but also, in the very "recesses of the office files," with Bartleby [14]. These are only a few among the writers who have warned us against the explosion of society, against the identification of person and social category. Surely, we are both persons and social beings, we make society as society makes us; but at a time when the social drowns out the human we must remember our faith in the human voice, no matter how pitiful, perhaps even unintelligible, its tune may be. Often it is not the courage to name that we lack, for the difficulty is far greater: we do not know what it is that we are expected to name or we do not know that we are expected to name anything at all. Courage takes only encouragement, but no matter how hard this may be to come by, to tear ourselves out of ignorance or pseudo-knowledge is much harder yet. In such a situation we have nothing to begin with but ourselves and therefore we must take ourselves seriously, trusting that the spirit to which we are devoted has not gone out of us. If it were not such a crisis, it would not be worthy of our unconditional effort and it would not be the extreme situation in which we are if it did not call on us whole.

# IV

Thus in my second effort on intellectuals they emerged as men devoted to the spirit amid the horror, men in a maelstrom threatened by drowning but trying to preserve the light by forcing it up above the waters, voices whispering "Man," breathing this word in the roar of society. In the end there was a hint—now I see it—that I did not know, or knew only vaguely, what I was talking about: "we do not know what it is that we are expected to name or we do not know that we are expected to name anything at all." There followed a blanket entreaty, perhaps a desperate but perhaps a blank shot, to entrust ourselves to ourselves, a plea for the faith "that the spirit to which we are devoted has not gone out of us." Ambiguity: was the salvation I implored nothing perhaps but cathartic withdrawal?

The very possibility shows the flawed conception, the misplaced sentimentality, the writer's misunderstanding of his place in the world, his misinsertion in the world. It did not feel so then; it feels so now. Why?

Was it possible a few years ago to find hope in the appeal to the man devoted to the spirit, who was to be resuscitated out of the fallen intellectual—academician, professor, teacher? That the moral plea—which had also characterized my previous attempt, whose strongest component it had been—was still passionately or desperately clung to to get into the world, even though it had since become or shown itself as far more horrible, and to make it feel less horrible?

# V

I must try to get over this ambiguity by consulting two searching and anguished descriptions of our world: Barrington Moore, Jr.'s "Revolution in America?" [15] and Herbert Marcuse's *An Essay on Liberation* [16].

Barrington Moore does not say whether he means that the question of the prospects for revolution in the United States must be asked in any diagnosis of this country today, but he would probably consider it inseparable from it—perhaps even more so than the diagnosis of the United States from that of mankind as a whole. At any rate, the result of his investigation is that although the prospects for revolution are dim "the prospects for any transformation of American society by purely peaceful and democratic means are dimmer still." Hence there is a very somber but not a passive and fatalistic sense of the world to come. Moore attributes, or recommends, it to the intellectual:

> One task of human thought is to try to perceive what the range of possibilities may be in a future that always carries on its back the burden of the present and the past. Though that is not the only task of the intellectual, it is a very important and very difficult one.

What possibilities emerge? Acting on his own injunction to intellectuals, Moore has reviewed those of revolution here. Is *this*—I find myself coming back to that hint in my earlier try—"what we are expected to name" if we would make our best diagnosis? What is the perception of possibilities based on? Optimally on a position in which the perceiver, the intellectual, takes as little for granted as he can manage. In the present instance he would *not*, for example, take for granted the limitation of possibilities to the alternative revolution or reform versus continuation of status quo or martial law or worse. He would not take for granted a traditional conception of revolution ("seizing and holding power") but would rather be guided by revolutionaries themselves who, Moore writes, to the extent that they "did succeed, . . . often did so in large measure by avoiding slavish adherence to past models and by displaying ingenuity in devising new policies for unprecedented situations." One reason for the thinker not to cling to the traditional definition of revolution might be the very "pathos of novelty," "the experience of man's faculty to begin something new" [17], that Hannah Arendt stresses as the essence of revolution.

I base this recommendation to take as little for granted as possible— or bearable—on at least three grounds. First is that we live in an unprecedented situation if only—to mention one of many reasons for saying this— because we can all be killed far more quickly and with greater probability than ever before in history. Second, the principles by which the student selects and orders his facts—as Barrington Moore himself writes elsewhere—"have political and moral consequences" [18]. The aspect of this proposition which justifies the advocacy of the maximum suspension of received notions is that the student's definition of his task, including the conceptualization of his subject matter, may also have consequences for the definitions, conceptualizations, and actions of his readers and for an unpredictable number of other persons: the kind of his understanding and the degree of his understanding make a difference; they are his awful responsibility. Third, the procedure argued makes the student who follows it perceive more than the more traditional student does. It is easy to understand, for instance, that in his frame of reference Moore has to say about "New Left semi-revolutionary movements" only that they cannot provide the "need for protection and continuing benefits" (furnished by "liberated areas" characteristic of peasant revolutions) "through such symbolic gestures as offering sanctuary to draft resisters or liberating a university through a student riot." Would a less traditional conception of revolution not predispose one to undertake a more expectant and dedicated exploration of possible influences on social change—let this term denote the broadest possible topic Moore is concerned with—which such phenomena as the "New Left semi-revolutionary movements," but many others as well, might have? Let their sphere be subjective or cultural, should it be a foregone conclusion that the subjective factor, the realm of culture, thought, the spirit, is irrelevant to social change, hence to its analysis—that there is no such thing as the cunning of reason?

# VI

In contrast to Barrington Moore's diagnosis, Herbert Marcuse's *An Essay on Liberation* focuses precisely on the problem of the relation between the subjective and the objective factor, between culture and politics, between sensibility and social structure, organization, change. In this analysis, Marcuse writes, neither "critical theory" nor "political practice," can

> orient itself on a concept of revolution which belongs to the nineteenth and early twentieth century . . . [and] envisages the "seizure of power" in the course of a mass upheaval . . . (p. 79),

whereas now, if

> in the rebellion of the young intelligentsia, the right and the truth of the imagination become the demands of political action, . . . this apparently insignificant development may indicate a fundamental change in the situation (p. 30).

Obviously Marcuse's implied conception of revolution and of what is happening to consciousness and within consciousness—in the subjective conditions, in culture—differs from Barrington Moore's. Marcuse's chapter on "The New Sensibility," from which the last quotation was taken, analyzes movements or occurrences relevant to consciousness: art, language, drugs, and music. The attendant refusal of our society, Marcuse writes, "is affirmative in that it envisages a new culture which fulfills the humanistic promises betrayed by the old culture" (p. 10).

> This is the vicious circle: the rupture with the self-propelling conservative continuum of needs must *precede* the revolution which is to usher in a free socity, but such rupture itself can be envisaged only in a revolution . . . (p. 18).

There is "the striking contrast between the radical and total character of the rebellion on the one hand and the absence of a class basis for this radicalism on the other" (p. 79), so that "every step in the struggle for radical change isolates the opposition from the masses and provokes intensified responses" (p. 68). Therefore "the radical is guilty—either of surrendering to the power of the status quo or of violating the Law and Order of the status quo" (p. 70)—of the status quo whose "insane fea-

tures" are the "expression of the ever more blatant contradiction between the available resources for liberation and their use for the perpetu-
ation of servitude" (p. 83).

Guided by his "consciousness and conscience" (p. 71), Marcuse arrives
at a point in front of an impossible landscape (of the kind we encountered before: the world)—it arrests him, and thus us, who have accompanied him. What does he do? He remembers himself as an intellectual
who has memories of impossible situations and, speaking biographically,
as one who has been accused of claiming the right to draw the limits of
tolerance, of recommending a dictatorship by intellectuals [19]:

> But who has the right to set himself up as judge of an estab-
> lished society, who other than the legally constituted agencies
> or agents, and the majority of the people? Other than these,
> it could only be a self-appointed elite. . . . Indeed, if the alter-
> native were between democracy and dictatorship . . . , the
> answer would be noncontroversial: democracy is preferable.
> However, this democracy does not exist. . . . The representa-
> tion is representative of the will shaped by the ruling minori-
> ties. Consequently, if the alternative is rule by an elite, it
> would only mean replacement of the present ruling elite by
> another; and if this other should be the dreaded intellectual
> elite, it may not be less qualified than the prevailing one. To
> be sure, this has never been the course of a revolution, but it
> is equally true that never before has a revolution occurred
> which had at its disposal the present achievements of produc-
> tivity and technical progress. . . . Prior to its realization, it is
> indeed only the individual, the individuals, who can judge,
> with no other legitimation than their consciousness and con-
> science. . . . Their judgment transends their subjectivity to
> the degree to which it is based on independent thought and
> information, on a rational analysis and evaluation of their
> society. The existence of a majority of individuals capable of
> such rationality has been the assumption on which democratic
> theory has been based (pp. 70–71).

A few years earlier he wrote:

> The question, who is qualified to make all these distinctions,
> definitions, identifications [among policies, opinions, move-
> ments] for the society as a whole, has now one logical answer,
> namely, everyone "in the maturity of his faculties" as a human
> being, everyone who has learned to think rationally and auton-
> omously. The answer to Plato's educational dictatorship is

the democratic dictatorship of free men. . . . In Plato, rationality is confined to the small number of philosopher-kings; in Mill, every rational human being participates in the discussion and decision—but only as a rational being. Where society has entered the phase of total administration and indoctrination, this would be a small number indeed, and not necessarily that of the elected representatives of the people. The problem is not that of an educational dictatorship, but that of breaking the tyranny of-public opinion and its makers in the closed society [20].

# VII

Thus the point is not a Platonic academy, not a dictatorship by intellectuals but—to argue at least one legitimate and justifiable reading of these passages—the elevation into consciousness of something spontaneous that is going on and that we must develop into a principle of conduct and policy; something that has long since been practiced but must be realized as the revolutionary lever it can become. The clue to it is that "the existence of a majority of individuals capable of such rationality has been the assumption on which democratic theory has been based." This, together with the sentence preceding it and with other ideas contained in the passages quoted, suggests that individuals, legitimated by their consciousness and conscscience and on the basis of independent thought and information, judge and assess their society, appealing to the reason in their fellowmen. Let the former be called intellectuals (echo of Socrates, rather than Plato); the latter are other people, unpredicated and unpredicable beyond their endowment with reason.

Questions arising out of Barrington Moore's paper led to the recommendation that we, intellectuals and other people, take as little for granted as possible—or bearable; thus that we not take a lowest common-denominator conception of revolution as the basis for speculating on the prospects for revolution now. Marcuse, we saw, does reject such a concept of revolution for both critical theory and political practice. In thus suspending or bracketing a received notion he is intellectually more radical than Moore, less deflected by tradition as he gropes for roots. Furthermore, his statement that *both* theory and practice must suspend received notions hints at the close connection between intellectual and political radicalness: they are two thrusts of one radicalism, for which practice, or praxis, must be informed by theory, which is given life by praxis. In Marcuse's words, both Moore and he engage, in the writings at issue and in others, in "a rational analysis and evaluation of their [our] society." For Marcuse, here and elsewhere [21], this is the analysis of "the problem of the relation between the subjective and the objective factor, between culture and politics." The devotion to this analysis defines him as the intellectual: as the man devoted to the spirit, yes, but who thus devoted, thus legitimated, rationally analyzes and assesses his society, his shudder stayed by his faith that his followmen are, as he is, endowed with reason.

# VIII

At this point we envisage the intellectual located between culture and politics—located in two senses: it is here that we must look for him in our search for a concept of the intellectual that we can answer for, and it is here that we would have him recall that he is active.

*Medias in res*: for me one of the most utterly unresolved questions— let everybody ask himself whether it is for him or her—is simply how to live with or without the daily news. I feel corrupt as I watch and hear continuous lying, killing, torturing, the evidence of insanity, obscenity, hypocrisy, crime, while doing no more than occasionally protesting in one form or another and sending money to fellow protesters or helpers, and I feel corrupt *not* watching and hearing, turning away from the horror. The only way I can imagine feeling less corrupt, just possibly even at peace, would be to devote all my waking hours and extending them as much as I could physically stand it to work on reducing at least one of the innumerable outrages that diminish the world. This is a piece of theoretical imagination; it does not change my practice, though surely my theory. That I am corrupt and not free is no more than a theoretical insight, for my arrogance—this *may* be a misnomer—lets me continue doing what I am doing instead of what that insight tells me would make me less corrupt: my arrogance, that is to say my conviction, that being as I am I must do what I do rather than what on *theoretic* grounds strikes me as morally superior. (There *is* comfort in knowing that others, too, do so.) Arrogance would be a misnomer if doing what one must because one is what one is were itself morally equal or superior to doing what one must on theoretic insight. To affirm doing because of one's being is morally the more bearable and justified, the more firmly it is based on the most thorough examination one can undertake of one's practice *and* theory as they impinge on one another—the more firmly it is based on the injunction, "know thyself" [22]—thyself as man, as "species being." To communicate this concept of theory and practice and this theory and practice is surely one meaning of the proposition that the "man devoted to the spirit rationally analyzes and assesses his society, his shudder stayed by his faith that his followmen are, as he is, endowed with reason." Communication with a partner or partners who suffer from similar unresolved questions as I do differs from communication with those who do not—in the first case it may and in the second it may not be indicated to discuss such questions, What in both cases is not only indicated but essential and what goes beyond communication in even the broadest accepted meaning is that we try with *all* partners to be at our best (which, of course, is not always the same) because we not only become better ourselves but make the world better, instead of diffusing our discontent that the world is not better than it is or that the better future has not yet arrived.

# IX

To be at our best means to be not only kind, gentle, and considerate but also critical, and there is no end of occasions on which to be kind and critical. The fate of kindness in our society requires a large essay, which this one cannot be. I wish to make only one point, which I think important. The kindness I am referring to has not only an ethical but also an aesthetic aspect. Marcuse, and not only in the essay touched on, has much to say on aesthetics, though not in relation to kindness. What I mean is that to look at a painting, to walk, to listen to music, or to watch a play or movie can, whatever else it may be, also be a joy, and to give oneself or others joy is also to be kind. The question when to enjoy is again an unprescribable one of one's best "consciousness and conscience."

The kindness intrinsic to the intellectual's task is indicated by the fact (or definition) that his shudder is "stayed by his faith that his fellowmen are, as he is, endowed with reason." In accordance with what is most special to his task, however, we must now turn to him as critic. In moving between culture and politics, he may cry out, for instance, with Brecht: "Erst kommt das Fressen, dann kommt die Moral" ("First comes the grub, then comes morality"), a cry heard in the Weimar Republic in the late twenties, or with the French students in May 1968: "Soyons réalistes, demandons l'impossible!" ("Let's be realistic; ask for the impossible!")— or whatever his biographically or historically resounding cries may be: all he has to do is remember and a cry will rise in him that should be heard. These cries beat against aspects of society or result from somebody's, perhaps his own, assessment of society, which, of course, need not be his nation. The cries may reverberate only within the sphere of culture. Politicians, and not only tyrants and dictators, can by definition not hear them, in contrast to political men, including their professional variant, statesmen.

The excitement some intellectuals felt when they heard a devastating song from *The Threepenny Opera* sung or whistled in the streets of Berlin in the late twenties often was over an alleged or expected change in consciousness of ordinary people—the same excitement over consciousness now so often discussed with reference, for instance, to The Beatles [23] and comparable groups. Politically, it may be as irrelevant today as it was then, when a few years after Brecht-Weill came Hitler.

There are indications, however, that we have learned to understand this irrelevance; one example from the present exploration is the truth in Barrington Moore's cautionary comments on New Left semirevolutionary movements. The difficulty is that the sphere of culture, hence its relation to politics and its impingement on politics, changes historically—a circumstance, we noted, that is much more in Marcuse's thought than in Moore's. As we had occasion to say in different terms in connection with each of the essays of these two thinkers, the task of ascertaining, and *by ascertaining helping to constitute*, the boundary between culture and politics, hence of analyzing *and testing* the influence of culture on politics, is a task that can be attacked not only frontally but also in innumerable investigations and experiments which would be guided by the individuals' engaging in them. Therefore, whatever the tasks are, they are based on or contribute to a rational analysis and evaluation of the society they are done in or refer to. In many cases the exploration of the nature of this contribution is a part of the investigator's or experimenter's task of which he is quite aware [24].

# X

Among the many areas of which we would do well to be critically conscious I mention only language—and no more than a single example: this morning—but any would do—I received an advertisement from the *Bulletin of the Atomic Scientists* which committed this offense against the merits of the journal and against language and people who speak and write:

> In the months ahead Bulletin readers will be enjoying such stimulating articles as
>
> RADIATION AND INCREASING INFANT MORTALITY [these words in red capital letters]—A horrifying (and probably controversial) assessment of a little-noticed phenomenon.

The entertainment value of the article on the consequences of radiation for the death of infants—the article is almost surely quite different—is heightened by the parenthetical wink at the potential reader's ambition to be an inside dopester. Such vicious babble, of course, also bombards us in almost every newscast, which in this country, furthermore, is inter-rupted, with inhuman timing, by the lies and idiocies of the commercials, the reaction to which seems not to be outrage—any more than it was the social-science professors' to Joseph McCarthy, as Lionel Trilling then observed—but indifference, apathy, cynicism, amusement, or the con-sumer's docile alertness: the news consumer *has* assimilated the message—never mind (*pace* McLuhan!) the medium. George Orwell is one of the few among the commentators on the decline of our language to relate it—a cultural phenomenon—to politics:

> one ought to recognize that the present [1946] political chaos is connected with the decay of language, and that one can probably bring about some improvement by starting at the verbal end. If you simplify your English, you are freed from the worst follies of orthodoxy. You cannot speak any of the necessary dialects, and when you make a stupid remark, its stupidity will be obvious, even to yourself [25].

Recognizing and rejecting cant and other sports of tradition, as well as traditions, as historically inadequate—sometimes because they feed on hypocrisy—a recognition and rejection that may be accompanied by the identification and acceptance of something else as real, seem to be at least an important part of the movement on the subjective, the cultural side of the change or revolution that industrialized and industrializing societies are variously undergoing. In the United States the two groups that exhibit these shifts in acceptance and rejection most obviously are students [26] (and an increasing number of teachers and other professionals [27]) and those who already as a result of these shifts call themselves blacks. In several places Marcuse has located our hope in these two groups [28]. Some of the rejection they share—of cant, hypocrisy, oppression, tutelage, exploitation, and mutilation—are even more manifest than are some of their common acceptances and affirmations, such as insistence on the search for new identities and the claim to them, shared and sometimes converging convictions and practices of liberation by music, dance, drugs, sex, love, free speech (and print), and attendent practices, new ways of living together ("pads," "communes," "communities"), membership in newly self-conscious groups [29], and stress on the importance of the body. Eldridge Cleaver so formulates part of this convergence: "Martin

Luther King, Jr., giving voice to the needs of the Body, and President Kennedy, speaking out of the needs of the Mind, made contact on that day" ("when the Birmingham revolt erupted in the summer of 1963") [30]. The importance of the body had, of course, been emphasized by philosophers and psychologists —among the most recent Wilhelm Reich, in particular, must not be forgotten—but it is only in the last few years that this attention has broken out of the sphere of culture into praxis and toward politics. That like other facets of student and black activities it also shows irrelevant and self-defeating features, both of fashion and destructiveness, is obvious, unfortunate, and understandable.

Even this insistence on the body is partly a reaction against the war in Vietnam. Its fundamental importance for our social change—clearly not only in the United States but all over the earth—has many more direct manifestations. The most immediate is simply its rejection by draft resistance, desertion, sabotage, and the refusal of participation whatever, but they range all the way to questioning our educational system at ever lower levels and by ever younger students—this system supports the war or is at least indifferent to it—and to analyses of our economy [31], including its science [32].

# XI

Here is a statement concerning the relation between culture and politics:

> Hitherto men have constantly made up for themselves false conceptions about themselves, about what they are and what they ought to be. . . . The phantoms of their brains have gained the mastery over them. . . . Let us teach men, says one, to exchange these imaginations for thoughts which correspond to the essence of man; says the second, to take up a critical attitude to them; says the third, to knock them out of their heads; and existing reality will collapse.
>
> . . . The first volume of this present publication has the aim of uncloaking these sheep, who take themselves and are taken for wolves; of showing . . . how the boasting of these philosophic commentators only mirrors the wretchedness of the real conditions . . . [33].

Compare this statement by Marx with one made 110 years later:

> As a type of social man, the intellectual does not have any one

> political direction, but . . . his work . . . does have a distinct
> kind of political relevance: his politics, in the first instance,
> are the politics of truth, for his job is the maintenance of an
> adequate definition of reality. . . . The intellectual ought to
> be the moral conscience of his society, at least with reference
> to the value of truth. . . . And he ought also to be a man
> absorbed in the attempt to know what is real and what is
> unreal. . . .
>
> . . . If you ask to what the intellectual belongs, you must
> answer that he belongs first of all to that minority which has
> carried on the big discourse of the rational mind. . . . This
> . . . is not a vague thing to which to belong—even if as lesser
> participants—and it is the beginning of any sense of belonging
> that free men in our time might have. And, just now, at this
> point in human history, that is quite difficult [34].

Now compare this statement by C. Wright Mills with one made twelve
years later still, in 1967, by Noam Chomsky:

> It is the responsibility of intellectuals to speak the truth and
> expose lies. This, at least, may seem enough of a truism to pass
> over without comment, Not so, however. For the modern intel-
> lectual, it is not at all obvious. Thus we have Martin Heideg-
> ger writing, in a pro-Hitler declaration of 1933, that "truth is
> the revelation of that which makes a people certain, clear, and
> strong in its action and knowledge"; it is only this kind of
> "truth" that one has a responsibility to speak. Americans tend
> to be more forthright. When Arthur Schlesinger was asked by
> *The New York Times* in November 1965 to explain the con-
> tradiction between his published account of the Bay of Pigs
> incident and the story he had given the press at the time of
> the attack, he simply remarked that he had lied. . . . It is of
> no particular interest that one man is quite happy to lie in
> behalf of a cause which he knows to be unjust; but it is sig-
> nificant that such events provoke so little response in the intel-
> lectual community . . . [35].

Out of the many things that could be said about these three statements
on the intellectual between culture and politics I take only what strikes
me as most relevant to our concern—both in this essay and in our world
today.

1. Marx debunks the arrogance of culture (the philosophy of the Young
Hegelians) as a ludicrous mask of politics (the cause of the wretchedness
of the real conditions to which it is as indifferent as is that philosophy);
and he uncloaks its exhibitors, to recall the terms of one of the types of

anti-intellectualism (so misnamed) suggested before, as misplacers, abusers, and squanderers of ideas.

2. Like Mills and Chomsky (and many others), Marx wants intellectuals to tell the truth and, like them (and fewer others), above all the truth about politics, society, economics, and—in a much longer range than Mills and Chomsky—history.

3. It is easy to see that in addition to many other passages from Marx this one shows him, or could show him, as one of the fathers of the sociology of knowledge,—which has been criticized most acrimoniously in its development by Karl Mannheim [36], for (to use our own terms) not turning its attention to politics, society, and economics, for not breaking out of the subjective or cultural sphere. Just as the philosophy of the Young Hegelians was an object of Marx's critique, so the sociology of knowledge itself would have been if Marx could have witnessed it.

4. The Marx quotation contains no explicit exemption of *some* thought from its general debunking. If, however, there were nothing else in Marx's writing—which on the contrary contains much—to convince us that he was not a general debunker of thought, it is enough to recall his "Theses on Feuerbach," written about the same time as the passage quoted, if not shortly before, especially the famous eleventh, the last: "The philosophers have only *interpreted* the world in various ways; but the point is to *change* it." Far from advocating the abolition of philosophy, let alone of philosophers, this on the contrary gives them—the intellectuals—a different and today more specific task than telling the truth. Both Mills and Chomsky are moving in the direction of Marx's eleventh thesis. Mills, in addition to pleading that intellectuals acknowledge and be loyal to their tradition, "the big discourse of the rational mind," urges the political relevance of truth, which is their politics. Chomsky does so more concretely by naming betrayers of this truth and this politics. The difference between Mills and Chomsky, which may well reflect a difference between the times in which they wrote, is that the later statement is more urgent and specific than the earlier. The theoretical justification—in contrast to the historical—of both Mills's and Chomsky's propositions can be found in Marx's eleventh thesis on Feuerbach.

Part of how I read this thesis has also been expressed by Mills (in the same essay), though without reference to Marx:

> In so far as he [the intellectual] is politically adroit, the main tenet of his politics is to find out as much of the truth as he can, and to tell it to the right people, at the right time, and in the right way. Or, stated negatively: to deny publicly what he knows to be false, whenever it appears in the assertions of

> no matter whom; and whether it be a direct lie or a lie by
> omission, whether it be by virtue of official secret or an honest
> error [37].

Marx's, Mills's, and Chomsky's message is this: get your culture into the
world and work in and at the world at whatever task your being, so
informed by the message, bids you do. Obviously, this need not be political in any technical sense; on the contrary, whatever you do as so defined
*becomes* political, at the very least, by contributing in this practice to a
new understanding of an old meaning of politics as activity for the common good.

In bringing my references even closer to today and to my home, the
university, I would argue that such an understanding informs a collection
of critical essays on the humanities and social sciences, *The Dissenting
Academy* [38]. It is at least as specific and concrete as Mills's critique of
sociology [39]; it contains incisive papers (some more than others) on
academic delinquency in general, on English, economics, history, international relations, anthropology, philosophy, the social consciousness of
the social sciences, political science, and the Catholic college, and a
reprint of Chomsky's "The Responsibility of Intellectuals." It illustrates
an expression of the desire—the historical necessity of this desire—to get
one's "culture into the world and work in and at the world."

One example must do. In her paper on anthropology, "World Revolution and the Science of Man," Kathleen Gough asks: "How can the
science of man help men to live more fully and creatively and to expand
their dignity, self-direction, and freedom?" and suggests

> that social science, like all science, becomes morally and so-
> cially either meaningless or harmful unless its skills and knowl-
> edge are periodically referred back to the question, "Science
> for what purpose and for whom?" If we cease to ask this
> question, we cease to seek wisdom and cease to be intellectuals
> in any meaningful sense of the word. With the loss of respon-
> sibility for our learning, we also cease to be fully social, and
> therefore human [40].

This is more consciously political than Robert S. Lynd's question almost
thirty years earlier, "knowledge for what?" [41]; several symposiasts, however, properly pay tribute to Lynd's book by that title.

# XII

What have we found? That the intellectual is the man devoted to the
spirit,

who thus devoted, thus legitimated, rationally analyzes and assesses his society, his shudder stayed by his faith that his fellowmen are, as he is, endowed with reason.

That he is the man who does what he does on the basis of the most thorough examination of his practice *and* theory as they impinge on one another; that he is the man who ascertains, and by ascertaining helps to constitute, the boundary between culture and politics, who analyzes and thus tests the influence of culture on politics; that he is the man who gets his culture into the world and works in and at the world, informed by the historical necessity of his desire to do so.

These propositions contain definitional and historically diagnostic elements. The essential definition of the intellectual as the man devoted to the spirit results from a taxonomic analysis undertaken to distinguish him from other types of man with which clarity demands he not be confused. The diagnostic elements concern our world: it is unprecedented in the sense that we have to invent our beginning, since traditions are no longer viable but must be suspended in the most thorough analysis of their status relative to our own existence, our own theory and practice. It is the outcome of such an analysis that has resulted in the further findings just passed in review: *here, now,* to be a man devoted to the spirit means to be between culture and politics and thus to test the influence of the former on the latter. I should add that failure to mention the reverse influence, of politics on culture, cannot mean denying its existence, which would be absurd, but results from the diagnosis undertaken by an intellectual and addressed to intellectuals and from the desire to alert himself and them to an unrealistic assessment of the power or the impotence of culture, to disregarding politics or cringing before it in hopelessness. The idea of "doing one's being" is again the outcome of the condition of doing anything at all in our unprecedented world. It is to invent our beginning—we have nothing to begin with but ourselves, as I said before; and I add a new piece of diagnosis, that "doing one's being" is informed by the historical necessity of the desire to get our culture into the world. I mean this to be another way of referring to the rational analysis and assessment of our society or the concern with the boundary between culture and politics, thus suggesting unforeseeable ways of implementing this activity, all of them to be invented.

This chapter is such a way. It is not political in any technical sense—I said in general that it need not be—but in the sense that it might contribute to activity for the common good. Now, then, let us talk with others who would be intellectuals and with political men and other people, unpredicated and unpredicable beyond their endowment with reason, so that *all* of us can come closer to being each other's moral conscience and consciousness.

*Acknowledgment.* This chapter has greatly benefited from an unusually critical reading by Charles Nathanson to whom I am much indebted. It was prepared in 1969 for a symposium on intellectuals and power, edited by Godfried van Benthem van der Bergh and David Kettler, and published by van Gennep, Amsterdam, 1973.

### NOTES

1. The Free Press of Glencoe, Ill., 1958. This review was printed in *The Ohio State Morning Lantern,* April 27, 1959.

2. See Wolfgang J. Mommsen, *Max Weber und die deutsche Politik, 1890–1920* (Tubingen: Mohr, 1959), especially Chapter IX.

3. In his essay on *The Academic Mind* in *The Griffin* (December 1958) p. 11.

4. *American Journal of Sociology* (July 1958).

5. "The Enemy Within: Anti-Intellectualism, *The Centennial Review,* 7 (Winter 1963), 46–63. An earlier version was presented at the annual faculty conference, Denison University, March 2, 1962. I acknowledge my indebtedness to George B. de Huszar, Ed., *The Intellectuals: A Controversial Portrait* (Glencoe, Ill.: Free Press, 1960), of which I made much use.

6. Bertrand Russell, quoted in Russell Kirk, "The American Intellectual: A Conservative View" (1965), in de Huszar, *ibid.,* p. 309.

7. Edward A. Shils, "The Tradition of Intellectuals" (1958), *ibid.,* p. 56.

8. Seymour Martin Lipset, "American Intellectuals: Their Politics and Status," *Daedalus* (Summer 1959), 460.

9. Karl W. Deutsch, "Comments on 'American Intellectuals: Their Politics and Status,' " *ibid.,* 489.

10. Arthur Schopenhauer, "The Art of Literature" (1851), in de Huszar, *op. cit.,* p. 116.

11. Jose Ortega y Gasset, *The Revolt of the Masses* (1930) (Mentor 1950), p. 82.

12. Harold Rosenberg, "The Orgamerican Phantasy," in *The Tradition of the New* (1959) (New York: Grove Press, 1961), p. 277.

13. Harold J. Laski, "The Limitations of the Expert," in de Huszar, *op. cit.,* p. 171.

14. Rosenberg, *op. cit.,* pp. 271, 282. (Rosenberg refers to Poe's story as "The Man Who Was Made Up.").

15. *The New York Review of Books,* January 30, 1969.

16. Beacon Press, Boston; 1969.

17. Hannah Arendt, *On Revolution* (New York: Viking, 1965), p. 27 and *passim.*

18. Barrington Moore, Jr., *Social Origins of Dictatorship and Democracy: Lord and Peasant in the Making of the Modern World* (Boston: Beacon, 1966), p. 521.

19. Particularly because of his essay, "Repressive Tolerance" (from which, however, note a quotation presently), in Robert Paul Wolff, Barrington Moore, Jr., and Herbert Marcuse, *A Critique of Pure Tolerance* (Boston: Beacon, 1965). See reviews by David Spitz (*Dissent*, September–October 1966), Nathan Glazer (*American Sociological Review*, June 1966), and Henry David Aiken (*The New York Review of Books*, June 9, 1966). For similar accusations see Herbert Marcuse *et al.*, *Das Ende der Utopie* (Berlin: v. Maikowski, 1967), pp. 39 f.; "Democracy Has/Hasn't a Future . . . A Present" (a discussion by Nat Hentoff, Norman Mailer, Arthur Schlesinger, Jr., and Herbert Marcuse), *The New York Times Magazine*, May 26, 1968, especially pp. 31, 98; "Marcuse Defines His New Left Line" (an interview with Jean-Louis Ferrier, Jacques Boetsch, and Françoise Giroud of *L'Express*), *The New York Times Magazine*, October 27, 1968, especially p. 100; Sidney Hook, *The New York Times*, December 29, 1968, p. 36, and his review of *An Essay on Liberation*, *The New York Times Book Review*, April 20, 1969; and Irving Howe in *Harper's Magazine*, July 1969.

20. Marcuse, in Wolff *et al.*, *op. cit.*, p. 106.

21. Above all in *One-Dimensional Man* and *Eros and Civilization.*

22. The alternative acting on theoretical insight and "doing because of one's being" is analogous to Stuart Hampshire's research "by rational calculation of directly useful and socially relevant results" and by "intellectual excitement," whereby the "law of displacement" may show retrospectively the relevance of the latter to the former. Hampshire's discussion, however, remains limited to cultural concerns without touching on politics. Stuart Hampshire, "Commitment and Imagination" in *The Morality of Scholarship*, by Northrop Frye, Stuart Hampshire, and Conor Cruise O'Brien, Max Black, Ed. (Ithaca: Cornell University Press, 1967), pp. 29–55.

23. See Richard Poirier, "Learning from the Beatles," *Partisan Review* (Fall 1967), reprinted in Jonathan Eisen, Ed., *The Age of Rock: Sounds of the American Cultural Revolution* (New York: Vintage, 1969).

24. This awareness appears to be more characteristic of Left radical than of liberal, conservative, or Right radical literature, for the first wishes to change the status quo, whereas the other three, depite obvious important differences, do not; cf. the importance given to the problem of the relation of the intellectual to the revolution by Marx, Kautsky, Lenin, Gramsci, and other Marxist theorists.

25. George Orwell, "Politics and the English Language" (1946) in *A Collection of Essays* (Doubleday, 1954), p. 177. Orwell has more specific advice in this article, although some of it borders on that given in style manuals. (In regard to German—Wilhelminian and Weimar-Republic—Karl Kraus is far more outraged and searching, but preoccupation with language was central to him and not to Orwell.) [Recall a reference to Kraus in Chapter 9.]

26.   An estimate of 12- to 25-year-olds on earth is 750 million now and a billion by 1980: Kathleen Teltsch, "Study Sees a Rise in Youth Protest," *The New York Times*, February 16, 1969, p. 10 (the reference is to a study by United Nations sociologists). The literature on the student movement is already large; cf. Alexander Cockburn and Robin Blackburn, Eds., *Student Power* (Penguin, 1969), with *Youth in Turmoil*, adapted from a special issue of *Fortune* (New York: Time-Life Books, 1969).

27.   Cf. *Radicals in Professions* (Ann Arbor, Mich.: Radical Education Project, 1967), especially the contribution by Barbara Haber and Al Haber.

28.   Cf. Chapter II of *An Essay on Liberation* and the end of *One-Dimensional Man*.

29.   Most recent at the time of this writing (June 1969)—to my knowledge—and potentially important is women's liberation (cf. Peter Babcox, "Meet the Women of the Revolution, 1969," *The New York Times Magazine*, February 9, 1969); Beverly Jones and Judith Brown, *Toward A Female Liberation Movement* (Boston: New England Free Press, 1969).

30.   Eldridge Cleaver, *Soul on Ice* (New York: McGraw-Hill, 1968), pp. 201, 200. Living through what has long preoccupied philosophers theoretically as the Mind-Body problem is related to the politicization of experience encountered by many young radicals, especially in the student movement, and above all convergence as well as contagion by Negroes who in the process and by virtue of it change into Blacks (or antecedent equivalents, particularly Black Muslims). See *The Autobiography of Malcolm X* (New York: Grove, 1964); Claude Brown, *Manchild in the Promised Land* (New York: Signet, 1965). A related experiential basis also underlies the therapeutic theory and practice of the British psychiatrist R. D. Laing; notice especially, including the title, *The Politics of Experience* (New York: Ballantine, 1967). Also related is the work of Norman O. Brown, from *Life Against Death* (Middletown, Conn.: Wesleyan University Press, 1959; Vintage) to *Love's Body* (New York: Random House, 1966); cf. Herbert Marcuse, "Love Mystified: A Critique of Norman O. Brown" (1967), and Brown's response (1967), both reprinted in Marcuse, *Negations*, with translations from the German by Jeremy J. Shapiro (Boston: Beacon, 1968), pp. 227–247.

31.   Only two of many especially illuminating examples: David Horowitz and Reese Erlich, "Big Brother as a Holding Company" (on Litton Industries), *Ramparts* (November 30, 1968), and William D. Phelan, Jr., "The 'Complex' Society Marches On," *Ripon Forum* (January, March, April, May 1969, and continuing at the time of this writing).

32.   Again only one of many examples: "What is it that these eminent dissenters [professors at M.I.T.] have in common with the student radicals at Berkeley, Columbia, and the Sorbonne or those quietly challenging the Soviet leadership in Moscow? It seems to be a conviction that the various societies of our planet are trapped in ruts of ideological dogma, nationalism, and power politics." Walter Sullivan, "Fighting the 'Misuse' of Knowledge," *The New York Times*, February 9, 1969, p. 7E. (The article deals with a day of research

stoppage, sponsored by a number of professors at M.I.T. and then planned to take place at various universities.)

33. Karl Marx, preface to Karl Marx and Friedrich Engels, *The German Ideology* (1845–1846), with an introduction by R. Pascal, Ed. (New York: International, 1939), pp. 1–2.

34. C. Wright Mills, "On Knowledge and Power" (1955), in *Power, Politics and People,* Irving Louis Horowitz, Ed. (New York: Oxford University Press, 1963), pp. 611, 612–613.

35. Noam Chomsky, "The Responsibility of Intellectuals," *The New York Review of Books,* February 23, 1967. (Regarding the last sentence of this quotation, cf. Lionel Trilling's similar observation.) See also Chomsky's incisive "The Menace of Liberal Scholarship," *ibid.,* January 2, 1969, responses, predominantly oppositional, by various writers, and Chomsky's rejoinder, "An Exchange on Liberal Scholarship," *ibid.,* February 13, 1969.

36. See many entries in the bibliography appended to Mannheim's *Ideology and Utopia,* translated by Louis Wirth and Edward Shils, preface by Louis Wirth (1936; Harvest, n.d.), IV. The Sociology of Knowledge, 2. Present Status. For a more recent example see Theodor W. Adorno, "The Sociology of Knowledge and Its Consciousness" (1935), in *Prisms,* translated by Samuel and Shierry Weber (London: Neville Spearman, 1967), pp. 35–49.

37. Mills, *op. cit.,* p. 611.

38. Theodore Roszak, Ed. (New York: Pantheon Books, 1967, 1968). By comparison, two thirds of *The Morality of Scholarship* (n. 22)—the articles by Frye and Hampshire—are written from a subjective or cultural point of view; only O'Brien's gets into politics: "The intellectual community to which we belong, and whose morality we are discussing, is that of the advanced, capitalist world" (p. 66). O'Brien's "Politics and the Morality of Scholarship" is a political analysis.

39. *The Sociological Imagination* (1959; Evergreen, Galaxy). (Its existence is used to justify the absence of a treatment of sociology in *The Dissenting Academy,* p. vii.)

40. Gough in Roszak, *op. cit.,* pp. 148–149. See also her (Kathleen Gough Aberle) *Anthropology and Imperialism: New Proposals for Anthropologists* (Ann Arbor, Mich.: Radical Educational Project, 1967). [See also Chapter 25.]

41. Robert S. Lynd, *Knowledge for What? The Place of Social Science in American Culture* (1939; Evergreen Black Cat). (The less consciously political nature of this book is suggested by its subtitle.)

---

Reprinted from the *International Journal of Contemporary Sociology,* 8 (1971), 13–34, and *The Centennial Review,* 7 (1963), 46–53, by permission of the publisher. The essay has been edited and partially revised by the author.

# IV

## · SOCIOLOGY

*To my fellow students and particularly to Egon Bittner, Franco Ferrarotti, Agnes Heller, Alberto Izzo, Mihailo Markovic, John O'Neill, Gajo Petrovic, Alessandro Pizzorno, and John R. Seeley.*

Among other things, *Trying Sociology* presents my own introduction to sociology, thus also an introductory offer to those who would accompany me on my voyage. After three major stops— (I) with the sociologists who helped initiate the journey, (II) inventories of received specializations and questions about them, an exercise in a received method, a reminder of the roots of sociology in mankind and of one of my own in Jewishness, and (III) investigations of another of my roots (Germany), of my new home (the United States), and of a type of person (the intellectual) now trying to come to terms with his world— there is a fourth— sociology itself. I entered into this phase of the voyage (like that which led to America) not long after my arrival in the New World, with which it was so closely connected (cf. introductions to Parts I and II). My first effort (Chapter 12) was the application to sociology (if in modified form) of one of Karl Mannheim's ideas, the need for a twofold interpretation of whatever one would seek to understand—Mannheim's ideological (here immanent) and sociological (sociocultural) interpretation (cf. Chapter 2, n. 4, and later chapters in this book). I have become aware only decades after that early piece that this distinction occupies a fundamental place in my epistemology: maximum understanding requires both intrinsic and extrinsic interpretation (as I have come to call the two aspects). Neither is possible without the other so that the relation between the

199

two is not that of mutual exclusion but of a "virtuous circle" (a variant of the philological or hermeneutic circle). Not all, but, on the contrary, only a few and extraordinary occasions of understanding (the most serious kind of study referred to from another angle in Chapter 16) require their maximally sustainable application—a "surrendering to" what is to be understood. Some of the later chapters make reference to, or make use of, this twofold interpretation, which, however, does find its most focused development in the analysis of surrender [1].

The first paper, in Part IV. Chapter 12, "Toward a Sociocultural Interpretation of American Sociology" (1946), shows the effort made to find my way into this sociology. It shows its influence especially in its methodological chest drumming, but it also bears witness to my Mannheimian background in the remarks about interpretation and in its general outlook, which is informed by the sociology of knowledge. In comparison with C. Wright Mills's even earlier writings, some of which I have made use of, as well as with my own later work (not only in Chapter 18, on *Sociology on Trial*), it is almost daintily cautious. This, I think, is so partly because I felt like a novice, partly because I wrote it during my first year at Ohio State (originally for oral delivery), and partly because the groping, mentioned in the introduction to Part III, between liberalism and radicalism must have begun even then: there are negative (muted) references to George A. Lundberg, the apostle of neopositivism, positive (scientifically restrained) references to Mills, and an allusion or two to Dwight Macdonald's *Politics*, which in those years I used to read from cover to cover. What I say substantively about American sociology now strikes me as child's play, though not without some of a child's sure instinct, despite the late Howard Becker's fatherly corrective remark that

> Wolff's contentions, which ran to the effect that marked class biases and sentimental attachments distorted the findings of many prominent American sociologists, were somewhat sweeping, and it is to be doubted whether he got much beyond the familiar *argumentum ad hominem*. Research comparable to Stahl's in its thoroughness [Margaret Smith Stahl, "Splits and Schisms: An Analysis of Atomic Energy Factions, "unpublished dissertation, University of Wisconsin, 1946] was clearly necessary if Wolff hoped to be taken seriously . . . [2].

Like this early attempt at a sociocultural interpretation of American sociology, "A Note on Morality and Society" (Chapter 13; written about ten years later, but not published until 1965) originated as a talk to fellow sociologists at Ohio State and might be called a "position paper."

Although very brief, it laid down one thesis after another, but for all its formal clarity it is an angry outcry far removed from the timid voice that had mumbled "sociocultural interpretation." (Here is a new variousness in the meaning of sociology.) It connects with the preceding chapter by its attention to values and argues for the elimination of the term from the vocabularies of social science and philosophy and from rational discourse altogether (except for its technical referents in economics, logic, and mathematics). In the next essay (Chapter 14) on Hannah Arendt's *The Human Condition,* I develop this argument. I contrast habit or custom with rational action—but "rational" is not what it is for Max Weber, even though he too, opposes it to "traditional"; nor is it Pareto's "logical," which he contrasts with "nonlogical." My emphasis is on the nonreflective character of the habitual, customary, and traditional, but above all on the maximally reflective as the essential characteristic of the rational, which can thus be seen to develop in its greatest purity in "surrender" (see also Chapter 15).

Indeed, my definition of thinking, utilizing Hannah Arendt's definition of rational (in rational action; see Chapter 14), defines a central aspect of surrender. Another affinity between Arendt's thought on solitude and mine on surrender is that it is in solitude, as I point out, that an individual is most human, most part of mankind (Chapter 14). This is akin to saying that in surrender, when one is most nearly oneself, one falls back on what he shares with mankind. [This coincidence, if not identity or at least synthesis, between the unique and the universal was formed much earlier, notably in "The Unique and the General" (Chapter 27).]

The genesis of my paper on Arendt's *The Human Condition* (Chapter 14) is mentioned in Note 1. It is an attentive reading of her book, although the reading is (by definition) selective, in part admittedly so. At the same time, it is a meeting with the book that I hope goes toward meeting its author as well and in which I also get acquainted with myself and my world and tell my fellow inhabitants some of what I have found. Once more, then, with all its analysis, this is predominantly a practical paper, as I have tried to make explicit in its structure.

The paper on Arendt was published in German translation in 1968. [3] I chose a section title, "Man's Historicity and Dualism," for my essay, and the theme, analyzed in terms of freedom, nonsovereignty, and necessity, will later, in my writing on surrender, develop into the notion of man as a mixed phenomenon. This notion is also shown in its consequences for conception and practice of the social sciences, which here, as the subtitle implies ("significance for sociology"), is my major concern. Despite—

better still, *in*—its furious analyticity this is a rhetorical, practical piece, perhaps weightier than the other papers which are critical of sociology and which I have assembled mainly in Parts IV and VI.

The paper on Hannah Arendt is followed by one written a few years earlier, "Before and After Sociology" (Chapter 15). It anticipates some of the critical questions about sociology that are developed, although this is not the reason why it is reprinted. In its critique of the widespread interest in creativity it records one reaction to it in the mid-fifties; it formulates the critique of sociology as one of scientism; and, perhaps more important, it expresses itself in terms of surrender, which, like creativity and scientism, is, self-critically, "before sociology," that is, "before" a politically and sociologically adequate sociology. Thus it contributes to an illumination of the genesis, both systematic and, much less important, biographical, of the idea of surrender. Because this idea has already come up (to my own instructive surprise) so many times in connection with preceding and in anticipation of later chapters, its more explicit appearance in the context of a critque of sociology should not be suppressed (even though the quotation on total experience, a synonym of surrender, presents an early version that I have since somewhat modified).

Another preoccupation with value, which has figured in Chapters 13 and 14, also appears in "Before and After Sociology"; I have elided some of the elaboration but have more fully developed it in "Man's Historicity and Dualism."

"Sociology and Evil," Chapter 16, combines "For a Sociology of Evil" (1969) and "Pour une sociologie du mal" (1967). Both resulted from an invitation by the *Journal of Social Issues* to contribute to a symposium (which did not materialize) on the social and psychological aspects of evil. In preparing for my contribution, I did a seminar on the topic at the University of Paris-Nanterre, where I did not limit myself strictly to the subject but took the opportunity to discuss some of my ideas about sociology, as I did in the paper that resulted from the seminar and appeared that summer in the recently launched *L'homme et la société*. In the fall I profited from a seminar on the sociology of evil at Brandeis, but in the English version of the assay I decided to eliminate the pages on social science that applied to *any* social-scientific topic and not only to evil. For this book, however, I have worked these pages into Chapter 16 because they develop some aspects of a concept of social science, more particularly sociology, that I have not (or not so fully) articulated elsewhere. These aspects are the analysis of nominalism and realism, of the inevitable presence of nominalist *and* realist, specifically, the scientific *and* existential, elements in research, even though the emphasis in less than maximal or optimal research may be on one or the other, and the distinction and the relation between scientific and existential truth. Also, although the term "surrender" does not occur in the paper, the reference to "unexpected extraordinary experiences . . . calling the world into question and reconstituting it" (cf. total experience in Chapter 15, a considerably earlier paper, which, of course, discusses surrender explicitly) is a reference to it. In surrender the world is bracketed, neither affirmed nor denied, but suspended. Here is a clue to the affinity between certain aspects of surrender and the phenomenological reduction.

The second half of Chapter 17, "Sociology and History; Theory and Practice," takes up the distinction applied to the structure of Chapter 14; it is a variant of the scientific-existential dichotomy also stressed in the essay on evil. In Chapter 17 it is connected with different characteristics of sociology and historiography, but the designation of sociology as theoretical (in the sense of the contrast developed here) is already changed in the only slightly later Chapter 14, in which I say that I consider it to be both theoretical and practical. At the time of this writing I find that the systematic or theoretical distinctions that one might make (such as this or between nomothetic and idiographic or still others) do not coincide with distinctions between disciplines, for example, sociology and historiography, because not only these two but all disciplines have those characteristics, which thus emerge as ideal-typical or logical rather than descriptive of disciplines as practiced. In any event, despite the insistence on sociology, in contrast to historiography, as theoretical, the major impetus of the chapter is to drive home the practical aspect of sociology—a complexity of aspect and contrast that I try to suggest by the semicolon in the title: a colon would have too bluntly, indeed misleadingly, declared sociology theoretical and history (historiography) practical.

Thinking as an example of atemporal (not timeless) activity now points, by hindsight, to a quality not only of the unexpected extraordinary or total experience (surrender) of Chapters 16 and 15, respectively, but to a feature common to all situations in which we forget time, psychically and because logic or reason, which apply atemporal standards of judgment rather than time, is the judge. This atemporality, which is shared by love, anxiety, solitude (cf. Chapter 14), meditation, creation (Chapter 16), and many other situations whose common denominator perhaps is focused attention or absorption, has struck me only in rereading, remembering, juxtaposing passages from various papers written at various times and is something that I have yet to clarify for myself. (What is the relation between the atemporality of the everyday world and that of extreme situations? Is it the same, has it the same bearing in the two worlds, or has it a different meaning? If so, what it is it?)

As Section II in Chapter 16, so the whole of Chapter 17, but most patently its last section, approximates a realist discussion—surely a practical one (cf. the introduction to Part III on the rhetorical and practical nature of some of my papers).

Part IV ends with a book review (published so far only in Italian, in 1964) which I include because of its possible historical interest as one person's assessment of the state of American sociology in the early sixties. (In thinking about a title for the present book, incidentally, I had forgotten that the editors of *Sociology on Trial* made a pun about trial-trying related to mine on *Trying Sociology*.) My review appropriately concludes this part, which began with remarks about the same topic eighteen years earlier. The tone of the more recent assessment still sounds a few years later in the essay on evil, which begins with Seeley's "social science is social action theorem" taken from his paper in *Sociology on Trial*.

My review snaps at sociologists as jobholders in a bureaucracy (cf. Arendt's society of jobholders, Chapter 14) and at the professionalization of sociology. On balance, I think, the situation has since improved, partly because word of the inanity and irrelevance of the sociology castigated in *Sociology on Trial* has got around—especially by protesting students—and has led, more or less directly, to a great variety of results, among them self-examination such as Alvin W. Gouldner's *The Coming Crisis of Western Sociology* [4] and Robert W. Friedrichs' *A Sociology of Sociology* [5], both 1970.

### NOTES

1.   At any rate, here is an illustration of my remark in the introduction to Part I: that Karl Mannheim has influenced my thinking in many areas, not only in sociology. I became aware of this long after I studied with him, even after my introduction to the United States and *its* sociology—really much later than that. Such awareness is never exhausted but perhaps only set aside.

2.   In Howard Becker and Harry Elmer Barnes, with the assistance of Emile Benoit-Smullyan and others, *Social Thoughts from Lore to Science*, 1938 (Washington, D.C.: Harren, 1952). "1937–1950 Appendix on Sociological Trends," p. xxiii (original dots).

3.   Kurt H. Wolff, *Versuch zu einer Wissenssoziologie* (Berlin: Luchterhand, 1968), Chapter VIII, *Die Geschichtlichkeit und der Dualismus des Menschen.* . . .

4.   New York: Basic Books.

5.   New York: Free Press.

# 12

# TOWARD A SOCIOCULTURAL INTERPRETATION OF AMERICAN SOCIOLOGY. 1946

The purpose of this chapter is to develop suggestions in regard to the sociocultural interpretation of American sociology [1].

## IMMANENT AND SOCIOCULTURAL INTERPRETATION

The concept of sociocultural interpretation is clarified when contrasted with that of immanent interpretation [2]. The two may be defined briefly as follows:

1. Immanent interpretation includes the logical examination of thought and the attitudinal structure [3] of the thinker.

2. Sociocultural interpretation consists in the development of hypotheses which serve to explain the results of the immanent interpretation in sociocultural terms, that is, with reference to the sociocultural phenomena that suggest themselves for fruitful examination: social background of the author of the work under consideration; classes, power distribution, and other structural aspects of the society concerned; and attitudes, beliefs, and knowledge of the author's and related cultures.

An example may clarify practical applications. If I wanted to interpret a book by Arthur Koestler, I would examine its implicational and attitudinal structure (immanent interpretation), I would try to understand the book better by relating the results of the immanent interpretation

205

to those of my investigation of the author's life history in terms of affiliations and contacts, and I would try to establish the relations between
Koestler's culture, that is, his attitudes, beliefs, and knowledge, and the
cultures of various groups that show similar and dissimilar cultures;
for example, liberals, frustrated liberals, ex-Communists, intelligentsia,
uprooted intellectuals, and the like (sociocultural interpretation) [4].


## AMERICAN SOCIOLOGY AS AN ORIENTATION OR CULTURE

For the purposes of this chapter it is not necessary to define American
sociology, although it is recognized that if more than mere suggestions for
an interpretation of American sociology were intended such a definition
would be of prime importance. It is further recognized that this definition
would raise the difficult question of the classification and analysis of
American sociology as an intellectual product and/or process. In the
present context, however, any referent of American sociology the reader
may have in mind will suffice. What follows will itself raise questions in
regard to the characteristics of American sociology and thus, indirectly,
questions of its definition.

It is proposed to consider American sociology not exclusively as a
science or as a discipline striving to become scientific (which it is also
assumed to be) but as an orientation, an outlook, a *Weltanschauung*,
a culture. Although as far as I know this has not been explicitly done
before, implications of several well-known considerations of American
sociology can easily be drawn and thus are likely to make the proposal
plausible. I call attention to three types of consideration—the relations
between values and research, changing contents of sociology, and sociological publication.

By and large, it is probably recognized by sociologists (as well as by
other scientists) that valuations enter into research—whether valuation
be taken as Myrdal's "ideas about how ... [reality] ought to be [5], in
Dewey's more general appraisal [6], or in other current significations.
Sociologists presumably will agree as well with the propositions that
values are "operating in the determination of what is significant for research" and can "themselves ... be the object of research" [7]. They will
concur also, I believe, with the thesis that science itself is a value or "the
expression and the fulfillment of a special human desire and interest" [8],
although this recognition is perhaps often lost by the emphasis on the
objective and nonevaluative character of science, including sociology [9].

Finally, it is surely undisputed that objectivity itself is a value that
entails other values. A good current definition of objectivity presumably

is that given by Hagood: objectivity is "a characteristic of results measured by the degree of agreement which there would be between these results and the results obtained by observation of the same phenomena by any other trained observer," [10]. Also, in Lundberg's words: "When an observer communicates his observations so that others can corroborate his reports, we call such data objective" [11]. Both quotations, to be sure, refer to the objectivity of *data*, but it is probably legitimate to infer that the scientist's objectivity would consist in gathering objective data. Furthermore, in doing so he is aided by the exclusion, or at least awareness, of the "personal equation" [12]. Last, it should be noted that objectivity produces a specific behavioral, personality, or role type:

> *As a human being*, the scientist may properly look to the social
> results of his conclusions. . . . But as a scientist his only
> ethical responsibility lies in seeing that the rules of scientific
> procedure have been complied with [13].

Because these propositions, then, are statements of values, it is logically permissible to conclude that to the extent that these values are held in common by sociologists they are part of their culture [14]. Some of them, to be sure, are part of the culture of science in general. Nor is it important to insist on the term value, for even if it were preferred to call these ideas beliefs, theses, tenets, or stimuli toward which sociologists respond with similar attitudes they are still part of their culture because they are something sociologists have learned in the process of preparing for their profession. There should be no quarrel, either, with the statement that both science in general and sociology in particular are part of American (as well as of other) culture (although an elaboration of this proposition would require a more precise definition of "part").

Another consideration of American sociology which points to its character as an orientation or outlook has to do with its contentual aspects, as witness both the attempts to assemble contentual principles on which American sociologists can agree [15] and to gather contents once adhered to but subsequently discarded [16].

Finally, a third angle on the cultural character of sociology is suggested by a passage toward the end of Cuber's article, in which the author points out that if his or similarly formulated principles could indeed be agreed on they would be likely to "demonstrate that there does exist an integrated 'body of knowledge' called sociology ... which will give some idea to intelligent persons concerning just what it is that we do agree upon [17]. This passage may serve as a reminder of the sociologist's consciousness of public relations—as a teacher, researcher [18], and often as a writer. A brief consideration of him in the capacity that among the three just mentioned comes closest to his role as a scientist shows that extrascientific, extraobjective factors enter into his work not only when he thinks about publishing a certain book or paper—where, in what form, with what emphases, for what public—but also when contemplating writing itself with the possibility of publishing. In other words, the *selection* of fields and topics of research and the nature, character, frame of reference, in brief, the *constitution* [19] of his work are codetermined by the consideration of publication. (Needless to say, this goes for the present paper as well.)

This brief look at values, contents, and public relations as characteristic of the culture and society of the sociologist and therefore of sociology should at least have made plausible the contention that sociology, in addition to being a science, is also an outlook, orientation, or culture; that sociology is determined by logical, intrascientific, and sociocultural factors (acting through the individual perhaps by way of idiosyncrasies [20] or the "basic personality structure" and "character structure" [21].)

By recalling the definitions of immanent and sociocultural interpretation given above we can see more clearly how we should have to proceed in trying to apply these interpretations to the work of an American sociologist. To repeat, we should try to ascertain the logical and intrascientific and the sociocultural elements in his work. A few examples of hunches are now given—that is, hunches of how sociocultural factors are operative in the scientific work of sociologists, *not* as they influence the sociologist as a teacher or citizen.


### EXAMPLES OF TRAITS OF AMERICAN SOCIOLOGY AS A CULTURE


These examples refer to only two aspects of American sociology—the question of its attitude toward the status quo and the problem of its selective character.

Can one speak of an attitude of American sociology toward the status quo? It is submitted that the agreement on sociology as the study of what *is*—an agreement necessarily following from the tenets of science—has nevertheless far-reaching attitudinal implications which in turn have their influence on the selection and the constitution of research. Three examples in support of this thesis are given.

Regarding social change, Mills found, on the basis of his study of social-pathology texts, at least strong evidence of the preference of slow to fast change—

> the slow, "evolutionary" pace of change is taken explicitly as normal and organized, whereas "discontinuity" is taken as problematic [22],

a preference that implies another preference, namely, for amelioration of the status quo as against viewing the status quo itself as problematical. The social pathologists, Mills writes,

> do not typically consider whether or not certain groups or individuals caught in economically underprivileged situations can possibly obtain the current goals without drastic shifts in the basic institutions which channel and promote them. [23]

Finally, the connotations of the concept of adjustment—itself highly specific in its attitudinal implications—are very selective.

> The ideally adjusted man of the social pathologists is "socialized." This term seems to operate ethically as the opposite of "selfish," it implies that the adjusted man conforms to middle-class morality and motives and "participates" in the gradual progress of respectable institutions [24].

It may be objected that the examples given refer not to scientific writings but to textbooks whose writers, even consciously, compromise with several extrascientific pressures—the public, the publishers, educational organizations, and so on. It is submitted, however, that it is not these forces that make for the character of the texts examined by Mills, but far subtler influences (such as Mills suggests). This assertion cannot be demonstrated; to do so would necessitate an examination of scientific writings of the textbook authors; but it would seem probable that features similar to those characterizing their texts also characterize their scientific writings.

Regarding social stratification, especially the problem of Negro-white relations, W. Lloyd Warner's caste-theory of the Negro in the South is instructive. As far as I know, this theory, divulged almost ten years ago [25], was not critically examined in published form for six years [26], when Oliver C. Cox wrote a critique of it [27]. Rather it has been taken over by at least one widely adopted introductory sociology text [28]. The important point for our purposes is not to examine the shortcomings of Warner's (and Cox's) theory but to stress the fact that Cox has demonstrated one questionable feature of Warner's theory and to ask why this had not been noted before (or hardly since, for that matter). This feature is Warner's failure to take into consideration the fact that a caste system is characterized also by its being *accepted* by the members of all castes, a situation that clearly does not obtain in the present-day South. "Caste barriers in the caste system are never challenged; they are sacred to caste and caste alike" [29]. The use of the term caste to refer to Negroes and whites has a reassuring connotation, although I am far from imputing to the founder of the school the *intention* to spread such soothing news— namely, that the Negroes just *are* an inferior caste. I am only suggesting that racial prejudice and discrimination have been structuralized into more or less static features of the status quo social system [30]. The attitude sketched by this suggestion is reminiscent of that of the white southerner who customarily simply denies the existence of a "Negro problem" because the relations between the two races

> a long time ago . . . had been stratified into "folkways and mores," known and respected by both races and taken for granted, or rather as self-evident, in view of the inferior endowments of the African race and the superior qualities of the Anglo-Saxon master race [31].

"Folkways" and "mores," in their universal and generally uncritical [32] use, are probably indicative of an unfavorable attitude toward induced change and of a *laissez-faire* attitude in general, to which Myrdal, in the first two appendices to the *Dilemma*, calls attention. Only one point may be mentioned here. Speaking of Robert E. Park, Myrdal writes:

> Not observing much in the way of conscious and organized planning in his contemporary America except that which was bungling and ineffective because it it did not take due account of the natural forces, he built up a sociological system in terms of "natural" causation and sequence. . . . we . . . find [in Park's writing] . . . a systematic tendency to ignore practically all possibilities of modifying—by conscious effort—the social effects of the natural forces [33].

Here, again, an objection can be raised—namely, that Park (and most of the other sociologists Myrdal discusses) is no longer representative of American sociologists in their attitude toward the status quo of American sociology. The question then becomes: who is? Those who, in the name of modern scientific sociology, are perhaps most likely to raise this objection would probably say that the neopositivists—Lundberg, Bain, Dodd, and others—represent American sociology today. If they do, the remarks about Lundberg that follow are all the more significant.

These examples must suffice, although others, which also bear on the attitude toward the status quo, could be produced One might examine whether a case could be made for the existence of sentimental, hence extrascientific and presumably socioculturally determined elements in Redfield's folk-urban [34] and in Becker's sacred-secular theories, in the differential treatment accorded the country and the city [35], or in the ecological concept of natural area. Important topics of research would also be the relative absence of the analysis of power in our society [36], the investigation of the theoretical foundations of the field of human relations in industry, and a study of the influence of mass-research tools, such as Hollerith and other machines, on both the selection and constitution of research.

Only one more suggestion bears on a further characteristic of American sociology—this time, a negative one: the absence of the recognition of a trait of man to which other cultures and disciplines have given a paramount place—that trait that may be called man's greatness or meanness or his tragic aspect—in fact, the whole field of the spiritual, and especially spiritual suffering [37]. There is theoretically no reason why this should not become the topic of sociological investigation [38]. It would seem that although (as our examples suggest) a hypothesis that such attitudes and concepts as middle-class morality and motives, head-in-the-sand politics, and subservience to power play a role in informing American sociological thought is worthwhile, the hypothesis that man's tragic nature informs it similarly does not seem capable of demonstration. I am not suggesting that the focus on man's tragic nature ought to inform American sociology as one of its concepts but only that insofar as it does not, American sociology, for reasons that a sociocultural interpretation might reveal, is not objective in its orientation because it overlooks one side of man which at least to some "trained observers" is important, that to the extent that it tries, consciously or just by growth, to provide "that unified and coherent theory which men have always craved," [39] it plans or develops a set of attitudes, beliefs, knowledge—a culture—that is as distinct as any other [40].

The definitions of two highly emotionally charged concepts—power and freedom—serve as illustrations. Both concepts have found definitions that are as objective as one could desire; their definitions can be applied to all or at least to a great many situations which one might want to characterize in their terms. Power, Lundberg says, is the "time-rate of doing work" [41]. It needs little imagination to see that this definition can be applied to analyze the power of the X family in Middletown, of the Nazis in Germany, of an American politician. The important point is that, however objective, it seems to have attitudinal implications that make it unlikely that the study of power as suggested above and exemplified in the examples quoted in note 36 is stimulated by it; it certainly is not mentioned in these examples nor is it probable that it has given rise to them.

Similarly with Lundberg's definition of freedom:

> Actually, the term ["freedom"] is used to designate that feeling-tone which an individual experiences when his habits are relatively in accord with the restrictions of his environment. In short, men are free when they feel free. They feel free when they are thoroughly habituated to their way of life. It follows that within the limits of human conditioning, the feeling of freedom is compatible with an almost unlimited variety of social conditions [42].

Again, this definition is bare of any historically colored connotations of "for," "from," and "of," hence is applicable to the consideration of the freedom, or unfreedom, for example, of Americans in the United States or Jews in Nazi Germany. Like the objective definition of power, it seems not to have produced studies of freedom or the lack of it [43].

It should be noted that these examples—these nonobjective aspects of American sociology, as well as concepts that seem to approach the limit of objectivity possible in our present universe of discourse but also seem to produce selective attitudes—raise the question of objectivity itself (a question hinted at before; cf. n. 30). More precisely, part of this question appears to be the problem of the thought model of various concepts of objectivity, the most widely adopted one certainly patterned after the natural sciences. It is possible to investigate implications of this model, or such models, in order to ascertain the socioculturally selective [44] character of objectivity. This investigation might benefit if it were asked to what demands the various concepts of objectivity are socially responsive [45].

## METHODOLOGICAL CONCLUSION

*Operations Performed.* In the foregoing sections an attempt has been made to do three things: to allude to a theory of interpreting intellectual-emotional phenomena; to point out in what sense it might be legitimate, for purposes of this theory, to consider American sociology as a phenomenon to which such interpretation could be applied by trying to show that existent considerations of science and sociology imply a view of sociology as not merely a science but also as an orientation or culture—considerations of the relations between value and research, of changing contents of sociology, and of its public relations; to suggest the codetermination of certain concepts in certain fields by aspects of American—or a wider, narrower, or overlapping—culture, the absence from the ongoing subject matter and awareness of American sociology of a characteristic of man and of human relations, and some implications of this absence (the selective nature of the concept of objectivity itself as a possible key with which to examine more systematically the culture of American sociology). In other words, beginnings of a sociocultural interpretation of American sociology have been shown.

*Inadequacies of the Operations Performed.*   The principles of selecting the features of American sociology in which its sociocultural codetermination is believed to be especially visible have not been stated; obviously these principles are somehow related to the recent appearance of writings that present piecemeal criticisms of American sociology (Mills, Myrdal, Hartung, etc.); thus, at least (and methodologically at the most modest), one of the common features of these writings have been shown and utilized within the framework suggested by the theory of interpretation. American sociology has not been defined. More especially, the question of the representativeness of the writings, concepts, ideas, and so on, used as examples has not been raised, much less answered. For purposes of this chapter, however, it is sufficient that these examples, according to the knowledge common among American sociologists, embody attitudes that are at least widely held among them; but if this common knowledge has been misjudged, the examples are irrelevant (which would not, however, destroy the suggestiveness of the theory itself). More probably, in fact, some readers will agree, others will agree in part, and still others will completely disagree with their choice [46].

*Operations Needed and Suggestions of Their Implementation.*   A definition of American sociology for the purposes of its sociocultural interpretation is paramount. Such a definition may be arrived at in a questionnaire designed to test previously formulated hypotheses regarding its nature or in an analysis to be worked out of books, magazines, magazine contents, courses, and course contents in sociology. If such a definition is established, it will serve to interpret American sociology immanently by methods largely articulated in the course of the work done to decide on the definition, thereby discovering aspects that suggest the sociocultural interpretation of American sociology which in turn may lead to, or even necessitate, a definition of the culture found to be operative in it. (Even the few notes presented in this chapter suggest that this will be not only American culture but will also contain elements of the culture of science in general, of Western civilization, and of the Christian tradition.)

*Functions of the Study Suggested.* The projected sociocultural interpretation of American sociology will serve to test the theory of interpretation, the core of which has been presented. It will help to develop a general theory of the sociology of knowledge, of which the theory of interpretation is a part. It may provide a greater self-awareness of American sociology by showing its empirically undemonstrable, socioculturally determined aspects, thus incidentally clarifying the theory of the cultural approach [47] and suggesting attitudinal changes on the part of American sociologists that may result in a greater understanding of their own and other cultures, in a more defensible evaluation of science and culture and their respective roles, and in a clarification of the relation between science and applied science. It may help to bring out and perhaps explain differences of various kinds between American sociology and sociologies of other countries as well as differences in the history and institutionalization of American sociology according to regions—for example, New England and the Middle West.

*Related Studies.* From the last suggestion rises the plausibility of a related study, namely, the development of a set of hypotheses regarding the nature of American sociology compared with the sociology of another country [48] without the necessity of a detailed study implied by the definition of immanent interpretation and with the related purpose (which can be less conclusively reached than by way of an intensive immanent interpretation) of arriving at the ascertainment of sociocultural forces. A point of attack of the original study envisaged could be, or might have to be, the study of behavior and role types of American sociologists as codetermined by their being engaged in their particular profession. Znaniecki's social roles of men of knowledge—technologists, sages, scholars, and explorers [49]—plus the types, at least, of the politician, promoter, and administrator in sociology, could serve as a lead to an investigation of the social backgrounds (biographies) of American sociologists and perhaps also to an investigation of the differential distribution of such types in other fields.

### NOTES

1. My thanks to John W. Bennett, John F. Cuber, Paul K. Hatt, and Cecil C. North for important criticisms and suggestions that I tried, no doubt inadequately, to incorporate into this chapter.
2. The first formulator of the difference between the two types of interpretation—under the terms sociological and ideological, respectively—was Karl

Mannheim ("Ideologische und soziologische Interpretation der geistigen Gebilde," *Jarbuch für Soziologie,* 2 (1926), 424–440 [translated in Wolff, *From Karl Mannheim, op. cit.,* pp. 116–131].

3. The term is borrowed from Arthur Child, *The Problems of the Sociology of Knowledge* [Berkeley: University of California (unpublished Ph.D. thesis), 1938], Chapter III.

4. This theory of interpretations—such brief indication must do—is based on G. H. Mead's social-behavioristic theory of mind as applied to the sociology of knowledge by Child ["The Theoretical Possibility of the Sociology of Knowledge," *Ethics,* 51 (July 1941): 392–418, especially 416–418], and more specifically on Child's discussion of "immanent" and "transcendent" interpretation (*The Problems of the Sociology of Knowledge, op. cit.,* Chapter VII). [For a related approach, also drawing on Mead, see C. Wright Mills, "Language, Logic, and Culture," *American Sociological Review,* 4 (October 1939), 670–680.]

5. Gunnar Myrdal, *An American Dilemma* (New York: Harper, 1944), p. 1027.

6. John Dewey, *Theory of Valuation* [Chicago: University of Chicago Press (International Encyclopedia of Unified Science, Vol. II, No. 4), 1939], *passim,* especially p. 25.

7. Gwynne Nettler, "A Note on Myrdal's 'Notes [sic] on Facts and Valuations,' Appendix 2 of *An American Dilemma,*" *American Sociological Review,* 9 (December 1944), 688.

8. Dewey, *op. cit.,* p. 66.

9. Presumably all scientists would agree that science is, or strives to be, objective and value-free but that it represents a value (whatever aspects of the implications of value they would single out), *if* the two propositions were put before them in juxtaposition, as done here. Their juxtaposition is probably not so much a part of current conceptions of science and its role as is each proposition separately, the first more so than the second.

10. Margaret Jarman Hagood, *Statistics for Sociologists* (New York: Reynal and Hitchcock, 1941), p. 20n.

11. George A. Lundberg, *Social Research* (New York: Longmans, Green, 1942) (2nd ed.), p. 90.

12. See, for example, Pauline V. Young, *Scientific Social Surveys and Research* (New York: Prentice-Hall, 1939). pp. 134–135.

13. Lundberg, *op. cit.,* p. 53. The explicit formulation of this split between scientist and human being or citizen is at least as old as Max Weber's *Science as a Vocation* (1918), in *From Max Weber: Essays in Sociology,* translated and edited and with an introduction by H. H. Gerth and C. Wright Mills (New York: Oxford University Press, 1947), especially pp. 145–147.

14. According to whatever definition of culture is preferred—for example, Tylor's, Albert Blumenthal's, Read Bain's, those discussed in Clyde Kluckhohn and William H. Kelly, "The Concept of Culture" [in Ralph Linton, Ed., *The Science of Man in the World Crisis* (New York: Columbia University Press, 1945), pp. 78–106].

15. Cf. John F. Cuber, "Are There 'Principles' of Sociology?" *American Sociological Review* (June 1941), 370–372.

16. Cf. Howard W. Odum, "The Errors of Sociology," *Social Forces*, 15 (March 1937), 327–342, and Earle Edward Eubank, "Errors of Sociology," *ibid.*, 16 (December 1937), 178–201.

17. Cuber, *op. cit.*, 372. For an explicit public-relations document, a plea for recognition of the social sciences, see Leo P. Crespi, "Social Science—a Stepchild," A.A.U.P. *Bulletin*, 31 (Summer 1945), 189–196.

18. For a description of the sociologist as a government-employed wartime researcher and the effect of this role on his research see Julian L. Woodward, "Making Government Opinion Research Bear Upon Operations," *American Sociological Review*, 9 (December 1944), 670 677.

19. The conception of the selective and constitutive character of social determination, which has had some significance in the German sociology of knowledge and which has been incorporated into the definition of immanent interpretation given here, is best presented in Child, *The Problems of the Sociology of Knowledge, op. cit.*, pp. 286–287.

20. In the sense of Clyde Kluckhohn and O. H. Maurer, "'Culture and Personality': A Conceptual Scheme," *American Anthropologist*, 46 (January–March 1944), 1–29.

21. Cf. Abram Kardiner, "The Concept of Basic Personality Structure as an Operational Tool in the Social Sciences," in Linton, Ed., *op. cit.*, pp. 107–122.

22. C. Wright, Mills, "The Professional Ideology of Social Pathologists," *American Journal of Sociology*, 49 (September 1943), 178.

23. *Ibid.*, 179.

24. *Ibid.*, 180.

25. W. Lloyd Warner, "American Caste and Class," *American Journal of Sociology*, 42 (September 1936), 234–237.

26. Here it may be objected that the reason why Warner's theory was not criticized was not that it was accepted but that it was considered outside the field of sociology, inasmuch as Warner is perhaps better known as an anthropologist than a sociologist (although the theory appeared in the foremost American sociological periodical). If this were the case, it would throw into relief another extrascientific factor that influences sociology, namely, intrasocial-science factions and feelings, a lead (even if the present case should be off the mark) well worth pursuing.

27. Oliver C. Cox, "The Modern Caste School of Race Relations," *Social Forces*, 21 (December 1942), 218–226. See also his further elaborations in "Race Relations," *Journal of Negro Education*, 12 (Spring 1943), 144–153; "Class and Caste: A Definition and a Distinction," *ibid.*, 13 (Spring 1944), 139–149; "The Racial Theories of Robert E. Park and Ruth Benedict," *ibid.*, 13 (Fall 1944), 452–463; "Race and Caste: A Distinction," *American Journal of Sociology*, 50 (March 1945), 360–368; "Estates, Social Classes, and Political Classes," *American Sociological Review*, 10 (August 1945), 464–469.

28. Ogburn and Nimkoff, *Sociology* (Boston: Houghton Mifflin, 1940), pp. 323–324. (It would be difficult to imagine that textbook considerations as suggested here are responsible for the inclusion of Warner's theory.) Perhaps best known among works that utilize Warner's theory—but not written by sociologists—are John Dollard (*Caste and Class in a Southern Town*) and Davis Gardner (*Deep South*). For other titles see Cox, "The Modern Caste School . . ." *op. cit.*, 218, n. 1. Myrdal's *Dilemma, loc. cit.*, is also informed by Warner's schema; *passim*, especially Chapter 31.

29. Cox, "The Modern Caste School . . . ," *op. cit.*, 222. This is precisely the characteristic of feudal society. It was largely true of the ante-bellum South and is still found in the stratification of aristocracy versus peasants or servants and even middle-class servants in most of Europe, at least until World War II. See some of Henry James's novels or the film *Mrs. Miniver* (i.e., its portrayal of the breakdown of caste); *in this respect* (only) these are examples of caste; whether other features make some of them examples of class need not be discussed here (cf. Cox, "Class and Caste," *loc. cit.*). On India, see, for example, Mason Olcott, "The Caste System of India," *American Sociological Review*, 9 (December 1944), 648–657.

30. Norman D. Humphrey ["American Race Relations and the Caste System," *Psychiatry*, 8 (November 1945), 380], in a critique of Cox, points out that the American caste system is breaking down but is for this no less a caste system. The question is, what kind of system or social structure will follow its complete breakdown—a question not raised by Humphrey but exemplifying a perspective other than that of friendliness toward the status quo (though probably similarly biased). This consideration shows the difficulty of objectivity in front of certain situations.

31. Myrdal's paraphrase of statements by an elderly, very distinguished doctor in the South: "Explorations in Escape," in *An American Dilemma, op. cit.*, p. 33.

32. It might be suggested that not only their use shows extrascientific influences but that the unclear definitions of the terms, especially their distinction, hint at such influences.

33. Myrdal, *op. cit.*, pp. 1049–1050. I do not find Nettler's critique (*loc. cit.*) of Myrdal's critique a proof that Sumner, Park, and Ogburn do *not* exhibit an attitude favorable to *laissez-faire* (although his statement has other merits). On *Folkways*, in the context of our discussion, see also Frank E. Hartung, "The Social Function of Positivism," *Philosophy of Science*, 12 (April 1945), 131–133.

34. It is true, of course, that Redfield is a cultural anthropologist, not a sociologist, but his theory is widely known and also used by sociologists.

35. "Whereas rural life in the United States has for a long time been a subject of considerable interest on the part of governmental bureaus, the most notable case of a comprehensive report being that submitted by the Country Life Commission to President Theodore Roosevelt in 1909, it is worthy of note that no equally comprehensive official inquiry into urban life was undertaken until . . ." 1937. Louis Wirth, "Urbanism as a Way of Life," *American Journal of Sociology*,

**44** (July 1938), 3n. It has been remarked that much of urban and rural sociology is permeated by the idea that the rural community is better than the city and that the city is a kind of deviation from the good old days. Perhaps some truth in this suggestion could be demonstrated.

36. See, however, the work of Robert S. and Helen M. Lynd (especially *Middletown in Transition,* Chapter III) and Robert S. Lynd's *Knowledge for What?* (Princeton, N.J.: Princeton University Press, 1939), especially pp. 74–79. See also Lynd's preface to R. A. Brady, *Business as a System of Power* (New York: Columbia University Press, 1943), and some recent sociological papers that have used the concept of power envisaged here: Reinhard Bendix, "Bureaucracy and the Problem of Power," *Public Administration Review,* **5** (Summer 1945), 194–209, and Robert K. Merton, "Role of the Intellectual in Public Bureaucracy," *Social Forces,* **23** (May 1945), 405–415. See also C. Wright Mills, "The Powerless People: The Social Role of the Intellectual," A.A.U.P. *Bulletin,* **31** (Summer 1945), 231–243 [originally in *Politics,* I (April 1944), 66–72].

37. It would be extraordinary for a sociologist to say or to investigate people who say what the philosopher Karl Jaspers said: "That we are still alive is our guilt." [See *Politics,* **3** (February 1946), 53.] Or Ellsworth Faris on Kierkegaard, *American Journal of Sociology,* **50** (March, 1945), 401–404.]

38. The absence is greater in the positivistic branch of American sociology than in the "understanding" branch represented by such sociologists as MacIver, Znaniecki, and Parsons. [For an impressive embodiment of the contrast between the two "branches" see Lundberg's and Znaniecki's papers in the Semicentennial Issue of *The American Journal of Sociology,* **50** (May 1945), 502–513, 514–521.] See also Lundberg's Presidential Address, "Sociologists and the Peace," *American Sociological Review,* **9** (February 1944), 1–13, especially p. 3, n. 2, Arthur Evans Wood's reaction to it [*ibid.* (June 1944), 319–320], and Lundberg's rejoinder [*ibid.* (August 1944), 435–436].

39. George A. Lundberg, *Foundations of Sociology* (New York: Macmillan, 1939), p. 534.

40. In this connection the recent appearance of the revival, in explicitly value-charged terms, of Sapir's distinction between genuine and spurious culture might be a symptom of greater cultural self-awareness on the part of some American sociologists: Melvin Tumin, "Culture, Genuine and Spurious: A Re-Evaluation," *American Sociological Review,* **10** (April 1945), 199–207, especially 207.

41. Lundberg, *op. cit.,* p. 236 (see also pp. 471–472).

42. Lundberg, "Sociologists and the Peace," *op. cit.,* 4b. (see also *Foundations, op. cit.,* pp. 405–406). On the basis of Lundberg's definition of freedom and his other statements, Hartung concludes that Lundberg's positivism ultimately prepares an attitude favorable to facism [Frank E. Hartung, "The Sociology of Positivism," *Science and Society,* **8** (Fall, 1944), 340] and thus goes considerably further than I do in imputing "attitudinal implications." I do not find Hartung's particular argument convincing, however.

43. For a similar controversy over the objective definition of the situation see Lundberg versus MacIver on fear and hate; cf. MacIver, *Society, op. cit.*, pp. 476–477, Lundberg, *Foundations, op. cit.*, pp. 12–13, and MacIver, *Social Causation* (Boston: Ginn, 1942), pp. 299–300.

44. In contrast with and in addition to the selective character of any concept [cf. Robert K. Merton, "Sociological Theory," *American Journal of Sociology,* 50 (May 1945), 465].

45. Cf. Thelma Z. Lavine, "Naturalism and the Sociological Analysis of Knowledge," in Yervant H. Krikorian, Ed., *Naturalism and the Human Spirit* (New York: Columbia University Press, 1944), pp. 198–200. The question whether science as such can be objective involves questions of the nature of logic and can be answered only on the basis of a theory of science, which cannot and need not be discussed here.

46. Some disagreements I have tried to anticipate and eliminate, but it is perhaps more difficult to show sociocultural influences at work in whole complexes of concepts and attitudes, as done here, than it would be to trace them by minute study of more specific sociological productions in the manner that Mills used in his study of social-pathology texts.

47. Cf. Kurt H. Wolff, "A Methodological Note on the Empirical Establishment of Culture Patterns," *American Sociological Review,* 10 (April 1945), 176–184 [Chapter 20].

48. Among the numerous materials bearing on this question may be mentioned Pitirim A. Sorokin, "Some Contrasts of Contemporary European and American Sociology," *Social Forces,* 8 (September 1929), 57–62, and various passages in other works of Sorokin; C. Wright Mills, "Methodological Consequences of the Sociology of Knowledge," *American Journal of Sociology*, 46 (November 1940), 330; Harry Elmer Barnes and Howard Becker, *Social Thought from Lore to Science* (Boston: Heath, 1938), Vol. II.

49. Cf. Florian Znaniecki, *The Social Role of the Man of Knowledge* (New York: Columbia University Press), 1940.

---

Reprinted from *American Sociological Review,* 11 (1946), 545–553, by permission of the publisher. The essay has been edited and partially revised by the author.

# 13

# A NOTE ON MORALITY
# AND SOCIETY. 1965

1. There is widespread agreement in contemporary social science concerning "values." Among the items of this agreement are the propositions that

values are important in the selection of problems for research;
values are important in the interpretation of findings;
social science itself is a value.

2. Such agreement is institutionalized or customary; that is, more than the result of rational examination of what is the case, it is a rationalization of what is the case.

How is a problem actually selected? Answer: Above all, institutionally or customarily—while seeking to obtain a degree in decorous and expeditious fashion, while trying to get into or stay in the market, or obtain or meet a research contract. The very conception of a problem is largely set by authority—scientific, social, economic, political.

To a considerable extent the interpretation of findings is likewise set by the institutional framework.

An explication of this item means that social science is useful, for it is the most realiable way of gaining knowledge—but knowledge about means, not ends, that is, social science is no guide to moral decision.

The question is whether it can be such a guide. Let us remember this question in the following, and after.

3. If (1) and (2) are correct, there is little or no clarity on the matters on which there seems to be agreement. Nor is there clarity, though related

220

agreement, on what constitutes a value. It tends to be anything of interest; anything toward which a person is not indifferent.

> The much deplored devaluation of all things, that is, the loss of all intrinsic worth, begins with their transformation into values or commodities, for from this moment on they exist only in relation to some other which can be acquired in their stead [1].

A pervasive meaning of value is its original meaning of (commercial) exchange value, constantly exhibited, for example, in the mass media of communication (an earthquake following or preceding a fashion show in the newsreels, advertisements distinguished from articles by the label "advertisement," etc.).

4. Another pervasive meaning of value is that as anything of interest it is a psychological phenomenon. Interest is a nonmoral concept. Interests may be economic, biological, psychological, social, or political. They are found in all cultures, although their articulations relate to the culture or cultures in which they occur. Universal value is a term that characteristically refers to such interests or, less specifically, to economic features (material needs), biological features (organic needs), psychological features (psychological needs), social and political features (power, stratification, etc.). In contemporary social science these needs or interests are not considered capable of settling moral issues. Morality is divorced from the economic, biological, psychological, social, and political features of man and society. It is as relative as the culture that contains it and as arbitrary, irrational, or idiosyncratic. The divorce between morality and the economic, biological, psychological, social, and political features of man and society engenders the social scientist's (and philosopher's) hopeless quest for universal values. Cultural relativism has become a substantive or philosophical problem, but it is a pseudo-problem which can be accounted for by reference to circumstances external to it. Here the reference is to semantics and society.

5. The agreement on values [see (1) above] is customary and therefore discourages reflection. Because customs are answers, they persuade in their favor. To think customarily is to think unscientifically. The views of values described are unscientific. The agreements on the relation between social science and values ned revision. The word value itself must be eliminated from the vocabularies of social science and philosophy and from rational discourse altogether (except for its technical referents in economics, logic, and mathematics).

6. The economic and highly specific historical origin of the word value

tends to be overlooked or slighted by many, if not most, contemporary social scientists (and philosophers). Its application to social science other than economics takes its significant development from Max Weber's value-free social science. Outside social science we still feel its economic or technical nature when we speak of a valuable person, and do not dream of applying the adjective valuable to individuals who are important to us personally or who point directions to us as members of a nation (e.g., Lincoln), of Western civilization (e.g., Shakespeare), or mankind (e.g., the founders of world religions). We do not call them valuable, but great, seminal, or we say that they teach us possibilities or dimensions of man. When we speak of individuals personally important to us, as parts of ourselves and the like, the word valuable would strike us as blasphemous, or as brutally commercial. The words we use to refer to these important persons are not social-scientific concepts. Nor are value and valuable, as used in social science, categories of everyday life, where they are used in their economic or technical sense.

7. The crux of morality is a moral decision. A moral decision is an action based on the recognition, by affective thinking, of what is right. It presupposes ignorance, confusion, and perplexity preceding the thinking which leads to the decision. A moral decision thus must be distinguished from a habitual or customary decision, which is action by authority (habit or custom), not action on the basis of thought. One of the functions of custom is to exempt people from having to make moral decisions. It tells them what to do and what not to do. To identify custom with morality (moral relativism) is to deny morality. Only when custom does not function is there the possibility of a moral decision. If he were consistent, the moral relativist would have to deny the fact that moral decisions exist (no matter how rare they may be). The most important American formulator of cultural relativism, William Graham Sumner, failed to draw theoretical conclusions from such remarks as this:

> The trained reason and conscience never have heavier tasks laid upon them than where questions of conformity to, or dissent from, the mores are raised. It is by dissent and free judgment of the best reason and conscience that the mores win flexibility and automatic readjustments [2].

Customary action, then, is not moral action. Custom, tradition, and habit must be distinguished from thought and morality. If we keep on discussing values as customarily defined, we are not thinking. We are elaborating custom.

8. If customs generally, in all societies, exempt people from having to make moral decisions, it is worthwhile to look at our own customs. When Western society is described as technological, materialistic, or commercialized, it means that many of our customs are no longer moral but economic and technological. Many of our decisions regarding social matters are economic and technological—whom to invite, how to spend time, what career to choose, whom to marry, how to choose a religion (religion as satisfying psychological needs). Two widely noted extraordinary developments are relevant. The first is that of a market economy. We are so bombarded with goods (values) that what is not advertised tends not to exist for us. The psychological effect is the coincidence between what exists and what we want: there is nothing we may want that does not exist, and wishes for what does not commercially exist tend to result in neuroses.

> The quantity of indiscriminately consumed goods becomes fatal. It makes it impossible to find one's way, and as one looks for a guide in the monstrous department store, just so the people at large, overwhelmed by offers from all sides, wait for their leader [3].

The second extraordinary development is that of science and technology, with its notions from "it can be done," to "man is a drag on progress," and "man is a faulty construction" (in comparison with the electronic computer or the rocket). Science fiction describes our desire for technological power, to which economic power is incidentally attached. The atomic physicists, who are most cognizant of scientific and technological developments, are the scientists who have raised moral problems. The control of nature has controlled the controllers. We have become parts of controlled nature; we are denied the status of moral beings.

9. Social science without social philosophy, as well as social philosophy without social science, tends to be ideological; that is, to elaborate customs, and to rationalize interests. By social philosophy I mean the inquiry into the problems of how truth, right, goodness, and beauty can exist in social organization. By social science I mean the critical analysis of what and why people act, think, feel, and speak the way they do. Both are moral enterprises. Critical analysis increases our capacity to make moral decisions. By analyzing customs, institutions, and pressures we become less dependent on them and more respectful of a practice that we can answer for.

NOTES

1.   Hannah Arendt, *The Human Condition* (Chicago: University of Chicago Press, 1958), pp. 165–166.
2.   William Graham Sumner, *Folkways* (Boston: Ginn, 1906), p. 95.
3.   Theodor W. Adorno, *Minima Moralia* (Berlin: Suhrkamp, 1951), p. 218.

Reprinted from *Estudios de sociología,* **9** (1965), 191–194, by permission of the publisher. The essay has been edited and partially revised by the author.

# 14

# MAN'S HISTORICITY
AND DUALISM:
The Significance
of Hannah Arendt's
*The Human Condition*
for Sociology. 1961

*EXPOSITORY*

The title of Hannah Arendt's book, *The Human Condition* [1], was to have been *Vita Activa* [2]. It is an analysis of the *vita activa*, of its vicissitudes in Western history, and therewith of much of the story of Western man.

# I

Arendt begins, however, with a systematic rather than historical description of the *vita activa*. This is the term she chooses to refer to the three human activities of labor, work, and action, each of which "corresponds to one of the basic conditions" (p. 7) of human existence.

Labor corresponds to life itself. It is the activity man must engage in if he would live on this earth, where he is neither immortal nor self-sufficient. In laboring, the human body "concentrates upon nothing but its own being alive, and remains imprisoned in its metabolism with nature" (p. 115; cf. 209) or "matter" (p. 183, n. 8).

Work, on the other hand—a term that Arendt uses synonymously with making and fabricating—corresponds to man's worldliness. It is the activity of producing the human artifice, that is, all the things that are used, enjoyed, revered, or contemplated. They are not consumed, however, for to be consumed is precisely the fate of the products of labor, not of work. Within the "artificial world of things" provided by work, "each individual life is housed, while this world itself is meant to outlast and transcend" (p. 7) the life of the individual.

The third human condition, plurality (simply the fact that man is not one but many), is the condition of action—"the only activity that goes on directly between men without the intermediary of things or matter" (p. 7)—hence of all political life. Plurality must not be confused with society, which is not a human condition but only one of the historical forms of plurality.

# II

To understand the distinction between plurality and society and to understand the rise of society itself we must explore the distinction Arendt makes between the public and private realms. It is the distinction between the *polis* and the family household, made in "all ancient political thought" (p. 28), in which the *polis* was the (public) realm of freedom, to which the mastery of the necessities of life in the household entitled one, and the household was the (private) realm of necessity, in which the man labored for individual maintenance and woman for the maintenance of the species.

The rise of society signifies the rise of economic activities—of private activities characteristic of the household—"to the public realm" (p. 33). Society is essentially a phenomenon of the modern age, which began "in the seventeenth century [and] came to an end at the beginning of the twentieth century" [in contrast to "the modern world, in which we live today" and which was born "with the first atomic explosion" (6)].

Society replaces action with behavior and it equates the individual with his social status (which determines his behavior)—rank in the eighteenth-century half-feudal society, title in the nineteenth-century class society, "or mere function in the mass society of today" (p. 41). In the earlier stages of society its science was economics, which introduced and developed statistics to describe behavior—but only parts of the behavior of the population. This germinal, though modest, beginning was to develop

> into the all-comprehensive pretension of the social sciences which, as "behavioral sciences," aim to reduce man as a whole, in all his activities, to the level of a conditioned and behaving animal (p. 45).

Members of modern societies are indeed laborers or jobholders, people who "consider whatever they do primarily as a way to sustain their own lives and those of their families" (p. 46). The society of jobholders, "the last stage of the laboring society" (p. 322), no longer belongs in the modern (p. 319), but in a later age (cf. p. 6).

As behavior and labor go with society, so does the division of labor, the organization of laboring, which presupposes (as image perhaps even more than as the individual's activity) a gigantic household wherein all members are harnessed to one or another of myriad mechanized labor processes. This mechanization of labor has gone so far that it allows us to forget "the verbal significance of the word [labor], which always had been connected with hardly bearable 'toil and trouble' " (p. 48) [3].

Public refers, first (as an adjective), to what "can be seen and heard by everybody" (p. 50), second (as a noun), to the man-made world common to men, including the affairs that go on among them; and this world contrasts with "our privately owned place in it" (p. 52). By virtue of this common man-made world men are related and separated; by virtue of it they *can* relate to one another and distinguish themselves from one another. Such a public, as against private, space "cannot be erected for one generation and planned for the living only; it must transcend the life-span of mortal man" (p. 55).

Historically, Arendt claims, the most conspicuous proof and exemplification of the private realm has been property, which had the same obscurity—as contrasted with publicity—as the other essential features of the household (the laboring of the man and woman). We are likely to forget this because of the modern identification of property with wealth. Wealth, however, is the individual's "share in the annual income of the society as a whole," whereas property, originally, meant "to have one's location in a particular part of the world and therefore to belong to the body politic" (p. 61). The interior of the household, as well as birth and death, remains hidden from the public, but its exterior appears as the boundary that separates one household from the next; and the original meaning of the law of the *polis* was the boundary line between the private and the public (pp. 63–64 and notes 63, 65).

Thus, in addition to labor (and the division of labor) and behavior, a third characteristic of modern society is wealth and propertylessness. Their simultaneous rise has meant the extinction of the difference between the public and private realms, hence their simultaneous disappearance in the social realm and their replacement by it. The modern age has emancipated both women and laborers, the two types of man who had not been part of public life but had been private, laborers in the two senses of the term; and "the few remnants of strict privacy even in our own civilization relate to 'necessities' in the original sense of being necessitated by having a body" ( p. 73).

# III

The products of labor are destined to be consumed; they are consumer goods. Hence to speak of our society as one of consumers or one of laborers is merely to single out one or the other phase of the same process. The "thing character" of our world is guaranteed by the work of our hands, the main products of which are use objects; and without use objects we might not even know what a thing is (cf. p. 94). Labor produces no things. It is a process, repetitive, self-perpetuating, and fertile, which has emerged for conceptualization ever since the seventeenth century. That was the time when political theorists were first "confronted with a hitherto unheard-of process of growing wealth, growing property, growing acquisition" and thus turned "to the phenomenon of a progressing process itself, so that . . . the concept of process became the very key term of the new age as well as the sciences, historical and natural, developed by it" (p. 105).

Labor is the only activity into which we can translate, and which corresponds to, the life process in our bodies that we know by introspection. The discovery of introspection in philosophy coincided with that of process in the natural sciences. Modern philosophies of labor, followed by philosophies of life, have equated productivity with fertility, but the philosophies of life have lost sight of labor, which is the activity needed to sustain the life process, and labor, having become more effortless than ever before, has indeed become "more similar to the automatically functioning life process" (p. 117).

To labor and to consume are so overwhelmingly the activities in whose terms we conceive of our lives that every other activity, all that is not making a living, is a hobby. This dichotomy is anticipated in the several types of modern labor theory, all of which contrast labor with play.

Leisure, which has increased and spread by the mechanization and division of labor, has engendered the crucial problem "how to provide enough opportunity for daily exhaustion to keep the capacity for consumption intact" (p. 131). Still, no matter what forms labor takes, it remains in the realm of necessity. Its elevation to unprecedented status is the elevation of necessity to such status.

# IV

*Homo faber*, the maker of things and objects—in contrast to the man of action—"is master of himself and his doings" (p. 144). Labor, as compared with making, has no beginning or end, and action inevitably involves others. *Homo faber* is different from both laborer and man of action also in distinguishing between means and ends in respect to his activity, making or fabricating. Both he and the laborer may use tools or machines. The *problem* of the machine, however, has developed with the function of the machine in the service of labor rather than in the service of fabrication. Because everything, natural or man-made, enters the conditions of man's existence, the problem of the machine is not one of adjustment: man adjusted himself to the machine the moment he designed it (cf. p. 147). Rather the problem of the machine is that "as long as the work at the machines lasts, the mechanical process has replaced the rhythm of the human body" (p. 147). If the present stage of machine technology channels "natural forces into the world of the human artifice, future technology may yet consist of channeling the universal forces of the cosmos around us into the nature of the earth" (p. 150). The tools and implements of *homo faber* primarily serve to erect a world of things. The question of machines today is not so much whether we are their masters or their slaves as whether they still serve such a world or whether, "on the contrary, they and the automatic motion of their processes have begun to rule and even destroy" it (p. 151).

It could be that the dialectic that governed the replacement of *homo faber*, man the maker, with *animal laborans*, man the laborer, was released by the failure of Western man to realize that, "while only fabrication with its instrumentality is capable of building a world, this same world becomes as worthless as the employed material . . . if the standards which governed its coming into being are permitted to rule it after its establishment" (p. 156); that is, the means-end scheme, which controls the making of the world of things, does not control it once it is made. Instead it controls the public realm of *homo faber*, namely, the exchange market (cf.

p. 160), which is the arena of values in the authentic historical, hence the only legitimate sense of this term:

> The much deplored devaluation of all things . . . begins with their transformation into values or commodities, for from this moment they exist only in relation to some other thing which can be acquired in their stead. Universal relativity, that a thing exists only in relation to other things, and loss of intrinsic worth, that nothing any longer possesses an "objective" value independent of the ever-changing estimations of supply and demand, are inherent in the very concept of value itself (pp. 165–166; cf. p. 235, n. 74).

The reason that every man-made thing once made (as contrasted with the thing-in-the-making) transcends the means-end scheme is that it "must appear, and nothing can appear without a shape of its own." Consequently everything in some way transcends "its functional use, and its transcendence, its beauty or ugliness, is identical with appearing publicly and being seen" (p. 173).

# V

Man may be human without laboring (but allowing others to labor) or working (but enjoying the things made by others); but a "life without speech and without action . . . is literally dead to the world; it has ceased to be a human life because it is no longer lived among men" (p. 176). To speak and act is to insert ourselves into the world, not by necessity, as when we labor, nor by utility, as when we work, but by virtue of that beginning which was our birth; it therefore is like a second birth (cf. p. 177 and n. 3).

Speech plays a much greater role in action than in any other human activity in which it has the function of communication. Indeed it must not be confused with communication, although in modern society, including much of modern social science and philosophy, the two are often, if not characteristically, no longer distinguished—just as labor and work and behavior and action have lost all clear differentiations. Unlike communication, which, along with making, is governed by the means-end scheme, speech and action are not. They disclose the person who engages in them and is willing to risk being disclosed. This can, however, be done only in the public realm: neither the doer of good works nor the criminal can, since their deeds and words must remain hidden. Neither is such revelation possible when people are for or against one another rather than simply together, for then speech and action become means to an end as, for example, in war.

Only a man's biography—the story in which he is the hero—tells us *who* he was or is; hence "we know much better and more intimately who" Socrates was "because we know his story than we know who Aristotle was, about whose opinions we are so much better informed" (p. 186).

We cannot know human nature or who man is because *his* story is history, or the storybook of mankind, and mankind is an unidentifiable agent (cf. p. 194). Even the individual agent cannot know the meaning of his action: it can be revealed only by the storyteller, who has the advantage of hindsight. The reason is that action is boundless and unpredictable: "it acts into a medium where every reaction becomes a chain reaction and where every process is the cause of new processes" (p. 190). The resulting frailty of human affairs was transcended by the Greek *polis*, which assured "the mortal actor that his passing existence and fleeting greatness . . . [would] never lack the reality that comes from being seen, being heard, and, generally, appearing before an audience of fellow men" (p. 198).

That which keeps the public realm, that is, the space in which acting and speaking men appear, in existence, is *power*. Power passes away when it is not actualized, and it

> is actualized only where word and deed have not parted company, . . . where words are not used to veil intentions but to disclose realities, and deeds are not used to violate and destroy but to establish relations and create new realities" (p. 200).

Power, inseparable from action and politics, is unknown to *homo faber*, who is convinced that man's products may be more than himself, and to the *animal laborans*, who believes that life is the highest of all goods. Power, instead, accrues to the man of action, for whom "the greatest that man can achieve is his own appearance and actualization" (p. 208).

Because action is unpredictable in its outcome, irreversible (products can be destroyed), and anonymous in its authorship, the attempt to substitute making for action is as old as recorded history. Fundamentally, it is the attempt to have one man, modeled after *homo faber*, *make* political life. This attempt is at the bottom of all arguments against democracy— the political form that most fully recognizes the human condition of plurality—and thus is "an argument against the essentials of politics" (p. 220) itself.

We have seen that in the modern age the seeming elimination of labor has resulted in work being performed in the mode of labor, and the products of work, that is, objects, being consumed like consumer goods. Similarly, the attempt at eliminating action and replacing it by producing has resulted "in channeling the human capacity for action ... into ... a [new] attitude toward nature" (p. 231)—the nature into which we have begun to act.

Still, the fact that man is both free and not sovereign, that is, he can act, start something new, and yet cannot control its consequences, does not justify the existentialist conclusion that human existence is absurd, for action is not only irreversible it is also forgivable, and the remedy for its unpredictability is "the faculty to make and keep promises" (p. 237). Forgiveness terminates a chain of action and reaction, when vengeance promotes such a chain, and forgiveness is as revelatory as action itself. The force of mutual promise, or contract, is the power that keeps the public space in which people can act together in existence. What is mastership in the realm of making and the world of things is sovereignty in the realm of action and human affairs, but although the former is conceivable only in isolation, the latter can only be achieved by the many bound together (p. 245).

# VI

Throughout most of the parts of her book on which I have expounded so far Arendt has written in a historical vein more implicitly than explicitly. She has told us, for instance, of the (historical) rise of society and of the (historical) confusion between private and public, property and wealth, behavior and action, labor and work, consumption and use, values and a great many things, communication and speech, power and strength, force, or violence, action and work (and, as we shall see, truth and truthfulness). In the last part of her book "The *Vita Activa* and the Modern Age" she faces, equipped with the frame of reference with which we have acquainted ourselves, more explicitly the nature of the modern age and its history.

The modern age is characterized by world alienation, or the loss of a common human world. In social life the first phase of this age was marked by the cruelty toward ever-increasing numbers of laborers deprived of family and property, of a place in the world; its second stage, by the rise of society that replaced the family as the subject of the new life process.

In physics and philosophy the center of the universe, at one time the earth, later the sun, has disappeared in the Einsteinian "centerless world view" (p. 263). We have transcended the age of natural science, which looks on nature from a universal standpoint and thus acquires complete mastery over her, and have entered that of a universal science, "which imports cosmic processes into nature even at the obvious risk of destroying her and, with her, man's mastership over her" (p. 268). Our thought is still dominated by the Cartesian doubt and its two nightmares: that reality may be a dream and that an evil spirit, rather than God, rules the world—a devil who has created a creature which harbors a notion of truth but which "will never be able to reach any truth, never be able to be certain of anything" (p. 277). Thus, in religion, Protestantism has resulted in the loss of the *certitudo salutis*, and, in regard to cognition, modern man has lost the certitude of truth (and has substituted for it the ideal of truthfulness). Introspection, or "the sheer cognitive concern of consciousness with its own content" (p. 280), has dissolved objective reality into subjective mental processes and has transformed common sense into "an inner faculty without any world relationship" (p. 283). Modern science deals exclusively "with a hypothetical nature" (p. 287); scientific and philosophical truth have parted company; and "the philosopher no longer turns from the world of deceptive perishability to another world of eternal truth, but turns away from both and withdraws into himself" (p. 293).

The loss of a common human world was first indicated by the elevation to predominance of making and fabricating. Man who made instruments and experiments no longer asked what or who but only how. The objects of his knowledge no longer were things or eternal motions, but processes; no longer nature or the universe, but their history. Ever since Vico the despair of human reason made itself felt in the conviction that only man-made things were understandable to man.

Yet there was a second shift or reversal: *homo faber* was replaced by *animal laborans*; making by laboring; means-end-product by process; the principle of utility by that of the "greatest happiness of the greatest number," that is, by the principle of life itself. The reason for this second reversal, a reversal in the *vita activa*, is the very medium within which it took place. This medium was the Christian society with its traditional immortality of the individual life, as against the pre-Christian immortality of the body politic. This medium, however, had been secularized, and secularization had deprived man of faith in individual immortality, which was still believed in during the Middle Ages. Now, the one thing of potential immortality "was life itself, that is, the possibly everlasting life proc-

ess of the species mankind" (p. 321). The concept of life unifies all processes, from subatomic through human to terrestrial and galactic. The
**reason**

> why the behavior of the infinitely small particle is not only
> similar in pattern to the planetary system as it appears to us
> but resembles the life and behavior patterns in human society
> is, of course, that we look and live in this society as though we
> were as far removed from our own human existence as we are
> from the infinitely small and the immensely large which, even
> if they could be perceived by the finest instruments, are too
> far away from us to be experienced (p. 323).

Nevertheless men keep on making things and have not even lost the
capacity to act, although this capacity is largely limited to the scientists.
The scientists, however, act into nature by releasing processes. Their
action therefore lacks, "the revelatory character of action as well as the
ability to produce stories and become historical" (p. 324).

In line with both the premodern and modern tradition Arendt has
omitted thought from her reconsideration of the *vita activa*, but she concludes her book with a few remarks on it. "As a living experience," she
writes,

> thought has always been assumed, perhaps wrongly, to be
> known only to the few. It may not be presumptious to believe
> that these few have not become fewer in our time. This may
> be irrelevant, or of restricted relevance, for the future of the
> world; it is not irrelevant for the future of man. For if no
> other test but the experience of being active, no other measure
> but the extent of sheer activity were to be applied to the
> various activities within the *vita activa*, it might well be that
> thinking as such would surpass them all. Whoever has any
> experience in this matter will know how right Cato was when
> he said: . . . "Never is he more active than when he does
> nothing, never is he less alone than when he is by himself"
> (p. 325).

In her end she thus comes back to her beginning: "What I propose,"
she then wrote,

> is a reconsideration of the human condition from the vantage
> point of our newest experiences and our most recent fears.
> This, obviously, is a matter of thought, and thoughtlessness—
> the needless recklessness or hopeless confusion or complacent

repetition of "truths" which have become trivial and empty—
seems to me among the outstanding characteristics of our time.
What I propose, therefore, is very simple: it is nothing more
than to think what we are doing (p. 5).

### INTERPRETIVE

We should miss the nature of Hannah Arendt's book were we not to
analyze it as communication *and* thinking. In respect to the former we
examine two facets: factual statements and theoretical claims [4]. For
purposes of this chapter I disregard Arendt's factual statements, although
many of them, especially those contained in her extensive comments on
Plato, Aristotle, Marx, and other thinkers, warrant sharp scrutiny. Nevertheless, they are of secondary importance in light of my purpose, which
is to bring home the significance of Arendt's book for contemporary
sociology. As I see it, this significance lies above all in the exemplification
of an attitude toward history and our time. The power of this attitude is
related to the viability of the theoretical claims that Arendt advances in
its behalf and, to be sure, but more indirectly, to the correctness of the
factual statements that she makes in support of her theoretical claims.
My interpretation, which omits the factual statements, thus is incomplete,
but incomplete, I think, in regard to the less important, the relatively
least important part of Arendt's work.

By interpreting this work I mean commenting on its theoretical claims,
which, along with its factual statements, here disregarded, make it up as
a piece of communication, and on its attitude, which, I hold and shall try
to show, far exceeds the author's factual and theoretical concerns and
reveals her to us as the thinker she is. To appreciate this second task of
interpretation we should recall, to paraphrase Arendt (pp. 170–172), that
thinking is autonomous, self-contained, without end (both without purpose and without terminal point), whereas communication, like cognition,
is patterned after the means-end scheme. Thinking, we go on, tries to
accept no distinctions man has ever made (including the many Arendt
makes); it is a maelstrom that engulfs whatever ordering the world may
exhibit; it shows man at his most unconditioned, and this means at his
most practical—as open and exposed to the world as he can be, with no
holds barred, no outcome certain, even the fact of any outcome at all
uncertain. Thus to think is the extreme meaning of the practical reaction,
including that of the sociologist, to Arendt's book.

As she says with Cato, however, to think is to be by oneself, and to
speak, and certainly to write, is to add an element of making to thinking—

an element that increases from speaking to writing. When in the following I enumerate some of the propositions I wish to submit for inspection, perhaps even thinking, by others, it is a sure sign that I am submitting cognitions and tentative outcomes, that is, interruptions of thinking yielded to under its onslaught, and made, but only somehow, into entertainable propositions—I cannot do the impossible, submit thinking itself.

The first part of these halts in thinking—all of which I consider relevant to the social scientist—concerns (we recall) theoretical questions, including the definitional and methodological, some of which require answers in order to decide the items in the second section, which are practical.

## *Theoretical*

THE RELATIONS AMONG THE CONDITIONS OF THE THREE ACTIVITIES OF THE VITA ACTIVA. To say that the human condition of *labor* is life itself means that man (though not necessarily every man) must labor if he wants to live. To say that the human condition of *work* is worldliness means that man (with the same qualification) must work if he wants a world beyond nature. Yet, of course, he must live in order to be able to work and must labor in order to live. It thus appears that the two human conditions, life and worldliness, are not coordinate and mutually irreducible but rather hierarchical: labor makes life possible, which in turn makes work possible; but although life is possible without work (though not without labor), work is possible only if there are labor *and* life. Furthermore, labor is biologically necessary, work is not.

As to plurality, the predicate "condition" does not mean what it does in life and worldliness. Man can choose not to live and not to be worldly, but he cannot choose not to be plural: plurality, as the word says, is not an individual trait, and its abolition is the abolition of mankind, which, on the contrary, is left intact by both the individual's death (including suicide and murder) and other-worldliness (in whatever sense of this term). Plurality, in fact, is the condition of the denial of life by man-made death, whether suicide or murder, and of other-worldliness. Durkheim has shown this in suicide. It is obvious in murder. Other-worldliness, even in the form of withdrawal from mankind, is a withdrawal, an activity "that goes on directly between men" and was preceded by similar activities [5]. Plurality, in fact, is the condition without which man cannot survive long enough to reach the maturity needed for choosing death or other-worldliness. Even if there were authenticated cases of feral children (I am not aware of any), they would not be of human children, who, like many other animals, need adults of their species to bring them up.

It turns out that all three of the human conditions—life, worldliness, and plurality—corresponding to the three human activities of labor, work, and action, are not coordinate and mutually irreducible for neither life nor labor is possible without the other. Both life and labor are necessary prerequisites of work, but not vice versa, and neither life nor worldliness is possible without plurality, which therefore is necessary not only for action but for labor and work as well.

LABOR AND WORK.  Labor is private, necessary, repetitive, and for consumption, whereas work is public, spontaneous, with a beginning and an end, and destined to last. Yet we have seen that work can be performed in the manner of labor and the products of work can be consumed like consumer goods, which suggests that the above predicates of labor (private or necessary) and work (public or spontaneous) are not intrinsic to these activities but dependent on man's attitudes; that a man is not laboring or working by virtue of what he does but by virtue of what he thinks he is doing. Thus an assembly-line laborer in an automobile factory is laboring if he expects that the car on the production of which his effort is expended will be consumed, but he is working if he thinks that he is contributing to making a use-object. Whether an item is a consumer good or a use-object likewise appears to depend on the attitude one has toward it. Thus, if I use my car as a vehicle in the service of my everyday life, including my occupation, it is a use-object, but what can it mean to say that I consume it, that it is a consumer good, other than that I feed it, as it were—not into my stomach but into my system of thrills or prestige? Something like voraciousness, whether literal or figurative, thus appears to be the attitude that determines an item's status as a consumer good. The only other entertainable criterion for distinguishing between use-object and consumer good is even more inarticulate. This is the matter of the time that an item is to last: if brief, it would be a consumer good; if longer, a use-object. This time element does enter into Arendt's distinction—things, for instance, have durability, but by this criterion how long must a car last to transcend its status as a consumer good and become a use-object?

The result of our questions seems to be that labor and work are ideal-typical extremes of a continuum which, as we move, in this order, from one to the other, decreases in privacy, necessity, repetitiveness, consumptive character, perishability, as well as in the intent for the product *not* to have these characteristics, or, to put it positively, which increases in public nature, spontaneity, beginning-and-end character, durability, as well as in the intent for the product to have *these* characteristics. In other words, labor and work are, in this view, not different in kind but different in the degree to which they possess not one but a number of characteristics [6].

Surely this is not what Arendt means. A reversal such as that from *homo faber* to *animal laborans* is not a quantitative affair. At least what Arendt wants to convey is the change in *kind* from one to the other, never mind the difficulties of formulation and demonstration that a more careful conceptual analysis might uncover. Hers is a practical, a rhetorical concern, and indeed, kind or quality is, above all, an inevitable category of practice. At this point (and we shall see others) Arendt's theory appears in the service of practice but much in need of clarification; she wants "to think what we are doing": the thinking and cognizing are for the sake of the doing.

ACTION.    Like work, action is public and spontaneous; like work, it has a beginning, but it has an end in a sense other than in which work has an end. Again, like work, it produces lasting things, its "stories," that correspond to work's use-objects. Although work is ended when its purpose is achieved, Arendt would probably admit that an action also has a terminal point, which is a feature of the empirical (though not the analytical) referent of Parsons' unit act [7]. This is quite irrelevant compared with the fact that action is boundless and unpredictable. It is difficult to understand the difference between these two attributes unless the first means infinitely interpretable. This reading is suggested as the result of juxtaposing the boundlessness of action with the idea that action, by virtue of being free and in this sense an absolute beginning (cf. p. 177 and n. 3), is part of a unique person who, being unique, cannot be exhaustively or definitively interpreted—cannot even tentatively be interpreted before his death, that is, before he ceases to act, before we have all his actions from which to make our stories. This reading, however, would make the story, or historiography, of any people not yet extinct impossible—not only that of mankind, as Arendt says. The death of a people, say, the Roman people, would, in turn, be a matter of interpretation: we might have no historiographies at all.

The meaning of boundlessness as infinite interpretability must not rest on the impossibility of historiography—after all, there *is* historiography—but on the initiatory character of action. I suggest that this character refers to the uniqueness of action, its sheer "thereness," to the total absence of the element of fabricating, making, working, purposing. To put it differently, action, like thinking, is the purest state of human elementarity we know of and for this reason we can "make" anything out of it, not just one thing—exactly as in thinking. The only difference between action and thought is what might be called externalization or objectification: action is externalized thought.

Arendt also calls action unpredictable, that is, it is unpredictable in both its occurrence and consequences. Let us take these two subjects of unpredictability in this order. Does the first mean that when a person does something that I predict he is not acting but, say, behaving? Does it mean that if he does something other than I predict he is acting? I predict that my friend will show up at noon. He does; hence, he does not act. He does not show up; hence he acts. This, of course, cannot be Arendt's meaning. Might it be that we have action when rather than any of the predictions we can entertain on the basis of our best knowledge something else happens? I can predict a number of things my friend might do other than show up; but he will have acted only if, instead of keeping his appointment with me, he does something I could not have predicted. This is tautologous; it merely says that the unpredictability of action means the unpredictability of action. Again this cannot be what Arendt means. Perhaps unpredictable does not mean not predictable at all but rather *that* in respect to which the question of predictability or unpredictability is irrelevant; that is, in action the dimension of predictability-unpredictability is overshadowed by another dimension: once more, by its uniqueness, "thereness," novelty, its initiatory character. The nature and location of the criterion of this characteristic remain to be worked out, but we shall see, on the basis of the fact that action presupposes plurality in a way that labor and work do not, that this criterion is located neither in the agent nor in the witness alone.

What about the unpredictability of the consequences of action? Because we do not know all causal laws, we cannot predict these consequences. For the same reason, however, we cannot predict the consequences of anything, including labor and work. Does Arendt mean that the regularity of labor and work eases their predictability and that the irregularity (if this term be permitted) of action makes its predictability more difficult? Probably not, for this again would be a quantitative matter to be discarded for the same reasons that we thought we had to discard it in distinguishing between labor and work. Here, too, we may surmise, the unpredictability of the consequences of action derives from its novelty: action brings something new into the world, something intrinsically unpredictable, not only difficult to predict. If predictable and unpredictable were understood as causal concepts, Arendt would probably mean not that action has no part in any causal matrix but that because of its novelty we can anticipate neither the emergence of its cause nor its effect. In this sense it is a miracle, as man as man of action himself is [8].

The counteragent of the boundlessness of action is that it can be forgiven; of its unpredictability that it can be hedged in by promise. The forgivableness of action raises problems in our interpretation of its boundlessness and unpredictability, for if these conditions are interpreted as infinity of interpretability and novelty, respectively, what then is to be forgiven about action? The unprecedented, unique, unforeseeable lies outside the realm of forgiving or not forgiving, which is the realm of ethics. It is at this point that we must remember plurality as the condition of action, and we realize that there *are* limits—precisely those set by plurality—to the uniqueness, the sheer "thereness" of action. Only when action exceeds these limits (recall that plurality is not society) does forgivability become a criterion applicable to it. Action then emerges, as it were, as an experiment in the ethical character of plurality such that, for instance, the prophet's action needs no forgiveness, although he transcends the ethics of plurality as grasped before his emergence, whereas a Raskolnikov does. It is clear that Arendt's conceptions of ethics, plurality, and action and their interrelations call for much more explicit treatment than she has given them.

In regard to the faculty to make and keep promises as the remedy for the unpredictability of action there is a related difficulty if we would preserve action's uniqueness, for contract, or the force of mutual promise, surely follows the means-end scheme and thus is more a case of making than of acting. Here, again, the way out of the apparent contradiction must lie in the fact that only *that* promised doing and not-doing is action which is limited, not by a purpose, by something to be achieved or avoided, but exclusively by the ethics of plurality as such.

Although this, too, obviously needs explication, it will be clear that the criterion of the uniqueness or novelty of action, that is, the question when a given activity is or is not action, lies *both* in the agent and his witness: this criterion itself is developed and applied by the plurality such as it exists at the moment when it confronts the activity. Thus it is a practical, and both a collective and a historical, criterion.

PUBLIC AND PRIVATE.    Action, we have heard, is public, whereas labor is private. Here, too, we must argue that both may appear to be matters of degree and of attitude. First, how public is "public," and how private is "private?" We do know from experience and observation of others in our own society and in other societies that here again there is a continuum that ranges between the poles of a completely public and a completely private character. This is true in either of the two senses of "public" that Arendt distinguishes—the adjective ("public" is what "can be seen and heard by everybody . . . by others as well as by ourselves," where the quantitative element is implied in the question *which* others and *which* ourselves) and the noun (the man-made world common to men, in which the quantitative element is implied in the question of *which* men, which how-brought-up men). The answer to the quantitative question is the attitude or intent of the doer, who wants his activity to be public or private within the limits that he intends to draw.

We can only repeat what we said after we brought out the quantitative and attitudinal character of work and labor. We did not think then that Arendt was engaged in an ideal-typical construction of a continuum but in persuading us of the reversal from work to labor, from *homo faber* to *animal laborans*. Similarly, now we think that she is concerned with driving home the emergence of the household as the organizing principle of society, the rise of the private to public recognition. Again the theory in the service of her practical concern needs clarification.

What about the identification of privacy with the household and with necessity? This may be an apt description of the *polis* but surely does not cover all meanings of privacy, notably the privacy of feeling [rather than only of feelings that issue into bodily activities, to which Arendt alludes (p. 73)], and of thinking [which she also mentions (p. 325)]. The necessity for labor as a condition of life (and vice versa) is one thing; the necessity of feeling by which one is overcome is quite another; the necessity of the thinking that is begun in freedom is different yet. Nevertheless, all three are private: my having to make a living is private, my love and hatred are private, my thinking is private. What makes us call these three things, all of which are necessary in three very different senses of the term, by one name, "private?" Surely only the first has anything to do with the household, and necessity has such different meanings for each of them that to take it as their common characteristic strikes me as playing with words. Private itself means something different in each of the three. In the first, it means, precisely, of no public concern, of no relevance to action or to history—a technical condition without which man can neither work nor act. In the second, it does not mean that man cannot work or act unless his bodily needs are met but that he cannot work or act unless he feels, that his feelings become of public concern only insofar as they become transformed into publicly inspectable works or deeds. Private in the first case refers to a necessary condition of work or deed but in the second only to a possible source. In the third, finally, private refers to that solitude in which man is least alone, for then he is most human, he is as close to being a representative of mankind as he can be. That we do apply the term private to all three—making a living, feeling, and thinking—suggests that we see man at once as an organism, as a potential maker, and as a member of mankind.

POLITICS AND POWER.    To be able to act demonstrates man's freedom. In our discussion of action we found it necessary to limit this freedom by the ethics of plurality. A further limitation is imposed by Arendt's locating the realm of freedom in politics, that is, by her tendency to equate action with political action (e.g., p. 220) [9]. Freedom in the sense of starting something new by virtue of one's birth (p. 177) and in the political sense of starting something new (by virtue of one's birth) in behalf of society surely is not the same thing; nor is it clear why man can act (the prerequisite for disclosing himself) only if he is with, rather than for or against, other men (p. 180). An unanalyzed infatuation with the *polis* or with an image of the *polis* may be at work here, but perhaps there is something of more than biographical interest, namely, the fact that, *polis* or no, man's freedom can be realized only in common with other men. This means that what has vaguely been called the ethics of plurality becomes explicated to some extent: it comes to mean that to act truly in freedom is to act for mankind's good. This, however, is difficult to reconcile with the discussion of the irreversibility of action (p. 220), its inevitable incurrence of guilt (pp. 223–235), and the attendant distinction between man's freedom and his nonsovereignty (pp. 234–235). In Arendt's conception of political action we have the desire for the demonstration of the continuity of mankind rather than the demonstration itself as we have it in the remembering of etymology [10], that is, in our speech and its history.

What is to be understood as political itself is not clear either. "The Latin usage of the word *societas*," Arendt writes (p. 23), "also originally had a clear though limited political meaning; it indicated an alliance between people for a specific purpose." She gives examples—*societas regni, societas sceleris*. Is it the character of what in contemporary sociology is often called an interest group that makes a group political or is it this character that makes it political in a limited sense? Surely, an interest group has a purpose and to achieve it uses certain means—all of which have the earmarks of making not of action. Perhaps the solution to the puzzle is that to the extent that the effect of the group's activities—to rule, to commit a crime, to do business—enters the surrounding plurality the group is political, even if its procedure is work rather than action. If so, it would have clarified matters if Arendt had made this argument explicit, although explication might not have validated it. At any rate, it would parallel our understanding of promise as action, despite its contractual, that is, means-end, character.

What keeps the public realm in existence, we are told, is power, the attribute of the man of action, but not of the maker, for whom his products, nor of the laborer, for whom life, is the highest good. Power, apparently, is engendered only by public action, by action publicly perceived, taken up, carried on, and transformed. Power is the power of freedom, of beginning, it would appear, and it is, as we saw, to an astonishing degree independent of material factors, either of numbers or means; it is a potentiality that can be actualized but not fully materialized (p. 200), and unlike force, Arendt says elsewhere [11], it grows rather than decreases if divided. Power, apparently, is the contagious humanness disclosed by action. There is nothing that man cannot do if the spirit moves him. Unfortunately, here again, the practical-rhetorical nature of Arendt's enterprise is indicated, among other things, by the imprecision of the concept. Applying it, as she does elsewhere, to the power of the federal government of the United States, which, she claims, is increased rather than diminished by the power of the states, she finds herself recommending that the matter of school segregation or desegregation be left in the private sphere, which, apparently, is meant to be championed by the states rather than nationally [12]. Such practice suffering from unclarified theory complements the withdrawal from practice that appears characteristic of much contemporary social science. If the latter shows what Arendt calls world alienation, perhaps the former betrays the desire for a world *à tout prix*—in her terms, it displays not so much power as violence.

SOCIETY AND BEHAVIOR. What are the social scientists' "societies" that existed before the rise of society and when was society formed? The two questions are interrelated; that is, the fact that Arendt does not propose a term to designate presociety "societies" is connected with her failure of clarity on the time period in which society itself emerged. We have heard that this happened in the modern age, with "the rise of the 'household' . . . or of economic activities to the public realm" (p. 33), when society replaced the family as the subject of the new life process (p. 256). Although society is a modern phenomenon, and the modern age began in the seventeenth century (p. 6), still Arendt speaks of the medieval "society of the faithful" (p. 31). Perhaps this is no contradiction but an easily corrected failure to explicate the beginnings and the history of society. If so, this failure, in turn, may have something to do with the importance Arendt gives to etymology. Is the historical and sociological significance of Livy's *societas regni*, of Cornelius Nepos' *societas sceleris*, of Aquinas' *societas* of risk-sharing investors, of the medieval society of the faithful, of Locke's society of property owners, of Hobbes' acquisitive society, of Marx's society of producers, of our society of jobholders, and of the totalitarian laboring society (p. 23, n. 3; p. 31) even comparable except in a distorted and misleading sense? Theoretically it is clear that a much more careful tracing of continuity and change is needed in which a terminology would accurately designate the results of the analysis. Perhaps even before that one would have to decide on what to call groupings (by one name, by many names?) that do *not* figure in this enterprise. Hence the interrelation between the vagueness concerning the rise of society and the failure to give presociety "societies" a name or names. It would also appear that Arendt has here succumbed to one of the dangers of etymology, namely, the tendency to assume that the same word means, if not the same thing, at least something related. The question of a defensible attitude toward etymology comes up in our consideration of what she has to say about values.

Similar observations must be made in respect to behavior, which, in society, as we have seen, replaces action. What other than laboring, working, acting, thinking, and contemplating does or can man do and what are the relations between his activities in the *vita activa* to whatever these other things may be? What were people engaged in (besides laboring, working, acting, thinking, and contemplating) before, with the rise of society, they started to behave? Both questions parallel one of those we raised about society itself, namely, that concerning the lack of nomenclature for presociety "societies," which corresponds to the lack of terms for both prebehavior "behavior" and human conduct other than that discussed. It is tedious to call attention once more to the practical nature of Arendt's undertaking—here to her desire to carry home the nature of our society, the nature of our behavior—and to her theoretical inadequacies.

Intrinsic to Arendt's observations on society, of course, are her observations on labor. Labor, we are told, is the only activity into which we can translate, and which corresponds to, the life process in our bodies that we know through introspection—hence (logically or psychologically and historically) the modern labor philosophies and their succession by the various philosophies of life (p. 117). Neither her argument nor experience shows that labor rather than thought (p. 325) is the only activity that corresponds to the introspectively perceived life process and the only activity into which we can translate this process. Is she not missing something to clinch her argument—a sociological rather than a psychological point? Might this point not be the distrust of thinking rather than the objective impossibility of discovering it through introspection (recall Descartes, otherwise so importantly drawn on by Arendt), which is relevant if we would account for the availability of life, and the fascination by it, in the various philosophies of life? In respect to labor philosophy might a quite different feature not be less intellectual than social and political, lying in the area, to use a Marxian term, of class struggle, of shifts in the relative claims and powers of labor and capital?

NATURE.   Arendt distinguishes between nature and the cosmos or universe (pp. 150, 268). Nature is not only that which is not man-made, for this also applies to the universe, but it is, most explicitly suggested by the equation of "terrestrial and 'natural' laws" (p. 268), the earth. Hence Arendt's distinction between natural and universal science, the former looking at nature—the earth or man's traditional habitat—from a universal standpoint, the latter importing cosmic processes into nature itself (*ibid.*). We have seen the considerations into which this distinction enters (VI, above) and thought it appropriate to record it explicitly rather than having to glean it from widely scattered passages in Arendt's book.

## *Practical*

The matters discussed in the section just concluded were theoretical, that is, largely questions of conceptual and, by implication, factual clarification. In our efforts to answer these questions we found ourselves led back, again and again, to Hannah Arendt's attitude and concern, which we have called predominantly practical and rhetorical. We have now come to a point in our preoccupation with her book at which we ourselves take a practical attitude, which focuses on what we must do—what we, as social scientists, must do.

Our focal points are behavior and action, value, the means-end scheme, and man's historicity and dualism.

BEHAVIOR AND ACTION. We have commented on some of the difficulties inherent in Arendt's use of these terms. Now we disregard these theoretical matters and instead consider the meanings of behavior and action as used by contemporary social scientists, on the one hand, and by Arendt, on the other. We have seen that Arendt holds behavior to be a historically specific term, which it is not in contemporary, nor for that matter in past, social science. There are other differences, however, between the two uses of these terms. A number of adjectives may serve to suggest them.

1. Noncommittal-committal. Social scientists do not commit themselves to pass judgment on the merits or demerits of man's activities which they call behavior and action, whereas Arendt does.

2. Operational-substantive. For them the terms are what their operational definitions stipulate; Arendt means to get at their nature.

3. Observational-participatory. The social scientists set up their definitions and observe the empirical referents of these definitions; Arendt's relation is more to behaving and active individuals with whom she is participating than with the behavior and action abstracted from them.

4. Theoretical-practical. For social science the terms are concepts in theory; for Arendt they refer to human fates.

5. Nonhuman-human. For social science behavior and action can be predicated of any item in the universe, even of concepts (not only of animals but of prices, rates, or telephones); the terms do not refer to exclusively human activities; hence the question concerning their place within a concept of man does not come up, whereas for Arendt it is central, no matter how implicit.

6. "Out-group—in-group." Social scientists are not members of a group of people or things that behave or act; Arendt is.

7. Extrasystemic-intrasystemic. Social scientists do not intend to conceptualize themselves and have the concepts thus obtained enter the system in which behavior and action are located; Arendt does.

8. External-existential. The terms refer to matters external to the social scientists; for Arendt, to characteristics of human existence, including her own.

9. Neutral-affective. These terms are affectively neutral, both intrinsically and regarding the social scientists' relation to them; the opposite is true in both respects of Arendt's use.

10. Scientific-humanistic. For social scientists behavior and action are abstracted from their apperception mass; for Arendt they are real and of real concern.

11. Non-normative—normative. In social science the referents of the terms lack any character of requirement or obligation; for Arendt they have such a character.

12. Systematic-historical. In social science the terms function not only in theories but in systematic theories (of man's social and psychological life); in Arendt the terms function in a concept, philosophy, or theory of history. They may also be called nomothetic and idiographic.

There is also, however, a difference between the distinctions that social science and Arendt make *between* behavior and action. If social scientists make one at all, it is in the form Max Weber gave it, for whom action was

> human behavior (no matter whether external or internal
> doing, failing to do, or suffering) if and insofar as the acting
> person or persons connect a subjective meaning with it [13].

which includes all but reflexive and other unconscious behavior under the category of action and within this category makes no contentual distinctions. What the two terms mean for Arendt, and consequently how she distinguishes between them, we saw in the preceding part of this section and in the last paragraph.

It is clear that as sociologists we have to make a decision about two competing concepts—we must reject or accept them both or accept the current or Arendt's use. I have gone to great lengths in assembling adjectives intended to show the differences between the two (many of these adjectives are synonyms or severally imply each other logically) in order to make the need for the decision more plausible. It is clear that most of the adjectives used to characterize the first of the two concepts of behavior and action mark it as scientific. To recognize this allows us to formulate the decision we have to make as that between being scientific-theoretical and not scientific but, say, practical, although the four options (accepting both, rejecting both, accepting the first, accepting the second) remain open. If we view social science, as I do [14], as both theoretical and practical, we must make our decision accordingly: we must choose the first option, that is, accept both conceptions.

This decision itself, however, changes their status, namely, from competitive to cooperative. The question now before us is, for what purpose, in what situation, must we use one or the other? The most immediate answer is that we use the theoretical concept for theoretical, the practical for practical, purposes. This answer needs a qualification that is entailed by our analysis of Arendt, who we found in her more practical orientation fell short on theoretical clarity, hence on scientific soundness. To reformulate our criticisms, even if in oversimplified fashion, Arendt's practical results would perhaps not have changed but would have been more persuasive or powerful if she had asked how far and in what ways theoretical weakness has influenced them. This observation illustrates the cooperative status of the components. As to the difference between behavior and action, which in social-scientific usage is, with some exceptions, comparatively unattended, we have been struck by the power of Arendt's propositions, despite their theoretical inadequacies. We must try to make up for them, although here, of course, we can only attempt to suggest the direction that improvement might take.

I propose to preserve the customary social-scientific use of behavior which answers a number of questions we asked about Arendt's application of the term. What Arendt calls behavior, then, might be qualified by an appropriate adjective, for example, administered, but before we can find one more accurate an inspection of the relevant literature on the difference between the behavior in "presociety societies" and contemporary society, and, depending on the outcome of such inspection, perhaps actual research, would seem indicated. To read the literature intelligently and engage in research, however, we must also be clear on Arendt's use of "society," which is the locus of her "behavior." Here I suggest something similar to the proposal concerning behavior itself: to preserve society in its social-scientific usage as the most general term to designate global human wholes and to refer to Arendt's society, once more, by a restrictive adjective, possibly the same as the one suggested for behavior, namely administered. As in that earlier case, however, corresponding preparatory inquiries are called for.

Action, because it has, on the whole, a hardly specific definitional status in social science (despite, of course, the antibehaviorist action theorists, notably Parsons), needs more conceptual work to become theoretically tenable. First, it must be distinguished precisely from behavior; then, when properly defined, Arendt's action must be further distinguished from it—whereas in the cases of behavior (as well as society) the first of these two steps had already been taken in social science itself.

Here it helps to recall Weber's typology of action (traditional, affective, purpose-rational, and value-rational). If we allow subjective meaning to be one of the requirements with which to distinguish action from behavior, then, strictly speaking, both traditional and affective action are not action but precisely behavior, as Weber himself admitted without, however, eliminating them from his typology [15]. We propose to speak, instead (conceptually or ideal-typically) of traditional and affective *behavior*. What is left of Weber's offerings are purpose-rational and value-rational actions. Let us ask ourselves—let everyone ask himself—when it is that we think we have acted. We shall probably find that we think we had either when we did something which at the time or in recall had more than customary meaning or when we did something that had what we considered, or have come to consider, important consequences—however we may define either meaning or consequences.

If this is correct, we have two quite different criteria of action: heightened meaning and important consequences. On the first criterion, for instance, I act when I think (in Arendt's sense of thinking), when I write a poem or perform a piece of music. We immediately have several, easily augmented kinds of action: thinking, artistic action, performing action, always provided, of course, that the first criterion is met. The feeling of particular meaningfulness may often be accompanied by a state of heightened consciousness or self-consciousness or the assignment of meaning may be accompanied by the recall of such consciousness. By the first criterion decisions that the agent considers especially meaningful are actions. On the second criterion, we have, perhaps more often than not, actions only in retrospective definition, and probably more often than not, we have chains of action or processes rather than single actions. Suppose a sociologist asks himself how he came to be one rather than something else he once planned to be: chances are that he will recall a number of things he did rather than any one, that one thing led to another, and that in his mind all together make up a sequence whose elements he may call actions, although none may have been particularly meaningful or a particularly meaningful decision (if he recalls any decisions at all).

Let the most generic term for behavior that is action by the first criterion (meaningfulness) be significant action. We have, almost at random, already listed several types (thinking, artistic action, and performing action). Let the most generic term for behavior that is action by the second criterion (important consequences) be consequential action.

Meaningfulness, clearly, is a subjective criterion. Again we can follow Weber's procedure [16] by introducing the distinction between analyzing *particular* cases that, if distinguished by heightened meaning felt or recalled about them, are actions and cases *typically* not so distinguished, which we therefore list under behavior. Thus the fact that yesterday Smith's piano practice was especially meaningful to him does not make American piano practicing an action, for, in reference to the United States (during a certain period), to practice the piano is for certain people (types of people) traditional, hence falls under the category of behavior. Similarly for consequential action. Aside from the fact that Harry's getting married was particularly meaningful for him, it is likely to have had considerable consequences for him, his bride, and perhaps others. Again this does not make marrying in the United States an action; in reference to the United States it is, once more, behavior.

We should note that, unlike meaningfulness, for whose presence or absence we have only the agent's word (although we can, within limits, check on his statement), important consequences is a criterion that can also be applied by the observer—most rigorously if it is understood in the causal sense of the term.

In short, whether certain behavior is an action depends on its intrinsic criteria, meaningfulness and consequences, as perceived by the agent, and on the social unit or period in reference to which the analyst considers it [17].

What about Arendt's action in the light of these suggestions? The element of special meaningfulness is contained in her associating action with freedom and disclosure. If we reconsider the unpredictability of her action, we discover still another dimension of this term (which caused us so much difficulty)—namely, that action is unpredictable in the sense that it may have important consequences. In our terms Arendt's action would appear to be such by virtue of its intrinsic properties—uniqueness, "thereness," initiatory character, novelty—just as our significant action is such by virtue of the intrinsic property of particular meaningfulness (rightly or wrongly located, as we said, by the agent himself).

When it comes to predicating this intrinsic property, there is an important difference between Arendt's action and our significant action. Our procedure is scientific or theoretical (in the sense of finding out what is the case), whereas for Arendt it is practical (in the sense of wanting to know what we must do in consequence of what we have found out). We must add that she has not told us the full story that made her try to persuade us that it is the intrinsic properties she discusses that transform behavior into action. Here we are led back to her theoretical insufficiency.

Within our framework we have to drop Arendt's properties of action and instead define, as the theoretical parallel to her action, the type that is characterized either by a maximum degree of meaningfulness, by maximum consequences, or both. The colloquial term "historical act" connotes both characteristics [18].

It is up to the interpreter to argue the term maximum. Theoretically the scientist reports what others have considered to be maximally meaningful and maximally consequential actions; practically, he arrives at his own commitment concerning them. In most instances most people, including scientists, cannot collect the scientific knowledge that would enable them to use it as a basis for commitment (they lack time, interest, energy, and competence); instead they use secondhand knowledge (obtained, for instance, from parents, teachers, or books).

VALUES.   The history of the term value and its occurrence in various contexts remains to be written. As far as I know the term originally meant exchange value, which is redundant for value, short and simple. The referents of the word have multiplied far beyond this clearly demarcated usage—conviction, norm, principle, standard, criterion, preference, rationalization, goal, aim, end, purpose, taste, things important, not indifferent, desired, desirable are surely not all of them. Such expressions as use values, intrinsic values, and ultimate values are self-contradictory. If my relation to an item is that of use, it is not that of exchange. Something intrinsically valuable is not valuable in relation to something else, and if something ultimate can be bartered for another ultimate neither of them is. To designate the many different things, not all of which have been mentioned, by the one term, value, suggests that they have something in common, precisely the element of exchangeability. Unawareness of this may account for the difficulty encountered by those more self-conscious users of the term who try to define it [19]. Such broad, relievingly broad, as it were, definitions as "any object of any interest" [20] or "a conception ... of the desirable" [21] homogenize not only all matters toward which one is not indifferent or which are desirable to one but also all ways in which something may be of interest or desirable. Finally, there is the ubiquitous use of the term and the difficulty, especially, it seems, for academic people, of getting along without it. All of this—the multiplicity and heterogeneity of referents, the vacuousness of definitions, and the compulsive character of the use—betrays the exchangeability element, the means element, in all things to which the term refers, whether we are aware of it or not. Values are difficult to distinguish from valuables.

This means-character accounts for what ever since Weber social scientists have called the irrationality of values, particularly when understood as ends. In this view a value or end has no intrinsic worth that can in any sense be rationally assessed, and all science can do, as Weber insisted, is to make clear that

> *If* you take such and such a stand, then, according to scientific experience, you have to use such and such a *means* in order to carry out your conviction practically [22].

In short, if you want X, you must pay Y for it, but X is only one of the many values available in the market, and I can tell you the price of each of them, but not which of them you ought to buy or sell. That is altogether your private business. The stand the person questioning the scientist takes is private; only the area of means, the commodities or exchange market, is public. It is a conversation between two brokers (a species of *homo faber*), the less experienced one asking, the more experienced one answering.

Max Weber was so experienced that he was tempted to consider a variety of progress, namely, technical progress, altogether outside the market, that is, to deny technical progress status as a value and to elevate it to that of fact [23]. Thus he held that if the historian of art means by progress in art the technical improvement of the materials the painter uses—canvas, pigments, and brushes—he does not cease to be a scientist; neither does he when he designates as progress the advent of perspectival drawing. The reason is that improved canvas, pigments, and brushes make painting more efficient; they are better means to an end. In perspectival composition the end in reference to which it constitutes progress is complexity of vision: to see perspectively adds depth to the previously available two-dimensional way.

Here, again, Weber is talking as *homo faber*, for whom the end of technology, that is, efficiency, is beyond analysis. Weber admittedly could not argue with another type of man for whom efficiency is not the end— say, a contemplative man, a man of action, or a poet. Weber did recommend that the term progress, even if it means technical progress, be dropped from the vocabulary of the scientist. He also recommended it for the wrong reason: in view of the great difficulty of being quite unambiguous about its purely technical meaning. The legitimate reason is that even this meaning does not transcend *homo faber*; hence the irrationality of his ends, including that of technical progress.

Our analysis of the term value suggests that what Weber in effect did was to warn social scientists not to be duped by the market. He allowed them to speculate there, of course, but only after hours, privately. In his own terms they must guard against values that parade as facts such as progress (other than technical), trends, and adaptation [24]. They were not to use these terms at all, but if there were any excuse for the use of progress it would be in its technical sense because there is universal agreement on *its* aim—efficiency. Thus Weber verged on getting into the market after all, both by applying an irrelevant criterion—universal agreement—to establish factual status and by declaring efficiency intrinsic to things [25].

The fact that social scientists should in recent years have gone all out for the study of values is quite in line with our analysis: they study what people in the market, as it were, what different kinds of people in different situations, are willing to pay for and how much they are willing to pay to get something else; value systems or value patterns are fashioned after economic or financial inventories and marketing habits [26]. The sociologist, like the market analyst, keeps himself entirely out of his own investigations; he studies other people's values, not his own. The reason is that the student's own values are scientifically irrelevant because they *are* private and irrational. Still, although the scientist does not intend to be part of the system he is studying but to remain external to it, purely theoretical and scientific, we have tried to show that he, along with the subjects he studies, is involved practically in a much larger system than he imagines, namely, the time in history in which he and they are located—the time that has given his activities meanings that he is not aware of and does not control.

What must we do? The first thing, I should think, would be to eliminate the term value from our vocabulary, except for its original meaning of exchange value. Second, whenever we are tempted to use the term we must ask ourselves what we mean, which might be one or more of the things already mentioned—convictions, norms, principles, and so on. Third, and in comparison the two preceding steps amount to no more than an imposed diet, we must change our concept of the world in which we live and practice our profession and recognize it as a common way of life of which we are part; that is, we must recognize, acknowledge, and act on our nature, hence our scientific enterprise, which is ineluctably both theoretical *and* practical.

We now raise the question about a "defensible attitude toward etymology that we anticipated. For in respect to the preceding discussion the objection may be lodged that it is beside the point, that in its contemporary usage value does not, of course, mean exchange value, and that everybody knows and understands it. The situation is the reverse of an aspect of that in which we analyzed behavior and action. There, among other things, we found that in one sense of their meaning both terms referred to the same phenomenon—what in Arendt's view is simply behavior. To call attention to it makes a plausible case for terminological revision—here, simplification. On the contrary, we now find that one term, value, stands for many different things and the need for advocating terminological revision, here, differentiation, would appear to be equally plausible. The objection anticipated is not based so much on theoretical as on practical argument. It urges—to continue its argument—that value is a term that has come to stay in our vocabulary and that no *theoretical* argument will ever be able to dislodge it, that our concern is unwarranted anyway because we have many other words that have changed their meanings, occasionally even into their opposites.

The question of a tenable attitude toward etymology raised by this argument is which one we should take toward linguistic change. The answer would seem to be that when we know of change and have an arguable interpretation of it we should act on this knowledge and interpretation. First, we should call attention to the change and its nature, as we see it; second, if, as in the case of values, the change reflects a trend we wish to control and alter, we should do so, rather than allowing it to victimize us. The minimum step in this procedure is to put our own terminology in order, hence to say more nearly what we mean, instead of what we don't know who means.

THE MEANS-END SCHEME. It is fair, if somewhat oversimplified, to say that the users of the means-end scheme in recent sociology—chiefly Max Weber and, developing him, Talcott Parsons [27]—do not focus on the question of its area of proper application and, particularly, nonapplication and nonapplicability. Rather it is a model to which to relate whatever action may be examined. Ends (other than as means to further ends) cannot be analyzed with its help; they fall outside its range of competence and in this sense are not subject to rational analysis. It should be noted that whatever modification of the scheme has been introduced by structural-functional analysis, notably in Parsons' own later writings, is no more than that, for the structural-functional analysis of ends changes them into means—means of maintaining, disturbing, and integrating the system in which they are located. In regard to the end of the system itself—typically it is its survival—it is an end cognate to the laborer-consumer's view of the world (or nonworld).

What those fascinated by the means-end scheme tend to forget is that, to repeat a quotation from Arendt,

> while only fabrication with its instrumentality is capable of building a world, this same world becomes as worthless as the employed material, a mere means for further ends, *if the standards which governed its coming into being are permitted to rule it after its establishment* (p. 156, italics added).

As she also puts it, utility is identified with meaningfulness; that is, meaningfulness is lost (cf. p. 158). *Homo faber*

> will judge every thing as though it belonged to the class . . . of use objects, so that, to follow Plato's own example, the wind will no longer be understood in its own right as a natural force but will be considered exclusively in accordance with human needs for warmth or refreshment—which, of course, means that the wind as something objectively given has been eliminated from human experience (p. 158).

It is clear that in the means-end scheme the wind figures only instrumentally or functionally. To this extent the scheme is authored by *homo faber*.

What happens as we move historically from *homo faber* to *animal laborans* is that to the former's lost understanding of meaning is added the latter's lost understanding even of instrumentality. Further,

> just as the implements and tools *homo faber* uses to erect the world become for the *animal laborans* the world itself, thus the meaningfulness of this world, which actually is beyond the reach of *homo faber*, becomes for him the paradoxical "end in itself" (p. 155).

The end in itself is the survival of the structural-functional system. In the society of *animal laborans* man labors in order to consume—regardless of how little and ever less he may have to labor. For him there is, strictly speaking, no longer any world, whether of durable things or of speech and stories; both work and action have disappeared, and necessity, the earmark of both labor and its counterpart, consumption, reigns more absolutely than it has ever before in history (cf. pp. 126–135, especially pp. 133–135).

Let us continue from here. We spoke of necessity once before, of its different referents when the term is used in connection with labor, with feelings, and with thinking. The meaning of instrumentality, of the means-end scheme, may receive new light once we realize that in relation to it necessity is located in the connection between means and end, this connection being causal and a causal connection being a necessary connection. As the man of action is free to act, so *homo faber* is free to make what he wants to; necessity enters once he has started fabrication. The *animal laborans*, on the other hand, is never free but always under the necessity to labor. Yet for man, the burden of necessity is relieved only by the freedom to choose necessity—in the activity of thinking and in creative action, the two are inseparably mixed. Hence the reports that thinking, or writing a poem, is at once the most glorious and the most gruelling experience.

It may be that the ascription of irrationality to value in contemporary social science, combined with the insistence on the means-end scheme, whether in the analysis of action or modified in structural-functional theory, wishes to preserve both freedom (in the irrationality of ends) and necessity (in the espousal of the means-end scheme). If so, however, the relation to both freedom and necessity is essentially a relation of consumption—to have one's cake and eat it, too. Once the means-end scheme is embraced as the most conspicuous avenue for exploring the world the sociological *homo faber*, forced as he is to espouse the idiosyncratic character of ends, transcends himself in the direction of *animal laborans*, and both meaningfulness and the instrumentality he celebrates are in danger of being lost to the necessity of labor.

MAN'S HISTORICITY AND DUALISM.   In *The Human Condition* Arendt shows in many instances how men have not so much penetrated, as having been penetrated by, their time and place. The question of man's historicity— the possibility of his transcending it and the nature and extent of this possibility—has, of course, been a major preoccupation of historicism, the sociology of knowledge, and, in a certain sense, cultural relativism. The new complexion this question takes on in Arendt's view gives it a new cogency. This view appears to be that we do not know the meaning of a story, of part or all of man's history, until it is over—but we must add that when it is over the question is not exclusively a matter of causal analysis but also one of interpretation, through which the end of the story reveals itself to us along with its meaning, as integral to this meaning. We must add this in view of Arendt's concept of action and our analysis of it as well as her discussion of the two major historical reversals she describes—the replacement of the *vita contemplativa* by fabrication, that is, one of the activities (that of *homo faber*) of the *vita activa* [28] and the replacement of *homo faber* by *animal laborans*. In fact, many of our preceding questions concerned the tenability of parts of her interpretation of Western man's history. Aside from these criticisms, however, to generalize from the two historical reversals as we did is another way of formulating her proposition that man is both free and nonsovereign, that is, not master of the meaning of what he is free to do.

Man is free within the world of necessity, but nonsovereign within the world of freedom. To realize this brings us closer to an answer to our question about the limits of man's historicity. Man is free to deal with the world to the extent that this world is characterized by necessity and he knows this. I am free to fell a tree, provided I have all that is necessary to do so (e.g., a keen axe and a strong body) and provided the infinite number of causal nexuses that result in the tree and its characteristics (e.g., its species, height, quality of timber) necessitate its falling under my axe. Furthermore, I am free to cut the tree down to the extent that the contract I made to do so is binding and thus enters the world of necessity (e.g., buying the land on which the tree stands, the purchasing contract containing no clause against tree feeling, or contracting with another person to cut the tree as a paid service or as a favor). On the other hand, I am not free to cut it down if I do so as a poacher because then I deny the world of social necessity, whether I try to escape or to change it (though not of natural necessity, as long as my body is strong and the axe keen). To generalize, I am free to act within that part of the world of necessity in which I find myself; let us call it the "relevant world of necessity." No matter how variable this world is—my private room in which I compose while having or not having a headache; the prison from which I try to escape; the mathematical problem that I am trying to work out; the necessary premises of my thought which set limits to it—it is always characterized by necessity.

I am neither sovereign within the world of freedom nor master of the meaning of what I am free to do. The important point here is not to confuse meaning with causal consequence [29], because causal consequence belongs in the world of necessity, and if I am not master of the consequences of my doing it is only because of insufficient knowledge of this world or insufficient interest in it. Meaning, on the other hand, belongs in the world of freedom and is uncontrollable, precisely, because not only I am free but all men are free, that is, free, within the limits of the world of necessity, to interpret and act on my actions in at least more than one way, for as soon as there is more than one way necessity no longer rules alone. How many ways there are is indeed codetermined by necessity, by all the causal nexuses, as in the case of the tree, that result in the particular persons that all the interpreter-actors are; but unlike trees, persons are also characterized by freedom, the freedom to raise questions, to imagine, to explore and try.

The historical moment is the conjuncture of the worlds of necessity and freedom at a given time. Our question concerning the limits of man's historicity can now be formulated as the question of the changing, as against permanent, nature of his freedom and his nonsovereignty. Both being characteristics of man, they are, in this sense, permanent. The question, therefore, is whether the *relevant* world of necessity within which he is free and the *relevant* world of freedom within which he is nonsovereign are, in turn, permanent or whether they change. Once we have formulated the question we see immediately that the relevant world of freedom is the world of freedom itself. Not being a world of necessity but of meaning, it is not located in space and time, as the world of necessity is; the world of freedom which enters the conjuncture of the historical moment as one of its two components does not change. Man is not only permanently nonsovereign, the very meaning of this nonsovereignty is permanent.

In other words, man's nonsovereignty is not subject to history; only his freedom is historical. The question regarding his historicity, therefore, is limited to that concerning the historicity of his freedom. It is subject to limitations from two sources, the relevant world of necessity and the world of freedom itself.

The relevant world of necessity is a source, in turn, of two kinds of limitation: those imposed by its own nature and those imposed by our ignorance of this nature. On the one hand, coal is such that we cannot eat it; on the other, we may not know its combustibility. In general, whenever we speak of beating our heads against a wall or use a similar expression, the chances are that we refer to the limitations imposed by the nature of things; when we speak of unexpected results, side effects, unanticipated consequences, and the like, chances are that we refer to the limitations imposed by our ignorance. Our freedom changes (i.e., increases) with our knowledge of the world of necessity which, insofar as it restricts us by virtue of our ignorance, decreases in relevance with our increasing knowledge. The nature of the world of necessity remains an ultimate source of limitations on our freedom, but its relevance depends on our knowledge. *Savoir est pouvoir* is qualified by the fact that both knowledge and strength are lodged in the world of necessity; it means "to know the necessary is to be able to find our bearings."

The world of freedom, of meaning, action, will, thought, and imagination, clearly is another source of limitations on our freedom. Examples are commands, intentions, decisions, and arrangements, made by other persons or by ourselves, which bind or hinder us, or our own beliefs, desires, ideologies, and prejudices; in short, large sections of our culture. The difference between our freedom *vis-à-vis* the world of necessity and our freedom *vis-à-vis* the world of freedom itself is the difference that results from the fact that the world of necessity is, precisely because it is not the world of freedom, nonhuman, whereas the world of freedom is human. Gravity we share with nature, and the necessities of our bodies with all organisms, but will, intent, and meaning are shared only with other men. *Vis-à-vis* necessity we can only accept (whether the necessary be a part of nature, like sunshine, or a man-made object, like a house), reject (escape a thunderstorm or fight a political régime), or know (sunshine and thunderstorm, house and political régime). *Vis-à-vis* freedom or, better, within the world of freedom, we can talk, think, act, persuade and be persuaded. Action and speech are closely akin and both are located in freedom, as we have already been told by Arendt.

Necessity and freedom, however, are mixed because man lives in the world of both, although, to repeat, only the latter is exclusively human. Determinisms of all kinds stress necessity or even deny freedom outright; some philosophies of life emphasize freedom. Although it seems incontrovertibly true that man is both free and limited by necessity—no matter how his situation has been formulated—the actual mixture of the two elements is subject to investigation in respect to individuals, groups, societies, and times. We have many proclamations on the subject but neither a scientific discipline nor even a program that is devoted to it. Yet myriad investigations exist in all disciplines, in the natural and social sciences and in the humanities which the enterprise could draw on; particularly important among them are efforts made in the sociology of knowledge [30].

To conclude, man's historicity is the changeability inherent in his freedom, which, with his unchangeable nonsovereignty, makes up his dual nature. Changeability inheres in his freedom because he lives in two worlds, those of necessity and freedom, and he is free to reduce the limitations from them with knowledge, acceptance, or rejection and thought, speech, or action. How he has done so in the past and may perhaps in the future, hence what is the nature of the relations between the two components of man and their relative weight, is the subject matter of a not yet existing science.

Our analysis of Arendt's *The Human Condition* has urged revisions that we must make as social scientists if we would clarify our practice, our place in the world, our attitude toward it, the nature of our chances to act in it—just as the failure to make such revisions would muddle our practice, giving theoretical sanction to our world alienation, to our point in history, exhibiting our time that we may have thought we were analyzing, and evincing, unbeknown to us, our loss of a common human world. These revisions would increase our freedom by shrinking the world of necessity relevant to us.

In line with our distinction of theory and practice which we stated at the beginning of this chapter and have maintained since (and which is related to that of freedom and nonsovereignty), we arranged our dealing with Arendt's book in theoretical and practical parts. In the part on theory we tried to signal some things, at least, that need determination. Many were matters of conceptual clarification, but some, as well as what we said at the very end of the part on practice just concluded, need little developing to appear in the form of areas (vast areas, to be sure) of research. I shall merely list them, in recapitulation, as the terminal point of our inquiry occasioned by Arendt's book.

1. Behavior in past societies and in contemporary society.

2. Past and contemporary societies analyzed in terms other than behavior.

3. History of the term value and its colloquial and academic uses.

4. Analysis of cybernetics, game theory, information and communication theory, operations research, and similar developments in contemporary social science in respect to elements of *homo faber* and *animal laborans* operative in them.

5. The nature and historically changing relative weights of freedom and necessity in man (this suggests the beginnings of a new science).

### NOTES

1. Hannah Arendt, *The Human Condition* (Chicago: University of Chicago Press), 1958. Figures in parentheses refer to pages of this book. An earlier version of this paper was developed in connection with a seminar on "The Means-End Scheme in Contemporary Sociology and Its Relation to an Analysis of Nonviolence," conducted at the Institute for Social Research, Oslo, August 1959; for helpful suggestions I am indebted to members of this seminar, particularly to Gene Sharp. An earlier version of the first part was presented at the annual meeting of the American Catholic Sociological Society, Notre Dame University, December 1958.

2. Personal communication from Hannah Arendt. *Vita Activa* is the title of the German edition of the book (Stuttgart: Kohlhammer, 1960).

3. In support of this point Arendt discusses the Latin, English, Greek, French, and German words for labor (pp. 48, n. 39; cf. 80, 81, n. 5; 101).

4. The beginning of such an examination has been made by Ralph Ross and

John W. Bennett in their respective reviews of the book in *The New Leader*, September 29, 1958, and *American Anthropologist*, August 1959.

5.  Arendt herself illustrates this with the case of the hermit (p. 22).

6.  The difficulties inherent in the logic of ideal-types have been well known, at least since Max Weber. See a recent essay, with bibliography, by Don Martindale: "Sociological Theory and the Ideal Type," in Llewellyn Gross, ed., *Symposium on Sociological Theory* (Evanston, Ill.: Row, Peterson, 1959), pp. 57–91.

7.  Talcott Parsons, *The Structure of Social Action* (New York; McGraw-Hill, 1937), pp. 733, 740 (henceforth *Structure*).

8.  On Arendt's conception of "miracle" (*Wunder*), see her "Freiheit und Politik," *Die neue Rundschau*, **69**, 4 (1958), 1–25, especially 20–22.

9.  More centrally and in more detailed and explicit argument in her article on freedom and politics, *ibid.*

10.  As in the remarks on the etymologies of *zöon politikon* versus *animal socialis* (p. 23), society (p. 23, n. 3), labor (referred to before), *polis*-"law"-city (pp. 63–64 and n. 65), *homo faber* (p. 136 and n. 1), object (p. 137, n. 2), nature (p. 150), action-beginning (referred to before), and power (p. 200).

11.  Hannah Arendt, "Reflections on Little Rock" *Dissent*, **6** (Winter 1959), 54.

12.  *Ibid*, 54–56.

13.  Max Weber, *Wirtschaft und Gesellschaft* [Tübingen: J. C. B. Mohr (Paul Siebeck), 1925], p. 1 (henceforth *WuG*); cf. *The Theory of Social and Economic Organization*, translated by A. M. Henderson and Talcott Parsons, Ed., with an introduction by Talcott Parsons (New York: Oxford University Press, 1947), p. 88 (henceforth *Theory*).

14.  Space limitations prevent me from doing more in support of this view than to refer to a paper in which I attempt to argue it: "The Sociology of Knowledge and Sociological Theory," in Llewellyn Gross, Ed., *op. cit.*, pp. 567–602 [Chapter 29].

15.  Cf. *WuG*, pp. 12–13; *Theory*, pp. 116–118.

16.  Developed in his comments on understanding; cf. *WuG*, p. 4, *Theory*, p. 96.

17.  The second point similarly applies to the question whether an event constitutes change. The birth of a child is almost certain to be so considered by the members of the child's immediate family, but it is not if, instead of the family, their country is the social unit in reference to which the event is assessed [cf. Chapter 5].

18.  It should also be noted that "*Wertheziehung*" and causal efficacy, the two predicates either of which determines a historical unit for Max Weber, are intimately related, respectively, to our meaningfulness and consequences; cf. Weber, "Critical Studies in the Logic of the Cultural Sciences" (1905), in *On the Methodology of the Social Sciences*, translated and edited by Edward A. Shils and Henry A. Finch (Glencoe, Ill.: Free Press, 1949), especially p. 59 (henceforth *Methodology*).

19.  See, for example, Ray Lepley, Ed., *Values: A Cooperative Inquiry* (New York: Columbia University Press, 1949), which contains the essays of 13 philosophers. A reading of this volume pointedly shows the divergence of opinion even among scholars of somewhat the same school of thought. The editor remarks, with a note of defeat, in his preface: "At one stage of the inquiry it was hoped that agreement might be reached upon a common glossary of fundamental value terms . . ." (Louis A. Ryan, O. P., *Value Judgments in Selected American Introductory Sociology Textbooks, 1947–1950*, Ph.D. dissertation, Ohio State University, 1957, p. 11, n. 5).

20.  Abraham Edel, "The Concept of Levels in Social Theory," in Llewellyn Gross, *op. cit.,* p. 189 (paraphrasing R. B. Perry).

21.  Clyde Kluckhohn and others, "Values and Value-Orientations in the Theory of Action," in Talcott Parsons and Edward A. Shils, Eds., *Toward a General Theory of Action* (Cambridge: Harvard University Press, 1951), p. 395.

22.  Max Weber, "Science as a Vocation" (1918), in *From Max Weber: Essays in Sociology,* translated and edited and with an introduction by H. H. Gerth and C. Wright Mills (London: Kegan Paul, Trench, Trubner, 1947), p. 151.

23.  Max Weber, "The Meaning of 'Ethical Neutrality' in Sociology and Economics" (1913–1917), *Methodology,* p. 38.

24.  *Ibid.,* pp. 22–27.

25.  See also "The Means-End Scheme" below.

26.  More recent developments in social science, especially cybernetics, game theory, information and communication theory, and operations research, need study in this connection. Note such pivotal terms as input-output, feedback, and strategies, all of which are taken from economics and engineering, the realms of various types of *homo faber*.

27.  For minimal references cf. *WuG,* pp. 12–13 *(Theory,* pp. 116–118); *Structure,* pp. 648, 733. For a less technical textbook presentation see Kingsley Davis, *Human Society* (New York: Macmillan, 1949), pp. 120–146.

28.  We have not discussed this first reversal in this paper; on the history of contemplation consult *The Human Condition,* index under "Contemplation," and especially pp. 14–17, 20–21, 291, 301–302.

29.  This is a distinction Weber took great pains to clarify; cf. *Methodology,* especially p. 158.

30.  Cf. Kurt H. Wolff, "A Preliminary Inquiry into the Sociology of Knowledge from the Standpoint of the Study of Man," *Scritti di Sociologia e politica in onore di Luigi Sturzo* (Bologna: Nicola Zanichelli, 1953), Vol. III, pp. 585–618 [Chapter 28]; "The Sociology of Knowledge and Sociological Theory," *loc. cit.*

---

Reprinted from *Inquiry,* **4** (1961), 67–106, published by Universitets-forlaget, Oslo, by permission of the publisher. The essay has been edited and partially revised by the author.

# 15

# BEFORE AND AFTER SOCIOLOGY. 1956

"Before and after sociology" [1] is a phrase that veils complex relations among the referents of its four words. In addition, each of the referents has more than one meaning. In part because of this complexity, the title of this chapter may, in retrospect, appear to have almost the character of a pun—almost—because, more than a play on words, it is the announcement of the arguments to be developed, even though only to a modest extent. They cannot be fully elaborated in any of their numerous ramifications.

## BEFORE SOCIOLOGY: SURRENDER

"Before" refers, first, to the prescientific phase of the process in which the student of sociology [2] engages in making a study. In this sense before is processual, not historical nor even temporal.

When beginning a study, it is possible to suspend the preconceived notions concerning subject matter, method, and theory that one has acquired in one's special education and throughout one's life. The extent to which such a divestment is possible is theoretically limited, but practically and psychologically it is so considerable that it may involve the most profound change in oneself, one's study, and one's philosophy of study. The occasion on which received notions are shed and, perhaps, subsequently questioned, modified, or replaced is not, of course, necessarily the embarkation on a particular study but may present itself at any time as a "total experience." Total experiences

> claim the whole being of the person and . . . change it. They
> have been described in the fiction, religious literature, poetry,

and philosophy of many periods and cultures; terms like "conversion," "transformation," "enchantment," and "mystical
union" are among those that hint at them. But . . . empirical
instances, no matter which, can be argued: "All that can be
proved can also be disputed. Only the unprovable is indisputable." [3]

The reader may have had such "total experiences" while listening to music or a speech, while seeing a play or movie, in
contact with an idea, a landscape, a book, a painting, a person,
a face, a body, in love, or in another "extreme situation,"
perhaps in a concentration camp; or caught, "confused," by a
profound moral, religious, or esthetic moment. These are only
examples, however, of "total experiences," which at the same
time call to mind some of the occasions on which we have
many reports that such "total experiences" occur—the occasions cannot be exhausted, since "the wind bloweth where it
listeth." . . . as the word "total" suggests, the totality of such
experiences also contains everything negative, such as uncertainty, danger, evil, death; and to appreciate this fact is to
have a realistic conception of "total experience"—of the kind
of experience which only man can have . . . and hence to
appreciate it, is to be man in the full sense of the word. . . .
Die so you may live; perish so you may be born; despair so
you may be able to hope. Although this dialectic, from the
negative to the positive, can be expressed in many ways, essential to it is the unreserved readiness to come face to face with
the extreme negative; for otherwise the dialectical process could
not be completed since the positive would not be possible. . . .
causes or contents (including ideas) which vitiate such "surrender" by their presence, in however various ways this presence may make itself felt—such ideas, such causes or contents,
are "not true." The implication, of course, is that under
other conditions they *can* be true: namely, when they exist,
not *against* the surrender, but *because* of it, when they are the
"catch" in consequence of the surrender, when they are "come
upon," "come into," "invented." [4].

These quotations place us, as it were, at the starting point of a number
of roads that may be followed, a number that must remain unspecified
because only one of them has been marked out by the intent of this
essay, the one that leads to the relevance of surrender as a prescientific
phase in the student's preoccupation with his study. On this road the
idea of surrender appears important as suggesting a conception of sociology in which this idea is incorporated as an attitude toward a projected

study, toward projected studies. This attitude is characterized by the faith that study is possible but must be attempted without the received tools—postulates, assumptions, concepts, theories—that are designed to aid in studies "of this kind," whatever the kind may be; that is, in consequence of surrender—both the experience and the concept—a projected study is conceived to be not "of a kind" or "general" but unique [5]. Existing tools of study therefore must withstand the surrender, must be tested by it, and out of it emerge either legitimated by reinvention or modified, replaced, or discarded.

The function of surrender in the process of scientific inquiry, then, is that of a crucible for the tools of an inquiry "of this kind." Having passed this crucial stage, the inquiry proceeds with the help of such tools, and from a logical and methodological standpoint it proceeds as it would without antecedent surrender [6]. Surrender has no implications for science as a method but only for the scientist's conception of the function of science, for his selection of studies, and for his interpretation of findings [7].


## BEFORE SOCIOLOGY: CREATIVITY AND SOCIAL SCIENTISM


A second meaning of "before" is pretheoretical, and in this second sense it *is* historical [8]. Unlike its first meaning, it refers to a particular [9], though powerful, kind of sociology, the predominantly American, positivistic, scientistic, administrative yet "value-free" kind.

A social-scientific investigation was the occasion on which the ideas of surrender and related notions and attendant procedures were originally developed and fused into a complex that has tentatively been called the study of man. As the preceding section of this chapter must have suggested, the study of man is critical of the concept of sociology that prevails, at least in the United States, today. It is especially critical of the image of man [10] implied by it, and it proposes a different concept and a different image of man [11]. To associate the prevailing sociology with smugness, false security or false certainty, ritualism or ceremonialism, routinization, the elaboration of the status quo, conservatism, group idolatry or group tyranny is to suggest some of the different but interrelated lines of argument along which this critique can be developed. One of the crucial features at which it is directed is the pretheoretical, that is, the not yet theoretical, character of this sociology—a feature it shares with the study of man.

In what sense are the prevailing sociology and the study of man (which was developed, also, in reaction to that sociology) not theoretical? The study of man is not, in the sense that the inquiries that follow its approach are not directed by a theory but, on the contrary, suspend theory (though in order to develop, in their own course, a more viable one). How can contemporary American sociology, which devotes so much attention to theory—notably and, in a certain sense, uniquely on the part of Talcott Parsons—be said not to be theoretical? The answer is because it lacks inspiration by a historical theory of society [12]. In the view that both the study of man and the prevailing sociology are not theoretical only for the time being, that their nontheoretical character is transitory or historical, they may be called pretheoretical.

They are pretheoretical in the same sense in which two other contemporary phenomena are pretheoretical. These two phenomena, which are otherwise very different, even contradictory, are interest in creativity and the practice of social scientism. The former is related to the study of man, the latter, to the predominant sociology. Interest in creativity—overwhelmingly manifested outside sociology—is an element in pragmatism and in progressive education but ranges all the way to sheer cult [13]; it also connects with important aspects of existentialism (especially Martin Heidegger), phenomenology (especially Max Scheler), and with neo-Freudian developments [14]. Scientism, an element in contemporary sociology, may be defined as "the unempirical faith that science can give us a complete philosophy for all our human needs," [15] as an "approach which, before it has considered its subject [human life], claims to know what is the most appropriate way of investigating it," [16] or as marked

> by three principal dogmas: (1) the assumption that the mathematized science of natural phenomena is a model science to which all other sciences ought to conform; (2) that all realms of being are accessible to the methods of the sciences of phenomena; and (3) that all reality which is not accessible to sciences of phenomena is either irrelevant or, in the more radical form of the dogma, illusionary [17].

Both creativity and social scientism may also be characterized by their common function of vicarious attempts at coming to terms with the defects of contemporary society and with the more or less inarticulate discontent over the state of this society. Both lack one of the bases of a corresponding realistic attempt: a theory of this society or, at least, the continuous consciousness of the relevance of such a theory.

An essential feature of the emphasis on creativity is the opposition to the compulsory (and often compulsive) closure of exploration that is practiced and would be imposed by scientism [18]. By its very intent, however, such emphasis on creativity ignores historical and sociological analysis. One of its functions is that of an escape from the very reality in protest against which it came into being. Preoccupation with creativity, indeed, is politically harmless, hence can be tolerated, even utilized, by any political system.

The escapist character of social scientism can best be introduced by a moment's consideration of natural science. Natural science is an asset to the material power and welfare of any society. The destructive application of nuclear physics, however, has called the attention of many people, foremost the physicists themselves [19], to the fact that nobody, neither the physicists nor the social scientists, has been prepared to handle the problems attendant on this application. The natural scientists have not because natural science is understood to be a specialty whose practice does not include action following from responsibility for the implications and consequences of this practice; the social scientists have not because their severe schooling in the avoidance of value judgments has been all too successful. This avoidance of value judgments is one feature of social scientism. It renders the social science that practices it politically as harmless, hence as tolerable and exploitable, as the preoccupation with creativity. Such social science is pretheoretical because it has not yet seen the need for a theory that could serve at least to defend it; and the interest in creativity is pretheoretical because it has not yet found the need for a theory of a society that would be commensurate with creativity.

### AFTER SOCIOLOGY: A POLITICALLY AND SOCIOLOGICALLY ADEQUATE SOCIOLOGY

In abandoning its concern with a historical theory of Western society in which sociology exists, sociology has become historically untrue to itself:

> Sociology [20] arose in the seventeenth century in opposition to the inextricable mixture of ethical and legal principles in the doctrine of Natural Law. This expression of an *empirical* attitude was an attempt, ultimately successful in certain respects, to distinguish between important elements of social behavior and outlook characteristic of Western society. The preoccupation with Western society constitutes the major unifying theme for problem, research, and theory of sociology throughout its history. It is reflected in many otherwise heterogeneous instances: in Hobbes' psychological approach to European politics; in Montesquieu's "structural-functional" examination of laws; in Comte's "positivism" set against the "negative" lingering-on of the French Revolution; in Spencer's elaborate doctrine of progress with its apologia for Victorian England; in Marx's concern with the redemption

of industrial society; in Weber's puzzlement over its essential features—capitalism, rationalization, bureaucracy; or in the involvement of American sociology with "social problems" such as racism, immigration, and urbanization.

The rise of "scientific sociology" in the present century . . . has modified somewhat this major concern with the West. Emphasis has shifted toward general laws of social relationships, processes, and forms, and away from involvement with the nature of Western society . . . [But] the injection of "science" contains an element of disguise and confusion: while professing to search for general laws, the sociologist continues indulging his concern with his own society, but as a "scientist" does not admit it. The positivistic phase of sociology thus belies the historical mission of the field: an *empirical* analysis of the nature and future of the Western world [21].

The pivotal concept, which has a specific though widely held and little analyzed meaning, is empirical [22]. Let one question about it be settled: let the term refer to attitude rather than subject matter. Let us speak of an empirical attitude without raising the issue of the empirical or non-empirical character of the world that is to be investigated. Essential among the various characteristics of the empirical attitude is its detachment from subject matter. Even if the subject matter relates to feelings, involvements, passions, or decisions, the social scientist's attitude remains that of the observer of what is external to him. He does not look at his subject matter to find out how he is and how we, his readers, are and, in one process, should be. He has learned to separate the Is from the Ought, although he is not always sophisticated enough to avoid the naturalistic fallacy and consequently is worried by the impossibility of deriving values from facts.

This specific separation of Is and Ought has its direct bearing on the problem of values which today is of so much concern to so many social scientists. It parallels that in creativity and the practice of social scientism. It, too, is a vicarious attempt at coming to terms with the defects of contemporary society; the means is attention to what is presumed to be above and beyond the sphere of these defects. But the values to which the attention is directed are merely a nobler edition of the commercialism that the persons interested in them often complain of so bitterly. If one function of the emphasis on creativity is escape from the reality in protest against which the interest arose and one function of social scientism is service of the status quo under a banner of high prestige which obscures this service, then one function of the preoccupation with values is the glorification of the existing value structure by elevated discourse on the nature of man.

The best-known and probably most influential single insistence on freedom from value judgments in social science—Max Weber's—actually was launched from a platform built of nonempirical certainty. Note this passage:

> . . . the identification of *ethical imperatives* with *"cultural values,"* even the highest of them, must be rejected. For there may be positions for which cultural values are "obligatory" even if they are in inevitable and insoluble conflict with every kind of ethic. And inversely . . . [23].

Merely consider Weber's distinction between ethical imperatives and cultural values, as well as his failure to draw any consequences that this distinction has for the attitude of the social scientist. Weber must have assumed uncritically that everybody understood what he meant by (universal or at least Western) ethical imperatives and that everybody could distinguish them, as a matter of course, from (in some sense relative) cultural values. Weber was not a mere observer of these ethical imperatives. Yet, unaware of the relevance that his unquestioned conviction of their existence and truth had for his concept of sociology, he could afford the luxury of advocating that this sociology be value-free [24].

A politically and sociologically adequate sociology is not a sociology that would proclaim particular values. This would be salesmanship, even less dignified than the veiled support of the status quo or the reflection or incorporation of its practices. Instead this chapter, itself, is an attempt to show the kind of *concern* that may lead to the conception of a sociology that is more adequate than those discussed. It points in the direction in which an effort toward a historical theory of our society may be made. Along the road in this direction lie the attempt at self-awareness and awareness of the past and present place of sociology in society, so that the ground for investigation and argument may become more solid, and the attempt at finding points from which a view of this society may be gained that shows it in its inseparable fusion of Is and Ought, hence makes the viewer not merely an observer but, inseparably from it, both a Socratic arguer and a critic whoc an say no and (probably more rarely) yes [25]. On such an unempirical, but actually more truly empirical, basis, he proceeds with his scientific investigations.

## CONCLUSIONS

I conclude by restating some of the major points made in this essay and drawing some consequences.

Neither the fascination of creativity for those who are tired or who despair of scientism nor the fascination of science for those whose loneliness has not been dispersed by the preoccupation with their own creativity (nor, for that matter, the hope that the study of values may transcend the realm of valuables) keeps its promise of eliminating their malaise and discontent because malaise and discontent cannot be eliminated by adopting a soothing stance but only by changing the society that produces them because they are part of it. One way—for the sociologist, *the* way—of changing this society is to prepare to change it (and thus actually to contribute, however small the degree, to changing it) by studying this society as it *is*—but "is" in the full sense of the word, which includes "is" ethically and politically. This would make his subject matter and his attitude, if it is commensurate with his subject matter, empirical in a truer than the positivistic sense. This attitude must be informed by the desire to get hold of the nature of the society in which he lives, and if he can argue its good, rather than its defective features, still as a sociologist he can do so only to the extent that he implements his desire by exploration [27]. A concrete beginning might be the question: What is important to investigate? This immediately leads to an unaccustomed seriousness and introduces unaccustomed concerns.

In the diagnosis of sociology presented sociology emerges as uneasily plodding between the dimly perceived and vaguely outlined creativity and its related philosophies (as well as value philosophy) on one side and the much closer service of the world "as is" (a *real* pun) on the other. In contemplating this vision, these propositions are formed:

1. The situation of sociology just suggested is a historical situation.
2. It can be overcome by being recognized.
3. One hope, or the hope, of approximating this recognition lies in the effort toward a historical theory of society (on which only some remarks could be made in this chapter).
4. Only by embarking on such an effort can sociology become politically and sociologically adequate.
5. No matter how far we may be from the theory envisaged we should know that a politically naïve sociologist is, at this point in history, a contradiction in terms.

### NOTES

1. I am deeply indebted to Miss Josephine L. Burroughs and Professors Herbert Marcuse and Alfred Schutz for critical readings of an earlier draft of this chapter and for their pertinent suggestions.

2. The following pages show, by implication, that this applies as well to students of other subjects.

3. Georg Simmel, *Fragmente und Aufsätze* (edited by Gertrud Kantorowicz), Munich, 1923, p. 4; quoted in *The Sociology of Georg Simmel*, p. xx.

4. Kurt H. Wolff, *Loma Culture Change: An Introduction to the Study of Man*, Columbus, Ohio (Ohio State University; mimeographed), 1952, pp. 22, 23–24, 25.

5. Kurt H. Wolff, "The Unique and the General: Toward a Philosophy of Sociology," *Philosophy of Science*, **15** (1948), 192–210 [Chapter 27].

6. Perhaps it need not be emphasized that the discussion of surrender by no means covers all prescientific phases of study but only one possible one. On the other hand, it should be re-emphasized that, in turn, the prescientific relevance of surrender is not at all its only one. Other implications of the idea of surrender are ontological, epistemological, moral, and therapeutic. (Some of them are treated in the introduction to the previously quoted *Loma Culture Change*.) To act as if surrender were exhausted by its prescientific function—especially to say that it is a conceptualization or formulation of the muddle that precedes the stage of clear-aimed, well-structured investigation—is to render it harmless by incorporating it, as an interesting addition, into the inventory of received notions; it is to rob it of its critical character and its power.

7. This is a second meaning of prescientific. The position sketched—no more than sketched—thus is not in conflict but in agreement with the phenomenologist concept of the scientific (as against the natural) attitude. Cf. Alfred Schutz, "On Multiple Realities," *Philosophy and Phenomenological Research*, **5** (1945), 533–576, especially 563–575, and "Common-Sense and Scientific Interpretation of Human Action," *ibid.*, **14** (1953), 1–38: also Kurt H. Wolff, "The Sociology of Knowledge: Emphasis on an Empirical Attitude," *Philosophy of Science*, **10** (1943), 104–123, especially 114–116, 118 [Chapter 26].

8. At least in the sense most relevant here. In another sense it is biographical; in still another, processual. This is one of the many matters, however, that cannot be developed in this chapter.

9. It also applies (though it will remain hardly more than an implication) to the other social sciences and even to aspects of the humanities.

10. Cf. Albert Salomon, "Prophets, Priests, and Social Scientists," *Commentary* (June 1949), and Reinhard Bendix, "The Image of Man in the Social Sciences," *ibid.* (February 1951).

11. Cf. Wolff, *Loma Culture Change, op. cit.*, pp. 29–30, 40–41.

12. It will become clearer later on what is meant by this theory, which inspired the work of most earlier sociologists, whether Comte or Marx, Spencer or Durkheim. In the form of the depoliticalized and—in this sense at least—dehistoricized concept of culture it still characterizes cultural anthropology. On various problems touched on here, cf. Herbert Marcuse, *Reason and Revolution* (1941) (New York: Humanities Press, 1954); Reinhard Bendix, *Social*

*Science and the Distrust of Reason* (Berkeley: University of California Press, 1951); Albert Salomon, *The Tyranny of Progress* (New York: Noonday Press, 1955), many articles in the *Zeitschrift für Sozialforschung* (later *Studies in Philosophy and Social Science*), 1932–1941; C. Wright Mills, "I.B.M. plus Reality plus Humanism Equals Sociology," *Saturday Review of Literature*, **37** (1953), 22–23; John W. Bennett and Kurt H. Wolff, "Toward Communication between Sociology and Anthropology," in William L. Thomas, Jr., Ed., *Yearbook of Anthropology—1955* (New York: Wenner-Gren Foundation for Anthropological Research, 1955), pp. 329–351 [reprinted in Thomas, Ed., *Current Anthropology* (Chicago: University of Chicago Press, 1956), same pagination].

13. There are the creative adult, creative camping, capitalism, chemistry, demobilization, education, experience, expression, freedom, intelligence, knowledge, man, mind, moments, personality, power, re-education, society, spirit, theater, unconscious, will, writing, and youth—among others. From the title catalog of Widener Library, Harvard University.

14. Cf. Max Horkheimer, *Eclipse of Reason* (New York: Oxford University Press, 1947); Max Horkheimer and Theodor W. Adorno, *Dialektik der Aufklärung* (Amsterdam: Querido, 1947); Theodor W. Adorno, *Minima Moralia* (Berlin: Suhrkamp, 1951); Herbert Marcuse, "The Social Implications of Freudian 'Revisionism,' " *Dissent*, **2** (1955), 221–240.

15. Eliseo Vivas, *The Moral Life and the Ethical Life* (Chicago: University of Chicago Press, 1950), p. 19.

16. F. A. Hayek, *The Counter-Revolution of Science* (Glencoe, Ill.: Free Press, 1952), p. 16.

17. Eric Voeglin, "The Origins of Scientism," *Social Research*, **15** (1948), 462–463. The phenomenologist stress on the scientific as one among other attitudes constitutes another criticism of scientism. See the papers by Alfred Schutz cited in n. 7; also Alfred Schutz, "Concept and Theory Formation in the Social Sciences," *Journal of Philosophy*, **51** (1954), 257–273. For a critique of what in the context of this paper is the scientistic nature of contemporary social science, especially sociology, see also George Simpson, *Science as Morality* (Yellow Springs, Ohio: American Humanist Association, 1953), Chapters I and III.

18. "Obscurantism is the refusal to speculate freely on the limitations of traditional methods. It is more than that: it is the negation of the importance of such speculation, the insistence on incidental dangers. . . . The obscurantists of any generation are in the main constituted by the greater part of the practitioners of the dominant methodology. Today, scientific methods are predominant, and scientists are the obscurantists." Alfred North Whitehead, *The Function of Reason* (Princeton: Princeton University Press, 1929), pp. 34–35. "Scientists" in the last sentence should perhaps be replaced by "scientificists."

19. See editorials and articles in the *Bulletin of the Atomic Scientists*, 1945 ff.

20. Cf. Albert Salomon, *History of Sociology, Abstracts* (n.p., n.d.; mimeographed), Abstract I, p. 1; Karl Mannheim, "The Problem of a Sociology of Knowledge" (1925), in his *Essays on the Sociology of Knowledge*, Paul Kecske-

meti, Ed. (New York: Oxford University Press, 1952), pp. 139 ff. [reprinted in *From Karl Mannheim*, pp. 64 ff.].

21. Bennett and Wolff, *op. cit.*, p. 330. Italics added.

22. Social scientists, especially cultural anthropologists, know that the empirical, in its nontechnical meaning of profane (as against sacred), practical, or common sense, and the like, varies widely in its application, though by no means without limits. The technical meaning of the term emerged relatively late in the history of Western science and philosophy [cf. George de Santillana and Edgar Zilsel, *The Development of Rationalism and Empiricism* (Chicago: University of Chicago Press, 1941)]. Here we are interested in what by comparison is a much more minute problem: the changes in the meaning of empirical in modern social science as not only proclaimed in methodological writings but also exhibited in empirical studies (cf. n. 24). To my knowledge this analysis has yet to be undertaken. (It goes without saying that it cannot be done in the present chapter.)

23. Max Weber, "Der Sinn der 'Wertfreiheit' der soziologischen und ökonomischen Wissenschaften" (1913–1917), in his *Gesammelte Aufsätze zur Wissenschaftslehre*, Tübingen, 1922, p. 466. Italics added. Cf. the translation by Edward A. Shils and Henry A. Finch, "The Meaning of 'Ethical Neutrality' in Sociology and Economics," in *Max Weber on the Methodology of the Social Sciences* (Glencoe , Ill.: Free Press, 1949), p. 15.

24. That Weber was not free from value judgments in his empirical studies (either), especially in his investigations in the field of sociology of religion, and that he could not be has been shown by Leo Strauss in "The Social Science of Max Weber," *Measure, 2* (1951), 204–230, reprinted in *Natural Right and History* (Chicago: University of Chicago Press, 1953), Chapter II, "Natural Right and the Distinction between Facts and Values."

25. Space limitations forbid further explication of this conception of the nature of society and of the scientist's several relations to society.

26. A related way of formulating the present situation of sociology as diagnosed in this essay is to say that there is a conflict between two types of sociological inquiry. The first is motivated by spontaneous concerns—say over problems connected with the horrible and puzzling phenomenon of totalitarianism [read Czeslaw Milosz, *The Captive Mind* (New York: Vintage, 1955), and Carl J. Friedrich, Ed., *Totalitarianism* (Cambridge: Harvard University Press, 1954)]. Here the investigator can endure much frustration because of the importance his topic of study has for him. The second type is motivated by institutionalized concerns, such as the desire to show results; here the goal is reduced to compatibility with minimum frustration (endurance of frustration probably being proportionate to the importance of the goal for the investigator). The unsatisfactory situation of sociology (as reflected, for example, in the dissatisfaction observed among certain graduate students) would be caused by the suppression of the first type of inquiry by the second. This is the individual-psychological side of the situation that this chapter tries to recognize more from

the historical and sociological angle. The weight of the first type of inquiry might increase to an extent that would force a revision of sociology, perhaps in the direction indicated in this essay as desirable. Without such pressure the reflection on the philosophical bases of sociology—for example, the recognition of society as essentially existential *and* normative—might emerge only when forced by unanticipated results of research. This is most unlikely, but it is a development that physical science seems to have gone through in its crisis at the end of the nineteenth century.

27.   This is not, as I have come to realize, what the study of man does. At this point I see the significance of the "study of man," or understand its meaning, to lie in the considerably developed (though of course not in this paper—cf. n. 6) argument in favor of "surrender" as an approach to reality, an approach that is neither offered nor institutionalized but is fought and punished in contemporary Western society (as shown by many institutions and practices), and as an experience in learning and in therapy of which there may be others (but which I do not know). I have come to see, however, that the study of man must be supplemented by the concern with theory that I have tried to argue in this paper. In other words, the "study of man" lacks the insight that the society hostile to "surrender" and threatened by it can be changed or that the idealism and romanticism of the "study of man" must be enriched and corrected by other attitudes and ideas, mainly those that were developed by the Enlightenment, Hegel, and Marx.

28.   Preparing sociologists emphasizes the How of investigation; and, if the What, then largely by taking the extant sociology for granted and asking "what" gaps are in it—not in the world. This is similar to the attitude of the physical scientists whose experiments, rather than any philosophical critique, forced the breakdown of the Newtonian system. To hope for something like it in the social sciences would be ideological; it would be to evince scientistic piousness; cf. n. 26.

---

Reprinted from *Transactions of the Third World Congress of Sociology,* **7** (1956), 151–160, by permission of the publisher. The essay has been edited and partially revised by the author.

# 16

# SOCIOLOGY AND EVIL. 1969, 1967

> Certainly in some, probably in most, very likely in all of his activities *as a social scientist,* the social scientist by what he does inevitably intervenes in, interferes with, meddles in the social process.

If this "social science is social action theorem" (Seeley, 1963, p. 56) is true, it follows also that social-science neglect makes itself felt in society. Such neglect exists in regard to evil: to my knowledge no social scientist, as a social scientist, has asked what evil is.

"What is evil?" is a question that has been raised (both in the East and West) by philosophers and theologians as well as by uncounted, unclassified, unrecorded people since time immemorial. Here, however, most social scientists, do not feel negligent but virtuous, and self-evidently so: "Of course," they might put it, "the exploration of the nature or essence or meaning of evil *obviously* is not our concern; it *is* the concern of the philosopher and the theologian! All we do and legitimately *can* do is ascertain (as well as possible) what men, what certain men *consider* evil. We study beliefs about evil, conceptions of it, attitudes toward it, the moral code of a given society or other group, and so on; in short, we explore what is *called* evil, but as social scientists we do not and cannot commit *ourselves* to a conception of evil, because if we did we would *by definition* no longer be social scientists but precisely become philosophers or theologians." As they might *not* put it, in their nominalism and the practice attendant on it social scientists commit themselves to a science that claims *not* to know what evil is, *not* to be responsible for knowing or seeking to know it, and would, they are convinced, indeed lose its scientific character if it founded its investigations of evil on its own conception of it.

274

This social science is characterized not only by its neglect in raising the question at issue—as well as many others it considers equally non-scientific—but also by certain related, typically unacknowledged, theoretical consequences of conceptions of truth, particularly scientific truth, and of the relations between student and subject matter, Is and Ought, theory and practice, knowledge and its application, science and history, society, politics, and ethics.

Even more conspicuous are two other relations between social science, especially sociology, and the investigation of evil. On the one hand, there is the "classical tradition" which puts sociology at the service of improving the society studied, whether we think of Marx, Comte, Spencer, Durkheim, Max Weber, or others among its representatives. On the other, there is the plethora of research into social problems, that is, into evil*s*, which are, however, conceived as such characteristically not by specified groups but by some sort of anonymous middle-of-the-road (American) society with which their student, probably in contradiction to the conception of sociology he would profess if he were pressed, might well agree. (For an attempt at specification, cf. Mills, 1963.)

The representatives of the classical tradition, no matter how different from one another, share an explicit conception of history. Both features, but particularly the latter, are not characteristic of the social pathologist. The one characteristic that the two groups have in common is a desire to ameliorate extant society—the classicists consciously and as an admitted task of their activity, the social pathologists blushingly, given their vaunted freedom from value judgments. The latter, and sociologists typically, in the United States probably more than elsewhere, do not judge what they study, or judge it unwittingly, but if they do at all it is more likely to be on the basis of their private views which, according to their conception of social science, ought not to contaminate it. They do not tell us, or do not tell us frankly, what they consider evil or, for that matter, evils: their conception of social science cannot tell *them*. Instead they take over the ideas of others and base their own studies on them, if not by contract or on order. Their position, role and professional type approach those of the "organization man."

# I

These social scientists are unaware that whatever they may be studying their nominalist position hides a twofold commitment. One of its aspects is evident: it is a commitment to a science that does not know what its subject matter is, does not hold itself responsible for such knowledge (to repeat), and fears to lose its character as a science if it bases its studies of evil (for instance) on its own conception of it. The second aspect may be less immediately obvious: it is that in his research, which he believes to be purely nominalistic, the sociologist (and, of course, not he alone) depends and cannot help depending on his own conceptions and convictions, not only concerning evil but quite generally whatever phenomena figure in the study he may be undertaking.

Suppose he is interested in the conceptions of evil existing in a given society. He tells himself that he does not know what they are, in any event that his own notion of evil, if he has one, neither matters nor enters his research. Because he is dealing with a society, he will have to use a sample. He finds, let us say, that he will have to choose between a random and a stratified sample. If he chooses a random sample, it means in his view that the distribution of concepts of evil is not tied, at least not significantly, to the social, economic, religious, or political characteristics that distinguish the groups or strata in his universe. That is, he bases the expected distribution on a notion of evil itself, namely, on one whose expressions vary more with individuals than with aggregates, which have other traits (age, sex, occupation, etc.) that might form the basis of a stratified sample. He expects these expressions to vary less between bankers and unemployed, between old and young, men and women, Catholics and Protestants, or painters and engineers than *among* bankers, unemployed, old, young, and so on, as *individuals*. Inversely, if he uses a stratified sample he is indicating his expectation of a stratified distribution of expressions or concepts. Moreover, regardless of his choice of sample, conceptions beyond those of distribution and evil itself necessarily play a role, particularly assumptions of the nature of the society he wishes to investigate and of the groups, strata, and individuals composing it. After all, it is on the basis of these assumptions that he justifies the kind of sample he has chosen. In short, even to begin nominalist research presupposes definitions, concepts, or convictions that are the researcher's own, even though he may fancy dealing only with other people's ideas for which he is not responsible.

The situation is the same if his universe is too small to require sampling, for here, also, figure notions of his own influence, the student's choice of technique (interview, questionnaire, scales, etc.), and so on.

The next question asks where these notions come from. Undoubtedly from socialization, including general and special education, and reflection. What distinguishes the social scientist is that in his professional education he has acquired the concept or concepts of social science that prevail in his society, among them, the one we have called nominalist.

Even in this approach, then, there is inevitably an element that might be called realist, a fact that may come to the student's attention if he finds that his concepts, which are based on his own socialization and education, are inadequate. Suppose he is troubled by the diversity of traditions that concern the very nature of the society he wants to study. He then has two options: either he chooses one of the traditions or reinterprets it in a way that is more acceptable to him or he feels that his trouble has less easily specifiable grounds—for instance, a diffuse distrust of tradition in general. Although the two cases differ, once the student comes up against the unavoidable presence of a realist element in his undertaking the basis of his concept can become a problem. If it does, once again he has two options: to affirm or to replace this basis. In the first case, if it is the plurality of traditions that bothers him, he may try to reaffirm a traditional basis. In the second, which is distrust of tradition in general, he may try to replace this basis altogether.

He proceeds by carefully examining the competing traditions in the hope of arriving at one of them, or at a synthesis of their elements, that strikes him as trustworthy. To reaffirm or affirm a basis means to take existing traditions for granted, not to call them into question, and to stay within their framework. What could it mean to leave their framework—what is there beyond tradition? How can the social scientist replace it instead of trying to affirm it as honestly as he can? It is possible to bracket the world (to use a phenomenological expression), that is, neither affirming nor denying but, precisely, calling it into question, suspending it. Such suspension of the world, which may be followed by its reaffirmation, redefinition, or reinvention, is an extraordinary experience, in which the whole being, not only the cognitive faculty, is at stake. The desire to have such an experience does not guarantee its occurrence because it is unforeseeable. The very consciousness that tradition no longer is viable may arouse the will to go beyond this consciousness to find in oneself the basis of his convictions. Because human beings are socialized, that is, because they would not be human beings without their traditions with which to orient themselves, it is clear that "oneself" cannot mean some kind of *tabula rasa*. Rather, it refers to that psychic state in which the question of tradition does not come up at all—that extraordinary state, that extreme situation, of which love, anxiety, solitude [cf. Chapter 14], meditation, creation, or other unexpected extraordinary experiences are examples—"extraordinary" meaning not ordinary, nonroutine, not everyday. If not simply enjoyed or suffered but undergone as cognitive experiences, they may be occasions of calling the world into question and reconstituting it; and this reconstituted, reinvented, new world gives the experiencer greater certainty about the world than he has had before. As far as he knows, what he has found is true, not in a nominalist sense of a truth for others that does not commit him, but true for himself. To distinguish this truth from scientific truth let us call it existential.

We saw that the researcher's own view also figures in the nominalist approach. He searches for scientific truth but cannot help availing himself of truths that, whatever their origin, are, for him, existential truths. Thus there is a relation between the two kinds of truth in the very act of research. This relation emerges as more systematic on the basis of the criteria for verifying the two kinds. We read [in Chapter 5] that the criterion for verifying existential truth is the outcome of the examination of received notions, which also include all the scientific truths at the examiner's command. They, too, consequently, are examined. It follows that existential truth, unverified by the examination of relevant scientific truth, is, properly speaking, merely idiosyncrasy. On the other hand, it also follows that scientific truth that disregards existential truth is empty. Let us come back to our example—research into the conepts of evil in a given society—in order to see concretely how these two kinds of truth, their relation and their interdependence, manifest themselves.

In this example scientific truth refers to concepts of evil found among certain people. We take it that the researcher has ignored what for him are existential truths, namely, a number of propositions he accepts as valid (propositions on the distribution of the concepts of evil in the society he wants to study, his own notions of evil, of that society, and of the groups, strata, and individuals making it up), for it is on the basis of these concepts that he has chosen his samples or adopted other techniques. He ignores them, however. It might be objected that the notions mentioned are not existential but scientific. If this is so, it is easy to understand that the researcher had to conceive them on the basis of decisions which, at some point, must be existential in nature, even though this point may not be the one envisaged here (the one at which the choice of sample or the interview, instead of the questionnaire, was made). Whatever the stage of the research, there is a moment, if only he is aware of it, when the student is bound to place his trust in existentially true propositions as the basis of his enterprise.

It is equally important to point out that existential truth that is indifferent to scientific truth is an idiosyncrasy. Suppose that in a study of concepts of evil a student bases the choice of his sample on the hypothesis (an existential truth for him) that his population must be classified by hair color, for he anticipates a significant correlation between the distributions of hair color and the concepts of evil. If such a hypothesis strikes us as idiosyncratic, if we do not believe it, it may be because we have the results of enough scientific studies to be convinced of its invalidity. If, instead of hair color we take ethnic or religious affiliation, we may in certain cases not know whether there is a correlation between ethnic and religious groups and evil. We may or may not be inclined to think so. In any event, we must examine our expectations, which can become existential truths provided they are controlled by the results of scientific investigation. Otherwise the growth of existential truth would be stunted.

Thus what is required is a conscious cooperative effort of the two kinds of truth, which figure in research anyway. We have seen that each suffers from the absence of the other and that each serves to correct the other. Their cooperation thus resembles a virtuous circle [recall in the comment on Chapter 12 in the introduction to this part the remarks about the virtuous circle between intrinsic and extrinsic interpretation], whereas if the student allows one of them to exploit the other, on the contrary, a vicious circle forms. It does if, instead of rigorously examining his existential truths, he chooses only those that he considers existentially valid. To give an absurd illustration: if he chooses among all his studies only that of a strange community in which redheads have an idea about evil that is different from that of all blonds and he generalizes on it in order to demonstrate his existential truth, the exploitation of scientific by existential truth, is nothing but the rationalization of a prejudice. There may, however, also be exploitation of existential by scientific truth. It occurs if the student assumes that scientific truth is all the truth there is: he may not distinguish between the two kinds or may believe that scientific truth can lead him to existential truth, or, far from not distinguishing them, he may maintain that existential truth cannot be analyzed rationally because it *is* idiosyncratic. The last is close to Max Weber's attitude, which, however, he prescribed more than he practiced [cf. Chapter 15]. The first two of the three positions are varieties of scientism; the third is one of nihilism or absolute relativism. All three produce a vicious circle.

We must distinguish clearly between these types of misalliance of scientific and existential truth and cases in which the two are not even meant to meet. If we now say that there are studies in which not both of them figure, we speak from a psychological point of view, from that of the student and no longer from the systematic. So far we have made reference only to the most serious form of study, from the student's standpoint, in which he tries as best he can to honor the claims of both truths. His own aim, however, may be only one of them. If it is scientific truth, he will discover and collect facts that do not personally concern him and which he will relate to other facts in order to determine their structure for the purpose of comparison or generalization. If, on the contrary, he is seeking existential truth, he may proceed in an analogous manner but with reference to facts that do concern him: he will want to find out what he can truly hold to be good or bad, beautiful or ugly, right or wrong—what he must do. From a systematic point of view the difference between these two types of study is only in the distribution and emphasis of the two kinds of truth which are always present—a difference of degree. From a psychological point of view the first type is that of a pragmatic, hypothetical, stipulative, propositional, external, objective, theoretical study [cf. the adjectives used to designate scientific knowledge in Chapter 5]. From a social point of view, and only with respect to the relation between the study and the society in which it is done, this relation depends, in both cases, on the existential truth on which the study is based, because it alone can bring to light an attitude (positive, negative, or neutral) toward the society and, combined with scientific truth, can have a social effect, for scientific truth by itself is neutral, ineffectual, impotent, like Max Scheler's ideal factors, his "logos."

# II

We began with the observation that the question "What is evil?" has been raised not in social science but in philosophy and theology. Why is this so? Perhaps we can try for an answer by glimpsing the history of the Western concept of evil and contemporary society.

This concept is marked, above all, by the Judaeo-Christian tradition, particularly its Christian component, whether original sin or glad tidings be considered the core of Christianity. The Western concept of evil would thus have dissipated with the dissolution of that tradition, especially of Christianity itself. Perhaps because of the personal and particular loyalties that characterize it—to Jesus, to saints and priests, to the Protestant's individual conscience—because of this "particularism," Christianity seems difficult to reconcile with the "universalism" (both terms in Talcott Parsons' sense) that characterizes industrial, technological, bureaucratic society, whether capitalist or socialist (despite the fact that a line connects certain features of universalism with certain features of Protestantism). This difficulty obviously accounts for much of the controversy and movement that has for some time agitated many churches—the Catholic Church notably since John XXIII. The heritage of the Christian concept of evil, at any rate, even though modified, diluted, and deformed, is rooted in us, and the combination of this heritage with the historical development that is hard to reconcile with it goes some way toward accounting for the incapacity of presumably a great many individuals today to form a viable concept of evil, one for which they—and we— could truly answer.

To put it differently, God has been replaced by other absolutes—state, race, the future of a given people, if not of mankind, to which the present generation must be sacrificed (cf. Camus, 1958, especially p. 282). Millions of men have been victimized by these absolutes and in their names have victimized others. The bad conscience or unease hovering about them remains to be ascertained. When infidels or witches were executed, bad conscience and unease were likely to have been covered up by the con- viction that these acts were done in the name of God—although the persecuted died as irrevocably as if they had fallen prey to Hitler, Stalin, a traffic crash, or napalm. Recognition of mishandling the name of God, however, played its role in the Reformation, which, among other things, was a secularization of Catholicism in that it questioned previously un- questioned aspects of God and their abusive institutionalization on earth.

Yet the suffering inflicted in the name of more recent absolutes is much less limited than that perpetrated in the name of God: the numbers and categories of people that punishment, misery, and death can attain have grown enormously with democratization and technology, especially communications, transportation, and destruction. Modern social control thus is more nearly total and far more cruel, and efficient than ever before, when crimes against mankind had not yet been recognized as such. They were first named and punished at Nuremberg but have also been perpetuated for years in Vietnam by American "fire power," "espe- cially air power (Harvey estimates . . . [its preponderance over the Viet- namese] at about 1000 to 1)." Crimes against mankind have not yet entered the consciousness and conscience of mankind, so that "American Huey troops at Vinh Long" (soldiers hovering in a Huey Hog, "a con- verted transport helicopter which has been remade into a floating firing platoon with the fire power of a World War II infantry battalion crammed aboard")

> didn't hurl impersonal thunderbolts from the heights in super- sonic jets. They came muttering down to the paddies and hootch lines ["rows of houses along a road or canal"], fired at close range and saw their opponents disintegrate to bloody rags 40 feet away (Harvey, 1967, quoted by Crichton, 1968).

If ever these men conceive of their actions as evil, they fail to act in accord with their conception. Thus if "no poetry after Auschwitz," what social science in the face of such bestiality? Will there be a Nuremberg for the American military and their Washington directors or will it be impossible to distinguish the Eichmanns among all of us? Yet to

> be silent about what we cannot grasp is the only adequate mode of being; the only adequate mode of being before that which we cannot grasp is *not* to be silent about it. Between these two contradictory truths lies our dilemma, for we can neither be silent nor speak; we must speak but we cannot speak. [Beginning of Chapter 8.]

This dilemma has taken historical body in our paralyzing suspension between two impossible worlds: one in which we can no longer believe, a world ordered by religious directives and moderations and one that we cannot bear, a world without these directives and moderations. We are alienated from both, yet there seem to be no others. This, perhaps, is the reason why we have not succeeded in articulating a concept of evil that would be adequate to the secularized world in which we live but which has left evil itself, in contrast to space, cancer, the Greenland Icecap, and innumerable other phenomena and problems, comparatively unexplored, ominously sacred and threatening. Evil is no longer committed in the name of God. It is less than ever legitimated by religious or even moral motives and is covered over for political, economic, and technological reasons on a larger scale than ever—but the cover can also be seen through, and is seen through, by more people than ever. There is evil, such as the suffering and death caused by famine and epidemics, that the technology and economy we have developed could eliminate if we applied them to this end instead of submitting to other orders we also have developed, notably the distribution of power and the distribution and, especially, the nondistribution of economic products.

The decisive difference between the two worlds is that the first is done with, whereas the second is there for us to work on to make it one we can affirm. Here Max Weber's work (Marcuse, 1968) can be helpful not only in its analytic power but also its symptomatic character. *The Protestant Ethic and the Spirit of Capitalism*, in particular, has a significance at once vaster and more specific than tends to be recognized, for it deals not only with the two phenomena indicated in its title but conjures up, for Weber as well as for us, a much larger complex, which profoundly troubled Weber himself, and which consists, in addition to the remnants of ascetic Protestantism and the spirit of capitalism, of the associated elements of bureaucracy, functional (technical, instrumental) rationality, secularization, impersonality, and control. In other words, it represents modern industrialized society, the second of the two worlds mentioned. It is this complex and those and related elements that make us feel frustrated, alienated, powerless, vicarious, or anonymous, as we so often say. Beyond analyses, discussions, and laments, however, are more active and practical responses, suffering, and political action. Max Weber's intent was to account for the rise of the spirit of capitalism, but what this account can mean for us was probably as unintended by him as was, from the point of view of Calvinism, capitalism itself [1].

Let us recall the features of the Protestant-capitalist complex: labor, work, making, producing, discipline, asceticism, control, specialization, bureaucracy, profit. Being parts of a whole, they are related, as are our responses to them. In terms of this list capitalism and the reaction to it, socialism, which has become the other variant of modern industrialized society, are much more alike than unlike.

This society goes back far beyond the present generation and so does its critique—it is enough the recall Marx, Kierkegaard, and Nietzsche, utopian communities, communist and socialist movements, and many other indications in the arts, philosophy, and theology. What is new is the extraordinarily accelerated development of this society during the last decades. Some of its results are Stalinism, nazism, and fascism, and, more generally, the A- and H-bombs, electronics, and the exploration of space. Perhaps the most common reaction to them is one of puzzlement, foreboding, and ignorance and, more recently, the protest against the proliferation of nuclear weapons and the war in Vietnam. There are many more indirect reactions that nevertheless are equally, if not more, instructive in regard to the society in which we live: the widespread feeling of alienation and concern with alienation; the resistance against control and manipulation on the part of younger people, particularly students; the distrust of their elders; the civil-rights struggle; the ecumenical movement; the formation of various groups who protest or withdraw, from Beats to Hippies and Diggers; developments in art—pop-art, happenings, and art in the service of politics; certain governmental programs, especially the antipoverty program; and developments in the social sciences—for instance, action anthropology [Chapter 24]. A few words about some of them will show their relevance in our context.

Alienation places a distance not only between the individual and his society but also between himself and whatever he might believe reality to be (Keniston, 1967). Much of what the alienated encounters, including himself, is unreal, and he longs for the real. He may try to find it in psychic states induced by drugs; he may be tired of the centuries-old sermon on deferred, indefinitely deferred, gratification and seek it now; he may "turn on" (but notice the mechanical metaphor) by letting music, turned on full-blast, invade him. He may be less pervasively alienated and instead reject more definable and particular aspects of his society, notably people, especially his parents and his elders in general, who he believes suffer from this world as he does but whom he may also hold responsible for its horror. He may rebel against certain of the features he resents as particularly objectionable, such as control and manipulation—despite the official veneration of science, as if science were nothing but the highest expression of this control [2], or he may do more than rebel by joining others in trying to leave his society physically, socially, emotionally—perhaps founding a community. This may be no more than withdrawal or, as in the case of the Diggers, it may also entail action on concern and kindness.

Others react to this society by attempting to improve it, working, for instance, for civil rights or in the ecumenical movement. A few try to understand how certain children and adults risk their lives doing what strikes them as right—how *they* fight evil (Coles, 1967), or they attempt—as did the late C. Wright Mills, Herbert Marcuse, Barrington Moore, or Kenneth Keniston—to understand this society historically and critically, or they engage in political actions of many kinds.

Concerning our society, various forms of art, most obviously caricature and cartoon but also certain mime and pantomime plays, use irony and sarcasm; in other forms expectations are broken—from the *trompe-l'œuil* to the happening ("it isn't as you think it is"), which may, like the social "no," pass into a "yes," into the effort to feel real or to have an experience, if only to be shocked out of numbness. This consideration points to antecedent developments in art—surrealism, dadaism, and expressionism—and in literature, from the contemporary "new novel," in which the object replaces the subject, to Kafka, Joyce, Henry James, imagism, and stream-of-consciousness writing. Marshall McLuhan, too, finds his place here, with his insistence in favor of the appeal to all the senses, or, in Norman O. Brown's words, polymorphism.

The most obvious problem of modern industrial society lies in international relations, though less, despite its magnitude, in the precarious connection between the two variants of this society, capitalist and communist, than between both and those that are neither—the "developing nations," the "third world." The truth of Marx's adage that the root is not society but man shows itself when man comes to the fore and fights—most dramatically as a guerrilla—against the whole military-industrial complex. The political outcome surely is uncertain; thus in Vietnam an increasing number even of observers who are members of that complex admit that our machinery is not equal to guerrilla warfare; in Latin America the success of the guerrillas appears to have been set back by

Che Guevara's assassination; in the United States itself the future seems impenetrable but of more importance than almost anywhere else.

Max Weber's methodological tenets, notably his misleading and widely misread insistence on a value-free social science but also his dangerously elliptic formulation of the ethics of responsibility and of principle, suggest his position at the end of a period during which men took it for granted that the nation was the largest unit of social organization. Characteristic of Weber's position was that he felt urged to diagnose his society and his time but that he insisted on doing so outside sociology. "No one knows"—to recall a famous passage at the end of *The Protestant Ethic*— "who will live in this cage of the future" (the "iron cage" that the "light cloak" of the Puritans' "care for external goods" had become),

> or whether at the end of this tremendous development entirely new prophets will arise, or there will be a great rebirth of old ideas and ideals, or if neither, mechanized petrification, embellished with a sort of convulsive self-importance. For of the last stage of this cultural development, it might well be truly said: "Specialists without spirit, sensualists without heart; this nullity imagines that it has attained a level of civilization never before achieved." But with this [Weber checks himself], we get into the field of value judgments and judgments of faith, with which this purely historical presentation shall not be burdened (Weber, 1958, p. 182; my translation of the last sentence).

If we take Weber, the whole man, and not only that part of him that he himself admitted into his sociology, then by bringing his diagnosis to bear on ourselves we are acting on his intent. We placed Protestantism and capitalism into the complex of which they are a part and from which Weber had isolated them for scientific analysis, and we are trying to understand the whole of this complex today. The reactions to it we have sketched, to which many could be added, suggest that we are closer to the end of Weber's period than he was or are already into the beginning of a new one, of which we know as little as Marx could know about the reign of freedom that was to follow the reign of necessity.

On the basis of the diagnosis suggested, the task of the sociologist is to analyze and interpret the responses to our society that have been illustrated. To vary Marx's formula of the change from necessity to freedom we can adopt Marcuse's (in *Eros and Civilization*) of the change from life under the performance principle, which we all know, to life under the pleasure principle, of which we have only the most fleeting notions. Under the guidance and compulsion of the former we have produced so many things and so much knowledge that we can afford the most radical change in man's history: to a society that would be acceptable to an unprecedented majority of men because they would consider it good on mature reflection. Not only this change, but also its outcome is almost impossible to imagine. Still, it is quite possible, if not likely, that in the short run we shall be dead but that the prospects for those who come after us, if we ourselves attend to this change with everything at our command, are unimaginably better than is the world in which we live.

# III

This suggests what one sociologist at least might argue as good: a necessary utopian society whose seed he recognizes in ours. *Evil*, therefore, would be the failure to recognize and fight all that would choke this seed: injustice, misery, and sham and the institutional arrangements that favor and facilitate them. A historically adequate concept of evil cannot locate it in the individual as evil deed, sin, or vice (which, of course, exist) nor in myth, religion, or philosophy (not that its mythical, religious, and philosophical dimensions are not relevant today) but must find it in society and in the individual's relations to society.

Hence the task of a *sociology of evil* is to study the various reactions to our society that have been mentioned, or others that are similar, in an effort to specify the corresponding characteristics of this society, thus the society itself, the changes it needs, and how they are to be made.

It may be stated that such an undertaking is possible without reference to evil, in another perspective or, indeed, without one that is explicitly formulated. It may also be stated that the undertaking, in whatever perspective, is superfluous because we know enough already and what is needed is not study but action. Both objections, if they are counter-suggestions, are to be welcomed. What recommends the proposal submitted here is this. It acknowledges and acts on sociology as morality and praxis, which has been neglected, thus helping to reconnect sociology with its historical task and thereby to re-establish, at least in one area of our intellectual concerns, a believable, affirmable continuity. It re-establishes a continuity also with the universal human preoccupation with good and evil. This continuity is expressed and denied—expressed, e.g., in nightmares, neuroses, psychoses, anxiety, aggression, violence; denied in the widely observable reluctance to use the word evil and to prefer, instead, less haunting words. The enterprise proposed thus has a therapeutic function for those who would act on it as well as for those who would in any way come in contact with it. The failure to study evil intervenes, and its study will intervene—if we recall Seeley's "social science is social action theorem"—in the social process. On the most modest scale those engaged in the study will find it meaningful, hence feel less alienated for it. This may also apply to some readers of their findings. Less modestly, the study may contribute to a change in the definition of the situation of contemporary society and thus perhaps to a change in the situation and the society.

I conclude with a few examples of study complexes that may serve to make the proposal more concrete by conveying its open and comprehensive character.

### An example of one of the investigations envisaged by the general diagnosis suggested

In all countries perhaps, there are people who recognize certain aspects of our historical situation and act accordingly: resisting, protesting, rebelling, fighting, destroying, killing, building, planning, constructing, helping, writing, marching, analyzing, proclaiming, and preaching. It is always a "No" to aspects they have recognized and a "Yes" to others whose seeds they discover and want to cultivate, whether a peasant revolt or a civil-rights struggle, whether the actors are colonials, ex-colonials, or students. Is a new concept of evil—less Christian or religious in general, more secularized and more in line with our One World—in the process of developing? We could try to find out by studying the leaders of many of these types of activity and the participants at all levels; we would probably arrive at a number of concepts of evil. What are the social sources of these concepts and what are their social and political effects? Which are their common traits? Is it possible to ascertain a rather limited number of types, or even one, that would be diffused everywhere? What purposes would such studies serve, how could their utilization be justified, how could they be used and what could the consequences of their use be?

### An example of research into sociology suggested by the sociology of evil proposed

The individual and sociologist who argues this sociology of evil is himself somebody who acts according to his recognition of certain aspects of the world in which he lives. His own concept of evil finds expression, for example, in his insistence that evil be recognized as a topic of social-scientific, especially sociological, research. What kind of sociologist is concerned with evil as a scientific topic; what kind is not? What has happened in the world that would account for the change from the second to the first? Is there, in addition to the precarious role of Christianity in a society partly described, partly predicted by George Orwell twenty years ago in *1984*, also the precarious situation of the white man and of Western domination predicted fifty years ago by Oswald Spengler in *The Decline of the West*? The social psychologist who studies socialization, aggression, resentment, and prejudice, the psychiatrist who studies neuroses and psychoses, the cultural anthropologist who studies the variety of cultures, including moral codes, and the sociologist who studies slums, crimes, and vice are probably more sensitive than others to the problematic and dangerous aspects of our world. Many of them separate their professions from their lives, hold on to a value-free social science, and try to practice it. What is the origin, beyond Max Weber, of this social science? (Recall the change from the Hegelian concept to positivism; Marcuse, 1960). Its practitioners have spread not only their knowledge but also their personal sensitivity to social phenomena far beyond the social sciences themselves. Is this, however, comparable to knowledge diffused by the mass media in having contributed less to the enlightenment than to the disorientation of the general social consciousness and to its increased disturbance?

*A few examples of sociological analyses of materials*
*not originally found in sociology but relevant to the inquiry*

*From sin to complex*

Origin and development of the psychological interpretation of the infraction of moral norms, including changes in attitude toward such infractions, especially the shift from judgment and condemnation to understanding and explanation. Development of efforts to correct and improve the behavior of those who breach norms. Changes in the significance attributed to the thought of infraction as against the act of infraction. All these aspects are to be investigated in relation to social situations and structures and their changes. One of the lessons of the research could be the answer to the question that both the author and his readers might ask: what is a justifiable attitude toward his or their own behavior and that of others—critical or understanding, moral or psychological?

*Mythology and practice of ordeals*

What concepts of evil can be deduced from ordeals described in myths; what concept of evil, from ordeals that have in fact been practiced? What can we infer about the nature of ordeals and corresponding concepts of evil from an analysis of the mythical against the practical context (circumstances, explanations, frequency, and consequences) of ordeals? What does the study of ordeals suggest if we compare them with investigations that suspected persons undergo in our own society (examinations and cross-examinations, lie detection, brainwashing, punishment, and humiliation to discover the truth or obtain a statement)? To what extent can such studies change our own attitudes toward these measures?

### Evil in dreams

Dreams about particular evils, their imagery of evil, inferences regarding the dreamer's concept of evil, and comparison of this concept with that of the awake person. Special attention should be paid to relations between evil and anxiety, fear, and the mechanisms by which what is feared becomes an evil or evil. What is the importance of these mechanisms to our understanding of the relations between anxiety, fear, mythical figures, and symbols of evil, of the phenomenon of the scapegoat and, more generally, of prejudice—including the importance to our understanding of these phenomena in ourselves?

### When does who think about evil?

We could begin by studying socialization in which people acquire their ideas of evil. What are these ideas and what importance for the individual is given them? For which manifestations of evil, which the researcher knows from other sources, does socialization inadequately prepare the individual? A comparison of what the student knows about concepts of evil acquired in socialization and what he knows about evil or evils that exist in the world can furnish him with hypotheses concerning evil(s) for which socialization does not prepare, or insufficiently prepares, the individual. These hypotheses can then be examined by studies of cases in which the individual thinks about evil or otherwise encounters it. We could also begin with these cases, wherever they are found—in scientific literature, in novels, or short stories, or by direct investigation—in order to find an answer to this question.

### What does the history of censorship teach us about the history of concepts of evil?

The inquiry that tries to answer this question should be accompanied, as far as available sources allow, by another into the diffusion of censored writings and their readers. Censorship, diffusion of censored books, and types of reader show perhaps marked changes according to the contents of the writings. Thus the history of pornographic books is possibly less variable, despite the variations in the criteria of pornography, than the history of books censored for theological or political reasons. In any case, what can we learn from such studies about the nature of evil that expresses itself in this fashion in its varied relations with social institutions and human traits—particularly in contemporary society?

Obviously, these examples could be vastly multiplied (for more, see Wolff, 1967, pp. 206–213). In addition to the concepts of evil and their differences and convergences, the examination of sociology and sociologists in regard to notions of evil and attitudes toward them, interpretations of the breaches of moral norms, ordeals, evil in dreams, occasions on which people think about evil, and censorship—what about comparative studies in the etymology and semantics of "evil" and cognate and contrasting words in one language, inquiries into the place of evil in the history of philosophy, into ideas of evil as counterconcepts to ideas of the good society in works of sociologists and other thinkers, into the antecedents, if they exist, of evil in prehuman animals, or into the vast relations between evil and technology or between evil and law—among many, many others? No matter how heterogeneous these areas of research may appear, drawing as they do on the literatures of sociology, social, child, and depth psychology and psychoanalysis, ethics and theology, cultural anthropology, law, linguistics, philosophy, history of ideas, social, economic, and intellectual history, animal sociology, ethology, and genetics, the histories of science and technology, literature and the other arts, and journalism—what makes them contributions to one central problem is the question that inspires them: the question concerning the seeds of a better society than ours. This, to put it mildly, is a *good* task for sociology.

*Acknowledgment.* Talks with Ruth Meyer, Juan E. Corradi, Roger Pritchard, Alice Stewart, and Barrie Thorne, friends and students, responses to the first version of this chapter in French (Wolff, 1967) by Carroll Bourg, S.J., Mihailo Marković, Barrington Moore, Jr., Paul Ricoeur, John R. Seeley, Hans Weil, and Walter A. Weisskopf, comments on an earlier draft in English by members of a seminar on the topic at Brandeis University, Fall 1967–1968, especially Stephen D. Berkowitz, Y. Michael Bodemann, Mario Montano, and Andrew Strickland, as well as by Milton Rokeach and Ralph K. White, and critical readings of this essay itself by Montano and Strickland have influenced and helped me. I wish to acknowledge my gratitude to all these persons.

## BIBLIOGRAPHY

Camus, Albert, *The Rebel*, translated by Anthony Bower (New York: Vintage, 1958).

Coles, Robert, *Children of Crisis* (Boston: Little, Brown, 1967).

Crichton, Robert, "Review of Harvey," *New York Review of Books*, **9** (January 4, 1968), 4.

Harvey, Frank, *Air War: Vietnam* (New York: Bantam, 1967).

Hirsch, Walter, "The Image of the Scientist in Science Fiction," in Bernard

Barber and Walter Hirsch, Eds., *The Sociology of Science* (New York: Free Press, 1962), pp. 259–268.

Keniston, Kenneth, *The Uncommitted* (New York: Delta, 1967).

Marcuse, Herbert, *Reason and Revolution* (1941), (Boston: Beacon, 1960).

Marcuse, Herbert, "Industrialization and Capitalism in the Work of Max Weber" (1964), translated by Kurt H. Wolff and Jeremy J. Shapiro, in Marcuse, *Negations,* translated by Shapiro (Boston: Beacon, 1968), pp. 201–226.

Mills, C. Wright, "The Professional Ideology of Social Pathologists" (1943), in Mills, *Power, Politics and People,* Irving Louis Horowitz, Ed. (New York: Oxford University Press, 1963), pp. 525–552.

Parsons, Talcott, *The Structure of Social Action,* (New York: McGraw-Hill, 1937).

Seeley, John R., "Social Science? Some Probative Problems," in Maurice Stein and Arthur Vidich, Eds., *Sociology on Trial* (Englewood Cliffs, N.J.: Prentice-Hall, 1963), pp. 53–65.

Weber, Max, *The Protestant Ethic and the Spirit of Capitalism* (1904–1905), translated by Talcott Parsons (1930) (New York: Scribner's, 1958).

Wolff, Kurt H., "Pour une sociologie du mal," *L'homme et la société,* 4 (April, May, June 1967), 197–213.

### NOTES

1.  Capitalism as what Robert K. Merton might call "an unintended consequence of purposeful social action" is suggested by Talcott Parsons: "one cannot say that the Calvinistic ethic or any of its legitimate derivatives ever approved money making for its own sake or as a means to self-indulgence, which was, indeed, one of the cardinal sins. What it did approve was rational, systematic labor in a useful calling which could be interpreted as acceptable to God. Money was, certainly in the beginning, regarded as a by-product and one by no means without its dangers. The attitude was, that is, an ascetic one. But even this served capitalistic interests since, on the one hand, work in economic callings would serve to increase earnings but, on the other, the fear of self-indulgence would prevent their full expenditure for consumption" (Parsons, 1937, pp. 526–527). Thus it looks like a double surprise: first, capitalism, then the meaning for us of Weber's analysis of it.

2.  Despite this veneration, its more spontaneous distrust is shown, for example, in science fiction in the decreasing confidence in the scientist as the human type who solves "social problems" which are rather left to the natives of other planets, suggesting that faith in the magic of science had resurrected the older magic of the *deus ex machina* (Hirsch, 1962, p. 267).

Reprinted from *L'homme et la société,* No. 4 (1967), 197–213, and *Journal of Social Issues,* 25 (1969), 111–125, by permission of the publishers. The essays have been edited and partially revised by the author.

# 17

## SOCIOLOGY
## AND HISTORY;
## Theory and Practice. 1959

In discussing the broad topics of sociology and history with sociologists it is hardly necessary, at least not at the start, to present an array of concepts of sociology. Instead, I shall begin with some observations on history.

# I

The most obvious is the distinction, sometimes overlooked, between history—in W. H. Walsh's formulation—as "the totality of past human actions," or history proper, and history as "the narrative or account we construct of them now" [1], or historiography. In this distinction the last word, "now," has an importance that Walsh seems not to have accorded it, for if it were left out of the second definition the distinction between it and the first would disappear, inasmuch as narratives or accounts surely belong among human actions. Thus historiography accomplished is part of history proper, or only historiography-in-the-making is historiography, for once made, it is history.

Now, in the first place the present moves ineluctably, not, as it is so often put, into the future, but into the past [2]. As you read this sentence, now—the "now," once spoken, no longer is—is becoming past. As I write the history of yesterday, even of today, my historiography is becoming part of the time in which it was written, part of history. Yet not all of me, not all of man and mankind, is historical; not all of us is composed of an ever receding present and an ever growing past; not all of us is intrinsically temporal. There are situations, for instance, in which we forget time, in which, were we reminded of it, we should be struck as if by an incongruous and irrelevant noise; for example, the situation in which we think. When we think, we make connections that are not temporal. They are logical. Their judge is not time but logic or reason, which apply atemporal standards of judgment. Thoughts, ideas, their connections, their judgment, and its standards are atemporal. This does not mean that they are timeless, for, obviously, they change in time. Ineluctably, they are located in time. Causal sequences are temporal; sequences of ideas are not [3].

In the second place we have just seen that ideas are parts not only of atemporal, acausal sequences but also of temporal, causal sequences, being causes and thus having effects, being effects and thus having causes. As I am thinking, my idea, willy-nilly, becomes part of the past and only thus takes on the character of a candidate in a causal sequence. While I am thinking it it is wholly atemporal, wholly caught in the realm of ideas, wholly outside the realm of time, but once thought it can be inspected—I or somebody else can inspect it and can ask not only logical but also causal, temporal questions about it. One can ask atemporal questions such as these: What are its premises? Is it consistent with them? What are its implications? Now that it is before us, no longer in the making but made past, we also can ask temporal questions: How did I get this idea? What effect may its communication have? In the present's moving into the past, ideas take on the dimensions of causality and temporality. If this were not so, historiography of whatever subject matter, including intellectual historiography or, as it is usually called, intellectual history, would not be possible. Historiography, as we have already seen, has this characteristic of all ideas, that in the making it is *only* an atemporal, acausal process of ideas but that once made it is also a temporal event which has its cause and effect.

A third observation which has to do with the movement of the present into the past concerns a distinction between theory and practice. Theory is looking, contemplating; practice is doing, acting, making. As attitudes, the two—theory and practice—are not differentiated in the present. They become differentiated only by the present's moving into the past. Whether I am thinking a thought or making a tool, my attitude is inextricably both watchful, inspecting, reflecting, and fashioning, changing, combining, recombining. Although my purpose may be predominantly theoretical or predominantly practical, in the present, even if I am conscious of it, purpose is an atemporal element in an atemporal complex. Once I have thought the idea or done or made the thing, the thought—as we have already seen—and the deed or product become links in a causal chain and may be inspected in reference to their effects in the realms of both ideas and actions. What is more, they may be inspected in reference to other men's ideas or actions or to my own. If I look at them wholly in reference to other men's, I am, whatever else I may be, not practical, for I exclude from my reference the core of the present, which is myself. Full practice is acting on theory, on my theory, my looking, my contemplating. This is expressed, even if elliptically or inaccurately, in the saying that the theorist is the most practical of men.

The past, then, with which historiography deals, may be approached as a reservoir of atemporal ideas or of causal sequences, and it may be approached theoretically or practically. If we take atemporal ideas out of the past in which we find them (rather than think them ourselves), we may deal with them either atemporally, in logical analysis, or in their temporal dimension, either in explicit causal analysis, that is, explanation, or implicit causal analysis, or, as we might call it, probability analysis. So for our dealings with causal sequences, for we may take them, too, as atemporal ideas or in their temporality. All are theoretical, for in all of them I look to see and understand relations and phenomena. They are practical if I undertake them in order to learn about myself as a person who must act. In this case I deal with ideas atemporally, yet not in logical analysis but in ontological, moral, or aesthetic analysis, and I deal with causal sequences, in explanations or probability analyses or other interpretations, in order to understand myself better as a person who must act and the time in which I live and must act. Intellectual disciplines, such as the various branches of philosophy, historiography, and social science, have, of course, not developed according to this scheme of distinctions and relations, for their development has surely not resulted, as this scheme has, from an observation of the relations between present and past and attendant observations of ideas and causal sequences and of theory and practice.

John C. McKinney writes:

> It is obvious that the research tasks of sociology and history are different as *disciplines,* for their procedures answer to their respective research purposes. Nevertheless, since all data are historical in one sense, the data of history and sociology are the same. The logical difference lies in what they do with the data. The research task of the sociologist is to generalize; that of the historian, to individualize. . . . The historian is concerned with processes and structures that are singular in their space-time occurrence; hence he does not conceive of

them as being repeatable, whereas the sociologist adopts the opposite view. The sociologist is concerned with the repetitive and constant factors, or tendencies to regularity, of human society [4].

# II

Many other writers who have discussed the relations between sociology and historiography likewise follow, more or less closely, the distinctions made by Windelband, Rickert, Dilthey, Troeltsch, and others between sociology as generalizing (nomothetic, a *Naturwissenschaft*) and history as particularizing or individualizing (idiographic, a *Geisteswissenschaft*) [5].

Still others are not so much concerned with analyzing the nature of the two disciplines as with pointing out or advocating the advantages of their cooperation. Thus Arnold M. Rose reminds sociologists that in some branches of their science (e.g., the study of social change, social movements, social trends, and migration), historical data alone provide content; that the investigation of national characteristics is impossible without recourse to history; that "a knowledge of history is essential . . . in providing . . . a cultural premise for any hypothesis" [6]; that is, in making us realize that our findings, based as they are on culture- and time-bound data, have no transcultural and transtemporal validity and that we can learn methods from historians, the use of documents, for example, and the synthesis of wide varieties of facts. On the other hand, historians may learn from sociologists the usefulness of such techniques as descriptive statistics and content analysis, some concepts and findings, and the relevance of grasping contemporary phenomena for studying past periods. Similarly, though in more general terms, Maurice Mandelbaum says:

> History . . . depends for the furtherance of its analysis upon principles which only sociology and the other theoretical social sciences can disclose; sociology depends upon historical investigation for the material upon which it works, examining and comparing historical instances in order to discover the laws which may be implicit within them [7].

What is common to all these disquisitions is their positing historiography and sociology as having coordinate status, neither occupying a position that is in any sense preferred. Not so, however, for Franz Oppenheimer. For him the two are not equally legitimate scientific enterprises, one seeking the particular or unique and past, the other, the regular or general and atemporal, for, in contrast to sociology, historiography is not a science at all, nor, for that matter, is it an art. Instead, it is a "descriptive doctrine of the ideal." This concept, Oppenheimer believes, "fits in beautifully with the very common idea that history should and can be the schoolmaster of mankind . . . [and] even better, with the utterances of important historians and philosophers of history" [8].

The distinction between Oppenheimer's concepts of history and historiography and those mentioned above is that Oppenheimer's is practical, whereas the others are theoretical. Oppenheimer's is the conception of a man who is "doing," "making," and "acting," who must act, whereas the concepts referred to previously are those of men who "look" and "contemplate." As Oppenheimer says, there are many historians and philosophers of history who hold a practical view of their subject. Thus for Arthur Child, a more recent writer, practical history is "an imitation of the processes of decision . . . a choosing once more among alternative lines of conduct which themselves, in deliberation, are evaluated," and the historian's assessments form a part "of that massive disputation, of that vaster dialectic, within which society as a whole discusses the problem of its practice" [9].

Of particular relevance for our purposes is R. G. Collingwood, who asks, "What is history for?" and answers:

> "for" human self-knowledge. . . . [And knowing] yourself means knowing, first, what it is to be a man; secondly, knowing what it is to be the kind of man you are; and thirdly, knowing what it is to be the man *you* are and nobody else is. Knowing yourself means knowing what you can do; and since nobody knows what he can do until he tries, the only clue to what man can do is what man has done. The value of history, then, is that it teaches us what man has done and thus what man is [10].

This statement assigns to the study of history the task of throwing light on man's house with its three mansions (mankind, group, and individual) and, by implication, of applying the changes that such illumination may entail. This is the same house that appears in another contemporary but ahistorical theory of personality in which we find the proposition that "every man is in certain respects a. like all other men, b. like some other men, c. like no other man" [11].

# III

To sharpen and enrich the distinction between practice and theory as it bears on the relations between history and sociology two other contrasts, in addition to that between a practical view of man and a theoretical view of personality, may be mentioned. The first is between a practical and a theoretical use of pluralism. In the context of Frederick Woodbridge's *The Purpose of History*, the pluralism of history means that a single purpose is not discoverable in history but that there are many purposes; that, for man, "the study of his own history is his congenial task to which all his knowledge of other histories is contributory; and for him the conscious, reflective, and intelligent living of his own history is his congenial purpose" [12]. Compare this with Mandelbaum's "historical pluralism" [13], which "consists in the view that . . . we shall always find that in themselves all of . . . [the] components [of the historical process] are not related to each other in any save a temporal manner." Clearly, Woodbridge's interest in the purpose of history, as serving a practical end, contrasts with the interest of Mandelbaum and others in the methodology of history as serving theoretical ends.

The second contrast is that between the typical contemporary social-scientific studies of national character on behalf of theoretical interests and Américo Castro's study of a given people's "dwelling-place of life" and "living structure" on behalf of practical interests. By "dwelling-place of life," Castro means *"the fact of living* within certain vital possibilities (preferences) and impossibilities (reluctances)"; by "living structure," *"the mode according to which* men live within this dwelling-place." It is his conception of history that imposes the investigation of these two aspects of a people, for, in history, in Castro's view, "are realized . . . man's possibilities for achieving great deeds and works that endure and radiate their values afield . . . that can affect the mind, the imagination, or the soul" [14]. Thus Castro is arguing that we study history in order to learn who we are by realizing what various kinds of men, of our own and other kinds, have been. This is what Collingwood and Woodbridge say, the former focusing on universal and particular man, the latter, on universal and particular history. The practical sides of these three contrasts show kinship—as do, from the standpoint of practice, their theoretical sides.

# IV

All this is not to suggest, not even indirectly, the abandoning of sociology conceived as a theoretical discipline or a plea for historical sociology. The first may be eliminated by saying that I advocate not the abandoning of theoretical concerns but their formulation on the basis of a historical diagnosis of our time [15], that is, on the basis of a practical concern. Such a program, far from contaminating or weakening the two components of sociology, purifies and strengthens each, and, although neither can be eliminated, either can be and has been played down, exaggerated, and otherwise sinned against. In the most recent past the sinning has been done more against the practical than the theoretical component, yet surely a practical concern gave rise to sociology in the first place, whether our disciplinie is said to have begun with Hobbes, Montesquieu, or Comte, with the eighteenth-century philosophers of history, with the economists [16], or whenever else. Always there were concrete phenomena of Western society that called for illumination and action, and this has been true for the further development of sociology until the last two or three decades [17]. (As to this view, one of the most outstanding American sociologists in this classical tradition is C. Wright Mills [18], and some writers who are not professional sociologists, such as David Riesman and William H. Whyte, Jr., share it more than many, if not the majority of, sociologists. The widespread interest in the work of these men is to the sociologist interested in a diagnosis of our time an obvious problem for sociological investigation, but I am not aware of its having been explored [19].)

The aims of historical sociology are not relevant here, except for the one that, in Raymond Aron's interpretation, characterizes some of its German representatives (Oppenheimer, Alfred Weber, Mannheim, and Scheler), who consider sociology as "akin to a theory of universal history and as undertaking the tasks of the philosophy of history; namely, the provision of the answer to present anxieties out of the experience of the past" [20]. In this country, to judge by the work of its foremost advocates, Howard Becker and Harry Elmer Barnes [21], historical sociology consists in the attempt to discover regularities in the past and to derive generalizations from them. Although in neither German nor American usage can one easily distinguish historical sociology from historiography or from philosophy of history [22], the Americans evidently see it as predominantly theoretical, whereas the Germans admit a practical component of much greater significance.

Oppenheimer—one of the German historical sociologists treated by Aron—concludes his analysis of the relations between history and sociology by saying that "the writing of history ceases to be the *opponent* of sociology and becomes its *subject of study*" [23]. Such a conception parallels Howard Jensen's concept of the sociology of knowledge, which must provide a sociological analysis of the history and present status of general epistemology. Jensen sees far more clearly than Oppenheimer (perhaps in part because of the intervening work of Karl Mannheim and the considerable critical discussion of it) that this concept presupposes the acceptance of "the autonomy of logical principles and the possibility that conceptual systems can transcend cultural relativity," for otherwise the sociology of knowledge (and, we may add, sociology in general) "undermines the basis of its own validity" [24]. Despite this acknowledgment, however, Jensen's argument is theoretical, as it intends to be. What would a practical argument look like here?

# V

I propose that the practical argument is a plea for raising questions in the face of recognition of the overwhelmingly and inescapably practical character of history. For we are historical in the most practical sense—not exhaustively so but much more profoundly and pervasively so than our historical moment will allow us to see. Even so, we may realize that one of its most practical manifestations is history as terror [25]. The terror of history follows from our failure to master our arsenal of machines. We have built it, but we understand it so little that it may terrorize us. This terror has not yet shown enough signs of passing for us to replace this concept of history with another toward which we are drawn with equal force. We are, as Hannah Arendt has put it, "where man, wherever he goes, encounters only himself," where

> the Kantian and Hegelian way of becoming reconciled to reality through understanding the innermost meaning of the entire historical process seems to be quite as much refuted by our experience as the simultaneous attempt of pragmatism and utilitarianism to "make history" and impose upon reality the preconceived meaning and law of man [26].

In grasping history, sociology appears both impotent and arrogant, in need, therefore, of both strength and humility. Not that there are no strong and humble sociologists—Max Weber, surely, is one of them. He could, wrote the historian Friedrich Meinecke, "motivate his unrealistic project of value-neutral historical research with the most value-laden goals: 'I wish to see how much I can endure.'" As a whole man even Weber was stronger and humbler than the prescriptions laid down in his methodological pronouncements [27].

In respect to the sociology of knowledge, a transformatino from theory into practice is suggested by Mircea Eliade:

> It is certain that none of the historicistic philosophies is able to defend . . . [man] from the terror of history. We could even

imagine a final attempt: [in order] to save history and establish an ontology of history, events would be regarded as a series of "situations" by virtue of which the human spirit should attain knowledge of levels of reality otherwise inaccessible to it . . . such a position affords a shelter from the terror of history only insofar as it postulates the existence at least of the Universal Spirit. . . . It is only through some such reasoning that it would be possible to found a sociology of knowledge that should not lead to relativism and skepticism. The "influences"—economic, social, national, cultural—that affect "ideologies" . . . would not annul their objective value any more than the fever or the intoxication that reveals to a poet a new poetic creation impairs the value of the latter. [They] . . . would, on the contrary, be occasions for envisaging a spiritual universe from new angles. But it goes without saying that a sociology of knowledge, that is, the study of the social conditioning of ideologies, could avoid relativism only by affirming the autonomy of the spirit—which, if we understand him aright, Karl Mannheim did not dare to affirm [28].

The theoretical autonomy of logical principles of Jensen and others among Mannheim's critics is being transformed here into the practical autonomy of the spirit, the attribute of a man who acts in a world that is common to men—past, present, and future. The former is what a man sees who looks and contemplates; the latter, what a man acts on who must act. How, as sociologists, must we learn to see? As practical men; but this means as reasonable men.

*Acknowledgment.* This chapter is a revision and expansion of a paper prepared for the meeting of the American Sociological Society, Seattle, Washington, August 1958.

## NOTES

1. W. H. Walsh, *An Introduction to Philosophy of History* (1951) (London: Hutchinson's University Library, n.d., 1956), p. 14. See also Michael Oakeshott, *Experience and Its Modes* (Cambridge: The University Press, 1933), p. 93, discussed by R. G. Collingwood in *The Idea of History* (1946) (New York: Oxford University Press, 1957), p. 153.

2. Cf. Frederick J. E. Woodbridge, *The Purpose of History* (New York: Columbia University Press, 1916), pp. 36–40.

3. Cf. Robert M. MacIver, *Social Causation* (Boston: Ginn, 1942), pp. 21–22.

4. John C. McKinney, "Methodology, Procedures, and Techniques in Sociology," in Howard Becker and Alvin Boskoff, Eds., *Modern Sociological Theory in Continuity and Change* (New York: Dryden Press, 1957), pp. 228–229.

5. See, for example, Nicholas S. Timasheff, *Sociological Theory: Its Nature and Growth* (Garden City, N.Y.: Doubleday, 1955), pp. 5–7; Karl R. Popper, *The Poverty of Historicism* (London: Routledge & Kegan Paul, 1957), especially pp. 143–147; Morris Ginsberg, "History and Sociology" (1932), in *On the Diversity of Morals* (New York: Macmillan, 1957), especially p. 179. See also S. F. Nadel, *The Foundations of Social Anthropology* (Glencoe, Ill.: Free Press, 1951), pp. 8–17 ("Anthropology, Sociology, and History"); Talcott Parsons, *The Structure of Social Action* (New York: McGraw-Hill, 1937), p. 771.

6. Arnold M. Rose, "The Relationship between History and Sociology," *Alpha Kappa Deltan*, **26** (Spring 1956), p. 33. See also Kenneth E. Bock's analysis of the pervasive and unexamined acceptance by social scientists of evolutionism in *The Acceptance of Histories: Toward a Perspective for Social Science* (Berkeley: University of California Press, 1956), especially Chapter VII, p. 116.

7. Maurice Mandelbaum, *The Problem of Historical Knowledge: An Answer to Relativism* (New York: Liveright, 1938), p. 265; see also Richard Hofstadter, "History and the Social Sciences," in Fritz Stern, Ed., *The Varieties of History: From Voltaire to the Present* (New York: Meredian, 1956), pp. 359–370.

8. Franz Oppenheimer, "History and Sociology," in William Fielding Ogburn and Alexander Goldenweise, Eds., *The Social Sciences and Their Interrelations* (Boston: Houghton Mifflin, 1927), pp. 227–228.

9. Arthur Child, "History as Practical," *Philosophical Quarterly*, **4** (July 1954), 209, 215. Important but little noted among similarly oriented writers is Georg Simmel, who is not treated in this respect by Mandelbaum (*op. cit.*, pp. 101–119). Among Simmel's writings on history see particularly "Vom Wesen des historischen Vertehens" (1918), reprinted in *Brücke und Tür*, Michael Landmann, Ed., in collaboration with Margarete Susman (Stuttgart: Koehler, 1957), specifically pp. 59–82. See also Child, "Five Conceptions of History," *Ethics*, **68** (October 1957), 28–38, and for "history as imitation" *ibid.*, 28–30; "History as Imitation," *Philosophical Quarterly*, **2** (July 1952), 193–208; Mircea Eliade, *The Myth of the Eternal Return* (1949), translated by Willard R. Trask (New York: Pantheon, 1954), especially pp. 34–35.

10. Collingwood, *op. cit.*, p. 10. See Karl Marx, *Selected Writings in Sociology and Social Philosophy*, with an introduction and notes by T. B. Bottomore and Maximilien Rubel, Eds., translated by T. B. Bottomore (London: Watts, 1956), p. 72; and Friedrich Nietzsche, "The Use and Abuse of History" (1874), in *Thoughts out of Season*, translated by Adrian Collins (Edinburgh: T. N. Foulis, 1910), p. 16.

11. Clyde Kluckhohn and Henry A. Murray, "Personality Formation: The Determinants," in Kluckhohn and Murray, Eds., *Personality in Nature, Society, and Culture* (New York: Knopf, 1948), p. 35.

12.  Woodbridge, *op. cit.*, pp. 49, 57.

13.  Mandelbaum, *op. cit.*, p. 274. Similarly, David Bidney, "On the So-called Anti-Evolutionary Fallacy: A Reply to Leslie White," *American Anthropologist*, **48** (April–June 1946), 293, quoted in Bock, *op. cit.*, p. 119.

14.  Américo Castro, *The Structure of Spanish History*, translated by Edmund L. King (Princeton, N.J.: Princeton University Press, 1954), pp. 33, 31.

15.  Cf. Kurt H. Wolff, "Before and after Sociology," *Transactions of the Third World Congress of Sociology* (1956), **7** , 157 [Chapter 15].

16.  Cf. Karl Polanyi, *The Great Transformation* (1944) (Boston: Beacon, 1957), pp. 111–129.

17.  Cf. John W. Bennett and Kurt H. Wolff, "Toward Communication between Sociology and Anthropology," in William L. Thomas, Jr., *Yearbook of Anthropology—1955* (New York: Wenner-Gren Foundation for Anthropological Research, 1955), p. 330; reprinted in Thomas, Ed., *Current Anthropology* (Chicago: University of Chicago Press, 1956), p. 330; and Wolff, *op. cit.*, p. 115.

18.  For his own assessment of the matter see his "IBM plus Reality plus Humanism Equals Sociology,"*Saturady Review of Literature* (May 1, 1954), 22 ff., and *The Sociological Imagination* (New York: Oxford University Press, 1959).

19.  Cf. Michael S. Olmsted's remarks at the end of his review of John Kenneth Galbraith's *The Affluent Society*, *American Sociological Review*, **23** (December 1958), 753.

20.  Raymond Aron, *German Sociology* (1936), translated by Mary and Thomas Bottomore (London: Heinemann, 1957), p. 37.

21.  Howard Becker, "Historical Sociology," in Harry Elmer Barnes, Howard Becker, and Frances Bennett Becker, Eds., *Contemporary Social Theory* (New York: Appleton-Century, 1940), pp. 491–542; Howard Becker, *Through Values to Social Interpretation* (Durham, N.C.: Duke University Press, 1950), pp. 128– 188; and Harry Elmer Barnes, *Historical Sociology: Its Origins and Developments* (New York: Philosophical Library, 1948). Similarly, Howard E. Jensen, "Developments in Analysis of Social Thought," in Becker and Boskoff, *op. cit.*, p. 53. Also W. J. H. Sprott, *Science and Social Action* (Glencoe, Ill.: Free Press, 1954), pp. 123–140.

22.  This, in several places in this brief essay, is perhaps the most plausible in which a more thoroughgoing discussion would require the analysis of some of Hans Freyer's writings, especially *Soziologie als Wirklichkeitswissenshaft* (1930). Cf. Ernest Manheim, "The Sociological Theories of Hans Freyer: Sociology as a Nationalistic Program of Social Action," in Harry Elmer Barnes, Ed., *An Introduction to the History of Sociology* (Chicago: University of Chicago Press, 1948), Chapter XVIII, pp. 362–373; also W. E. Mühlmann, "Sociology in Germany: Shift in Alignment," in Becker and Boskoff, *op. cit.*, Chapter XXIII, pp. 664–665; René König, "Germany," in Joseph S. Roucek, Ed., *Contemporary Sociology* (New York: Philosophical Library, 1958), pp. 788–789.

23.  Oppenheimer, *op. cit.*, p. 230.

24.   Jensen, *op. cit.*, p. 58. See also his lucid critique of Mannheim's perspectivism, pp. 55–56.

25.   Cf. Eliade, "The Terror of History," *op. cit.*, Chapter IV, pp. 139–162.

26.   Hannah Arendt, "History and Immortality," *Partisan Review*, **24** (Winter 1957), 31 and 34.

27.   Friedrich Meinecke, "Values and Causalities in History" (1928), translated by Julian H. Franklin, in Stern, *op. cit.*, p. 284. The prescriptions may have had more influence on contemporary sociology than has that part of the man Max Weber which he himself did not admit into them; that part of Weber is alluded to by Meinecke when he contrasts Weber's neutral project with his passionate goal. Cf. Leo Strauss, *Natural Right and History* (Chicago: University of Chicago Press, 1953), pp. 35–80.

28.   Eliade, *op. cit.*, p. 159 and n. 15. This position is closer to Scheler's than to Mannheim's. See also Kurt H. Wolff, "A Preliminary Inquiry into the Sociology of Knowledge from the Standpoint of the Study of Man," in *Scritti di sociologia e politica in onore di Luigi Sturzo* (Bologna: Nicola Zanichelli, 1953), Chapter III, especialy pp. 612–618 [Chapter 28].

---

Reprinted from *The American Journal of Sociology*, **65** (1959), 32–38, published by the University of Chicago, by permission of the publisher. The essay has been edited and partially revised by the author.

# 18

# SOCIOLOGY ON TRIAL. 1964

This chapter deals with a paperback of only 182 pages, a wedge between the fat textbooks and readers in American sociology or a stick of dynamite on the luxury liner *Sociology*, ready to explode her as she sails along a path warned against more than thirty years ago by Karl Mannheim, her list of passengers to be drawn up later, as they became more visible, by C. Wright Mills (to whose memory the book is dedicated and who is referred to often in its pages): Grand Theorizers (with a close-up of Talcott Parsons), Abstract Empiricists, Liberal Scatterers, Illiberal Practitioners, but also the innumerable offspring of Max Weber, the value-free Minotaur. Yet the whole alienated crew gets thrown overboard, the ahistoricity on which they float is caught and analyzed, and the possibilities of getting off course are strongly suggested. In fact, there is considerable doubt that the ship and passengers are there at all. Still there is a description of the land, once sighted, and art, history, and the stage are suggested as points of departure for sociologists.

By now, surely, there is a metaphoric fog, that resembles the fog the book has tried to penetrate, and thus we have made some progress toward appreciating the present state of American sociology. First we must catch our breath. *Sociology on Trial* [1], then, consists of an introduction and eleven papers, all but three published between 1932 and 1962. The one early paper (Mannheim's) is unique in its antiquity and its anticipation. All others are recent (Barrington Moore, 1958; C. Wright Mills, and Hans Gerth and Saul Landau, 1959; Joseph Bensman and Arthur Vidich, 1960; Alvin W. Gouldner, Lewis Feuer, and Robert A. Nisbet, 1962). The three previously unpublished were written in the last two years. Note where the published essays appeared originally: none in the official *American Sociological Review*; two (Mannheim and Bensman-Vidich) in the *Amer-*

*ican Journal of Sociology*, the oldest American and one of the oldest periodicals dedicated to sociology; two in books by their authors (Mills's *The Sociological Imagination* and Moore's *Political Power and Social Theory*); the rest in recent leftwing "little magazines" (Gerth-Landau in the first issue of *Studies on the Left*, Feuer in the third of *New Politics*) and in smaller sociological periodicals (Gouldner in *Social Problems*, Nisbet in the *Pacific Sociological Review*).

The editors of *Sociology on Trial* can by no means be defined exhaustively as dynamiters. Maurice R. Stein wrote *The Eclipse of Community* with passion but also with circumspection and he is coeditor with Vidich of the important *Identity and Anxiety*. Arthur Vidich is coauthor with Bensman of *Small Town in Mass Society*, a careful study (on which Vidich and Bensman have drawn for a chapter here). The editors did not look only for material that was meant to be dynamite, of which Daniel Foss's "The World View of Talcott Parsons" is an even more unadulterated stick than Mills's "The Bureaucratic Ethos," but more broadly for potential dynamite, for writing that questions, criticizes, and condemns the stubborn features of contemporary American sociology—its bureaucratization, its ahistoricity, its obsession with value-neutrality, systematicity, quantifiability, and exactitude—as well as for material, such as Nisbet, Stein himself, and, most clearly, John R. Seeley present, that goes beyond what Mannheim would have called intrinsic criticism and verges on asking how sociology is possible at all. I don't think it was too difficult for the editors to find these essays, for American orthodoxy in sociology, though far from monolithic and in fact luxuriating in subtle variants, has nevertheless allowed, compelled, or perhaps inveigled the heterodox and the heretics to develop considerable knowledge of one another, possibly even a modicum of group consciousness, which has, of course, nothing to do with any class consciousness because all of them are university professors, present, past, or future. (Still, it would be misleading to say that the American university is a house of many mansions; rather is it a house with several clearly graded floors as well as a basement and attic, backstairs, and, to hide the backstairs, sunny balconies.)

In their introduction Stein and Vidich argue against sociology as a boundary-maintaining field (to use a Parsonian term) against professionalized knowledge, against sociology as a job and the sociologist as a jobholder, and against the noise of recent celebrations of the discipline. They identify "the sociology of sociology" presented in their book as "an expression of conscience for sociology as a whole." "While it is clear," they write, "that no trial has been held, these essays have made the sociologists' world more trying than it would otherwise have been."

The papers are arranged in four parts, The Ethos of American Sociology, Value Neutrality as Disguise and Defense, The Suppression of Historical Concerns, and The Rediscovery of Sociology. The first contains articles that do deal with features of American sociology, but at least one in each of the other three parts has little in common with the part title. Thus Seeley's "Social Science? Some Probative Problems," which is one of the two chapters in Part II, hardly touches on the topic of value neutrality. Mannheim's and Gerth-Landau's contributions to Part I deal as much with the suppression of historical concerns, the theme of Part III, as do Moore's and Foss's, whereas it is difficult to justify the third paper under this headline. Feuer's "What Is Alienation? The Career of a Concept," no matter how important, deals with just what the title promises. These remarks, however, are meant less as strictures than as characterizations of the book, whose impact would be none the less if the contributions were arranged differently or without any subdivisions at all.

This *is* a collection of essays. If it were longer, it would be called a reader or a symposium—not one man's work. Otherwise there would probably have been an analysis of the aspects of the ethos of American sociology beyond those treated in the papers of Part I—even if the imaginary author had not offered a definition of the term itself. Two of the three papers in this part are well-known—Mannheim's review of *Methods in Social Science*, edited by Stuart A. Rice, and reprinted in Mannheim's *Essays on Sociology and Social Psychology*, and "The Bureaucratic Ethos" from Mills's *The Sociological Imagination*; one less known is "The Relevance of History to the Sociological Ethos" by Gerth and Landau. Mannheim's analysis is still surprisingly timely, although some of it needs to be brought up to date. Thus, although "the limited scope of the questions to which . . . [American sociology] confines itself" continues to be complained of in other chapters of the book, and, indeed, elsewhere and not only by professional enemies of sociology but also by students of it, perhaps more by undergraduates than graduates, the "excessive fear of theories" has since been replaced by an excessive fear, often made palatable as admiration and emulation, of leading theorists. Still largely true, however, are sociology's mistrust of philosophy or metaphysics, a certain, one-sided, ideal of exactness, the fact "that typical American studies start from questions in nowise connected with those problems which arouse our passions in everyday political and social struggle," "the false modesty of the empirical scholar whom his 'exactitude complex' prompts to ignore the genuine basis of his own questioning, which alone makes a scientific occupation worthwhile," the tendency to conclude "from the existence of ready documentary evidence, of statistical material, etc., that social research is worthwhile," "the absence of the viewpoint of *Wissenssoziologie*," and thus of "an element of self-control."

Some of these strictures are made again and again in other contributions to this book, although the next one, by Mills, helps to bring Mannheim's up to date. Mills observes "that precisely the people most urgently concerned to develop morally antiseptic methods are among those most deeply engaged in 'applied social science' and 'human engineering,' " and explains the seeming irony by reference to the nature of their work, which is expensive, hence requires large institutions that depend on or are part of the Establishment and that have developed two types of man new to the academic scene: the intellectual administrators or research promoters and the research technicians. Gerth and Landau point out that

> Just as United States leaders began to realize their dream of a world economic empire headed by American corporate power, the American sociologists dispensed with world concepts. . . . The integration of the world was left to the businessmen and politicians. The sociologist wanted to routinize the functioning of the good society at home, and labored to perfect "statistical and survey techniques, and small precision group work," developing specializations within sociology and betraying "the original sociologists' ethos."

> It was not until 1940, after the hot war was underway, that the *American Journal of Sociology* decided to publish an article on the Nazi Party. In all, from 1933 to 1947, only two articles on National Socialism appeared in the *Journal*. A fifty-year index of the *Journal* shows exactly three listings under Marx or Marxism, and under Lenin (or Leninism) there are no citations. By and large, the sociologists of today have shut 'the world crisis out of their vision, focusing their intellectual energy on the crisis of the family, while the Chinese revolution, involving 600,000,000 people—perhaps the greatest mass movement of mankind—is totally neglected.

Part II opens with Gouldner's "Anti-Minotaur: The Myth of a Value-Free Sociology," an excellent and urgently needed analysis of the historical circumstances of Max Weber's position on the topic, of its place in Western intellectual history, even of its psychological constellation in Weber himself. The essay applies what Mannheim said he missed when he reviewed American sociology: an approach inspired by the sociology of knowledge. In Gouldner's words:

> . . . what I will do is to view the belief in a value-free sociology in the same manner that sociologists examine any element in the ideology of any group. . . . I will look at . . . [it] as part

of the ideology of a working group and from the standpoint
of the sociology of occupations.

Although for Weber the advocacy of a sociology free from value judgments was "a proposal for an academic truce ... among academicians
whose political commitments were often intensely felt and in violent
opposition," our situation today is such that "it seems odd to prescribe
self-suppression as a way of avoiding external suppression" (for "suicide
does not appear to be a reasonable way to avoid being murdered"). Today,
the image of a value-free sociology is an anodyne that changes the alienation of many sociologists from the larger community "into an intellectual
principle; it evokes the soothing illusion ... that ... [it] is a self-imposed
duty rather than an externally imposed constraint." To give up the critical impulse is less a callous sell-out than a slow process of accommodation.
In Weber, instead, the position was the outcome of an excruciating effort
to resolve the old problem of the relation between reason, particularly as
manifested in science and bureaucracy, and faith, as expressed in charisma
and conscience.

Seeley's paper takes less for granted than any other in the book and
indeed than most papers on social science anywhere. His probative problems are presented as theorems; for example, the "uniqueness theorem."
Unique among all role-players, the social scientist has the right and duty
to study the whole society, but who or what, in a secular age, gives him
his mandate or supplies him with his point of view outside the social?
Surely not science, which is "not, or not sufficiently, trans-social, as any
student of the psychology or sociology of science (let alone the politics or
sociology of sociology) will tell us." The problem becomes especially
haunting in view of the closely related "social science is social action
theorem," which formulates the fact that by his very activity the social
scientist intervenes in the social process, and in view of the "freedom
theorem," which says that theories of human behavior enter human behavior so that it cannot be said to be definitely determined. Seeley discusses
several other fundamental questions of this kind; indeed, there are so
many of them, he writes, "that I am often left with the feeling that the
house of social science is still largely founded on sand." Even though it is
evident that men increasingly turn to social science, he concludes that

> Before we have to take the strain that must ensue as our style
> of perception and explanation becomes the dominant style, as
> they shortly may, I should like to know more surely that we
> know, at least in large outline, what we are about.

The title of Moore's "Strategy in Social Science," the first of the three papers in Part II, is more optimistic than its text. Contemporary social science, Moore writes, is acritical, ahistorical, abstract, and formal; Parsons, Merton, Stouffer, and Lazarsfeld have less to say about society than Marx, Durkheim, Weber, or Mosca. The outcome of Moore's inquiry is that we seem to be left with a radical historicism of an antiquarian or overly voluntaristic-optimistic variant or with an absurd and trivial social science in the image of mathematics or natural science. "At this point we seem to have reached a dead end. If one rejects both the major positions . . . , what is left? . . . It is tempting to . . . write: *Finis*." Yet man continues to want to understand himself and his world and has had some success in his effort. Our hope today lies in trying to do right by the unique (roughly, the province of the historian) and the general (roughly, the province of the scientist) by seeing the general manifested in the unique or, more particularly, by entertaining a revised idea of social evolution.

Foss's paper on Parsons is the only analysis among the articles of the book that is addressed to a single author and only to those of Parsons' writings that deal with "the goals and objectives of an industrial society, the industrialization of the underdeveloped world . . . , and the structure of power in industrial and industrializing societies," which may attest to the fascination Parsons exerts even over his most passionate critics. Foss manages to read him in a shattering fashion. Thus of the United States Parsons writes:

> Economic growth is highly valued as the most immediate focus
> of adaptive capacity. Beyond that, we value particularly tech-
> nology and science as means to productivity, and the maximi-
> zation of opportunity for individuals and subcollectivities.

In the same paper by Parsons ("Voting and the Equilibrium of the American Party System") there is a sentence which, its critic comments, "deserves to live forever in sociological infamy": "Whether there is opposition or not is an empirically very important but theoretically secondary matter." In Parsons' extended review of Mills's *The Power Elite*, we read:

> If genuine and, in some sense, effective controls had not been
> imposed, I find it impossible to understand the bitter and con-
> tinuing opposition on the part of business to the measures
> which have been taken.

His analysis of Parsons' writings in the three areas mentioned leads Foss to conclude that Parsons' "sociology of complacency is a failure in dealing with the experiential reality of industrial society," and "What may be needed is a 'sociology of horror' in which social science tries to be honest with the industrial world and with itself."

Like Gouldner's analysis of value-free social science, Feuer's of alienation is a study in the sociology of knowledge. Feuer traces the concept from Calvin through Hegel, Feuerbach, Marx, and Engels to contemporary social science—a rich and dramatic story—and finds that today its referents are so varied that all they have in common is the frustration of basic emotional desire. The term is used to convey the emotional tone that accompanies any behavior in which the person is compelled to act self-destructively, and Feuer asks why just this term should designate the phenomenon. His answer:

> Alienation is the dramatic metaphor of the intellectual who has left the Political Garden of Eden and projects his experience as the exemplar of all human frustrations. The frustrations are immense and universal, but are they not misdescribed in the projective metaphor of a very small section of humanity?

If Foss destroys an idol, Feuer achieves even more, he lays a ghost, and a general invitation to the funeral should follow.

We have seen, especially in Part III, a serious dissatisfaction with sociology, even grief and pessimism, but just as Moore cannot end his paper on such a note neither can the editors end their book; therefore they add Part IV, "The Rediscovery of Sociology: Some Straws in the Wind." In "Sociology as an Art Form" Nisbet, somewhat reminiscent of Robert Redfield in "The Art of Social Science," points out that some of the most distinctive ideas that sociology has contributed to modern thought—mass society, alienation, anomie, rationalization, community, disorganization—are not the outcome of logico-empirical analysis as this is understood today but rather are visions that had their earliest and most far-reaching appeal in Romantic art. In "Social Theory and Field Research," Bensman and Vidich describe the interaction between theory and research in the study of social phenomena, especially during the field phase. This interaction includes the evocation of theory from observation, the exhausting of theories in accounting for observation, their substitution, and their use to criticize field work. If it is difficult to determine what constitutes a straw in the wind in Nisbet's article, except perhaps a sentimental comfort that vision may not yet be exhausted, here the encouragement comes from the honest report of work at a craft—comparable to the encouragement that may be derived from Mills's "On Intellectual Craftsmanship."

Stein's concluding essay, "The Poetic Metaphors of Sociology," declares history, drama, and system to be the "three root metaphors from which sociological inquiry can spring," laments the undue monopoly of the third, argues that a

> full sociological vision must include . . . (1) concern with the interpretation of the history of modern society; (2) concern with interpreting major modern crises; (3) concern with developing decisive value judgments leading when possible to effective action; and (4) concern with systematic ordering of concepts, propositions, and techniques to stimulate further inquiry,

and comments briefly on Lewis Mumford, Hannah Arendt, Paul Goodman, Marshall McLuhan, Harold Rosenberg, Herbert Marcuse, Norman Brown, Raymond Williams, and Erik Erikson, in addition to the sociologists David Riesman and C. Wright Mills, as promising alternatives to systematic sociology. The solace here, I take it, derives from the fact that there is some important writing, a little of it within, and more of it outside sociology, but all highly relevant to it.

This last part is the weakest and its inclusion strikes me as a bow to optimism, Nisbet exclaiming how beautiful art is and how artistic good sociology, Bensman and Vidich contributing an essay certainly not meant as a straw in the wind but as an analysis of field work, and Stein condensing several chapters of a forthcoming book to make up a third paper. The volume thus ends with a pious ritual, which makes one reconsider the depth of the bite of what precedes it. The editors should have let it go at page 147.

This is all relatively unimportant in comparison with the critical analysis of "value-free" sociology, of Parsons as a commentator on contemporary politics and economics, of alienation, of the bureaucratization of sociology, of its detachment from history and indeed from the world in which we live, and of its dubious logical and epistemological foundations. It is probably symptomatic that the constructive part of the book is so inferior to its critical parts. A parallel that comes to mind is Erich Kahler's *The Tower and the Abyss*, in which a highly perceptive and complex analysis of contemporary consciousness had results that must have so troubled the author that it imposed on him the need for some hopeful conclusion. We may think also of earlier works, for example, Durkheim's proposal to overcome the anomie he had discovered or Mannheim's *Man and Society in an Age of Reconstruction* as a response to his earlier studies in the sociology of knowledge.

What the first three parts of this book call for, it seems to me, is not Part IV as printed but instead a synthesis of the elements toward a phenomenology of contemporary American sociology that are laid out in them. Whether it would contain its own corrective I find it difficult to foresee, but if it did it would obviously not be tacked on. In the meantime it remains to be seen what the reaction to this book will be; it, too (remembering Seeley's "freedom theorem") will be part of that phenomenology and we shall be able so to analyze it.

### NOTE

1.   Maurice Stein and Arthur Vidich, Eds., *Sociology on Trial* (Englewood Cliffs, N.J.: Prentice-Hall, 1963).

---

This chapter has not been published previously in English.

# V

# CULTURAL
# ANTHROPOLOGY

*For Dorothy Lee, obviously—for Paul Riesman,*
*and in memory of Robert Redfield*

There is neither a systematic nor a theoretical reason that I can make out for separating sociology from cultural anthropology as a field of study. There are, of course, historical reasons, but putting together some of my papers under the present heading has a more narrowly historical, perhaps a biographical, justification. My acquaintance with cultural anthropology, such as it is, goes back to the work I did in 1943 and 1944 at the University of Chicago with Sol Tax and the late Robert Redfield, more particularly in a course in methods of anthropology given by Redfield (out of which came Chapter 19). It also goes back to what has turned out to be more lasting and far reaching: my experience in the field, in "Loma" (New Mexico), when Redfield and Tax acted as my severest critics, to whom I regularly sent field notes on which they commented. I say something on this in Chapter 23, "The Collection and Organization of Field Materials." It was in Loma, more specifically in the five months of the summer of 1944 (I had been there on my own twice before, in 1940 and 1942), that the first notions concerning surrender originated, much helped by correspondence, usually polemical, with Redfield and Tax, even though the word itself occurred to me only six years later, when, in the summer of 1950, I taught a course on the study of the small community at the New School which focused above all on my research in Loma.

Substantively, Chapters 20 to 23 deal with various aspects of Loma. The problem that figures importantly in Chapter 19, an analysis of Gregory Bateson's *Naven*, but is central in Chapter 20, which describes a way of establishing culture patterns empirically, is how the student of people with other cultures can get at their point of view and mediate it to himself and his readers. The problem first of all presupposes the recognition of the difference between the two points of view, the student's and that of his subjects, and this recognition and the problems attendant on it had struck me, as the paper on *Naven* shows, even before I went into the field in 1944—years before I came to consider in the analysis of the two view-Alfred Schutz. Schutz first undertook this analysis in a critique of Max points one of the fundamental contributions made to social science by Weber's concept of subjective meaning [1]. He showed that Weber had not seen the importance of the problem and tried to remedy this far-reaching defect. Perhaps like the problem of evil (Chapter 16), it is one that has long been recognized by philosophers (as that of knowledge of other minds, for instance) rather than by social scientists. Why this should be so—if it is—deserves illumination, also because unlike some other traditional philosophical problems it is one whose neglect is coconstitutive of social-scientific theory and practice as well as of their consequences beyond social science itself.

None of this was on my mind when I wrote "A Critique of Bateson's *Naven*," but, as before, in reflecting on Chapter 17 (on history and sociology), something became clear to me (suggesting, as it did then, a problem for investigation) as I reread these pieces and tried to understand the cultural-anthropological component in my writing, this phase of the voyage, and its relation to other components and phases. In Chapter 19 surrender comes up again in the context as the maximum effort one can make to understand the other: one of the characteristics of surrender is identification (although not in Bateson's meaning).

My reading of *Naven* was as attentive (and, of course, as selective) as that of Arendt's *The Human Condition* many years later (or that of Arthur Child's work—see especially Chapter 28—which I studied at about the same time as *Naven*). The differences in my attention to Arendt and Bateson are clear, however. My interest is much more practical in respect to *The Human Condition*, more concerned with its consequences for outlook and attendant conduct. In *Naven* it is focused on theory, on presenting and trying to clarify the author's theories and concepts, or at least on suggesting steps for doing so. Thus it makes far less of an effort to reach out to the author and join him, and for him to join us, in a common venture of setting the world straight. At that time I was still a novice, certainly in anthropology, and accepted things more implicitly and readily than I did when I read *The Human Condition*. In this sense the analysis of *Naven* is more intrinsic (cf. the discussion of Chapter 12 in the introduction to Part IV) than that of Arendt.

Chapters 20 to 23 on Loma belong together in other ways as well, but 21 and 22 (on culture change and leadership) are much more closely related than 20 and 23 (on culture patterns and on the collection and organization of field materials).

The "first notions of 'surrender' originated" in 1944 during my (longest) stay in Loma assisted by correspondence with my severest critics, especially Robert Redfield. I had been sent to find out (Chapter 23)

> whether "culture patterns" could be established empirically so that another student could go back and check point by point. But [and here comes the turn that was to lead to surrender] eventually I found that I could not accept this assignment because it presupposed a conceptualization that I could not be sure was appropriate to my Loma experience. Finally, I became skeptical of received notions as guides in research generally . . . I advocated, instead, that in the field the student hold as many of these notions as possible in abeyance and expect the organization and presentation of his materials to emerge in the study itself.

Still I gave in to pressure by Redfield and Tax to come up with a structure and to report on whatever I might be able concerning my original assignment. At about the midpoint of my stay in Loma, in August 1944, I followed their invitation to present a paper at the Summer Institute of the Society for Social Research in Chicago. Chapter 20, "A Methodological Note on the Empirical Establishment of Culture Patterns," is the result. It begins with the distinction between the cultural and the objective approach, which I now perceive as an implicit defense of my developing position, a halfway house between the traditional way of doing field work (entering the scene equipped with hypotheses that are largely derived from the current state of the discipline in which the student was "trained") and the one that had barely begun to articulate itself, chiefly under the impact of my experience in Loma. The cultural approach was also drawn from other sources, from my own upbringing in Europe, and more particularly from my studies in the sociology of knowledge, to which there are references, and which makes itself felt even in some of my earlier work in the New World, such as the essays on Pareto (Chapter 1) and the sociocultural interpretation of American sociology (Chapter 12), written shortly after the one under discussion.

This study of culture patterns takes much more for granted than I have subsequently come to accept. I should not now write, for instance, that "a preliminary classification of the culture under study" provides the student with a "theoretical, or rational, framework," which in the field he is to "fill empirically," nor would I say without decisive qualifications that "I am also aware, of course, that one cannot proceed without hypotheses." In the ordinary meaning of a proposition formulated with a view to testability it is entirely possible to proceed without hypotheses; it is probably more common to start with vaguely articulated hypotheses. The question is to what extent one would wish to suspend, question, or hold in abeyance *whatever* formulations, articulations, or conceptualizations may, to the utmost of one's grasp and imagination, appear to bear on the investigation; to what extent one would be capable of standing such suspension and be likely to try it—how far one could surrender to the situation. In this radical sense it is indeed *not* possible to proceed without hypotheses: one cannot go behind or beyond one's ultimate, basic, or primitive propositions concerning the world or those of the unique-universal human being one is (cf. introduction to Part IV).

Chapter 20 is still far from this position. It is still as defensively scientific as some of my early writing in general (the two surveys, Chapters 4 and 5, and the remarks on Chapter 12 in the introduction to Part IV), including the remaining chapters on Loma (21 to 23). It repeatedly insists on the task of research as understanding and predicting. On the other hand, the conceptualization of background materials (on which there is considerable technical detail in Chapter 23) already points in the direction of something (which again I would not formulate in this way now) that cuts across or transcends all particular cultures, something universal—universal, however, not because it is exclusively human but because it is shared by man with other contents of the cosmos (as I put it later in some of my papers on surrender). It points toward the formulation of man as a mixed phenomenon (cf. the discussion of the chapter on Arendt in the introduction to Part IV). In the remarks on the immanent interpretation of a culture the idea of identification, a component of surrender, comes up, as it already had in the earlier paper on *Naven*.

The style of these chapters on Loma, again especially 21 and 22, betrays their cautious character, also typical of some other early writing (e.g., Chapters 4, 5, 7, and 12).

I had not thought of Chapter 20 as a contribution to the sociology of knowledge and was surprised when more than twenty years after its publication the editors of the first reader in the field in English asked to reprint it. Presumably the reason was that it carefully describes one person's effort to get at the minds of others.

The difference between "A Preliminary Research Report" as the subtitle of Chapters 21 and 22 and "A Research Report" as that of Chapter 23 is that I had thought of the first two (1950) as interim efforts but by the time of the third (1952) had considered the collection and organization of field materials over with and had abandoned the expectation of finishing some of the tasks described in that paper. More particularly, in the first note to Chapter 21, "Culture Change in Loma," I refer to the forthcoming monograph on Loma in which the full documentation of what appears to be largely impressionistic will be found. That paper is still concerned with developing "theory" and "theories," as is Chapter 22, on "Leadership in Loma" (see especially the last pages and in particular n. 8)—theories concerning culture change and leadership. I did not find it necessary to say what I meant by theory nor to justify or even question the notions of culture change and leadership, as I had already done in regard to culture pattern, although not, or hardly, in the paper dealing with it. Later my interest moved toward the nature of the ground of conceptualization and its process in general, and this is at least one of the reasons why the research reports remained preliminary, despite several drafts, even years after Chapter 23, of the monograph referred to. Chapters 21 and 22 may be of some interest because of the methods used to ascertain culture change (historical, life histories, school compositions), because of some aspects of the typology of leadership, including various types and their changes, or, despite the theoretical impetus and perhaps unwittingly, because of what the two papers drive home about some individual Lomans and Loma as a "dwelling-place of life" (Américo Castro; see Chapter 17).

As I said, I considered Chapter 23, "The Collection and Organization of Field Materials," no longer preliminary but more nearly terminal. The last section on "Writing up the Materials" is a report on the changes I found it necessary to make (or undergo) when I moved from collecting and classifying to writing (and never getting beyond the first two of the seven categories under which I had subsumed the topics that I had devised. These two resulted in more than one draft of that monograph, *Loma Culture Change*). Thus by the time I wrote this chapter I suspected that this was *not* the way in which I could do justice to my experience in Loma. The first formulation of the idea of surrender had occurred in 1950, in a short piece, even now only published in part in English, called, precisely, "Surrender and Catch." The beginnings of the idea are described in the first two paragraphs of the section on the "Collection of Field Notes and Their Classification by Topics" from which I quoted earlier in this introduction. I start the paper with the strong conviction that a student, who "is, after all, a man" and whose "subject matter, too, is man," must be as cognizant as he can of what he is doing and what is done to him in the process of his study and fully relate it, and complain

that there is so little written or known on this process between field work
and publication. At that time, it now appears, I took a step preparatory
to the notion of surrender, namely, emphasizing the importance of utmost
honesty so that the reader would be in the best possible position to follow,
examine, and assess the course of study and its findings. In the meantime,
I rather think that because the report itself is the "catch" of surrender—
the catch in the net, the yield, harvest, outcome, result, necessarily emerging structure—requirements such as honesty, too (other than, obviously,
in its "everyday" sense), should not be prescribed but called into question,
for it is only *post factum* that the characteristics of both surrender and
catch can be discerned and judged. It is like a story that can be told only
after its subject has ceased to exist, as Hannah Arendt reminds us
(Chapter 14).

"A New Reality in Social Science," Chapter 24, began as described in
n. 1, but was published originally in Italian (under the title, *Note sul
profilarsi di una nuova scienza sociale,* "Notes on the Emergence of a
New Social Science"). In the translation I have shortened it somewhat
and given it a new title.

I had been much impressed by the reports at anthropologists' meetings
in 1957 and 1958 on field experiences and conclusions drawn from them
and had discerned in them elements that converged toward a new social
science, a new concept of the world of the social scientist. I tried to explicate these in my comments at those meetings, later put together as the
Italian article. The emphasis (in the last pages) is on a diagnosis of our
time encountered more than once before (more specifically in Chapter 16
on the sociology of evil); veiled reference is made to "history as terror,"
explicit in Chapter 17 on sociology and history written about that time,
and attention is given to the particular nature and applicability of the
means-end scheme that *homo faber* would universalize (on which there is
more in the roughly contemporaneous Chapter 14). Despite the emphasis
on history, no connection is made between it and social change, as there
is in the papers on sociology and history and on social change (Chapters
17 and 5), the latter written shortly before the Italian version on the "new
social science." Since then, however, I have not tried seriously to work out
the differences and relations between the two studies. I now think that the
approach to take, if I were to attempt it, would lie in the Schutzian idea
of "world"; that is, I should try to identify the worlds of the student of
social change and the historian, and the first expectation that occurs to
me is that we must distinguish the former as described in Chapter 24
(active, in the present) from the one in Chapter 5 (analyst of the past).
This suggests a comparison between the meaning of practicality in relation to the active student of social change and the historian (cf. Chapter

17), as well as questions about the time dimensions of the worlds of these various types (which may not be two, as I expected, but three).

At any rate, even if I should have been aware of the problems of studying social change in relation to studying history when I drafted the essay in Italian (and I was more likely to have been than not, as the chronological observations above would seem to suggest), I did not touch on them. Whatever the reason, another concept I did work with is that of received notions: the action anthropologists whose writings I analyze came to their new reality having found many of their received notions inadequate to their experiences in the field and the articulation of their aims. This facet of surrender came to the fore spontaneously.

Chapter 24, of course, is a critical paper, but differs from others in being more constructive than negative as well as in taking its point of departure from cultural anthropology rather than sociology (as do Chapters 2, 5, and 12 to 18). As I said at the beginning of this introduction, I see no systematic or theoretical distinction between the two, and the understanding of our time, as inviting or requiring the suspension of received notions, surely does not bear exclusively on one or both nor on social science as a whole.

Five years after the Italian version of Chapter 24, in "This Is the Time for Radical Anthropology" (Chapter 25), the emphasis on suspending received notions has come to figure even more prominently as the definition of radicalism, both human and political. The two are distinguished by the different classes of received notions they suspend or, in terms most faithful to the paper, by the different classes of received notions they do *not* suspend, the former thereby running the risk of political, the latter of human mystification. The message in this rhetorical and practical paper points to the twofold danger and urges its avoidance by fusing the two radicalisms. This device-advice is based on the view of man as a mixed phenomenon (which is only hinted at here and of which we had earlier indications in the discussion of "Man's Historicity and Dualism" in the introduction to Part IV), both unique in the cosmos and sharing many features with innumerable other contents or inhabitants of the cosmos, of which man is a companion. Thus various strains come together in this chapter: among them are the problem of the two radicalisms, also discussed in Chapter 11 on the intellectual, and referred to in commenting on that chapter in the introduction to Part III; the vaster preoccupation, in which that with radicalism, even the movement toward it from liberalism (cf. remarks in connection with Chapter 10, "A Memorandum on the United States of America," in the same introduction), is embedded; and the preoccupation with surrender, which, to my continuing and growing surprise, becomes ever more distinct as I examine my own words in the work submitted. This is the last thing I want to say in my introduction to Part V on cultural anthropology, in which phase of the voyage the idea of surrender first emerged in my thoughts on my experience in Loma.

### NOTE

1.   Alfred Schutz, *The Phenomenology of the Social World* (1932), translated by George Walsh and Frederick Lehnert, with an introduction by George Walsh (Evanston, Ill.: Northwestern University Press, 1967), Chapter I.

# 19

# A CRITIQUE OF
# BATESON'S *NAVEN.*
# 1944

*Naven* [1] is a work that, in essence, represents the exposition of a theory formulated in the observation of a Iatmul ceremony which Mr. Bateson considered strange. The book is named after that ceremony, which takes place between the *wau* (mother's brother) and his *laua* (sister's child). The theory, which originally had the purpose of explaining *naven* within its own culture, makes use of concepts applicable to other phenomena and cultures. These concepts had been developed in part by Bateson before he went to New Guinea or knew anything of *naven,* but there they were further developed and partly applied without change to the materials found. Because *Naven* is presented as a book of science (p. 1), I give first an outline of Bateson's theory, that is, of the system of his concepts, and in Section II I show its method of application. In Section III I consider the book in terms of Mr. Bateson's development as a scientist and make some evaluative remarks.

# I

In an early chapter of *Naven* Bateson defines two basic concepts—structure and function. Cultural structure, he says, is

a collective term for the coherent "logical" scheme which may
be constructed by the scientist, fitting together the various
premises of the culture (p. 25).

In a note he insists that logic must be interpreted differently in every
culture, and before his definition of structure he gave one of premise,
another key term in this definition.

A premise is a generalised statement of a particular assumption or implication recognisable in a number of details of
cultural behaviour (p. 24).

It will be noted that both structure and premise are constructs in the
mind of the student of a given culture and that nothing is said in answer
to the various questions inherent in this position; for example, whether
all cultures are *Dinge an sich*, which cannot be understood on their own
terms but can only be appropriated by their students by virtue of mental
constructs built or modified for the purpose; or (if the answer is negative)
what the relation actually is between the student's construct and the facts,
material, or data as he finds them in studying a given culture. Later I try
to show that some of Bateson's definitions can be understood more clearly
if they are not taken literally but rather in the light of other definitions
or the exposition of the material.

Bateson does not define function, although he points out the insuffi-
ciencies of the various uses of the term in anthropological literature (pp.
26–29). He does, however, define five different types of function: structural, affective, ethological, eidological, and sociological (pp. 29 ff.). In
these definitions function is used synonymously with relationship:

1. *Structural* or "logical" relationships, between the cognitive
aspects of the various details of cultural behaviour: the cognitive reasons for behaviour.

2. *Affective* relationships, between details of cultural behaviour and the basic or derived emotional needs and desires of
the individuals: the affective motivation of details of behaviour.

3. *Ethological* relationships, between the emotional aspects of
details of cultural behaviour and the emotional emphases of
the culture as a whole.

4. *Eidological* relationships, between the cognitive aspects of
details of cultural behaviour and the general patterning of the
cultural structure.

> 5. *Sociological* relationships, between the cultural behaviour
> of the individuals and the needs of the group as a whole: the
> maintenance of solidarity, etc.

If these definitions are not to contradict Bateson's former ones, we must assume that all five relationships are again mental constructs of the investigator and, as such, elaborations of premise and structure, enriched by the elements of emotion and sociology. If I understand correctly, I am trying to establish a structural or logical relationship between such details of cultural behavior as a mother singing her child to sleep and Mr. Smith, a member of the same society or culture, going to the cinema, when I attempt to relate to them the cognitive aspects of each act: for instance, the mother's knowledge that the child will fall asleep more quickly if sung to and Mr. Smith's knowledge that he will broaden his mental horizon by seeing the picture in question. A large enough collection of relationships of this sort would then enable me to formulate the cognitive premises of the society of which the mother and Mr. Smith are members. I fail to understand, however, why these relationships are also called the cognitive reasons for behavior, for the mother's knowledge of the sleeping habits of her child is clearly not the reason for Mr. Smith's knowledge of the film he is interested in, or vice versa [1]. Hence the cognitive aspect should not mean anybody's knowledge of anything but rather the student's knowledge of how to fit observed details of behavior (the mother's or Mr. Smith's, for instance) into a coherent cognitive construct of the culture he is examining.

The definition of affective relationships is, in contrast, much clearer. To take the same details of cultural behavior, this time examining their affective aspects, I shall try to establish an affective relationship between the mother's love of her child (which moves her to sing to him) and Mr. Smith's craving for new experience (which moves him to prefer a visit to a theater to domestic boredom). Again I might arrive at a typology of emotional needs if I collect enough examples of affective motivations. In other words, an affective relationship is one between what people do and what they feel. Is it not possible that, analogously, a cognitive relationship is one between what people do and what they think? Perhaps I have taken Bateson's definition of cognitive relations too literally, this simple explanation being what he really means. In neither case, however, is anything said about how the student arrives at his mental construct or how he ascertains what people think and feel, nor do the subsequent definitions contribute answers. When, with reference to eidological relationships, Bateson uses the word patterning (which, I think, stands for premises), we are not informed in what way the student discovers a pattern. The failure to illuminate these problems is especially evident in a definition much less adorned with special terminology than the four preceding, namely, that of sociological relationships. How is the student to determine the needs of the group he is studying and how is he to distinguish between group needs and cultural needs? Where is he to draw the line between sociological and nonsociological types of knowledge and affection, that is, between those that affect, positively or negatively, the satisfaction of group needs and those that do not (if, indeed, there be any)?

More important than the concepts discussed are two others derived from them—ethos and eidos. Ethos and eidos have found subsequent application in Bateson and Mead's *Balinese Character* [2], whereas the others, I believe, have not. Furthermore (and this is more significant), ethos and eidos represent two of the three viewpoints alluded to in the subtitle of *Naven*, the third being sociology; that is, the *naven* ceremony, and to some extent the whole of Iatmul culture, are considered in their ethos, in their eidos, and in their sociology. Ethos is the sum of the emotional emphases of the culture, eidos, the "general picture of the cognitive processes" (p. 32). With reference to ethos and eidos Bateson does say something about the method by which the student may establish them in a given culture:

> . . . though the relationship between eidos and structural premises is so closely analogous to that between ethos and affective functions, . . . the study of ethos is a necessary preliminary to any conclusions about pragmatic functions [Malinowski's term]. But in the case of structure and eidos . . . the details of the cultural structure are to be first studied and from these the eidos is deduced. . . . in studying cultural structure we are concerned with the manifest cognitive content of behaviour, whereas in studying pragmatic functions we are concerned with the much more obscure emotional content. The manifest content can be *described* piece by piece and the underlying system deduced from the resulting description. But emotional significance can only be *ascribed* after the culture as a whole has been examined (pp. 32 f.).

This implies, if I understand Bateson correctly, that observation or understanding of the people under study is the prerequisite for both the ethos and eidos constructs, but I cannot follow his reasoning when he maintains that it is easier to construct the eidos than the ethos because the former is abstracted from description, whereas the latter is abstracted from ascription or imputation, the former being manifest, the latter, much more obscure. A statement purporting to be a piece of knowledge, although it makes no sense in the student's universe of discourse (such as "April is this afternoon"), can be more readily described in words, because it was itself originally expressed in words, than can an emotion, which may not be expressed in words but rather in facial or bodily movements. A mere description of either contributes as much or little to the reader's understanding of the culture. Whether we wish to understand the function of a piece of knowledge or a piece of affective behavior, a grasp of the culture as a whole (i.e., an ascriptive act) is required. In either case description and logically subsequent ascription are needed. Bateson's parceling out of one to eidos and the other to ethos appears to me to have resulted from confusion between forms of data (words and nonverbal behavior), on the one hand, and logical functions on the part of the student (words calling for their description, nonverbal behavior calling for its imputation) on the other. I return to this point later.

Sociology, finally, is the study of social functions, that is, of the effects of behavior in satisfying the needs of groups of individuals (p. 34). This definition, however, removes none of the difficulties arising from the former definition of sociological relationships.

Before some additional Batesonian concepts are discussed two other passages that refer to ethos must be mentioned. Ethos is also defined (p. 118) as "the expression of a culturally standardised system of organisation of the instincts and emotions of the individuals," a definition that formulates, in different terms, the one given before and introduces the problematical concept of instinct. The relative looseness with which Bateson delimits his terms is an example, I think, of his experimental method of procedure. This new definition of ethos is immediately followed by another: the ethos of a given culture is "an abstraction from the whole mass of its institutions and formulations." Bateson then suggests that

> it might therefore be expected that ethoses would be infinitely various from culture to culture—as various as the institutions themselves. Actually, however, it is possible that in this infinite variousness it is the *content* of affective life which alters from culture to culture, while the underlying systems or ethoses are continually repeating themselves. . . . we may ultimately be able to classify the types of ethos (*ibid.*).

Although here Bateson does not relate his ethos to Ruth Benedict's configurations, he does so in connection with the passage that distinguishes between the description of eidos and the ascription of ethos, already quoted, and again in his discussion of eidos and ethos as aspects of personality. In the first instance Bateson says:

> The sum of ethos and eidos, *plus* such general characteristics of a culture as may be due to other types of standardisation, together make up the configuration (p. 33).

From this statement it would appear that he considers the configuration to be conceptually broader than the ethos and eidos combined, although it is not clear what other types of standardization he has in mind; his own sociology might be understood as such, but if he had wished to, presumably he would have said so explicitly. In the other passage that refers to configurations the term obviously implies something else:

> I have stated that ethos and eidos are an expression of the affective and cognitive aspects of personality, but it is worth stressing that other aspects of the personality may also be standardised, and we may here very briefly consider some of these aspects:
>
> 1. Apollonian and Dionysian. Dr. Benedict has described two extreme poles of a possible variation in personality, and has shown that these extremes may be standardised in culture. It is not perfectly clear, however, how the syndromes which she has called Apollonian and Dionysian are related to ethos and eidos. My own impression is that in Apollonian personality we have a standardisation which might occur with many types of organisation of the emotions and sentiments. But until the phenomena of dissociation have been properly related to other psychological phenomena, and especially until we have some idea of what we mean by consciousness, it will not be possible to define these poles of variation more precisely (p. 255).

It is difficult to understand why other aspects of the personality are referred to, for Apollonian and Dionysian seem to be only certain ethological-eidological syntheses standardized in certain cultures. Furthermore, I do not believe that the concept of configurations (and in this context it does not matter whether they are used for defining cultures or personalities) suffers in distinctness from our lack of knowledge of such psychological phenomena as dissociation, consciousness, and coconsciousness any more than do ethos and, for that matter, eidos. All these concepts are affected by the relation between the culture studied and the mental construct produced by the student who interprets this culture in accordance with his own universe of discourse (that is, the universe of discourse of his general and scientific culture). No member of any culture looks at his own culture in terms of ethos, eidos, or configuration, whether in those general terms or in Bateson's or Benedict's specific applications, unless he be a disciple of such a school of thought and modify his relatively natural optics. Thus as long as we are contented with our own mental constructs as instruments of understanding a culture, without essentially paying attention to the subjective meaning of any example of cultural behavior to the people under study, the present state of our knowledge of psychology will not constitute a problem. Neither Bateson nor Benedict has raised, much less solved, the question of imputation, in spite of Bateson's distinction between description and ascription.

In addition to Apollonian and Dionysian, the other aspects of the personality which may also be standardized are tempo, perseveration, and the orientation to the world in terms of the past or the present (pp. 255 f.) One would think that a student who approached a culture in terms of ethos and eidos would conceive of these additional aspects as ethological, eidological, or mixed, yet Bateson mentions them only as heuristic tools in the understanding of cultures. Thus, if we identify the tempo of a culture (however this may be defined more specifically), note the way in which startling news is delayed or precipitated (given as an illustration of perseveration or its reverse), or diagnose the manner in which a culture is viewed by its members "either as a product of the past or as a mechanism working in the present," we may learn significant things about the culture without bothering, in theory at least, with the place of this insight in a more general system, such as that of ethos-eidos or of configurations. To leave tempo systematically undetermined is in my opinion as stimulating as making it (or, more precisely, sociocultural time) a referential principle of integralist sociology, as Professor Sorokin has done in *Sociocultural Causality, Space, Time.* Whether or not perseveration is logically an aspect of tempo, it appears to me to fit in with the idea of Dionysian and Apollonian configurations; the precipitous type could be provisionally associated with the former, and the delaying type with the latter; singling out this element of perseveration for special analysis might also lead to a refinement of the concept of configuration and of its application. Finally, in regard to the emphasis on orientation toward the past or toward the present (why not toward the future?), it is worth noting that an orientation conceptualized in similar terms may be found in the "*mañana* configuration" which Dr. Florence Kluckhohn has described as instrumental in the culture of the Atarqueños. It may be mentioned that the theoretical framework she and Professor Clyde Kluckhohn have evolved presents an important improvement, especially in the distinction between pattern and configuration, over Benedict's and (by implication) Bateson's schemes because it bears witness to the recognition of the distinction between fact and mental construct.

The remaining concepts that Bateson introduces may be dealt with more briefly; although those discussed were created to comprehend in one term phenomena not usually taken together in anthropological theory, the others are rather new labels for phenomena that had hitherto been given no label, or a different one. These are centripetal and peripheral social organizations and the terms complementary schismogenesis and symmetrical schismogenesis.

Social organization is centripetal "if it depends upon a single central authority or upon some form of hierarchy" (p. 281). It is peripheral "if it depends for its sanctions not upon a higher authority but upon the behaviour of other equivalent groups" (p. 285). These are glossary definitions, and no others are given in connection with the description of the field data that led Bateson to distinguish between the two types of organization. Commoner terms, for instance authoritarian or hierarchical, might have been used instead of centripetal and equalitarian or democratic instead of peripheral, but it would be unfair to consider Bateson's neologisms, outside their genetic context, which is discussed in the following section.

Schismogenesis is a term described by Bateson before the publication of *Naven* in his "Culture Contact and Schismogenesis" [3], a paper stimuated by "A Memorandum for the Study of Acculturation," written by Redfield, Linton, and Herskovits [4]. As developed in *Naven*, however, schismogenesis is a clearer concept, more closely applied to the facts under study, than in the earlier article; it has also been deprived of some of its earlier elaborate ramifications and distinctions. Schismogenesis is defined in *Naven* as

> a process of differentiation in the norms of individual behaviour resulting from cumulative interaction between individuals (p. 175).

Although this is a process closely related to acculturation and social differentiation, Bateson's distinction between two main types of schismogenesis is, I believe, new:

> If . . . one of the patterns of cultural behaviour, considered appropriate in individual *A*, is culturally labelled as an assertive pattern, while *B* is expected to reply to this with what is culturally regarded as submission, it is likely that this submission will encourage a further assertion, and that this assertion will demand still further submission. We have thus a poten-

tially progressive state of affairs, and unless other factors are
present to restrain the excesses of assertive and submissive
behaviour, *A* must necessarily become more and more assertive, while *B* will become more and more submissive; and this
progressive change will occur whether *A* and *B* are separate
individuals or members of complementary groups.

Progressive changes of this sort we may describe as *complementary* schismogenesis. But there is another pattern of relationships between individuals or groups of individuals which
equally contains the germs of progressive change. If, for example, we find boasting as the cultural pattern of behaviour in
one group, and that the other group replies to this with
boasting, a competitive situation may develop in which boasting leads to more boasting, and so on. This type of progressive
change we may call *symmetrical* schismogenesis (pp. 176 f.).

Thus schismogenesis is complementary if the process of differentiation in
the norms of individual or group behavior (resulting from cumulative
interaction between the individuals or groups) generates behavior in the
two individuals or groups culturally regarded as of two different (complementary) sorts, whereas it is symmetrical if it generates behavior in
the two individuals or groups culturally regarded as the same kind. The
usefulness of the two terms is again examined in connection with their
application to the field material, but a minor objection to the general
term schismogenesis would be that not all schismogeneses are characterized by the kind of personal conflict "schism" suggests nor is a schism
necessarily implied in Bateson's definition.

The *Naven* glossary lists the more technical terms used, and in part
defined, in the text. I introduce them only when the analysis of the application of Bateson's conceptual framework to the understanding of Iatmul
culture calls for them.

# II

In Section I I have tried to summarize Bateson's theory insofar as I
thought it could be detached from the context of the present study; we
must now see how the concepts presented have been applied to the
analysis of the problems with which *Naven* deals. Because Bateson illustrates this in a personal way, a concurrent description of the organization
of the book is unavoidable.

The Foreword consists mainly of acknowledgments, but a detailed

Table of Contents and a little explanatory note (p. ix) indicate the experimental character of the book:

> This Table is provided to help those who may be interested in dissecting the arguments contained in this book. Every heading in the book is listed in the Table, and, in addition, a number of finer sub-divisions, not specially marked in the text, are here given the dignity of headings.

In "Methods of Presentation" (Chapter I) Bateson distinguishes between artistic and scientific techniques and briefly discusses among the latter the functional school in anthropology. The scope and the limitations of his own book are set forth as follows (pp. 2 f.):

> The present work is a description of certain ceremonial behaviour of the Iatmul people of New Guinea in which men dress as women and women dress as men, and an attempt—crude and imperfect, since the technique is new—to relate this behaviour, not only to the structure and pragmatic functioning of Iatmul culture, but also to its ethos.

> This enquiry will involve me in a perhaps tedious discussion of abstractions, and to those who have some difficulty with, or a distaste for, epistemology I would recommend that they read first the descriptive chapters, especially those on the ethos of Iatmul culture, so that a preliminary study of concrete examples may make clear my abstractions. Others may find that the Epilogue, in which I have recounted some of the theoretical errors into which I fell in the course of my enquiry, will help them to understand my present theoretical position.

It is announced that the study is synchronic only and that therefore causal explanations are in terms of conditional, not of precipitating, causes. A brief sketch of the geographical position and of the social organization of the Iatmul is presented. The Iatmul, among whom Mr. Bateson spent more than fifteen months, live on the middle reaches of the Sepik River [5].

After this miscellaneous but concise introduction Bateson proceeds directly to describe the *naven* ceremonies (Chapter II). *Naven* is performed by the *wau* (mother's brother) in honor of his *laua* (sister's child). The numerous occasions on which a *naven* may be called for a boy or man are grouped by Bateson into five classes. First is major achievements, such as homicide or help toward homicide, which are celebrated with an elaborate *naven* when they occur for the first time in the life of the particular *laua* and with a simpler one when repeated. Second, most standard cultural acts, when performed for the first time (but not when repeated) are honored by a *naven*—the killing of certain animals, planting certain plants, felling a sago palm, using a spear-thrower, and many other activities. Third, the *wau* exhibits some *naven* behavior whenever his *laua* performs an act characteristic of his position as *laua*—the exhibition of totemic ancestors of the *wau*'s clan or beating secret slit-gongs; these acts are conceived as representing a mixture of the duties, services, and privileges of the *laua*. Fourth, if the *laua* boasts in the presence of his *wau*, the *wau* will show some *naven* behavior, but if the boasting goes too far the *naven* behavior is carried out in a spirit of anger or annoyance rather than in one of congratulation. Fifth, changes in the social status of the boy—the boring of his ears or his nasal septum, his initiation, and his marriage (but neither his birth nor his death)—are celebrated by a *naven*. The number of and typical occasions for *naven* are fewer for girls than for boys; however, catching fish with hook and line, washing sago, bearing a child, and other acts may call for a celebration.

Bateson has witnessed only five *naven* "in which any of the ritual was carried out" (p. 11); the most frequent *naven* behavior, shown on the numerous occasions when the *laua*'s achievement is brought to the attention of his *wau*, is limited to gestures only. The *wau*

> exclaims: "*Lan men to!*" (husband thou indeed!), throws some lime over his *laua* and hails him ceremonially with a string of names of ancestors of *wau*'s clan (p. 10).

Quite different are the large *naven* ceremonies. In those witnessed by Bateson the *wau* were dressed as filthy and decrepit women (more exactly as widows) and the female relatives as smartly dressed men. The ceremonies involved a presentation of gifts to the *laua*, some of them including the formulas for dances and other symbolic acts, and always concluded with the *laua*'s gift of valuables to his *wau*. The larger the ceremony, the more *wau*, *laua*, and other persons that participate, the groups sometimes extending to the entire village and even to classificatory *laua* residing in other villages. It may last an hour or longer or a whole day. The behavior of the various relatives, as observed on several occasions taken together, is summarized as follows:

> *Wau* (mother's brother) wears grotesque female attire; offers his buttocks to male *laua*; in pantomime gives birth to female *laua* who looses his bonds; supports himself on the adze presented by her; presents food to *laua* of either sex and receives in return shell valuables; acts as female in grotesque copulation with *mbora*. These ceremonial acts may be performed either by own *wau* or classificatory *wau*—most usually the latter.

*Mbora* (mother's brother's wife) wears either grotesque female attire or (probably grotesque) male attire; dances with digging stick behind her head; takes male part in mimic copulation with *wau*; like *wau*, she presents food to the hero of the *naven* and receives valuables in return.

*Iau* (father's sister) wears splendid male attire; beats the boy for whom *naven* is celebrated; steps across his prostrate *mbora*; participates in mimic contest between *mbora* and *iau* in which the former snatch the feather headdress from the latter.

*Nyame* (mother) removes her skirt but is not transvestite; lies prostrate with other women when the homicide steps across them all.

*Nyanggai* (sister) wears splendid male attire; accompanies the homicide, her brother, when he steps across the women; he is ashamed but she attacks their genitals, especially that of *tshaishi*; weeps when *wau* displays anal clitoris [represented by an orange-coloured fruit].

*Tshaishi* (elder brother's wife) wears splendid male attire; beats husband's younger brother and her vulva is attacked by his sister.

*Tawontu* (wife's brother, *i.e.*, *wau* of ego's children) presents food to sister's husband (*lando*) and receives valuables in return. *Tawontu* may, I believe, rub his buttocks on *lando's* shin, when the latter marries *tawontu's* own sister (pp. 21f.).

It is obvious that these roles and activities make no sense and, as already pointed out, Bateson has introduced a number of concepts in the hope that they will make the ceremony comprehensible. In the following chapter he deals with the concepts of structure and function, which I have discussed in general terms. Bateson says (p. 23):

> I have described the *naven* ceremonies with a minimum of references to the culture in which they are set; and any attempt to *explain* them must take the form of relating the ceremonies to their setting. Even to construct an historical theory of their origin would require an exhaustive examination of the remainder of the culture, and this is still more true of any theorising which would account for the *naven* in terms of the structure or of the functioning mechanisms of the culture. Since I shall try to give analyses of the position of *naven* from both structural and functional points of view, it will be well to state definitely what I mean at this stage by the two concepts, Structure and Function.

In a footnote Bateson explains what he means by this stage:

> This chapter contains a statement of my theoretical position
> when I was writing the body of this book. The various de-
> scriptive chapters were a series of experiments in the use of
> the different abstractions which are here discriminated and
> defined. On the whole these abstractions have stood the test
> of experiment, and their use has led to generalisations which
> I have thought interesting.
>
> The meaning which I attach to the terms *affective* and *cogni-
> tive* is here left vague, and the whole book was written with
> a vague use of these terms. I hoped that experiments in the
> description of culture might clear up this matter which the
> study of individual psychology has left obscure. In the
> Epilogue from a comparison of my various methods I have
> gone on to attempt the solution of this problem, and the
> position at which I finally arrive is slightly different from that
> which is outlined in this chapter. To re-write my statement
> of working hypotheses in terms of the results of my experi-
> ments would take away from the "detective interest" of the
> theoretical chapters.

This quotation shows very clearly the character of *Naven* as conceived
by its author, and it also shows the developmental position, so to speak,
of Bateson's concepts, even of concepts as central to his theory as structure and function. Nevertheless, because their definitions, reported earlier
in this chapter, are final within the limits of the present book, it seemed
to me reasonable to criticize them as scientific concepts, regardless of their
place in the development of Bateson's scientific attitude.

In the following three chapters on "Cultural Premises Relevant to the
*Wau-laua* Relationship," "Sorcery and Vengeance," and "Structural Analysis of the *Wau-laua* Relationship" Bateson discusses Iatmul culture
from the structural point of view. In the first of these chapters the technique of arriving at the premises underlying the *wau-laua* relation is
described as the ascertainment of identifications (and discriminations) in
relations between individuals, especially relatives. Identification (a term
adopted from Radcliffe-Brown) between two individuals is characterized
by the fact that many details of their behavior are similar, that many
details of the behavior of other individuals are similar to both, and that
usually each of them behaves as if he had performed acts that were
actually performed by the other.

With reference to *naven*, Bateson describes one discrimination and four types of identification. The discrimination is between the *wau* and *nyai'* (father's brother or father), in regard to kinship terms and many behavior patterns toward these relatives. Certain identities obtain between father and son, between mother's clan and child (this seeming paradox is resolved if the kind of behavior exemplifying one or the other identity is taken into consideration), between brother and sister, and between a woman and her husband. Bateson illustrates these identities or elements of identity abundantly. Father-son identity is shown in the patrilineal system of clans and in a number of kinship terms which are compounds that refer to a whole group of patrilineal ancestors or to patrilineal ancestors in general. Father and son are thus largely identified by and for the outsider, but they are sharply differentiated as one to the other by a number of tabus that make intimacy impossible. The fact that the child is in some way also linked with its mother's clan is

> symbolically expressed in the native theory of gestation. It is supposed that the bones of the child are a product of the father's semen, while its flesh and blood (somewhat less important) are provided by the mother's menstrual blood. . . . [Thus] the child is in one way a member of its father's clan, but at the same time it is in quite a different way a member of its mother's clan (p. 42).

The child is given two sets of names belonging to the totemic ancestors of his paternal and maternal clans. These names apparently represent two different aspects of the personality and much ritual behavior is distinguished by the use of one or the other set. The elements of identity between brother and sister are again revealed in certain kinship terms and compounds, in important ceremonies connected with the passing-on of clan names, and in the fact that both, except for the gender termination, are frequently given the same name. Finally, the element of identification between a woman and her husband, which is not reciprocal, is indicated in their home, labor, and economic activity and in their usual behavior toward outsiders, but it can also be noted in some of the terms applied to less important ramifications of kinship.

The next chapter illustrates these identifications according to the ideas and practices of sorcery and retribution. An important concept, which recurs in the cases of vindictive sorcery cited by Bateson, is *ngglambi*. It designates both a feeling of dangerous and infectious guilt and a dark cloud enveloping the house of a man who has committed some outrage. The first case reported indicates that "*ngglambi* infection comes typically down the patrilineal line and illustrates the identification of father and son" (p. 58). The second story describes elements of identification between brother and sister, woman and husband, sorcerer (child) and his mother, and father and son. The remaining nine cases show similar identifications.

The concept of identification is an important element in making the "Structural Analysis of the *Wau-laua* Relationship" (Chapter VI) comprehensible. The *wau* (mother's brother) is to some extent identified with the mother; hence some of the *laua*'s behavior toward the *wau* is that of a child toward his mother. A man is also to some extent identified with his father; hence some of the *wau*'s behavior toward his *laua* is the same as if the *laua* were the *wau*'s sister's husband.

> Lastly it is possible that the *wau-laua* relationship has features which are due to other identifications which we have not considered, or that the relationship may have certain features *sui generis* (p.75).

The position of the mother in Iatmul culture is characterized by providing food, pride and self-negation, and comforting. These same aspects are stressed in the behavior of the *wau* towards his *laua*. That he gives him food has already been mentioned. Pride and self-negation are expressed when the *wau* hails his *laua* with a string of names of outstanding totems of the maternal clan, when he throws lime over him, and when he wears filthy female garments to shame himself. At the *laua*'s initiation the *wau*—then actually called "mother"—comforts him. Similarly, the typical child-mother behavior patterns of loyalty and boasting are expressed by the *laua* toward his *wau*. The relation between brothers-in-law, explicable mainly because the sister is sold to her future husband and revealing a mixture of indebtedness, distrust, and co-operation, can also be traced in the *wau-laua* and *laua-wau* behavior. Nevertheless, some features of the *wau*'s behavior remain unexplained; for example, the *wau* may not take fire from his *laua*'s house, recalling the tabu that prevents a father from eating food collected by his son. If in this instance the role of the *wau* resembles that of the father, this resemblance may likewise underlie the fact that he does not engage in crude commercial transactions with his *laua*.

The residual details of behavior are mentioned in the following summary:

> Our experiment has shown that almost the whole of the *wau*'s cultural behaviour can be analysed in terms of two identifications. Of the details which remain unaccounted for some can

be referred to a third identification but a few still defy anal-
lysis in these terms. We still do not know why the *wau's*
behaviour tends to be exaggerated and comical, why the
*laua* is regarded as the ancestors of the maternal clan, and
why this culture has followed the logic of its identifications to
such extreme conclusions. These problems must be left for
solution in terms of aspects of Iatmul culture other than the
purely structural (p. 85).

After the discussion of the structural point of view Chapter VII expounds
the sociological. The decisive question, according to the Batesonian definition of sociology, is whether the *naven* ceremony has any effect on the
integration of society. Because the *wau-laua* relationship is strengthened
by the *naven*, the question may be narrowed by asking what effects this
strengthening has on the integration of society. At this point Bateson
interpolates the remark that the statistics required to answer sociological
questions were not collected by him, and that

the [present] chapter itself is only included for the sake of
giving an illustration of the problems and methods of approach of sociology in the strict sense of the word (p. 87, note).

To understand the sociological repercussions of the *wau-laua* relation
we should recall that it is usually the classificatory *wau* who performs
*naven*; the integrating aspect of the ceremony therefore extends to more
individuals than if it were limited to the consanguineous *wau* only. Moreover, the *wau-laua* relation itself is particularly important as an integrating force because the marriage regulation, in other societies often the
chief integrating factor, is extremely weak among the Iatmul. Equally
weak, in comparison with the *wau-laua* relation, is the only other affinal
link that is culturally stressed at all, that between a man and his *lanoa
nampa* ("husband people," including sister's husband, sister's husband's
brother, sister's husband's father, and sister's husband's son). Only by
appeal to these two relations (which are based, respectively, on marriages
in the past and in the present) can cooperation be obtained. Even so,
quarrels are not rare, and integration in general is low. Villages are also
frequently too large to be integrated and consequently split. The particular maner of these fissions adds to the disintegrating effect of the fissions
themselves, for

. . . when they occur [they] invariably follow the lines of the
patrilineal groups—a clan, a phratry or a moiety splitting off
from the parent community and thereby rending the system

of affinal linkages. From this pattern of cleavage it is evident
that the patrilineal linkages are stronger than the affinal, the
latter presenting as it were a plane of weakness of the community. Under these circumstances the importance of any factor
which strengthens the affinal links becomes apparent and we
are justified in saying that the villages could not be as big as
they are if it were not for *naven* ceremonies or some analogous
phenomenon (p. 97).

In this conection it must be mentioned that the Iatmul have no sanctions
*ex officio* (in the name of the community), only personal sanctions for
personal offenses. These offenses may lead to quarrels among groups
defined by affinal or clan linkages, and it is the major disputes that gen-
erate the community fissions. In discussing these phenomena, Bateson
describes the Iatmul system as peripheral, in contrast to most Western
societies, which are organized centripetally:

> . . . always the offender expects his own people to be active
> on his side and the quarrel remains one between two *periph-
> eral* groups, never taking the *cenripetal* form which we might
> phrase as "Rex or State *versus* So-and-so." Such a form is in-
> deed precluded by the considerable feeling which exists in the
> Itamul community against any participation of outside per-
> sons in quarrels which do not concern them (p. 99).

I have suggested above that Bateson's definitions of peripheral and centripetal did not seem to warrant a new terminology, but viewed in the
present context it seems plausible that these neologisms are preferable,
as ideologically and emotionally more neutral, to commoner terms such
as authoritarian and equalitarian.

Before describing the Iatmul ethos, Bateson surveys, in Chapter VIII,
"Problems and Methods of Approach," the results of considering his
material structurally and sociologically and discusses some other problems. He returns here to the unresolved questions raised by the exaggerated and burlesque behavior of the *wau*, by the large size of the
villages, and by the *wau*'s motive in gaining the allegiance of his *laua*
with *naven*. He suggests that "all these questions might be answered
[by the ethological method] in terms of emotional satisfaction given to
the individuals by the various phenomena, buffoonery, large villages and
*naven*" (p. 111). Most of the chapter is devoted to a discussion of the
relation between this method and various concepts from which ethos is
derived, especially *Zeitgeist* and Ruth Benedict's configuration.

Both holistic approaches to the study of cultures emphasize systems of thought and scales of values whose carriers are, of course, the individuals living in a given culture. The mentality of the individuals is standardized by the culture in which they participate (the term standardized subsuming both the selection and the education of these individuals and assuming that both processes are effective). These ideas have been fused and transformed in a concept of ethos which, as the basis of culture study, can be defined as follows:

> The essence of the [ethological] method is . . . that we first determine the system of sentiments which is normal to the culture and emphasised in its institutions; and when this system is identified we are justified in referring to it as a factor which has been active in shaping the institutions (p. 116).

Although Bateson has much to say in justification of this circular argument, he does not tell us how we can determine the system of sentiments normal to the culture unless by inferring it from an observation of the institutions. The institutions, however, are not stressed by Bateson in order to compare their functions with those of the same institutions in other cultures because any one institution, marriage for example, may have so many different functions that its comparative study would not verify any statement of its function in any one culture. Rather, on the basis of the definition of ethos previously quoted (Section I), Bateson hopes to arrive at verifiable types of ethos, similar to the types of personality distinguished by psychologists, perhaps, indeed, with the help of personality types. To illustrate further the concept of ethos two examples of contemporary English ethos are adduced. One is the temporary ethos characteristic of a casual conversation, the other more permanent and typical of an army mess or a college high table, in which the significance of tradition is stressed. In these examples the terms mood, atmosphere, casual, and traditional appear to me quite adequate and no more vaguely defined by usage than is ethos by Bateson. It is more important, however, to examine the application of ethological theory to the analysis of Iatmul culture, and this is a task to which the next six chapters of *Naven* are devoted.

In the first, in which the ethos of the men is discussed, it is pointed out that the ethological sex division is indeed the most important differentiation in Iatmul culture. The masculine ethos can best be observed in three complexes: the ceremonial house and its activities, initiation, and head hunting. The ceremonial houses are proud and impressive, richly ornamented buildings which serve as club houses for debate and quarrel as well as for rituals calculated to impress the women. The debates of the men are highly histrionic, erudite, and ironical. The most frequent topics are extracts from totemic history, and the debaters try to outdo one another in esoteric knowledge, which may have as many as twenty thousand polysyllabic names, or by revealing some secret about the totemic ancestors of the other side. This frequently leads to brawls and even to long-term quarrels and subsequent feuds that involve killing by sorcery. The less erudite a man, the more he relies on boasting and abuse, and both the erudite and the abusive types are accepted, but a third type, the nervous and apologetic speaker who tries in vain to be erudite, is despised. Pride, buffoonery, erudition, and self-congratulation are clearly shown in the men's behavior, whether in connection with ritual ceremonies or with everyday work, much of which is also planned in the ceremonial house.

> Each man of spirit struts and shouts, play-acting to convince himself and others of the reality of a prestige which in this culture receives but little formal recognition (p. 129).

The spirit prevailing in initiation is that of bullying and swagger. On one occasion

> one moiety of the initiators decided that the novices had been bullied as much as they could stand and were for omitting one of the ritual episodes. The other moiety then began to brag that the lenient ones were afraid of the fine fashion in which *they* would carry out the bullying; and the lenient party hardened their hearts and performed the episode with some extra savagery (p. 131).

Several observations and considerations lead Bateson to the assumption that during the course of the initiation ceremonies the novices change their ethos from feminine to masculine.

In addition to the characteristics mentioned, Iatmul men are distinguished by their tendency to "cut off their own noses to spite the other fellow's face" (p. 135), that is, to throw "the whole initiatory system open to men, women and children, showing everything to everybody," whenever a serious situation develops in the initiatory enclosure (e.g., when a woman sees some of the secret objects, such as the sacred flutes, or when a critical quarrel breaks out). This tendency is more often threatened verbally than carried out in action, but Bateson cites some examples of a general breakdown of the initiatory system accomplished by such "breaking of the screens."

Head hunting is extinct among the Iatmul, but descriptions show that in it the masculine ethos was perhaps most completely expressed. Head hunting was a sport without rules of sportsmanship: its two main motives were the personal pride of the hunter and his satisfaction in the prosperity and strength of his community. Failure was associated with shame and followed by savage vengeance.

The ethos of the women (Chapter X) contrasts sharply with that of the men. The Iatmul woman is unostentatious, jolly, and cooperative, yet she is independent in many household and bargaining matters and frequently takes the initiative in love affairs. This double emphasis is especially evident in ceremonial activities, the friendly and cooperative spirit being manifest in the celebrations that women hold by themselves, as distinguished from the pride shown in the celebrations they hold publicly, in the dancing ground, with men in the audience. In these public performances the women exhibit a mild transvesticism, wearing, among other things, ornaments usually worn by men.

The contrast between the masculine and the feminine ethos emerges even more distinctly in events highly charged with emotion than in everyday and ceremonial life. This is especially clear when attitudes toward death are considered (Chapter XI). Although the reaction of the women appears to be a natural expression of sorrow, that of the men is to take death as an occasion for exhibiting the competitive pride of the initiatory moieties. Describing the men's behavior in one particular case, Bateson says:

> They escaped entirely from a situation which was embarrassing because it seemed to demand a sincere expression of personal loss, an expression which their pride could scarcely brook. From this situation they took refuge in a cultural stunt. They re-phrased their attitude towards the dead and expressed it satisfactorily in terms of spectacular pride, the emotional language in which they are at ease (pp. 155 f.).

Bateson cautions, however, against too facile a description of such ethological contrasts and, for that matter, of culture traits in general.

> I have described the ethos of the men as histrionic, dramatising, over-compensating, etc., but these words are only a description of the men's behaviour as seen by me, with my personality moulded to a European pattern. My comments are in no sense absolute statements. The men themselves would no doubt describe their own behaviour as "natural"; while they would probably describe that of the women as "sentimental."

> It is difficult, too, to describe a pair of contrasting ethoses
> without so weighting the descriptions that one or the other
> appears preferable or more "natural." The business of the
> scientist is to describe relationships between phenomena, and
> any ethos which he finds in a culture must be regarded not as
> "natural" but as normal to the culture. Unfortunately what
> is normal to one culture may well be abnormal to another,
> and the anthropologist has at his disposal only the adjectives
> and phrases of his own culture. Thus it has happened that
> English people with whom I have discussed Iatmul ethos
> have sometimes remarked that the women appear to be "well
> adjusted" while the men appear to be "strained" and "psy-
> chopathic." My friends forget that the values assigned by
> European psychiatrists to various mental conditions are either
> *cultural* values based upon European ethos or estimates of
> the fitness of the individual for life in a European community
> (pp. 157 f.).

This caveat is of course not new, but because Bateson gives it this
importance we look for an attempt to change his method in order to
arrive at a higher degree of objectivity. Relevant to this is a later passage
from the Epilogue (Section III).

In the following chapter on "The Preferred Types" Bateson shows
that two male types are admired in Iatmul culture: the man of violence
and the man of discretion. The violent man is more highly esteemed, but
the esoteric knowledge of the discreet man is considered more trustworthy. Bateson attempts to relate these preferred types to Kretschmer's
cyclothyme and schizothyme personalities. He did not collect field data
with this theory in mind, for he first read Kretschmer only after returning
to England. Hence his admittedly inconclusive remarks are designed to
call attention to the possibilities of this approach to the study of cultures
and, in particular, to the study of acculturation:

> I suggest that a very great deal of the action of culture con-
> tact in destroying institutions may be due to mechanisms of
> this kind—the contact upsetting the delicate adjustment be-
> tween the temperaments of deviant individuals and the ethos
> of the culture (p. 170).

"Ethological Contrast, Competition and *Schismogenesis*" (Chapter
XIII) is essentially an exposition of the theory of schismogenesis, which
I have already discussed. Bateson has asked himself how ethological contrasts, such as the one described for Iatmul men and women, originate,
and his assumption is that in Iatmul culture the ethos is acquired in the

later training of boys and girls rather than in earlier childhood experiences. Complementary schismogenesis is exemplified in the exhibitionism of the men versus the showing of admiration by the women, in the behavior of the initiators versus that of the novices, and possibly in the *laua*'s boasting versus the *wau*'s attitude in shaming himself. Symmetrical schismogenesis appears most clearly in the competitive bullying of rival moieties at initiation.

To show the importance of the concept of schismogenesis Bateson points out that certain forms of marital, neurotic, prepsychotic, and paranoiac maladjustment in our own culture might be understood or even cured if they were treated as schismogenic phenomena. Carrying his remarks on the significance of schismogenesis for the study of culture contact beyond the preliminary description in *Man*, Bateson says:

> The process . . . by which two groups whose respective cultures are mutually irrelevant evolve a complementary or symmetrical relationship in terms of behaviour which is normal to neither group, has never been investigated. It should, if susceptible of study, give us clues to the process of establishment of schismogenic pairs.
>
> Once complementary patterns of behaviour have been established, it is my opinion that subsequent schismogenesis is responsible for many of the antipathies and misunderstandings which occur between groups in contact. Hand in hand with the ethological divergence we find the development of structural premises which give permanence and fixity to the split. But it is not clear to what extent these formulations, of "colour-bar," "racial antipathy," and mutual avoidance contribute to promoting the schismogenesis. It is possible that some of these formulations prevent it from going too far. These are problems which need investigation (pp. 185 f.).

Finally, in the field of politics symmetrical schismogenesis is typical of international conflicts, whereas complementary schismogenesis characterizes class war.

It will be noticed that schismogenesis is a concept that brings together a number of phenomena which, without it, would remain in different fields of knowledge. Whether these phenomena can also be explained and the kind of explanation that could be achieved in terms of schismogenesis are problems whose treatment would require a special paper, but I believe that the merits inherent in Bateson's concept could thereby be established.

In the remainder of the chapter Bateson discusses the nature of the progress and control of schismogenesis. In Iatmul culture, for instance, the masculine ethos cannot develop unchecked. Thus

> if a man specialises too far in violence, his wives will run away from his house, his brothers-in-law will turn against him, and he will live under a threat of perhaps violent death, but certainly sorcery (p. 192).

There seem to be several processes that in general counteract the infinite progression of schismogenesis. It is possible, Bateson argues, that inherent balancing features are present in every type, so that none is purely symmetrical or purely complementary. Further, in one complementary schismogenesis there may be elements of another that prevent the first from excessive growth.

> To give a hypothetical case, it is likely that, in a marriage in which there is a complementary schismogenesis based upon assertion-submission, illness or accident may shift the contrast to one based on fostering and feebleness. Such a shift may bring instant relief to the schismogenic strain, even though the schismogenesis had previously reached the limits of cultural tolerance (p. 194).

The strain may also be relieved by a sudden shift in the terms of a symmetrical schismogenesis (e.g., from harshness to buffoonery among the Iatmul) or by outside elements, to face which the two parties unite in loyalty or hostility.

In the last of the chapters dealing with ethos all previous concepts are applied to the discussion of "The Expression of Ethos in *Naven*" (Chapter XIV). The ethological theory of *naven* is, briefly, as follows. *Naven* is the expression of pride in the achievements of the *laua*; since men cannot express it themselves, pride in someone else's success being contrary to their ethos, they (i.e., the *wau*) dress as women. At the same time the exhibitionism of the masculine ethos makes it more appropriate for men than for women to act on such an occasion. The transvesticism is explained by the men's contempt for the feminine ethos, especially for open grieving at death; hence the *wau* dresses in the filthiest of widow's garments. On the other hand, women express no contempt for the men's ethos, and their dressing in the best male attire, when they exhibit themselves publicly, is understandable merely in terms of transvesticism itself, by which they take over from the male ethos not only their activities (in this case, public performance) but also other aspects of behavior, such as dress. Although the *wau* acts as a woman, his buffoonery and exaggeration—inexplicable in structural terms—is normal to the male ethos. In a similar way Bateson interprets details of the behavior of the other relatives participating in *naven* (cf. earlier in this section) as expressions of sex ethos.

The chapter before the Epilogue concerns "The Eidos of Iatmul Culture." The primary task of the eidological approach is to explain the presence in Iatmul culture of so much structural detail, such as elaborate heraldry and totemism, and to elucidate this same hypertrophy in the initiation and *naven* plexuses:

> I said that cultural structure was a system built up by the scientist, and we may phrase our present problem in these terms: why should the materials of Iatmul culture drive the abstracting scientist to greater complexities of exposition than are demanded by, for example, the culture of the Arapesh? Is this complexity of exposition the reflection of a real complexity in the culture, or is it only an accidental product resulting perhaps from a disparity between the language and culture of the ethnographer and those of the community he is describing?
>
> Here we are on very difficult ground, and the scientist who has set out the exposition is perhaps the man least fitted to judge of the origin of its complexity. I can only say, first, that the Iatmul culture appeared to me complex and rich before I even attempted a structural analysis, and secondly, that the result of analysis has been to cause the culture to appear, to me at least, not more complex, but simpler. I can only trust to these impressions as evidence that the complexity is now entirely a creation of my own methods of thinking (p. 219).

Bateson adds the following in a note (*ibid.*):

> To some extent my methods of thinking—structural, ethological and sociological—are followed by the natives themselves. This matter is discussed at the end of this chapter (p. 250).

Here we return to the problem of the relation between the scientist's mental construct and the reality he tries to explain in terms of it; but Bateson seems to be translating a field experience or emotion, namely that of bewilderment, confusion, or complexity, into an objective quality inherent either in the culture under study or in the scientist's exposition of this culture.

Yet this comment is not relevant to eidos except as it records the reflection that led to the concept's formation and to the discovery of the most important characteristic of Iatmul eidos—high degree of intellectual activity unusual among primitive peoples. Memory, the basis of the vast and detailed erudition highly esteemed among the Iatmul, is, however, cultivated not as rote learning (to which the polysyllabic and usually paired names do not seem to lend themselves) but as a process of imagery or word-association, as shown by the continual slight changes in the order of recitation and by the debates which depend on hints at details and on the exhibition of objects rather than on the narration of chronological wholes. Proneness to kinesthetic thought is also shown "in the continual tendency to diagrammatise social organisation" (p. 225); that is, in ceremonies individuals are physically placed according to their positions in the totemistic or moiety systems of groupings.

Erudition is not confined to specialists but is found in almost all men (Bateson has no data on women), although there are, of course, great differences of degree, and all are proud of their knowledge.

> In the younger men, however, this passion for showing off even weakly developed erudition is almost completely checked by the feeling that erudition is only appropriate in senior men. I had three very intelligent youths who consistently avoided giving me names, and who referred me to their seniors when I pressed them. But I was told by other people in their absence that two of these youths were already well on the way towards erudition, and would be great debaters when they were older. Thus the reticence of the younger men on the subject of names does not imply that they are not, like their seniors, keen on this form of mental virtuosity (p. 227).

The most erudite men purport to be and are accepted as judges in matters concerning initiation or land tenure and many others, and thus contribute to the elaboration and maintenance of the culture. Similarly, the erudition exhibited chiefly in the debates pervades all other cultural institutions and activities. Spells, songs, the shamans' utterances, and agricultural products are given names, and marriages are often concluded in order to gain names.

Trying to characterize Iatmul thought further, Bateson says that much of it is intellectual (in "that slang sense in which it is used to imply that people are 'intellectual' rather than intelligent," p. 229), that is, concerned with questions that (to us) seem totally unreal. A long-standing controversy between two moieties regarding the nature of night is mentioned; another example is a dispute about the sun and the settlement of this dispute in favor of two suns, one of which is rotting in the plains; or an inquiry into the nature of ripples and waves, solved by one of

Bateson's informants (who had been present when he did some photographic developing, and who then implored him not to reveal the secret to members of clans other than his own). One final illustration (p. 232):

> A lunar eclipse occurred while I was in Kankanamun and I discussed this with my informants. I was rather surprised to find them but little interested in the phenomenon. They ascribed it to magic performed by the Tshuosh people. One informant, Iowimet, seemed rather doubtful about this theory, and asked me what we Europeans believed. I hedged for a while, and then explained the secret. The moon during the eclipse had turned red, and my informant had told me some days previously that the sun was a cannibal. I ascribed the redness of the moon to blood in the sun's excrement, and said that this material was between the moon and the earth obscuring the moon's brightness. This secret was quite a useful bond of understanding between my informant and me, and several times later he referred to it as "that matter we both know about."

Iatmul thought is also characterized "by a tendency to insist that what is symbolically, sociologically, or emotionally true, is also cognitively true" (*ibid.*) or, expressed in other terms, by a predilection for what to the outsider sounds like a paradox; for example, persons have various and often contradictory aspects, according to their identifications with the paternal and maternal clans, with the classificatory *wau*, and with their status as initiates. This contradictoriness is revealed even more clearly in the case of *wagan*, the most important type of spiritual being; certain of its identities are esoteric secrets known only to a few men. Again, a certain palm is believed also to be a fish (a statement that is sociologically but not cognitively explicable). Further, there is a tendency to emphasize the cognitively more obscure of two truths.

> In the *naven* ceremonies we can see the same sort of twisted thinking acted out in ceremonial. In a social and economic and emotional sense, the *wau* is a mother and wife of his *laua*. But in a strictly cognitive sense he is not anything of the sort. In the carrying out of the ceremonial, it is the emotional truth which is stressed, which, of the two, is the more difficult of cognitive assimilation (p. 235).

Bateson, however, does not demonstrate that the cognitive aspect of *naven* is easier than the emotional and does not even prove that for the Iatmul two aspects really exist.

Other patterns of Iatmul thought, some of which are logically contradictory, are described (*ibid.*):

> (*a*) A sense of pluralism: of the multiplicity and differentia-
> tion of the objects, people, and spiritual beings in the world.
>
> (*b*) A sense of monism; that everything is fundamentally one
> or at least is derived from one origin.
>
> (*c*) A sense of *direct* dualism: that everything has a sibling.
>
> (*d*) A sense of *diagonal* dualism—that everything has a sym-
> metrical counterpart.
>
> (*e*) Patterns of thought which govern the seriation of indi-
> viduals and groups; these patterns being apparently based
> upon (*c*) and (*d*).

Bateson gives convincing examples of these various patterns of thought;
it is necessary, however, to explain what he means by the two kinds of
dualism. Direct-dualism relations are established by analogy with two
siblings of the same sex; symmetrical dualism has an analogy in the relation of two opposite corners of a rhombus and is exemplified in the
brothers-in-law relationship and in the relation in the *naven* ceremony
between the father's sister, who dresses up as a man and is identified with
the father, and the mother's brother, who dresses up as a woman and is
identified with the mother. The seriation of individuals and groups (*e*)
is shown in the alternation of generations, of initiatory grades, and of
siblings; for instance, a *mbapma* (line) consists of one's own, one's paternal
grandfather's, and patrilineal grandson's generations; opposed to it is the
line formed by father's and son's generations.

Toward the end of this chapter the question whether the Iatmul themselves think in sociological, structural, and ethological terms and which
of them have the major emphases in their eidos is discussed. In Iatmul
culture most sociological concepts are represented symbolically; for example, the well-being of the community is ascribed to spiritual beings or the
fighting force of the community is symbolized by an eagle. This fact,
Bateson explains, shows that sociological behavior is not emphasized in
Iatmul culture nor are phrasings in terms of emotions. Structural phrasings, however, are heavily stressed; thus the *wau* is explicitly stated to
be a mother, much cultural behavior is viewed as being carried out
because it always has been, and stereotypes betray the structural viewpoint.

The chapter ends with a discussion of personality aspects other than
affective and cognitive on which I have already commented in Section I.

The book itself concludes with an Epilogue in which Bateson evaluates his work, especially the central theory, by explaining how it was evolved. The largely personal character of the epilogue makes it appropriate to treat it in a separate section.

# III

In what precedes I have tried to show the application of Bateson's concepts to his materials, my critique referring to questions of methodology and logic rather than subject matter. In this section I discuss some of the evaluative remarks. Bateson introduces the epilogue as follows:

> The writing of this book has been an experiment, or rather a series of experiments, in methods of thinking about anthropological material, and it remains to report upon how I was led to carry out these experiments, to evaluate the techniques which I devised, and to stress what I regard as my most important results.
>
> My field work was scrappy and disconnected—perhaps more so than that of other anthropologists. After all, we set out to do the impossible, to collect an exceedingly complex and entirely foreign culture in a few months; and every sincere anthropologist when he comes back to England discovers shocking gaps in his field work. But my case was somewhat worse. The average anthropologist has some definite interest in some one aspect of the culture he is studying, whether it be in historical reconstruction, in material culture, in economics, or in functional analysis, and he will at least collect an adequate supply of material for a book permeated by his particular point of view. But I had no such guiding interest when I was in the field. . . .
>
> I did not clearly see any reason why I should enquire into one matter rather than another. If an informant told me a tale of sorcery and murder, I did not know what question to ask next —and this not so much from lack of training as from excess of scepticism. In general, therefore, apart from a few standard procedures such as the collection of genealogies and kinship terminology, I either let my informants run on freely from subject to subject, or asked the first question which came into my head. Occasionally I made an informant go back to some previous subject of conversation, but I should have found it hard to give theoretical reasons for such special attention to certain subjects.

> This method, or lack of it, was wasteful, but it has its compensations. I know, for example, how great a value the natives set upon their enormous system of totemic names; and I know this, not from some colourless statement, but from the curious experience of writing down thousands, literally, of names at my informants' bidding; and I know it too from the more bitter experience of finding my note books full of names when I searched them for information about preferred types (pp. 257 f.).

Bateson then relates how the arrival of part of the manuscript of Benedict's *Patterns of Culture* and conversations with Fortune and Margaret Mead helped him to find out what he wanted to do, how his decision directed the later stages of his field work but still left him with only "bunches of facts" on his return to England, and, finally, how he came to organize *Naven* by starting from his theory of Iatmul transvesticism (Chapter XIV), to which other methods of approach were added until "it has become the present book" (p. 260).

Bateson places considerable emphasis on the process by which he had disposed of the fallacy of "misplaced concreteness" (the fallacy of taking points of view, or aspects, for things): ethos, eidos, and sociology are not parts of a culture, he learned, but aspects in terms of which the natives, or the student of the culture, think. In comparison with this the formulation of abstractions was relatively easy, but he gives the biographical history of their formulation. He summarizes this history by saying that he has now found a general approach to the study of human beings in society, namely, the application of five major points of view: "structural (and eidological), emotional (and ethological), economic, developmental and sociological" (p. 266); but the third and fourth of these points have not been illustrated in the study of Iatmul culture. In reviewing the application of the ethological and logical-eidological approaches to it Bateson discusses the significance of the sequence in which they are brought to bear. He reminds us that the general description of the ethos has preceded the analysis of the emotions displayed in connection with the *naven* ceremonies, whereas the discussion of the premises of Iatmul culture has preceded the general picture of Iatmul eidos. He then asks,

> why, if it is not justifiable to guess at motives before the whole ethos has been studied, is it permissible to attribute behaviour to specific premises before the eidos of the culture has been sketched (p. 267)?

Bateson's answer to this question includes his most specific discussion of the problem of the relation between the investigator's mental construct of a culture and that culture itself.

> This question is, I suspect, one of considerable importance, and its answer may well reflect upon the relation between the affective and cognitive aspects of the personality. At present I can only suggest two possible answers: the order of procedure which I have been forced to adopt may be a result either of my own psychology or of that of my informants. I have stated that in my own conscious mental processes, the structural and logical aspects of behaviour are more clearly seen than the emotional, and I believe that the same is true of the Iatmul men. If this observation be correct, then in attributing emotional value to details of behaviour I was speculating about the more unconscious processes and therefore needed the supporting material which could only be provided by a preliminary study of Iatmul ethos. But in the case of the logical aspects of behaviour I could hope for some degree of articulateness in my informants and could proceed directly to the statement of consistency between different details of behaviour (*ibid.*).

Thus Bateson has answered the question of the relation between the student's mental construct of the culture and the culture itself with the belief that the two coincide, a belief the reader may accept or reject in this particular case, whether or not he is convinced by the preceding exposition of Iatmul culture. I am inclined to think that if another anthropologist studied the Iatmul without being acquainted with Bateson's theories concerning this culture he would not arrive at the same picture of it in general, and of *naven*, that would necessitate the creation of the same concepts, for these concepts originated not only under the impact of Iatmul culture but under its impact on an individual with individual knowledge. Some of the constellations of this knowledge were unique; for example, the conversations with Fortune and Mead and the acquaintance with Benedict's theory at a particular point in the field work. A confirmation of Bateson's impressions by another anthropologist, however, would prove only that a second anthropologist thought about the Iatmul as the first did. Essentially this is true of any interpretation of cultures. These extracts—acts, ceremonies, and institutions—can be convincingly interpreted, but any attempt to make a whole of all the extracts is necessarily our own creation, except when it is a whole created by the members of those cultures, in which case we may report them. This, however, occurs in few cultures, if any, yet such creations may be regarded as more or less valid, and their validity increases with the number of extracts thereby interpreted, that is, by the application of concepts. The more clearly the concepts are understood by both the man who applies them and by the reader who is invited to assess the application, the more convincing the interpretation. The clarity of concepts is not only a function of their definition because each definition involves other concepts that must in turn be clear; the concept is the clearer, the more familiar we are with its component concepts through use in our daily discourse, both general and special. Most of Bateson's concepts are his own creations or represent nuances of the more common ones, and thus his definitions acquire a significance they would lack if he had been able to do without neologisms. That his definitions are largely unsatisfactory I sought to show in Section I. My quotation from Bateson's own biographical sketch of the history of his concepts reveals two things: first, that he is aware of this difficulty and, second, that his book, which we have hitherto considered solely as a work of science, can also be considered as something more personal and literary, for Bateson's theory still includes too many personal elements to be called scientific without qualification. In the passage last quoted, for instance, light is thrown on the scientifically debatable assertion that ethos must be ascribed whereas eidos can be described. In this assertion Bateson seems to project the characteristics of his own thinking processes rather uncritically in order to make of them a general principle.

Autobiographical aspects of *Naven* are, however, best elucidated by reference to Bateson's later article, "Experiments in Thinking about Observed Ethnological Material" [6], in which he extols the virtues of hunches on the ground that they are often obtained by analogies gleaned from other disciplines with which the ethnographer may be familiar— zoology, in his own case. Bateson's view concerning advances in science is expressed *in nuce* in the following passage:

> I want to emphasize that whenever we pride ourselves upon finding a newer, stricter way of thought or exposition; whenever we start insisting too hard upon "operationalism" or symbolic logic or any other of these very essential systems of tramlines, we lose something of the ability to think new thoughts. And equally, of course, whenever we rebel against the sterile rigidity of formal thought and exposition and let our ideas run wild, we likewise lose. As I see it, the advances in scientific thought come from a *combination of loose and strict thinking*, and this combination is the most precious tool of science ("Experiments . . . ," 55).

Ethos, one of the main concepts of *Naven*, is shown in its evolution from a hunch to a mistaken entity to a point of view, and some other concepts are similarly treated. Bateson further emphasizes the fact that important contributions to science can be made by theories expressed in clumsy concepts, and he cites psychoanalysis as a striking case in point. Nevertheless, the implication with reference to the concepts and theories put forth in *Naven* is that the author still approves of them (cf. "Experiments...", 66) five years later. Thus, having applied an initial critique I might call literal, I may now evaluate them in a way that Bateson himself would approve. To make this meaning clearer I quote from the end of the same article, in which he refers again to the alternation between loose and strict thinking:

> And if you ask me for a recipe for speeding up this process, I would say first that we ought to accept and enjoy this dual nature of scientific thought and be willing to value the way in which the two processes work together to give us advances in understanding of the world. We ought not to frown too much on either process, or at least to frown equally on either process when it is unsupplemented by the other. There is, I think, a delay in science when we start to specialise for too long either in strict or in loose thinking. I suspect, for example, that the Freudian edifice has been allowed to grow too big before the corrective of strict thought is applied to it— and now when investigators start rephrasing the Freudian dogmas in new stricter terms there may be a lot of ill feeling, which is wasteful. (At this point I might perhaps throw out a word of comfort to the orthodox in psychoanalysis. When the formulators begin rootling about among the most basic of analytic premises and questioning the concrete reality of such concepts as the "ego" or "wishes" or the "id" or the "libido" —as indeed they are already beginning to rootle—there is no need to get alarmed and to start having terror dreams of chaos and storms at sea. It is certain that most of the old fabric of analysis will still be left standing after the new underpinning has been inserted. And when the concepts, postulates, and premises have been straightened out, analysts will be able to embark upon a new and still more fruitful orgy of loose thinking, until they reach a stage at which again the results of their thinking must be strictly conceptualized. . . .) ("Experiments . . . ," 67 f.).

It is still not clear whether Bateson classes his concepts among examples of loose or of strict thinking, but my own verdict would be that his attempt to interpret Iatmul culture belongs in the latter category, whereas some of his individual concepts seem to have remained in the role in which they originated—as expedients for explaining this culture—and as such do not conform to the strictness of the pursuit itself. Bateson would probably welcome the application of these concepts to the study of cultures other than the Iatmul, and I would group ethos and eidos (rather than sociology and schismogenesis) with other concepts that are being used experimentally, all for the same purpose of understanding cultures or, more precisely, of understanding more of their aspects than is possible with the older approaches in anthropology, such as the institutional or even the functional. I am thinking here especially of Redfield's folk-urban theory and of what might be called the configurational approach. With reference to the latter Florence Kluckhohn remarks [7],

> the specific use of the term [configuration] and its correlative terms of sub-configuration and integration is . . . an integration in itself *for purposes of analyses in particular culture areas* of the concept of "logico-meaningful integration" developed by Professor Sorokin in his analyses of whole cultural eras, and such other concepts as Pareto's "residues," Professor Parsons' "ultimate value attitudes," Professor Sapir's "system of unconscious meaning," and Dr. Benedict's "unconscious canons of choice." There has been a remarkable convergence in social theory upon conceptions of this . . . order.

It is obvious that a culture study which combined the three frames of reference developed by Redfield, the "configurationalists," and Bateson would be fruitful. Although it seems to me that the ultimate result of the folk-urban theory is the establishment of laws of acculturation, our information regarding acculturation, as well as types of folk and urban society, would undoubtedly be enriched by knowledge of configurational variations among either type, of the process of change (and especially acculturative change) in terms of configurations, and of types and parts of configurations with respect to their degree of susceptibility to acculturative influences. It would likewise be enriched if we could test the usefulness of ethos and eidos by applying these concepts to folk and urban societies in order to ascertain their ethological and eidological characteristics. If such are established, the acculturative influences on these types of ethos and eidos might again be studied. Similarly, our knowledge of configurations would be enhanced if we examined what permits us to speak of a rural or folk type and to contrast it with an urban type, in spite of configurational differences found (or rather hitherto largely assumed) in various rural and urban cultures. At the same time it might prove profitable to break down configurations not only into patterns but also into ethological and eidological traits. Finally, the concepts of ethos and eidos could be more sharply defined if they were analyzed, as indicated, in terms of the folk-urban theory and configurations.

In alluding to these trends I have overlooked others, among which some might be used profitably in connection with the remaining Batesonian concepts, such as sociology and schismogenesis. Schismogenesis, moreover, may well become a familiar concept in anthropology, regardless of particular interests within this field, although perhaps especially for those engaged in psychiatry and studying the relations between the individual and society [8].

Finally, we may consider the place of Bateson's book among the varied interests represented in anthropology. The influence of Malinowski, Radcliffe-Brown, and Benedict as well as Fortune and Mead, who belong chiefly on what may be called the generalizing side of science rather than on the historical, is acknowledged by the author. What of Bateson himself? *Naven* is a synchronic study of Iatmul culture, as its author explicitly states. Thus it is a history, although not a diachronic history. The concepts Bateson develops in order to construct this synchronic picture of Iatmul culture, or rather the interests he exhibits in developing these concepts, betray an orientation toward generalizations and more specifically toward generalizations designed ultimately to yield relations between the individual and culture and thus also types of culture. Yet the concepts are for the present no more than methodological tools to be applied in attempts to establish these types, Bateson's five points of view—structural-eidological, ethological, economic, developmental, and sociological—refer to aspects of culture in terms of which a methodological program for the establishment of types is drawn up; and there is still only a program. Thus I should conclude that it is too early to ascribe to Bateson a fixed place among the trends of modern anthropology.

### NOTES

1.   Gregory Bateson, *Naven: A Survey of the Problems by a Composite Picture of the Culture of a New Guinea Tribe Drawn from Three Points of View* (Cambridge: University Press, 1936), 286 pp., with 28 plates, 6 figures, and a glossary.

2.   Gregory Bateson and Margaret Mead, *Balinese Character: A Photographic Analysis* (New York: New York Academy of Science, 1942).

3.   *Man*, 35 (1935), No. 199, 178–183.

4.   *American Anthropologist*, 38 (1936), 149–152.

5. A people almost adjacent to the Iatmul are the Arapesh, studied by Dr. Margaret Mead.

6. *Philosophy of Science*, 8 (January 1941), 53–68.

7. *Los Atarqueños; A Study of Patterns and Configurations in a New Mexico Village* (Ph.D. dissertation, unpublished, Cambridge, Mass., Radcliffe College), 1941, Vol. I, p. 13.

8. It is noteworthy, however, that in *Balinese Character* Bateson and Mead made no use of this concept.

---

Reprinted from *Journal of the Royal Anthropological Institute,* **74** (1944), 59–74, by permission of the publisher. The essay has been edited and partially revised by the author.

# 20

# A METHODOLOGICAL NOTE
# ON THE EMPIRICAL
# ESTABLISHMENT OF
# CULTURE PATTERNS. [1] 1945, 1970

## THE CULTURAL APPROACH

Fundamentally, the scientific study of a culture exemplifies one of two approaches. One is followed in most of the monographic anthropological literature. The other is implied in some of the more theoretically oriented anthropological writings [2] and especially in certain concepts of the sociology of knowledge [3], yet it has not, to my knowledge, been made the explicit theoretical basis of the empirical study of a culture or community. The two approaches may be distinguished, first, on the philosophical-methodological level and, second, on what may be called the contentual level.

Philosophically, and therefore methodologically, the first approach proceeds on the assumption that a person can and should study a culture as the natural scientist studies nature [4]. The culture is *there*—the task is to learn about it; and we learn about it with the help of rules that will be perfected in the course of scientific progress. It is true that many students of this school are aware of the personal equation, which refers to the investigator's biases, emotions, prejudgments, or even to his own cultural mold [5]. Yet this personal equation is considered merely a flaw that each student must try his best to eliminate so that objectivity may be preserved as much as possible [6]. For this process of elimination he relies on rules of science that are widely held and often taken for granted, such as the careful formulation of a hypothesis, the systematic search for the negative case, various pragmatic aspects, and others [7]. By contrast, for the second approach to the scientific study of cultures the personal equation is not a necessary evil but the explicitly acknowledged basis. The personal, or better, cultural equation determines what *can be* perceived and interpreted of the culture under study and *how* it can be perceived and interpreted. For reasons of simplified reference I call the first, the objective approach, and the second, the cultural approach. On the philosophical-methodological level, then, the contrast between the two can be pointedly summarized: For the former, the objective approach, the relation between the student and the culture he is examining is taken for granted and the central concept is that of scientific procedure, under which problematical aspects of the relation between the student and the culture under study are subsumed as technicalities. For the latter, the cultural approach, the scientific procedure is taken for granted and the central concept is that of cultural equation, under which problematical aspects of scientific procedure are subsumed as technicalities.

Furthermore, the follower of the objective school not only finds his work largely predetermined by scientific rules but also by what may be labeled "contentual" rules. His teachers have not only told him *how* to study a culture but also *what* to study. If he is a sociologist, he may, for instance, take *Middletown* as a model and study his community by beginning with "Getting a Living" and following the chapters down the line until he comes to an outlook on the future. If he is an anthropologist, he probably has in mind a number of important aspects of a culture, such as economics, social relations, child rearing, and education. He takes it for granted that some sort of division obtains in the culture he wants to study, no matter which, because such a division makes sense in his own culture [8]. Yet suppose a Tasmanian, or even a Spanish-American, were studying the culture of New York or Seattle [9]; would he take for granted the same aspects that an American student of a Tasmanian tribe or Mexican or New Mexican community takes for granted? I imagine he would not. I cannot prove it because to my knowledge either no Tasmanian or even Spanish-American has studied an American community or he was "trained" in the objective school. Unless he were so trained, we might be inclined not to consider his study scientific but merely a curious and naïve document. This reflection, though in a roundabout way, proves the highly specific, that is, cultural, character of our social science and should therefore at least make it clear that its approach is only one among others [10].

Perhaps the contrast with the second approach can be pointed out most sharply on this contentual level. Instead of treating a culture by contentual divisions [11] the cultural approach proposes to treat it in terms of its patterns. The concept of pattern overrides contentual distinctions. Rather it considers any contents as materials that may be patterned. From the standpoint of the members of the culture under study the contentual is that to which patterns may apply; from the standpoint of the student of the culture the contentual is the heuristic sphere of observation in which patterns may be discerned. Clyde Kluckhohn [12] has presented clearly a list of pattern types. Yet two decisive questions have not been raised, much less answered. One is the question of selection; that is, which observations of materials, inferences, or constructs does the student call patterns and which does he not call so? The other is the question of method; that is, how does the student establish patterns empirically [13] so that another student can check on them and how does he prove that his patterns are adequate as an interpretation of the culture under study? In the following section preliminary answers to these two questions based on five months of field work in "Loma," a small Anglo-Spanish community in New Mexico, are given.

### SELECTION OF PATTERNS

Tentative answers to both questions may be found if it is remembered, first, that the pattern concept is typical of the cultural approach and that the central concept of this approach is the cultural equation; second, that the cultural equation determines what *can be* perceived and interpreted in the culture under study and *how* it can be perceived and interpreted. It may be assumed that in any culture a certain type of phenomena calls for interpretation. It is these phenomena that strike the student as different from those that form part of his and his group's universe of discourse [14], phenomena that are not readily incorporable into this universe of discourse and consequently call for some procedure by means of which they can be. This picture seems to be the more clearly cut the more different the two universes of discourse or cultures—that under study and that of the student. A ritual among the Iatmul undoubtedly and at once appears to be part of a culture not shared by the student, hence calls for subsumption under a larger whole which in turn is incorporated into the student's own culture. To express the same thought in more customary terms, the student tries to understand the ritual within that larger complex and in turn tries to understand the complex itself. The picture seems least clearly cut when the two cultures are most similar. In contrast to the study of an exotic culture we have the sociological community study, in which the student is struck by relatively minor nuances of his own culture [15]. The middle is held by folk cultures [16]. They partake of the urban civilization of which the student is a member but also of another culture he wants to detect and describe in its fusion with his own. In many cases, therefore, it is difficult to ascertain whether an observation belongs to a whole that has the same significance as it has in his own culture or whether it betrays hitherto unsuspected or suspected features. This is but to say that in folk cultures, diversities are not so striking as in exotic cultures and likenesses not so striking as in urban communities.

The first step, then, toward an answer to the question which observations are dignified by the term pattern is a preliminary classification of the culture under study in such terms as exotic, folk, or urban. This classification is usually performed spontaneously and without much or any regard for the methodological consequences discussed here. The awareness of its methodological implications, however, results in a sharper focus on the selection of patterns. Suppose the culture under consideration is classified as belonging to the broad category of folk culture. The student thus expects to find patterns that this culture shares with his own—perhaps in the attitudes toward money and the manipulation of it—and others not shared by the urban culture—perhaps in certain beliefs about planting or stars. Now it must never be forgotten that this division of potential patterns is the student's own division—very likely not that of the members of the culture under study. It is a theoretical distinction on the level of classification and heuristic hypothesis or, to use a term of Karl Mannheim's [17], of sociological interpretation. It has not proceeded to the level of understanding or of immanent interpretation. It does not yet interpret the culture under study in terms of its members [18]. The real difficulty, or the proper task, of the student of a folk culture is to study the mutual interdependence and shaping of patterns he has preliminarily ascribed to urban or to "native" influences. Thus patterns that express attitudes toward money, for example, must be examined with reference to their possible relation to, or influence on, patterns that express beliefs in stars. The empirical ascertainment of interactions of this kind allows the student to describe the uniqueness of the folk culture he is examining [19].

Aware of a preliminary classification of the culture he wants to study and of the difference between a classificatory and an immanent interpretation of what he will observe, the student now proceeds to the actual field work: he is about to fill his theoretical or rational framework empirically. He is interested in answering the question how this particular folk culture is made up in terms of his theoretical approach. According to his individual disposition, he may quickly formulate hypotheses and search for checks on them or he may record anything that comes under his observation and try to piece together patterns in a slower manner. In either case his cultural and personal sensitivity, enriched and sharpened by theoretical thinking, puts the limit on what he can perceive and interpret [20].

In the field, then, the question of selection is answered in the following order: avid collection of empirical materials, immanent interpretation of these materials, their classification, and classification of the culture. This is the reverse order of that characterizing the theorizing stage preceding the field work. The three last steps in the field—immanent interpretation of materials, their classification, and classification of the culture—answer the question of selection. They determine (a) what patterns appear when the materials are interpreted as constituents of a meaningful presentation of the culture, (b) how the materials are to be classified—because constituents of this presentation—as imputable to other presentations (types) of culture, and (c) how the culture itself is to be classified. When each of these steps is taken probably depends on the investigator's disposition [21].

## EMPIRICAL ESTABLISHMENT OF PATTERNS

The answer to the first question—of selection—remains not quite clear as long as there is none to the second; that is, how the student establishes patterns empirically and how he proves them to be adequate as an interpretation of the culture. In other words, after it has been shown how patterns are found it must be demonstrated how they can be ascertained. Although the preceding discussion did justice to any meaning the reader may reasonably have been expected to attribute to pattern, it now becomes necessary to introduce a formal though still provisional definition.

A pattern is uniformity of emotion, attitude, thoughtway, or knowledge [22]. In this definition it is implied that a pattern may be characteristic of an individual, a group, or all members of the culture under study. Therefore to find out to which of the three categories the pattern applies is a statistical proposition. Theoretically this is all that has to be said in answer to the question how patterns are established empirically—by statistics [23]. In practice, however, there is more to it. In most cases a sample technique must be devised not only because it would be impossible, even in a culture shared by few individuals, to test all patterns by a complete coverage but also because it is not necessary to do so. It is often scientifically legitimate to do without a statistically valid sample, as I shall try to show. When this is possible depends on the nature of the pattern under examination and on the purpose of the study.

If we want to know how many members of a culture are married, own a house, belong to a certain organization, have given occupations, or similar uniformities, there is no substitute for a statistically valid sample count. According to the concept of society and culture current in our universe of discourse, counts of this sort are necessary for the presentation of a general picture of the culture under study. They are customarily dealt with under such contentual models as property, marriage and family, organizations and institutions, and occupational distribution. It is not important here to answer the question whether uniformities of this nature should be called patterns; they could be only by stretching our definition considerably [24]. If the task of the student is to give a total picture of the culture, they are not of primary importance [25], yet they bridge the two cultures or universes of discourse (the student's and his readers' and the one to be studied) to function as background materials for the culture to be incorporated. They can be readily understood by the same means as they would be in the study of a culture similar to that of the student's and readers'—an American urban or even rural community.

At this point the implication of immanent interpretation must be more closely examined. Immanent interpretation has two referents, of which Mannheim has discussed only one [26]. Immanent interpretation of patterns is, first, the description of the meaning that an individual or group gives to the uniformity of emotion, attitude, thoughtway, or knowledge. In this sense it is the description of what meaning a person or group gives, for example, to being in a reverent mood in church (emotion), to liking beer, children, and nature, to hating Negroes, Jews, or Mexicans (attitude), to conceptions of war, time, or money (thoughtways), to orientation in time and space, to an acquaintance with and use of herbs, sewing machines, wells, or radios (knowledge). In other words, it is the recording of interpretations given by the members of the culture under study (and in some cases interpretations may be rationalizations). This is the referent Mannheim discusses, but immanent interpretation has another more important one denoted in the expression, the "immanent interpretation of the materials." This expression was used to designate the first step taken by the student toward a presentation of the culture he is studying. When this step was discussed, it was defined as the interpretation of the materials "as constituents of a meaningful presentation of the culture." The significance of this statement must be made more explicit.

The meaningful presentation of the culture is its reinterpretation to make its uniqueness incorporable into the universe of discourse of the student and his readers. The ideal-theoretical extreme of meaningfulness is identification with this culture [27]. However, this is not only almost impossible to attain but such identification would also be unformulable objectively, hence unscientific (but rather artistic-intuitive). Yet even if we do not go beyond the establishment of patterns, their scientifically desirable statistical bases are not always either obtainable or called for. I have discussed the types of uniformity (usually not called patterns) for which they are obtainable as well as called for—for those which, in the cultural approach, make up background materials. For patterns, that is, uniformities of emotion, attitude, thoughtway, or knowledge, something else is both obtainable and called for—the presentation of the interrelatedness of patterns that will enable us to understand and predict the culture under study.

Suppose [28] the student has observed that an eight-year-old girl is afraid to cross a small creek. He has also observed fear in other individuals of the same culture on other occasions. He tentatively formulates fear as a pattern of reaction to certain things. It is impossible for him to ascertain statistically all things to which all members of the culture react with fear. Rather he keeps his preliminary fear pattern—a uniformity of emotion and/or attitude—in mind while continuing his observations and preliminary formulations of other patterns. One he observes, is the economical handling of language in speech and its unaccomplished semi-illiterate handling in writing—a uniformity of thoughtways. He also remembers, from his background materials, statistical figures on literacy, formal education, and the like. Again it is impossible for him to ascertain statistically all situations in which all members of the culture express themselves linguistically, nor is it called for, for what the student is interested in is the question of the interrelatedness of the fear and language patterns. Is there a connection between fear as a norm of reacting to certain things accepted by the members of this culture and the similarly accepted economic handling of language as norm of manipulating (expressing, withholding, implying) one's thoughts? Is economic insecurity perhaps a link between the two patterns? Here again the student adduces his background figures on property, income, indebtedness, and budgets.

In this example a number of methodological questions have been ignored, but it is hoped that the answer to the first part of our second question will now become clearer: the student establishes patterns empirically by the presentation of the interrelatedness of patterns that enable us to understand and predict the culture we are studying. It should be added that in establishing the interrelatedness of patterns the student makes use, as much as his sensitivity and integrity as a scientist force him to, of scientific rule. He will try to obtain some statistical basis that alone enables him to ascertain whether the pattern he has hypothetically formulated applies to an individual, a group, or to all members of the culture. Both for this purpose and for the purpose of throwing light on the inter-relatedness of patterns it is necessary to search for negative cases. These two examples once more illustrate what is meant, with reference to the empirical establishment of patterns, by the fact that scientific rule is taken for granted in the cultural approach.

It will have been seen that the answer to the question how patterns are established empirically is intimately connected with the answer to the question of their selection. Even more closely related to the problem of empirical ascertainment of patterns is the last question, namely, how the student proves that the patterns he has established are indeed adequate as an interpretation of the culture. In fact, the answer is implied in the statement that he establishes patterns empirically by the presentation of their interrelatedness. The answer only needs to be made explicit. His patterns are proved adequate when they make it possible to understand and predict the culture presented in their terms. What is meant by predictability, that is, the anticipation of the reaction of the culture to certain changes and its change with these changes, is connoted by the colloquial meaning of the term. The predictive quality of the presentation can be judged only by the future. As regards understanding, the meaning of this term has been made clear by the discussion of the pattern approach: it is precisely this approach that is held to be most appropriate to our understanding of a culture. It should be noted, however, that the understanding of certain aspects of a culture, made possible by the presentation of certain patterns, does not guarantee the understanding of other aspects. In other words, the fact that a presentation makes sense or is plausible does not prove that important things have not been over-looked—the future may, or may not, find the student out. Other than this, his only probability of having understood the culture is the maximum collection of materials, the most rigorous search for negative cases, and the most imaginative testing of varieties of other explanations and pattern combinations. Here again his sensitivity, disciplined by theoretical thinking, is essentially important.

In comparison with the immanent interpretation of a culture, its classification is easier, less urgent, and less exclusively the responsibility of the student, for once he has presented the culture others may classify it according to their own theories. The original presentation may enrich a relatively wide universe of discourse with a new concept of human society and culture. The classification will enrich the universe of discourse of a more specialized public—those interested in sociological and anthropological theory and, especially, in types or continua of cultures. This is not to say, however, that the classificatory phase is less important. For science itself it is the most important aspect of the study because science progresses by a refinement of theory. Therefore the decisive contribution to the advancement of science, made by the cultural approach in the presentation of a culture, is its contribution to scientific theory.

### SUMMARY

A summary of the contrast between the two approaches to the study of a culture and of the methodological bases of the cultural approach may be given as follows:

Two approaches to the scientific study of a culture.

1. Objective: central concept, the scientific (natural-science) procedure; personal equation taken for granted and sought to be eliminated as far as possible.
2. Cultural: central concept, the cultural equation; scientific procedure taken for granted and followed as far as possible.

Characteristics of the cultural approach.

1. Overriding of models of contentual aspects of cultures by the pattern concept.

2. Steps in the study of a culture:

   (a) Preliminary comparison of the culture with that of the student's; hence its preliminary classification; hence expectations regarding types of pattern.
   (b) Establishment of patterns. Hypothetical patterns arrived at by observation and tentative interpretation; their immanent interpretation, that is, recording of interpretations given by the members of the culture, plus the establishment of the interrelatedness of the patterns to make possible the understanding and predicting of the culture.

3. Methodological elements characterizing the cultural-approach study:

   (a) Presentation of statistically reliable background materials and the connection between these and the patterns.

(*b*) Presentation of patterns and their immanent interpretation.

(*c*) Demonstration of the application of the patterns to individuals, groups, or all members of the culture.

(*d*) Demonstration of the connection between the patterns and culture types (cf. 2*a*); the problems of history and culture change (especially important in the study of folk cultures).

(*e*) Demonstration of the adequacy of the patterns for understanding and predicting the culture, by discussion of negative cases and of other interpretations of materials and patterns.

(*f*) Classification of the culture in terms of types of cultures or of other theories.

## AN ILLUSTRATION: PRELIMINARY HYPOTHESES REGARDING THE CULTURE OF THE SPANISH-SPEAKING PEOPLE OF LOMA

It may be useful to illustrate some of the ideas expressed in this chapter with a few remarks about the culture of Loma. These remarks are made at the stage of investigation described in the preceding summary. They contain (a) a list of some features of Loman culture that are thought to be patterns (although it cannot yet be demonstrated that they are, much material collected in the field points in this direction); (b) an attempt to show the interrelatedness of these features or possibly patterns in a way that would make possible the understanding and predicting of the culture, and also some remarks on change. It should be emphasized once more and it should be kept in mind while reading what follows that it is preliminary, fragmentary, and presented only by way of illustration.

*Some Hypothetical Patterns of Loman Culture* [29].

ACCEPTANCE. Preliminary definition [30]: the unreflective acceptance of what comes or is. Illustrations [31]:

> *J* [Anglo] very kindly brought us [my wife and me] a pound-box of candies . . . which we produced again yesterday after *lonche* [lunch] and of course offered *R* [our maid]. The candies are individually packed in the customary brown folded paper cups. *R* ate hers with a spoon out of the paper cup using it as a kind of plate and said from time to time "*muy dulce*" [how sweet], "*dulcito*," and similar. This struck me as the acceptance of life—sweet or bitter, good or bad, not much fuss about anything. Other example: when I stopped in at *P*'s

waiting for *Fr* [Anglo] to bring me to . . . [the county seat]
to pick up the family, *P* said a nephew of hers . . . was *enfermo*
[sick], *en la cabeza, tumor* [in the head, a tumor]— *muy triste*
[very sad]; he had been in Italy (which I had learned the day
before), but now in *Norte America*, and what that was, and
I said that must be this country. Later *Fr* told me they [the
*M*'s] had just received a telegram from the War Department
that he was seriously ill, cerebral tumor, was in the North
American area . . . They had not indicated to me that they
had just received the wire that mornnig. *R* mentioned nothing about this yesterday after she had undoubtedly learned
of it [32].

*C* [my wife] had picked up an ant which had gotten into her
bed. Called *R*'s attention to it. *R* suggested it might be
*chinches* [bedbugs]. *C* showed terror, quite in contrast to *R*,
who wiped a wooden board in her bed (otherwise iron bed)
with vinegar. Hence *C* mentioned that *E* and *P* [visiting
friends of ours who had spent a night in the *M* house] had
found bedbugs in *A*'s [*R*'s brother] bed [in which *E* and *P*, in
*A*'s absence, had slept]. *"Siento mucho"* [I am very sorry], but
*A* sleeps outside for this reason—every night he takes his
blankets and sleeps under a tree. Not the slightest moral indignation was mixed in *R*'s reaction—as it would have been in
that of a *Hausfrau* or even an American housewife . . . Are
bedbugs necessary evils which are accepted similar to the
death of five out of fourteen children, say, lacking knowledge
of birth control and disease prevention? [33]

ECONOMICS.    P.d.: a social institution, that is, a phenomenon virtually
composed of heterogeneous elements but constituting a unit in the universe of discourse of the members of the culture under study. Ills.:

*R* came later today with the news that *A* had suddenly arrived.
The FSA [Farm Security Administration; see next chapter]
to which he has owed $170 for 2–3 years . . . wired his com-
pany in . . . ordering him back because he had to attend to his
farm. . . . *R* rightly said that the farm is well taken care of and
that *A* can pay his debt much better working for wages than
staying here. In fact, he already sent $130 home . . . [This sum]
was, as *A* wrote, for their (family's) use, but when he now
came they told him that they hadn't used a cent of it, keeping
it for the payment of the debts, since *"tenemos suficiente"* [we
have enough anyway]. Aside from the FSA loan, *A* also owes
. . . the county and the state taxes since 1931; although in
some years he managed to pay back a little. *R* said he had

nothing to do at home; of course, they were glad he is with them . . . Now that he makes no more money, *R* said, *"Yo no sé como lo haremos, pero ahora que está* A, *lo arreglará todo —y si no, todavia estamos muy contentos que esté"* [I don't know how we shall do it, but now. that *A* is here he'll set everything straight—and if not, still we're very glad that he is here]. This remark most clearly shows how the family relation at least counterbalances economic stress. [34]

FAMILY. P.d.: as under economics. Ills.: last part of preceding quotation and the following:

> It is very bad when families separate, *P* likes it when all stay together, but nowadays many go away, yet almost all come back. I said how happy she must be with her large family, and she broke out into almost a hymn to *el Señor* [the Lord] who blessed her with so good and large a family—and it was the *menor* [*youngest* (daughter)] who produced so many children . . . she counted on her fingers all . . . children by name, first the seven sons, then the three daughters. She repeated, hymn-like, *"por eso que estoy tan contenta, contenta, contenta"* [it is for this that I am so happy, happy, happy]—what more can I ask for but that I am here with my family all together? *"Bueno es estar juntos, pero cuando van afuera se debe andar al correo"* [It is good to stay together, but when they leave one has to go to the post office]—as now regarding *A* [35].

HAPPINESS. P.d.: happy state of mind, in the colloquial sense of the expression, induced by certain culture elements, such as physical presence of kin in the family's house. Ills.: preceding quotation and the following:

> The *M*'s were having supper when I came back, and of course invited me, finally pressed a cup of coffee upon me. The family . . . was obviously very happy. *A* said to me that he had wanted to eat *quelite* [kind of spinach] . . . , which he got . . . *R* [had] beamed all day long as if the arrival of the brother [*A*], in spite of the [negative] economic implications, were the fulfillment of her wishes, which it most likely is . . . [36].

> When the baby [ours] laughs, *R* laughs quite cordially too. This is probably an occasion engendering happiness because fitting in their own culture set-up (laughter of children, fine weather, flowers, and the like) . . . *R*, beaming, brought a telegram from *F* [her nephew] saying he is in this country, fine, and expecting to come to a hospital nearer home where he expects his parents to visit him. *"Que buenas nuevas—ayer*

A, *y en la tarde la nueva de* F. [What good news—yesterday
A, and this afternoon the news from F] [37].

HOSPITALITY.    Ills.: beginning of first quotation under Happiness and the
following:

> C asked R yesterday whether she could take a few apricots
> from the tree, to cook for the child. R, after a moment of sur-
> prise at the question, so it seemed to C, opened her arms and
> said, but that *todo, todo* [everything] was ours—what a ques-
> tion. She then expanded that at this time of the year one
> didn't have to buy fruit; that after the apricots came the
> plums . . . This is another instance of . . . the instant trans-
> formation of persons when acting as hosts [38].

HOUSES.    P.d.: as under Economics; the fact that acting in one's own
house with fellow residents (usually family) or toward a stranger promotes
a feeling of security, pride, and contentment not enjoyed outside the
house. Ills.: preceding quotation and the following:

> R thanked me after we were through with the door work
> [done at my suggestion and for my convenience] as if I had
> helped her improve the house. That she found it an improve-
> ment was obvious, for she commented most favorably to C
> and me about it. Also, after I came home I suggested to put a
> . . . [curtain] in front of my clothes, and while we were look-
> ing for rods, etc., she called to C, "*ya tenemos una nueva
> idea*" [already we have another new (good) idea] . . . C asked
> her in connection with this and with the door how A [her
> brother, the owner of the house] would like it (that we made
> so many changes in the house), and she said of course he
> would, for he liked air and sun, which now could enter more
> easily than before [39].

> The house in which one lives seems to be part of the happi-
> ness complex. At coffee we talked about things R and I had
> planned to do, such as the cleaning of the well. A inquired
> whether the roof had leaked. This set off a number of things
> he wanted to do in case he stays *algunos dias* [for several days]
> —put new dirt on the roof, dig a well near the kitchen (*no
> más 12 o 15 pies, no más dos, tres días de trabajo* [no more
> than 12 or 15 feet (to dig), no more than two, three days of
> labor]) . . . He was greatly interested [40].

MAÑANA.    P.d.: enjoyment of the present; acting on impulse relatively
freer from other considerations than is true in our culture; absence of

time-is-money complex. Cf. also under Organization, Time, To the Point.
Ills.:

> When I'd just started typing . . ., *A* came in with a bunch
> of herbs, sat down murmuring something about my being
> busy, but then started explaining [the herbs] [41].

> *A* came twice today to bring me more herbs, no matter
> whether I was busy or not, but immediately understanding
> that the first time I had to go to the post office, the second
> up to *Fr* [42].

> *C's* [our child's] birthday . . . There is some truth to Campa's
> "Mañana is today"[43], but it is journalistic in that it does not
> attempt, even, to determine how far the today extends: there
> is some provision for the future, some planning among the
> people here . . . [Although] *Cr* made the quilt for the baby
> only last night (*Fr* saw it unfinished yesterday), and badly
> enough . . . , it was ready, as were her cake (paid for) and one
> (gift) made by *Pa* and *Cl*, . . . while *R* had even as long as a
> week ago bought three flower-painted drinking glasses (for
> baby and his parents) [44].

ORGANIZATION.   P.d.: greater lack of capacity for coordination of thoughts,
activities, persons, functions, than is found in our culture. Cf. also under
Mañana, Time, To the Point. Ills.:

> *J* and *Fr* [Anglos] reported that . . . [their dog] had died;
> they found him dead this morning and think, as does *JA*,
> that he was poisoned by eating some bran which some people
> put on their alfalfa against grasshoppers: it is mixed with
> arsenic lead. They remarked upon the fact that there was
> no notice posted of the spread poison with shrugging shoul-
> ders. *A* explained how it was *tirado con la mano* [scattered
> with the hand] and that it was only within *cercos* [fences],
> but that *un animal mediano* [a (small) medium-sized animal]
> could pass through [the fence] and be poisoned [45].

> *R* said she had told yesterday . . . [the store-keeper] to direct
> the doctor to her (*P's*) house. This remarkable foresight is
> probably due to the importance of the case—her mother's
> health, . . . the lack of organization is overcome through the
> significance of the event. In other words, here Mañana in-
> cludes the tomorrow [46].

> She [*P*] said she went to see the doctor [in the county seat],
> but he was away for two weeks. (Re "Organization": she

made a trip, difficult for her, only to find that it was in vain, since she hadn't made sure before going whether the doctor was available. However, . . . the lack of organization is observed by me in terms of what we—members of "my" culture —think about organization. In other words, it is a lack of organization or of planning in terms of our, not of their, culture. What is it in terms of their culture? The answer to this question could be approached only by "immanent interpretation," i.e., by what *P* herself says about this unsuccessful trip. The trouble is that she cannot interpret it. All she could . . . interpret she has already said: she went, and the doctor wasn't there, and that it is too bad [47]).

TIME. P.d.: conceptions of time exemplified in unpunctuality, vague knowledge, and designation of periods of time; psychological distribution of events in time [48]. Cf. under Mañana, Organization, To the Point. Ills.:

I asked *R*, *"no está muy lejos para andar a* Fr" [it isn't very far to go to *Fr*] . . . , and she answered, *"no, no está muy lejos"* [no, it isn't very far] . . . but since I was anxious to get there and was tired and hungry, I asked further, *"Como diez minutos?"* [about ten minutes?], and she answered, *"O si, como diez minutos, veinte"* [O yes, something like 10 minutes, 20]. . . . The fact is it is at least 20 minutes to go up there, crossing four fence gates . . . I remember . . . when I asked old Mrs. *P* how old *Cr* and *R* [her daughters] were, and she didn't know it and had to figure it out asking them, asking *A* [her son], reckoning by other dates, etc.; or, when I asked *MM* yesterday how old her son was, of whom she was so proud, and she hesitated and asked her husband—19 months [49].

I was waiting for *Fr* and observed to the *M's* that their clock (alarm) was about half an hour late . . . To my surprise, *P*, who very probably can't read the clock, asked me how I *arreglo mi reloj* [regulate my watch]—thus "imprecision" re time does not preclude awareness of it, and chronological at that, even in the . . . illiterate *P*. I explained that some days before I had adjusted it [my watch] after the *V*'s radio time. Yet they didn't do a thing about adjusting their clock. *Cr* remarked that when the school bell rang at nine (it rings at nine and at one) theirs showed . . . [about half past eight]— but nothing was done about it [50].

Mrs. *H* has to go to . . . [the county seat] for her OAA [Old Age Assistance] insurance to be transferred to her name [her husband having died a few days before]. She was there Saturday, but thought she was only 60 or 61 years old. She looked up her *fé de bautismo* [certificate of baptism] and found she was 71 and hence entitled to OAA; therefore she has to go and produce the certificate of baptism at the "welle-fare" [51].

TO THE POINT.    P.d.: the relation of what is immediately given and what the given implies is different in Loman culture from what it is in ours so that it appears that in Loman culture there is only a reaction to and grasp of the given rather than of its implications. Cf. under Mañana, Organization, Time. Ills.:

This morning, *R*, upon my question re the San Ysidro service today, said that there wasn't going to be any; Mrs. *S* (in posses-sion of the church keys) told her that Mrs. *AS* was in . . . [the county seat] and hadn't come back yet. So I asked about the significance of Mrs. *AS*, and *R* said she was *mayordoma de la iglesia* [church stewardess], which she hadn't told me yesterday. Gradually then I found out that there are always not two persons, as I thought yesterday, but two couples who make the *mayordomos* . . . Tentatively stated, the "pattern" would be to give information only to the point, but not thinking in terms of "complexes" or, better, "topics" [52].

WASTE.    P.d.: the almost automatic conservation of waste matters which in our culture would more generally be thrown away. At the same time, the frequent forgetting that something has been preserved and its conse-quent spoiling. Ills.:

*R* today cleaned a head of lettuce which was about to spoil, conserving small still-fresh particles and putting the whole saved into a jar [53].

*R* saves the tin lids removed, with the can opener, from sar-dine cans and the like, to use them as curl rollers for her hair, since curl rollers are no longer available [54].

*C*'s information . . . Example: I left a potato on a shelf, raw and cut in half—I forgot it, having taken the other half for the baby. Although *R* sees the shelf many times a day, she didn't throw this potato away but left it there because she thought I could use it. Finally I threw it away into a bucket which she brings to the hogs. Example: she had *cuajada* [clabber] stand around for days till it got moldy and then told me she thought we couldn't use it any more; she asked me

whether I didn't think she should throw it away. Example:
she thinks I am utterly wasteful ("oh, you can use those
things") if I throw away the green points of onions—she fries
them with potatoes or meat, etc. Example: everywhere I see
folded-up paper conserved [55].

*Attempt at Interrelating the Features or Patterns and Some Others* [56].
Acceptance, that is, the unreflective acceptance of what comes or is;
hence the conception of time as something of relatively minor importance; time orientation is relatively vague. Therefore Campa [57] is
right, but he overlooks the limitation of the mañana pattern by events
that tradition has made outstanding and the meeting of which therefore
calls for planning. Tradition is, of course, also a check on acceptance.
On the other hand, tradition enhances what little organization there is
patterned. Readiness to conceive of nontraditional complexes is slight:
the to-the-point pattern. Perhaps one could say that acceptance, mañana,
and lack of organization are expressions of what might be called the
*hic-et-nunc* configuration [58]. It is based on a profound optimism, which
is also shown in spontaneous friendliness, hospitality, and confidence, and
it finds its most literal expression in the picture of happiness, which
might be labeled "here," "together," in the significance of the family and
the home. It is possible also that the careful preservation of waste matter,
checked by lack of organization (so that much of what has been preserved
spoils or is forgotten), is an expression of *hic-et-nuc*, in part channeled
through precarious economics.

If this picture of the emotional setup of Loman culture (optimism,
etc.) easily follows from that of the intellectual-conceptual setup (acceptance, time, etc.) [59], it must not be forgotten that important changes
have taken place and are taking place in all these patterns and therefore
in the interrelatedness of the patterns (configuration or configurations).

On the whole the patterns have been changing in the direction of
those prevailing in the Anglo culture which surrounds that of Loma.
Loman culture would therefore appear to have undergone a process of
losing its characteristics (perhaps only ideal-typically) as outlined above.
Probably some of the original patterns can be more clearly observed in
this process of change than they could if it did not exist—for example,
the traditionally fixed temporal events such as the *fiesta* [60], when contrasted with present-day instability. At the same time, the vague time
conception and acceptance pattern appear to be predisposing to this
change. The integrating role of the family, even of the home, has de-
creased; the concepts of happiness, hospitality, and mañana have changed
in the direction of the money-accentuated urban-American culture. Least

changed are those patterns that were characterized in negative terms: they are tending to become liabilities in competing with the Anglos—lack of organization and planning (Organization) and inability to see new complexes (To the Point) [61]. Even the conservation of waste may show the heavier stress of the second aspect of this pattern, namely, wasting conserved matter by spoiling or even forgetting that it has been conserved.

The great amount of petty thievery (cigarettes, small change, and food) practiced by Spanish-speaking persons against Anglos, even against those with whom they are connected by the most cordial relations and friendships, as well as against other Spanish-speaking persons, may be a reaction to the competitive aspects of the change, a kind of stereotyped (patterned) revenge based on frustration, which in turn would be due mainly to a feeling of economic inferiority [62]. At any rate, petty thievery must be examined with reference to each pattern sketched.

In conclusion it should be reiterated that the whole of the foregoing "illustration" has been given only to make the theoretical part of this chapter more concrete—not to produce a sketch of the culture of Loma. Otherwise two points in it would appear to invalidate it: the failure to utilize *all* materials for the discussion of patterns (e.g., religion, kinship, language, education, knowledge of herbs, magic, witchcrafts, sex, and others for which voluminous field notes have been gathered) and the remaining conceptual insufficiency, especially in regard to a distinction between patterns, traits, complexes, and configurations.

### NOTES

1. Revision of a paper presented at the Summer Institute of the Society for Social Research at the University of Chicago, August 4, 1944. The research on which this paper is based was made possible by a postdoctoral fellowship of the Social Science Research Council. I am indebted to Dr. Sol Tax, University of Chicago, and to Dr. Melvin M. Tumin, Wayne University, for valuable criticisms and suggestions.

2. For example, Gregory Bateson, *Naven* (Cambridge: University Press, 1936), or E. E. Evans-Pritchard, *Witchcraft. Oracles and Magic Among the Azande* (Oxford: Clarendon Press, 1937), and the "culture pattern" school. See also Gregory Bateson, "Experiments in Thinking about Observed Ethnological Material," *Philosophy of Science*, 8 (January 1941), 53–68, and Clyde Kluckhohn, "The Place of Theory in Anthropological Studies," *Philosophy of Science*, 6 (July 1939), 328–344.

3. See the works of George A. Lundberg and Read Bain.

4. Especially Karl Mannheim's concept of "existential determination of knowledge," in *Ideology and Utopia*, translated by Louis Wirth and Edward

Shils (New York: Harcourt, Brace, 1936), pp. 237–240, especially p. 239 and note and its discussion by Robert K. Merton, "Karl Mannheim and the Sociology of nowledge," unpaged reprint from *The Journal of Liberal Religion*, **2**, No. 3 (Winter 1941); see also further discussion of Mannheim in Virgil G. Hinshaw, Jr., "The Epistemological Relevance of Mannheim's Sociology of Knowledge," *The Journal of Philosophy*, **2** (February 4, 1943), 57–72, and in H. Otto Dahlke, "The Sociology of Knowledge," in Barnes, Becker, and Becker, *Contemporary Social Theory* (New York: Appleton-Century, 1940), especially pp. 82–85. For a concise general treatment of the problems of the sociology of knowledge (although with little attention to Mannheim) see Gerard DeGré, *Society and Ideology* (New York: Columbia University Bookstore, 1943).

5. Cf. Pauline V. Young, *Scientific Social Surveys and Research* (New York: Prentice-Hall, 1939), pp. 134–135.

6. Cf. the general attitude expressed by L. L. Bernard, "The Sources and Methods of Cultural and Folk Sociology," in L. L. Bernard, Ed., *The Fields and Methods of Sociology* (New York: Farrar and Rinehart, 1934), especially pp. 354–355; also the whole literature on evaluation versus fact in the social sciences, from Rickert and Max Weber to Gunnar Myrdal, *An American Dilemma* (New York and London: Harper, 1944), pp. 1035–1064.

7. Cf. M. R. Cohen and E. Nagel, *An Introduction to Logic and Scientific Method* (New York: Harcourt, Brace, 1934); John Dewey, *Logic: The Theory of Inquiry* (New York: Holt, 1938); A. D. Ritchie, *Scientific Method* (London: Kegan Paul, 1933); A. N. Whitehead, *Science and the Modern World* (New York: Macmillan, 1925); A. C. Benjamin, *The Logical Structure of Science* (London: Paul, Trench, Trubner, 1936); G. H. Mead, "The Nature of Scientific Knowledge," in *The Philosophy of the Act* (Chicago: University of Chicago Press, 1938), pp. 45–62.

8. In this connection Gunnar Myrdal's suggestion is highly stimulating (*An American Dilemma*, p. 3): "America, compared to every other country in Western civilization, large or small, has the *most explicitly expressed* system of general ideals in reference to human interrelations. This body of ideals is more widely understood and appreciated than similar ideals are anywhere else."

9. Cf. R. H. Tawney's suggestion that a Maori anthropologist undertake a study of the British, in reciprocation of Firth's study of the Maori [in the preface to Raymond Firth, *Primitive Economics of the New Zealand Maori* (New York: Dutton, 1929), p. xvii].

10. Following the presentation of the first draft of this paper, Robert J. Havighurst suggested that this line of thought necessarily leads to the question whether in our own society a middle-class sociologist could adequately study a lower-class group. A thorough answer to this question needs, first, a distinct and comprehensive theory of "class" and, second, a distinct and comprehensive theory of the relations between our subcultures and our culture. I do not think at present we have either. As to the first, certainly W. Lloyd Warner's and his followers' class theory is inadequate; cf. C. Wright Mills's review of Warner and Lunt, *The Social Life of a Modern Community* (New Haven: Yale Uni-

versity Press, 1941), in *American Sociological Review,* **7** (April 1942), 263–271. On subcultures see the stimulating discussion in Ralph Linton, *The Study of Man* (New York: Appleton-Century, 1936), pp. 275–276. My offhand answer to the question raised by Professor Havighurst is that recent presentations of American culture, especially in Robert S. Lynd, *Knowledge for What?* (Princeton: Princeton University Press, 1939, Clyde Kluckhohn, "The Way of Life," *The Kenyon Review,* **3** (Spring, 1941), 160–179, Margaret Mead, *And Keep Your Powder Dry* (New York: Morrow, 1942), would indicate that what our culture has in common is more pervasive than what differentiates it, so that the case of the middle-class sociologist studying a lower class group would not seem to be an example in point of my thought and that such documents as Shaw's studies of delinquents, Anderson's studies of the hobo, Thrasher's *The Gang,* and Whyte's *Street Corner Society* are not fundamentally vitiated by the shortcoming that Professor Havighurst envisaged [cf. the critiques of Adler, Rank, Freud, Thomas and Znaniecki, Shaw, and others by John Dollard in his *Criteria for the Life History* (New Haven: Yale University Press, 1935)].

11. The closeness of the cultural approach to Malinowski's functionalism is obvious; functional anthropology "holds that the . . . laws of the cultural process are to be found in the function of the real elements of culture. The atomizing or isolating treatment of cultural traits is regarded as sterile because the significance of culture consists in the relation between its elements . . ." [cf. Bronislaw Malinowski, "Culture," in *Encyclopedia of the Social Sciences,* **4** (1931), 625]. However, although Malinowski is predominently interested in an explanation of culture as a human characteristic and, proceeding on this basis, comes on the concepts of need and institution [cf. his "Man's Culture and Man's Behavior," *Sigma Chi Quarterly,* **29** (October 1941), 182–196, and **20** (January 1942), 66–78, and *A Scientific Theory of Culture and Other Essays* (Chapel Hill: University of North Carolina Press, 1944)], the cultural approach lies in studying cultures and the concept of pattern.

12. Clyde Kluckhohn, "Patterning as Exemplified in Navaho Culture," in Leslie Spier, A. Irving Hallowell, Stanley S. Newman, Eds., *Language, Culture, and Personality, Essays in Memory of Edward Sapir* (Menasha, Wis.: Sapir Memorial Publication Fund, 1941), pp. 109–130, especially 114–129. This exposition by far surpasses the methodology of preceding studies, especially Ruth Benedict's pioneering *Patterns of Culture* (Boston: Houghton Mifflin, 1934) or Carle C. Zimmerman's *The Changing Community* (New York: Harper, 1938), especially 155–157, as well as philosophically related works, from Nietzsche's *Birth of Tragedy* to Sorokin's *Social and Cultural Dynamics* and Morris's *Paths of Life.*

13. Kluckhohn *op. cit.,* pp. 120 and 124, seems to answer this question in terms of statistics.

14. "Universe of discourse" (of an individual or a group) is the totality of concepts used (by that individual or group), plus their implications. Cf. Kurt H. Wolff, "The Sociology of Knowledge: Emphasis on an Empirical Attitude," *Philosophy of Science,* **10** (April 1943), 109, n. 19 [Chapter 16]. See also George

H. Mead, *Mind, Self, and Society*, Charles Morris, Ed. (Chicago: University of Chicago Press, 1934), p. 269.

15.   See the remarks made in n. 10.

16.   The most recent systematic presentation of folk culture known to me is Robert Redfield, *The Folk Society* (Chicago, August 12, 1942), hectographed.

17.   Karl Mannheim, "Ideologische und soziologische Interpretation der geistigen Gebilde" (1926) [cf. Chapter 2, n. 4].

18.   It is from the latter standpoint, however, that Kluckhohn, in "Patterning as Exemplified in Navaho Culture," has classified patterns.

19.   It should be noted that the two elements of a folk culture, designated here in an oversimplified form as urban and nonurban, may of course need to be seen as consisting of various cultural strains. Thus the culture of the New Mexican community previously referred to combines in its urban aspects strains of a culture colored by international industrialization, of the average American city culture, of regional cultural peculiarities, and of cultures of still more nearby semiurban centers; in its nonurban aspects it combines strains of Spanish, Mexican, rural, and Indian cultures, and all strains are differentiated in terms of the two main (and other) types of the members of this culture: Spanish-speaking and English-speaking persons.

20.   My own experience is that for an initial period of field work I prefer the slower, more chaotic manner of recording anything that comes under my observation to the method of rapidly formulating hypotheses because I am aware that a premature hypothesis, although checkable and corrigible, shapes one's chances of perception and interpretation. I am also aware, of course, that one cannot proceed without hypotheses, but those that I have advanced as a general theoretical approach to the study of cultures appear to me to be the minimal limitations-enrichments of my sensitivity.

21.   From my own experience I should say that the initial period of avidly collecting materials comes to an end when their sheer quantity forces the student to begin his interpretation. It may be noted that this interpretation is likely to be based on a topical breakdown of the materials, a breakdown that has probably accompanied their collection [cf. Chapter 23].

22.   Kluckhohn, "Patterning as Exemplified in Navaho Culture," unfortunately gives no explicit definition of pattern. In contrast to custom and trait, which are contentual, it is structural (pp. 114, 116); in contrast to configuration, which applies to covert culture, it applies to overt culture (pp. 114, 124, 129); overt and covert are not defined, however.

23.   It is understood (as is all scientific rule) that the method by which statistical data are arrived at depends on the nature of the pattern (it may be interview, casual conversation, questionnaire, or any of their combinations).

24.   Namely, if Kluckhohn's distinction between structural (patterns) and contentual (traits) regularities were obliterated and house ownership (i.e., something in which the student is interested as in a contentual item) were considered in its interrelation with (structural) patterns. The study in which this is done has not to my knowledge been written.

25. They are paid no, or very little, attention in Benedict, *loc. cit.*

26. With reference to intellectual productions exclusively.

27. Cf. Wolff, *op. cit.*, 113.

28. The following discussion is simplified by overlooking a classification of the patterns mentioned according to Kluckhohn's scheme in Spier et al., *op. cit.* 114–129.

29. The following analytical features are omitted in this list or introduced only unsystematically: number and characteristics of population sharing these patterns, including the question whether they are shared by individuals or populations outside Loma, whether they are typical of Spanish-speaking New Mexico or of rural people elsewhere, and classification of patterns according to Kluckhohn.

30. Henceforth P.d. Given only if the concept used here deviates specifically from its colloquial usage.

31. Henceforth Ills. These illustrations deal almost exclusively with members of one family, the *M*'s. For the sake of concreteness, quotations are copied literally from my field notes (with the exception of the entry referred to in n. 56). Omissions are indicated by ellipses; additions (mainly English renditions of Spanish expressions), by brackets. Parentheses, except those within brackets, are in the original notes. "Anglo" is a traditionally and customarily English-speaking person. Spanish spelling is in accordance with Appleton's *New English-Spanish and Spanish-English Dictionary* (New York and London: Appleton-Century, 1943).

32. My field notes (ms.), p. 6, May 5, 1944.

33. *Ibid.*, pp. 173–174, June 26, 1944.

34. *Ibid.*, p. 127, June 12, 1944.

35. *Ibid.*, p. 26, May 9, 1944.

36. *Ibid.*, p. 130, June 12, 1944.

37. *Ibid.*, p. 133, June 13, 1944.

38. *Ibid.*, p. 398, August 25, 1944.

39. *Ibid.*, p. 65, May 22, 1944.

40. *Ibid.*, p. 131, June 12, 1944.

41. *Ibid.*, p. 290, July 23, 1944.

42. *Ibid.*, pp. 297, July 24, 1944.

43. Arthur L. Campa, "Mañana Is Today," *The New Mexico Quarterly*, 9 (February 1939), 3–11.

44. My field notes, p. 288, July 22, 1944.

45. *Ibid.*, p. 327, July 29, 1944.

46. *Ibid.*, p. 362, August 17, 1944.

47. *Ibid.*, p. 337–338, August 13, 1944.

48. Cf. Pitirim A. Sorokin, *Sociocultural Causality, Space, Time* (Durham, N.C.: Duke University Press, 1943), pp. 158–225.

49.   My field notes, pp. 4–5, May 5, 1944.

50.   *Ibid.*, p. 49, May 15, 1944.

51.   *Ibid.*, p. 345, August 14, 1944.

52.   *Ibid.*, p. 47, May 15, 1944.

53.   *Ibid.*, p. 126, June 11, 1944.

54.   *Ibid.*, p. 200, July 3, 1944.

55.   *Ibid.*, p. 335, August 12, 1944.

56.   This paragraph is a slightly revised field-note entry (pp. 334–335, August 12, 1944).

57.   Campa, "Mañana Is Today."

58.   It will be noted that the term configuration is used here for the first time as a possible structural concept because the relation between patterns and configurations has not yet become clear to me nor does the justification of configuration as a concept denoting a step at which one can arrive empirically yet appear to me to be demonstrated. Cf. n. 22. On configurations cf. Kluckhohn in Spier, *op. cit.*, pp. 124–129, and Florence R. Kluckhohn, *Los Atarqueños: A Study of Patterns and Configurations in a New Mexico Village* (Ph.D. dissertation, unpublished, Cambridge, Mass., Radcliffe College, 1941), pp. 9, 12–31.

59.   It would be inviting to develop a presentation of Loman culture in terms of a more systematic development of its emotional (ethos) and intellectual (eidos) aspects, as Bateson (in *Naven*) has attempted it for Iatmul culture, but at this stage of the investigaiton I am not yet sure whether such a framework is ideal for the study of Loma. For a comparison of the early-stage pattern approach (Benedict) with Bateson (and Margaret Mead) cf. S. F. Nadel, "The Typological Approach to Culture," *Character and Personality*, **5** (June 1937), 267–284.

60.   Cf. the information on the San Ysidro celebration in 1944 in the illustration of To the Point.

61.   Florence R. Kluckhohn (in *Los Atarqueños*, pp. 27–28) discusses fear as one of the configurations of the Atarque culture. Although I have material on fear in Loma, I do not yet know what role it plays or whether it has been accentuated only along with economic insecurity (and the inadequacy of "Spanish knowledge," i.e., knowledge regarding herbs, craft, witchcraft, and cures, to meet this insecurity).

62.   For the theory underlying this sequence see John Dollard et al., *Frustration and Aggression* (New Haven: Yale University Press, 1939).

Reprinted from James E. Curtis and John W. Petras, Eds., *The Sociology of Knowledge: A Reader,* by permission of the publisher. In the British Commonwealth published by Gerald Duckworth. In New York published by Praeger, pp. 320–341. The essay has been edited and partially revised by the author.

# 21

## CULTURE CHANGE
## IN LOMA:
## A Preliminary Research
## Report. 1950

"Loma," [1] "Justino" County, Southwest, is a relatively isolated community of some 200 people (40 families). Most of them are Spanish-speaking; the rest are "Anglos," non-Spanish, English-speaking whites. The community lies 7000 feet high in a little valley stretching across a state road, which, in rainy weather, takes a special art to travel.

Almost all the Spanish inhabitants were born in Justino County and a majority in Loma itself. The Anglos are more heterogeneous in this respect, as well as in many others, even occupationally: one is a trader and store owner, whose wife runs the post-office, another rents cabins, but all also farm. The Spanish people make their living farming and doing wage work outside Loma (most combine the two), especially sheepherding, sheepshearing, and potato picking. Land is the chief property. Anglo acreages and values are higher than the Spanish but there is much variation within each class.

For about 40 years Loma has had a public grade school. The church (Catholic), only some ten years old, is a mission of the Justino parish. Mass is held once a month, not on a Sunday, by an Anglo priest. The Anglos belong to various non-Catholic denominations or to none.

People look lean and many are bony, for the Spanish diet is deficient and sickness is widespread, much of it undiagnosed. Infant mortality is high and birth control is practically unknown.

Loma history has few specific dates, although tenants lived in the locality as long as 120 years ago when water rights were granted by the Mexican government. Soon the first irrigation ditch was dug, and about 60 years ago an Anglo pioneer dug the first well. The most far-reaching event was the establishment of the National Forest early in this century. It eliminated sheep and goats by pre-empting grazing lands and pasture, thus depriving the Lomans (*Lomeños*) of basic sources of income, of meat, milk, and cheese for food, of wool for spinning and weaving, and, indirectly, of spinning, weaving, and related skills. The next important change factors, more difficult to date, were the introduction of the automobile and the less directly significant contacts with other urban inventions—radio, magazines, dance halls with their nickelodeons in Alta (the nearest community to the south), the movie in Justino, and latest of all, electricity. In most of these diffusions federal and county agencies and the Loma Institute were instrumental.

The defunct Farm Security Administration was the most important federal agency economically and, in conjunction with other farm-improving services, for reforms in agriculture as well. People recognized this: the FSA made more sense to them than any other effort. Individuals who benefited from it also rated WPA highly. The Soil Conservation Service has met with some interest, but most of the plans discussed in connection with the district have not yet materialized. The county agent, according to the individual who occupies the office, may function as merely one of the numerous vague entities called government officials or as an intimate friend and adviser.

Justino, the seat of all these and other governmental agencies, also houses the tax authorities. On the whole, they are felt to be functionaries of a vast and fateful power. In 1940 more than half the farms in the county had become the property of the state for back taxes, often without the knowledge of the original owner. For Loma the figure may be as high as one-fourth. In 1941 the percentages of incomes represented by taxes ranged from one to 75.

Directly or indirectly, the agencies have tried to introduce a foreign-imposed kind of community organization of a nontraditional, nonreligious, nonfeudal, non-Spanish kind. Yet it was the Justino Plan and the Loma Institute that were most intent on improving conditions by rational measures. The Plan, which operated for about three years during the early 1940s, obtained "problem lists" from representatives of all communities in the county. It cooperated with the other agencies, public and private, and with the people in the communities themselves. In Loma in 1942 the most urgent problems, according to the residents, were water scarcity, for which the building of a reservoir and the adjustment of ditches were given the highest rating as a suggested solution, inadequate education, for which additional teachers were named as a measure of improvement, and poor health. The Justino Plan did various things to alleviate these and other problems, and ever since its demise several efforts have continued.

The Loma Institute, created and directed by a midwestern Anglo teacher and his wife, was more intimately connected with the community. It was developed with money collected by the operation of summer camps, frequented by boys and girls from as far away as New York. Later, a year-round grade and high school was opened mainly for local Spanish students. Because of the scarcity of personnel, decimated by military service, and shifting interests on the part of the few individuals left, the Institute lasted only five years, yet while it ran it engaged not only in formal education but also in various other community activities, such as the 4-H Club, health clinics, the establishment and supervision of a community center, dances, and the like. Aside from direct give and take, the most outstanding means of communication between the Institute and the community was a newspaper, *The Lomeño*. Written and mimeographed by staff and students, it gave expression in particular to the Institute's emphasis on participation in political life—local, county, state, and national.

Yet in spite of these efforts planning and organized cooperation in matters not traditional (such as irrigation) remained foreign to the people. Here, however, the narrative must be interrupted, in order to insert a methodological note or perhaps to confirm an observation made by the reader, namely, that what has been said so far refers mainly to the Spanish people of Loma. Beyond showing this awareness, it is not possible to do more than to point out, rather peremptorily, that the reason for this preferential treatment is that Loma is a predominantly Spanish community in more than one respect and to state that from now on the Spanish society and culture of Loma are dealt with exclusively. To resume the argument, then, how much planning and organized cooperation remained foreign to the *Lomeños* is suggested by the answers to questions concerning their community, asked of them in 1942. One question was: "How much land do you think is needed for raising enough animals and crops to supply yourself and your family without having to go outside for wage-work?" Answers to it ranged from 15 to 250 acres. Another was: "Given the cultivable land and the water available, how many families do you believe can make a living in Loma without having to go outside for work?" Replies ran from two to 25 families. Still other questions resulted in comparable answers: all showed polite compliance with the kind of request made but did not go beyond it toward a more empirical preoccupation with the topics brought up.

Almost all that has been said illustrates Loma culture change. Anglo-carried phenomena—economic, technological, industrial, urban—act on a culture formerly not so impressed. This impact is both local and pervasive (cf. Figure 1). Among the local elements, in chronological order, are Anglo-derived education, the National Forest, the Anglo-operated

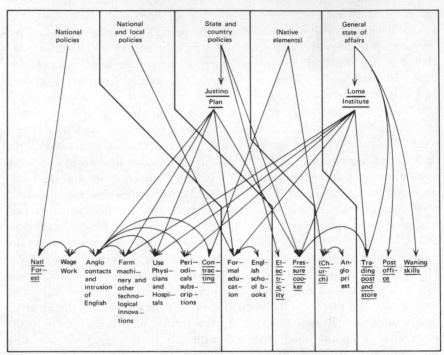

*Figure 1. Elements in the process of Loma culture change. The top line lists influences (whose preponderant direction is indicated by arrows) outside the local change system, with the possible exception of the vague last, "General State of Affairs." The bottom line lists elements operating in the Loma culture as of 1948 (and thereafter). These elements are shown in their connections with one another, as well as with the influences listed on the top line. Two elements (Justino Plan and Loma Institute) are placed in an intermediate position to indicate that they were no longer in existence in 1948. Underscoring indicates the fact that the item can be traced only to an influence outside the local change system; non-underscored items can be traced to influences within this system. The—undoubtedly existing—influences of items on the bottom line are not indicated except for a few specific ones (the chain leading from National Forest to Contracting; the introduction of English School Books through Formal Education; of the Anglo Priest through the Church; and of Pressure Cooker and Post Office through the Trading Post and Store). The parentheses around "Church" indicate that this element is native.*

trading post and store, the post office, the Anglo priest, and the short-lived Justino Plan and Loma Institute. More pervasive elements, in approximately chronological order, are the intrusion of English and English school books, the appearance of outside wage work, the waning of handicrafts, contracting, farm machinery, the services of physicians and hospitals, the introduction of sewing machines, pressure cookers, and other household appliances, magazine and newspaper subscriptions, and electricity.

In a much more intimate fashion the process of this change is shown in life histories (Figure 2) and in compositions written by upper-grade school children. Lotario Rodriguez, a twenty-year old boy who graduated from

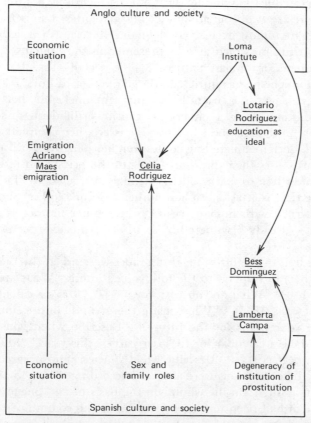

*Figure 2. Elements in the process of culture change on the part of five Lomans. The positions of the five individuals diagrammed symbolize their respective "nearness" to Anglo and Spanish culture and society, respectively. Arrows indicate preponderant direction of influence.*

the state university( so far the only Spanish Loman to do so), exemplifies a change in Loman culture by the incorporation of (Anglo) education as ideal. Another type results from socioeconomic change. It is illustrated by several young married men, for instance, Adriano Maes, who emigrated, probably for good, preponderantly on economic grounds. A third type, perhaps, is represented by Lotario's younger sister Celia. Although her brother may be said to participate in two worlds, Spanish and Anglo, Celia's outlook seems little Anglicized in spite of her equally good English and other participations in American culture. In part, this is so because she is a girl. As her most impressive experience she recalled the onset of menstruation and the fatal accident of a younger sister, whereas the brother's most fundamental change, as interpreted by him, consisted in the process of education and he did not even mention the sibling's death. Finally, there are two women, mother and daughter, Lamberta and Bess, whose lives are almost exclusively definable in terms of a decaying insti-tution, prostitution, which may be presented as the Lomans' handling of one component of human nature—evil, especially sex. Lamberta, the mother, although she has initiated a large number of boys, is treated like any other villager, in a friendly, ordinary manner, but her role is no longer stable and clear. Lamberta is cautious, diffident, and confused. Furthermore, although she emphatically asserts her complete agreement with church doctrine, including confession, her daughter, still unmarried, favors divorce, uses the expression "none of the priest's business," prefers Anglos, would like to marry one, is strongly attracted by the "city" but at the same time is attached to her mother and the "folks." She nc longer seems concerned with human nature, whereas her mother is still bewil-dered by it—already bewildered by it if, in turn, she is seen against the past.

The children in the fifth to eighth grades were asked (by the substitute Anglo teacher) to respond to the following stimuli: "What are you look-ing forward to?" "What do you wish for most?" "Make a calendar for the rest of this year (1944)." "What made the greatest impression on you?" "What are your plans for the future?" "Describe when you were most happy." "Make a calendar for the past part of this year." "Make a calen-dar for last year (1943)." "Describe when you were most scared" [2]. The answers to these questions were analyzed according to Anglo and Spanish components posited, on the whole, on the basis of an "image" of Loman culture which had been formed by staying in the community and which is subject to checks yet to be applied. The list just given is in the order of decreasing Anglo percentages. In the "looking forward to" question they amounted to 77 percent, the then current war figuring overwhelmingly.

Next (72 percent) came the "wish," with the war likewise preponderant, but with a close-by tie between desires for spatial movement, mainly trips, and material possessions. Next (57 percent) came the calendar for the end of 1944, with war once more strongly in the lead. Next (46 percent), the "most impressive experience," with the reflection of industrialization and urbanization in various respects being most clear. Next (40 percent), "future plans," with spatial movement outstanding. Next (33 percent), "happiness," with the war slightly surpassing industrialization and urbanization. Next, the calendars of the past part of 1944 (30 percent) and of 1943 (26 percent), with school experiences ranking uppermost; finally, 18 percent of the children's "scare" memories were Anglo components, equally connected with the war and with aspects of industrialization.

Among the complementary Spanish elements fantasy was most important in 23 percent of the "looking forward to" questions; personal relations in 28 percent of the "wish" questions; farm matters in 43 percent of the calendar for the end of 1944; nature in 54 percent of the "most impressive experience" questions; farm matters again in 60 percent of the "future plans"; personal relations in 67 percent of the "happiness" category; the farm once more in the calendars of the past part of 1944 (70 percent) and of 1943 (74 percent); and nature in 82 percent of the "scare" memories.

If the overpowering influence of World War II as well as all items amounting to less than three percent each of the components in either the Anglo or the Spanish class are eliminated, the children's answers can be classified exhaustively into three Anglo items totaling 37 percent of all components, namely, the school, spatial movement, and industrialization and urbanization, and into four Spanish items totaling 63 percent, namely, personal relations, the farm, nature, and self. The Anglo components reflect interest in an institution, expressions of attitudes, and impacts of a process. The Spanish components reflect social relations (personal relations and, as an inspection of the children's answers indicates, self) and institutions (farm and nature [3]).

The analysis of cultural change has thus led to a confrontation with Loman culture. As this culture emerges from an analysis of the children's compositions and from the life histories, it would appear to be a culture that in the way described has both Anglo and Spanish components. This statement anticipates a good deal, for it is based also on answers to questions that have not been discussed here as well as on the largely unknown impact of the situation in which the questions were asked on the answers given. The validity of statements concerning Loman culture can be increased only if it is possible to formulate them in a less tentative and more intelligent and justifiable fashion. This, in turn, can be done only if Anglo-Spanish relations are more intimately studied—if, that is, the structure of the Loman social system is better understood.

At this stage of analyzing the data neither this study nor the many other things that need to be worked out and clarified have been done. What has been presented, therefore, stands pending the solution of these tasks, for it has been elaborated to the point, it would seem, at which it can be revised only on their completion.

### NOTES

1.  This paper, read at the Twenty-fifth Annual Meeting of the Central States Branch, American Anthropological Association, Indiana University, Bloomington, May 13 and 14, 1949, is a concentrated synopsis of some parts of a large-scale monograph on Loma designed to develop and document a concept of social science, especially sociology and cultural anthropology and the study of culture. (Other parts of the monograph already published are "A Methodological Note on the Empirical Establishment of Culture Patterns," *American Sociological Review*, **10** (April 1945), 176–184, and "The Unique and the General: Toward a Philosophy of Sociology," *Philosophy of Science*, **15** (July 1948), 192–210. Field work in Loma was done in 1942 and 1944, in 1944 on a Social Science Research Council fellowship. Writing was begun in 1948 and 1949 under grants from The Viking Fund, Inc., and the Graduate School of The Ohio State University. In the summer of 1947 Mrs. Morgan Bissette, a graduate student, spent several weeks in Loma under my and Dr. John W. Bennett's supervision (all of Ohio State University). Material collected by Mrs. Bissette is employed here as well as in the first volume of the monograph written up so far. To these organizations and persons I gratefully acknowledge my indebtness. This paper will probably appear to be largely impressionistic, due overwhelmingly, if not wholly, to the impossibility of anything more than very slight documentation in view of the time limitations under which it had to be presented. Even the methodology could be indicated, if at all, only by implication. Reference for full documentation must therefore be made to the forthcoming monograph.

2.  A good deal of explaining was necessary to make these questions understandable. This, along with the classroom context, the teacher's personality, and similar factors, made an important situational impact on the answers which, however, could not be measured. A consideration such as this is only one among many that went into the technique of analyzing the children's answers in regard to Spanish and Anglo components. The techniques cannot be described here.

3.  By institution is meant a unit within a sociocultural context that contains social and cultural elements (individuals and their relations and their interpre-

tations) and that also may contain elements of the natural environment; a unit that must "be counted with" by the participant individuals. It may be suggested that, although in Loman culture Nature is an institution in this sense, it is not an institution in the typical urban culture, although it is one (however, with variable contents) perhaps in rural culture generally and very probably in the Anglo culture of Loma.

---

Reprinted from *The Ohio Journal of Science,* **50** (1950), 53–59, by permission of the publisher. The essay has been edited and partially revised by the author.

# 22

# LEADERSHIP IN LOMA:
## A Preliminary Research Report. 1950

In Chapter 21 the Spanish culture of Loma appeared to be changing in the direction of the surrounding Anglo culture, with a concomitant loss of its original characteristics. The topic of this chapter [1], leadership, suggests the adoption of an explicitly diachronic view: the new Anglo-influenced Loma system is contrasted with the old, the almost purely Spanish.

At this stage of investigation fifteen leadership types have tentatively been established. Eight of them function within the old system, seven within the new. Old types are the religious leader, the community leader, the man of knowledge and wisdom, the *patrón*, the *médico*, the *curandera*, the *hechicero (brujo)*, and the prostitute; new types are the contractor, the creditor, the priest, the physician, the nurse, the educator, and the community planner. Some of the old leaders still figure, if in attenuated form, in the present setup.

The religious leader is Sigismundo Campa. Some of his characteristics of leadership include his organizing role in home services, his instrumentality in the building of the church (after which home services nearly ceased), his influential functioning as a member and official of various religious organizations, and his wife's teaching of the catechism. His activity is thus the development or articulation of a certain institution, religion, by which in some respects (one has already been mentioned) his influence is enhanced by sharing it with his wife. She, however, is regarded by the Lomans merely as a person to whom some of her husband's duties have been delegated. The religious leader does not occupy an "office" of leadership: there is in Loma no such office or position. It is rather the personality of this particular individual that give certain activities within the institution of religion the quality of leadership. In answer to the question whether the religious leader belongs to the old or the new Loma it should be noted that an individual's seizure of available institutional opportunities for leadership is, by itself, no more characteristic of the old than the new system. What does characterize the old is the fact that the institution chosen is religion. Other leaders use other institutions more characteristic of the new system.

The community leader's role is similar, for he, too, is without office and develops existing institutions. He differs not only because the area within which he exercises influence is different but also because it contains a variety of institutions rather than one or two that are closely related. In the case of Alejandro Maes these institutions are education, economics, and justice. Maes gave the land on which the first schoolhouse was built and for many years he was a member of the school board. For some time he was considered the best farmer. He organized cooperative work at the seasonal times it was carried on by tradition and took a lead in the administration of irrigation. For many years he was the justice of the peace. Yet, although school-board member, water commissioner, and justice of the peace are well-defined offices in Loma, Alejandro is a leader not because he occupies these offices but, once more like Sigismundo Campa, because of his personality and particularly because of his wide interest in Loma and the qualities that endow his official actions with an importance that other office holders do not derive from their occupancy.

The same individual also is the man of knowledge and wisdom, a designation that refers to no office whatever, for the only related position is that of teacher (which has always been filled by a woman). The area in which Maes exercises leadership in his capacity of man of knowledge includes that of community leader, but it is broader than the fields of economics, education, and justice, for it covers other miscellaneous matters. His influence consists in inspiring confidence and security with his wisdom. He neither participates in nor articulates existing institutions; rather he perpetuates the character of tradition.

Actions committed by others may be observed by the outsider as similar to those of both leaders and may be classified as leadership acts but they are not so defined by the Lomans. Religious and community leadership is granted only to Campa and Maes.

The *patrón* represents a type different from those considered so far. Not only is his office clearly established, but its nature is such that it gives economic power to the holder. Unfortunately, little else is as certain about the office of *patrón*; for instance, it is not known whether the *patrón* was merely the largest landholder who had hired men or tenants working for him or whether he was a full-fledged feudal baron, on however modest a scale. In either case, because of the office he occupies, he exerts economic power. Adriano Orlando Maes, Alejandro Maes' father, at any rate the only known (perhaps the only) *patrón* Loma ever had, was a leader as well in many other respects, several of which were probably not included in the definition of his office but again were due to his personality. Adriano seems to have played a role similar to that of his son, inasmuch as he, in his day, was an over-all leader in an even larger way than Alejandro: he preceded Sigismundo Campa in religious affairs; he had the welfare of the community at heart (he donated the land for the cemetery and made and planted the first cross); he had influence in matters of education, health, various customs, and, of course, economics, and he was generally the man of knowledge and wisdom. In the course of economic change the office of *patrón* itself has disappeared and the leadership associated with it has been transmitted to other personalities. It is safe to assume that in becoming plural these offices have also become specialized but not to the point of institutionalization. It is true that now there are the offices of teacher, county agent (agricultural-economic), priest, physician, and more, but they have not developed historically from the *patrón*: all are imported.

Because of the power connected with the office of *patrón,* its occupant holds a position of leadership regardless of personality. The *patrón* may therefore be called an office leader and his office may be said to give its occupant office leadership. Three leadership types that are characteristic of the old Loma system have certain similarities with that of the *patrón*. It is not clear, however, whether *médico, curandera*, and *hechicero (brujo)* are leaders merely by virtue of their offices, or whether anybody who exercises their functions and thus articulates the institutions of health and witchcraft, thereby becomes a leader. It is not clear, in other words, whether healing and witchcraft are units in the institutions of health and, say, the sacred or the magical, or whether they themselves are institutions. In the case of the first two it is not economic power, and in the case of the *hechicero* it is not secular but sacred power that makes a leader. The *médico* performs the functions of physician, particularly in psychosomatic medicine, which, with the addition of midwife, is also the function of the *curandera*. Although the patients of the *curandera* are almost entirely women and children, those of the *médico* are nearly always men. Both satisfy health needs but also wield some measure of sacred power. This is truer of the *médico* than of the *curandera*, for the former more clearly than the latter is the counteragent of the *hechicero (brujo)*, the witch or sorcerer. Witchcraft is as little a full-time occupation as leadership in matters of religion, the community, and general knowledge and wisdom. Nor is witchcraft altogether a specialty monopolized by the witch, for certain arts of witchcraft, particularly casting the evil eye, are exercised by a number of others, men and women. In a similar fashion not all cases of bewitchery require the services of the *médico* or *curandera*; familiarity with the witch's tricks or special piety, often possessed by several persons of both sexes, suffices to exorcise the spell. To repeat, it is difficult to decide before the pertinent data are more carefully analyzed whether the *hechicero* holds office or whether anybody who commits an act of witchcraft thereby, and for that time [2], becomes a leader merely by virtue of his skill. A parallel question must be raised in regard to the *médico* and the *curandera*.

The prostitute's influence consists in the introduction of the young to sex life and in the channelization of the evil in human nature. The former refers to boys but the latter to mature people and, though differentially to men and women, not to men alone. It is uncertain whether Lamberta had many or even any regular customers among those whose sex life was settled, especially in marriage, but her influence is felt nevertheless among the villagers in their treatment of her, which takes cognizance of her role, yet is friendly and respectful. There are good grounds for believing that prostitution is, or rather was, an institution. If this is correct, there is a further case of office or institutional leadership.

In Table 1 five aspects of leadership characteristic of the old Loman system are brought toward greater, even though still preliminary and tentative, systematization. Two of these aspects, entered in the last two columns, have not been specifically discussed but will be understood from the discussion presented. It should be observed that the office of *patrón*, rather than Antonio Orlando Maes' occupancy of it, has been analyzed. It will be noted further that status, a concept so often discussed in connection with leadership, has not been specifically treated. By implication, however, a certain aspect of it can easily be inferred from the fourth column, which, in effect, says that within the area described the respective leader has the highest status, although other individuals may also exercise influence. Thus in religion the religious leader has the highest status, but other persons may have religious influence as well—as is true, for instance, not only of particularly religious individuals but also of more institutionally defined persons like the officials of religious organizations who, however, are not considered leaders. The peculiarity of the first three leaderships is that their respective areas are defined by the Lomans in terms of the leaders' personalities. "Highest status," therefore, is synonymous here with "only status," inasmuch as no other person has status at all. Com-

*Table 1.  Aspects of Leadership in the Old Socio-Cultural System of Loma*

| Leadership | Relation to Institution (s) | Personal, Office, and Institutional Aspects | Area of Influence | Means of Influence | Ethical Aspect |
|---|---|---|---|---|---|
| Religious | Articulating available institution(s) (religion, church) | Personal | Religion | Precept and interpretation | Good |
| Community | Articulating available institutions (economics, education, justice) | Personal | Community affairs | Precept and advice | Same |
| Knowledge and wisdom | Perpetuating perceptive and orienting aspects of tradition | Personal | Knowledge and wisdom | Advice | Same |

| Patrón | Fixing power distribution | Office | Power | Economic power | Neutral |
|---|---|---|---|---|---|
| Médico | Articulating institution of health | Office or Institutional | Men's health | Superior knowledge and sacred power | Good |
| Curandera | Same | Same | Women's and children's health | Same | Same |
| Hechicero | Articulating institution of witchcraft | Same | Magic | Sacred power | Bad |
| Prostitute | Channelizing aspects of sex and of evil | Institutional | Sex and ethics and morals | Potential and actual physical contact | Compensated; choice of the relatively better for the relatively worse |

parable ramifications could be formulated in regard to the other areas of influence. At any rate, status refers to a leader within a given area, not to leadership [3].

Before presenting new-system leaderships several questions must be discussed. One concerns a definition of leadership itself: it refers to the exercises of significant influence within a sociocultural system—Loma is conceived as such a system. If the leadership types discussed are inspected, it appears that significant influence refers to one that affects the system itself—corroborating it by confirmation or articulation, questioning it, or changing it. (Here there are instances only of corroborating influence. The system has changed, not because of leadership but for other reasons, as indicated, especially in Chapter 21.) Leadership must not be confused with other influences in a system, which, of course, are innumerable. In the first place, in addition to affecting the system, it must also be concentrated rather than diffused. It may be concentrated in an office, institution, or person, all of which are found in Loma. Farmers, fathers, mothers, and so on, exert influence and thereby affect the system—in Loma once more in the corroborating sense. They are not considered leaders because their influence is not concentrated. Thus one connotation of the fact that prostitution is breaking down as an institution is the diffusion of the occupant's influence, a phenomenon more widely observed in contemporary urban cultures than in Loma.

In the second place no leadership office stands alone. Suppose the office of *patrón* were vacant. Leadership by mere occupancy will have been replaced by an impersonal portion of the sociocultural system, the distribution of power and land (and concomitant customs, beliefs, etc.). It may be added that because this particular portion of the system involves power, it will, after a relatively short time, either be personalized (by occupancy) or abolished (by some socioeconomic change). By itself it constitutes no leadership, although it does, even without the occupant's cooperation, bestow it on him. Thus leadership is seen to have a further requirement, namely, that it be exercised by an individual [4]. Moreover, the leader must be a living individual. If, for instance, a person says, "Christ is my leader," he may actually have no leader whatever (if he should really "live by" nothing but Christian doctrine, which is extremely improbable) but is talking about a normative system or a religious conviction, in short, about an aspect of his culture; or he actually has other leaders, such as his wife, a teacher, or a minister. With his death Christ ceased to be a leader. He was later replaced by the church, an institution with many offices and office leaderships in numerous sociocultural systems other than itself—among them, in Loma (though in a more articulate, even if weaker, fashion, only in its new phase).

How does the student of a system know—it may be asked—what leadership positions meet the requirements developed? Obviously, he must have a certain knowledge of the system itself before he can even formulate hypotheses regarding the concentration of influences that act on it. Space permits no more than a few, rather apodictic remarks, which are, however, necessary to further the argument. [Cf. Chapter 20.] The student identifies himself as best he can with the system he is studying. Thus he will eventually get some sort of picture with elements relating to the participants in the system and others relating to himself. The presentation of the picture he has gained amounts to its translation into his and his readers' culture. No Loman, for instance, would ever dream of thinking up Table 1, nor could he understand it, unless he were familiar with anthropological or sociological thought, in which case his culture would have been enriched or replaced by another, precisely, by the current social-science universe of discourse [5].

In the new Loma system, the leaderships—to repeat—are contractor, creditor, priest, physician, nurse, leader in education, and community planner. They can be discussed much more briefly, in part because they are more like one another than the old types, in part because they are well known to the readers of this chapter. With the exception of the last two, they are office leaderships. The contractor (Patricio Campa, a nephew of Sigismundo, the "old" religious leader) and the creditor (the Anglo trader) have taken over most of the economic functions, and therefore the power, that once were part of the *patrón's* leadership. The priest (an Anglo) has to a considerable extent replaced the religious leader; the physician, the *médico*, and the nurse, the *curandera*. Sigismundo Campa still plays some role, and the officials of the religious organizations combine minor office leadership with reminiscences, both of their own and of those with whom they interact, of a less institutionalized, more spontaneous, and personal religious life. Neither have the old-time representatives of health and un-health completely died out; some old people still resort to traditional medicines and cures, with or without the help of *médico* or *curandera*, believe in witchcraft, especially the evil eye, and take prophylactic and therapeutic measures against it, although a *hechicero* has not been known in the community for a long time.

The leader in education is represented most often by the public school teacher but also by government officials (such as the county agent), whose efforts on the whole consist in using educational measures to bridge the gap between the old and the new systems. During the existence of the Loma Institute some of its staff members, especially the president and his wife, exercised a tenuous and short-lived personal leadership, largely if not wholly irrespective of the institution of education or of the newly created Institute. Although there is educational leadership owing to the permanent existence of school and various government agencies, there was community planning only during the existence of the Loma Institute and the Justino Plan, and here again the leadership was assumed by the Institute's president and his immediate staff. He took it over from the Plan in Justino, exercised it locally, and began to delegate some of it to certain villagers. With the demise of the two organizations, however, the function of community planning died out.

If this is correct, why should these processes have occurred? This question suggests a further analysis of the relation between leadership and the sociocultural system of Loma. The system, it has been shown over and over, has been changing to the extent of imposing on its student the distinction between an old and a new phase. Yet, despite the fact (documented in Chapter 21) that the contemporary Spanish culture of Loma— at least of the younger generation—is indeed a mixture of Spanish and Anglo elements, leadership in the old system strikes one as somehow more effective than in the new. One suspects something that is common to all the old-system leadership types, in spite of the differences among them that have been pointed out; conversely, one suspects something common to all the new types. The common features may be described tentatively in the old system as an "end" relation to the leader because leadership, whether of office or of person, is the implementation of an unquestioned common normative system. In contrast, in the new system the relation to the leader is a "means" relation not because leadership is in conflict with (or irrelevant to) a normative system that would correspond to the new system but because there is no unquestioned common normative system developed to a point of which it could be implemented by leadership. The personal leaderships in religion, the community, and knowledge were accorded their representatives because the practice and promotion of religious tenets and rituals, the solution of community problems or of individuals' problems that bore on the community's welfare, and the dispensation of knowledge and wisdom by personally skillful resort to tradition were ends in Loman culture, sought for their own sake. It was good to be pious, to have questions answered that referred to one's own welfare in its relation to that of the community as well as to many other matters concerning which knowledge or wisdom were deemed helpful. It was good to be or to serve the *patrón*—merely to resent him as an oppressive power would not have made for stability [6]. It was good that there should have been a *médico* and a *curandera*, for both helped to restore health, and even though they were used as means to attain this end their occasional failure showed that they were God's instruments for showing his will and thus they had to be dealt with as ends in themselves. It is likely that the sacred power attributed to witchcraft and to the *hechicero* permits the application of a similar dialectic by which he, too, is seen to have become an end, but the precise process in which this might have been brought about is not known, at least not at this stage of analysis. Finally, although it was bad that man should have an evil component which shows itself especially in his sex appetite, it was good that there should have been a prostitute, for this institution controlled the appetite, and the person who performed this function therefore imposed respect.

Further implications of the old leadership type must be brought out before it is contrasted with the new. One is that the old leader had to make little use of coercion. The other is that the possibility of maintaining end relations with the leader was facilitated by the smallness of the community. This also provides the opportunity for over-all relations with him. People knew the religious leader, the community leader, the man of knowledge, even the *patrón* and the prostitute, not only in these capacities (it has been mentioned that the second and third leaderships were lodged in the same individual) but in many others as well, and they knew them as fellow citizens. The concomitance of over-all and end relations does not apply so clearly to the *médico*, the *curandera*, and the *hechicero*, because their specializations usually were too expensive for one community to support. It is probable, therefore, that end relations were maintained with them in several communities, whereas over-all relations developed in only one of them, in their places of residence.

A third point concerns political leaders. It will be noted that they are listed neither in the old nor in the new system. Yet *políticos* have been known to individual Lomans since long before the old system began to change. In spite of this familiarity with the type, the politician seems never to have played a leader's role, perhaps because there has never been a local *político*. The *político* is defined as an individual who plays politics on the side, as a part-time specialist. He gives parties and hands out liquor and is paid for it by the political machine, but he is not a boss, and no trace of bossism has been found that would have reached into Loma, much less have centered there. He can be called a leader only if the area within which he functions is clearly understood not to be connected with the common normative system, although the common norms apply as much to the treatment of the politician as a person as they do to that of all others, leaders or not. The politician, along with the *patrón* and the religious leader, tied (however tenuously) Loma to the outside Spanish world which was governed by politics and by comparatively far-flung economic, power, and religious relations. How little politics is part of the common normative system is shown by the fact that even one of the most specifically political acts, casting the ballot, is not governed by it but by other directives, especially by family and similar traditions [7].

Behavior of this sort has been labeled individualism, but this is a misnomer, for it is governed not by self-relying decisions but by common, though not by political, norms. Nevertheless there is individualism in Loma, that is, behavior based on personal rather than on common premises. Individualism governs personal relations that are not affected by the common norms—religious, familial, or communal. It does not govern relations that have the capacity of maintaining the social order. The order is accepted; the individual is appraised according to the appraiser's own normative system. Mr. McIntire, the trader, is not highly esteemed, but he is often chosen as a water official because both the regulation of the water and harmony with the creditor are important and also because Mr. McIntire has proved satisfactory in the office of ditch boss and water commissioner. Lomans thus distinguish various roles of the same person. Office roles are defined, and a given individual, if the system makes him a candidate for a certain office, achieves it by rules that are part of the system. Office roles are probably more numerous than personal roles, which, in turn, are considerably less clearly defined. Their attainment depends much less on the system, for here the system limits the range of individual achievement of role player and participant or participants only in the relation to which the role is relevant.

All this is pertinent to leadership not only in the old but also in the new system. The most general statement that can be made about the new order is that all the characteristics of the old are either absent or in a state of confusion. That there is no common normative system implemented in leadership types has been anticipated. There are no leaders, in other words, to whom relations constitute ends rather than means. It may be added that the relatively neat distinction between office and personal roles, with their different ascription and achievement and their relations to common and personal normative systems, has disappeared because the cohesive principle of the old society and culture, a common normative system, has been succeeded by another principle, the desire to overcome insecurity or impotence and to gain security or power. Because this is not a cohesive principle, it cannot function as the old one did.

The contractor and the public school teacher (and sometimes a doctor or nurse) are the only Spanish leaders characteristic of the new system. For this reason they are less mere means than are the remaining leaders, all of whom are Anglos and, except for the creditor and the Institute president while he was functioning, nonresidents. It is understandable, therefore, that the relations with the contractor and the teacher should be less specialized and more over-all than are those with the other types. Although the office and personal roles of Patricio Campa, the contractor, and corresponding relations with him can be clearly distinguished from one another, his office itself has not gained the dignity of the older offices. The contractor does not implement a norm; he provides a job. On the other hand, Filiberta Tejada, the teacher, is merely a specialist who otherwise is a Loman woman. Attitudes toward her as a specialist vary with the concept of education as something uninspiring that is taken for granted, as an imported imposition of doubtful merit, or as a prestige-giving acquisition. In no case is it a common norm that the teacher could implement.

Relations with the remaining types are predominantly though not exclusively office relations. To the extent that they are, they are specialized rather than over-all. The purest exemplification of a means relation concerns Mr. McIntire. Although differing from individual to individual, it is characterized both by the Spanish people and his own by bargaining. It is perhaps because of economics, the area in which this relation obtains, that is shows the new type of leadership in such purity, for it is harder to reduce relations with the priest, the physician, and the nurse to pure bargaining. The priest's office has all the dignity required to implement a common norm, but here it is the present occupant who falls short of his office. Yet it must be observed that already the priest's is no longer only an office leadership, for the office itself has lost significance. Church attendance is an indication, as are statements made by the priest and by numerous Lomans of both sexes and various ages. Religion is no longer something common to all Lomans. Those who participate least in the old system (a group composed to a considerable extent, but not entirely, of the younger men) find religion least satisfying and are either confused or motivated individually by a quest for economic security or power.

The physician and the nurse are used (if at all) as means to attain the specific ends for which their respective offices equip them (though not with the bargaining characteristics of the creditor relation) or are received or consulted with diffidence and suspicion as foreign importations (somewhat less so when they are Spanish), or treated as if they were *médicos* or *curanderas*. Relations thus are either specialized or confused. Finally, what influence the short-lived educator and community planner from the Loma Institute had was based on personal relations rather than on the establishment of and participation in common norms. What, if anything, he had created in the way of offices thus disappeared with the removal of his person.

Before coming to a conclusion regarding leadership in Loma and implications for our own society it may be clarifying to summarize the characteristics of leadership discussed in reference to Loma but perhaps more widely applicable.

1. Definition of leadership: the exercise of influence within a socio-cultural system, which influence (a) affects (corroborates, questions, changes) the system, (b) is concentrated in an office (institution) or person(s) rather than diffused, and (c) is exercised by a person (or persons) living in (or possibly outside) the sociocultural system at the time the system is a going concern.

2. The type of leadership is determined by its (a) relations to an institution or institutions in (or outside) the system, (b) by its being office (institutional) or personal leadership, (c) its area of influence, (d) its means of influence, (e) its ethical aspect or aspects by which (c) through (e) must be analyzed as office and personal characteristics in accordance with the information required under (b).

3. The type of leader himself is determined by (a) the relations obtaining between him and other differential individuals and groups, whereby end and means, over-all and specialized, and social and personal relations must be distinguished; (b) the roles played by him, which may be office roles or personal roles; (c) his status, which, by definition, is the highest (or only) one within a given area (or areas) of influence and which may be analyzed further (a step not taken in the present chapter) in regard to subjective status (the leader's definition of his status), accorded status (the status given the leader by differential individuals and groups), and system status (the status accorded the leader by the student of the sociocultural system in which the leader functions, on the basis of the student's construction and presentation of this system); (d) the way in which the leader attains leadership, for which knowledge of (a), (b), and (c) is pertinent, particularly in regard to the application of ascription and achievement to (a), (b), and (c) and their subdivisions [8].

Table I sketched 2a through e for all leadership types of the old Loma system. Subsequent discussion, set by 1, arrived at 1a, b, and c and discussion transitional to a presentation of leadership in the new system; this discussion itself yielded 3a through d and subdivisions, though without tabulation and even without analysis of all points. Yet a further aspect of leadership has been touched on at length but does not appear in the above schema because it is not yet clear even to the point at which it could be incorporated. This aspect is the relation between the system of common norms (as a part of culture, which in turn is part of the socio-cultural system) and leadership. All that can be done at the present stage concerning this aspect is to clarify its theoretical and methodological status.

1. To grasp the relation between a common normative system and leadership is extremely important to an understanding of (a) culture change,

(b) the failure or success of change measures introduced into a system, and (c) the stability or instability of a system.

2. The relation between the common normative system and leadership is not clear beyond the observation in which the latter seems or does not seem to implement the former; nor is the connection between end relations and a common normative system obvious beyond the suggestion that both seem to go together.

3. The relation between the common normative system and culture is not clear beyond the suggestions, (a) that the former is the most important part of the latter and (b) that it may be absent from it; nor is the connection between common normative system, area (of influence), and culture evident.

4. Stability and instability of a culture need definitions that must be undertaken in conjunction with efforts to define the relations between culture, common normative system, and area, because it may be hoped that a combined attack will lead to satisfying the quest for understanding indicated under (1) above.

This quest has been at least one of the motives for studying Loma in general and its aspects, among them leadership, in particular. The idea has been, and still is, that once a unique culture is grasped—and the culture of Loma, like any culture, is conceived as unique—an understanding of others that are unique, including our own, will be furthered. [Cf. Chapter 27.] The hope is for more tenable generalizations to emerge than are those derived from viewing Loma as a mere variant of our own set-up —a view that is based on the notion that people are generally alike, no matter where they are. It will have been noted that throughout the last portions of this chapter, and particularly in some passages in the descriptions of religious change and voting behavior, problems have been discussed that can be seen, even at this stage in the analysis of the Loma materials, to be our own. More specifically, one of the most important problems that not only we and Loma but the major part of the world have been facing is how to create a common normative system (whatever the definition of this term) to implement types of leadership. Closely related to this problem is the question how long a sociocultural system can exist without doing more about it than asking how it might be solved [9].

### NOTES

1. My thanks go to Richard T. Morris and Melvin Seeman for their most helpful discussion and to Mrs. Bissette, mentioned in Chapter 21, n.1, for stimulating correspondence regarding a first draft of this chapter.

2.   Leadership does not imply continuous action but only the recognized availability (of person or office) for such action.

3.   In the latter case status could only denote the position of a particular leadership within an order of leaderships. This usage is not employed in the present paper, although some of the discussion may suggest it. Furthermore, no more refined analysis of the leader's status has been undertaken, such as would be entailed by a differentiation of statuses into "subjective," "objective," "specific," "general" or what other subdivisions might seem desirable. The reason for this failure is not skepticism of the utility of such subdivision but once again the present stage of analyzing the data. Toward the end of this paper, however (n. 8 and text preceding it), a scheme is presented that suggests a certain classification of leader statuses.

4.   There is no reason why it could not be exercised by a group, a clique, perhaps, but no such instance was found in Loma.

5.   The old-system leadership presented can be contrasted not only with that of the new but also with systems outside Loma. The most fruitful manner of undertaking a more general comparison would probably be to refine the dimensions described in the columns of Table 1 in order to make them more clearly defined; this almost certainly would involve revisions and additions. Once improvement is achieved, however (and it is hoped that the further analysis of the Loma materials will contribute to it), a usable typology of leadership may be looked forward to. Yet the variables and their articulations as suggested in Table 1 are so numerous that from the standpoint of economy a more advisable procedure might be to begin with a typology of sociocultural systems, for in this manner the multidimensionality of the leadership typology might be reduced in consideration of empirical requirements. The possibility of sociocultural systems without leadership (in the specific sense defined) should not be overlooked in such an undertaking.

6.   This statement illustrates (rather than contradicts) the ethical characterization, "neutral," of the *patrón* office, as given in Table 1. The office itself is neutral but may be defined in a given culture as good or bad, depending on whether it is accepted or resented. It can be accepted (rather than merely accommodated for a time) only if it is incorporated as desirable into the culture: that is, presumably, in a certain number of certain individuals.

7.   Thus one of the women who were in sympathy with the Institute's viewpoint, who was most interested in national affairs, who, in fact, had assumed some leadership in putting over communal, educational, and health plans originated by the Loma Institute and Justino Plan, and who had consistently expressed her agreement with the New Deal and with President Roosevelt, voted the straight Republican ticket because her nephew ran for county office.

8.   The following schema is an abridgement of the last three paragraphs:
1.   Leadership defined as influence in a socio-cultural system which
(a) affects system,
(b) is concentrated (office, person),
(c) is exercised by living person(s).

2. Leadership type determined by
    (a) institutional relations,
    (b) office- or personal nature,
    (c) influence area, ⎫
    (d) influence means, ⎬ to be analyzed as office and personal characteristics.
    (e) ethical aspect, ⎭
3. Leader type determined by
    (a) relation:
        (1) end, means,
        (2) over-all, specialized,
        (3) social, personal;
    (b) role:
        (1) office,
        (2) personal;
    (c) status:
        (1) subjective,
        (2) accorded,
        (3) system;
    (d) manner of attainment

9. A further methodological-theoretical note may be in order. If this chapter makes any contribution to the study of leadership, it is in whatever theoretical suggestiveness it may possess rather than in the rigorous application of a fully developed theory to empirical materials (for many Loma materials have not yet been analyzed) or in methodological stimulation (hardly any methodology has been indicated). The following comments are offered to show a partial awareness of these shortcomings. The chapter is descriptive rather than explanatory or analytical. To mention only a few of the many questions never raised, why was no common normative system the outcome of concerted efforts made by the Loma Institute and the Justino Plan? Why did the *patrón's* son become a leader? Analytically, is there such a thing as inheritance of leadership? Is there conversion of leadership from one area to another? Most concepts in addition to those discussed in the last pages require further clarification as well as interrelation.

---

Reprinted from *The Ohio Journal of Science,* **50** (1950), 210–220, by permission of the publisher. The essay has been edited and partially revised by the author.

# 23

# THE COLLECTION
# AND ORGANIZATION
# OF FIELD MATERIALS:
## A Research Report. 1952, 1960

Relatively few sociological and anthropological monographs throw light on the process by which the student's experience in the field is transformed into his published statement [1]. Yet, because it is, after all, a man—and not some impersonal scientific apparatus who makes the study and because the student's subject matter is also man, however complexly abstracted he may be, it would seem to be exceedingly important that the student become aware of this process, examine it, and submit his findings to his readers.

I have tried to do so in a preliminary fashion (Wolff, 1952) in respect to my own experience in Loma without going, however, into the actual operations that governed the collection and organization of field materials. To describe these operations—a task much more modest than the larger enterprise mentioned, though intimately related to it—is the purpose of the present chapter, which contains only a brief allusion to that more comprehensive enterprise and only a brief reference (in the last section) to the writing up of the materials gathered.

### COLLECTION OF FIELD NOTES AND THEIR CLASSIFICATION BY TOPICS

In 1942, as an employee of the Loma Institute, I made a house-to-house survey of the community, largely for census-type information. When I returned in 1944 as a Social Science Research Council fellow, under the supervision of the late Professor Robert Redfield and Professor Sol Tax of the Department of Anthropology at the University of Chicago, I was to find out whether culture patterns could be established empirically so that another student could go back and check point by point. Eventually I found that I could not accept this assignment because it presupposed a conceptualization that I could not be sure was appropriate to my Loma experience. Finally, I became skeptical of received notions as guides to research in general, including those codified in *Notes and Queries* or the Human Relations Areas Files. I advocated, instead, that in the field the student hold as many of these notions as possible in abeyance and expect the organization and presentation of his materials to emerge in the study itself.

Although not all this was clear to me in the first stages of my field work, it accounted—satisfactorily to me—for the fact that I had begun to observe and record my observations at once, without any attempt at order or selection. My field notes thus resembled a diary, expanding page by page, immediately typed from short notes, memory, or dictation. As writing accumulated, however, some sort of structuring became imperative, and I proceeded to break down my notes by topics. I started only after having produced about 80 single-spaced pages of typescript, but once I had completed the classification (at a point at which the pages had increased to approximately 140—I had continued to write down notes even while going on with the breakdown), I kept it up to date. From the beginning I made two carbons of all notes, keeping the original as a running account, sending the first copy to Professor Redfield, at certain intervals, and using the second for clippings. I wrote the names of the topics on the margins, clipped the page or pages, and placed the clippings in envelopes, each bearing the name of the topic under which I classified a particular passage. Thus there were as many envelopes as there were topics—66 (Table 1).

### EXPLANATIONS AND ILLUSTRATIONS OF SOME TOPICS

The meaning of some of these topics needs clarification. *Acceptance* covers materials bearing on the unreflective acceptance of what comes or is (cf. Chapter 20); *Compañero* refers to the habit of two or more persons doing things together (e.g., walking); *Correspondence*, to letters dealing with the Loma study between various persons and myself; *Emotionally*, to the affective channeling of experience; *Happiness*, to its conceptions and criteria; *Indian*, to Indians and things Indian; *Investigator*, to evaluations, by Lomans, of myself or my activities; *Knowledge, Anglo*, and *Knowledge,*

*Table 1.    Classification of Field Notes by Topics: Loma, 1944*[1]

| | |
|---|---|
| 1. *Acceptance* | 34. Investigator |
| 2. Agriculture | 35. Isolation |
| 3. Anglo-Anglo Relations | 36. Kinship and Genealogy |
| 4. Anglos re Anglos | 37. Knowledge, Anglo |
| 5. Anglos re Spanish | 38. Knowledge, Spanish |
| 6. Change | 39. Language |
| 7. Children | 40. Life History |
| 8. Clothing | 41. Mail |
| 9. Community Organizations | 42. *Mañana* |
| 10. *Compañero* | 43. Marriage |
| 11. Cooperation | 44. Methodology |
| 12. Correspondence | 45. Organization |
| 13. Craft | 46. Politics |
| 14. Crime | 47. Population |
| 15. Death | 48. Race |
| 16. Economics | 49. Religion |
| 17. Education | 50. Self |
| 18. (Emotionality) | 51. Shame |
| 19. Family | 52. Smoking |
| 20. Farmers' Union | 53. (Sociology of knowledge) |
| 21. Fear | 54. Spanish-Anglo Relations |
| 22. Feudalism | 55. Spanish re Anglos |
| 23. Food | 56. Spanish re Spanish |
| 24. (Gestures) | 57. Spanish-Spanish Relations |
| 25. Happiness | 58. Status and Prestige |
| 26. Health | 59. Time |
| 27. History | 60. *To the Point* |
| 28. Hospitality | 61. Transportation |
| 29. Houses | 62. Visiting |
| 30. Indian | 63. War |
| 31. Individuals, Anglo | 64. Waste |
| 32. Individuals, Spanish | 65. Water |
| 33. Informants | 66. Weather |

[1] Parentheses around the name of a topic indicate that field-note passages relevant to it can be found only under other topics. See discussion of *Also under* list below. Italicized topics appear to be patterns (see Chapter 20).

*Spanish*, to concepts by English-speaking and Spanish-speaking individuals of miscellaneous phenomena; *"Mañana"* labels particular attitudes toward the immediate present (*ibid.*); *Methodology* covers items of sociological methodology and theory; *Organization* refers to concepts and practices of coordinating thoughts, activities, and persons (*ibid.*); *Race, Self, Shame,* and *Time* cover notes relevant to the conception of these phenomena; *To the Point* refers to relations between the immediate occasion and its possible implications (*ibid.*); and *Waste* includes clippings that describe the conception and handling of waste materials.

### CROSS-REFERENCING THE TOPICS

I provided the topics with a twofold index. Each envelope that contained clippings relevant to a particular topic carried, in addition to the name of that topic, two lists of others: (a) those for which some of the clippings contained in the envelope were also relevant (*Also* list) and (b) those under which additional clippings relevant to the topic could also be found (*Also under* list). An illustration:

> C [my wife] told me that when she remarked . . . that so many people die here, S answered, "Nadie muere de enfermedad aqui (nobody dies of sickness here)!" C pointed to [young] David Armijo's death, but S said this was pneumonia. I'll find out about this; perhaps it was only a reaction in terms of community pride to say that people here die only of old age (as S elaborated); or it might—less likely—indicate belief in death causes other than sickness and old age. [Field notes, p. 351, August 15, 1944.]

I classified this field-note clipping under *Death,* but cross-referenced it, in the manner indicated, with the topic *Knowledge, Spanish.* (Clippings, of course, varied greatly in length, from a line or two to several pages. On the whole, the longer they were, the more likely that they would be relevant to topics in addition to the one under which they were classified.)

### CLASSIFICATION OF TOPICS BY CATEGORIES

I brought back from the field 66 envelopes containing 500 pages of single-spaced typescript. When I tried to write up these materials [2], the need for further classification became obvious. In other words, I found that I had to proceed with the topics as I had with the field notes—to arrange them under fewer and broader headings, of which there emerged seven: the six categories of *Background Materials, Culture Change, Social Relations, Social Institutions, Evaluations and/or Interpretations* (on the part of Lomans), and *Clues to Patterns* and a seventh section on *Theory and Methodology: Concluding,* the latter corresponding to a similar introductory section. Furthermore, I found it useful to distinguish between a primary and a secondary relevance the topics had to these headings. In Table 2 the names of the topics of primary relevance follow the category directly; those of secondary relevance are listed by numbers in parentheses. (For the identification of these numbers see Table 1.) Appendix A provides an inventory of all topics, with their Also and Also Under lists, that are relevant to the first two categories (Nos. 1 and 2 in Table 2).

The definitions of the categories, which guided the classification of the topics, are most concisely presented in tabular form (Table 3). These definitions were tentative for preliminary organizational purposes, but as I began to write up my materials the seven headings or categories seemed well suited to serve as titles of the seven parts in which the study could be presented; and while drafting the first two—which is all I have completed so far (for the second, see Wolff, 1956 and 1957)—I found no reason for questioning this decision. In discussing the topics and their

Table 2.  *Classification of Topics by Categories: Loma, 1944*

| Category | Topics |
|---|---|
| 1. Background Materials | Agriculture; Clothing; Craft, Food; History; Isolation; Population; Transportation; Water (16; 20; 26; 29; 36; 46; 49; 52; 63; 66) |
| 2. Culture Change | Change (20; 22; 27; 63; 65) |
| 3. Social Relations | Anglo-Anglo Relations; *Compañero*; Cooperation; Hospitality; Kinship and Genealogy; Mail; Spanish-Anglo Relations; Spanish-Spanish Relations; Visiting (4; 5; 55; 56) |
| 4. Social Institutions | Children; Community Organizations; Crime; Economics; Education Family; Farmers' Union; Houses; Language; Marriage; Politics; Smoking; Status and Prestige (22; 49) |
| 5. Evaluations and/or Interpretations | Anglos re Anglos; Anglos re Spanish; Death; Fear; Feudalism; Happiness; Health; Indian; Individuals, Anglo; Individuals, Spanish; Informants; Investigator; Knowledge, Anglo; Knowledge, Spanish; Life History; Organization; Race; Religion; Self; Shame; Spanish re Anglos; Spanish re Spanish; Time; War; Waste; Weather (7; 17; 19; 28; 29; 35; 39; 58) |
| 6. Clues to Patterns | *Acceptance*; Emotionaltiy; Gestures; *Mañana; To the Point* (10; 21; 25; 28; 39; 41; 45; 50; 51; 59; 64) |
| 7. Theory and Methodology | Correspondence; Methodology; Sociology of Knowledge (31; 32; 33; 34) |

*Table 3.   Definitions of Categories: Loma, 1944*

| Category | Definition |
|---|---|
| 1. Background Materials | Aspects of a culture that can be readily understood by the same means as they would be in the study of a culture similar to that of the student[1]; those materials that strike the student as not presenting methodological problems[2] |
| 2. Culture Change | Change in culture; presupposes, for its apperception, a conception of the culture under study as different, or as methodologically assumed to be different, from that of the student[3] |
| 3. Social Relations | Relations between individuals as individuals and as members of groups |
| 4. Social Institutions | Phenomena virtually composed of heterogeneous elements but constituting units in the universe of discourse of the members of the culture under study[4] |
| 5. Evaluations and/or Interpretations | Evaluations, conceptions, and/or interpretations of phenomena by the members of the culture under study |
| 6. Clues to Patterns | Materials bearing on culture patterns |
| 7. Theory and Methodology | Materials used as current checks on formulations of uniformities and on other generalizations and as sources of experimentation with scientific rule |

[1] Cf. Wolff (1945, p. 181) [Chapter 20].
[2] Cf. a similar definition of "general" (as against "unique") in Wolff (1948, p. 208 [Chapter 27].
[3] See discussion of "Culture Change" below.
[4] Cf. Wolff (1950, p. 59, n. 3) [Chapter 21, n. 3].

subsumption under the categories I have limited myself to them—Background Materials and Culture Change.

### BACKGROUND MATERIALS AND CULTURE CHANGE

The first, Background Materials, is the only or primary place for the following topics: *Agriculture, Clothing, Craft, Food, History, Isolation, Population, Transportation,* and *Water.* This subsumption suggests the *factual* character of the information gathered under these labels. Agriculture deals with the kinds, cultivation, and history of crops, with sharecropping, tenancy, marketing, and the like—the latter items also classifiable under Economics, a topic, however, to be found primarily under Social Institutions and only secondarily here under Background Materials—16 (figures refer to numbers in parentheses in Table 2). Clothing describes what people wear and where they buy it but also contains clues to Evaluations and/or Interpretations of clothing. Craft deals with crafts and skills practiced in Loma but is relevant as well to Culture Change. Food treats dietary and culinary items but also indicates changes in food habits and Spanish-Anglo and Indian-Spanish customs dealing with foodstuffs, recipes, and relevant nomenclature. History is largely a chronological concept but also covers data bearing on Culture Change: hence it is listed under that category—27. Isolation functions as an element in the physical aspects of the community, but the label also describes the influence of this element on people; therefore it appears (35) under Evaluations and/or Interpretations. Population refers to the customary statistical conception. Transportation and Water are descriptive; under the latter topic, however (cf. Isolation) are reactions to the water situation and ideas concerning its improvement; hence Water also figures under Culture Change (65).

Topics of secondary relevance as background materials (cf. the numbers in parentheses in Table 2) are *Economics* (16), *Farmers' Union* (20), *Health* (26), *Houses* (29), *Kinship and Genealogy* (36), *Politics* (46), *Religion* (49), *Smoking* (52), *War* (63) and *Weather* (66); that is, the primary relevance of these topics is to other categories (as shown in Table 2). Some of their aspects, important here in regard to Background Materials, are Economics (income, property, wagework); Farmers' Union (its history, activities, membership); Health (disease statistics, mortality, therapies); Houses (structure and equipment); Kinship and Genealogy (kinship terms, overt kinship behavior, genealogy); Politics (Loman officeholders, especially in the county, election procedures, and other mechanics); Religion (the church and the cemetery, church membership and attendance, religious societies); Smoking (usage and extent); War (its bearing on population changes); and Weather (meteorological data).

When I looked at the topics under Culture Change, I was struck by the fact that I had listed only one topic, Change itself, as of primary relevance and only five others as of secondary relevance to this category. On the other hand, I realized that almost all topics contained some information on "how it used to be" as compared with "how it is now." Thus, instead of asking myself why there were no more topics under Culture Change, I soon wondered why I had set aside any at all. The answer I found was that I had been guided in my arrangement by a conception of the culture under study as different, or as methodologically assumed by me to be different, from my own; that is to say, changes in the cultivation of crops, clothing, craft, population, transportation, or the water system were dealt with under topics relevant to Background Materials, whereas Culture Change covered these changes as viewed by the Lomans and thus as challenging the student to an interpretation of their view. It was these materials that I must have set aside under the special topic Change. Such materials are also contained under the topics listed as secondary in relevance to Culture Change, Farmers' Union (20), Feudalism (22) [cf. Chapter 22], History (27), War (63), and Water (65). Although Change contains recordings of conversations with individuals who had changed their evaluations, concepts, and goals, Farmers' Union covers data concerning an imported institution that modified the outlook of certain Lomans on agriculture, education, government, community organization, and the like; Feudalism is significant as a label for clues to an earlier social system and to its present-day traces; and History mainly describes factual changes in terms of which changes in a more interpretive sense may be understood. War affects changes in the cognitive, emotional, and moral horizons (in the knowledge of geography and, to some extent, of history; in the preoccupation with family members in the services, and in identification with the fate of the nation). Water illustrates the efforts to improve the agricultural and economic situation in the direction of greater initiative and organization, thus indicating changes in attitudes toward nature.

The exposition of Background Materials and Culture Change is summarized in Table 4, in which only the topics of primary or secondary relevance to these first two categories (21 out of the 66) are contained.

## WRITING UP THE MATERIALS

I conclude by mentioning an important problem that, along with others, forced me to reconsider my procedure and my role in the Loma study. The problem resulted from a discrepancy between the utilization of my field notes as anticipated (and detailed here) and their actual use when I wrote them up. I illustrate this discrepancy by referring to the part on Culture Change because I have committed myself to it, having already published a summary [Chapter 21]. I found myself using not so much the materials that pertained to the topics subsumed under Culture Change, but only part of them and, in addition, two other types of material: life histories (Wolff, 1956) and compositions by Loma school children (Wolff, 1957). Life History (as Table 1 shows) was a topic not originally listed under Culture Change, not even as secondarily relevant to it, but under Evaluations and/or Interpretations (cf. Table 2). Furthermore, I made

*Table 4.   Description of Topics in Terms of Their Primary (P) and Secondary (S) Relevance to Background Materials and Culture Change: Loma, 1944*[1]

| Topic | Background Materials | Culture Change |
|---|---|---|
| 2. Agriculture | Crops, sharecropping, marketing: P | |
| 6. Change | | Changes in culture: P |
| 8. Clothing | Who wears what: P | |
| 13. Craft | Crafts and skills: P | |
| 16. Economics | Income, property, wage-work: S | |
| 20. Farmers' Union | History, activities: S | Change in agricultural outlook: S |
| 22. Feudalism | | Past *vs.* present social system: S |
| 23. Food | Who eats what: P | |
| 26. Health | Health statistics: S | |
| 27. History | History: P | Material and broader changes: S |
| 29. Houses | Structure: S | |
| 35. Isolation | Element in physical aspects of culture: P | |
| 36. Kinship and Genealogy | Kinship terms: S | |
| 46. Politics | Officeholders, procedures, mechanics: S | |
| 47. Population | Statistical category: P | |
| 49. Religion | Church, cemetery: S | |
| 52. Smoking | Usage and extent: S | |
| 61. Transportation | Transportation: P | |
| 63. War | Bearing on population changes: S | Bearing on intellectual horizon: S |
| 65. Water | Description of water situation: P | Changes in attitudes: S |
| 66. Weather | Meteorological aspects: S | |

[1] The relevance (primary of secondary) of these topics to categories other than Background Materials and Cultural Change is not indicated. Items listed under topics are not exhaustive but only illustrative, most important, or typical.

use of materials not contained in my field notes but had not considered their importance to the organization of my data. Most significant among them were the life histories obtained by another person who spent several weeks in Loma in 1947 [3] and the school compositions I had the local Spanish-speaking school children write in 1944, with the cooperation of the public school teacher. I tried to clarify my procedures when I deviated from the earlier plan described here; and this clarification is reflected in the study. What I learned led to a new introduction (Wolff, 1952), analyzing the process by which my Loma experience was transformed into my objective statements and defining my position regarding the study of man more generally. It also led me to make other changes in the text, especially in Background Materials.

The foregoing discussion, although brief in some respects, indicates the manner in which unforeseen factors in the organizing of data can influence the analytical process of field research. These features of methodological operations and experience are usually not prominently treated in research reports, hence can only rarely be inspected and evaluated. Yet they often have considerable influence on the final product.

*Appendix A. Topics, with Their Also and Also Under Lists, Relevant to Background Materials and Culture Change: Loma, 1944*[1]

| Topic | Also | Also under |
|---|---|---|
| 2. Agriculture | *Acceptance* | Anglos re Spanish |
| | Anglos re Spanish | Crime |
| | Economics | Economics |
| | Hospitality | Family |
| | Individuals, Anglo | Happiness |
| | Knowledge, Spanish | Individuals, Spanish |
| | Methodology | Spanish-Anglo relations |
| | Spanish-Anglo relations | Spanish-Spanish relations |
| | Spanish-Spanish relations | Transportation |
| | Transportation | |
| | Water | |

[1] *Topic* is the topic under which certain field-note passages are classified. The *Also* column lists topics for which certain field-note passages classified under the *Topic* are also relevant. The *Also under* column is the reverse of the *Also* column: it lists topics under which field-note passages relevant to the *Topic* may also be found. Thus, some parts of field-note passages classified under *Agriculture* (*Topic*) are *Also* relevant to "*Acceptance*," and some parts of field-note passages classified under *Anglos re Spanish* (*Also under*) also contain material relevant to *Agriculture*.

| Topic | Also | Also under |
|---|---|---|
| 6. Change | Economics | *Acceptance* |
| | Spanish-Spanish relations | Children |
| | Visiting | Clothing |
| | | Correspondence |
| | | Craft |
| | | Death |
| | | Economics |
| | | Family |
| | | Farmers' Union |
| | | Food |
| | | Individuals, Spanish |
| | | Kinship and genealogy |
| | | Knowledge, Spanish |
| | | Language |
| | | Marriage |
| | | Politics |
| | | Religion |
| | | Water |
| 8. Clothing | Change | Crime |
| | Children | Individuals, Spanish |
| | Time | |
| | Weather | |
| 13. Craft | *Acceptance* | Correspondence |
| | Change | Economics |
| | Death | Family |
| | Economics | Food |
| | Family | Health |
| | Fear | Hospitality |
| | Hospitality | Houses |
| | Knowledge, Spanish | Individuals, Spanish |
| | Language | Knowledge, Spanish |
| | Religion | Religion |
| | Spanish-Anglo Relations | Spanish-Anglo Relations |
| | | Time |
| | | Visiting |
| 16. Economics | *Acceptance* | *Acceptance* |
| | Agriculture | Agriculture |
| | Change | Anglo-Anglo relations |
| | Craft | Anglos re Spanish |
| | Crime | Change |
| | Family | Children |
| | Food | Community Organizations |
| | Individuals, Spanish | Craft |
| | Language | Death |
| | Mail | Family |
| | Methodology | Farmers' Union |

| Topic | Also | Also under |
|-------|------|-----------|
| | Politics | Health |
| | Spanish-Anglo Relations | Houses |
| | Spanish re Anglos | Individuals, Anglo |
| | Spanish re Spanish | Individuals, Spanish |
| | Status and Prestige | Life History |
| | Water | Religion |
| | | Time |
| | | Transportation |
| | | Water |
| 20. Farmers' Union | Anglo-Anglo Relations | |
| | Change | |
| | Community Organizations | |
| | Crime | |
| | Economics | |
| | Education | |
| | Family | |
| | Health | |
| | Individuals, Anglo | |
| | Individuals, Spanish | |
| | Informants | |
| | Language | |
| | Marriage | |
| | Organization | |
| | Politics | |
| | Race | |
| | Spanish-Anglo Relations | |
| | Spanish-Spanish Relations | |
| | Time | |
| | *To the Point* | |
| | Visiting | |
| | War | |
| | Waste | |
| 22. Feudalism | History | Health |
| | | Spanish-Anglo Relations |
| | | Spanish-Spanish Relations |
| 23. Food | Change | Correspondence |
| | Children | Economics |
| | Craft | Knowledge, Spanish |
| | Hospitality | Language |
| | Kinship and Genealogy | Methodology |
| | Knowledge, Spanish | Religion |
| | Language | Spanish-Anglo Relations |
| | Race | Visiting |
| | Spanish-Anglo Relations | |
| | Visiting | |
| | Weather | |

| Topic | Also | Also under |
|-------|------|------------|
| 26. Health | *Acceptance*<br>Craft<br>Economics<br>Emotionality<br>Family<br>Feudalism<br>Happiness<br>Individuals, Spanish<br>Isolation<br>Kinship and Genealogy<br>Knowledge, Spanish<br>Language<br>Methodology<br>Organization<br>Shame<br>Spanish-Anglo Relations<br>Spanish-Spanish Relations | *Acceptance*<br>Anglos re Spanish<br>Children<br>Family<br>Farmers' Union<br>Individuals, Anglo<br>Individuals, Spanish<br>Knowledge, Spanish<br>Language<br>Religion<br>Self<br>Spanish-Anglo Relations<br>Visiting<br>War<br>Water |
| 27. History | Indian<br>Knowledge, Spanish<br>Language<br>Population<br>Spanish-Anglo Relations | Correspondence<br>Feudalism<br>Language<br>Politics<br>Spanish-Anglo Relations<br>Spanish-Spanish Relations |
| 29. Houses | Craft<br>Economics<br>Indian<br>Knowledge, Spanish<br>Spanish-Anglo Relations<br>Transportation | *Acceptance*<br>Family<br>Hospitality<br>Individuals, Spanish<br>Religion<br>Spanish-Anglo Relations<br>Time<br>Weather |
| 35. Isolation | Hospitality<br>Individuals, Anglo<br>Methodology<br>Spanish-Anglo Relations | *Acceptance*<br>Health<br>Individuals, Anglo<br>Transportation |
| 36. Kinship and genealogy | Change<br>Family<br>Individuals, Spanish<br>Knowledge, Spanish<br>Language<br>Marriage<br>Methodology<br>Religion<br>Spanish-Spanish Relations<br>Visiting | Correspondence<br>Death<br>Food<br>Health<br>Informants<br>Marriage<br>Religion<br>Spanish-Anglo Relations<br>Visiting |

| Topic | Also | Also under |
|---|---|---|
| 46. Politics | Change | Economics |
| | History | Farmers' Union |
| | Individuals, Spanish | Individuals, Anglo |
| | Investigator | Individuals, Spanish |
| | Knowledge, Spanish | Spanish-Anglo Relations |
| | Language | Visiting |
| | Religion | Weather |
| | Spanish-Anglo Relations | |
| | Spanish re Spanish | |
| | Spanish-Spanish Relations | |
| 47. Population | | History |
| 49. Religion | *Acceptance* | Anglos re Spanish |
| | Change | Correspondence |
| | Children | Death |
| | *Compañero* | Informants |
| | Craft | Kinship and Genealogy |
| | Economics | Life History |
| | Education | Politics |
| | Family | Spanish-Anglo Relations |
| | Food | Status and Prestige |
| | Gestures | Time |
| | Health | *To the Point* |
| | Hospitality | |
| | Houses | |
| | Indian | |
| | Individuals, Spanish | |
| | Kinship and Genealogy | |
| | Knowledge, Spanish | |
| | Language | |
| | Organization | |
| | Spanish-Anglo Relations | |
| | Spanish-Spanish Relations | |
| | Status and Prestige | |
| | Time | |
| | Visiting | |
| 52. Smoking | | Crime |
| 61. Transportation | *Acceptance* | Agriculture |
| | Agriculture | Houses |
| | Cooperation | Individuals, Spanish |
| | Economics | Spanish-Anglo Relations |
| | Family | *To the Point* |
| | Hospitality | |
| | Individuals, Anglo | |
| | Isolation | |
| | Knowledge, Anglo | |
| | Mail | |

| Topic | Also | Also under |
|-------|------|------------|
| | Spanish-Anglo relations | |
| | Time | |
| | Visiting | |
| | War | |
| 63. War | Health | Anglos re Spanish |
| | Knowledge, Anglo | Family |
| | Mail | Farmers' Union |
| | | Individuals, Anglo |
| | | Individuals, Spanish |
| | | Language |
| | | Spanish-Spanish Relations |
| | | Transportation |
| 65. Water | *Acceptance* | Agriculture |
| | Anglos re Spanish | Economics |
| | Change | |
| | Cooperation | |
| | Economics | |
| | Fear | |
| | Health | |
| | Individuals, Anglo | |
| | Sociology of Knowledge | |
| | Spanish-Anglo Relations | |
| 66. Weather | Fear | Clothing |
| | Houses | Food |
| | Individuals, Spanish | Spanish-Anglo Relations |
| | Informants | |
| | Knowledge, Spanish | |
| | Language | |
| | Politics | |
| | Spanish-Anglo Relations | |

## NOTES

1. Most of those I know—all of them anthropological—are referred to in Herskovits (1948), Chapter 6, "The Ethnographer's Laboratory," in which the first pages (81–83) of Section 2 give an excellent example of the transformation of field experience into generalized statements. Among the references contained in that chapter the most important are certain passages from M. J. and F. S. Herskovits (1934), Malinowski (1922), the relevant section of which is reprinted under the title "How an Anthropologist Works" in Haring (1949), Evans-Pritchard (1940), and Mead (1940). Cf. Bateson [1932, especially pp. 441–444, and 1936 (2nd. ed., 1958), especially Chapters 1, 8, 16]. See also pertinent passages in Wolff (1944, 1951), Mead (1949, Chapter 2), and Bennett (1959). Radin (1957, pp. xxi–xli, "Methods of Approach") and Mead and Métraux (1953)

contain statements and considerations that, when attention is specifically focused on this problem, might promote questions and answers relevant to it. The related problem of the bearing of the student's expectations on his eventual report leads, if pursued systematically, into the whole problem area of the sociology of knowledge. As a case in point, cf. the studies of Tepoztlán by Redfield (1930, 1953, pp. 155–157, 1955, pp. 133–136) and Lewis (1951, pp. 428–448). For another case see Bennett (1946). For an approach to the sociology of knowledge, which, in Bennett's words, includes "the observer in the frame of reference"—that is, it applies some of the lessons of the Loma study to this field; cf. Wolff (1953). For an attempt to apply them to the whole problem of interpretation, exemplified by the interpretations of two texts (Spitzer, 1949, and Simmel, 1950) and a cartoon (Steinberg, 1947), cf. Wolff (1951).

2. The opportunity to do so was given me by grants from the Wenner-Gren Foundation for Anthropological Research (then The Viking Fund), and the Graduate School, The Ohio State Univesrity, in 1947 and 1949, to which institutions I gratefully acknowledge my indebtedness.

3. After briefly acquainting herself with my 1944 field notes, Mrs. Morgan Bissette spent approximately seven weeks in the field under Professor John W. Bennett's and my joint supervision. She was instructed to secure information on topics to which she, as a young, then unmarried, woman, would have more access than I. These matters mainly concerned children and related subjects; insight into them was to be obtained from girls of about Mrs. Bissette's age with whom it was hoped (rightly) that she could establish friendly relations.

## REFERENCES

Adams, Richard N., and Jack J. Preiss, Eds. (1960), *Human Organization Research* (Homewood, Ill.: Dorsey).

Bateson, Gregory (1932), "The Social Structure of the Iatmul People of Sepik River." *Oceania*, 2.

—— (1936), *Naven* (Cambridge: The University Press).

—— (1958), *Naven*, 2nd ed. (Stanford, Calif.: Stanford University Press).

Bennett, John W. (1946), "The Interpretation of Pueblo Culture: A Question of Values." *Southwestern Journal of Anthropology*, 2, 361–374.

—— (1959), "Individual Perspective in Field Work," in Adams and Preiss, 1960, 431–440.

Evans-Pritchard, E. E. (1940), *The Nuer* (Oxford: Oxford University Press).

Haring, Douglas G., Ed. (1949), *Personal Character and Cultural Milieu* (Syracuse, N.Y.: Syracuse University Press).

Herskovits, Melville J. (1948), *Man and His Works* (New York: Knopf).

——, and Frances S. Herskovits (1934), *Rebel Destiny* (New York: McGraw-Hill).

Lewis, Oscar (1951), *Life in a Mexican Village* (Urbana: University of Illinois Press).

Malinowski, Bronislaw (1922), *Argonauts of the Western Pacific* (London: Routledge).

Mead, Margaret (1940), "The Mountain Arapesh. II. Supernaturalism," *American Museum of Natural History Anthropological Papers*, **37**, Part 3.

—————— (1949), *Male and Female* (New York: Morrow).

——————, and Rhoda Métraux (1953), *The Study of Culture at a Distance* (Chicago: University of Chicago Press).

Radin, Paul [1957 (1927)], *Primitive Man as Philosopher*, 2nd rev. ed. (New York: Dover).

Redfield, Robert (1930), *Tepoztlán* (Chicago: University of Chicago Press).

—————— (1953), *The Primitive World and Its Transformations* (Ithaca, N.Y.: Cornell University Press).

—————— (1955), *The Little Community* (Chicago: University of Chicago Press).

Simmel, Georg [1908 (1950)], "The Stranger" (1908), in *The Sociology of Georg Simmel*, translated, edited, and with an introduction by Kurt H. Wolff (Glencoe, Ill.: Free Press), 509–512.

Spitzer, Leo. (1949), "American Advertising as Popular Art," in *A Method of Interpreting Literature* (Northampton, Mass.: Smith College).

Steinberg, Saul (1947), "But It *Is* Half Man and Half Horse," in *All in Line* (New York: Duell, Sloane and Pearce).

Wolff, Kurt H. (1944), "A Critique of Bateson's *Naven*" [Chapter 19].

—————— (1951), *Experiments in Interpretation* [Columbia: Ohio State University, Department of Philosophy (mimeographed)].

—————— (1952), *Loma Culture Change: A Contribution to the Study of Man* [Columbus: Ohio State University, Department of Sociology (mimeographed)].

—————— (1953), "A Preliminary Inquiry into the Sociology of Knowledge from the Standpoint of the Study of Man" [Chapter 28].

—————— (1956), *Life Histories of a Spanish-American Man and 2 Women*. Microcard Publications of Primary Records in Culture and Personality (Madison, Wis.) **1**, 18.

—————— (1957), *School Compositions of 25 Spanish-American Children. Ibid.*, **2**, 15.

Reprinted from *The Ohio Journal of Science*, **52** (1952), 49–61, and Richard N. Adams and Jack J. Preiss, Eds., *Human Organization Research: Relations and Techniques* (Homewood, Ill.: Irwin, 1960), 240–254, by permission of the publishers. The essays have been edited and partially revised by the author.

# 24

# A NEW REALITY
# IN SOCIAL SCIENCE.
# 1958, 1959, 1964

Discernible in action anthropology [1] are the elements of a new reality
in the process of being discovered by its practitioners, a reality that can
be traced in doubts of a number of received ideas as well as in new
affirmations. Both doubts and affirmations rise from the individual field
experiences of authors, hence perhaps do not promise commonality.
Nevertheless, as I hope to show, they contain the outline of and approach
to a new social science.

Three aspects of this new social science stand out: a concept of social
science itself, the relation between Is and Ought, and an idea about the
nature of society.

### SOCIAL SCIENCE

The new concept of social science may be described under six headings:
prediction, the means-end scheme, the nature of the social scientist and
of the relation to his subject matter, cultural relativism, the systematic
and the historical approach, and the relation between theory and practice.

*Prediction.* The anthropologist works at the same time with the people
he is studying. His problem of prediction, Tax (I) argues, resembles that
of the clinical psychologist more than the scientist's in the laboratory.
For the clinical psychologist, as for the anthropologist in the field, prob-

lems of prediction are spontaneously translated into language expressive of the feelings of the persons participating—psychologist and patient, anthropologist and his "subjects." In the field, more particularly, that language expresses current group sentiments which embody, for both anthropologist and group, an intuition that cannot be considered a reliable basis for planned intervention. In the clinical attitude affirmed by Tax the acts of learning and helping have equal importance, but "to camouflage an uncalculable probability prediction as an absolute prediction . . . is ethically questionable," whereas "to rest content, as a matter of course, with a probability prediction would . . . be to rank helping below learning." If one wants to help, probability is not enough; nor must one claim full understanding if all one actually has is probable understanding or an understanding of what is probable. In other words, prediction yields to learning from the people one wants to help, to helping and teaching them, whereby learning, helping, and teaching are aspects of a single process.

*The Means-End Scheme.*   According to Tax (I), means and end, especially if separated and contrasted, lose most of their thrust. We do not tell people with whom we work, Tax writes, that if they do *A*, then *X*—which is what they desire—will necessarily follow; we do not tell them that if they want to reach a certain end they must act in such and such a way, adopt this or that means. Instead, the action anthropologist asks (by word and deed) the person(s) he works with whether they want the combination *AX*. The meaning is that once the ends are supplied not only the means but the ends themselves must be discussed because we know that the two are not so independent of each other as we thought having been taught—especially in Max Weber's famous lecture on "Science as a Vocation" [2]—that science can discuss and supply means but never ends, for ends are not rational. Tax reports that the North American Indians he studied and worked with, but perhaps also people in general, cannot immediately say with any precision what they want, for there are always aspects and consequences of the combination *AX*—ends desired and means required to attain them—that are not foreseen but emerge only in the course of action.

*The Nature of the Student and of the Relation to His Subject Matter.* The action anthropologist does not construct proofs—nor a closed, demonstrable, perhaps even elegant system—but a "structure of convictions" (Tax I). He cooperates in articulating a complex of convictions that emerges from the cooperative exploration in which he and the people he works with are engaged. This structure of convictions, however, is not his own esoteric possession, for it is submitted, as always in science, to the criticism of his peers.

Regarding the relation between the anthropologist and his subject matter—often the subjects he studies—Tax (I) writes that clinical study (in the context of community development) requires a trusting and candid atmosphere of interaction between the student and the people he helps and from and with whom he learns. They are not objects or things but persons—subjects, precisely. This is an implicit consequence of the means-end scheme conceived here. It becomes manifest to the student as a necessary atmosphere that is human and not cold, neutral, or objective.

For Holmberg (I) the anthropologist who adopts the research-and-development approach (the two converging in one process), which Holmberg himself articulated in the course of his practice, has as his goal the realization of basic human dignity to which every individual is entitled. Thus for Holmberg, too, the people he is studying and whose conditions he wishes to improve are persons. No matter what the differences between their culture and his own, the basic human dignity is shared by both parties and by almost all human beings.

*Cultural Relativism.* One of the limits of cultural relativism is asserted by Holmberg (I) as basic human dignity, which is *not* relative to culture (even though its expressions are) and must always be respected, promoted, defended, and protected. Another article by Holmberg (II), and one by Steward, shows that human dignity is not a matter of assertion but is brought home to the student by the practice of action anthropology. The experience of both Holmberg and Steward has been—and if we think about it even for a moment, we must expect that it has also been for others who have taken part in comparable situations—that the preferences associated with certain lines of action exist only within the limits of given problems and moral principles which at once exclude certain options that are acceptable or at least entertainable in other moral systems. It follows that the anthropologist or the social planner can consider actions he contemplates only within the moral code of the people among whom he is working. It also means that in his work a moral system develops, no matter how inarticulate it may be empirically, which is a synthesis between his own and that of the society he is studying. This means, in turn, that we have a clue to the possibility of resolving the theoretical problem of a shared, potentially universal, and universally binding ethical code. This is the problem over whose solution the cultural relativist agonizes, for, indeed, he has no hope of attaining it and occasionally makes fun of its very possibility, as if it were nonsense. Holmberg (II) and Steward do not report serious moral dilemmas—

which nevertheless exist. If faced with them, the anthropologist has three options for affirming a moral code. He may succeed in articulating the synthesis mentioned between his own ethic and that of his subjects; he may feel strong and sure enough about his own convictions to persuade those he works with; or he may feel sufficiently open to be persuaded by *them*. In all three cases the dilemma is overcome. It thus appears fair to conclude that the cultural relativist does not see clearly what all men have in common (what is *not* relative) or has insufficient faith in his own ability to identify it. (If so, the sources of such an attitude may be found in the culture in which cultural relativism itself emerged and has grown.)

*The Systematic and the Historical Approach.*   The neatness of the distinction between these two approaches is also called into question by the new reality the students cited have encountered as well as by the nature of their encounter. Steward suggests that we understand

> The problem of identifying acculturational trends and predicting the emergence of subcultural types . . . as the interaction of three variables: first, the traditional culture or base line from which change is reckoned; second, the processes of change which originate in an emerging world industrial culture; and third, the specific regional, national, or international context within which the processes operate to bring about a variety of local subcultural types.

Although the local acculturative effects may differ, "the processes of acculturation generated by the industrial culture are everywhere extraordinarily similar" and can be predicted "in terms of the operation of processes, not as the emergence of specific subcultures." Such processes follow a rather orderly progression of stages, each presupposing prior developments. Steward thus underlines the possibility of attaining knowledge of processes rather than of particular cultures; he appears to put his trust more in form than in content, more in systematicity than in history. We should realize that the constellation of the three variables from which such knowledge is to be gained is particular and historical. The first two variables are specific cultures, the "traditional culture or base line from which change is reckoned" and the "emerging world industrial culture." The third is equally particular, namely, "the specific . . . context within which the processes operate to bring about a variety of local subcultural types." What is more, the fact that "the processes of acculturation generated by the industrial culture [the second variable] are everywhere extraordinarily similar" also reflects a historical observation, that is, that we find ourselves in a time in which this observation is valid, in which, in other words, we have, at least in respect to industrialization, only one world.

Steward's paper suggests the possibility of an additional characteristic of the action anthropologist or social planner which distinguishes him from the traditional social scientist: the possibility of revising the distinction (in social science) between the systematic-formal and the historical-contentual approaches. This revision might be formulated as the proposition that the best generalization or systematization is based on a historical diagnosis which the generalizing or systematizing student undertakes in the most explicit manner possible.

*Theory and Practice.* The action anthropologist and the student of social change try to find out what they are concerned with in the process of acting, and not from a detached position, and they act in the process of trying to find out. This means that two distinctions fundamental to the tradition of the social sciences are no longer valid: first, that between theory and practice, more particularly between academic and applied science, and second, and related, that between the Is, which alone is usually considered the domain of the sicentist (cf. the earlier discussion of the means-end scheme), and the Ought, which is declared forbidden territory. The revision of this second distinction, however—in contrast to the revisions already discussed—is not limited to the conception and practice of the social sciences, for it also bears on problems traditionally considered philosophical—above all, on those of the nature of fact and value and their relations, of the reality of facts and their moral implications (if any), of science and ethics, and factual statements and value judgments—that is, precisely, of Is and Ought. I have mentioned this in order to justify the treatment of the revision of the relation between Is and Ought in a separate section rather than as another aspect of the emerging social science.

### THE RELATION BETWEEN IS AND OUGHT

Like the other revisions, this one originated in field experience. Once more we refer in particular to the writings of Holmberg (II) and Steward, which deal with planned social changes in which their authors have participated. It is not, they say, that Ought problems, or normative problems, do not come up in research, but they do so as questions of feasibility, preference, or option, that is, as practical questions, answers to which are found, or at least sought, with intelligence, knowledge, and imagination, not by fiat. In other words—those used already in regard to the limits of cultural relativism that are brought to light by these authors—moral problems operate to fix the limits within which feasibility, preference, or option can emerge. If this is so, we have taken a second path toward that other characteristic of the new social scientist: the possibility of bringing about a revision of cultural relativism, which hitherto has constituted a pervasive feature of recent social science in general and of cultural anthropology in particular.

There is more. Some anthropologists at least, writes Lisa Peattie, "feel somehow a *duty* to act" when they are faced with "Nazi racism, government policy towards the American Indian, and racial segregation in education"; and thus acting, they "do in fact draw value deductions from their science—even when they claim the impossibility of doing so on a logical basis." In analogous fashion, Tax (II) supports both truth and freedom and sees no contradiction between them. More generally, he disapproves of deciding on questions of values unless they concern us, and it is in action that we must confront and try to resolve them. Holmberg (I) maintains that "human traits are such that progress can be made toward the realization of human dignity."

### THE NATURE OF SOCIETY

In the writings analyzed here indications of the third aspect of the new reality are least common. In the beginning of the next section I make some suggestions why this may be so. Nevertheless, there *are* elements of a concept of society, notably two, one more specific, the other more general.

The more specific element concerns a question about Redfield's folk-urban dichotomy [3], one among a number in which societies are divided into two types. Some of the authors of these dichotomies see them in a morphological sense; others explicitly claim one of the two types to be the historical predecessor of the other. Among the characteristics of Redfield's urban society is the importance of rational choice in individual conduct; correspondingly, in the folk society there is the relative absence of choice and the prevalence instead of traditional or habitual conduct. Similar contrasts are found in almost all related nineteenth- and twentieth-century dichotomies, including those, for example, of Spencer, Durkheim, and Tönnies [cf. Chapter 5]. On this point Tax (1) observes the importance of choice among the Mesquakie (Fox Indians in central

Iowa), who in other respects approximate a folk society. Tax therefore asks whether it is proper to consider choice a particular characteristic of the urban society, thus questioning the validity or appropriateness of (at least) this element in Redfield's dichotomy. One could go beyond this and ask whether the tendency to dichotomize history and to place one's own society into the second type is as scientific an undertaking as the dichotomists think or whether it also contains an ideological element, namely, celebration of the progress from the first to the second type, even if it is muted by apprehensions concerning the latter (the best-known example probably being Durkheim's worry about "anomie," which he found in his own "organic society" whose complex division of labor he affirmed [cf. Chapter 5]).

In a more general perspective action anthropology adds to traditional anthropology a greater interest in process and dynamics (Peattie). Its primary subject of study is social change, Barnett observes, even though it is aware of its limits, which are indicated by resistance if it threatens social death or the violation of certain values. The new anthropologist wishes to study communities by the method of trying to help them (Tax I): here we discern the tendency to produce or, at any rate, reconstruct—on the basis of experience rather than on acceptance of ideas developed in the past and deposited in books—a concept of community itself and, on a larger scale, of society.

### CONCLUSION: SUMMARY AND DEVELOPMENT

What are the elements of the new reality and of its conception? It is understandable, it must be said first, that most of what the students discovering it have to say concerns the part represented by themselves, the researchers, and their activity, science. Furthermore, because they are anthropologists living in a society whose relation to history is problematical—that is, in the United States (but in a certain sense this also applies to Western society or culture in general)—and because they have been brought up in a predominantly ahistorical if not antihistorical social science it is easy to understand why they should have comparatively little to say about the nature of society.

Their main interest is not prediction but learning and helping or research and development in one process. They launch this process together with those they want to help, from whom they want to learn, and whom they want to teach—together with other fellow human beings who, like them and with them, improve in this common undertaking, by being led to greater human dignity. A means-end scheme is as unsuitable to guide such an undertaking as the related position according to which facts and values Is and Ought are irreconcilably divorced, for the enterprise is dynamic and dialogical. Neither the anthropologist nor the people being studied are calculating men who can formulate their ends and the means most conducive to them. Instead, they devote themselves fully to examining their situations before acting with all the intuition and knowledge of normative beings. If proof is a term applicable (in Martin Buber's [4] language) to the I-It relation, Tax's "structure of convictions" belongs in the I-Thou relation. The structure of convictions is an important, perhaps the most important, part of the endowment of a speaker, of one who participates in discussion, because he uses it in his dialogue with those with whom he initiates the common search for what is true. In his Socratic endeavor he places it at the service of persuasion and being persuaded. In such a situation doubts about received notions are likely to arise in him, and exposed to these doubts he may be convinced that society is dynamic but that the limits of its dynamics are set by the dignity of man—that is, of those with whom he would initiate a dialogical relation and who must be allowed the capacity or possibility of self-determination (Tax I).

But are *all* human beings to be allowed self-determination? Is action anthropology possible, Tax (I) asks, among people rent by conflicts admitting of no compromise, among groups oppressed by colonial administration, among tribes practicing cannibalism, infanticide, or ordeals? Why does the action anthropologist, asks Peattie, promote the introduction of new plows but not of a new religion? Why does he not wish to meddle with kinship systems but would *like* to reduce witchcraft? "Applied anthropology," Peattie writes, "will always continue to raise the great unsolvable questions of ethics." What is a satisfactory life? To what extent is the suffering of the present generation justified by the good that may come from it to future generations? The argument that the community knows better than its student what is good for it, that "what . . . is best for . . . [people] involves what they want to be" (Tax I), may mean that Tax is less preoccupied than Peattie with the great unsolvable questions of ethics, which, as Tax perhaps holds, can and must be confronted when they confront *us*, as it were, not abstractly but in practice, in concrete situations.

All of these characteristics distinguish the action anthropologist or the social-scientific planner from the traditional social scientist: the revisions of the conceptions of prediction, of the means-end scheme, of the nature of the student and the relation to his subject matter, of cultural relativism, of the systematic and the historical approach, of the relations between theory and practice and Is and Ought, and of the nature of society. All of these are interrelated, as should no longer surprise us. All reflect a common experience of human beings by human beings. Perhaps what connects them all has its source in the historical moment that has brought them into being in the experience just mentioned.

The new reality pointed to by the characteristics enumerated must be rendered explicit and related to various other phenomena indicative of this historical moment. We might begin by recognizing the necessity of diagnosing it, and diagnosing it in a historical perspective. We might ask what time this is in which action anthropology has developed and promoted the convictions that emerge in the writings analyzed. What images of man, society, major social institutions, and history are affirmed in these convictions? Under which aspects, in what sense can these images be reconciled with images that are accepted elsewhere, as a diagnosis of our time might show? What can we do if we find incompatibilities? What role can dialogue play compared with other procedures?

I conclude by hinting at two additional considerations that I think are called for by our historical moment. The first concerns the problem of how much time we have for immersing ourselves in the study of planned social change; the other concerns the possibility of applying this study to our own society—our own national and all of Western society, indeed the earth.

Our moment is characterized also by the technical possibility of our total destruction. This possibility, it seems to me, imposes on the student of social phenomena the duty of investigating the social and cultural changes that could eliminate it. Here, I believe, is the most distinct aspect of the situation in which some of the traditional concepts in process of revision—above all, those of cultural relativism and of the relations between Is and Ought, theory and practice, historical and systematic study—no longer make sense. From a consideration of the time— or the lack of it—at our disposal derives the second consideration of applying the study of planned social change to our society, the earth society, mankind. Once we have focused on this we will realize immediately that not only the need for a study is at stake but also the diffusion of its results to make them useful for attaining the end that inspired the study in the first place. There re-emerges, therefore, but on a much larger scale, another characteristic of the work of the social planner with which he is familiar from his experience in community development: the inseparability of attaining knowledge and acting collectively on it. This may well be the greatest significance of the inseparability of theory and practice, Is and Ought, systematicity and historicity, or history itself.

NOTES

1. This chapter is based on the following publications: *A Reader in Action Anthropology* [Chicago: University of Chicago), n.d., p. 115, multilith (introduction by Tax and three chapters by Fred Gearing), here referred to as Tax I], and two symposia, "Values in Action," organized by Melvin Tumin, and "Planned Change," organized by John W. Bennett, held at the annual meetings of the American Anthropological Association in 1957 and 1958. The first, published in *Human Organization,* 17, No. 1 (1958), contains Melvin Tumin, "Introduction"; Lisa Peattie, "Interventionism and Applied Science in Anthropology"; Homer G. Barnett, "Anthropology as an Applied Science"; Allan R. Holmberg, "The Research and Development Approach to the Study of Change" (Holmberg I); Tax, "The Fox Project" (Tax II); and comments by Robert Redfield, Kurt H. Wolff, and Conrad Arensberg. The second, published in *Human Organization,* 18, No. 1 (1969), contains John W. Bennett, "Introduction: Planned Change in Perspective"; Julian H. Steward, "Prediction and Planning in Cultural Change"; Holmberg, "Land Tenure and Planned Social Change: A Case from Vicos, Peru" (Holmberg II); and a comment by Wolff. (This symposium also contains three other articles and a comment, of which, however, I have not made use here.)

2. Max Weber, "Science as a Vocation" (1918), in *From Max Weber,* translated and edited and with an introduction by H. H. Gerth and C. Wright Mills (New York: Oxford University Press, 1946, pp. 129–156.

3. See Robert Redfield, *The Primitive World and Its Transformations* (Ithaca, N.Y.: Cornell University Press, 1953), Chapter 2, or "The Natural History of the Folk Society," *Social Forces,* 31 (March 1953), 224–228.

4. Cf. Martin Buber, *I and Thou* (1923), translated by Ronald Gregor Smith (Edinburgh: Clark, 1937).

This chapter has not been published previously in English.

# 25

# THIS IS THE TIME
# FOR RADICAL
# ANTHROPOLOGY. 1973

The task of this chapter is to explicate its title [1] and to convey its trust. Its seven words—"this is the time for radical anthropology"—reflect three inseparably connected concepts: *this time, radical, anthropology.* Although inseparably connected, their exposition, which is to tell their story, is necessarily consecutive; it begins with "anthropology."

The anthropology that is relevant at this time is radical, but the justification of this assessment must wait until we come to "this time." What radical anthropology exists is, as far as I know, either humanly or politically radical. Among the major representatives of humanly radical anthropology, although in most other respects they are quite different from one another, are Paul Radin, Edward Sapir, Ruth Benedict (in at least one of her writings), and Dorothy Lee. A representative of politically radical anthropology is Kathleen Gough. We must find out what is common to these two radicalisms [2].

Paul Radin, in contrast to Lévy-Bruhl, for instance, thought and felt that the Winnebago—his Winnebago—were human beings like himself; he listened in a manner as unprejudiced as possible to what Crashing Thunder (Radin, 1920, 1926) had to say and incidentally, as Robert Redfield wrote, "stimulated the now widespread use of autobiographies..." (Redfield, 1960, p. 3); he also found primitive philosophers (Radin, 1927). Joseph Campbell's observation is pertinent: whereas

> any science that takes into consideration only or even primarily the vulgar, tough-minded interpretation of symbols will inevitably be committed to a study largely of local differen-

tiations, while, on the other hand, one addressed to the views
of thinkers will find that the ultimate references of their
cogitations are few and of universal distribution [will, I paraphrase, seek and come closer to what is universal, radical in
man, what is the root of man]. Anthropologists, by and large
(or, at least, those of the American variety) are notoriously
tough-minded. . . . They have tended to give reductive interpretations to the symbols of primitive thought and to find
references only in the particularities of the local scene (Campbell, 1960, p. 381).

Not, of course, Paul Radin, nor Edward Sapir, as we can see in his search
for genuine culture (Sapir, 1919, 1922, 1924), which is

inherently harmonious, balanced, self-satisfactory. . . . It would
be too much to say that even the purest examples yet known
. . . have been free of spiritual discords, of the dry rot of
social habit, devitalized. But the great cultures, those that we
instinctively feel to have been healthy spiritual organisms,
such as the Athenian culture of the Age of Pericles and, to a
less extent perhaps, the English culture of Elizabethan days,
have at least tended to such harmony (*ibid.*, pp. 314–315).

To be cultured, it follows, is to be honest with onself, for spurious
harmony is a contradiction in terms:

Sooner or later we shall have to get down to the humble task
of exploring the depths of our consciousness and dragging to
the light what sincere bits of reflected experience we can find.
These bits will not always be beautiful, they will not always
be pleasing, but they will be genuine (*ibid.*, p. 331).

Sapir saw the implications of this view of culture and the cultured individual for what has since been called applied anthropology. He warns or
reminds us that

the deliberate attempt to impose a culture directly and speed-
ily, no matter how backed by good will, is an affront to the
human spirit. When such an attempt is backed, not by good
will, but by military ruthlessness, it is the greatest conceivable
crime against the human spirit, it is the very denial of culture
(*ibid.*, p. 328).

from this warning or reminder follows the call for a world civilization:

> Such transnational problems as the distribution of economic
> goods, the transportation of commodities, the control of
> highways, the coinage, and numerous others, must eventually
> pass into the hands of international organizations for the
> simple reason that men will not eternally give their loyalty to
> the uselessly national administration of functions that are of
> inherently international scope. As this international scope gets
> to be thoroughly realized, our present infatuations with na-
> tional prestige in the economic sphere will show themselves
> for the spiritual imbecilities that they are (*ibid.*, p. 329).

In other words, we have reached a stage at which we must realize our
immediate ends on a world-wide scale, precisely in order to devote our
cultural activity to the remoter ends that we have come to envisage (cf.
*ibid.*, pp. 319–321). This argument hints at a possible connection between
human and political radicalism and we shall come back to it.

Ruth Benedict's human radicalism shows itself above all in her paper,
"Anthropology and the Humanities" (Benedict, 1948). Witness, for
instance, her observation or insistence that the anthropologist should
follow "the critic's surrender to the text itself," for he

> knows that he will succeed in his work if he takes into account
> whatever is said and done, discarding nothing he sees to be
> relevant; if he tries to understand the interrelations of discrete
> bits; if he surrenders himself to his data and uses all the
> insights of which he is capable.

Concretely, therefore, life histories should not be used so much for items
of ethnographic knowledge as for

> that fraction of the material which shows what repercussions
> the experiences of a man's life . . . have upon him as a human
> being. . . . Such information, as it were, tests out a culture
> by showing its workings in the life of a carrier of that culture;
> we can watch in an individual case, in Bradley's words, "*what
> is,* seeing that so it happened and must have happened"
> (Benedict, 1948, p. 592).

Dorothy Lee is humanly more radical than Radin, Sapir, or Benedict.
Some of the crucial elements of her position are contained in the following passage:

> I believe that it is value, not a series of needs, which is at the
> basis of human behavior. The main difference between the

two lies in the conception of the good which underlies them. The premise that man acts so as to satisfy needs presupposes a negative conception of the good as amelioration or the correction of an undesirable state. According to this view, man acts to relieve tension; good is the removal of evil and welfare the correction of ills; satisfaction is the meeting of a need; good functioning comes from adjustment, survival from adaptation; peace is the resolution of conflict; fear, of the supernatural or of adverse public opinion, is the incentive to good conduct; the happy individual is the well-adjusted individual.

Perhaps this view of what constitutes the good is natural and applicable in a culture which also holds that man was born in sin, whether in Biblical or in psychoanalytic terms. But should we, who believe that other cultures should be assessed according to their own categories and premises, impose upon them our own unexamined conception of the good, and thus always see them as striving to remove or avoid ills? It seems to me that, when we do not take this negative view of the good for granted, other cultures often appear to be maintaining "justment" rather than striving to attain adjustment. For example, for the Hopi, the good is present and positive. An individual is "born in hopiness," so to speak, and strives throughout life to maintain and enhance this hopiness. There is no external reward for being good, as this is taken for granted. It is evil which is external and intrusive, making a man kahopi, or unhopi; that is, un-peaceful, un-good.

In my opinion, the motivation underlying Hopi behavior is *value*. To the Hopi, there is value in acting as a Hopi within a Hopi situation; there is satisfaction in the situation itself, not in the solution of it or the resolution of tension. . . . the notion of value is incompatible with that of a list of needs, or adjustive responses, or drives; so that, wherever it is held, the list must go (Lee [1948], 1959, pp. 72–73).

Inasmuch as the term value so often smacks of, if it is not short for, exchange value, although it is for the most part used unwittingly, it risks contributing to the commercialization of our language and outlook, even though we may protest this commercialization by invoking values. (Cf. Arendt, 1958, pp. 163–167 [Chapter 14]. Clearly, Dorothy Lee (also see Lee [1954], 1959, p. 88) does *not* mean exchange value but rather its opposite, something inalienable, intrinsic, and essential: *worth*. The student of the Hopi must look for "hopiness"; the anthropologist, in general, must determine what corresponds to "hopiness" in any culture he may wish to study [3]. To say that this conception of anthropology is humanly radical means to stress the injunction inferred in Dorothy Lee's writing, namely, that the student of man get at the root of man as it has grown (or is growing) in a given culture, as it is mediated by this culture, for it is never found ungrown or unmediated, and it is this grasp of a *unique* growth that is the grasp of man's root, that is, of the *universally* human [cf. introduction to Part IV]. This view, on which cultures and culture are relative to man, the absolute, is the opposite of that cultural relativism for which cultures are relative and monadic and culture itself is absolute (cf. Gibson, 1966, 56).

Dorothy Lee does not examine the relation between man's worth and his religiosity, but she writes: "To describe a way of life in its totality is to describe a religious way of life" (Lee [1952], 1959, p. 165). The paragraph that ends with this sentence reads as follows:

> In these societies [Wintu, Kaingang, Arapesh, Tikopia, and presumably other "primitive" societies], where religion is an everpresent dimension of experience, it is doubtful that religion as such is given a name; Kluckhohn reports that the Navaho have no such word, but most ethnographers never thought to inquire. Many of these cultures, however, recognized and named the spiritual ingredient or attribute, the special quality of the wonderful, the very, the beyondness, in nature. This was sometimes considered personal, sometimes not. We have from the American Indians terms such as *manitou,* or *wakan,* or *yapaitu,* often translated as power; and we have the well-known Melanisian term *mana.* But this is what they reach through faith, the other end of the relationship; the relationship itself is unnamed. Apparently, to behave and think religiously, is to behave and think. [Hence] To describe a way of life in its totality is to describe a religious way of life.

The relation between man's worth and the power experienced in religious experience is a topic for particular studies. Dorothy Lee's message is to remember both powers, or at least one or the other, if we would come into them, our heritage. Implied in this message is a contrast between primitive and contemporary society; for instance, with reference to freedom she has the following to say:

> As a concept or as a recognized value, freedom is rarely if ever present in non-Western cultures; but the thing itself, freedom, is certainly often present and carefully implemented—as

autonomy, or otherwise as a dimension of the self. In this country, on the other hand, we do have the notion of freedom, and an ideal image of ourselves as "free." Ours is the "land of the free," we are born "free and equal": and certainly, when these phrases were originally used, *free* referred to something of value beyond price, worth fighting and dying for.

A few years ago, with this in mind, I proceeded to find out how we use the term *free* in the mid-twentieth century. . . . I came reluctantly to the conclusion that the term *free* was almost never used, except by people whose function it was to evoke or facilitate freedom, or to remind people about freedom, or to prod people into being concerned about it—that is, by people such as social scientists, politicians, psychoanalysts, and educators. Otherwise, the term *free* was not applied to the freedom of the self. When used at all, it was used occasionally to refer to freedom from entanglement, and more frequently, to free time and free objects, that is, objects which could be acquired or enjoyed without being paid for, such as free lectures or free cigars. *Free* here referred merely to a condition of the situation, a negative condition; to something that was not there. It referred to a welcome lack of requirement, to an absence of *have to*. I *do not have to* pay for the cigars, or for a ticket to attend the lecture; my time is free because I *do not have to do* anything now (Lee [1958], 1959, pp. 53–54).

This passage does more than contrast primitive and contemporary society: it implies a historical judgment ("when these phrases were originally used, *free* referred to something of value beyond price"; when Dorothy Lee made her observations, "free" referred merely . . . to an absence of "have to"). To explicate "This Is the Time for Radical Anthropology" a historical judgment of the kind must be developed. For the moment let us realize that Dorothy Lee's idea of worth-*mana*-power has close kinship with Hannah Arendt's concept of power.

Power and violence are opposites; where the one rules absolutely, the other is absent. Violence appears where power is in jeopardy, but left to its own course its end is the disappearance of power (Arendt, 1969, p. 27).

Perhaps we might add already that today have gained in violence what we have lost in power.

Before we venture more forthrightly into historical judgment—before we come to "this time"—we must turn to the politically radical anthropologist Kathleen Gough.

Gough sees the tasks of anthropology in a political perspective (Gough, 1967–1968) in which four new proposals for anthropologists emerge (Gough, 1968; for an earlier version, Gough, 1967; and for a sharp critique of the bias in her political perspective, Gould, 1968; see also comments by various authors on Gough, 1968, appended there): (1) A comparison between capitalist agricultural production in underdeveloped countries and socialist production to ascertain which is better. (2) Comparisons of the structure and efficiency of socialist and capitalist foreign aid. (3) Comparative studies of types of modern intersocietal political and economic dominance which would help us to define and refine such concepts as imperialism and neocolonialism (4) Comparisons of revolutionary and protorevolutionary movements for what they can teach us about social change (Gough, 1968, 406–407). "I may be accused," Kathleen Gough adds,

> of asking for Project Camelot, but I am not. I am asking that we should do these studies in *our* way, as we would study a cargo cult or kula ring, without the built-in biases of tainted financing, without the assumption that counter-revolution, and not revolution, is the best answer, and with the ultimate economic and spiritual welfare of our informants and of the international community, rather than the short run military or industrial profits of the Western nations, before us (Gough, 1968, 407).

Such proposals, it would appear, are in response to the question about its purpose and its beneficiaries that science, including anthropology, must periodically ask itself lest its practioners cease being fully social and fully human intellectuals (cf. Gough, 1967–1968, pp. 148–149). Gough also sees her proposals as contributions to the maturing of anthropology

> into an interconnected body of empirical knowledge and theory, continually being revised, about the total process and main directions of the evolution of human societies and cultures, geared ultimately, although not at every point directly and immediately, to a search for the enhancement of human happiness and dignity. Such a view of the ultimate goals of anthropology [she adds] does lead to criteria of relevance or, as I would prefer to put it, significance (Gough, 1968, "Replies," 429).

Now, then, to "this time." Although Edward Sapir wrote the essay from which I quoted earlier almost fifty years ago and although *that* time is, indeed, not *this*, much of Sapir's paper still applies to *us*. I repeat a passage:

> Sooner or later we shall have to get down to the humble task of exploring the depths of our consciousness and dragging to the light what sincere bits of reflected experience we can find. These bits will not always be beautiful, they will not always be pleasing, but they will be genuine.

Sapir continues: "And then we can build." He meant to build culture, but the last half century has shown this to be a historically inadequate formulation. Since Sapir launched his plea we have experienced—witnessed, contributed to, fought, turned away from, been enthused or terrified, victimized, or killed by—fascism, Stalinism, nazism, an incomparably vaster world war than the first, at the end of which Sapir wrote, nuclear explosion, and much else that is unprecedented and still impossible radically to come to terms with. Impossible radically to come to terms with means that we have to go deeper than culture if there is to be any hope that we *can* come to terms with it. Sapir, we saw, envisaged something of the sort in his idea of international organizations and in his judgment of infatuations with national prestige as spiritual imbecilities. Without explicating the concepts needed for distinguishing international organizations from culture and for relating the two, he paid attention to the former and separated their discussion from that of the latter. Today, and indeed already yesterday, something seems even more promising and urgent than to engage in the conceptual clarification of these phenomena. This is that our time is so unprecedented that we cannot hope to do justice to it by relying on, as it were, precedented concepts, or received notions. Instead we must suspend or bracket received notions as best we can, for only in this way, by not relying on them, can we hope to come on a concept and on concepts that may be less inadequate (cf. Kurt H. Wolff, 1964, 1967). This is what being radical, what seeking the root of man now means.

In this view it appears that the humanly radical anthropologists we have recalled are far more radical than the one politically radical anthropologist we have considered. If their position were carried to its logical consequence, the former would in their study suspend their received notions as much as possible, whereas Kathleen Gough has rejected rather than suspended the received notions that make up capitalist-bourgeois ideology (and not without replacing them with a strong dose of equally received neo-Marxism). The decisive difference between the two radical-isms, however, is not this matter of degree. It lies, instead, in what our authors do not even perceive as relevant to their tasks, hence in what they neither work with in traditional fashion nor suspend. This, greatly over-simplified, is politics in the case of the humanly radical anthropologists, which Gough, on the contrary, is concerned with, and in Gough's case the relation of the student to the people he studies, which is in the fore-front of Radin's, Sapir's, Benedict's, and above all Dorothy Lee's atten-tion. Yet again, for one who is seeking an anthropology more adequate to this time, more commensurate with it, neither difference is nearly so pertinent as the fact that both radicalisms, though variously and un-evenly, indeed, do suspend received notions: this is what humanly radical and politically radical anthropology share. To become aware of it calls for pleading with the former that it recognize the relevance of politics, with the latter, that it recognize the relevance of the relations between student and persons studied, and with both that they practice the max-imal suspension of received notions. Both kinds of anthropologists would then come closer to the root and to perhaps unsuspected roots of man, hence closer to doing right by our unprecedented time.

A given anthropologist, however, may find it impossible to be radical in both senses; for instance, the investigation of a particular group may so draw him into political problems, if not into politics, that he will not be able to remain true to his goal, which is to come as close as possible to the people he studies. Conversely, he may be so concerned with the clari-fication of a given political problem that he will find it irrelevant if not frivolous to be humanly radical ("What poetry after Auschwitz?"). Thus the two radicalisms have complementary limitations. They may be ex-pressed by saying that to explore while being moved only by the desire to get at the root of man and thus failing to analyze his social setting with its institutions and arrangements that diminish him is to engage in political mystification, whereas the analysis of a social setting without trying to surrender to the people involved in it is an exercise in *human* mystification. Once more, to say this cannot imply that one must be expected to be both humanly and politically radical; it only invites us to be aware of the difficult if not impossible *demand to be both* and to do our best within the difficulties this demand imposes [4].

Underlying the difference between the two radicalisms may be a differ-ence in attitude toward our time—the humanly radical faith and hope in man's worth; the politically radical insistence on the compelling need for great change. This is a serious difference, but it is as nothing (I repeat) compared with what the two attitudes have in common, which distin-guishes both from the attitudes characteristic of social scientists and other men who have *not* examined life as both kinds of radicals have. It is in the light of our time that the two radicalisms appear far more similar than different, or we might say that it is more pertinent to stress what they have in common than what separates them.

To understand our time we must realize that unprecedented refers to our experience of it, here, now: it cannot mean that our time has not developed in time. In fact, if we would understand it, we must consider the processes that have brought it about.

Among social scientists, Max Weber was probably the most devoted and far-sighted explorer of these processes. One of many passages in his writings—dating from about the same year as Sapir's essay—may serve to illustrate Weber's reading of this time and the historical processes at work in it:

> The fate of our times is characterized by rationalization and intellectualization and, above all, by the "disenchantment of the world." Precisely the ultimate and most sublime values have retreated from public life either into the transcendental realm of mystic life or into the brotherliness of direct and personal human relations. It is not accidental that . . . today only within the smallest and intimate circles, in personal human situations, in *pianissimo*, that something is pulsating that corresponds to the prophetic *pneuma*, which in former times swept through the great communities like a firebrand, welding them together (Weber [1918], 1946, p. 155).

For our purposes, we may omit the prophetic from pneuma (in view of Weber's fascination with prophecy) and add pneuma to Dorothy Lee's worth-*mana*-power and Hannah Arendt's power as characteristics of primitive societies or of earlier times—which, of course, remain to be specified; or we may, with similar intent, concentrate on Weber's insistence on disenchantment, which marks our time, as does the absence of worth-*mana*-power-*pneuma*.

Long before these authors Rousseau expressed a similar idea:

> The savage lives within himself, while social man lives constantly outside himself, and only knows how to live in the opinion of others, so that he seems to receive the consciousness of his own existence merely from the judgment of others concerning him (Rousseau [1755], 1941, p. 237).

Indeed, Rousseau held that advances beyond the savages

have been apparently so many steps towards the perfection of the individual, but in reality towards the decrepitude of the species (*ibid.*, p. 214).

And inequalities and men's obsession by them may lead to such flagrant despotism that all private persons return to their first equality, because they are nothing; and, subjects having no law but the will of their master, and their master no restraint but his passions, all notions of good and all principles of equity again vanish. There is here a complete return to the law of the strongest, and so to a new state of nature, differing from that we set out from; for the one was a state of nature in its first purity, while this is the consequence of excessive corruption (*ibid.*, p. 235) [5].

This vision leaves no hope, in stark contrast to most of the Enlightenment philosophy of history or to Hegel's or Marx's. It may strike us as all the more plausible for its bleakness and tempt us to succumb to it, but we know that this can be only a mood of desperation. Indeed, we can read another text, far less well known in the English-speaking world, less desperate, and more realistic, thus bearing more directly on the historical diagnosis in which we are engaged.

In 1810 Heinrich von Kleist (a year before his suicide at the age of 34) published a story, "On the Puppet Theater." It relates a conversation between the narrator and a dancer who praises the excellence of puppets and their superiority to human dancers.

". . . what advantage would this puppet have over living dancers?"

"What advantage? First of all, a negative one, my excellent friend, namely this one, that it would never give itself airs. For airs, as you know, appear when the soul (*vis motrix*) finds itself at any point other than the point of gravity of the movement. Since the puppeteer, simply by means of the wire or thread, holds no other point in his power but this one, all other limbs are what they ought to be, dead; pure pendula; and follow the mere law of gravitation; an excellent quality, which one seeks in vain among most of our dancers. . . ."

"Such mistakes [as human dancers make]," he added, stopping short, "are unavoidable ever since we have eaten from the tree of knowledge. But paradise is bolted, and the cherub is behind us; we must make the trip around the world and see if it is perhaps somehow open again at the back. . . ."

"We see that in the measure in which in the organic world reflection becomes darker and feebler, grace appears ever more radiant and dominant. . . . when knowledge has gone through an infinitude, as it were, grace re-emerges, so that it appears in its purest form in that frame of the human body which has either no consciousness at all or an infinite consciousness— that is, in the puppet or in the god."

"'Thus," I said, a bit distracted, "we should have to eat once more of the tree of knowledge to fall back into the state of innocence?"

"Exactly," he answered; "that is the last chapter in the history of the world" (Kleist [1810], n.d., IV, pp. 136–137, 140; cf. Kleist [1941], 1947, 69–70, 72).

It may be worth reading this story, written more than a century and a half ago, as a parable that refers to *us*, people of the most advanced historical consciousness, living in the most advanced industrial and technological societies. Laboring, working, acting (for these three activities, cf. Arendt, 1958 [Chapter 14]), creating, experiencing, enjoying, despairing—in short, being (cf. Kurt H. Wolff, 1967). For tens of thousands of years we and our predecessors have produced an unmastered artifice [6]. We have traded our worth-*mana*-power-*pneuma* (and, to add Kleist's word, our grace, whether read as gracefulness or as gift as in charisma) for a struggle with disenchantment and alienation, for compulsive domination, for an indifferent, cynical, hypocritical, or desperate play with life and death, for, when we feel driven to it, a global sneer [7]. We must emerge from this condition into such innocence as man is capable of, through whatever "opening at the back" human and political radicalism can jointly discover.

Thus seen, we are not at the end but, if we can become conscious of it and act on our consciousness, if, as Kleist put it, we realize that we must once more eat of the tree of knowledge and have the courage to do so, we may become able, in Marx's terms, to leave our prehistory and begin our history, for we have reached a time when we can hardly bear our failure to master our disenchantment, because this failure has resulted in masks, machines, and deceptive substitutes whose character reveals itself to us by their capacity to destroy us even physically. The great inventions of science and technology have seduced us to use them also for controlling, manipulating, exploiting, and destroying ourselves and everything else. The liberal glory has become bankruptcy, destitute either in its continued insistence on tolerance at all costs, even of hate mongering and racism, or in its untutored and fearful casting about for grounds on which to qualify it (Robert Paul Wolff, Moore, Marcuse, 1965); the epistemological and ethical companion of liberal bankruptcy is cultural and moral relativism (cf. Mannheim [1946], 1959 [Chapter 29], for a moving illustration).

In his effort to define primitive societies, which he intends "as a means of furthering our critical understanding and, hopefully, our humane shaping of the processes of civilization" (Diamond, 1967, p. 22), Stanley Diamond writes that

> the sanguine and terrifying aspects of primitive life, which civilized individuals could hardly sustain, precisely because of the immediate personal contexts in which they occur, do not begin to compete with the mass, impersonal, rationalized slaughter that increases in scope as civilization spreads and deepens. . . . Certain ritual dramas or aspects of them acknowledge, express and symbolize the most destructive, ambivalent, and demoniacal aspects of human nature; in so doing, they are left limited and finite; that is, they become self-limiting. For this, as yet, we have no civilized parallel, no funcitonal equivalent (*ibid.*, p. 26).

To generalize from this we have not learned to civilize or to sublimate without loss the primitive oneness of confrontation and harmony. There is a largely instinctive effort to re-enact this oneness in the confrontations of war by love of contemporary young men and women—the hippies and flower children—as if they believed in Freud's conviction:

> All that brings out the significant resemblances between men calls into play this feeling of community, identification, where-upon is founded, in large measure, the whole edifice of human society (Freud [1932], 1964, p. 78).

They correspond outside the academy, although many are or were students, to the humanly radical anthropologists whose attention is to their relations with the people they study, and they act out or live much of what radical philosophers—existentialists, including for many the early Marx, and phenomenologists—have thought and think. The other chief group of critics of our society, the militant Blacks and representatives of the Third World, correspond outside the academy (and fewer of them are or were students) to the politically radical anthropologists whose attention is focused on the injustices of the *status quo*.

These two groups constitute, on this diagnosis of our time, the main hope for us of entering history, of realizing in knowledge, rather than in primitive innocence of it, worth, *mana,* power, grace, *pneuma.* By virtue of their education and attendant experience, radical anthropologists have a better chance than sheer individual talent to acquire a consciousness that would make them ally themselves with these two groups and make them seek others among comparably favored individuals, such as philosophers, theologians, historians, and other social scientists, anywhere at all. This alliance, that is to say, *we,* we constitute the vanguard of history who must diffuse our worth that we remember so that others, too, remember their own lest all that they, all that we, are left with be violence. This proposition, obviously, resolves none of our excruciating political problems, but it is prepolitical to the extent and in the sense that the maximal suspension of received notions is the precondition of knowing what we must do—*whatever* this may be. Men of critical mind and good will, we everywhere, must unite, for we realize that we may have nothing to lose but our lives.

## BIBLIOGRAPHY

Arendt, Hannah (1958), *The Human Condition* (Chicago: University of Chicago Press).
—— (1969), "Reflections on Violence," *The New York Review of Books,* **12,** 4 (February 27), 19–31.
Benedict, Ruth (1948), "Anthropology and the Humanities," *American Anthropologist,* **50,** 585–593.
Bramson, Leon, and George W. Goethals, Eds. (1964), *War: Studies from Psychology, Sociology, Anthropology* (New York: Basic Books).
Campbell, Joseph (1960), "Primitive Man as Metaphysician," in Diamond, 1960, pp. 380–392.
Chomsky, Noan (1966), *Cartesian Linguistics: A Chapter in the History of Rationalist Thought* (New York: Harper and Row).
Diamond, Stanley, Ed. (1960), *Culture in History: Essays in Honor of Paul Radin* (New York: Columbia University Press for Brandeis University).
—— (1967), "Primitive Society in Its Many Dimensions," in Wolff, Moore, and Marcuse, 1967, pp. 21–30.
—— (1964), "What History Is," in Manners, 1964, pp. 29–46.
Freud, Sigmund (1932), "Why War?," in Bramson and Goethals, 1964, pp. 71–80.
Gerth, H. H., and C. Wright Mills (1946), translated, edited, and with an introduction, *From Max Weber: Essays in Sociology* (New York: Oxford University Press).
Gibson, Mickey (1966), "The Image of Man in Social Anthropology," *Review of Existential Psychology and Psychiatry,* **6,** 51–62.
Gough, Kathleen (1967), "New Proposals for Anthropologists," *Economic and Political Weekly* (Bombay) (September 9), 1653–1658.

—————— (1967–1968), "World Revolution and the Science of Man," in Roszak, 1967–1968, pp. 135–158.

—————— (1968), "New Proposals for Anthropologists," *Current Anthropology*, 9, 403–407.

Gould, Harold A. (1968), "New Proposals for Anthropologists: A Comment," *Economic and Political Weekly* (Bombay) (April 27), 682–685.

Gross, Llewelln, Ed., (1959), *Symposium on Sociological Theory* (Evanston, Ill.: Row, Peterson).

Kleist, Heinrich von (1810), "Über das Marionettentheater," *Werke* (Leipzig: Bibliographisches Institut, n.d.), Vol. IV, pp. 133–141.

—————— (1941), "Essay on the Puppet Theater," translated by Eugene Jolas, *Partisan Review*, 14 *(*1947), 67–72.

Lee, Dorothy (1948), "Are Basic Needs Ultimate?", in Lee, 1959, pp. 70–77.

—————— (1952), "The Religious Dimension of Human Experience," in Lee, 1959, pp. 162–174.

—————— (1954), "Symbolization and Value," in Lee, 1959, pp. 78–88.

—————— (1958), "What Kind of Freedom?" in Lee, 1959, pp. 53–58.

—————— (1959), *Freedom and Culture* (Englewood Cliffs, N.J.: Prentice-Hall).

Lévi-Strauss, Claude (1963), "Rousseau, Father of Anthropology," *UNESCO Courier*, 16, 3 (March), 10–14.

Mandelbaum, David, Ed. (1949), *Selected Writings of Edward Sapir* (Berkeley: University of California Press).

Manners, Robert A., Ed. (1964), *Process and Pattern in Culture: Essays in Honor of Julian H. Steward* (Chicago: Aldine).

Mannheim, Karl (1946), letter in Chapter 29.

Partridge, Eric (1958), *Origins: A Short Etymological Dictionary of Modern English* (New York: Macmillan, 1959).

Radin, Paul (1920), "The Autobiography of a Winnebago Indian," *University of California Publications in American Archaeology and Ethnology*, 16, 381–473.

—————— Ed. (1926), *Crashing Thunder: The Autobiography of an American Indian* (New York: Appleton) (commercial publication of Radin, 1920).

—————— (1927), *Primitive Man as Philosopher*, foreword by John Dewey (New York: Appleton).

Redfield, Robert (1960), "Thinker and Intellectual in Primitive Society," in Diamond, 1960, pp. 3–18.

Roszak, Theodore, Ed. (1967–1968), *The Dissenting Academy* (New York: Pantheon).

Rousseau, Jean-Jacques (1755), "A Discourse on . . . the Origin of Inequality among Men . . . ," in Rousseau, 1941, pp. 155–238.

—————— (1941), *The Social Contract* and other writings (London: Dent, Everyman's Library).

Sapir, Edward (1919, 1922, 1924), "Culture, Genuine and Spurious," in Mandelbaum, 1949, pp. 308–331.

Spitzer, Leo (1948), *"Ratio > Race," Essays in Historical Semantics* (New York: S. F. Vanni), pp. 147–169.

Vidich, Arthur J., Joseph Bensman, and Maurice R. Stein, Eds. (1964), *Reflections on Community Studies* (New York: Wiley).

Weber, Max (1918), "Science as a Vocation," in Gerth and Mills, 1946, pp. 129–156.

Wolff, Kurt H. (1964), "Surrender and Community Study: The Study of Loma," in Vidich, Bensman, and Stein, 1964, pp. 233–263.

——— (1967), "Beginning: In Hegel and Today," in Wolff, Moore et al., 1967, pp. 72–105.

———, and Barrington Moore, Jr., with the assistance of Heinz Lubasz, Maurice R. Stein, and E. V. Walter, Eds. (1967), *The Critical Spirit: Essays in Honor of Herbert Marcuse* (Boston: Beacon Press).

Wolff, Robert Paul, Barrington Moore Jr., and Herbert Marcuse (1965), *A Critique of Pure Tolerance* (Boston: Beacon Press).

## NOTES

1. This chapter was written in 1969 as a contribution to a *festschrift* for Dorothy Lee. The *festschrift* did not materialize, but *Reinventing Anthropology* (edited by Dell Hymes and published by Pantheon Books) is at least as good a place in which to honor her. I wish to thank Dell Hymes for his criticisms and suggestions of an earlier draft.

2. To avoid misunderstandings I want to stress that all authors named in this chapter are referred to not as private individuals but as types construed from their concepts of study gleaned from some of their writings. I make no statement whatever concerning their personal interactions or lack of them with the people they have studied or reported on.

3. If "hopiness" is the exclusively human, as exemplified in the Hopi, its study does not exhaust the student's task, which also includes aspects of man he shares with other contents of the cosmos, because man is a mixed phenomenon. In passing, it may be pointed out that this conception of man as a mixed phenomenon militates against the romanticization of primitives inasmuch as it invites attention to dismal aspects of their conditions. (Cf. Kurt H. Wolff, 1964, especially pp. 244–246. For the examination of some community studies in regard to their adequacy to exclusive and shared human features, *ibid.*, pp. 251–261.)

4. Much in this paragraph was stimulated by comments on an earlier draft of this chapter that I was fortunate to receive from Paul Riesman and Kewal Motwani, to whom I am grateful.

5. In "Rousseau, Father of Anthropology," Claude Lévi-Strauss (1963) celebrates Rousseau as the father of what is referred to here as humanly radical anthropology. See also Chomsky, 1966, pp. 91–93, n. 51.

6. This view is compatible with, if not a variant of, Stanley Diamond's (1964, p. 45) answer to the question, "What History *Is*": "the spectacle of a people forming out of their natural, material, and spiritual resources, their 'fate.' "

7. A comparable process of disenchantment or degeneration may be found if we move from *ratio* to race in the eighteenth- and nineteenth-century use of the term: the former appears to be the etymon of the latter [Spitzer, 1948; Partridge (1958), 1959, p. 546a, v. race (2)].

---

# VI

# SOCIOLOGY
# OF KNOWLEDGE

*In memory of Hermann Broch and Erich Kahler; for Mildred and David Bakan, Arthur Child, and Virgil Hinshaw*

Rereading the titles of the parts that make up this book, I find that the first three refer to more varied matters than the last. Still, the time spans in which the chapters assembled under each of the six parts were published—27, 21, 15, 23, 29, and 28 years—do not clearly reflect this variation, as they might if there had been periods of predominant viewpoints or concern with particular areas or problems. There are surveys, for instance, in 1940, 1946, 1958, and 1963 (Part II), but also in 1967 (Chapter 31, "The Sociology of Knowledge in the United States of America," in Part VI). Nevertheless, the last three parts are the longest, each containing, as it happens, seven chapters: aspects of what was defined as cultural anthropology, sociology, and sociology of knowledge have been more outstanding, having made me write papers over the years from 1946 to 1969, 1944 to 1973, and 1943 to 1971. The last part goes back even earlier to my study with Karl Mannheim in 1930 to 1933 and my Italian dissertation in 1935, as I indicated in the introduction to Part I. It is proper that I return to the sociology of knowledge in Part VI, the last.

In the New World I wrote my first paper on it (Chapter 26) less than two years after arriving, shortly after the study of the Jewish population of Dallas (Chapter 7) and Pareto (Chapter 1). These two papers were stimulated by other people to help me find a place in American academia.

449

I must have then felt secure enough to want to take up and develop what had so attracted me to Karl Mannheim. His influence makes itself clearly felt in that first paper, but so does that of the new environment; for instance, toward the end of the introduction I refer approvingly to the "relatively natural *Weltanschauung*" of the (American) social scientist. I even use, if not pejoratively, then at least residually, the adjective metaphysical (n. 16) without analyzing it in the least, even though the whole paper is a plea for an "empirical attitude," that is, for a postponement of theoretical closure until the subject matter can be investigated more thoroughly than is customary in the "speculative attitude." It also urges (n. 18) that the use of terms (but these include "metaphysical!") be specified in concrete research whenever a doubt rises in the mind of the investigator about the unambiguousness of a term employed (this recommendation was developed in Chapter 27 into the notion of the unique a few years later). There is also the optimism, if not smugness, of scientific method, most striking in the way the paper recalls the optimism of Chapter 10, "A Memorandum on the United States of America" the beginnings of which go back to about the same time.

Although I do not bracket the term metaphysical, I do argue for a much broader subject matter in the sociology of knowledge than knowledge itself because, as I did not then realize but can see now, knowledge is one of the terms that must be questioned, the meaning of which must be suspended. There are other anticipations: the notion of central attitude, which is applied a few years later also to culture, personality, and intellectual product (Chapter 27), is related to that of pattern, developed soon afterward (Chapter 20), and to similar concepts devised to grasp the whole of a culture (cf. Chapter 20, but also the interest in Bateson's holistic concepts in Chapter 19), as well as much later to identification as a component of surrender (cf. the comment in the discussion of Chapter 19 in the introduction to Part V). Closely connected (see the first point under "Interest and Method" in Chapter 26) is the emphasis on immanent versus sociological interpretation (encountered before in Chapters 2 [1958], n. 4, and 12 [1946] and comments in the introduction to Part IV). Both figure in the central-attitude-mode of understanding (characteristic of the sociology of knowledge) which, therefore, might displace them as alternatives: soon (1948, Chapter 27; 1953, Chapter 28) I shall indeed no longer be able to consider them as alternatives but find both indispensable components or phases of maximum understanding. Some years later in developing the notion of man as a mixed phenomenon (hinted at before mainly in the discussion of Chapter 14 in the introduction to Part IV), although by no means dropping this requirement for maximum understanding, the stress above all is on the importance of intrinsic interpretation for grasping the exclusively human and of extrinsic interpretation for grasping what man shares with other contents of the cosmos. It is a warning against the danger of treating man as a unique phenomenon—against the romanticization, etherealization, and angelization of human beings—and at the same time, against the danger of treating him as just another part of the cosmos—against making him into a thing, against reification (in this sense), objectification, and cynicism. In other words, there develops a critical thrust against corrupting seduction by idealism, and scientistic positivism—all this in the analyses of various aspects of surrender.

Already there is the distinction between the practical and theoretical attitudes (cf. the discussion of Chapters 14, 1961, and 17, 1959, in the introduction to Part IV), which are oriented, respectively, "toward concrete facts or conditions, in defense of, or adaptation, or opposition to them," and "toward the solution of a mental task, irrespective of the question of the cause, the use, and the effect of this solution in the practical sphere" (subsection "The concept of 'typical central attitude'"). This understanding of the distinction now strikes me as theoretical (or academic) in the pejorative sense of the term, even when compared with later formulations I developed. One aspect I find interesting but have not taken up again, however, is the designation of the student's knowledge in the area of the taken-for-granted as practical, and knowledge in the area of discussion and distance as theoretical. This seems worth analyzing in its meaning and in its conceptual and ontological, implications.

There are other continuities found in this paper. One is the anticipation (in the subsection "Magical") of the problem of the two viewpoints (cf. the introduction to Part V), the student's and his subjects', which are developed further in the studies in cultural anthropology. Later, in the first writings on surrender, when I use the quotation from Hugo von Hofmannsthal (subsection "Artistic") to convey an idea of surrender, I forget its appearance in this early paper on the sociology of knowledge. Here I quote it in an effort to have certain readers recall their own experiences in the artistic attitude, which I would later come to understand as surrender to an aesthetic object; that is to say, the rapture (*Entzückung*), the deepest enchantment, in which "the whole soul is . . . fully integrated," in which "thy self . . . [can] be found" (Hofmannsthal), in which a person is most real, most "self," and thus most (universally) human, describes surrender. Willed to one's utmost, surrender is surrender *to something*, whatever it may be. Among the infinitude of objects, there also is the aesthetic object—whether in the making (the artist's surrender to it), in attention to it (the listener's, reader's, or spectator's), or in its performance (the musician's, actor's, or dancer's). This change from using the quotation from Hofmannsthal to point to the artistic (typical central) attitude to using it to point to surrender now shows me one of the sources of the idea of surrender: my relation to art. I have again learned something about myself, not as a private person but as the locus of a developing idea. (On other realizations that have occurred in the course of writing this book see the discussion of Chapter 15 and the end of the discussion of Chapter 17 in the introduction to Part IV and discussions of Chapters 19, 20, 23, and 24 in the introduction to Part V.)

In the last section I mention, at random, some complexes of projects of research, a large net, full of small and big fish, which now reminds me of the avid random collection of field materials detailed in Chapter 23. It is as if in throwing out this net I had followed what only years later was to become a matter of self-conscious methodology, a methodological *desideratum*, namely, the postponement of hypotheses until the imagination could extend to all possibly pertinent candidates for the study at hand—a rule I also went by years later in Chapter 16 (on the research areas for a sociology of evil). The rule is anticipated already in this chapter in the advocacy of postponing theoretical closure, alluded to in n. 18.

Chapter 27, "The Unique and the General: Toward a Philosophy of Sociology" (1948), was not meant as a study in the sociology of knowledge (but was translated for a Spanish reader in the field [1]) any more than was the paper on culture patterns (Chapter 20, discussed in the introduction to Part V). Still, like much of my work from the beginning, it shows its Mannheimian provenience. Like the preceding chapter and other early writings, it also shows eagerness to be properly scientific. It repeats the distinction between immanent and transcendent interpretation but, unlike before or after, defines the former as dealing with the intellectual structure or methodology of an *interpretandum* and the latter as dealing with its presuppositions or approach. This arrangement leads to the epistemological question how understanding and communication are possible in spite of unique experience. The appropriateness of the (received) distinction between scientific and epistemological concerns is questioned (see also ns. 39 and 43). Here, then, we have what will develop into two aspects of surrender. One is obvious: the suspension of received notions. ("When he studies the unique, the student drops as much of his scientific and general-cultural cloak as he can in order to 'expose' himself ["surrender"] to his 'subject matter.' ") The other emerges when I say that I will no longer speak of understanding in spite of unique experience but will rather insist that understanding (the "catch" of surrender) cannot exhaust experience (surrender).

I characterize the student who takes the human-studies approach (cf. the "cultural approach" in Chapter 12, which is a variant of it) as accepting the continuous challenge to remain aware of the relation between scientific pursuit and spontaneous experience. This, of course, reflects my own experience, including Loma. According to this challenge, subject matter is not ready-made (received) but emerges in the process of understanding, as it will in action anthropology and planned social change (Chapter 24). An approach that makes such awareness part of its own definition is that much more scientific for it. Indeed, scientific understanding, "that in which identification with the unique is counterbalanced by testable communicability" (Chapter 26), is synonymous with maximum understanding. This will develop into the conception of surrender as maximum rationality (mentioned in connection with Chapter 14 in the introduction to Part IV). The advocacy of "greater scientific concern with the unique than is customary in order to enrich materials from which to hypothesize and eventually to establish uniformities" will be radicalized into the idea of surrender entailing the "catch," just as terms like those I use to help the reader to recall situations in which he may have experienced the unique will later be used to help recall surrender.

I amplify the methodological rule formulated in Chapter 26 (especially n. 18) by urging that the scientist consider those possible topics of understanding as uniques about which he has doubts that the development of the methodology of his discipline has satisfactorily reduced to mere crosspoints of uniformities. Although the unique is a notion of far more comprehensive significance than for scientific methodology alone, still, human beings cannot live continuously in its experience: "not everything can, for psychological reasons, be so considered: nobody can live without routine." About twenty years later, in an effort to locate surrender in the everyday world, I gave names to the common stretches of men's lives ("leading a life") and to the rare and unusual interstices between them ("being").

Chronologically, this is the first paper in which the problem of cultural relativism comes up. In the arrangement of this book it has figured already in Chapters 13 (1965), 15 (1956), and 24 (1958, 1959, 1964), and will do so again in later chapters. Here its context is understanding: cultural relativism is incompatible with the possibility of understanding. Its correction is attempted with the help of Arthur Child's "theory of the categories." I cannot, indeed, reconcile it with my conviction that understanding *is* possible, even though it sometimes is very difficult. From the point of view of surrender it can intrinsically be no more than approximate, precisely because the catch can never exhaust surrender. Nevertheless, to say it again in slightly different words, cultural relativism is incompatible with the "fundamental methodological question of the human approach, . . . how we can investigate unilluminated aspects of man."

An intimate connection exists between surrender and the sociology of knowledge. In commenting on Chapter 26, which is explicitly devoted to the latter, we found one of the sources of surrender in its affinity to art. In this chapter the several anticipations of surrender rise out of a concern for the philosophy of science, particularly problems of understanding. The recurring and modulated theme of interpretation, both intrinsic and extrinsic, here sociological, and their relations, a theme at the center of the problem of understanding itself, is an essential preoccupation of the sociologist of knowledge who, like the student following "surrender to" as his guide to maximum understanding, wishes to do right by both intrinsic and extrinsic interpretation as best he can, rather than to fall short of either of them. This link between the sociology of knowledge and surrender presents another lesson, to me at least, that I must learn.

The connection between the sociology of knowledge and surrender is far more easily recognized in Chapter 28 (1953), "A Preliminary Inquiry into the Sociology of Knowledge from the Standpoint of the Study of Man" [2]. I called it preliminary because at the time I wrote it I was at work on the study of Loma, which I also considered the first articulation of an understanding of sociology or social science that I called the study of man. Over the twenty years since I wrote Chapter 28 this understanding has developed, although not quite as anticipated: not as the more explicit analysis of the methodological, epistemological, and ontological problems then formulated but in a radical way, as the continuing analysis of surrender. Because of this, I tried (many years later) to reassess Chapter 28. The result was "Presuppositions of the Sociology of Knowledge and a Task for It" (Chapter 28 [Supplement]), written in 1967, revised in 1971 (and previously published only in German).

The use of background materials to introduce the sociology of knowledge is taken over from their use in the study of a culture (cf. Chapter 23), and the exposition of the study of man is explicitly derived from the Loma experience: now I tell of my surrender to the sociology of knowledge (in its presentation by Arthur Child) as I had surrendered to Loma, except that in Loma I really had had only the first glimpses of the notion [3].

Concern with understanding imbues the praise of Child's conception of the categories (already sketched in Chapter 27), particularly because it invites us to ascertain the "line between primal and supervenient sources in categories" or, as I might have said, to identify the unique-universal in the particular-general. I am rather cavalier in accounting for the existence of primal categories. I merely expound Child, for whom their basis is biological ("biotic"). It had not occurred to me that one might argue another basis—in the transcendental subject—that the relation between the two foundations constitutes a problem. I now see that this neglect is especially embarrassing because the study of man clearly aims at a philosophical anthropology. Even now the problem still remains to be worked out: one more lesson.

In discussing the methodological in connection with the metaphysical premises of the sociology of knowledge and their different verifications, I present an early sketch of the distinction between theoretical-scientific and practical-existential truth [4]. I come, as I say, to find dualism (and naturalism) as metaphysical premises of the sociology of knowledge. A few years later, in the paper on Hannah Arendt's *The Human Condition* (Chapter 14), I mean by man's dualism his being free within the world of necessity, but nonsovereign within the world of freedom. Let us compare these two meanings of dualism. Translating the phenomenon from a premise (of the sociology of knowledge) into an attribute of man, we find that man seeks social relatedness but also validity, maximum intrinsic and extrinsic interpretation, understanding phenomena in their own terms and as instances of laws. The source of these variations is man's desire for both the unique (-universal) and the particular (-general) because he himself is both unique-universal (endowed, for instance, with primal categories) and particular-general (endowed, for instance, with supervenient categories): he is a "mixed phenomenon." (Cf. the discussion of Chapter 14 in the introduction to Part IV and the comments on Chapter 26 earlier in this introduction.)

Cultural relativism has figured several times before (cf. comments on Chapter 26) but is connected here with the experience of our time. It is a historically new experience, an ingredient of what the sociology of knowledge defines as a new situation. Through the sociology of knowledge

> man adapts himself to living in one world and through it he
> transcends cultural relativism toward the view of himself as
> dual and inexhaustibly challenging his own exploration.

Instead of sociology of knowledge, we may also read surrender. Again a new lesson I have to learn.

Now to the reassessment, the recasting of Chapter 28 (28 [Supplement]). It begins by tracking down the hidden subject of the question, "What is the sociology of knowledge?" Thus I act on the requirement to distinguish

between points of view, which came up in the papers on cultural anthropology and in Chapter 26 (cf. comments earlier in this introduction). I
challenge the anonymous asker to come forward: I challenge us, my
readers and myself, to come forward rather than hiding behind tradition,
in which we have at best a problematical trust, given once more the time
in which we live. It is the time (I might have already said in Chapter 13)
when we no longer believe in customs, which (as I do say there) "generally, that is, in all societies, exempt people from having to make moral
decisions" (or any other decisions), when therefore we must try to suspend
them and other received notions as best we can (see also Chapter 16).
I refer to Chapter 28 as an exemplification of surrender to the sociology
of knowledge (on the occasion of Arthur Child's work) and in this sense
reinterpret it by bringing to bear considerations that come out of the
papers on surrender written since that chapter (see n. 4 and other references to them) and ending with a concrete if enormously vast task for the
sociology of knowledge. The contrast between this task and the large
number of complexes of projects with which I concluded my first paper
in the field (Chapter 26) is striking. In that paper there is a diligent if
open-minded gatherer, a collector, of materials, the relevance of which
he does not know but is confident of finding [5]. Here there is one who
is assaulted by myriad evidences of the lives the majority of his fellow
men lead. Between writing the two chapters, he has come to recognize
man as a mixed phenomenon and human products as mixed phenomena.
In his surrender to one among them, the sociology of knowledge, he
cannot be concerned only with what is exclusively human but must also
do justice to what man shares with other beings and things. He wishes
to improve the mixture that man is so that man may be able to lessen his
distance from the image as the being capable of surrender and catch.

Chapter 29, "The Sociology of Knowledge and Sociological Theory,"
announces itself as a joint venture of author and readers, as do Chapter
28 (Supplement) and, most emphatically, Chapter 30. All of the several
papers that deal with existential truth or knowledge implicitly appeal to
the reader for his participation and assessment, for existential knowledge
is intersubjective in the dialogical sense, whereas scientific knowledge
might better be called "interobjective," inasmuch as its testing is less by
interacting than by comparing observations of the same object by a
number of individuals.

The first section, "What Is the Sociology of Knowledge?," has its title
in quotation marks to indicate the unanalyzed nature of the question.
Whoever has asked it (as in Chapter 28 [Supplement]) has not come
forward; the question is indistinct, imprecise, inaccurate, anonymous (as
I say in that later chapter), asked by an outsider (as I say here). I con-

trast the outsider with the insider, whom Karl Mannheim, most poignantly in a letter, exemplifies. Unlike the outsider, the insider takes risks. He engages in a venture whose outcome he cannot foresee; he surrenders. Indeed, here is the first time in this book that risk, another characteristic of surrender, is introduced (also see n. 49).

I again take up the question of Is and Ought (which also figures in Chapters 14, 15, 25, and most of all, 16) and of the diagnosis of our time (which we also find in Chapters 15, 28, and 28 [Supplement]), according to which we are underdeveloped (having lost worth-*mana*-power-*pneuma*, as Chapter 25 has it), and one characteristic of which is one world and cultural relativism, suggested in Chapter 28. There is the postulate of a transcultural human nature (especially in Chapter 28); the question raised in this introduction in discussing this phenomenon in connection with Chapter 28 (biological organism versus transcendental subject) is now at least mentioned (if not quite in these terms) but is considered of secondary importance in the context in which it comes up ("In the pursuit of understanding it is of secondary importance whether by our 'transcendental selves' we mean a supracultural core or residue, biological or spiritual...."). There again it is the task of the sociology of knowledge to transform a new and shattering experience into a problem. The various premises of the sociology of knowledge are developed in Chapter 28, but here they are even more intimately related to our time; there is the distinction between scientific and existential truth (cf. the discussion of Chapter 28 earlier in this introduction for references to it in Chapters 17, 29, 14, and 15), and there is the preoccupation with nineteenth- and twentieth-century civilizational-historical dichotomies, as in Chapter 5, but here in the context of modern American sociology and the sociology of knowledge.

There also is the anticipation of an idea, much further developed in Chapter 16, when I say:

> It is . . . widely recognized that it is important to distinguish between talking about one's own views of truth, which is considered a philosophical enterprise, and about somebody else's, which is accepted as a legitimate scientific enterprise.

In Chapter 16 the former case is coordinated with realism, the latter with nominalism, but these terms must not be confused as used in Chapter 29, for they characterize the conception of subject matter, whereas in Chapter 16 they characterize the student's relation to subject matter.

This chapter contains so much about American sociology, particularly in its variation from the European, that it might also have been located in Part IV, were it not that its focus is unmistakably that of the sociology of knowledge. It appears to me at least compatible with if not supplementary to the one chapter in this book (Chapter 10) that is devoted to American culture and to Chapter 12, which is explicitly concerned with American sociology.

There are two more allusions to surrender, in addition to those already remarked on. In "On Our Place and Time" (on the world as underdeveloped) I say "we may help reason in its cunning, recognizing in our befuddlement a reminder of objective reason and of the relation of objective to subjective reason." Some ten years later, without remembering this, I wrote a paper, "On the Cunning of Reason in Our Time" (see reference in Chapter 28 [Supplement], n. 4), in which I ask whether talking about the cunning of reason is at all tolerable in the face of, say, Auschwitz or Vietnam—and am once more led back to surrender as the highest exercise of man's reason (cf. comment on Chapter 14 in the introduction to Part IV). And in "one-world-and-cultural-relativism" I say that the "pursuit of understanding . . . perpetually challenges us to keep to the fine line between the belief of being in grace and the sin of pride"— which I will say of surrender. Again I did not remember the earlier passage just quoted, but am not surprised that I have used it to characterize surrender because I define surrender as cognitive love and consider it the closest to understanding that man can come.

The subtitle of Chapter 30, "Ernst Grünwald and the Sociology of Knowledge: A Collective Venture in Interpretation," tells what this paper is meant to be. I still think it *can* be a venture for a reader who opens himself to it and thus might actually experience, "at the very end, a perhaps unexpected climax," better yet, a shock—the worm of a question. This chapter is more constitutionally a surrender paper than any other in this book, far more than Chapter 28 or even 28 (Supplement), for it is not a *post-factum* report on surrender to (the sociology of knowledge, as in the chapters just named) but is surrender to (Grünwald's sociology of knowledge) *in actu*. It is, as it were, the wording of its process. It is so not despite but by means of its analyticity, just as analyticity was in the service of the practical-rhetorical thrust of Chapter 14, "Man's Historicity and Dualism" (pointed out in the discussion of that chapter in the introduction to Part IV).

I find that there is need here for stressing only two components of the analysis presented. One is, once more, the distinction between scientific-theoretical and (historical-)practical-existential truth. The other is the nature of the existentiality of knowledge, that is, the question whether this existentiality is selective or constitutive. This question has not yet come up in these terms but actually pervades the whole of the sociology of knowledge, notably Mannheim's, Scheler's, and Child's, and indeed much of contemporary Western consciousness. For it is a harmless sounding, esoteric way of asking whether we can be sure that there are objects at all, whether if there are we can know them, whether there is truth other than fundamentally arbitrary, relative, conditional truth. The analysis of Grünwald (the "documentary Grünwald") shows that for him the answers to all these questions are negative, and the perhaps unexpected climax of the paper is the reader's sudden confrontation with them when, as he is surrendering to them, he is on his own, thus falling back on what he shares with mankind. In less haunting terms the questions concern the nature of subject and object and their relation. We see Grünwald claiming the categories of thought and the laws of formal logic to be oriented exclusively toward the object of knowledge *(objektadäquat)*, claiming, that is, that there are at least *some* objects and that these can be truly known. We also see that he draws no conclusions, apparently not trusting himself [6]. Here, the matter must be left, dangling indeed.

Chapter 31, "The Sociology of Knowledge in the United States of America" (1967), is another survey similar to that of a few years earlier (1963) on social change (Chapter 5) in limiting itself to explicit statements. Also, like the earlier one, it cannot help emerging from the bibliographical web toward an assessment of the scene surveyed. The tone of the two surveys, however, differs, the present one being more judicious and poised, as behooves an almost officious document, similar in this respect to contributions to encyclopaedias or dictionaries (cf. introduction to Part II). For this reason, to show how they appear in such a document. I let some passages stand which are substantively repetitions of similar ones in Chapters 28 (on Child) and 29 (on the Hinkles' interpretation of American sociology). Chapter 31 is concise, a severe condensation more to be consulted perhaps than read or perhaps read first for the vertigiousness of the compression and then consulted occasionally.

This chapter, of course is the last, but introducing it here I hesitated to call it so for fear of the *tristitia post partum* following the making of this book—which now that it is made I must inspect (following Part VI). Yet whatever it turns out to look like, it comforts me to recall what I wrote in approaching it: it "represents an *attempt* (not yet, I hope, completed)."

### NOTES

1. "Lo singular y lo general: hacia una filosofía de la sociología," in Irving Louis Horowitz, Ed., *Historia y elementos de la sociología del conocimiento* (Buenos Aires: Editorial Universitaria de Buenos Airest, 1964), Vol. II, pp. 275–296.

2.  I have incorporated in it a short paper, "On the Scientific Relevance of 'Imputation' " (1950).

3.  The difference just indicated took me years to recognize. In several drafts of the study of Loma I tried to write it up in two parts, the first dealing with surrender, the second exemplifying it by the study of Loma itself. What took me so long to realize was that the study could be no such exemplification, for I had not done it while acting on the idea of surrender. I had to abandon the write up in that form and have proceeded in another, yet to be completed.

4.  This I was to develop in Chapters 17 and 29 (1959), 14 (1961), and 15 (1969, 1967); cf. the discussion in the introduction to Part IV, but see also Chapter 26 and discussion on p. 471 on theoretical versus practical attitudes.

5.  See earlier in this introduction the reminder in the discussion of Chapter 26 of Chapters 23 and 16.

6.  Since I wrote that paper I have in my preoccupation with surrender been led to begin exploring the epistemological and, indeed, the ontological subject-object problem in "Sociology, Phenomenology, and Surrender-and-Catch," mentioned in Chapter 28 (Supplement).

# 26

# THE SOCIOLOGY
# OF KNOWLEDGE:
Emphasis on an Empirical Attitude. 1943

## INTRODUCTION

Two distinct attitudes have been adopted by investigators in the field of the sociology of knowledge [1]. One may be called speculative, the other, empirical. The central interest of an investigator having the speculative attitude lies in developing a theory of the sociology of knowledge [2]. The central interest of an investigator having the empirical attitude lies in finding out or explaining concrete phenomena; the theory is employed, implicitly or explicitly, for this purpose [3]. The existence of the two attitudes may be explained in part, as far as the German sociology of knowledge is concerned, by reference to the history of this school, which has grown out of and been determined by a Marxist and materialistic philosophy and especially by the use of this philosophy as a political instrument in the struggle of the emerging proletariat against the bourgeoisie [4]. This statement, however, must be supplemented by a short location of the four most important contributors to the theory of the German sociology of knowledge. Max Scheler approaches the problem phenomenologically; he was the first and only one to ask the fundamental question, "What is knowledge?" [5]. Karl Mannheim, though markedly influenced by the Marxist viewpoint, particularly by Lukács, seems to me more adequately characterized by stressing his development from a more exclusively speculative to a more decidedly empirical attitude, which latter is especially evident in his most recent book, *Man and Society in an Age of Reconstruction* (1940). Alexander von Schelting's main contribution is his thorough logical analysis of Mannheim's theory in the light of Max Weber's methodology. Ernst Grünwald has given the most complete survey of the forerunners, the history, and the various contributions of the sociology of knowledge [6]. These four thinkers are indirectly dependent on the historically determined emphasis of the movement on ideology in that they remain on the level of a theoretical discussion without arriving at factual research [7].

The historical setting sketched above accounts for the fact that the sociology of knowledge has continued (rather anachronistically) to limit its subject matter to ideologies, theories, and, at most, ideas [8]. Even after the public at large had accepted the fact of the existence of a limited and characteristic bourgeois ideology the sociology of knowledge has not undertaken a general examination of the nature of knowledge and of the social element as it possibly determines this nature [9]. Such historically intelligible one-sidedness, which results in a lessening of its chances of perception (Mannheim's "*Sichtchancen*"), does not mean, of course, that this discipline has not discovered and formulated important problems; without it, we should not have had the basis for the particular form of the empirical attitude, an outline of which I am trying to give in this chapter.

The empirical sociologist of knowledge believes that the subject matter of his discipline will become ever clearer and more differentiated with a great number of empirical investigations. He is conscious that the basic concepts occurring in his field must be treated as hypotheses which have to be verified by research. He therefore includes a large number of projects that might be claimed as belonging to other disciplines, but he meets the objection of imperialism by pointing out that only the completion of his projects will determine whether they belong to his field or should be ascribed to other fields. He thus proceeds according to the principle of inclusion and exclusion. This must be kept in mind when the subject matter and the method of the sociology of knowledge, as typical of the empirical attitude, are dealt with later in this paper.

This brief introductory statement may have sufficiently indicated the character of the empirical attitude, which seems to me at once more general and more concrete than the speculative. Unless, however, I am to seem just as naively determined by history as the observers whose historical conditions I have described (assuming my particular use of the word empirical to be universal), I must qualify the adjective empirical. I do not deny my own inability to escape historical determination, but I do believe that my proposal belongs to the "relatively natural *Weltan-schauung*" [10] of the (American) social scientist today, that is, to what we accept as an unquestionable basis for discussion, namely, that the task of science is to find out things of defined interest [11].

In further discussion of this empirical attitude in the sociology of knowledge I develop an outline of the system of this discipline. This outline is divided into four parts: Range of the Subject Matter, Interest and Method, Suggestions of Concepts to Be Tested in Research, and Conclusion.

### RANGE OF THE SUBJECT MATTER

"Range of the subject matter," as I use the term here, describes the totality of the phenomena in which the sociology of knowledge may do research, that is, concerning which a sociologist of knowledge may want to find an explanation with respect to a particular problem in question and thus to make a contribution toward the solution of the fundamental problem of the sociology of knowledge, which may be characterized as the relation between knowledge and social setting [12].

Within the subject matter we have to distinguish between facts (understood as phenomena capable of sense perception, "literal facts") [13] and relations. For the sociology of knowledge the facts are communicated mental events; the relations [14] are those existing between communicated mental events and social units [15].

Mental event is a term that serves as a general denominator for all emotional-intellectual processes, productive or not, ranging from a flash-like feeling, association, or intuition to the creation of a philosophical system or a painting. "Communicated" is a term that serves as a general denominator for all ways of conveying a mental event, ranging from an observer's inference of an observee's flashlike feeling (on the basis of the observee's behavior) to the reading of a book in which a philosophical system is printed or to the contemplation of a painting. The term mental event, which covers, roughly speaking, all acts of knowing, thinking, and feeling, does not imply, by any means, the proposition of its identity with knowledge. If, however, the sociology of knowledge limits its investigations to manifestations of knowledge—as the mental presence of contents of the consciousness or as contents of the consciousness to which the qualification of "I know" can be attached—it excludes thinking and feeling from the beginning. This is unfortunate because in its attempt to contribute, through investigation of concrete phenomena, to the solution of the problem of the relation between knowledge and social setting it pretends, by means of an anticipating hypothesis, to be able to solve this problem on the basis of the limited research material offered by manifestations of knowledge alone. Any research in the sociology also involves manifestations of thinking and feeling. This fact may indeed explain why no sociologist of knowledge has yet attempted to define knowledge from a sociological standpoint, and it may also explain, in particular, why thinking and knowing have not been distinguished in the existing contributions to this discipline. We may even say that, although the workers in this field pretended to be founding a sociology of *knowledge*, actually they were developing a sociology of *thinking* or rather of certain types of thinking [16].

The expression of a mental event, when communicated, may become susceptible of sense perception, and, if so, becomes factual. A list of types of factual communicated mental events includes written communications (books, magazines, newspapers, leaflets, posters, manuscripts of all kinds, including diaries and notes, inscriptions, statistical and other tables, maps, charts, and diagrams); oral communications (conversations, interviews, speeches, addresses, lectures, and sermons); works of the fine arts and of music (paintings, drawings, prints, etchings, illustrations, ornaments, architecture, sculpture, and of instrumental, vocal, and mixed music, photographs, and moving pictures); and, if these are looked on as communicated mental events, also implements made by craft or industry (tools, instruments, and other objects) [17].

A social unit is an individual, a group (i.e., a numerical aggregate as well as a social group, from family to nation and culture), or an institution [18].

The subject matter of the sociology of knowledge is the material with which it has to deal according to its interest and method. Interest and method determine the selection of this material in a double sense: they guide the choice of the facts on which to operate in a specific research task as well as the aspects of each fact, that is, the conceptual scheme on the basis of which the sociologist of knowledge sees the facts and with which he operates on them. The two types of selection are interdependent.

### INTEREST AND METHOD

The method of the sociology of knowledge is that of understanding as realized by its interest in the huge and vague complex of knowledge and social setting. It may be explained as (1) the appropriation of the subjectively intended (immanent [19]) meaning of a given communicated mental event for the universe of discourse [20] of the investigator and of his public, and (2) the sociological interpretation of the results of (1), that is, their direct or indirect reference to social units as selected on the basis of the particular problem under examination—again within the universe of discourse of the investigator and of his public [21].

The typical chronological course of this process of understanding is as follows.

1. The sociologist of knowledge finds himself in a situation in which he discovers a certain object [22].

EXAMPLES. (a) He is listening to a statement by an acquaintance which tempts him to examine it with respect to other topics treated by the same person in order to obtain a fuller picture of his attitudes or of the status of his rational knowledge in a certain field. (b) The sociologist is reading a newspaper and is struck by the similarity between an article and a statement made sometime before by one of his friends.

2. He formulates the facts, those elements in his still vague enterprise that he takes for granted as a basis from which to start his research. Facts in this sense are psychological facts, as distinguished from the literal facts mentioned above; that is, they are items of the content of consciousness which are accepted as such in a specific situation or which are taken for granted after they have been examined as thoroughly as possible [23]. Thus a relation can be, and frequently is, a psychological fact.

EXAMPLES. (a) the sociologist of knowledge takes it for granted that he has discovered a certain attitude toward a value in his acquaintance's remarks and examines other comments made by this person with respect to this attitude, trying to establish a relation between them and the nature of this relation. (b) The sociologist has found out that there is no personal relation between anybody connected with the newspaper in which the article appeared and his friend; he is trying to collect similar statements and to determine how he can characterize the individuals who have made them and how he can classify the relations, personal and other, that obtain among them. (This will not be possible without clarifying a number of concepts that will thus indirectly contribute to the establishment of a scheme of the sociology of knowledge in that their applicability can be tested in further research.) Many similar steps follow, but their common property, readily seen, is the passing from facts and relations to new facts and relations within the limits of the situation as it determines and is determined by the developing problem and the simultaneously developing solution, including specific methodological questions. It may be stated that the solution is not always a definitive answer to the eventually clear-cut formulation of the problem but may also consist in the satisfaction of the investigator's desire for penetration so that he finds himself in a new problemless situation. Throughout this process the investigator uses concepts he assumes are understood unambiguously by his public in close connection with the contexts in which they appear and which he otherwise endeavors to define. (In these illustrations, for instance, the concept of attitude may need elucidation.)

The objection may be made that the process of understanding as indicated here is not exclusive to the sociology of knowledge, just as the range of the subject matter was shown to be shared by other sciences (cf. n. 17). All I can answer to this objection is that I think that the method— that is, *the logical and psychological operations evolved in carrying out research*—is indeed the same in the sociology of knowledge as in other social sciences. It is the synthesis of method, interest, and conceptual apparatus that is distinctive and will eventually produce a distinctive method—that is, *mental operations plus conceptual tools*—and a distinctive subject matter of the sociology of knowledge. I cannot see how, from the empirical, that is, scientific, viewpoint both can ever be more than temporarily definite (though ever more thoroughly analyzed), for there will always remain some new concept to be tested and some new type of material to be examined [24].

### SUGGESTIONS OF CONCEPTS TO BE TESTED IN RESEARCH

The concepts that can be found in the literature of the sociology of knowledge (and elsewhere), especially in Max Weber, Scheler, and Mannheim, as well as those mentioned in various passages of this chapter, must, in my opinion, be tested in research before they can be considered part of the conceptual apparatus of the sociology of knowledge and thus of its method in the empirical sense. The same certainly holds true for the concepts I propose in the following paragraphs.

*Concepts Pertaining to the Methodology of Understanding.* The concept of central attitude may best be introduced by an extract:

> The first pages of philosophical books are held by the reader in special respect. . . . He thinks they [philosophical books] ought to be "especially logical," and by this he means that each sentence depends on the one that precedes it, so that if the famous one stone is pulled, "the whole tumbles." Actually this is nowhere less the case than in philosophical books. Here a sentence does not follow from its predecessor, but much more probably from its successor. If one has not understood a

> sentence or a paragraph, he is helped but little by reading it
> again and again, or even by starting all over, in the conscien-
> tious belief that he is not allowed to leave anything behind
> that he has not understood. Philosophical books refuse such
> methodical ancien-régime strategy; they must be conquered
> à la Napoleon, in a bold thrust against the main body of the
> enemy; and after the victory at this point, the small frontier
> fortresses will fall of themselves. Therefore, if one does not
> understand a certain point, he may most securely expect an
> elucidation if he courageously goes on reading . . . [It is] as
> Schopenhauer said: his whole book contained only a single
> thought, but he could not convey it in any shorter way than
> in the whole book [25].

This extract may be freed from its restriction to philosophical writings
and applied to mental events in general. It implies the distinction between
the literal understanding of a specific element in a communicated mental
event (a word, sentence, gesture, or any other single part of a whole) and
an understanding of the entire context in which that element occurs that
will, in the same act of understanding, make understandable the function
of that element in the whole (communicated mental event). I propose
attitude as a term in the frame of reference for the understanding of an
element.

If by attitude we mean a prefixed selective scheme of action and reaction (including mental actions and reactions), each time we study a single
element we touch an attitude that we consider more comprehensive than
this single element, for we conceive of the latter as a function of the
former. The central attitude, then, is one that through our continuous
efforts in the process of understanding a given communicated mental
event reveals itself as that which renders understandable all single attitudes (each of which, in its turn, renders understandable single elements).
Concrete acts of understanding deviate from this scheme of gradual
understanding in that the central attitude is determined also by our individual approach, including the intensity of our interest, our logical capacity, and our own attitudes engaged, and by the general, though individually varying, capacity for intuition by means of which we jump from
elements to whole complexes of attitudes or even, in rare cases (of poetic
inspiration and, possibly, of "love at first sight"), directly into the grasping of the entire central attitude, or as much as we could probably ever
grasp in a patient step-by-step process.

The extremes of this process of understanding, irrespective of its actual
course, are the feeling of complete strangeness in front of the communicated mental event in question and that of identification with it (which

implies the capicity of re-creating it). In most concrete acts of understanding neither extreme is attained; usually there is some element that we understand from the beginning and some elements that we cannot understand even after the most careful study. (If we think we understand all, we usually have not examined some elements carefully or have overlooked some.) Often, we implicitly or explicitly carry out our study of a phenomenon from a standpoint that is less comprehensive than we are capable of adopting, the comprehensiveness of our standpoint being determined by the particular character of the study in which we are involved. Frequently, too, we are interested in studying only certain properties or aspects of a phenomenon. If, however, as sociologists of knowledge we wish to study something for which the highest degree of understanding is desirable, this aim may be more clearly envisaged if the central attitude is kept in mind as a frame of reference for our efforts. If, for example, we want to understand why a thinker developed a certain theory, we will only in the rarest cases have enough patience, time and interest to acquire the enormous amount of factual knowledge and methodical thoroughness that would enable us to follow the above indicated theoretical outline. Even in less consequential studies we may more easily become conscious of what our task *might* be and what we have *left out* if we keep the concept of central attitude in mind. The concept may help in developing a more conscious method and a greater capacity for the organization of studies [26].

Objections may be raised against my use of the term attitude (in the concepts of central attitude and typical central attitude, discussed later) because this concept claims a much more inclusive aspect of a personality and of a mental event than is customary in current sociological and psychological literature. I have, however, not been able to find a better term. "Position," which might be suggested, seems to point out a physical as well as deliberate characteristic. "Structure of assumptions" again seems to be limited to the sphere of the conscious, if not rational. I should be very grateful for suggestions of a better term.

Two remarks may broaden the aspect of the concept of central attitude.

1. If we keep in mind the concept of central attitude while trying to understand the behavior of a person (starting from his communicated mental event), we concentrate our efforts on becoming capable of forecasting attitudes that are not present in the communicated mental event in question. If, for example, we "know" a theory, we can forecast how it will deal with a subject matter not covered by it; or if we "know" an individual, we can forecast his behavior in situations still unobserved by us. The more factual knowledge about elements and attitudes we possess

and the more conscious a method we adopt, the more we are likely to attain such a degree of understanding, but the more shall we be unable to *formulate* the central attitude we are approaching because we are increasingly identifying ourselves with it. Somewhere along the line of this process of identification lies the scientific understanding that holds the balance between identification and distance through conceptual ties [27].

In our everyday social interactions we constantly practice the central-attitude approach without which we could not know how to behave toward other persons or how to read a book, to see a picture, or to play or listen to a piece of music (because we should not know what to expect of a person in any given situation or how to understand a book or a picture or a piece of music as a whole). An example of a certain type of social interaction which illustrates my point is offered in Ernest Hemingway's *For Whom the Bell Tolls*. Pilar, the Spanish woman, speaks of the "smell of death" and of her own capacity for perceiving it, hence foreseeing the death of the person that has that peculiar smell. She is describing to Robert Jordan, the American Republican soldier in the Spanish war, what nauseating things a person must do to acquire it.

> "But Pilar," Fernando said. "Surely you could not expect one of Don Roberto's education to do such vile things."—"No," Pilar agreed.—"You would not expect him actually to perform those degrading acts?"—"No," Pilar said [28].

Pilar (in spite of her vivid interest in telling her tale) knew that Jordan's attitude was too different from hers to expect him to accept her own central attitude which alone would enable him to accept also her belief in the "smell of death," which is an element in it. In everyday social interaction the case illustrated is less frequent than the case in which we perceive not differences in central attitudes (although likenesses are the exception) but differences in specific attitudes that can be overcome either by a discussion of the matter in question or by orienting our behavior toward individual attitudes of the other person. Differences in central attitudes probably become relevant to everyday social interaction in cases of greater cultural distance.

2. The particular relevance of the concept of central attitude for the sociology of knowledge lies in the possibility that this concept might displace the alternative between the immanent and the sociological interpretation of a communicated mental event, for both interpretations are contained in it. In order to understand an element in the sense of the central-attitude approach, I must be thoroughly acquainted with its intended

(immanent) sense; otherwise I shall have no clue to the understanding of its function within the whole of a mental event. Likewise, I must understand the immanent sense of a whole mental event in order to be able to understand its function in a still more comprehensive whole. (This logical order does not contradict the recipe of the chronological "Napoleonic" method in the quotation from Rosenzweig.) In our analysis we are always dealing, implicitly or explicitly, with the social units that condition or have conditioned a mental event.

If indeed further research should bring about the displacement of the immanent-sociological interpretation in favor of the central-attitude mode of understanding, we should have an example of how a new situation solves a problem (which development, in its turn, could be studied from the standpoint of the sociology of knowledge), how the chances of perception (immanent-sociological interpretation and its subject matter) can be changed (into the central-attitude approach and *its* subject matter), and why [29]. The consideration made in (2) holds true for studies in which the primary interest lies in *understanding* communicated mental events [30].

The scientist, in incorporating central attitudes into his universe of discourse and then in describing them, uses concepts that are current in, or that he must translate into, his public's universe of discourse. With these concepts he rationalizes his approach and his findings; therefore his interest in understanding communicated mental events is limited compared with the extreme of its possible attainment, which includes also nonscientific forms of understanding. This observation leads us to the concept of typical central attitude and to a tentative classification of typical central attitudes.

A typical central attitude (or, shorter, typical attitude) is a concept obtained by the reduction of an empirically traceable attitude to a defined type. This reduction is achieved by the elimination of empirical characteristics as deviations from the type [31]. This definition does not imply that the typical central attitude must necessarily be nonempirical, but it allows us to treat (empirically traceable) mixed attitudes as deviations of typical attitudes. Such concepts as "religious man," "scientist," "efficient business man," are ideal-typical structures of the same class as the structure of typical central attitude. In most empirical individuals whom we characterize as religious men, scientists, or efficient business men we can detect attitudes that are not religious, not scientific, not characteristic of an efficient business man, but which we treat as deviations from the ideal-typical structures. Likewise, when examining a communicated mental event, we facilitate our understanding by operating with typical attitudes [32].

Typical attitudes are autonomous insofar as they have to be understood according to their own structure [33]. At the present stage of methodological development I do not believe it is possible to determine the number of typical attitudes; the concept of typical central attitude itself must first be tested in research. We may assume that all attitudes have developed in historicosociological processes and that each pervades, as it were, all elements of the mental event that led us to become aware of it [34]. As sociologists of knowledge we may divide typical central attitudes into two main classes, the practical and the theoretical. A *practical* attitude is oriented toward concrete facts or conditions, in defense of, or adaptation or opposition to them. The criterion of a practical attitude is the very fact that there are always three possible attitudes toward one concrete condition, one defending it, the other opposing it, the third accepting it. Frequently, but not always, the representatives of the extreme (defending and opposing) attitudes are more easily identifiable with specific social groups than are those of the attitude of mere acceptance. Taking practical attitudes at random from our contemporary scene, I may mention the feudal attitude as adopted by the lord and the slave, the democratic versus the totalitarian, the imperialistic versus the anarchistic, and the capitalist versus the socialist or communist attitudes. A *theoretical* attitude is oriented toward the solution of a mental task, irrespective of the question of the cause, the use, and the effect of this solution in the practical sphere. The criterion of a theoretical attitude is that its corresponding attitudes of opposition and acceptance do not necessarily exist, but if they do they are likewise oriented toward a mental, not a practical task.

There are not only a great many typical attitudes but also an undefined number of empirical and typical combinations of theoretical, practical, and theoretical-practical attitudes (among them many in which the characterization as theoretical or practical may obstruct rather than facilitate understanding). Furthermore, the impact of emotion and mood is an element of first importance in understanding attitudes.

It must also be noted that attitudes determined by the application of theoretical solutions to practical tasks are practical attitudes (applied magic, applied science, etc.), but they may be considered identical with the social-activity attitude of those who represent them; thus we obtain the magician's attitude, the technologist's attitude, the priest's attitude, and so forth, as well as the corresponding attitudes that oppose or accept the concrete facts or conditions toward which they are oriented.

The most readily distinguishable among theoretical attitudes are the magical, the religious, the artistic, the philosophical, and the scientific. Although there are many practical typical attitudes, I cannot think of more than these five, or combinations among them, in which man can approach any mental task. As a tentative hypothesis we may therefore call them fundamental human (central) attitudes [35].

MAGICAL.   In attempting to define an attitude we observe or discuss we must try to avoid the confusion of our own interpretation with the feelings that the participants in the attitude may have themselves. Thus in the case of the magical attitude, which is usually far from our own, we must not confuse our interpretation of the magical performance with its meaning to the performer. The main emphasis in my listing typical central attitudes lies in their distinctness as autonomous frames of reference for our understanding of concrete communicated mental events. If we are excited, curious, scornful, or filled with dread when observing a magical performance, we must control our inclination to suppose that our feelings are shared by the performer; however, our emotional participation may be the basis of a successive understanding that can eventually be communicated to others in conceptualized form, whereas a mere analysis of the logical structure of magical performance—especially if referred to some system of our own—certainly neglects the emotional aspect of that performance. The investigation of magic through field work or field-work reports (mainly books by anthropologists and ethnologists), if undertaken with the intention of identifying ourselves with the magical attitude observed or described, will bring about a much more meaningful presentation than the one given by an attempt at defining it, for example, as "mistaking an ideal connection for a real one" [36], which definition is correct only from the standpoint of our own conception of reality and ideality. Probably one of the difficulties in understanding the magical attitude is that when magic has become the attitude of a minority, that is, in most civilized (as contrasted to preliterate) peoples, it becomes esoteric and disguises itself in opaque codelike formulas [37].

RELIGIOUS.   Having in mind the reservations that must be remembered when trying to define attitudes, I may attempt a hypothetical definition of the religious attitude (which is drawn from certain terms of Max Scheler): the nature or the fundamental assumption of the religious attitude is the attempt, or the success of this attempt, at getting in some kind of contact with some kind of a reality conceived of as powerful and sacred [38].

ARTISTIC.   To say that art (practice, enjoyment, and reproduction) is aesthetic and inspirational-intuitive is only expanding the term art, and conveys little to those who have not experienced the artistic attitude. This does not mean, of course, that certain concepts may not lead toward its understanding. The statement "To so enter into . . . [the object] in nature and in art that the enjoyed meanings of life may become a part of living is the attitude of aesthetic appreciation" [39], may well recall, in certain readers, recollections of their own experiences which greatly enhance the understanding of the autonomy of the artistic attitude. Hugo von Hofmannsthal may convey the specific character of the artistic, or of the romantic-artistic, attitude when he says, "The whole soul is never fully integrated (*beisammen*), except in rapture (*Entzückung*)" [40], or, "Where can thy self be found? Always in the deepest enchantment which thou hast undergone" [41]. According to my conception of the artistic attitude, knowledge exemplified in or knowledge about the nature of lyric, fiction, drama, fine arts, and music or of artistic techniques—literary, fine-arts, and musical productions—cannot be acquired or understood outside the artistic attitude.

PHILOSOPHICAL. Martin Heidegger's formulation of the fundamental metaphysical question seems to me a formula of the typical question of the philosophical attitude: "Why is there being (*Seiendes*) at all, and not rather nothing (*Nichts*)?" [42].

> Philosophy, according to Aristotle's striking remark, begins with . . . "wonder" that anything of "this" constant nature is there. . . . [It] *ultimately* drives at the question of how the ground and the cause of the world totality must be qualified so that "such a thing" . . . might be possible [43].

All metaphysical, ethical, logical, and aesthetic theories are ultimately conceived and understood in the philosophical attitude.

SCIENTIFIC. The most striking illustration I know of the scientific attitude is Galileo's *Eppur si muove!* Dewey thus circumscribes the scientific attitude:

> Scientific subject-matter and procedures grow out of the direct problems and methods of common sense . . . , and . . . react into the latter in a way that enormously refines, expands and liberates the contents and the agencies at the disposal of common sense. . . . Scientific subject-matter is intermediate, not final and complete in itself [44].

This statement leaves open the question whether the sociological function of science as indicated here is universally true or only in modern civilization. It may well be essential to science that its findings are being aimed at with the understanding of their accessibility and control through future research [45].

Although the concepts of central attitude and of typical central attitude belong to the methodology of understanding as it may be developed in research in the sociology of knowledge, I now wish to introduce briefly some tentative concepts that may eventually be of value in determining more accurately the nation of social setting.

*Concepts Concerning the Relationship of the Author of a Mental Event to That Event.*   I wish to begin with the concept of distance and again to introduce it with a quotation.

> . . . it is to be observed that it is the same with time as it is with place; . . . as beyond a certain limit we can form no distinct imagination of distance—that is to say, as we usually imagine all objects to be equally distant from us, and as if they were on the same plane, if their distance from us exceeds 200 feet, or if their distance from the position we occupy is greater than we can distinctly imagine—so we imagine all objects to be equally distant from the present time, and refer them as if to one moment, if the period to which their existence belongs is separated from the present by a longer interval than we can usually imagine distinctly [46].

> . . . it follows that all objects which are separated from the present time by a longer interval than our imagination has any power to determine affect us equally slightly, although we know them to be separated from one another by a large space of time [47].

Here we are less interested in the element of distance as pertaining to human thinking than in its variability in different mental events. We may define distance as the intensity of participation of the author of a mental event in certain elements of that event. Because distance is a relative concept, we must have at our disposal at least two comparable examples in order to be able to discover it; these examples can be within the same communicated mental event or distributed among various events or one of them may be theoretically constructed by the investigator for reasons of comparison. The nature of the participation of the author of a mental event in certain of its elements varies with the magical, religious, artistic, philosophical, and scientific attitudes. I should like to illustrate the case of the scientific attitude (thus myself offering an example of distance in that I am not illustrating other attitudes).

The participation of the scientist in his work takes the form of the conceptual penetration of and the selection of elements in his subject matter. The sociologist of knowledge can discover distance in scientific work by examining the definiteness of concepts in use, as well as aspects of certain elements in the subject matter covered by the scientist. I want to show the significance of the concept of distance by considering the phenomenon of conceptual penetration.

We must distinguish among three areas involved in any scientific work, namely, the area of the taken-for-granted, the area of distance, and the residual area. First, the *area of the taken-for-granted* includes the unwitting assumptions of the scientist, his and his groups' folkways, mores, laws, beliefs, preferences, and feelings, in short, his undiscussed or "natural" *Weltanschauung*. Here we cannot speak of distance, because the scientist identifies himself with it imaginatively. Second, the *area of distance* is of varying definiteness, of discussed concepts, of doubt, examination, penetration, definition, arrangement, rearrangement, illustration, and opinion. Here the outsider can discover distance by observing how the area of the taken-for-granted interferes with the interest in conceptual penetration, how personal experiences of the author, his scientific, logical, and specialized training, as well as circumstances of the publication of the work under examination (the author's mood, emotion, physical and psychic endurance, plus all kinds of conditions of the publication itself), and how specific attitudes or the central attitude of the author influence the degree of his conceptual penetration [48]. Third, the *residual area* [49], in which the concept of distance again cannot be applied, covers undiscussed aspects of the phenomena, concepts discussed by the scientist, or aspects that might be considered relevant but have been overlooked or deliberately omitted from discussion. The reasons why these unexamined aspects are considered relevant must be defined by the investigator in each case. It should be pointed out further that the failure of the scientist to consider some aspects of his subject matter is not to be attributed to his taking them for granted but rather to a conscious or unconscious refusal to bring them into the discussion. An illustration may be found in the current sociology of knowledge in general [50]—and particularly in the work of Mannheim—in which works of literature are discussed or mentioned without taking into account their aesthetic qualities. This procedure is quite distinct from taking aesthetic qualities for granted in that the question whether these qualities can be factors in certain situations involving works of literature does not even occur, nor is there any awareness of a significant omission among these factors. (In this example, of course, I intend only to give an illustration of the concept of residual area, but I can neither prove my statement regarding the lack of concern with aesthetic qualities in the current sociology of knowledge nor can I suggest reasons for this lack. All this, however, would have to be done if one tried to apply the concept of residual area in a concrete research case.)

With respect to types of knowledge, we may call the type we find in the area of the taken-for-granted naïve or practical; that within the area of discussion and of distance, reflective or theoretical; nonknowledge dominates the residual area. To summarize drastically the three concepts discussed, we might say that the area of the taken-for-granted covers things that are there, but the scientist does not know it; the area of distance covers things the scientist sees with varying clarity; and the residual area covers all that might be there but is not.


### CONCLUSION

It might be permissible to call this paper the first outline of a new attitude if it were not for a possible objection to the term "new"—an objection that might be raised by pointing out that an empirical attitude is characteristic already of the French and some other studies in the sociology of knowledge. I am disregarding this possible objection for the moment in order to develop the following line of thought. By characterizing the attitude outlined as empirical (as contrasted to speculative) its place in the history of the sociology of knowledge may be located, but this location does not familiarize the reader with this attitude in a way that will enable him to identify himself with it and to forecast how it will deal with a subject matter not covered by it [51]. *This* is indeed the purpose of this chapter—In this sense it conveys a "single thought." If this attitude takes root and is shared by other students and taken as a basis for research, it may possibly be identified as an attitude characteristic of the sociology of knowledge. We must recognize that all sciences correspond to specific attitudes that are hardly accessible to outsiders. It may be that the peculiar viewpoint of the sociology of knowledge, which sees mental events in their relative social settings, has already enabled us to recognize the peculiarities of our own attitude at a stage of early development, whereas we deal with the attitudes of other sciences at a stage of relative stabilization (after they have shaped their outwardly accepted folkways) [52].

I conclude with two remarks. First, I propose that psychology and psychoanalysis should be considered with respect to concepts that might be of immediate use in research in the sociology of knowledge [53]. Furthermore, I wish to mention a few conceptual complexes (which only for the reason of their being mentioned are not residual in my paper); I think these complexes might be treated for the purpose of obtaining additional conceptual tools useful for research. One is the concept of the *literal versus the symbolic aspect* in mental events [54]. Another is that of *language,* both in specific slang and terminology, and in a more fundamental consideration of the significance of language as a medium of communicating mental events [55]. A further complex is the relation between the *purpose* (overt as well as latent) of the communication of a mental event and the purposes of the groups to which its author belongs and the effects of his communication on various groups, including the question whether a rule obtaining between these relations can be established. Finally we may investigate the relation of *logical contradictions* in communicated mental events to central attitudes, and it may be possible to treat these contradictions as indices of (typical) attitudes.

Second, I mention at random some projects, or rather complexes of projects, that may show the breadth of the field of research in the sociology of knowledge.

1. A study of the Nazi movement with emphasis on the question how knowledge, attitudes, beliefs, preferences, viewpoints, the areas of the taken-for-granted, the residual, and distances in the conceptual penetration exhibited by which people are influenced in what way, by which means, and with what effects; what the differences are in regard to the role knowledge in totalitarianism and in democracy; what suggestions for eventual educational and other social reforms in the American democracy can be made if and as they seem to be warranted on the basis of such a study. (This last point may fall under the name of applied sociology of knowledge.)

2. A biography of a sociologist, possibly a living man who could cooperate. The following points should be investigated in particular: approach to his central attitude; deviations (and their explanations) from the scientific character (to be defined) of his writings; investigation of his social setting through his work (including articles and reviews) and of its presence in his work and in his own statements in interviews, reports of conversations with him, diaries, letters, unpublished manuscripts; effect of his personality and his work on precisely defined individuals, groups, and institutions. Those sources that should have been used according to the scope of the study but were not accessible would have to be stated and the reasons for their inaccessibility explained. (This last remark applies to any research project in the sociology of knowledge.)

3. A preliminary typology of American sociologists with reference to their social backgrounds, their official and private research interests, their methods, their influences on defined individuals, groups, and institutions and through these—not directly—on sociological thought, or with reference to other viewpoints.

4. Who reads what, when, how, why, and with what effect on what and whom? (To be made specific as a sample study.)

5. Who sees which moving pictures, how often, when, why, and with what effect on what and whom? (To be made specific as a sample study.)

6. Propaganda, including commercial advertising, is a vast field for research in the sociology of knowledge. An arbitrary example: What are the processes of thought that lead a banker, a seamstress, a grade-school teacher, an army officer, a college professor, an unemployed Texan, or an unemployed European refugee to buy a certain type of clothes? What is the methodological significance —adequacy or insufficiency—of these occupational and national categories within this research?

7. Who spells "through" "thru," "though" "tho," "thought" "thot," etc.? For how long has he been doing it, under the influence of whom or what, for which reasons, under which circumstances, and to what extent has this usage become a habit or folkway (taken-for-granted) with him? Can we detect any influence of this orthographic custom on the thought of such a person?

8. How do (certain selected and defined) individuals write book reviews? For which papers? Why? Who determines the selection of the books and according to what principles? Is there something that might be called monopolization in connection with the reviewing of certain books for certain publications? How do these reviewers obtain their information about the books to be reviewed? How frequently and how intensively is a book read before it is reviewed? What influence has the reviewer's mood, the amount of time at his disposal, his expectation with regard to the printing of the review, and his relations with the publiher, the author, the newspaper or magazine owner, and certain readers on the nature of his review? What are the effects of his review on selected groups

with respect to their purchase, opinion, and commendation of the book reviewed?

9. What differences are there in the roles played by material objects, folkways, institutions, emotions, metaphors, and symbols in the poetry of various contemporary poets or of selected poets of various defined epochs and cultures? Can any definable relation be established between these roles and the social backgrounds and central attitudes of these poets? Can any definable relation be established between these roles and certain epochs and cultures?

10. A parallel study with regard to musical forms; for example, what is the role of the triplet in selected pieces of Beethoven, Wagner, or Gershwin? [Questions corresponding to those in (9).]

11. What do selected individuals mean by "chair," "beauty," "nazism?" Which elements in their statements are stable, which vary? What are the relations between certain elements of these statements and various defined characteristics of the individuals who have made them?

12. A study of magical and religious texts and usages to determine the particular character of knowledge embodied in them. (To be made specific.)

13. A comparative study of translations by various persons into the same language or into different languages of an identical text, with special attention given to the relation between literalness and symbolic character determined by the interplay between the areas of the taken-for-granted observed in the translators (as expressed in terms of their respective individualities or cultures—both terms to be defined) and linguistic demands of the technical task (likewise a term to be defined), and, furthermore, with attention to the question of the selection of the elements in the original text which are transformed, preserved, and lost in the translation and to the effect of the translation on defined groups [56].

Such projects might contribute toward the demonstration of the usefulness or uselessness of concepts that are part of the theory of the sociology of knowledge. Studies of this kind will suggest not only other conceptual approaches in the field but also many other projects for further study so that eventually the objective, analytical methods developed by the sociology of knowledge may become a part of our more general thought and folkways.

*NOTES*

1. Part of this chapter was presented to the Sociology Section of the South-western Social Science Association, Dallas, Texas, April 11, 1941.

2. The most important works in this regard are those by Max Scheler, Karl Mannheim, Alexander von Schelting, and Ernst Grünwald. It would, however, be an immense task to collect all philosophical and other writing that, explicitly or implicitly, has some bearing on the sociology of knowledge and to build up a philosophical system of this discipline. Cf. Ernst Grünwald, *Das Problem der Soziologie des Wissens* (Wien: Braumüller, 1934), Chapter II, especially pp. 52–55.

3. Talcott Parsons, "The Role of Theory in Social Research," *American Sociological Review, 2* (1938), 15; Robert S. Lynd, *Knowledge for What?* (Princeton, N.J.: Princeton University Press, 1939), especially Sections IV and V. Robert K. Merton, in his review of Znaniecki's *The Social Role of the Man of Knowledge, American Sociological Review, 6* (1941), 112, distinguishes between sociology of knowledge and sociological theory of knowledge; cf. Arthur O. Lovejoy "Reflections on the History of Ideas," *Journal of the History of Ideas, I* (1940), 17–18 and Gerard De Gré, "The Sociology of Knowledge and the Problem of Truth," *ibid., 2* (1941), 115. Among empirical contributions, in addition to those listed in Karl Mannheim, *Ideology and Utopia* (New York: Harcourt, Brace, 1936), pp. 303–304, and, in addition to some of the well-known works of Durkheim, Lévy-Bruhl, Halbwachs, Granet, and others, Mannheim's own "Das konservative Denken. Soziologische Beiträge zum Werden des politisch-historischen Denkens in Deutschland," *Archiv für Sozialwissenschaft und Sozialpolitik,* 57 (1927), 68–142, 470–495, and Ernst Kohn-Bramstedt, *Aristocracy and the Middle-Classes in Germany: Social Types in German Literature, 1830–1900* (London: King, 1937) may be mentioned. Among works of the pre-*wissenssoziologischen* phase an outstanding approach to the sociology of knowledge which has decidedly influenced the entire discussion in the field is exemplified in Max Weber's *Gesammelte Aufsätze zur Religionssoziologie,* 3 vols. (Tübingen: Mohr, 1920, 1921, 1921), a famous part of which has been translated by Talcott Parsons as *The Protestant Ethic and the Spirit of Capitalism* (New York: Scribner, 1930). The listing of a large number of "implicit" American contributions would require a special study, for "what the sociology of knowledge deals with systematically and explicitly has been touched on only incidentally within the framework of the special discipline of social psychology or has been an unexploited by-product of empirical research." (Louis Wirth, Preface to Mannheim's *Ideology and Utopia, op. cit.,* pp. xx–xxi.)

4. Cf. Grünwald, *op. cit.,* pp. 1–51, especially 32–42, and 60–61; Mannheim, *Ideology and Utopia, op. cit.,* pp. 278–280; Gottfried Salomon, "Historischer Materialismus und Ideologienlehre," in *Jahrbuch für Soziologie,* Vol. II (Karlsruhe: Braun, 1926), pp. 386–423; Helmuth Plessner, "Abwandlungen des

Ideologiegedankens," *Kölner Vierteljahrshefte für Soziologie*, **10** (1931), 147–170.

5. Max Scheler, "Die Formen des Wissens und die Bildung," in *Philosophische Weltanschauung* (Bonn: Cohen, 1929), p. 113.

6. In regard to pre-Marxist thinkers who were expressly interested in the "social determination" of knowledge see Hans Speier, "The Social Determination of Ideas," *Social Research*, **5** (1938), 203–205, 198; Hans Speier, "Militarism in the Eighteenth Century," *Social Research*, **3** (1936), 330; Grünwald, *op. cit.*, pp. 4 ff.; Mannheim, *op. cit.*, p. 55; Werner Sombart, "Die Anfänge der Soziologie," in Melchior Palyi, Ed., *Hauptprobleme der Soziologie: Erinnerungsgabe für Max Weber* (München: Duncker und Humblot, 1923), p. 15. I extend my thanks to Dr. Harry Estill Moore, University of Texas, for suggesting a study of the work of the English institutional historians such as Maine, Maitland, Harris, Hobhouse, Toynbee, and Tawney, with reference to their possible contributions to the sociology of knowledge.

7. Scheler, of course, must not be interpreted as a sociologist but as a philosopher. The controversy between Scheler and the Marxist Max Adler strikingly reveals the two contrasting positions of the metaphysical and the Marxist ideologist [*Verhandlungen des Vierten Deutschen Soziologentages* (Tübingen: Mohr, 1925), pp. 118–237].

8. Talcott Parsons, *The Structure of Social Action* (New York: McGraw-Hill, 1937), p. 14, n. 1. Hans Speier ("The Social Determination of Ideas," *loc. cit.*, *passim*) implies that his technical and promotive or theoretical ideas are rational and fully conscious. C. Wright Mills, "Methodological Consequences of the Sociology of Knowledge," *American Journal of Sociology*, **46** (1940), 316–330, speaks of inquiries (*passim*) as the subject matter of the sociology of knowledge but seems to imply also that certain types of language (p. 322) and, more generally, verbal components of actions (p. 329) are within its field. Alexander von Schelting, *Max Webers Wissenschaftslehre* (Tübingen: Mohr, 1934), p. 85, insists that the sociology of knowledge has to distinguish between two spheres: (1) knowledge of empirical data, epistemology, and methodology, and (2) "those structures of thought . . . in which this . . . empirical world . . . is transcended." He does not decide, however, whether one or both spheres are the subject matter of the sociology of knowledge; neither does he do so in his earlier article, "Zum Streit um die Wissenssoziologie," *Archiv für Sozialwissenschaft und Sozialpolitik*, **62** (1929), 1–65, in which he develops this distinction more extensively on the basis of the categories of Alfred Weber's *Kultursoziologie*.

9. With the exception of Scheler; cf. n. 15. This limitation of the sociology of knowledge has hardly been changed by the highly significant contributions of the French school (mainly Durkheim) or by the irrational-naturalistic thought of Nietzsche, Pareto, Sorel, probably Freud, and others. For an excellent general characterization of the German compared with the Anglo-French thinker type and the former's peculiar atmosphere see Ernst Troeltsch, *Der Historismus und seine Probleme* (Tübingen: Mohr, 1922), pp. 141–143 (Vol. III of *Gesammelte Schriften*); see also Pitirim A. Sorokin, "Some Contrasts of Contemporary European and American Sociology, *Social Forces*, **8** (1929), 57–62.

10. Max Scheler's term: "Probleme einer Soziologie des Wissens," in *Die Wissensformen und die Gesellschaft* (Leipzig: Neue-Geist, 1926), p. 59.

11. Cf. John Dewey, *Logic: The Theory of Inquiry* (New York: Holt, 1938), p. 66. My forthcoming attempt at a theory that could account for the interest in the sociology of knowledge and the role of this discipline—both lasting after and far more significant than its historical incipiency—cannot be outlined here; it has to do with the gradual breakdown of traditions and norms and the possibility of nihilism in the last hundred years in European development as typified in a psychologically accessible process I call labilization.

12. It is probably Mannheim whose theories have been most widely discussed, and he may therefore be taken as representative in indicating the ultimate inconclusiveness of attempts at a clear definition of the concepts of knowledge and social setting (or however else these phenomena may be designated) and their relation. Mannheim's own terms (cf. *Ideology and Utopia, op. cit.*, pp. 239–256) have received much criticism that has revealed their ambiguity and logical insufficiency; the most thorough analysis was made by von Schelting (*Max Webers Wissenschaftslehre, op. cit.*, pp. 94–167). This gist of the extensive discussion of the general problem of the sociology of knowledge (see bibliography in Mannheim, *op. cit.*, pp. 300–303) lies in the relation between the social process and knowledge and in the clarification of these two concepts; particularly, it lies in the determination of imputation, that is, in the question how a specific piece of knowledge can be ascribed to a specific group or class and what exactly is meant by such terms as imputation or ascription. Even the most recent treatment of this theme with which I am acquainted [Arthur Child, "The Problem of Imputation in the Sociology of Knowledge," *Ethics*, **51** (1941), 200–219] does not put the question generally, as the title of the article might suggests, but limits it to the internal criticism (p. 200) of Lukács, Grünwald, and Mannheim, thus remaining within the historical boundaries mentioned before in this paper.

13. Cf. Morris R. Cohen and Ernest Nagel, *An Introduction to Logic and Scientific Method* (New York: Harcourt, Brace, 1934), p. 217.

14. In the process of understanding relations may become psychological facts.

15. The only purpose of this terms is to serve as a one-word name for individuals, groups, and institutions.

16. Cf. von Schelting, *op. cit.*, pp. 78, 85–87. The most inclusive definition of knowing is, I think, that of Max Scheler. Knowing is "the participation of a being (*Seiendes*) in the existence (*Sosein*) of another being" ("Erkenntnis und Arbeit," in *Die Wissensformen und die Gesellschaft, op. cit.*, p. 247). If, however, we try to find the empirical phenomenon, or fact, corresponding to these metaphysical units mentioned, we again must stop at general mental events and investigate concrete problems in order to arrive not only at an empirically controllable definition of knowledge but also at the relations between knowledge and other mental processes and their results.

17. This list of phenomena accessible to sense perception (facts) about which

the sociologist of knowledge wants to find out something is, of course, not peculiar to this discipline; the specific character of the sociology of knowledge lies in its selection and its treatment of these facts.

18. Among the social units listed only "individual" and "numerical aggregate" are capable of sense perception, and "social group" and "institution" are mental units that may be facts psychologically in the minds of the observers of and participants in them. See Eric Voegelin, "The Growth of the Race Idea," *The Review of Politics*, 2 (1940), 284. Almost no term used in sociology, and thus none of the abovementioned, has found a definition that is generally agreed on. My use of these terms is based on their current conception in American sociology, but this use must be specified in concrete research whenever any doubt occurs in the mind of the investigator about the unambiguosness of a term adopted.

19. Cf. Karl Mannheim, "Ideologische und soziologische Interpretation der geistigen Gebilde" ["The Ideological and the Sociological Interpretation of Intellectual Phenomena"], in *Jahrbuch für Soziologie, op. cit.*, Vol. II, pp. 424 ff.

20. My definition of the universe of discourse (of an individual or a group) is the totality of concepts used (by that individual or group) plus their implications.

21. I have made no attempt at a definition of understanding; this would transcend the scope of this chapter. In accordance with the empirical attitude in the sociology of knowledge, I believe in the necessity of concrete research before a logical system (as evolved in such research) can be defined. I fully realize that in any such attempt the problem of understanding will be of the greatest importance.. The attack on it, I think, will be based largely on Max Weber's conception as contained, especially, in "Ueber einige Kategorien der verstehenden Soziologie" [1913], in *Gesammelte Aufsätze zur Wissenschaftslehre* (Tübingen: Mohr, 1922), pp. 403–450, and "Methodische Grundlagen der Soziologie" (1920), *ibid.*, pp. 503–523, and on its analyses by von Schelting, *loc. cit.*, and Talcott Parsons, *The Structure of Social Action, op. cit.*, pp. 610–639. Special attention is likely to be given to such concepts as causal reference, ideal-types, *aktuelles* and *motivationsmassiges Verstehen*, and acausal complexes of meaning. Strictly speaking, we must distinguish between the primary method of the sociology of knowledge—that of understanding—and various secondary methods whose use has the purpose of enhancing understanding and of checking the results reached in the process of understanding. The selection of these auxiliary methods is determined by the particular problem under examination. They may involve the use of statistical devices and various tests, scores, and scales. In the discussion of the chronological course of the process of understanding I proceed without regard to possible auxiliary methods.

22. Cf. John Dewey, *op. cit.*, p. 67.

23. Cf. a similar aspect of fact in Cohen and Nagel, *op. cit.*, p. 218.

24. "This is the *fate*, more, this is the *sense* of scientific work . . . : every scientific 'fulfillment' means new 'questions' and *wants* to be 'surpassed' and

become obsolete . . . Fundamentally, this process is infinite." [Max Weber, "Wissenschaft als Beruf" (1918), in *Gesammelte Aufsätze zur Wissenschaftslehre, op. cit.*, pp. 534–535.] (Cf. "Science as a Vocation, in *From Max Weber, op. cit.*, p. 138.)

25. Franz Rosenzweig, "Das neue Denken" (1925), in *Kleinere Schriften* (Berlin: Schocken, 1937), pp. 375–376.

26. This presentation of the "central attitude" is itself an example of an attempt to convey a "single thought." The concept—still speaking by way of illustration—is an element that can be understood as a function of an attitude to be coordinated with other elements and attitudes. This process of understanding eventually leads the investigator to the central attitude of the concept's author which gave rise to his study.

27. See the discussion of a typical central attitude, pp. 470 ff.

28. Ernest Hemingway, *For Whom the Bell Tolls* (New York: Scribner, 1940), p. 257.

29. On chances of perception see n. 48.

30. Thus my general characterization of the process of understanding might become obsolete, but see my reference to scientific progress in n. 24.

31. Typical central attitude is an ideal-typical structure; on ideal type (Max Weber's term) see Max Weber, "Methodische Grundlagen der Soziologie," *op. cit.*, pp. 505–506; Talcott Parsons, *op. cit.*, pp. 653 ff., 716; von Schelting, *op. cit.*, pp. 329 ff.; Marcel Weinreich, *Max Weber, l'homme et le savant* (Paris: Vrin, 1938), pp. 96–113.

32. Typical central attitude—a concept—has nothing to do with a discussion of human nature which aims at establishing variable and invariable human properties.

33. This statement does not imply that we do not have to assume changeless components in mental processes, such as certain processes of thought or of feeling (a syllogism, the feeling of anxiety). The important problem of changeless versus changeable elements in mental processes has to my knowledge not yet found a detailed examination with respect to the establishment of a sociology of knowledge (in spite of the works of Durkheim, Lévy-Bruhl, and Granet). The most explicit statement about it has been made, I think, by von Schelting ("Zum Streit um die Wissenssoziologie," *op. cit*, p. 31). According to him, nobody has yet succeeded in proving "that the fundamental forms of apperception and categories and the basic forms of the contemplative, explicatory, concluding, and systematizing forms of the human intellect . . . have . . . changed." As a hypothesis I assume that there are certain logical and emotional processes whose function, rather than nature, changes with the typical central attitudes in which they appear. See also Francis M. Cornford, *The Laws of Motion in Ancient Thought* (Cambridge: University Press, 1931) and other works of his. Alvin P. Bradford's forthcoming thesis (University of Texas), "An Approach to the Philosophy of Adjustment: A Consideration of Organic Categories and the Sociology of Knowledge," should throw light on this problem.

34. This hypothesis, of course, does not concern a fundamental assumption of the sociology of knowledge as well as of sociology and psychology, namely, the possibility of explaining how attitudes originate in a given case and, eventually, of establishing a typology of attitudes and coordinated causes. In attempting such an explanation and such a typology on the basis of research, however, the process of understanding the attitude itself comes first.

35. Without daring to answer the question regarding human nature raised in n. 32. Of course, actions are performed in the spirit of these attitudes, but we can understand them, at least more easily, by understanding these attitudes. In many cases understanding may be attained by reference to the attitude of social activity (a practical attitude).

36. E. B. Tylor, quoted in Sigmund Freud, "Totem and Taboo" (1913) in *The Basic Writings of Sigmund Freud* (New York: Modern Library) p. 868.

37. See Eliphas Lévi, *Histoire de la magie* (Paris: Alcan, 1892), p. 1. This book, as well as Lévi's two others—*Dogme et rituel de la haute magie*, 2 vols. (Paris: Alcan, 1894), and *La clef des grands mystères* (Paris: Alcan, n.d.)—contains a multitude of descriptions of magical practices among civilized peoples. Being themselves magically biased, the three works are likely to familiarize the reader with the magical attitude.

38. Cf. Max Scheler, "Probleme einer Soziologie des Wissens," *op. cit.*, p. 64.

39. G. H. Mead, "The Nature of Aesthetic Experience," *International Journal of Ethics,* **36** (1926), 384.

40. Hugo von Hofmannsthal, *Buch der Freunde*, 2nd. ed. (Leipzig: Insel, 1929), p. 36.

41. *Ibid.*, p. 39.

42. Martin Heidegger, *Was ist Metaphysik?* [1929] (Bonn: Cohen, 1931), p. 28. Similarly Max Scheler, *Man's Place in Nature*, translated and with an introduction by Hans Meyerhoff (New York: Noonday Press, 1961) pp. 88–90. A position that stresses the constructive aspect of the philosophical shock is adopted by Karl Jaspers; see his *Existenzphilosophie* (Berlin: de Gruyter, 1938), p. 1, and his *Man in the Modern Age* (1931), translated by Eden and Cedar Paul (London: Routledge and Kegan Paul, 1933), p. 186.

43. Max Scheler, "Erkenntnis und Arbeit," *op. cit.*, p. 253. It is obvious that these quotations and references refer to an attitude entirely different from that of American pragmatic philosophy, especially C. S. Peirce and John Dewey, which is determined in part by the emphasis on practice as against reflection; see John Dewey, *The Quest for Certainty: A Study of the Relation of Knowledge and Action* (New York: Putnam, 1929), p. 37. For a discussion of pragmatism, especially Peirce and William James, from the Schelerian position, see Max Scheler, *op. cit.*, pp. 259–324. The autonomy of the philosophical attitude is more evident in the former quotations (with their philosophy for philosophy's sake) than in the pragmatic, less self-sufficient position.

44. John Dewey, *Logic, op. cit.*, p. 66.

45. See the quotation from Max Weber in n. 24: it continues to discuss the

meaning of science in the light of occidental intellectualization and rationalization (*op. cit.*, pp. 535–536). For the development of science in the occident cf. Wilhelm Dilthey, *Einleitung in die Geisteswissenschaften* (1883), 3rd ed. (Leipzig: Teubner, 1933), pp. 150–386.

46.   Spinoza, *Ethic* [1677] (London: Frowde, 1910), p. 181.

47.   *Ibid.*, p. 188.

48.   It may be noted that sufficient research with respect to distance may enable us to find typical distances that may be ordered according to the degree of their frequency (with the possible result of finding relatively permanent and variable distances) within certain historical periods or according to types of scientist and science. The distance-taken-for-granted-residual approach seems to me more specific, that is, more easily verifiable by research, than Mills's utilization of G. H. Mead's concept of the generalized other ("Language, Logic, and Culture," *American Sociological Review*, 4 (1939), 672–676, or Mannheim's "chances of perception" (*Ideology and Utopia,* op cit., pp. 237–238, *passim*). I cannot, however, enter into an examination here of the relatedness of these concepts.

49.   I owe this expression to Talcott Parsons' term residual category (*op. cit.*, pp. 16–20); however, the meanings of residual category and residual area are different.

50.   Again with the exception of Scheler and certain scholars of the French school.

51.   Cf. the discussion of central attitude above.

52.   This consideration might be taken into account in an examination of the conditions that were necessary for the rise of the sociology of knowledge in addition to what Mannheim wrote about this question (in *Ideology and Utopia, op. cit.*, pp. 252–253, "The Acquisition of Perspective as a Pre-Condition for the Sociology of Knowledge").

53.   Perhaps similar to the way in which Harold D. Lasswell has utilized psychoanalysis in his consideration of politics.

54.   One suggestion how to develop this problem may be found in the distinction between symbolic and actual behavior as indicated in Richard T. LaPiere and Paul R. Farnsworth, *Social Psychology* (New York: McGraw-Hill, 1936), pp. 232–233.

55.   In the direction of such studies as Ogden and Richards, *The Meaning of Meaning.*

56.   It is obvious that much literature that is useful, directly or indirectly, already exists in connection with these projects or with certain of their aspects and should be consulted with respect to their eventual formulation and execution.

Reprinted from *Philosophy of Science,* 10 (1943), 104–123, by permission of the publisher. The essay has been edited and partially revised by the author.

# 27

## THE UNIQUE
## AND THE GENERAL:
Toward a Philosophy of Sociology. 1948

### PHILOSOPHY OF SCIENCE

The term philosophy of science is used here to refer to the study of the approaches and methodologies of the sciences [1]. By approach is understood the totality of the *presuppositions* of a given science (body of sciences or scientific product): more precisely, both philosophical and scientific presuppositions, that is, categories, postulates, and premises as *conditions*, and existential presuppositions (organic, geographic, and sociocultural). By methodology is understood the *intellectual-emotional structure* of a given science; that is, its categories, postulates, and premises as *characteristics* and its concepts, methods, and techniques. Further, I advocate investigating a given science (body of sciences or scientific product) in a study of its approach and methodology. Finally, I submit that the best understanding of either of the two is impossible without the study of the other. More specifically, I advocate the interpretation of the intellectual structure or methodology of a particular science (body of sciences, e.g., the social sciences, or scientific product) (immanent interpretation [2]), followed by the study of its presuppositions or underlying approach (transcendent interpretation).

## THE NATURAL-SCIENCE AND THE HUMAN-STUDIES
## CONCEPTIONS OF SOCIOLOGY

Two conceptions of sociology have been in existence for some time. The first conceives of sociology as one among the natural sciences. The second sees considerable methodological implications in the fact that sociology, along with social psychology, cultural anthropology, political science, economics, and perhaps history, is a social science [3]. The difference between the two concepts lies not so much in research techniques (as part of methodology) as in approach. More particularly, it lies in the fact that each bases its methodology on a different premise regarding the nature of the subject matter of sociology (hence regarding its methodology other than research techniques). The only feature shared by the two concepts is precisely the conviction that sociological research should be executed by scientific methods. What research is to be carried on; why, and because of what nature of sociology? These and many other questions are answered differently by the two concepts and their schools.

It is hazardous and easily misleading to compress even the outstanding features of the approaches of these two concepts into formulas. Nevertheless, this is what we must attempt if we would carry the discussion further. To make this discussion possible is the only purpose of what at best is an oversimplified classification. Remembering this serious qualification, we characterize the two concepts as follows:

1. The *natural-science concept* postulates that sociology can and should study its subject matter as other natural sciences study other parts of nature which are *their* subject matters. However this subject matter is defined—as social relations, social processes, social interaction, group relations or processes, and the like—it exists outside the sociologist, is external to him, and he has but to discover, study, and learn about it [4]. Thus perhaps the most outstanding assumption of the natural-science approach, from which all its other assumptions and methodological tenets seem to derive, is the axiom that the subject matter of sociology, inasmuch as is natural or part of nature, is given and given alike to all investigators. It is this same assumption that is *not* shared but replaced by a very different one in the other concept of sociology.

2. This other concept may be called the *human* or the *human-studies concept*. Its postulate, which corresponds to that of the common-givenness of the natural-science concept, may be formulated by saying that the subject matter of sociology is given only in the sense that it emerges in the process of understanding, a process that (according to this concept) is, both individually and historically, never completed or completable.

Thus the human approach does not emphasize subject matter and givenness (in the methodology of science a correlate of subject matter) but rather the investigator as an agent and his investigation as action, as creative action. The fundamental methodological question of the human approach is therefore to ask how we can investigate unilluminated aspects of man and of men's living together.

The human approach is still reticent to delimit the area within which the subject matter of sociology should be confined because it feels that it has not itself been sufficiently exemplified or even articulated in theory or research to outline a classification of the social sciences that would be commensurate with it—that is, adequately independent of traditional historical classifications. This reticence, of course, is not in conflict with the fact that the human concept of sociology could not have developed, nor feel the sort of sophisticated reticence just alluded to, without the antecedent development of science, social and natural, by which it has been stimulated. More specifically, it could not react against the natural-science concept of sociology unless this concept itself existed [5].

In the natural-science approach [6] the role of scientific method is pivotal; in the human approach it is taken for granted. As has been said in a facetious manner, the former is interested in a refinement of scientific techniques and procedures at the exepense of human relevance, whereas the latter may pursue significant questions but cannot test what it is doing; or the former gets remarkably wise to increasingly dull matters, the latter knows less and less about more and more; and so on. Yet in spite of the differences in the concepts of science and scientific method that distinguish the two approaches, it must be emphasized that the human approach, where it has not yet developed scientific methods, endeavors to do so; that in terms of creativity, that is, in terms of the perception of problems and methods for solving them and in the breadth of its interests—hence in its function in the development of the study of man—it is more scientific than the natural science approach; that it thus has at least equal claim to being scientific, particularly as an expression of increasing secularization and an increasing secular attitude.

It is thus erroneous to maintain, as some seem to do, that anything but the natural-science approach, and more specifically the human approach, is unscientific or less scientific than itself. It is true, on the other hand, that many among the antecedents of the human approach, and thus Dilthey as well as much of the humanities, notably all that has to do with interpretation (e.g., literary criticism), suffer from a lack of rigorous method and systematicity in comparison with much of the natural sciences. This, I think, need not be so. I should regard it rather as an invitation to devise more scientific methods in the human studies (both in the social sciences and in the humanities) than as a suggestion to abstain from investigating problems that by some at least are felt to be important, only because we have not yet developed scientific methods for investigating them.

Both the natural-science and the human-studies concepts of sociology, then, have a scientific character. Yet the problems to which identical or similar research techniques are applied and the role of these problems in the general approach vary with the approach itself: the approach at least codetermines the problem selection. The differential concept of scientific character and method is an element in the approach.

Regarding this differential concept I am able to make only fragmentary statements. I hope, however, that these statements will enlighten, and will be enlightened by, those already made on the two approaches to sociology themselves. It should also be noted that the partial analysis that I have tried to undertake will be implemented by examples discussed in a later section.

It is not necessary to offer a definition of science. For our purposes its customary conceptions are adequate. Rather, that aspect of science stressed in the human approach must be emphasized. This aspect has, I think, been unduly neglected, but perhaps it can, if appreciated, lead to a less one-sided, hence more fruitful and more economical, sociology than we have at present. This aspect, which may be called the human equation [7], refers to the continuous challenge to remain aware of the relation between scientific pursuit and spontaneous experience, and consequently it refers to the inclusion of this awareness in the definition of the scientist [8]. I am convinced that it is not only useful but necessary for the development of sociology to include this awareness in the definition of the sociologist. This conviction rests on a concept of man that stresses, more than American sociology does, his irrational as well as creative, hence inexhaustible [9], qualities. With Cassirer [10] it emphasizes man as a symbol- and myth-making animal or, with Durkheim [11], man as an ideal-making animal, both ethically and cognitively. In Western civilization this notion of man has informed the artist, the religious, and the philosopher more often and more typically than the scientist. Yet I consider its incorporation into his approach a challenge to the scientist at the same time that I regard the incorporation of science and of scientific method into the study of man's creative efforts—artistic, religious, philosophical (and scientific)—a challenge to their traditional disciplines, mainly the humanities.

The following discussion of some concerns that so far have not, or only scarcely, been studied sociologically or, for that matter, scientifically, will serve to implement the general outlines of the human concept of sociology. This discussion suggests how sociology can study three phenomena that are important on the basis of the concept of man sketched, that illustrate the notion of the human equation of science, and that have hitherto been the almost exclusive domain of the humanities. The three phenomena chosen are the study of the unique, of the meaning of history, and of aesthetic experience. I begin with a description of the unique, then consider its study, and finally, more specifically though much more briefly, deal with the sociology of the meaning of history and of aesthetic experience.

### THE UNIQUE

The human concept of sociology here advocated and developed agrees with the well-known tenet of science according to which science aims at the establishment of uniformities—whether the avowed purpose of this establishment is to understand the structure of the universe, to make predictions, or both. The human conception of science, however, advocates greater scientific concern with the unique than is customary in order to enrich materials from which to hypothesize and eventually to establish uniformities.

After anticipating this emphasis of the human conception, it is necessary to explain it; that is, it is necessary to define or at least circumscribe "unique." In the first place unique is *not* a logical or ontological concept. Logically, there is either no unique, inasmuch as everything is homogeneous in some respect to everything else, or nothing but uniques exist, inasmuch as nothing is homogeneous in all respects or identical with anything but itself. Hence logically speaking, unique is better replaced by single, and single is *not* the referent of unique as used here. Ontologically, unique makes sense only in reference to something that is, on the basis of some concept of the nature of being, in fact, unique, that is, outstanding in a particular way in reality or value. This is a use of the term that points to a frame of reference outside any discussion in this paper.

In the second place, although unique is neither a logical nor an ontological concept, it is, positively speaking, a psychological (teleological, creative) concept. More specifically, the unique belongs to the process of understanding (see below). In the third place, the unique is suggested by such terms as empathy, intuition, insight, apprehension, grasp, mystical union, trance, identification, love (most obviously at first sight), vision, inspiration, flash, and revelation, all of which refer to experiences that to the experiencer are characterized, cognitively [12] by a sudden passive-creative incorporation of elements, which he believes to be important, into his universe of discourse. This is by no means to suggest that any of these terms is synonymous with understanding. Understanding, rather, is conceived here as a process that lies on a continuum extending between the two extremes. One is complete strangeness toward its object, the other, complete identification with it. The object changes with the process of its understanding and, in this sense, is the subject matter or given of understanding [13].

In the fourth place, most concrete understanding lies between the extremes indicated, and this is true also of scientific understanding. Scientific understanding may be defined more precisely as that in which identification with the unique is counterbalanced by testable communicability. If the scale is weighted in favor of identification, testability and even communicability suffer (as, characteristically, in studies done in the humanities); if it is weighted in favor of testable communicability, the grasp of the unique suffers (as in many studies by positivistic sociologists). Maximum understanding, a synonym for scientific understanding, is thus seen to result from the combination of a sense for the unique with scientific training, but what do grasp of the unique and sense for the unique refer to?

It is here that the experiences of empathy and intuition, may help to further the argument. The human concept advocates that its followers consider certain possible topics of understanding as uniques [14] by approaching them, actually or typologically (a question decided by the scientist's own psychological make-up), in such experiences as have been listed; that is, any student will entertain possible topics of understanding on the basis of his personality and the culture in which he lives. His culture, if he is a scientist, includes his scientific training, and his scientific training is particularly significant for his scientific pursuit, of which the selection of a topic of understanding and an approach toward such a topic are elements. More specifically, then, the human concept advocates that the scientist consider those possible topics of understanding as uniques about which he has doubts that the development of the methodology of his discipline has satisfactorily reduced to mere crosspoints of uniformities [15], and he must make explicit the reasons for his doubts. Even this statement, however, must be qualified, for if, as is held here with Pareto [16] and many others, science can be concerned only with successive approximation to reality (an ontological proposition), the degree of approximation held satisfactory at any given time is determined not only by the development of scientific techniques or methodology but also by extrascientific factors, such as the intellectual interests of a student or his time. Hence the above statement appeals to the whole personality of the scientist; at any rate, in the social sciences much less than in the natural sciences can he point to available objective criteria by which to justify his advocacy of the understanding of certain topics as uniques. Nevertheless he has more to go by than his feelings. It is my belief that at the present stage in the development of sociology three such possible topics—or complexes of topics—are culture, personality, and intellectual products. In the next section of this paper an outline of their study as uniques is given in an effort to justify my doubt, that is, to suggest the superiority of their study as uniques to other ways of studying them. This is done in a discussion of the study of the unique, with culture, personality, and intellectual products as examples, and is followed by an application of the method suggested to the more specific topics of the meaning of history and aesthetic experience.

In the fifth place, then, there is the question of what is to be considered as a unique. The scope of this paper allows no more than the suggestion of an answer. Moreover, this suggestion has already been implied in the preceding paragraph. Inasmuch as unique is a psychological concept, not everything can, for psychological reasons, be so considered: nobody can live without routine. Furthermore, what is to be so considered depends on the personality and the culture, general and scientific, of the student. We can now say that the unique emerges in such instances in which (for reasons he must endeavor to become aware of and state) the student stops taking his methodology for granted and begins to question his approach.

This more than commonly questioning attitude is one illustration of the greater scientific character in the sense of greater secularization which has been asserted as a characteristic of the human conception. To use a metaphor, when he studies the unique, the student drops as much of his scientific and general-cultural cloak as he can in order to expose himself to his subject matter. (He cannot drop it all inasmuch as he is a human being who by definition has culture.) To use Alfred Weber's terms, he realizes the civilizational character of his routine pursuits and enters the sphere of culture [17].

The introduction of the concept of the unique is thus seen to be an appeal to greater self-awareness and skepticism, or secularization, on the part of the scientist. The purpose of such appeal is, as has been anticipated, to enrich materials from which to hypothesize uniformities. It may be added that the human conception may also lead to the elimination of errors, factual as well as methodological. How this may be done, that is, what the scientist does after he emerges from the unique or how he studies it is our next concern.

The nature of the unique may be clarified further by contrasting it with the logical (rather than psychological) concept of ideal-type. (This is especially useful in view of the discussion of culture in the next section.) In speaking of Pareto's "abstract rationalistic type of society," Talcott Parsons [18] writes:

> . . . it is clearly understood that "integration" in this complete sense applies only to the abstract society; in this as in other respects it is a limiting case. Certainly neither Pareto nor the present author means to imply that concrete societies are in general or even approximately perfectly integrated in this sense, or that their members are normally, the majority, conscious that there is any system of common ends. But whether this system be explicit or implicit, whether integration be closely or only very distantly approached, does not affect the theoretical importance of this theorem, any more than the fact that feathers fall slowly and irregularly affects the importance of the law governing the falling of bodies in a vacuum. A concrete example which comes relatively close to the experimental conditions of the theorem is that of the Calvinists of Geneva in Calvin's own time who might be said to be pursuing the common end of establishing the Kingdom of God on Earth.

Here, then, as in Tönnies's *Gemeinschaft and Gesellschaft* [19], in Max Weber's conception of ideal-type [20], in Redfield's folk and urban societies [21], or in Howard Becker's sacred and secular societies [22], we are dealing with ideal-types in the sense of constructs in terms of which elements of reality (here, specifically, actual societies) can be understood. This is all well known, but what must be pointed out is that when cultures are designated as uniques (as in the following section of this paper) it does not imply that they are conceived as completely integrated wholes and that the ideal-type method should not be considered applicable to the study under discussion when the student, following the human concept advocated, embarks on the elaboration of his materials. In other words, the ideal-type method is logically and psychologically irrelevant to, and thus compatible with, the human concept, inasmuch as it moves in the sphere of methodology, whereas concern with the unique is a concern with approach.

### SCIENTIFIC STUDY OF THE UNIQUE: THE SOCIOLOGY OF THE "MEANING OF HISTORY" AND OF AESTHETIC EXPERIENCE

It should be remembered that naming is one phase of understanding and, further, that each culture possesses psychologically irreducible phenomena, or named uniques, which the individual in the culture usually takes for granted but which, as cultural anthropology has taught us, often strike the outsider precisely as uniques. Even if these uniques should occur in other cultures—and a variation of the question thus suggested will occupy us in the next section—their respective integrations in given cultures make them uniques. Hence each culture is unique, and for similar reasons and in a similar (always psychological, not ontological) sense each personality and each intellectual product is unique.

We are now in a position to suggest the basis of a methodology for the scientific study of the unique, a methodology I believe applicable to the study of cultures, personalities, and intellectual products, and perhaps to the study of other uniques. In the following discussion, at any rate, unique stands promiscuously for culture, personality, and intellectual product.

I submit that scientific understanding of the unique can be obtained by studing its central attitude. This term probably does not sound strange if the unique refers to a personality or even to an intellectual product, but it seems quite inappropriate if it refers to a culture. In the case of culture, therefore, such terms as pattern, configuration, and ethos, terms that are indeed closely related to central attitude, may be preferred to it and may be substituted for it in the following discussion, if this facilitates the argument.

The central attitude, then, refers to the attitude that reveals itself during the process of understanding a given unique as rendering understandable all single attitudes [23]. In order to show the relation of the unique to the general by way of the communicable—to call attention, that is, to the process of understanding as it overcomes the extremes of complete strangeness toward its object and of complete identification with it—I may be allowed to use my own statements as an example: obviously, on the basis of what has been said so far, the question is whether there is anything in what I am saying, whether there is anything in the concept of central attitude advocated. This question itself is one of the ways of introducing the understanding process—the most literal way but not the only one. Whether the process of understanding this (my) intellectual product is inaugurated in the manner indicated or in another manner, it is clear that the previously mentioned combination of a sense for the unique with scientific training produces maximum understanding of this intellectual product. It should be noted that both the inspector of an intellectual product and its (immediate) author enrich their respective universes of discourse with this product. They enrich it both additively and creatively: in the former sense the process involved is a relatively passive one of learning; in the latter sense it is a relatively active one of developing [24].

Does the concept of central attitude, then, give us the basis of a methodology for the scientific study of cultures, personalities, and intellectual products? I believe it does because it combines the highest degree of identification with the object of understanding which is compatible with testable communicability. This combination, it will be remembered, was posited as a necessity for maximum understanding.

It will probably be granted that the central-attitude method surpasses other methods of understanding in terms of intimacy (identification) with its object, but its testability and even its communicability will be considered with skepticism. It is true that its testability is precarious and its communicability probably limited to persons attitudinally predisposed toward it. This is not a condemning statement, for more than precariousness can be predicated of its testability, hence of its communicability. Positively, it can be stated that testability and therefore communicability obtain to the degree that the student of a unique making use of the central-attitude method is aware of, and makes explicit, the processes by which he arrives at the central attitude—a task for his mastery of the human equation of science, and that his approach incorporates into his and his public's universe of discourse (or explains) demonstrably *no fewer*, or demonstrably *more*, aspects of the phenomenon under study than does any other competing approach.

The second of these criteria of testability is one in all understanding, whether in its everyday or scientific forms. The first, reflecting the scientific tenet of public inspection, is usually replaced by the public inspection of the scientific method but, in keeping with our suggestions regarding the human concept of sociology, is extended here to include the approach inherent in a given investigation and not only its methodology. It is hoped and expected that as this human concept becomes more clearly developed (perhaps even formalized) it can be spotted at once, labeled, and taken for granted in future investigations, at which time public inspection may be limited to methodology. Such a situation is certainly far off, yet it can already be formulated as a development within science.

Let us now apply these general considerations of the study of the unique to the sociological study of the meaning of history and aesthetic experience. Two theses are submitted. The meaning of history, as an object of scientific understanding in the sense advocated here, can be one or both of two things. It can be a datum for scientific understanding, namely, some group's, some school's, or some culture's meaning of history, that is, as conceived by somebody, or it can be a concept emerging in the scientist himself, but as such it is scientific only in the measure in which the scientist developing it is aware of and makes explicit the processes by which he has arrived at it. It will be noted that I have just repeated one of the two criteria of testability and communicability (as among criteria of scientific procedure) mentioned in connection with the discussion of the scientific character of the central-attitude method. The explanation of this repetition is the hypothesis that to emphasize or make explicit this criterion of scientific procedure allows us to implement the extension of scientific procedure to the study of phenomena which, as has been pointed out, have hitherto been the exclusive domain of the humanities—at best, that is, of students deeply concerned with the identification of the unique but less so with testability. The same considerations apply to aesthetic experience: it, too, can be an object of scientific understanding either as a datum (somebody's aesthetic experience) or as a concept emerging in the scientist himself. Enough has been said concerning the second sense in which the meaning of history, aesthetic experience, and other uniques can become objects of scientific understanding, for this discussion was prepared for in the discussion of the study of the unique in general and the central attitude in particular. A second thesis dealing with the meaning of history and aesthetic experience as data [25] and. more precisely, as data for sociological rather than for generally scientific study remains to be stated.

At the present juncture of scientific development it is indispensable for the maximum understanding of the meaning of history, aesthetic experience, and other uniques that they be studied sociologically. Otherwise the fact that they are historical phenomena, that is, phenomena in a specific social time and space—a fact that we know or at least postulate and are therefore compelled to incorporate into our scientific universe of discourse—is left unanalyzed, hence uncontrolled by our understanding of them. This thesis calls for a discussion of the methodology of their sociological study. We may generalize and insist on a discussion of the methodology of the sociological study of intellectual products in general —intellectual products understood as a class of uniques. In other words, we are inquiring into the methodology of what has customarily gone under the name sociology of knowledge [26] and what may perhaps better be called the sociology of intellectual behavior.

Some elements of the *approach* of the sociology of knowledge have been indicated: it is sufficient to recall that this approach ought to be informed by the recognition of the importance of the unique or by the human equation of science. The fundamental problem, or at least one of the fundamental problems, of the *methodology* of the sociology of intellectual behavior is the interpretation and, more precisely, the sociological interpretation of its data. This problem has received a great deal of attention [27]. It is made more complex, however, by the approach suggested here. Yet before we come to this added difficulty we must briefly expound the difference between immanent and sociological [28] interpretation (the latter as one among possible transcendent interpretations). It should be noted that for the moment we must assume that the question of *what* is to be interpreted is settled, but this is a question to which we shall have to return presently in connection with the difficulty suggested above. At any rate, the immanent interpretation of an intellectual product uses as its source this product exclusively; transcendent interpretation uses other sources as well in order to throw light on the product, and, more specifically, sociocultural interpretation undertakes to explain the results of immanent interpretation in sociocultural terms [28].

The added difficulty becomes obvious when we ask what it is we want to interpret and beyond which we are not allowed to go if we would stay within the limits of immanent interpretation. The question, in the light of foregoing discussion, becomes synonymous with the question how something becomes a datum or given. The answer to it lies in the empirical study of the processes by which something does become a given, and this study is greatly facilitated by the scientist's report of these processes, a report to which he is committed by our first criterion of testability (applied to the central-attitude method and to the meaning of history and aesthetic experience as emergents). Thus, on the empirical level the question is answered [30], but it also has its epistemological implication, which, precisely, is the added difficulty that was anticipated, for we must also ask how it is *possible* that something becomes a given to be understood. This well-known question which, in another formulation, was one of the main concerns of Kant, cannot and need not be treated here. It should be remembered, however, that the unique by definition is incommunicable and that, on the other hand, it has in this paper been made the object of understanding. To remember this is to realize a contradiction that calls for a resolution, and it is this resolution that is an epistemological concern and to which we must now turn. This concern may also be formulated as the question how understanding and communication are possible in spite of unique experience, the postulate (leading to an answer) being that they are, in some sense, possible. In other words, what is it that all human beings have in common in spite of cultural differences? The very formulation of this question suggests the impossibility of absolute cultural relativism—epistemological, ethical, and aesthetic.

### SOCIOLOGY AND CULTURAL RELATIVISM

It is submitted that for sociology, and what is particularly relevant here, for the sociology of intellectual behavior, to be possible as a discipline that understands something other than itself—in other words, it is not (culturally) solipsistic—it must accept as a hypothesis the epistemological postulate that human intellectual-affective behavior exhibits both cultural variability and biologically founded identity. Earlier students of this problem tended to overemphasize one or the other of these components [31], whereas the consensus in recent sociology-of-knowledge and related literature [32] seems to lie in the direction of the postulate stated. Yet a completely satisfactory formulation of the two components has to my knowledge not yet been attained.

Child's recent attempt [33], however, seems to me to have great promise. Child begins with an analysis of the question whether the categories of thought are universal or culturally relative. Neither alternative, he points out, can be answered unreservedly in the affirmative, for on the one hand the inherence of categories in the nature of man has not been demonstrated, inasmuch as allegedly universal and necessary categories have not been proved, but on the other hand we cannot conceive of categories arising from experience, because such a postulate implies the structuralization, that is, the categorization, of experience itself. Rather we must postulate two kinds of category: primal, or biotic or socially underived categories and supervenient, or sociotic or socially derived categories [34]. Categories, Child emphasizes, are forms "not of the mind but of the whole responding organism" [35]; and they are cognitive, emotive, or conative according to their orientation or preponderate intent.

> Cognitive predispositions are simply organic potencies of response as oriented toward knowledge of the world rather than toward some feeling of it or some action upon it [36].

More precisely, in regard to the distinction between categories and other elements of thought, hence in regard to universal identity against cultural relativity in human behavior, Child writes as follows:

> While the primal categories are presumably invariable in essence, the concepts correlated with them continue, when once formulated, to develop and to undergo theoretical formulation and concatenation. And the conceptual correlates of the primal predispositions react upon these predispositions in the sense, at least, of acquiring themselves predispositional correlates which cluster around the original primal predispositions and which, in consequence, affect the apprehension, as well as the understanding, which occurs in the sphere of the predispositions concerned. Indeed, *it is in and through this process of accretion that the primal categories exhibit their primordiality.* As example of the way in which the con-

cepts of the understanding may condition or provide the mode
within which the primal categories operate, consider the fact
that space and time may be differently felt in different cultures
while the basic biotic forms of apprehension remain the same
in the individuals of all different cultures. But, in so far as
concepts function in this way, they do so as functionalized in
supervenient categories. These categories, the *a priori* formalizing factors which do not inhere in men as animals, are
those persistent and powerful tendencies to take the world as
such-and-such which, under certain circumstances, in certain
people or certain groups of people, have become compulsions.
By becoming compulsions they become categories [37].

Although several questions can be raised in regard to this theory (the
discussion of which, however, would far exceed the scope of this chapter),
it seems to me that Child has made it exceedingly difficult to maintain
absolute epistemological relativism and, because of his conception of the
categories, has at the same time made it exceedingly difficult to maintain
absolute ethical and aesthetic relativism.

If, then, we accept Child's distinction between primal and supervenient
categories, we are able to resolve the seeming contradiction between the
incommunicability of the unique, and the unique as the object of understanding. Now we can say that unique is a primal category that has been
conceptualized and probably functionalized into a supervenient category
on the basis of certain cultural circumstances and more precisely, even if
still vaguely, on the basis of certain developments in philosophy and the
social sciences, some elements of which have been alluded to in this paper
[38]. If we accept these developments, what follows for the relation
between epistemology and sociology or sociology of intellectual behavior?

To answer this question we would do well to act on the postulated
principle of becoming aware of the processes by which we have arrived at
our position, to the limited extent, at least, of retracing our major steps
to this point. We began by distinguishing approach from methodology.
We then sketched two concepts of sociology, the natural science and the
human-studies concepts, and in clarification and defense of the human
concept we circumscribed a concept of science which is characterized by
what was called the human equation. In this concept our attention was
called to some phenomena—the unique, the meaning of history, and
aesthetic experience—which we maintained were not studied as scientifically as our concept of scientific study would warrant. We gave a general
description of the unique and indicated the outlines of the scientific study
of the phenomena mentioned by introducing the notion of the central-
attitude method. We suggested their study as both data and emergents

and expanded on their study as data by requesting that it include their sociological investigation. This led us to one of the fundamental problems of the sociology of intellectual behavior, that of interpretation. The question of the object of interpretation itself, whether immanent or sociocultural, led further to the formulation of the contradiction between the incommunicable unique, and the unique as an object of understanding and to the resolution of this contradiction with the help of Child's statements regarding categories. The formulation of this contradiction and its resolution were recognized as an epistemological concern, but epistemological concerns, we now continue, are not sociological concerns, or, more generally, they are the business of the philosopher (particularly of the theorist of knowledge or epistemologist) not the scientist.

One can admit this and maintain [39] that whenever the behavior scientist deals with epistemological questions he no longer functions as a scientist but as an epistemologist. Yet the question may be raised whether we should stop at this recognition or rather consider the foregoing discussion of the philosophy of sociology as a challenge to undertake an even more radical reclassification of our intellectual efforts. This reclassification would be based on the twofold proposition, which is derived from the preceding discussion, that it requires the articulation of the relation between epistemology and intellectual efforts and that, inversely, the articulation of the relation between epistemology and intellectual efforts requires the classification of the latter. It is beyond the scope of this paper to undertake these articulations: here it must suffice to suggest their place and the need for them [40].

## SUMMARY: IMPLICATIONS FOR SOCIOLOGICAL PRACTICE

In this last section an attempt is made to point out the implications of this chapter for the practice of sociological study. This is done on a twofold application of the general concept presented. First I outline a specific research example that shows how the human concept of sociology, more particularly, the central-attitude method, applies to the study of a culture. Second, I make some general methodological observations that are primarily designed to dispel possible misconceptions of points raised in the present essay.

It has been suggested that in the study of a culture the aim of sociological understanding is terminologically more conveniently designated as culture pattern (or the like) than as central attitude. If the goal of the study is maximum understanding, the culture under examination must be conceived as a unique, even if its student (or other students) uses the results of the study of the culture as a unique as material from which to hypothesize and eventually to establish uniformities. In following the cultural approach—the variant, relevant to the study of cultures, of the more general human approach—the student is aware of the cultural equation. This awareness makes him suspicious of analyzing the culture in terms of contentual divisions such as child rearing, marriage, and death customs because he fears that they are naively, that is, relatively unaware, taken over from his own (general and special scientific) culture. He therefore discards this approach in favor of the pattern method, which he finds more in keeping with the study of the culture as a unique [41]. The two fundamental tasks of any scientific study of uniques—to grasp them to the highest degree compatible with testability and communicability—formulate themselves for the study of a culture as the question of ascertaining or selecting patterns to present a testable interpretation of the culture that is superior to all competing interpretations; that is, the student must present patterns and their interrelations in a manner that will enable him and his public to understand and predict the culture under study. The two criteria of understanding have been formulated as the demonstration of the degree to which the student is aware of the processes underlying his study and as the demonstration of the degree to which his study can compete with other studies. The criterion of prediction is the degree to which the propositions made in his study are confirmed in the future [42].

Similar remarks, as already suggested, could obviously be made in regard to the study of personalities and of intellectual products. It will also be recognized that they could generally be made concerning the investigation of any kind of human behavior. To recognize this amounts to admitting that this paper suggests the beginnings of a philosophy of the study of man as a sociocultural animal—a study to which social sciences other than sociology have made claims. It has been impossible to do more here than to show the relevance of this philosophy to sociology by taking examples from sociology and noting challenges to sociology rather than taking them from other social sciences and challenging them: sociology has not been defined nor has it been delimited in regard to other disciplines. To repeat, therefore [43], the next step is to develop the concept outlined by determining whether—and if so, how—it lends itself as an instrument for classifying subdivisions of the study of man. In line with this concept such a classification itself is seen as a vehicle toward a greater understanding of ourselves.

Fundamentally this paper advocates both the application of scientific method to topics traditionally outside the domain of sociology and a greater awareness in the scientific treatment of traditional topics (as here exemplified particularly by the topic culture). Furthermore, it suggests several tools designed to translate this advocacy into research practice. To avoid misunderstanding it is appropriate to conclude with a few clarifying remarks.

In the first place numerous questions dealt with in methodological literature have remained unanswered because they are irrelevant to the arguments expounded in this chapter. One is the applicability of the ideal-type method. Among many others, the following may be mentioned: what, in theory and in research, is the line between description and explanation, between idiographic and nomothetic study, between structure and content or structure and function? [44] All that can be said here in regard to these problems is that although they are irrelevant to the present discussion, inasmuch as they are methodological questions, they nevertheless require investigation in the framework of the approach presented and will, it is hoped, receive clarification from such discussion. The same goes for the various aspects of the relation between the unique and the general. Yet, in the latter case it must be noted that although the unique has been defined here according to its status both in the approach and in the methodology of sociology it is still necessary to define "general," at least in one of its various denotations, and more precisely in the denotation that supplements that of unique. The general, like the unique, is a psychological concept. Logical and ontological questions are as irrelevant to the concept of general as a concept within the approach of sociology as they are in regard to unique. More precisely, general refers to the methodologically *un*questioned, whereas (as stated earlier) the unique emerges exactly where methodology is questioned [45]. It becomes obvious that contemporary sociology (like any intellectual effort at any given time) is full of (conceptualized) generals, as well as of general areas, such as population, family, or "urban" [46]. This chapter, far from advocating the abandonment of these generals, merely urges an examination of the legitimacy with which their methodologies have been established; it urges a questioning of the division of sociology into these and similar branches, even as it urges, more articulately, that of our intellectual efforts in general [47].

In the second place a general placement of the conception of sociology advocated here ought to be worked out. It is enough to state that the one single concept to which it comes closest is that of Max Weber [48]. It is evident, however, that it would greatly benefit from a systematic investigation of similarities and differences between itself and Weber's concept, as well as those of Dilthey, Simmel, Znaniecki, Parsons, and of various recent cultural anthropologists.

It is hoped that the remarks in the last section place this paper within current problem complexes. Clearly, the paper entails two tasks. One is to solve the problems presented or merely mentioned in it theoretically. The other is to translate these problems into research as far as possible at present and to further their translation into research. It is in the hope that response to this paper will contribute to the solution of one or both of these tasks that it is submitted at this time.


## NOTES

1.   A first draft of this paper was presented early in 1947 in a Methodology of Science seminar conducted at Ohio State University by Dr. Virgil G. Hinshaw, Jr., to whom I am indebted for many stimulating and clarifying discussions. The revision of this essay (and its incorporation into a forthcoming monograph—cf. n. 42) was made possible by a grant from The Viking Fund, which is herewith gratefully acknowledged.

2.   See (2) [Chapter 12].

3.   For a recent convenient exhibition of the contrasts between the two conceptions see (17) and (34).

4.   Cf. (29) [Chapter 20].

5.   The claim to (as well as the exemplification of) some sort of human concept of sociology is, as has been suggested, well known: it goes back to the German controversy over *Naturwissenschaften* versus *Geisteswissenschaften.* Obviously the natural-science approach is related to the former, the human approach, to the latter. "Human studies" is a translation by H. A. Hodges (13), here adopted, of *Geisteswissenschaften,* particularly as used by Dilthey (13, p. 157). Moreover there seems to be evidence of a considerable approximation to the human approach, on the one hand, in the theoretical work of Znaciecki [see (33), (34), and (35)] and of some other contemporary American sociologists, particularly T. Parsons and R. M. MacIver, and, on the other, in certain recent anthropological literature; see (29), p. 176a, n. 2 [Chapter 20, n. 2], for some references.

6.   It will be noted that I have been using "approach" where I earlier used "concept" or "position." Approach, consistent with its definition given at the beginning of this chapter, is short for "approach characteristic of the (natural-science, or the human) conception of, or position in, sociology."

7.   In parallel to the cultural equation pertinent to the study of cultures specifically; cf. (29) [Chapter 20].

8.   The question whether it is useful to include this awareness in the definition of the natural scientist may be left unanalyzed here. An affirmative, though modified, answer would seem to be adequate in this case.

9.   In the sense of the assumption that man can never be definitively defined.

10.   Cf. (4) and (5). See also my review of the latter, *American Sociological Review,* **12** (June 1947), 372–373.

11.   Cf. (9), especially pp. 139–140.

12.   If they are, to the experiencer, cognitively relevant at all. At least, these experiences are not merely cognitive but involve affect and volition as well. This point is not important in the present context, however, inasmuch as at the moment we are concerned with developing the relevance of the unique in regard to the process of understanding. Although understanding, too, involves other than cognitive elements, it is nevertheless here (as is commonly done) regarded as a significantly cognitive process. The participation of affective and conative elements in understanding is not discussed in this chapter except that the question is touched on once again in connection with the discussion of categories (in the context of the discussion of cultural relativism).

13.   Whether the unique is the predicate of the object of understanding or of the understander is an ontological question that is irrelevant here, inasmuch as the unique, as pointed out in the first instance, is a psychological concept.

14.   Note the invitation to *consider* them as uniques, which consideration leaves the unique a psychological concept; that is, it does not make it ontological.

15.   Cf. (22), paragraph 99.

16.   *Ibid.*, paragraph 106.

17.   Cf. (28), especially pp. 31–47; also (20) and (18), pp. 272–281. It should be noted that the use here of Weber's concepts as metaphors implies neither agreement nor disagreement with the conception underlying them.

18.   Cf. (24), pp. 247–248.

19.   Cf. (27).

20.   The best succinct analysis of which is to be found in (23), pp. 12–15.

21.   See, for example, (25).

22.   See (2) and (3); also (1).

23.   Cf. (32) [Chapter 26]. For the formulation of a further degree of awareness in appraising this concept, *ibid.*, n. 25 [Chapter 26, n. 26].

24.   Thus in the example at hand the author of this intellectual product developed from the concept of central attitude that of typical central attitude (32) [Chapter 26]. For fuller presentations of central attitude and typical central attitude and for other concepts believed to be useful for the study of (certain) uniques, *ibid.*

25.   It should not be forgotten that they become data or givens in the sense indicated earlier.

26.   It is well known that this is a misnomer. See, for example, (21), 379–380.

27.   For a good summary and analysis of relevant literature see (6), Chapter VII.

28.   "Sociological interpretation" is used here synonymously with "sociocultural," "social," or "cultural interpretation." The differences among these various types are irrelevant to the present discussion and may therefore remain unanalyzed.

29.  Cf. (30) [Chapter 12]. Earlier in the present chapter "immanent interpretation" more specifically of a science was used to refer to the study of its intellectual structure or methodology as given and its "transcendent interpretation" to the study of its approach as not given with, but inferable from ("outside"), its methodology. On the two modes of interpretation in regard to culture patterns see (29) [Chapter 20]. For a deliberate attempt at excluding all transcendent (and some elements of immanent) interpretation (an attempt that shows the striking paucity of the result in terms of the understanding of the object examined) see (31).

30.  Cf. also (32) [Chapter 26].

31.  The instinctivists, Freud, and the Kantians, in their stress of instincts, supposedly universal psychological complexes, and a priori categories of thought, respectively, neglected cultural relativity, whereas the modern discoverers of cultural relativity, particularly Sumner and Westermarck, failed to raise the question whether men had anything in common in spite of it.

32.  See especially (26), (16), Chapter IV, (6), Chapter III, (15), and (14). For a more extensive treatment, see Chapter 28.

33.  (7).

34.  (7), 316–318.

35.  *Ibid.*, 323.

36.  *Ibid.*, 322.

37.  *Ibid.*, 327–328. First italics added.

38.  This concept of the unique not only allows us to resolve the contradiction just discussed but also throws light on our concept of understanding as an epistemological concept: epistemologically speaking, the aim of understanding is now seen to be the primal category of the unique by means of its culturally relative expressions, such as supervenient categories, concepts, and attitudes. The empirical vehicle of understanding is still the central-attitude method discussed earlier.

39.  As has most explicitly been done by Virgil G. Hinshaw, Jr.: see (12) and (11).

40.  It should be noted that lines of thought similar to those developed in regard to epistemology could (and should) also be articulated in respect to other traditional fields of philosophy such as logic, metaphysics, ethics, and aesthetics.

41.  In a definition that is inadequate but sufficient for the present purpose "culture patterns" may be designated as *certain types* of uniformity of emotion, attitude, thought, knowledge, and overt action; in short, as *certain types* of uniformity of behavior.

42.  For a considerably fuller presentation of the empirical establishment of culture patterns, see (29) [Chapter 20]. (The application of the concept outlined here and in the paper cited is the topic of a monograph [in preparation] on

the culture of a small, relatively isolated, largely Spanish-speaking community in northern New Mexico.)

43. Cf. the end of the preceding section of this chapter in which (in the discussion of the relation between philosophy, particularly epistemology, and behavioral sciences, particularly sociology) some clues to such a classification are presented.

44. There is a similarity—which cannot be analyzed here—between the utilization of unique as emphasized and what Clerk Maxwell called the dynamical method. The following quotation (which I owe to Dr. J. N. Spuhler, Department of Sociology, The Ohio State University) may be reproduced as an example of the numerous passages found in methodological literature that need analysis in terms of the approach suggested. (This passage is especially noteworthy for coming from the pen of such an eminent natural scientist.) In the "statistical method of investigating social questions . . . [persons] are grouped according to some characteristic, and the number of persons forming the group is set down under that characteristic. This is the raw material from which the statist endeavours to deduce general theorems in sociology. Other students of human nature proceed on a different plan. They observe individual men, ascertain their history, analyse their motives, and compare their expectations of what they will do with their actual conduct. This may be called the dynamical method of study as applied to man. *However imperfect the dynamical study of man may be in practice, it evidently is the only perfect method in principle* . . . If we betake ourselves to the statistical method, we do so confessing that we are unable to follow details of each case and expecting that the effects of wide-spread causes, though different in each individual, will produce an average result on the whole nation, from a study of which we may estimate the character and propensities of an imaginary being called the Mean Man" (19), pp. 219–220. Italics added.

45. It may be said that structurally the two concepts belong in the same category, whereas contentually they are opposite and complementary.

46. It is interesting to note that Durkheim, both in (10) and again 13 years later in (8), p. 419, n. 1., suspects that the economic sphere—to use the terminology employed here—is the only one that sociology may have to leave unquestioned, whereas all other social spheres must be redefined (as religiously derived).

47. Cf. the end of the preceding section.

48. Cf. (23), especially "Weber's Methodology of Social Science," pp. 8–29.

## REFERENCES

1. Howard Becker, "Constructive Typology in the Social Sciences," in Harry Elmer Barnes, Howard Becker, and Frances Bennett Becker, Eds., *Contemporary Social Theory* (New York: Appleton-Century, 1940), pp. 17–46.

2.   Howard Becker, "Processes of Secularisation, An Ideal-Typical Analysis with Special Reference to Personality Change as Affected by Population Movement," *Sociological Review*, 24 (April–July 1932), 138–154; (October 1932), 266–286.

3.   Howard Becker and Robert C. Myers, "Sacred and Secular Aspects of Human Sociation," *Sociometry*, 5 (August 1942), 207–229; (November 1942), 355–370.

4.   Ernst Cassirer, *An Assay on Man* (New Haven: Yale University Press) 1944.

5.   Ernst Cassirer, *Language and Myth* (New York: Harper, 1946).

6.   Arthur Child, *The Problems of the Sociology of Knowledge* [Berkeley; University of California (unpublished Ph.D. thesis), 1938].

7.   Arthur Child, "On the Theory of the Categories," *Philosophy and Phenomenological Research*, 7 (December 1946), 316–335.

8.   Emile Durkheim, *The Elementary Forms of the Religious Life* (1912), translated by Joseph Ward Swain (London: Allen and Unwin; New York: Macmillan, 1915).

9.   Emile Durkheim, "Jugements de valeur et jugements de réalité" (1911), in *Sociologie et philosophie* (Paris: Alcan, 1924), pp. 117–142.

10.  Emile Durkheim, "Preface," *Année sociologique*, Vol. 2 (Paris: Alcan, 1899).

11.  Virgil G. Hinshaw, Jr., "Epistemological Relativism and the Sociology of Knowledge," *Philosophy of Science*, 15 (January 1948), 4–10.

12.  Virgil G. Hinshaw, Jr., "The Epistemological Relevance of Mannheim's Sociology of Knowledge," *Journal of Philosophy*, 40 (February 4, 1943), 57–72.

13.  H. A. Hodges, *Wilhelm Dilthey: An Introduction* (New York: Oxford University Press, 1944).

14.  Thelma Z. Lavine, "Naturalism and the Sociological Analysis of Knowledge," in Yervant H. Krikorian, Ed., *Naturalism and the Human Spirit* (New York: Columbia University Press, 1944), pp. 183–209.

15.  Thelma Z. Lavine, "Sociological Analysis of Cognitive Norms," *Journal of Philosophy*, 39 (June 18, 1942), 342–356.

16.  Clarence Irving Lewis, *Mind and the World-Order* (New York: Scribner, 1929).

17.  George A. Lundberg, "The Proximate Future of American Sociology: The Growth of Scientific Method," *American Journal of Sociology*, 50 (May 1945), 502–513.

18.  R. M. MacIver, *Society: A Textbook of Sociology* (New York: Farrar and Rinehart, 1937).

19.  Appendix, Clerk Maxwell on Determinism and Free Will [1873], in Lawrence J. Henderson, *The Order of Nature* (Cambridge: Harvard University Press, 1917).

20.  Robert K. Merton, "Civilization and Culture," *Sociology and Social Research*, 21 (November-December 1936), 103–113.

21. Robert K. Merton, "The Sociology of Knowledge," in Georges Gurvitch and Wilbert E. Moore, Eds., *Twentieth Century Sociology* (New York: Philosophical Library, 1945), pp. 366–405.

22. Vilfredo Pareto, *The Mind and Society*, translated by Andrew Bongiorno and Arthur Livingston (New York: Harcourt, Brace, 1935), 4 vols.

23. Talcott Parsons, Introduction to his and A. M. Henderson's translation of Max Weber, *The Theory of Social and Economic Organization* (New York: Oxford University Press, 1947).

24. Talcott Parsons, *The Structure of Social Action* (New York: McGraw-Hill, 1937).

25. Robert Redfield, "The Folk Society," *American Journal of Sociology,* **52** (January 1947), 293–308.

26. Alexander von Schelting, "Zum Streit um die Wissenssoziologie," *Archiv für Sozialwissenschaft und Sozialpolitik,* **57** (1929), especially 31–32.

27. Ferdinand Tönnies, *Gemeinschaft und Gesellschaft, Abhandlung des Communismus und des Socialismus als empirischer Culturformen* [1887], translated and supplemented by Charles P. Loomis: *Fundamental Concepts of Sociology (Gemeinschaft und Gesellschaft)* (New York: American Book, 1940).

28. Alfred Weber, *Ideen zur Staats-und Kultursoziologie* (Karlsruhe: Braun, 1927).

29. Kurt H. Wolff, "A Methodological Note on the Empirical Establishment of Culture Patterns," *American Sociological Review,* **10** (April 1945), 176–184 [Chapter 20].

30. Kurt H. Wolff, "Notes Toward A Sociocultural Interpretation of American Sociology," *American Sociological Review,* **11** (October 1946), 545–553 [Chapter 12].

31. Kurt H. Wolff, "A Partial Analysis of Student Reactions to President Roosevelt's Death," *Journal of Social Psychology,* **26** (August 1947), 35–53.

32. Kurt H. Wolff, "The Sociology of Knowledge: Emphasis on an Empirical Attitude," *Philosophy of Science,* **10** (April 1943), 104–123 [Chapter 26].

33. Florian Znaniecki, *The Method of Sociology* (New York: Farrar and Rinehart, 1934).

34. Florian Znaniecki, "The Proximate Future of Sociology: Controversies in Doctrine and Method," *American Journal of Sociology,* **50** (May 1945), 514–521.

35. Florian Znaniecki, "Social Organization and Institutions," in Georges Gurvitch and Wilbert E. Moore, Eds., *Twentieth Century Sociology* (New York: Philosophical Library, 1945), pp. 172–217.

---

Reprinted in modified form from *Philosophy of Science,* **15** (1948), 192–210, by permission of the publisher. The essay has been edited and partially revised by the author.

# 28

# A PRELIMINARY INQUIRY
# INTO THE SOCIOLOGY
# OF KNOWLEDGE
# FROM THE STANDPOINT
# OF THE STUDY OF MAN.
## 1953, 1950

### BACKGROUND MATERIALS

The sociology of knowledge [1] is usually considered the branch of sociology that studies relations between society and knowledge or knowledge in its social setting. The term itself, a translation of the German *Wissenssoziologie*, is widely recognized as a misnomer; actual contributions in the field have been concerned not so much with knowledge in the sense of scientific or positive knowledge as with ideologies, political doctrines, types or models of thought, and various other intellectual phenomena.

The two main antecedents of the sociology of knowledge are Marxism and Durkheimian sociology. Marxism (its vulgarized forms more notably than Marx's own writings) has tended to debunk intellectual behavior (except its own tenets) as ideological, that is, as rooted in the social, particularly the class, position of its exponents. Durkheimian sociology has concentrated on the relations between forms of society (chiefly primitive society) and forms or categories of thought. Neither Marx-Engels nor Durkheim and his followers used the term sociology of knowledge or its German or French equivalents. *Wissenssoziologie* itself, nourished by

Marxism more than by any other single source, flourished in Germany in the 1920s and, after the rise of Hitler, was transplanted mainly to the United States.

The two outstanding representatives of *Wissenssoziologie* were Max Scheler and Karl Mannheim. Scheler, a philosopher of phenomenologist inclination, tried to incorporate the sociology of knowledge into a system of philosophical anthropology, which, however, remained uncompleted. Mannheim formulated the difference between the sociology of knowledge and a sociological theory of knowledge but failed to solve the epistemological problems involved in this distinction. At the time that the sociology of knowledge was introduced in the United States, mainly through Wirth and Shils's translation of Mannheim's *Ideologie und Utopie*, closely related American efforts had been in existence for decades (and continue to exist, with little, though perhaps increasing, contact with the sociology of knowledge). These efforts are embodied, especially, in pragmatism and social behaviorism. Most American students interested in the field have based their labors on a combination of pragmatist and social-behaviorist ideas with German and, particularly, French ideas. In addition, the most systematic survey of the philosophical problems inherent in the sociology of knowledge, the most convenient summary of its sociological and research problems, and the most concise sketch of its background and its American relations stem from Americans—from Arthur Child, Robert K. Merton, and Louis Wirth, respectively [2].

The sociology of knowledge has been more speculative and theoretical than empirical, although it boasts some outstanding research. It has been both a scientific and a philosophical concern. Its heterogeneous antecedents and concepts have not been synthesized into a comprehensive theory designed to be tested empirically but instead, on the whole, have resulted in *more* (often polemic) formulations and conceptions. This state of affairs has discouraged acquaintance with the sociology of knowledge and its cultivation on the part of some students who are familiar with it. Its promise, as a scientific concern, would seem to lie in its liberation from those historical fetters that have kept it from developing into a general and systematic *sociology of intellectual-emotional behavior.*

If one were to undertake such a task, he would have to assemble the knowledge that has been gathered by a great many students in a great many fields, all of which bear on the central problem-complex of the sociology of knowledge—the relations between society and intellectual life. Obviously this applies to much work in the social sciences other than sociology and in the humanities but also in certain biological sciences. Overlooking all particular works and names, some of the most important areas of research and theory seem to be these: in the social sciences, in addition to general sociological findings and to more specialized findings (as in communication, public opinion, and propaganda), social psychology in a very broad sense (including child psychology, abnormal psychology and psychiatry, psychoanalysis and related movements, psychological testing, learning theory, and the study of social perception, attitudes, and social norms); cultural anthropology, particularly linguistics with its various subdivisions, the study of culture and personality, and the study of culture itself; in the humanities social and cultural history, literary criticism, historical linguistics, and the methodological and empirical aspects of philosophy—epistemology, semiotics, logic, metaphysics, ethics, and aesthetics; and, finally in the biological sciences, whatever throws light on the biological dimensions of intellectual behavior (i.e., especially the field of human genetics). All are sources of knowledge relevant to the problem of the relations between society and intellectual life. To assemble and dovetail them, obviously, is a tremendous task, but also, it would seem, a tremendous challenge.

What has just been presented is the kind of answer one might give to an outsider who asks: what is the sociology of knowledge? It is a commonsense description of it as a historical phenomenon. One might continue in a similar vein in reply to a closely related question: what has the sociology of knowledge given us by way of fruitful concepts or of scientific inquiries? Perhaps Mannheim's distinction between immanent (intrinsic) and transcendent (extrinsic) interpretation [3] or Znaniecki's typology of men of knowledge and of the social circle, self, social status, and social function of the man of knowledge [4] would be mentioned. Among scientific inquiries outstanding (but rather arbitrary) illustrations are Mannheim's earlier studies in historicism and conservative thought [5], Kohn-Bramstedt's work in the sociology of literature [6], Merton's investigation of seventeenth-century English science and technology [7], or Zilsel's explorations in the sociology of science [8]. Thus a vast and exciting panorama would be opened but to do so is not the purpose of this chapter. Its purpose is something I believe to be even more important. It is implied in the phrase "the study of man," from the standpoint of which the sociology of knowledge is to be considered.


### THE STUDY OF MAN


The concept of social science that I call the study of man emerged chiefly out of the research done in Loma [9]. In this chapter I am trying to act on one of the tenets of this study by addressing myself to the sociology of knowledge. I do it by foresight, in the same way in which I found by hindsight that Loma was the occasion for the emergence and application of the study of man. This tenet is the need for emphasizing the interaction between the student of man and his subject matter—which in the present case is the sociology of knowledge— by which both become clarified and thus change. Put differently, I am now asking a question similar to the one or to the whole row of questions I found myself asking in Loma: What does it mean for me to study the sociology of knowledge? What is the nature of my research, of my contact with it? Who am I to approach the sociology of knowledge, what am I to do with it or to inquire into [10]? What is the sociology of knowledge as an interpretation of the world, its historical and symptomatic significance? What sort of a man is the man who invents it and is fascinated by it?

The first step toward answers to these questions, to this one question, is to define the sociology of knowledge operationally so that it is clear what I am inquiring into. To do this it is important to realize that the sociology of knowledge has been an enterprise that has not limited itself to scientific concerns but has also run into philosophical, especially epistemological, problems, and that this is most transparent in its philosophical assertions and claims—most pointedly when they were not meant to be but were held to be scientific or were not clearly distinguished from scientific statements. The best known case in point is Karl Mannheim [11].

I take Arthur Child's summary of the philosophical problems of the sociology of knoweldge [12] as the operational definition of my inquiry into this field. I am aware of the limitation imposed on my undertaking by this choice; most notably I shall not do full justice to Scheler, but I feel sure I catch significant aspects of the area and at least am able to show how I can apply an important tenet of the study of man. This is more pertinent at this time than to make the undertaking more comprehensive and definitive.

Thus I shall present the occasion of my inquiry by expounding and questioning as briefly as possible Child's conception with the sole purpose of equipping myself better for answers to the questions on my mind. Hence the elaboration of the problems posed by Child in the following section is only an incidental by-product of pursuing my principal quest.

## ARTHUR CHILD'S SOCIOLOGY OF KNOWLEDGE

The basis of Child's studies in the sociology of knowledge is his doctoral dissertation [13], which is divided into eight chapters: Preliminary Approach, The Possibility of a Sociology of Knowledge, The Categorical Structure, The Relation Between Being and Thought, The Problem of

Imputation, The Problem of Truth, Immanent and Transcendent Interpretation, and Summary. Five of these chapters exist in revised form as published articles [14]. For convenience' sake, exposition and appraisal follow the chapter sequence of the dissertation.

*Ideology.* Child begins his dissertation with the "principal philosophical problems that arise out of a consideration of . . . [the] basic premises of the sociology of knowledge" *(Problems,* p. 1). After a brief discussion of the philosophical and historical origins of the field, the major portion of Chapter 1, Preliminary Approach, is devoted to a clarification of the concept of ideology. Two groups of theorists of ideology are distinguished. One holds that ideology is by its nature falsifying [15]; the other emphasizes the functional character of ideologies, and the function of an ideology may or may not be falsifying [16]. On the basis of the studies surveyed Child offers his own definition of ideology as

> a system of ideas which consciously or unconsciously tends to advance the interests—or reflect the class position—of some social class or section of such class *(Problems,* p. 22.)

Unfortunately, social class, one of the key terms in this definition is not defined.

*Legitimacy of the Sociology of Knowledge.* The title of the paper, which is a revision of the second dissertation chapter, «The Theoretical Possibility of the Sociology of Knowledge» [17], suggests a fundamental problem which, as Child points out, has been largely neglected.

> This problem may be formulated as follows: Is the sociology of knowledge, from a theoretical standpoint, even possible? And how, especially, can that possibility obtain a theoretical ground? . . . Unless one can establish the legitimacy of the sociology of knowledge, there would appear to be little reason in discussing the problems that can arise only on the presupposition of its legitimacy *(Possibility,* p. 392).

Child finds that the answers these and related questions have received in the extant literature are seldom explicit. Nevertheless he classifies their authors into three basic groups: those who altogether deny the possibility of the sociology of knowledge [18], those who deny its possibility as a science [19], and those who attempt a logical proof of the social determination of thought [20]. Yet the examination of these numerous efforts leads Child to make the statement that if most of the refutations of the sociology of knowledge depend on dogma and confusion, the sociologists of knowledge, on their side, have thus far advanced no coercive ground for the objectivity of social determination (*ibid.*, p. 413).

To provide such ground is the task Child has set for himself. In this undertaking, he starts from the premise that

no one with the slightest regard for the facts would deny that to some extent, in some fashion or other, thought does exhibit the influence of society. We shall therefore take this vague and indefinite sort of social determination as admitted; it is at least some kind of determination by a transcendent factor (*ibid.*, p. 414).

By which factor or factors, and in which way, is social determination effected? In answering these questions, three hypotheses may be entertained: thought is determined by one factor; it is determined by several factors acting individually; it is determined by several factors acting through one. Now, because it would appear that thought varies with geography, nationality, and race, the first possibility—the one-factor hypothesis—is ruled out, but so is the second alternative, for

it is within highly particularized social-historical contexts that factors of geography and race, for instance, exert their hardly deniable influence on mentality (*ibid.*, p. 415).

Hence, the third possibility is left, and this factor through which several others act

could hardly be other than the social. . . . If the last alternative could receive an adequate ground, therefore, as specified to the social, the arguments of postulational skepticism [21] would be met, at last, in the measure and in the sense in which it is at all possible to meet them (*ibid.*).

Thus Child arrives at his proper task—to advance a coercive ground for the objectivity of social determination. The only way in which this can be done, he writes, is to show that mind itself is social; and this, in fact, *has* been shown by George H. Mead [22]:

If mind itself has a social origin . . . and if thinking consists . . . in the manipulation of generalized attitudes . . . then

> there can be no question of the social determination . . . of
> knowledge and thought. And there can be no question, conse-
> quently, of the validity of the interpretation of thought from
> a social standpoint. Furthermore, if thought is indeed a social
> process, . . . then neither can there be any question that, what-
> ever transcendent determinants may exist besides society, they
> can determine mind only through the intermediation of social
> reality *(ibid.,* p. 416).

Yet, even if Mead's theory were accepted, Child continues, three qualifications must be made. First; the theory may justify the social interpretation of thought, but it is insufficient to justify the sociology of
knowledge because to do so assumptions are required in addition to
those needed to establish social interpretation itself. Yet, although Child
differentiates [23] between the social interpretation of thought and the
sociology of knowledge, he does not define the difference. Nevertheless,
however we would define it—even if we followed the qualification just
mentioned—Child has failed in his undertaking to ground the sociology
of knowledge theoretically, as he himself explicitly admits *(Possibility*,
p. 417).

Second, Mead's theory may justify social interpretation, but it

> leaves untouched the question of *the meaning and the extent*
> of social determination, as well as the problem of the inter-
> action between this objective determination, the inherent
> logic of thought itself, and the spontaneous activity of the
> organically individualized mind *(ibid.,* p. 417; italics added).

Inasmuch as these three interacting variables (social factors, logic, and
the individual) are neither defined nor shown to follow from Child's
preceding discussion, their interaction, indeed, calls for investigation, an
investigation that is not forthcoming in Child's work [24]. Third, Mead's
theory contains no research suggestions (cf. *Possibility,* p. 417). Nor
does Child stop his self-criticism at this point. He not only admits his
failure to demonstrate the theoretical possibility of the sociology of
knowledge but he also points out that Mead's theory itself (which would,
at least, demonstrate the possibility of social interpretation) has not been
proved:

> . . . there is a last, unavoidable reckoning with postulational
> skepticism—a reckoning, perhaps, which in a measure par-
> takes of concession. For even if, in the view of social be-
> haviorism, the theory of postulational skepticism has been

undermined, the invincible skeptic might retort that social behaviorism itself appears only on the assumption of the social postulate. But we can argue with the skeptic no further: here, it would seem, we have come to one of those ultimate philosophical oppositions beyond which no additional analysis can avail. At such a point, indeed, the thinker must make a decisive and unambiguous choice as to the postulates from which his constructive reasoning will flow, as to his final—and only in that sense metaphysical—assumptions (*ibid.*, p. 417).

In appraising Child's statements concerning the legitimacy of the sociology of knowledge, it must be pointed out that these statements suffer from the lack of a definition of legitimacy. This term may refer to the appropriateness of the sociology of knowledge as an instrument for ascertaining properties of knowledge (or intellectual behavior), society, and their relations. Such appropriateness can be established only on the basis of a metaphysical (more precisely, an ontological) theory [25]. Legitimacy may also refer to the appropriateness of the sociology of knowledge as an instrument for studying concrete phenomena that fall within its province, according to the definition of this field. Such appropriateness, by contrast to the former, can be established only through the empirical testing of a theory of the discipline [26].

Child fails to distinguish between these two referents of legitimacy—the metaphysical and the methodological. His admission that he has not demonstrated the legitimacy of the sociology of knowledge because he has not met Grünwald's objection actually refers only to his failure to demonstrate its metaphysical legitimacy, and he has failed to do so because he has not developed a metaphysic in which it alone could be grounded. His weakness thus is the same as Grünwald's. Unlike Grünwald, however, Child continues to examine problems of the sociology of knowledge as if he *had* established its legitimacy. The logical justification of this procedure lies in the fact that these problems are methodologically relevant irrespective of the question of ontological legitimacy. In other words, Child shifts from a failure in metaphysics to a heuristic approach in methodology.

*Categories.* Although Child has not established the (metaphysical) legitimacy of the sociology of knowledge and although (it will be remembered) he has said that without such legitimation "there would appear to be little reason to discuss the problems of the presupposition of its legitimacy," he does go on, as has just been anticipated, with this discussion. More precisely, in the next two chapters of his dissertation he undertakes to deal with the questions of what in thought is socially determined and what in society determines thought [27].

Child answers the first of these two questions by developing his concept of the categorical structure. This he conceives as intermediary between the substructure (a system of certain objective relationships at a specific time in history [*Problems*, pp. 85–86], that is, the economic-social-historical structure of a given period) and the superstructure, which is erected over the substructure [28]. The categorical structure, then, is the instrument with which the substructure determines the superstructure; it is the means for the transmission of social determination (*Problems*, p. 90).

This categorical structure—sometimes, in the terminology of other writers, called by such terms as standpoint, position, world view, attitude, and *Weltanschauung*—must be sharply distinguished from the Kantian categories of thought. Kant's categories, inherent in the mind, form all thought perpetually in the same way and in the same way for all men. By contrast, the categories, in the terminology of the sociology of knowledge, "are themselves formed by the substructure and therefore differ with different substructures and change as the substructure changes" (*ibid.*, p. 89). Despite the significance of the categorical structure, it has been explicitly considered (if not always by this name) by only three contributors to the sociology of knowledge—Scheler, Mannheim, and Grünwald. Their analyses, however, prove unsatisfactory to Child. He therefore turns elsewhere—again to Mead [29]—for a more satisfactory answer. Because, however, Child abandoned this Meadian elaboration in his later, more definitive, treatment of the question of the categories, it is not reviewed here.

This more definitive treatment [30] begins with the proposition that both types of theory dealing with the categories—those that posit the inherence of categories in human nature (e.g., Kant's) and those that, on the contrary, posit their social experiential origin (e.g., Mead's)—must be rejected. For on the one hand Kant failed to establish the universality and necessity of his categories. On the other, it must be recognized that categories cannot develop from experience unless experience itself is structured, that is, categorized.

The way out of this dilemma is the postulation of two types of category—primal and supervenient. The primal categories are biotic, that is, socially underived; the supervenient categories are sociotic, "originating within a social context except insofar as they grow out of the experiential foundation provided by, or in the sense that they follow the guidance of, the primal categories" (*Categories*, p. 318).

In accounting for the existence of these two types of category, Child (thus deviating from Mead [31] and from his own earlier position) defines them, in act, "as formalizing intentions" (*ibid.*, p. 320) which, translated into concepts, appear "as some mode, manner, or order of being" (*ibid.*, p. 321), and, in potency, as predispositions.

> The term "predisposition" denotes any typified potency of response, any latent organization of organic processes with reference to a type of stimulus (*ibid.*).

By implication, this definition admits that inframental responses may possess categoriality; and far from denying this admission, Child writes,

> . . . we say that mind is simply a special range of organically unified organic response and that, while the categories become mental forms when they function within the response-range designated as mental, they are primarily forms not of the mind but of the whole responding organism (*ibid.*, pp. 322–323).

Nor is the notion of predisposition in conflict with a distinction between the cognitive, the emotive, and the conative: these three functions

> can be distinguished only by the criterion of orientation or of preponderate intent. Cognitive predispositions are simply organic potencies of response as oriented toward knowledge of the world rather than toward some feeling of it or some action upon it (*ibid.*, p. 322).

However, "predispositions . . . may actualize in non-categorical ways; and formalizing intentions . . . need not formalize categorically" (*ibid.*, p. 323). The specific characteristic of categories, as compared with noncategorical dispositions, is that they function apriorily [32]. More precisely, the primal categories possess both Kantian marks of apriority—universality and necessity, whereas the supervenient categories possess only necessity. Lest his discussion of apriority be misunderstood, Child points out that although it is commonly associated with concepts, a sharp distinction must nevertheless be made between categories and concepts, including aprioric concepts: "concepts can have categorical relevance only if they derive from, or become funded in, those predispositions toward the world which we distinguish as categorical" (*ibid.*, p. 326). Thus the nonconceptualization of a category does not prove its nonexistence, and neither does the assertion that a given concept is the translation of a category prove the existence of that category, for although

the primal categories are presumably invariable in essence, the
concepts correlated with them continue, when once formulated, to develop and to undergo theoretical elaboration and
concatenation. And the conceptual correlates of the primal predispositions react upon those predispositions in the sense, at
least, of acquiring themselves predispositional correlates which
cluster around the original primal predispositions and which,
in consequence, affect the apprehension, as well as the understanding, which occurs in the sphere of the predisposition
concerned. Indeed, *it is in and through this process of accre-
tion that the primal categories exhibit their primordiality.* As
example of the way in which the concepts of the understanding may condition or provide the mode within which the
primal categories operate, consider the fact that space and
time may be differently felt in different cultures while the
basic biotic forms of apprehension remain the same in the
individuals of all different cultures. But, in so far as concepts
function in this way, they do so as functionalized in supervenient categories. These categories, the *a priori* formalizing
factors which do not inhere in men as animals, are those persistent and powerful tendencies to take the world as such-
and-such which, under certain circumstances, in certain people
or certain groups of people, have become compulsions. By
becoming compulsions they become categories. And it is not
at all surprising that these compulsions should sometimes
originate in concepts, for it is clear that essence and existence
stand, by and large, in a reciprocal relationship: we believe
according to our responses and we respond according to our
beliefs (*ibid.*, pp. 327–328; first italics added [in this connection, Child refers to Granet's work on Chinese thought]).

Although the question whether categories change has already been dealt
with indirectly in Child's paper, the last part of it is devoted to an
explicit discussion of that question. The crux of the answer is that biotic
(primal) categories do not change but sociotic (supervenient) categories
do—as well within an individual as interindividually, that is, both inter-
culturally and interepochally (*ibid.*, pp. 330–335).

In a brief appraisal of Child's theory of the categories it should, above
all, be pointed out that he has given us an entertainable description of
the nature of human thought. If we accept his distinction between primal
and supervenient categories, we can understand why the former should
be universal (because biotic) and why the latter should be specific, partic-
ularistic, relative (because socially or culturally [33] conditioned). This
concept throws considerable light on the difficult problem of understand-

ing in the sociology of knowledge or intellectual behavior: it presents a constant challenge not to confuse primal with supervenient categories [34] and to distinguish, in analyzing any case of empirical validity (and of other, at least hypothetically, primal categories), what is primal and what is supervenient. More broadly speaking, Child's theory promises well for research to establish empirically where the line between primal and supervenient sources in categories must be drawn (both individually and typically).

Despite this great achievement, there are at least two areas, pertinent in this context, with respect to which some questions must be raised. In the first place, Child does not incorporate the postulated compulsory character of the categories into the rest of his theory. In the second place, and probably more important, Child fails to relate attitudes to categories, a relation of which he makes much in the first version of his treatment of the categories (in *Problems,* Chapter III). Although, for reasons stated, that version has not been summarized here, the chief questions it raises must now be recorded.

1. It is not clear in what sense implicit behavior patterns are identical with attitudinal structure (*Problems,* pp. 114–116).

2. Attitude itself is not defined. This lack is especially regrettable because it precludes the elucidation of attitudinal structure, a term that would seem to imply (cf. the reference to standpoint and world view in the third paragraph of this section) that it is not a mere sum of attitudes but rather a particular organization of them.

3. The arrangement of attitudes in the attitudinal structure is left unanalyzed. As just observed, both the term attitudinal structure and the general context in which its discussion occurs point to the assumption that attitudes are not homogeneous but distinct in terms of importance or in similar terms.

4. The merely psychological treatment of the question of the categories fails to meet the problems of validity and logic.

The first three of these questions, it will be seen, are not answered by Child's second version of his theory of the categories. The reason is, as has been suggested, that Child leaves an analysis of attitudes out of consideration. In other words, Child has given a highly suggestive answer to the problems of validity and logic but he has discussed neither the nature of attitudes nor their relations to categories [35].

*Existential Determination of Thought.* We saw how Child deals with the question of what element in thought is socially determined. After answering this question—in the dissertation, in the concept of attitudinal structure, and later in his theory of the categories—Child discusses the complementary question, namely, what element in society determines thought. He again begins with an examination of relevant theories [36] and then undertakes to develop his own.

An analysis of the notion that class interests determine thought leads him to point out the difficulties with which this notion is afflicted. These difficulties concern the nature of class, the character of the relations between class interests and individual interests, the conflict between the diversity of individual interests, on the one hand, and the postulated unity of class interests, on the other, and similar problems. Child asks why should social context be at all identified with class? Although the individual admittedly exists in some social context, class is only one among several conceptualizations of social contexts, only one element of the social situation.

After thus reducing the range of class, Child proceeds to narrow that of interests. It must be remembered, he tells us, that

> the social determination of thought involves much more than
> a mere conformity to interests. How, by the theory of interests,
> could one explain the fact that in certain periods virtually all
> theoretical fields . . . become permeated by some conception,
> some intellectual tendency, some style of thought, which mani-
> festly possesses a social relevance but which cannot be derived,
> with any measure of conviction, from pure interests? [37]

In view of this consideration, Child subsumes the concept of interests— again following Mead—under that of "group attitudes as incorporated into the structure of the individual mind" (*Determination*, p. 182). More specifically, although interests, as Child admits, in some cases, at some time, determine group attitudes, there are other factors that determine these attitudes—factors such as social-historical tradition and social heredity,

> group emotion from whatever cause—whether from natural or
> social catastrophe, from movements of national aspiration,
> regeneration, triumph, from rivalry with other groups or
> co-operation with other groups (*ibid.*, p. 182),

and "the force of the individual genius" (*ibid.*, p. 183). Child emphasizes the advantages of elevating the concept of group attitudes (cf. *ibid.*, pp. 183–185) to the place often previously held by that of class interests.

In evaluating Child's notions concerning the existential determination of thought, it must be noted, in the first place, that although Child set out to ascertain what element in society determines thought, he again lands among the attitudes, that is, where he arrived when he discussed that other question [38], namely, what element in thought it is that is determined by society. In the second place, if group attitudes determine thought, the question of the precise relation between these two elements of intellectual-emotional behavior is not answered by Child. In this connection Mead's identification of thinking with the taking of attitudes [39] is of no help: are logic and validity merely attitudes, and if so, how are they distinguished from others? If they are not attitudes, what are they? In other words, Child has failed to incorporate the concept of attitudes into his theory of the existential determination of thought—as he has failed to do so (it will be remembered) in regard to his theory of the categories. Finally, it is not shown that the disadvantages of the concepts of class and class interest necessarily result in the abandonment, for a theory of social determination, of any typical social context whatsoever. Do these disadvantages indeed lead to the thesis (which seems to be implied by Child's statements) that the conceptualization of particular social contexts must be undertaken merely in the course of research? In some of his statements on imputation, Child himself operates with typical uniformities in social contexts when he speaks of ruling class, and so on. One may well think that typical uniformities in social contexts lend themselves to heuristic hypotheses if one remembers only, for instance, the uniformities correlated with the distribution of power and with other aspects of stratification. Thus Child, even if indirectly, has formulated another problem for the theory of the sociology of intellectual behavior to resolve.

*Imputation.*   Among the various problems evolved in the literature of the sociology of knowledge imputation is noteworthy for three reasons. One is that it can be handled as a nonphilosophical problem: for the scientist its most relevant aspect is his understanding of it in regard to his research. Another reason follows from the first: it takes perhaps less effort to clarify the problem of imputation and thus to aid the scientist than is true of most other problems in the field. Finally, Child's treatment of imputation results from a critique of the major writers on the topic and can thus be taken as an authoritative and up-to-date statement. Its presentation and analysis, therefore, should yield relatively conclusive arguments.

Child has discussed the problem on three occasions [40]. In his earliest statement he clearly links the phenomenon of imputation to that of ideology; nor is this link repudiated subsequently. Despite this and despite the historical background of the linkage, it will be shown that the connection must be rejected.

> We can impute a given ideology to a definite class . . . by discriminating the attitudes that have produced it and by then assigning the ideology to the class to which the attitudes belong. That is the foundation of social behaviorist imputation (*Problems*, p. 190).

In order, however, for the imputer to know how to relate attitudes to classes, the concepts of attitudinal structure, simple and ideal, are needed.

> A simple attitudinal structure . . . is an implicit behavior pattern determined by the position of a class with relation to the total social process, by the interests resulting therefrom and by the natural drives as modified through social interaction (*ibid.*, p. 191).

The ideal attitudinal structure, on the other hand, is *"rationally suited* to a definite, typical position in the process of production"; it is "a situationally adequate behavior pattern" (*ibid.*) and

> is the structure that *would* prevail if the actual implicit behaviour pattern of the class in question *did* in fact correspond to the objective position of the class in reference to the totality of the social structure (*ibid.*, p. 192).

Hence one can speak of an ideological representative of a class other than his own as of a person whose actual attitudinal structure is identical with the ideal attitudinal structure of the class (cf. *ibid.*, p. 193).

The revision (*Imputation*) of Child's first inquiry into imputation is limited to an appraisal of Szende's, Mannheim's, Grünwald's, and Lukács's theories concerning the topic. The result is a convincing statement of their inadequacy, followed by an allusion to future analysis of the questions raised. This analysis is presented in Child's third study of imputation (*Resolved*).

The crux of the relevant literature, Child argues, is the assumption, shared by all contributors discussed in his second paper but not stated explicitly by any of them, that it is valid to impute ideas to socioeconomic classes. An investigation of this assumption is Child's prime motive, and from this investigation flow nine theses relative to imputation. These theses are not explicitly stated, but they may be construed profitably as such on the basis of a study of Child's propositions. They are briefly expounded here in the approximate order of their occurrence.

1. Imputation must be to "groups as they are rather than . . . to an ideal . . . class consciousness" (*Resolved*, p. 97). The reason, Child points out, is that ideal-typical class consciousness (Lukács's concept) is ideal not only in the traditional sense of being true to a type constructed as a limit of purity from atypical admixtures but also in the sense "of an end of personal or group desire" (*ibid.*) on the part of the imputer. In other words, despite the fact that ideal, as used in the term ideal type, customarily refers to empirically unattainable purity, Child suggests that the word, in this same concept, also partakes of the more colloquial referent of ideal—goal, aim, or challenge: the imputer vaguely entertains some such ideal and constructs his ideal type in conformance with it [41].

2. "The primary concern of imputation . . . lies . . . with the level of systematic theory"; for, in regard to perceptions they agree in general for practical purposes; and as for simple judgments they can be imputed only to some integral mode of interpretation as fragments thereof. In this case "the process of imputation would consist merely in the formation and verification of a hypothesis as to the implicit systematic relationship between simple judgments," (*ibid.*, p. 98).

3. Imputation is directed toward the constitutive function of the categories of thought; that is, it has as its subject matter different interpretations of approximately identical parts of reality. These interpretations are co-constituted by different categorical structures. Negatively, imputation is not concerned with the selective function of the categorical structure; it does not have as its subject matter interpretations of different parts of reality. The reason is that conflict occurs not among interpretations of different things but among different interpretations of the same thing. In practice, therefore, it is only in this second case that the need for (as well as the difficulties of) imputation develops (*ibid.*, pp. 98–99).

4. "For an idea to be imputable to any given class, sub-class, or stratum, it must so prevail among the members of that group . . . as recognizably to constitute the norm." Inversely, "the thought of any member of the group who does not have as his own that particular idea (or, more exactly, who does not think in such fashion that he has, or in principal could have, that particular idea as his own when the appropriate occasion arises) must . . . be recognizable as a deviation from the norm" (*ibid.*, p. 99). This is so because to be imputable to a group an idea must derive from "categories that are either peculiar to or primary to the given group" (*ibid.*).

5. Under normal conditions (i.e., under conditions not characterized by far-reaching changes in the power structure of the society under discussion) only a ruling class has "any considerable body of ideas—[that is, a] ... more or less systematically articulated set of convictions, principles, beliefs, and opinions—of the nature which one terms 'ideological'" (*ibid.*). The question how one can determine whether a given ideology belongs to a given ruling class is answered as follows: "if the members of a ruling class reward the person who thinks in certain ways, if, that is, they encourage such thinking; if they themselves, insofar as they are themselves ideologically fertile, produce ideology of the type in question; if such ideology, by whomever produced, appears acceptable to, and vital in the lives of, the normal members of that class—then the imputation of the ideological tendency to the particular class in question seems quite justified" (*ibid.*).

6. Subordinate or nonruling classes have ideologies only in the midst of some great social crisis, especially in times of revolution. Although "the categories of critical or revolutionary periods may exist implicitly in, and develop from, earlier vague tendencies of thought," they "would not be systematically elaborated ... into an integrated ideological structure; for the ideology actually prevalent in that class during a normal period would be the ideology of the dominant social class" (*ibid.*, p. 102).

7. "In a full and primary sense, the imputation of an integrated, systematically elaborated ideology can be made only to a group which is organized deliberately and ideologically ... —not to the class or classes which that specialized group attempts to lead" (*ibid.*, p. 104), for, "because of its necessarily critical, expanded, additive, and organized nature" (*ibid.*, p. 103), an ideology is really possessed only by particular individuals making up an organization "which, while usually composed in the main by members of the class in question, is, nevertheless, an organization quite distinct from the class itself" (*ibid.*). This holds good for both normal and critical periods: in either case it is only an elite, not the mass of people making up a class, which can properly be said to have an ideology [42].

8. Although "in the case of a socioeconomic class, an ideology can legitimately be imputed only in the sense of prevailing among what appears to be the majority of the members of the class ... , in the case of ideologically organized groups, ... imputation proceeds on the basis of the acknowledged ideal of the members as organized" (*ibid.*, pp. 105–106).

9. According to G. H. Mead, all ideas have a group origin: even if an idea is developed by an individual, the mind of this individual is itself

the result of social interaction. Ideologies, as a particular kind of ideas, must therefore be shown to have a particular social origin. We have seen Child's early definition to ideology. Now he writes that "the individual origination of ideologies does seem to involve a quite explicit and conscious group reference" (*Resolved*, p. 106). An examination of this group reference shows that the ideologist refers in his ideology not necessarily to the group to which he belongs (in some one of the various senses of belonging), but to the group he represents. In consequence, imputation, too, is concerned only with the group a thinker represents, that is, with the group with which the thinker "actively identifies himself . . . , whose interests, whose aims, whose desires, whose ideals . . . he attempts to make his own" (*ibid.*, p. 107) and which, in addition, recognizes his leadership: representation refers to a reciprocal process. Further, "it is . . . the ideologically organized group alone of which the ideologist can be a representative; and it is only such an affiliational group . . . to which in general the ideas of the ideologist can legitimately be imputed" (*ibid.*, p. 108).

Child's linkage of imputation to ideology requires an appraisal of his concept of ideology before his statements on imputation can be appreciated. The definition of ideology recalled in connection with Thesis 9 suffers from relatively unanalyzed terms. Nor is this definition clarified when it is applied to other relevant passages in Child's writings on imputation. A comparison of these passages raises the questions whether any or only a ruling class can have an ideology; what unconscious ideology refers to; whether the ideas about a class's position in society which are taken for granted both by that class and by members of other classes are ideological (as they are according to the earlier definition of ideology) or not (as they seem to be according to several among the theses on imputation); whether, ideological or not, they can be imputed and, if so, how and to which class.

An inspection of Child's statements on imputation itself shows a shift of interest from methodology (cf. the emphasis on such concepts as simple attitudinal structure and ideal attitudinal structure) to social structure (cf. the discussion of class, affiliational group, and elite in regard to imputation). The chief unsolved problems of the earlier phase concern the interrelated conceptualizations and the operational definitions of class and of similar group (structural) terms, of simple and ideal attitudinal structure, and of class (etc.) with relation to the total social process or structure.

In the later phase these problems are omitted from consideration rather than solved. A study of this later phase—of *Resolved* or of its exposition in the form of the nine theses presented—shows that the range of imputation is ever more narrowed down in the course of the argument: ever more qualifications are admitted until at the end Child states: "The notion of imputation, indeed, perhaps obscures considerably more than it illuminates" (*Resolved*, p. 109). An examination of this skeptical statement may help to determine the sense in which the term imputation may legitimately be used at all.

Child employs this term in a number of ways. Thus a comparison of Theses 4, 7, and 8 shows that in Thesis 8 Child draws on the first two and distinguishes between their applications. Concretely, which of their applications are possible? They would seem to be as follows: An ideological statement (always provided a statement can be identified as ideological) can be imputed to a class (to that of the person making the statement or to some other class) if the statement made is subscribed to by the majority of the members of that class—regardless, it would appear, of whether the person making the statement is aware of its being subscribed to by those others. If he is aware, imputation becomes synonymous with the imputer's discovery of social solidarity, social cohesion, *esprit de corps*, or the like—but why should this discovery be called imputation? If the person making the statement is not aware of its being subscribed to by other members of that class, imputation becomes synonymous with enunciating a classificatory proposition, which is different in no way from other classificatory propositions; hence, again, there is no justification for applying the term imputation.

An ideological statement, however, can also be imputed to an ideologically organized group, provided the statement made is part of the ideology of that group. In this situation there would appear to be three possibilities.

1. The student may impute the statement to the group of which the person making it is a member or with which he otherwise identifies himself. In this case imputation becomes synonymous with the discovery of affiliation, membership, solidarity, or the like.

2. The student may impute the statement to a group of whose existence —or of his own relation to which—the person making the statement is not aware. In this case imputation becomes synonymous with enunciating a classificatory proposition.

3. The student may impute the statement to some group other than the group whose ideology the person making the statement erroneously believes himself to share. In this case, imputation becomes synonymous with the ascertainment of an error. In none of these cases, clearly, is the term imputation anything but misleading.

In accordance with Thesis 2, Child makes still another use of the concept of imputation: he uses it in the sense of Mannheim's *sinngemässe Zurechnung*. Is there, this time, any justification for using the term? The kind of inquiry within which such imputation has its place is the social interpretation (however this may be understood) of an intellectual product. While proceeding with a given social interpretation I am stimulated by certain elements, which I encounter in the intellectual product, to construct a *Weltanschauung* or attitudinal structure or similar construct and to test it by using it as a frame of reference for as many other elements (thoughts, concepts, etc.) as possible. In this procedure, according to the fate of my hypothesis, I find elements that explicitly contain their own relationship to the structure hypothesized. I find elements that can implicationally be related to this structure—which confirm, contradict, support, and qualify it (and the tracing of such implicational relations is part of "immanent interpretation" [43], or I find relations by analogy. Here again, and for reasons parallelling those mentioned in the preceding analysis of comparable cases, the concept of imputation has no specific referent.

It follows that imputation is not, hence should not be used as, a concept denoting fact. It is therefore proposed to use it only as a concept that refers to a heuristic-hypothetical relation between an element of thought, emotion, or volition, on the one hand, and a group, institution, time, *Weltanschauung*, or attitudinal structure, on the other. It will now be clear why it was anticipated that a concept of imputation is unrelated to that of ideology, for imputation, as understood here, applies equally well to all cognitive, affective, and conative phenomena and in no way preferentially, much less exclusively, to ideologies, however they may be defined.

In attempting to expound the Childian concept of imputation in its essentials (the nine theses), I did not comment on all of them, most notably parts of Thesis 2 and Thesis 3. The reason for this was implied earlier when it was suggested that for the practicing sociologist of intellectual behavior imputation need not be a philosophical problem (as largely implied in Theses 2 and 3).

In the Marxian tradition imputation has overwhelmingly had a polemic, debunking function for which there is no room in scientific procedure. This historical background suggests why the problem of imputation should have been tied up with such problems as the relativity of truth and validity and with other philosophical, especially epistemological, concerns. The present discussion, on the basis of Child's views, tries to separate it from such problems, which are not, of course, solved thereby. What, if any, is their scientific relevance?

It is submitted that their chief scientific relevance lies in the attention that such problems—as illustrated by the history of the concept of imputation and of its ramifications—have called to the existence of, and to the historical failure to distinguish between, the unavoidable scientific postulate of both fact (as the intended subject matter of the scientist) and interpretation (as his relation to fact). Here I have tried to show that imputation has been used as an untenable bridge between the two, and have advocated its use as a frankly interpretive concept. The same kind of confusion also besets, for example, the use of the concept of social class; it is not clear whether this concept is a factually vague term employed in the course of evincing an interpretation of social structure or of history (not only Marxian) or an interpretively barren exercise in statistics. Similar observations could be made in regard to ideology. Both facts and interpretation as well as an ever refined reflection on both these tools are needed for optimal science. I hope that this need has become plausible, in a preliminary form, through an appraisal of imputation.

*Truth.* The discussion of Lukács's, Scheler's, Mannheim's, and Grünwald's treatments of truth [44] according to Child raises at least three questions regarding the concept of truth:

> First, there is the question of the sense in which, if at all, the concept of truth can apply to propositions assertive of concrete relationships between society and thought. With this question we shall not deal further, for our position . . . would follow, in any event, from our later discussion. There is the matter, second, of the relationship between the genesis of an idea and its truth; this question we shall presently take up with the idea of dismissing it. And then, third, there is the problem of the manner in which, the extent to which, and, perhaps, the social position from which, valid knowing can occur. The essence of the third problem, which we find the central and the only real problem, we prefer to re-formulate in its sharpest form as, namely, the problem of the possibility of a common and objective truth. To this we shall devote our attention as soon as we can dismiss the pseudo-problem of origin and validity (*Truth,* p. 22).

The origin-validity problem is a pseudo-problem because it can appear only if possible-accidental relations are confused with necessary-essential relations [45]. More particularly, if summarily,

> the relevance of origin to validity in this and only this: By investigating the origin of an idea, the student may be able to establish how it was, in some particular instance, that a spe-

cific ideologist, given his personal abilities and limitations, was socially enabled to develop an idea that was valid or was socially restricted to the development of an idea that was not valid. Or, conversely, departing from some social situation, the student may predict whether valid theories or invalid theories should be developed by the ideologists of the situation; and he may then proceed to test his prediction by the theories that actually were, or actually will be, developed. But in neither case does the genesis of an idea in any sense establish validity or invalidity; it can do no more than to explain the social possibility or to allow a prediction based on social probability. Always, therefore, *the validity of an idea—as well as its origin —is a matter for concrete and specific investigation; and the mere social derivation of an idea proves nothing whatsoever, one way or another, about its factual validity (ibid.,* p. 24; italics added).

The second question concerning truth, then, is how a common objective truth is possible. In answering this question, Child makes use of his conception of categories as predispositions and of his distinction between primal and supervenient categories. Error is possible only by social accretions (to the primal categories):

> . . . one of the chief causes of . . . error is . . . that the supervenient categories develop in part, too, under the influence of social determinants, the diversity of society being accompanied by a diversity in the interpretations of the same objective world. Still, these categories which yield error are also the only means to a more than primitive truth [i.e., to a truth other than that given by the primal categories]. Hence the problem of how a common objective truth . . . is possible in spite of, and yet through, the socially co-determined categories (*ibid.,* p. 32).

The resolution of this lies in the concept of creativity, of the independent directive power of mind, by virtue of which the individual "can and does criticize certain of his predispostions through the medium of others" (*ibid.*).

In an effort to appraise Child's concept of truth as related to the sociology of knowledge, several points must be made. Regarding the origin-validity problem, we noted that Child views it as a mere pseudo-problem, a problem that cannot and need not be solved on the basis of a theory of truth but only empirically from case to case. We can also formulate this view by saying that social origins and criteria of validity are two distinct classes of phenomena which, moreover, are related not logically but only empirically. It would seem, however, that one could, by empirical study, establish typical situations in which typical approximations to valid thought have a typical chance of occurring [46]. Although one must agree with Child's definition of the origin-validity problem as a theoretical pseudo-problem, it must be pointed out that empirical analysis could be carried considerably further than he has indicated. It must be added, also, that both in this context and in his inquiry into the problem of a common and objective truth Child has failed to define validity and, to relate specifically the problem of how universal validity is possible to the problem of how a common and objective truth is possible. (It is indicated above that his theory of primal and supervenient categories lends itself to a solution of the problem of universal validity but the theory does not explicitly offer this solution).

After anticipating so much of the problem of a common and objective truth it remains only to recall the relation between Child's distinction of primal from supervenient categories and truth. Primal categories, by their very definition, are incapable of error; error is due to the fact that we necessarily, because of our social heritage, operate with supervenient, socially codetermined categories. Hence we ask how we can correct error. The answer is the postulate of the creativity of mind [47]. Child, however, fails to analyze the normative concept of validity in relation to the other, structural, concepts. Does validity emerge from the interaction of primal and supervenient categories with the creativity and critical faculty of mind? Child's statements would seem to point to an affirmative answer but they do not give it explicitly.

Still another observation must be made. Child, without saying so, actually deals with only one type of truth—scientific truth [48]. It would appear, however, that there are other types of truth as well, types that must be accounted for by a theory of truth as needed by a sociology of knowledge and of intellectual behavior [49]. Such a theory will have to resolve the problems indicated here—categories and validity, validity and truth, types of truth—and it will probably do well to draw on Child's highly suggestive propositions.

*Immanent and Transcendent Interpretation.*   The last problem taken up in Child's dissertation is that of the nature and relation of immanent and transcendent interpretation. To begin with, Child states that the sociology of knowledge, like the histories of science, literature, or philosophy, is knowledge about knowledge and, in that capacity, is bound to interpret its data. Further, the mode of interpretation of the sociology of knowledge is not immanent but transcendent and, more specifically, sociological [50].

The two explicit statements regarding interpretation come from Mannheim and Grünwald. Mannheim's weakness, Child points out, lies in his presentation of ideological and sociological interpretation as alternatives —to which, of course, other optional interpretations might be added. This fact opens Mannheim's position to Grünwald's skeptical strictures. To overcome the objections of Grünwald's postulational skepticism is, in Child's view, indeed the major problem of a theory of interpretation. In other words, it must be demonstrated that both types of interpretation—immanent and transcendent—are objectively warranted. Child's solution of the problem is the proposition of the objectively-real dual causation of thought. That is, thought is caused immanently and this warrants immanent interpretation. It is also caused socially (if one accepts Mead's theory of mind) and this warrants social or sociological interpretation. Hence the two interpretations are more than optional in Grünwalds' sense.

It remains only to show the nature of the relations between these two interpretations. This can be done by a closer analysis of the two aspects of thought. Immanent causation of thought refers to its immanent logic or implicational consistency, and this is what immanent interpretation examines. Social causation, or determination, of thought has in turn a dual aspect, selective and constitutive: social existence selects, but it also, through the medium of the attitudinal structure, coconstitutes what is selected. The implicit behavior patterns

> so select and so integrate that . . . the realized mental-structures . . . represent a perspectival apprehension of reality (*Problems*, p. 286).
>
> . . . social determination determines precisely what, out of the vast realm of objectivity, . . . [the thinking individual] does attempt to know. And various of the possible conceptual aggregates represent emphases—and often distorted and distorting emphases—upon certain isolated elements of the objective truth. It results, therefore, . . . that despite . . . [the] search for reality, the sociological determination of the thought of some particular group can inform the mental-structures of that group in a peculiar manner. And it is this ensuing characteristic tone of the thought of any group that signifies the constitutive relevance of social existence.
>
> Selective relevance is not incompatible, then, with constitutive relevance. And on the basis of the view of the sociology of

knowledge here presented, they tend, indeed, to merge into one (*ibid.*, pp. 286–287).

This analysis leads Child back to the problem of truth and to a supplementation of the statements made earlier in his dissertation [51]. "We noted," Child writes,

> that any thinker, no matter of what class, can think only with the aid of the already existing thought materials. He can rework them, he can modify them greatly, he can add to them; but use them he must: the sociology of knowledge is not needed to tell us this . . . Now the sociology of knowledge teaches that some position in society . . . possesses superior truth-capabilities; that social determination of a certain sort or sorts affords superior opportunities for the genuine cognition of reality. But consider this contention alongside of the undeniable fact of the intellectual dependence of all thinkers upon the past. Do not these two propositions imply that no one position can stake out the exclusive potentialities for the cognition of truth? For the fact that elements not merely from the thought of the past, but also from the contemporaneous thought of other and even very antagonistic groups, become inextricably incorporated in the thought of that more favored social-historical position—this fact means that considerable sections of the thought of previous as well as of less favored contemporaneous groups must actually penetrate through the veil of class illusion and apprehend the structure of the objective world. The possibility of truth, then, is not confined to any one class even at a particular period in the development of society (*ibid.*, pp. 288–289).

Child concludes his chapter [52] with an allocation of the two modes of interpretation among the efforts of understanding human thought.

> If, as we have shown, the immanent and transcendent processes [of thought] interact; if the search for reality (and the flight from reality) in which all men, in their various degrees and manners, are engaged, necessitates that interaction of both immanent and transcendent processes; if mental-structures represent an amalgamation, through the selective and constitutive activities of the categorical apparatus, of both immanent and transcendent elements—then to split immanent and transcendent interpretation away from each other, and to forbid their cooperation in the momentous task of understanding the development of thought, constitutes a vi-

cious bifurcation, an illegitimate dichotomy, a violation of that integral unity which reality itself has created (*ibid.*, p. 291).

This combination of the two interpretations, Child intimates, will not be easy; on the contrary, it will be more difficult than either interpretation alone, but the necessity of performing the twofold interpretation is the unavoidable consequence of the foregoing considerations. These considerations lead to one more conclusion, which Child states as follows:

> . . . a correct understanding of those basic concepts of the sociology of knowledge—immanent and transcendent interpretation—leads, when that understanding is carried to its limits, to the abolition of the sociology of knowledge itself and to its reconciliation with the historical school in opposition to which it arose.

> Standing before a higher synthesis, we must not regret the inevitable mortality of its partial and abstract moments (*ibid.*, p. 292).

Child has not incorporated his theory of interpretation into his late papers on categories and truth. Hence there is no statement from him concerning (above all) the connection between the categories and the dual nature and causation of thought, immanent and social. The tracing of this connection therefore appears as another task and as a task to be handled in the context of the closely related inquiry into the nature of interpretation itself. Such an inquiry, furthermore, will have to face and elucidate Child's conclusion that the correct understanding of the sociology of intellectual behavior, on his view of interpretation, leads to its own abolition and reconciliation with historicist immanent interpretation.

### THE SOCIOLOGY OF KNOWLEDGE
### FROM THE STANDPOINT OF THE STUDY OF MAN

In accordance with the intent of this paper, I now argue—instead of tackling any of the problems just mentioned—that we are ready to begin inquiring into the meaning of the sociology of knowledge as an interpretion of the world, as a way of looking at the world, into its historical significance and symptomatic character, and into the image of the man who has invented it and is fascinated by it.

*Tasks Left by Child.* My first step is to recapitulate the major tasks [53] that Child, explicitly or implicitly, has set for a concept, entailed by his own work, of the sociology of knowledge and of intellectual-emotional behavior in general:

1. Definition of ideology, in which terms themselves are defined (p. 514) [54].

2. Typology of intellectual-emotional products, with allocation of ideologies (p. 514).

3. Metaphysical theory in which to ground the appropriateness of the sociology of intellectual-emotional behavior as an instrument for ascertaining properties of intellectual-emotional behavior, including knowledge, of society, and of their interrelations (pp. 514–517).

4. Definitions of attitude, attitudinal structure, thought, and knowledge, and of their interrelations (pp. 517–521).

5. Elucidation of the compulsory character of the categories of thought (pp. 517–521).

6. Definition of "social" and "cultural" and elucidation of their interrelations (pp. 517–521).

7. Definition of (social) class (possibly in relation to 1 above)(pp. 521–523).

8. Definition of "interests" and elucidation of their relations to other types of intellectual-emotional behavior (pp. 521–523).

9. Typology of social contexts (pp. 521–523).

10. Typology of social positions in regard to accessibility (and to other relations) to truth (pp. 530–532).

11. An epistemology; particularly, a theory concerning the relations between categories, truth, and validity, and the social relations of all these (to be handled in relation to 3 above) (pp. 530–532).

12. Typology of knowledge (pp. 530–532).

13. Theory of interpretation as related to all preceding problems (pp. 532–535) [55].

This list contains several kinds of problem, among which are methodological and metaphysical. The various tasks regarding definitions and typologies belong to the former; certainly the task to develop a metaphysical theory in which to ground the appropriateness of the sociology of knowledge and probably the task to articulate a theory concerning the relations between categories, truth, and validity, to the latter. By a methodological problem I mean one that is concerned with procedure of inquiry and to which statements on the nature of reality are irrelevant. By a metaphysical problem I mean one that is concerned with the nature of reality. The different purposes and subject matters of methodological and metaphysical problems entail different criteria of confirmation. For the former the criterion is pragmatic with reference to a given inquiry or type of inquiry (e.g., scientific or philosophical): it is a means criterion. For the latter it is agreement with the result of the most rigorously imaginable intrasubjective dialectical examination of one's most important experiences at one's most honest: it is an end criterion [56].

*Methodological Premises of the Sociology of Knowledge.* This is suggested in order to lend greater weight to the list of methodological premises of the sociology of knowledge as it is presented by Arthur Child (and, although certainly not always in Childian terms, by most other writers in the field), that is, to the list of propositions accepted as useful guides in the pursuit of (scientific) research. In a roughly descending order of certainty and clarity these premises appear to be the following:

1. The validity of thought has nothing to do with its origin.

2. There are logical and there are social aspects of thought; they can be illuminated by immanent (intrinsic) and transcendent (extrinsic) interpretation, respectively.

3. Man's thought is in some sense determined by attitudes, which in turn are incorporated into the structure of the individual mind. Further methodological statements could be added with respect to the kinds of group in which the individual develops his attitudes (family, play group, etc.) and with respect to the relations between attitudes and thoughts (cf. Pareto and Cooley).

4. There are primal and there are supervenient categories.

5. The social component in the supervenient categories accounts for the possibility of (factual and/or logical?) error; and the creativity or independent directive power of mind accounts for the corrigibility of error.

It may be noted that a satisfactory definition of all these terms (and, of course, of several others) will go a long way toward producing a methodological framework of the sociology of knowledge; that is, it will contribute much toward establishing the sociology of knowledge as a *science*.

*Volitional Premises of the Sociology of Knowledge.* I suggest that these methodological premises, these propositions accepted as useful guides in the pursuit of scientific research, are based on other premises, which are volitional. Both methodological and metaphysical concerns, I submit, are in the service of interpreting the world in which man (and society) engaged in interpreting lives; and interpretation is both a cognitive and a volitional enterprise. In my interpretation I come to *know* something and to *want* something. The methodological premises of the sociology of knowledge which I have listed indicate some of the subject matter about which the sociologist of knowledge who acts on these premises expects to come to know something (scientifically). I suggest that it is what he *wants* that has led him to find these methodological premises and these subject matters. What do I, as a sociologist of knowledge, want? A list of my wishes might look like this:

1. Origin-Validity. I want social relevance, but I also want unimpeachable validity. I do not want absolute relativism.

2. Interpretation. I want maximum intrinsic interpretation and I want maximum extrinsic interpretation.

3. Thought-Attitude-Group. I want to see man as logical (rational) and emotional (irrational); hence I investigate the interaction of thought and attitude. I want to see man as a social being, whose even innermost thought is socially codetermined.

4. Categories. I want to understand as many different thoughts as I can, but in order to do so, I must postulate universal features of thought (the primal categories). At the same time I want to preserve the specificity of thought. I therefore seek to guarantee this specificity by raising it to categorical status (the supervenient categories).

5. Error. I want to account for error and its corrigibility—could I do so in terms of my notions about the categories?

6. Social Interpretation versus Sociology of Knowledge. Although social interpretation makes sense, I have not yet found grounds for institutionalizing the sociology of knowledge as a discipline. Might not the reason be that it is a latecomer and that (comparable to sociology itself) it thus does not have the tradition that would allocate a place for it among the disciplines? Might this not suggest a reconsideration of our whole classi-

fication of disciplines, with a view to revising it in terms of methodological considerations, not of historical contingencies, and (I add *as* a sociologist of knowledge, that is, a person who is aware of some of his metaphysical premises and abides by them) in terms of metaphysical considerations?

*Metaphysical Premises of the Sociology of Knowledge.* I now go a step further and ask: What do I find out about the nature of reality, about my own reality, from an analysis of these wishes? I restate these wishes in fewer and more comprehensive terms:

1. I want social relatedness but I also want validity. I want to acknowledge the fact and to account for this fact, which is real to me, that matters are relative (socially, culturally, and biologically) and that they are true, irrespective of their relativity.

2. In slightly different terms: I want maximum intrinsic interpretation and I want maximum extrinsic interpretation. A poem is a poem, but it also has an origin, has come to be, and there is a relation between its origin and what it is. What is it? I want to push both intrinsic and extrinsic interpretation to the limit in order to find out.

3. A third variant: I want to understand phenomena in their own terms and I want to understand them as instances of laws. I want to carry each of these wishes to its extreme in order to do right by both.

I am discovering that these are indeed variations on two themes. I identify one of them by the form of these wish variations: the wishes are contrasting and complementary, based on the fact that matters are both relative and absolute—with the variations of this theme. The theme is dualism. I am discovering that I am espousing dualism, a metaphysical premise of the sociology of knowledge as an interpretation of the world, and this metaphysical premise is confirmed by the most rigorous examination of my most important experiences: as a student of man who wants to find out what the sociology of knowledge is and thus who *he* is, I find that I espouse dualism.

I identify the other theme by the content of my wish variations, which is the value placed on inquiry. I call this theme naturalism, in the sense of continuity of analysis [57]: I do not hesitate before an inquiry. On the contrary, I insist on investigating anything that may come to my attention as long as I have a hunch that it might be relevant to my inquiry. Furthermore, I try to enlist methodological aids that will make me more alert to investigable objects and to relevance [58].

*Dualism and Naturalism as Metaphysical Premises.* Once more I ask
what it means to say that dualism and naturalism are *metaphysical* premises of the sociology of knowledge as I have come to recognize in my
inquiry. A metaphysical problem, I said, is a problem concerned with
the nature of reality, with ascertaining what is real; and the criterion for
confirming a solution of a metaphysical problem is agreement with the
result of the most rigorously imaginable intrasubjective dialectical examination of that solution in the light of one's most important experiences
at his most honest. I must make the description of this criterion more
exact and find that it is more accurate to say that the criterion of confirmation is the illumination and confirmation of one's experiences that
one considers intrinsic to one's reality. What attainment of reality I have
experienced tells me such and such—namely, a metaphysical statement—
about reality. In the life of a person who has such a view of metaphysical
statements these statements will never be static: the absolute is relative
to his inquiry, which is life-long. And metaphysical statements can be
discussed; the dialectical method for their examination can be applied
intersubjectively.

I have said that this very continuity of inquiry, naturalism, is also a
metaphysical premise. If my definition of a metaphysical statement holds,
the metaphysical premise of continuity of inquiry is derived from some
statement about the nature of reality, namely, that reality is investigable.
This statement does not make investigation desirable. The desirability of
investigation again follows from my experience: what attainment of reality I have experienced tells me that surrender [59] to reality is the
method of attaining it and, furthermore, that inquiry into anything that
comes to my attention, as long as I have a hunch that it might be relevant to it, is inseparable from the idea and practice of surrender. To say
so is to articulate a valuation, which valuation, as this case clearly shows,
is conducive to the investigation of reality. Both predications of reality
and valuations of reality are thus metaphysical acts. The former may be
called ontological, the latter, valuational.

Metaphysical statements, both ontological and valuational, are relatively absolute, that is, absolute relative to experience which, relative to a
given stage of the individual's life, is absolute. This formulation allows us
to distinguish valuational from volitional statements. I believe it is no
accident that the list of volitional premises of the sociology of knowledge
given above is longer and more particular than that of its metaphysical
premises, which are three closely related statements that turned out to be
variations on two themes. There is more to the difference between the
two sets than is appreciated by calling the second, as I did, a restatement
of the first in fewer and more comprehensive terms. The volitional prem-

ises of the sociology of knowledge, I suggested, lead the student to his methodological premises, which in turn help him to learn something about the subject matters he wants to know about. Why does he want to know about these subject matters? Because of the time in which he lives. His time is the occasion on which he develops wishes and methods, but when he takes this occasion, in the form of his methodological and volitional premises, to attain reality which is not time-bound and historical, he begins to make metaphysical statements, ontological and valuational. The relation between both the methodological and volitional premises of the sociology of knowledge and its metaphysical premises parallels that between the historical occasion as a means and experience and exemplification of man as an end.

*Dualism and Naturalism and the Sociology of Knowledge.* It is the historical situation that must be envisaged to appreciate the specific function of the metaphysical premises of dualism and naturalism in the sociology of knowledge. Why is the sociologist of knowledge the man who is committed to dualism and naturalism and who has emerged at this time? What is this time? This question about our time is indeed another occasion for surrender, but such surrender cannot be exemplified here (in the way in which surrender to the sociology of knowledge has been exemplified, even though hardly more than didactically); instead, a tentative result of surrender to our time must do if we would answer the first question, thereby knitting together even more firmly the methodological-volitional (historical) and metaphysical (human) premises of the sociology of knowledge. As I took Child's treatment of the sociology of knowledge as my occasion for inquiry into it, for surrender to it, so I now take "one world and cultural relativism" as the occasion our time gives me, as my operational definition of our time—except (to repeat) that this is an outcome rather than the beginning of a demonstration of my inquiry into our time, of my surrender to it. "One world and cultural relativism" is a fact that has never before in man's history been a fact. By it I refer to the partly actual, partly potential fact that we now live in one world, in which whatever matters anywhere matters everywhere, most obviously in a political and economic sense but also, perhaps more dimly but yet compellingly, in a moral and cognitive and metaphysical sense. This extraordinary, hardly grasped fact of one world and cultural relativism goes far to explain, I suggest, the sociologist of knowledge as the type of man I have tried to identify.

By cultural relativism I mean the terrifying and confusing realization that men everywhere have values, social orders, ways of life, of love and hate, holiness and contempt, fear and trust, ignorance and knowledge, and the questions resulting therefrom: what, if we realize this fact, are we to do with our own way of life, with our own values? I suggest that the immediate answers are methodological and volitional and the more indirect answers, ontological and valuational, the answers that emerged in the present inquiry as premises of the sociology of knowledge. In having and articulating these premises, the sociology of knowledge appears, indeed, as a revision of our way of life, of our way of looking at ourselves and the world, of our attitude toward the world, of our interpretation of it. It defines a new situation—one world and cultural relativism. Before this self-realization of the sociology of knowledge the situation was merely new, profoundly fascinating, and profoundly threatening. The sociology of knowledge therefore may be called an elucidation of a new experience man has had and is still having. Through it, man adapts himself to living in one world and transcends cultural relativism. This transcendence takes the direction of a view of himself as dual and forever challenging his own exploration.

## NOTES

1. An earlier draft of parts of this paper was presented at the Annual Institute, Society for Social Research, The University of Chicago, August 5, 1949. I am indebted to Arthur Child, Virgil G. Hinshaw, Jr., Richard T. Morris, and Eliseo Vivas for their helpful criticisms of that draft.

2. For a selected Child bibliography sees ns. 13, 14, and 32. Robert K. Merton, "The Sociology of Knowledge," in Georges Gurvitch and Wilbert S. Moore, Eds., *Twentieth Century Sociology* (New York: Philosophical Library, 1945); Louis Wirth, "Preface" to Karl Mannheim, *Ideology and Utopia* [1929], translated by Louis Wirth and Edward A. Shils (New York: Harcourt, Brace, 1936).

3. Karl Mannheim, "Ideologische und soziologische Interpretation der geistigen Gebilde," *Jahrbuch für Soziologie*, 2 (1926), pp. 424–440. [*From Karl Mannheim* (New York: Oxford University Press, 1971), pp. 116–131.]

4. Florian Znaniecki, *The Social Role of the Man of Knowledge* (New York: Columbia University Press, 1940).

5. Karl Mannheim, "Historismus," *Archiv für Sozialwissenschaft und Sozialpolitik*, 52 (1924), 1–60 ["Historicism," translated by Paul Kecskemeti, *Essays on the Sociology of Knowledge*, London: Routledge and Kegan Paul, 1952, pp. 84–133]: "Das konservative Denken; soziologische Beiträge zum Werden des politisch-historischen Denkens in Deutschland," *ibid.*, 57 (1927): 68–142, 470–495 ["Conservative Thought," translated by Ernest Mannheim and Paul Kecskemeti, *From Karl Mannheim*, *op. cit.*, pp. 132–222].

6. Ernst Kohn-Bramstedt, *Aristocracy and the Middle-Classes in Germany. Social Types in German Literature, 1830–1900* (London: King, 1937).

7. Robert K. Merton, "Science, Technology and Society in Seventeenth-Century England," *Osiris*, **4** (1938), 360–632.

8. As a summary see Edgar Zilsel, "The Sociological Roots of Science," *American Journal of Sociology*, **47** (1942), 544–562.

9. Kurt H. Wolff, *Loma Culture Change: A Contribution to the Study of Man* (Columbus, Ohio, 1952) [mimeographed].

10. *Ibid.*, p. 12.

11. Among the numerous critiques of Mannheim Child's work and Virgil G. Hinshaw, Jr., "The Epistemological Relevance of Mannheim's Sociology of Knowledge," *Journal of Philosophy*, **40** (1943), 57–72, are especially noteworthy.

12. In addition to giving us this summary of the problems, Child has offered answers to some of them and has astutely criticized many of the German sociologists of knowledge, particularly Ernst Grünwald, Georg Lukács, Karl Mannheim, Max Scheler, Alexander von Schelting, and Paul Szende.

13. Arthur Child, *The Problems of the Sociology of Knowledge: A Critical and Philosophical Study*, Ph.D. dissertation, unpublished (Berkeley; University of California, 1938). This work is henceforth referred to as *Problems*.

14. Four (of five articles) in *Ethics*: "The Theoretical Possibility of the Sociology of Knowledge," **51** (July 1941), 392–418 (Chapter II of the dissertation); "The Existential Determination of Thought," **52** (January 1942), 153–185 (Chapter IV); "The Problem of Imputation in the Sociology of Knowledge," **51** (January 1941), 200–219, and "The Problem of Imputation Resolved," **54** (January 1944), 96–109 (Chapter V); "The Problem of Truth in the Sociology of Knowledge, **58** (October 1947), 18–34 (Chapter VI); and "On the Theory of the Categories," *Philosophy and Phenomenological Research*, **7** (December 1946), 316–335 (Chapter III). When a revision (which is often fundamental) exists, we shall go by it rather than by the formulation presented in the dissertation.

15. Child discusses Scheler, von Scheling, Günther Stern, Mannheim, and Siegfried Marck.

16. Here Child appraises Heinz O. Ziegler, Hans Freyer, Hans Speier, and, again, Szende and Mannheim. (A feature common to the last three of these authors is the effort to develop a social theory of ideology rather than a biologistic one, as Ziegler and, to a certain extent, Scheler attempt to do.)

17. *Loc. cit.*, henceforth referred to as *Possibility*.

18. Julius Kraft, Ziegler, and Stern.

19. Grünwald and Helmuth Plessner.

20. Scheler, Mannheim, and Szende.

21. Among the thinkers discussed in the present context, Grünwald, to Child, is the most serious. Hence Child's constructive efforts are pointed toward a refutation of Grünwald's "postulational skepticism" (Child's coinage: *ibid.*, p. 404). Briefly, Grünwald's position is that the sociology of knowledge "is not a science whose propositions are unconditionally valid for any thinking individual, but only an optional scheme of interpretation" [Ernst Grünwald, *Das*

*Problem der Soziologie des Wisses, Versuch einer kritischen Darstellung der wissenssoziologischen Theorien,* Walther Eckstein, Ed. (Wien-Leipzig: Braumuller, 1934), p. 66]. "Postulational" refers to the many different postulates—determination by society, race, and climate—on each of which depends a different type of interpretation. "Skepticism" represents Child's judgment on Grünwald's claim that each interpretation, on the assumption of its basic postulate, has the same validity as every other; that is, in view of their incompatibility, the assertion of their equal validity amounts to skepticism of the validity of any of them. One might derive the term postulational skepticism by pointing out that Grünwald's position hides the skeptical postulate that there can be only one reality which must determine knowledge and intellectual behavior in general. [See also the quotation from Child (pp. 516–517) and Chapter 30].

22.  G. H. Mead, *Mind, Self and Society*, Charles W. Morris, Ed. (Chicago: University of Chicago Press, 1934), especially pp. 6–8, 46–47, 90, 133–134, 155--158, 191–192, 270. (Cf. Child, *Problems,* p. 78.) Mead's concepts relevant to his theory of mind, are communication as conversation of meaningful gestures, significant symbol, generalized other. His crucial thesis: "Mind arises through communication by a conversation of gestures in a social process or context of experience—not communication through mind" (Mead, *op. cit.,* p. 50).

23.  On two occasions, *Possibility,* pp. 392–393 and 417.

24.  It may be noted that two of the three possible pairs in which these three variables can be arranged have received much attention in contemporary social-scientific literature, namely, social factors and logic (which involves basic epistemological problems of the sociology of knowledge) and social factors and the individual (which, under various labels, especially that of personality and culture, has aroused widespread discussion). The third possible pair—logic and the individual—has been dealt with mainly in connection with the other two complexes.

25.  For the concept of "metaphysical" and "ontological" acted on in this paper, see below.

26.  Cf. the indirectly relevant discussion of methodological premises of the sociology of knowledge; see pp. 537–538 and 539–542.

27.  Inasmuch as both chapters have been published in considerably revised form, the original dissertation drafts are largely neglected here.

28.  "We are well aware," Child writes, "that for Marx, the concept of the superstructure comprehends institutions—legal, political, religious—no less than the 'forms of consciousness' which 'correspond' to these superstructures built on the 'real foundation.' But in the sociology of knowledge, the term, 'superstructure,' apparently refers only to the ideologies; while institutions— as contrasted with their ideological expressions or reflections—seem to fall under the heading of the substructure or social-historical structure. If pursued far enough, this difference in the line of demarcation would perhaps reveal a basic difference in attitude between historical materialism and the sociology of

knowledge" (*Problems,* p. 87 n.). Aside from the value of the suggestion implied, this quotation also has the significance of showing that Child's main interest here is in the analysis of the categorical structure rather than in that of the other two structures: their vague definitions and the admitted indecision in their use in the sense of historical materialism or of the sociology of knowledge would indicate this. The same concentration of interest may also explain the lack of attention to still another concept, that of ideology. Child does not tell us whether he uses this term as previously defined or in a broader sense. Either use would have significant implications, also, for the definitions of the two concepts of structure.

29.  Cf. Mead, *op. cit.,* pp. 125, 128, 129, 132, 156–157.

30.  Arthur Child, "On the Theory of the Categories," *loc. cit.,* henceforth referred to as *Categories.*

31.  *Categories,* pp. 319–320; Mead, *op. cit.,* p. 125.

32.  Cf. Arthur Child, "Toward a Functional Definition of the 'a priori,'" *Journal of Philosophy,* **41** (March 16, 1944), 155–160.

33.  Child, in common with most contributors to the sociology of knowledge, fails to distinguish between social and cultural. As a contrast to biotic he could have chosen, instead of sociotic, some term like culture-derived (culturotic); that is, he does not specifically define sociotic.

34.  Cf. Arthur Child, "The Problem of Truth in the Sociology of Knowledge," *op. cit.,* p. 31.

35.  For a briefer exposition of Child's conception of the categories in the context of the problem of sociology and cultural relativism and related problems, see Kurt H. Wolff, "The Unique and the General: Toward a Philosophy of Sociology," *Philosophy of Science,* **15** (July 1948), 203–205 [Chapter 27]. See also pp. 541–542.

36.  Scheler's, Lukács's, and Grünwald's.

37.  Arthur Child, "The Existential Determination of Thought," *op. cit.,* p. 181. This paper is henceforth referred to as *Determination*

38.  Cf. "Problems," Chapter III, and the last paragraph in the preceding section.

39.  Of which Child makes use in his dissertation; cf. *Problems,* p. 114.

40.  *Problems,* Chapter V, "The Problem of Imputation"; "The Problem of Imputation in the Sociology of Knowledge," *loc. cit.* (henceforth referred to as *Imputation,* a revision of the former); and "The Problem of Imputation Resolved" (hereafter, *Resolved*).

41.  It may be noted in passing that this notion, if applied to the history of the ideal-type concept, from Max Weber to Howard Becker and Robert Redfield, would probably yield significant insights.

42.  Cf. Child's more casual use of the term imputation in a different content "One might select a group so large that the excessive breadth and pervasiveness, the excessive generality, of the esthetically relevant predispositions would exclude the legitimate imputation to them of any concrete and particular

esthetic response" [Arthur Child, "The Social-Historical Relativity of Esthetic Value," *Philosophical Review*, **53** (January 1944), 6]. Here Child seems to envisage, as prerequisites of imputing aesthetic matters, well-organized groups and well-organized aesthetic predispositions, paralleling the ideologically organized groups and the articulated ideologies in the case of imputing ideologies.

43.  Cf. Kurt H. Wolff, "Notes toward a Sociocultural Interpretation of Amercan Sociology," *American Sociological Review*, **11** (October 1946), 545 [Chapter 12].

44.  Arthur Child, "The Problem of Truth in the Sociology of Knowledge," *op. cit.*, pp. 18–22. This paper is henceforth referred to as *Truth*.

45.  Such an elementary confusion, Child maintains (*ibid.*, p. 23), characterizes the four types of erroneous theory dealing with origin-validity which he discusses, among them, Scheler's and Dewey's. Lukács is exculpated from any of these errors (*ibid.*, pp. 22–23).

46.  Pareto's statements on nonlogical conduct, Max Weber's analyses of types of power and authority, and Znaniecki's theory of social actions and social types, especially social types of men of knowledge, contain rich suggestions for the typology envisaged.

47.  The latter is a notion, evidently not taken from, but clearly inherent in, Dilthey's conception of understanding.

48.   A common truth is defined by Child as "a socially agreed-upon proposition . . . which . . . does in fact reconstitute its object in mind in the measure and sense in which it claims to do so" (*Truth*, p. 25).

49.  Note the relevance of the next section.

50.  Child does not raise the question whether the sociology of knowledge shares transcendent interpretation with the related efforts just mentioned.

51.  It will be recalled that Child's concept of truth, as presented in his dissertation, was superseded by his later *Truth*, which has been discussed here. The supplementation presently reported on, however, is not invalidated by this subsequent development.

52.  And thus the dissertation, for the last chapter is merely a summary of the findings arrived at throughout the work.

53.  Only the most important problems mentioned in the summary are listed here. Even this limited list, however, shows the scope of a theory of the sociology of intellectual-emotional behavior that can be envisaged on the basis of Child's work.

54.   Page numbers in parentheses following the items in this list refer to the preceding part on Child. It is obvious that all these tasks are more or less intimately interrelated, but these interrelations have been indicated in only three instances.

55.  Since the Spring of 1951 experiments in interpretation have been in progress at Ohio State University (so far three: Leo Spitzer's "American Adver-

tising Explained as Popular Art," a cartoon by Saul Steinberg, and "The Stranger" by Georg Simmel). They are promising as a basis on which to build a theory.

56.   Cf. Wolff, *Loma Culture Change, op cit.*, "Introduction." Sections 12, 13, and 15, on respectively, scientific, philosophical, and religious elements in the study of man. This is an apodictic and elliptic formulation, an elaboration of which would exceed the scope of this chapter. It is designed merely to make what follows plausible.

57.   In John Dewey's sense, as developed by Thelma Z. Lavine in her "Naturalism and the Sociological Analysis of Knowledge," in Yervant H. Krikorian, Ed., *Naturalism and the Human Spirit* (New York: Columbia University Press, 1944), p. 184.

58.   I am not asserting that the metaphysical premises of dualism and naturalism, as defined here, are not found outside the sociology of knowledge, in other types of man, or in other enterprises, but I do suggest that their specific combination, as indicated, is an essential feature of the sociology of knowledge.

59.   Wolff, *Loma Culture Change, op. cit.*, "Introduction," pp. 11–12 and Sections 5–7.

---

Reprinted in modified form from *Scritti di sociologia e politica in onore di Luigi Sturzo*, Vol. III (Bologna: Nicola Zanichelli, 1953), pp. 583–625, and *Ethics*, **61** (1950), 69–73, published by The University of Chicago, by permission of the publishers. The essay has been edited and partially revised by the author.

# 28 (Supplement)

## PRESUPPOSITIONS OF THE SOCIOLOGY OF KNOWLEDGE AND A TASK FOR IT. 1967, 1971

To begin the discussion of this topic, the presuppositions of the sociology of knowledge (and a task for it) [1], I shall try to show how it has come up for me. I found myself impressed by the fact that if one asks about the sociology of knowledge—for instance, what it is, where it comes from, who its main representatives are—the one who asks is a wholly unanalyzed subject. Possibly, or probably, it is the neutral *Man* of Heidegger [2], or it represents the public interpretation—Mannheim's term, taken over from Heidegger [3]—or Scheler's relatively natural *Weltanschauung* [4]. Let us imagine what would happen if we were not to ask in this fashion, if we did not take for granted the *Man*, the public interpretation, the relatively natural world view, with which in our uncritical unawareness we make common cause, but instead called them into question, neither denying or rejecting nor affirming or accepting but suspending or bracketing them? Would we then not come closer to what we are after than if we were separated from it by the opacity of the unidentified subject who does the asking, that is to say, if we were not separated from it by the veil of tradition? Can we lift this veil? How can we become conscious of the tradition, which we shared by our acceptance of the unanalyzed nature of that anonymous *Man*—by our identification with it? We must, of course, *wish* to lift the veil, a wish that may have various sources. To simplify the argument let us suppose that the source is our feeling of dissatisfaction with tradition, our feeling that there is something more real than what we have inherited in tradition: our wish is to come closer to that reality. How do we proceed if we call into question the only guide we were taught and were convinced we had, that is to say, tradition? If our wish to come closer to the reality we anticipate behind what tradition has taught us is strong enough, this wish will give us a new courage for our inquiry. It will give us the strength required of human beings who would face this time in which tradition has weakened and become problematic. We may realize that between this process of self-enlightenment, which is commensurate with the present time, and the sociology of knowledge there is a specific affinity, for the sociology of knowledge, too, especially as it was conceived by Karl Mannheim, calls into question, relativizes, particularizes, and transcends.

This act or state which comes out of our time and in which whatever emerges is questioned as thoroughly as a person engaged in such inquiry can bear I call *surrender,* and the structure that emerges from it I call *catch,* for it is a new, more trustworthy, more believable, more warranted catching or conceiving than could even be expected before the experience of surrender or the desire for it. The idea of surrender and catch itself comes out of our time; it is diagnostic; it has a not yet foreseeable area of meaning and application. So far I have tried to outline its relation to religion, the crisis of mankind today, to aesthetic experience, community study and social science in general, to rebellion, autonomy, to "beginning" as meant in Hegel and what it may mean today, to Hegel's "cunning of reason," and aspects of phenomenology [5]. Almost every one of these efforts has been a new beginning, and the more so, the more efforts it followed.

At this time, then, I shall try to clarify the relation between surrender and the sociology of knowledge or rather to develop a previous attempt [6], for early in the course of my preoccupation with the idea of surrender I tried to demonstrate it on the occasion of the sociology of knowledge itself. The occasion of that surrender, in turn, was the analysis of Arthur Child's presentation of the philosophic problems he found in the sociology of knowledge [7]. I now present in incomplete form the catch of that surrender.

In the first place Child—implicitly rather than explicitly—sets *tasks* [8] that must be met before a sociology of knowledge or of intellectual-affective life more generally, entailed by his study, can be worked out. Among these tasks are at least two different kinds: methodological and metaphysical. The methodological include demands for typologies; the metaphysical, for metaphysical and epistemological theories. The criterion for testing the solution of methodological problems is pragmatic, a means criterion; that for testing the solution of metaphysical problems is an end criterion, namely, the examination of the catch of the student's surrender.

I then moved on from tasks to premises from which the tasks can be shown to derive: methodological, volitional, and metaphysical. The latter I discovered to be *dualism* and *naturalism*, that is, I insist on investigating anything within the range of my attention that I feel, no matter how vaguely, might be relevant to my inquiry and try to be alert to whatever may make me more sensitive to the range of attention pertinent to an inquiry, to what is relevant within that range, and to the relevancies of the inquiry itself. In short, I found that I espoused surrender [9].

The relation between the methodological and volitional premises of the sociology of knowledge and its metaphysical premises parallels the relation between the means, the historical occasion of inquiry, and its end, the experience and exemplification of man as the being capable of surrender and catch. From the point of view of the inquirer the "world" [10] in which he focuses on methodological or volitional premises (and other methodological or volitional matters) is the mundane or everyday world; when he focuses on metaphysical premises, he has bracketed the world of everyday life and entered that of surrender, of "being" [11]. In the first he seeks scientific, in the second, existential truth [12]. In our own investigation we ourselves have moved from the first to the second, from the everyday world into the world of being: surrendering.

We may say, quite simply, that this world of being is not the world of everyday, but we may also do more than distinguish between the two, more than observe that moments of being are comparatively rare. We may express regret and pain, bewail the fate of man but bless those individuals, who, aware or not of their rootedness in being in whatever way, also lead their lives more nobly [13]. To advocate the experience of being or surrender is to espouse an image of man; that of the being who is capable of surrender and catch. It is an image of essential man, as he is revealed if he suspends as best he can his received notions, affirming only those he *can* affirm, that is, those that withstand the test of such surrender. It also follows from this image of man that these notions, which are the catch of surrender, are as truly and universally human as is possible within the unalterable limits of man's historicity, but these limits to universal truth are widened by surrender, for in surrender, man, whoever he may be, is thrown back on what he really is, which is what he shares with mankind [14].

To call this image of man an image of essential man means the postulation of a transcultural and transhistorical human nature and, at the same time, the invitation not only to support this image but to emulate it, that is, to lead lives that will do right by it [15]. What this entails is something every one of us must come to know. This question may well be an occasion for surrender. It might be to make music, as Pablo Casals did all his life, for peace, against totalitarianism; to put one's body on the line against oppression as Jean-Paul Sartre would like to do; to persevere in the pursuit of science on the faith in knowledge [16]; or many other things, including the study of the sociology of knowledge. I conclude by suggesting a direction in which research in the sociology of knowledge might go if it would translate what precedes into a concrete inquiry.

It would be an effort to increase our knowledge of people's desires, aspirations, fears, indifference, and ignorance in the hope of learning what social, political, and economic conditions would be favorable or unfavorable to the rise, development, decline, and other changes in their concerns. The purpose of this research would be to heighten our understanding of what we can do to bring about a society more conducive to a better life for more kinds of people and to a more widely diffused aspiration for being, as against leading a life, than are the societies in which we live. This goal is so ambitious that it may sound dreamy, frivolous, pious, or really irrelevant. I therefore add that the expectation on which the inquiry proposed is based is that in order to come closer to realizing the purpose in the service of which it is undertaken the world, the world of everyday, must be changed, an expectation that results from the critical nature of the idea of surrender [17]. The inquiry would focus not so much on the identification of desirable changes—a better distribution of wealth, health, education, and justice—on which research is hardly needed, as on the identification of the justifiable local or situational modes of these changes and above all the ways of bringing them about.

## NOTES

1. In this chapter I modify and develop "Über die Voraussetzungen der Wissenssoziologie," *Praxis*, **1967**, 3, 373–384, which is based on my earlier writing, mainly, "A Preliminary Inquiry into the Sociology of Knowledge from the Standpoint of the Study of Man," *Scritti di sociologia e politica in onore di Luigi Sturzo*, Vol. III (Bologna: Zanichelli, 1953), pp. 583–623 [Chapter 28].

2. Martin Heidegger, *Sein und Zeit* (1927) (Tübingen: Niemeyer, 1963), especially paragraph 27, p. 126.

3. Karl Mannheim, "Competition as a Cultural Phenomenon" (1928), translated by Paul Kecskemeti, in *From Karl Mannheim*, edited and with an introduction by Kurt H. Wolff (New York: Oxford University Press, 1971), p. 228.

4. Max Scheler, "The Sociology of Knowledge: Formal Problems" (1926), translated by Rainer Koehne, in James E. Curtis and John W. Petras, Eds., *The Sociology of Knowledge: A Reader* (New York: Praeger, 1970), p. 177.

5. "Surrender and Religion," *Journal for the Scientific Study of Religion,* **2** (1962), 36–50; "Surrender as a Response to Our Crisis," *Journal of Humanistic Psychology,* **2** (1962), 16–30; "Surrender and Aesthetic Experience," *Review of Existential Psychology and Psychiatry,* **3** (1963), 209–226; "Surrender and Community Study: The Study of Loma," in Arthur J. Vidich, Joseph Bensman, and Maurice R. Stein, Eds., *Reflections on Community Studies* (New York: Wiley, 1964), pp. 233–263; "Surrender and Autonomy and Community," *Humanitas,* **1** (1965),173–181; "Beginning: In Hegel and Today," in Kurt H. Wolff and Barrington Moore, Jr., with the assistance of Heinz Lubasz, Maurice R. Stein, and E. V. Walter, Eds., *The Critical Spirit: Essays in Honor of Herbert Marcuse* (Boston: Beacon, 1967), pp. 72–103; "Surrender and Rebellion: A Reading of Camus' *The Rebel*," *Indian Journal of Social Research,* **11** (1970). 167–184; "On the Cunning of Reason in our Time," *Praxis,* **1971**, 1–2, 129–137; "Sociology, Phenomenology, and Surrender-and-Catch," *Synthese,* **24** (1972), 439–471; *Surrender and Catch: A Palimpsest Story* (Sorokin Lectures, No. 3, Saskatoon: University of Saskatchewan, 1972). Also *Hingebung und Begriff* (Neuwied: Luchterhand, 1968).

6. "A Preliminary Inquiry into the Sociology of Knowledge from the Standpoint of the Study of Man" [Chapter 28]; see also "The Sociology of Knowledge and Sociological Theory," in Llewellyn Gross, Ed., *Symposium on Sociological Theory* (Evanston, Ill.: Row, Peterson, 1959), pp. 567–602 [Chapter 29].

7. [Chapter 28, n. 14.]

8. One of them, it may be recalled from Chapter 28, is a theory of interpretation that Child wrote himself, but he did so much later than his major work on the sociology of knowledge and hardly with reference to it, as suggested here. Arthur Child, *Interpretation: A General Theory* (Berkeley: University of California Press, 1965).

9. Neither dualism nor naturalism-surrender as a metaphysical premise but their combination [described in Chapter 28] defines the sociology of knowledge at this time in history. Metaphysical statements can be (rationally) discussed and the method of their intrasubjective examination, mentioned above, can be modified for intersubjective application. Cf. "Beginning: In Hegel and Today," *op. cit.,* pp. 91–95 ("The possibility of intersubjective existential truth").

10. Cf. Alfred Schutz, "On Multiple Realities" (1945), in *Collected Papers, Vol. I, The Problem of Social Reality,* edited and with an introduction by Maurice Natanson (The Hague: Nijhoff, 1962), pp. 207–259.

11. Cf. "Beginning: In Hegel and Today," *op. cit.,* pp. 85–90 ("Beginning and experience of being"), and "Sociology, Phenomenology, and Surrender-and-Catch," *op. cit.,* paragraphs 16–22 and 27.

12. Cf. "The Sociology of Knowledge and Sociological Theory" [Chapter 29], pp. 579–580; "Beginning: In Hegel and Today," *op. cit.,* pp. 99–102 ("Truth:

existential, everyday, scientific"). Scientific truth is more closely related to theoretical and everyday or "commonsensical" truth and existential truth is more closely related to practical and philosophical truth than the first group (or typology) is to the second, despite important differences within each of them (each of which also contains additional types).

13. Cf. "Beginning: In Hegel and Today," *op. cit.*, pp. 88–90; "Sociology, Phenomenology, and Surrender-and-Catch," paragraphs 22 and 27.

14. "Surrender and Religion," *op. cit.*, p. 40.

15. Cf. "Beginning: In Hegel and Today," *op. cit.*, p. 94 (paragraph 39).

16. It happens that a recent issue of *The New York Times Magazine* (October 17, 1971) contains relevant material on these last two options (hence my mentioning them here): an interview of Sartre by John Gerassi and an article on René Dubos by John Culhane.

17. On which see "Surrender and Rebellion," *loc. cit.*, above all.

---

This chapter has not been published previously in English.

# 29

# THE SOCIOLOGY
# OF KNOWLEDGE
# AND SOCIOLOGICAL
# THEORY. 1959

*In memory of Karl Mannheim*

The chapter that follows is a very personal paper [1]. It is, however, neither private nor idiosyncratic but, on the contrary, an experiment in communication—with myself and with those whom I hope to draw into it. You and I will be participating in a joint venture. We shall start in an expository mood, but as we proceed we shall find ourselves in a more pleading mood, and there will be points in our journey at which we may attain unexpected balances between exposition and rhetoric.

We shall visit much longer with the sociology of knowledge and sociology than with sociological theory, to which we shall come only at the end of our journey. When we look back then, our itinerary should lie clearly traced on the map that we shall realize we have used for our trip.

We start, naturally, from home, with the familiar. We begin with a standard review of the sociology of knowledge. We ask for information and receive it.

554

## "WHAT IS THE SOCIOLOGY OF KNOWLEDGE?"

We are told, or we remember, that it takes only a slight acquaintance with the subject to suspect or know that the term sociology of knowledge is a misnomer, namely, a translation of the German *Wissenssoziologie*. *Wissen*, however, is broader than "knowledge" [1]. Knowledge usually refers to scientific or positive knowledge. *Wissen*, on the other hand, is at least noncommittal on the inclusion of other kinds of knowledge. *Soziologie* is closer to social philosophy and thus broader than "sociology," which, particularly in its American usage, is more closely linked to a natural-science model. Indeed, efforts carried on in the name of the sociology of knowledge, no matter in what language, have been concerned less with scientific knowledge than with outlooks, world views, concepts, and categories of thought. Furthermore, these efforts have been made less in a self-conscious sociological perspective than in the moods of philosophy of history, epistemology, or philosophical anthropology.

The two immediate antecedents of the sociology of knowledge are Marxism [2] and Durkheimian sociology. What is usually referred to as sociology of knowledge, however, is the *Wissenssoziologie* [3] that flourished in Germany in the 1920s and was predominantly Marxist or anti-Marxist. Since 1933 it has led a precarious, transplanted existence, mainly in the United States, although since the end of World War II it has also been revived in Germany [4]. Its two outstanding representatives were Max Scheler (1874–1928) and Karl Mannheim (1893–1947), its two signal publications, Scheler's "Problems of a Sociology of Knowledge" (1924) and Mannheim's *Ideology and Utopia* (1929) [5]. Durkheim has had his greatest effect, outside France, in the United States, where the sociology of knowledge, nevertheless, was introduced chiefly by the English edition of Mannheim's book (1936) [6].

In the United States movements theoretically similar to the sociology of knowledge had existed for roughly half a century. Historically, however, and thus in their general intellectual significance, these movements [7] were different. Pragmatism, social behaviorism, and instrumentalism are, among other things, distillates of a more general and pervasive American outlook: practical, amelioristic, and future-oriented [8]. American students of the sociology of knowledge have combined these American orientations with the German and French. Among the results of their efforts are the most orderly survey of important philosophical problems of the field yet achieved (Arthur Child's [9]), the most succinct summary of its sociological research problems (Robert K. Merton's [10]), and the most concise sketch of its background and its American relations (Louis Wirth's [11]).

One way of characterizing the writings that have been produced in the name of the sociology of knowledge in general and of *Wissenssoziologie* in particular is to call them more speculative and theoretical than empirical and to consider them in need of systematization into a general sociology of intellectual-emotional behavior [12], intellectual life [13], mental productions [14], the mind [15], or gnosio-sociology [16] (to mention some of the few attempts at improving on the term sociology of knowledge). Such systematizing, however, would have to be preceded by inventories of considerable bodies of knowledge and theory, which, though accumulated outside the sociology of knowledge, nevertheless bear on its central problem, the relations between society and intellectual life. They lie scattered in the social sciences, the humanities, and certain biological sciences [17].

We might add to the answer to our question, "What is the sociology of knowledge?," some observations, such as these: despite its predominantly speculative and theoretical character, the sociology of knowledge has produced some outstanding empirical investigations [18]. It has given us useful (though not too widely used) concepts—for example, Mannheim's typology of interpretations [19] or Znaniecki's of men of knowledge [20]. It has had a continuing effect as a latent frame of reference [21] in other disciplines. Some of its American students, both sociologists [22] and philosophers [23], have later in their careers turned to work in other areas; the selection of this work, however, or the approaches to it, have probably been influenced by their previous preoccupation with the sociology of knowledge, and they may yet return to such preoccupation, for their careers are still going on.

The foregoing answer to our question, "What is the sociology of knowledge?," is what we referred to as a standard review of the field. Now we are going a step further. We shall take such a step when we realize, first, that in our question and in the answer to it we paid no attention to the persons who did the asking and answering; second, that not to have done so is a serious omission, which we must now try to make good. Let us attempt to identify these persons—first as types of men and then historically, that is, in respect to place and time.

### OUTSIDERS AND PARTICIPANTS

We did say something about the types of men who inquired into the sociology of knowledge and who expounded it by referring to them as seeking and receiving information. They were outsiders to the sociology of knowledge. They talked from the standpoint of some unarticulated version of the contemporary academic tradition in social science. Not only were they not among the developers of the sociology of knowledge, they betrayed no awareness that to ask and be given information about an intellectual endeavor is one thing but that to develop it and participate in it is quite another. It involves a much greater risk.

In our asking and answering there was no risk. There was no risk of participation in which the two activities of asking and answering and the two roles of asker and answerer might have fused and been transformed into one joint venture. The outcome would not have been certain—the kind of outcome, in fact, quite unforeseeable. Yet the sociology of knowledge, like any intellectual endeavor worth its salt, has had its participants; it could not have come into being without them. Unlike the asker and answerer of the question with which we started on our journey, these participants were startled, puzzled, bewildered, and troubled by novel problems. Among them, Karl Mannheim perhaps took the greatest chances of becoming confused and stymied, accepted the fewest among the received notions at his disposal, and staked the most of himself: he was the most unconditional participant. This may be gathered, even more palpably perhaps than from his published writings, from a letter written (April 15, 1946) to me in response to a critical analysis of Mannheim's work by members of a seminar on the sociology of knowledge. Mannheim wrote:

> . . . If there are contradictions and inconsistencies in my paper this is, I think, not so much due to the fact that I overlooked them but because I make a point of developing a theme to its end even if it contradicts some other statements. I use this method because I think that in this marginal field of human knowledge we should not conceal inconsistencies, so to speak covering up the wounds, but our duty is to show the sore spots in human thinking at its present stage.

> In a simple empirical investigation or straightforward logical argument, contradictions are mistakes; but when the task is to show that our whole thought system in its various parts leads to inconsistencies, these inconsistencies are the thorn in the flesh from which we have to start.

> The inconsistencies in our whole outlook, which in my presentation only become more visible, are due to the fact that we have two approaches which move on a different plane [*sic*].

> On the one hand, our most advanced empirical investigations, especially those which come from history, psychology, and sociology, show that the human mind with its whole categorical apparatus is a dynamic entity. Whereas our predominant

epistemology derives from an age, the hidden desire and ideal of which was stability, the traditional epistemology still thinks of concepts as reflecting eternal ideas. The premium is put on absoluteness and supertemporaneousness and accordingly, no other knowledge and truth can be conceived . . . [than] the static one. . . .

Now, whereas one part of our progressive insight convinces us that language and logic are also a part of culture which, in its turn—most people will agree on that—is different with different tribes and in different epochs and therefore nothing can be stated but in relation to a frame of reference; the other part of our intellectual orientation through its traditional epistemology cannot put up with this insight. The latter is reluctant to accept this because it failed to build into its theory the fact of the essential perspectivism of human knowledge.

To use a simple analogy, what happens is that in our empirical investigation we become aware of the fact that we are observing the world from a moving staircase, from a dynamic platform, and, therefore, the image of the world changes with the changing frames of reference which various cultures create. On the other hand, epistemology still only knows of a static platform where one doesn't become aware of the possibility of various perspectives and, from this angle, it tries to deny the existence and the right of such dynamic thinking. There is a culture lag between our empirical insight into the nature of knowing and the premises upon which the traditional idealist epistemology is built. Instead of perspectivism, the out-of-date epistemology wants to set up a veto against the emerging new insights, according to which man can only see the world in perspective, and there is no view which is absolute in the sense that it represents the thing in itself beyond perspective.

In the world of visual objects, we acknowledge that completely. That you can only see various perspectives of a house and there is no view among them which is absolutely the house and in spite of that there is knowing because the various perspectives are not arbitrary. The one can be understood from the other. What we, without any difficulty, admit for the apperception of the visual world, we ought to admit for knowledge in general.

I hope this is intelligible and it at least convinces you and your seminar that if there are contradictions they are not due to my shortsightedness but to the fact that I want to break through the old epistemology radically but have not succeeded yet fully. But the latter is not one man's work. I think our whole generation will have to work on it as nothing is more obvious than that we transcended in every field the idea that man's mind is equal to an absolute Ratio in favour of a theory that we think on the basis of changing frames of reference, the elaboration of which is one of the most exciting tasks of the near future. . . [24].

Mannheim's letter has been quoted exclusively as the document of an insider and is commented on in this respect alone. It suggests that, for the insider, problems of the sociology of knowledge—leading toward it or issuing from it—are more or less faithful formulations of his craving for an ordered world: they are existential problems for him. In the case of Mannheim, in particular, most of the work he did (not only that explicitly devoted to the sociology of knowledge) could be characterized as a diagnosis of our time (the title he gave one of his books): for him, existential problems were above all historical problems. They were the questions: "Where have we come from?" "Where are we?" "What, therefore, must we do?" Though never as clear on the matter as some might have desired him to be, Mannheim appears to have held that if we know who we are we know what we must do.

This is an old proposition. We do well to realize, however, that it is incompatible with the much newer, though almost all-pervasive, total separation between the Is and the Ought. For more than two millennia men had been saying that our existence itself, our "Is," is normative, that it includes the "Ought"; hence that if we recognize ourselves we know what we must do. What is new, now, about this Socratic position is the place and time of its rediscovery—of, perhaps, its fermenting.

We have touched only lightly on the place and time of the outsider who inquires into the sociology of knowledge. All we have said is that he seeks information, raising his question on the basis of some unarticulated version of the contemporary academic tradition in social science in which he has grown up but has hardly examined. Mannheim's example suggests an additional distinction between outsider and insider. It is that, unlike the outsider, the insider finds that he cannot inquire into the sociology of knowledge short of examining this tradition and that examining this tradition includes exploring his place and time. We shall now attempt to visualize such an exploration.

### ON OUR PLACE AND TIME

We begin with the place and the time: the West, now. This includes something on Western tradition, and later we shall examine some features of our tradition in sociology in particular. In our inspection of place and time we limit ourselves to three interrelated aspects: the administered nature of our lives, the world as underdeveloped; and one-world-and-cultural-relativism.

1. The part of the social structure that administers our lives is bureaucracy, "the type of organization designed to accomplish large-scale administrative tasks by systematically co-ordinating the work of many individuals" [25]. This part is so important that much of our outlook and conduct is the outlook and conduct of the administered life: not spontaneous interaction, but control, and the fear of its failing. If this is so, the reason may be that we have not come to terms with secularization and rationalization [26], but that we are ambivalent toward them. On this we shall have more to say below. Now, we put the matter by stating that we find ourselves having to pay for the recession of objective reason [27]. What do we mean by this?

Objective must be distinguished from subjective reason. Subjective reason is part of our mental equipment. It is our faculty of thinking, notably that of adapting means to ends [28]. Objective reason is the rational order of the cosmos (nature, society, history), which also contains *us*. This order is normative, teleological; it includes ends. Yet when we employ our subjective reason in a manner that lets us forget objective reason we lose our very capacity to assess ends. One effect of this forgetting and this loss is that ends turn sour, and we may declare them to be matters of taste, irrational [29]. Is and Ought have become divorced. Once this divorce has occurred, all our efforts to derive Ought from Is are vain [30].

The last sentence expresses a logically correct proposition. Its empirical applications, however—such as doubt and worry over the Ought or attempts at obtaining it from the Is—are so frequent that they may be said to characterize our contemporary consciousness [31]. To recognize the recession of objective reason may help us understand another phenomenon of our time, the simultaneous spurt in science and technology and the emergence of totalitarianism. It may come to appear less paradoxical that this period of unprecedented rise in the standard of living, of democratization, of decreasing superstition, of proliferating options should also be the period, not only of totalitarianism, but also of Western feelings that traditional ideals have lost significance, and the goal of a higher standard of living has become a barren one.

The administered nature of our lives has been hinted at in many expressions—for example, "brave new world," "1984," "other-directedness" (David Riesman), "escape from freedom" (Erich Fromm), but it could be that the contrasts or solutions, such as Riesman's "autonomy" or Fromm's "productive personality" [32], will be confined to the status of options in addition to those already available, thus contributing to their proliferation. As long as ninety years ago, Dostoyevsky wrote:

> In those days people seem to have been animated by one idea, but now they are much more nervous, more developed, more sensitive—they seem to be animated by two or three ideas at a time—modern man is more diffuse and, I assure you, it is this that prevents him from being such a complete human being as they were in those days [33].

2. We in the West have not, perhaps not yet, recognized the objectively rational status of man's desire to be free from hunger, sickness, fear, and ignorance. We have not recognized that from this desire we might develop the world. Instead, we tend to single out some areas of it as needing a push in the direction of Western development. On this view, the current notion of underdeveloped peoples or countries appears as a distortion of what should read "the world as underdeveloped" [34]. It is a corrupted text, the corrupting element being a Western projection. *We* are underdeveloped, as witness our helpless, administered lives, our helplessness in front of totalitarianism, the climax of administeredness, of derationalization and, at the same time, detraditionalization, of ahistoricity and, at the same time, amorality.

No matter how much our projectionism is attenuated—not least by the spontaneous understanding and puzzlement of social scientists, among them some of those active in underdeveloped countries [35]—we are glad, nevertheless, and understandably so, to repress our own dilemma. We tend to hold on to the essentially nineteenth-century dichotomies of sacred, folk, traditional versus secular, urban, rational societies, believing ourselves to belong to the latter, with which we want to dominate the nascent one world. Instead, we might cling to such nonprojective ideas as that the science and technology we have mastered under the very guide of subjective reason and its stubborn insistence on control (and in only precarious relation with objective reason), if deliberately applied to our economies, can reduce hunger and sickness faster than they have been; that return to trust in objective reason can increase knowledge and alleviate fear [36], and that, acting on these insights, we may help reason in its "cunning," recognizing in our very befuddlement a reminder of objective reason and of the relation of objective to subjective reason.

3. Such help to reason may be help to us at this time when one of the most palpable meanings of one world is the feeling of global claustro-

phobia. On the one hand, our science and technology have made our destruction feasible and thus a possibility. On the other, our social science in particular (especially cultural anthropology) has so overwhelmed us with a range of cultures that are strange, yet human—and, being human, ours—that we are terrified and confused. We may feel relief when we can transcend our terror and confusion by transforming them into questions such as these: What can we do with our own ways of life? How can we reinterpret our traditions so that we can all live together not by compromise but by being truer to ourselves? In the light or mood of such questions the idea of one world and cultural relativism may impress us as a democratized version of the idea of the brotherhood of man and the immortality of the soul. If developments under the sway of subjective reason have disenchanted us to the point of being haunted by our own disappearance, we may revive by insisting that these developments, despite world wars, death camps, atom bombs, genocide, and the administered life, are a phase of secularization and rationalization whose enchantment we have yet to discover. We may revive if we realize that this phase challenges us to reinvent ourselves so that we may learn how we can *live* in one world. We must get hold of our *trans*cultural selves after we have been so fascinated by cultural relativism, by our cultural unselves.

Without postulating a transcultural human nature, we could not account for the possibility of understanding between two persons of different cultures [37]—but this means between any two persons, even myself today and yesterday, here and in another place. The pursuit of understanding others and ourselves evinces faith in their dignity and our own, in the dignity of man. It is incompatible with condescension, toward underdeveloped man and ourselves alike and perpetually challenges us to keep to the fine line between the belief of being in grace and the sin of pride. In the pursuit of understanding it is of secondary importance whether by our "transcultural selves" we mean a supracultural core or residue, biological or spiritual, and whether, accordingly, we engage in the investigation of the physiological processes of thought, of intellectual history, or of the sociology of knowledge. In all these endeavors we further our understanding by the awareness that we are embracing both transcultural human nature and human culture, both man, or human nature, and unique cultures, and must be wary lest we confuse the first with the second or the second with the first—learning with biology, acquired with innate traits, nurture with nature, environment with heredity, or supervenient with primal categories [38].

*METHODOLOGICAL, VOLITIONAL, AND METAPHYSICAL*
*PREMISES OF THE SOCIOLOGY OF KNOWLEDGE:*
*ITS DUALISM AND NATURALISM*

We may seem to have strayed from the sociology of knowledge. Actually, we are in the process of becoming insiders, of participating in it. For that matter it has come up in the course of reflections on our time as one among various endeavors in the pursuit of understanding; it was also referred to, by implication, in the warning not to take supervenient for primal categories (and vice versa): we may recall this distinction as Arthur Child's attempt to solve one of the crucial philosophical problems of the sociology of knowledge, precisely that of the categories of thought. It is now necessary to show that the connection between the sociology of knowledge and our time is not casual, that it can be analyzed, and that it can be argued to be of a determinable kind and importance.

In his first explicit paper on the subject (1925) [39] Karl Mannheim examined four ultimate, fundamental factors which constitute the problem constellation of the sociology of knowledge. These are (1) the "self-transcendence" or "self-relativization of thought," that is, the possibility of not taking thought at its face value; (2) "the emergence of the 'unmasking' turn of mind" (or debunking); (3) the transcendence of thought toward the historical and social sphere, which is hypostatized as the ontological absolute or emerges as a new system of reference; in other words, the understanding of thought as the expression of or in relation to history and society; and (4) the social relativization of the totality of the mental world, not only of *some* thoughts. Without these four factors, Mannheim held, the historical emergence of the sociology of knowledge is unthinkable, but once in existence these factors make for a constellation which necessarily gives "rise to [its] problems" [40]. More succinctly, the sociology of knowledge tackles the question of what happens if intellectual processes and products are unmasked as the expression of, or in relation to, social-historical circumstance—if intellectual life as such is so unmasked. The sociology of knowledge must come to terms with this question because this is precisely what has actually happened. It has to come to terms with what it realizes has happened in the modern world. It must transform a new and shattering experience into a problem.

This does not mean that the theoretical distillate of this historical experience depends for its emergence exclusively on that experience. Theoretical preoccupations with the sociology of knowledge are at least as old as Xenophanes of Colophon (sixth century B.C.) and Sextus Empiricus (A.D. third century), to mention only two [41] of many theoretically relevant writers throughout the ages, but, as in the case of the American predecessors, their general intellectual significance is different from that of the historically conscious sociology of knowledge.

Mannheim's previously quoted letter, written more than twenty years after the paper referred to, shows that even then he was still struggling with the problem of intellectual life unmasked; that problem had not lost its humbling magnitude. Already the early source presents him engaged in a diagnosis of our time: he asks where we have come from, where we are, what, therefore, we must do, and he looks for an answer in the exploration of the modern (Western) consciousness.

Such a concept of consciousness is Hegelian-Marxian. Possibly for this reason it is absent from American preoccupations with the sociology of knowledge. Even the few American comments on the time and place in which the sociology of knowledge originated do not imply it, let alone explicitly use it. Those by Louis Wirth and Robert K. Merton may serve as illustrations.

Wirth describes that time and place, our period, as one of increasing secularization. As such, it has come to question "norms and truths which were once believed to be absolute," and to recognize that thought itself is disturbing because it is "capable of unsettling routines, disorganizing habits, breaking up customs, undermining faiths, and generating skepticism." Certain "facts" of the social life may not be investigated because this would impinge on vested interests. Mannheim, says Wirth, has gone beyond this insight into the reflection of interest "in all thought, including that part of it which is called science." Mannheim has tried "to trace out the specific connection between actual interest groups in society and the ideas and modes of thought which they espoused" [42].

Thus Wirth, in his attempt to locate our time historically, in effect praises Mannheim as a modern representative of the Enlightenment, particularly of the Enlightenment theory of interests. We saw, however, that Mannheim himself, even before publishing the book to which Wirth wrote the introduction just quoted, had no longer operated with such a theory but with the social relativization of the totality of the mental world. As to the Enlightenment itself, Mannheim argued, in the earlier paper, that it was a phase in the development of the modern consciousness we have left far behind. It was a phase endowing Reason with autonomy and thus "least likely to effect a relativization of thought." Rather it pointed "in the opposite direction, that is, toward an absolute self-hypostatization of Reason" [43].

Merton remarks that in an era of increasing social conflict and distrust, inquiry into the validity of ideas tends to shift toward preoccupation with their origin. "Thought becomes functionalized; it is interpreted in terms of its psychological or economic or social or racial sources and functions": witness not only the sociology of knowledge but also "psycho-analysis, Marxism, semanticism, propaganda analysis, Paretanism, and, to some extent, functional analysis" [44]. Merton no more than Wirth operates with a conception of history in which the notion of a consciousness either commensurate with or reflective of a period is a constitutive element.

The exploration of our time and place undertaken in the preceding section suggests the hope of an understanding that presupposes the acceptance of the dualism of man and his unique cultures. An analysis of recurring problems of the sociology of knowledge undertaken elsewhere [45] has shown the same dualism as one of the metaphysical premises of the sociology of knowledge—and naturalism as the other. As this is explained, it will become evident that naturalism, too, is a presupposition of the understanding in which we have found the hope of transcending our time.

Besides metaphysical, there are two other kinds of premise: methodological and volitional. The distinctions among the three may be made as follows: A *methodological premise* is a proposition accepted because of its usefulness as a guide to inquiry. A *volitional premise* is an affect or desire that animates the researcher. A *metaphysical premise* is a proposition concerning the nature of reality.

Among the methodological premises of the sociology of knowledge are the propositions that the scientific validity of intellectual phenomena has nothing to do with their origin, that intellectual phenomena have logical as well as social aspects. The corresponding volitional premises of the sociology of knowledge are the desires for unimpeachable validity, on the one hand, and social relevance, on the other. They are the desires for maximum intrinsic interpretation, which illuminates the logical aspects of intellectual phenomena, and for maximum extrinsic interpretation, which illuminates their social aspects. The nature of these wishes presupposes a certain conception of reality, which is expressed in the metaphysical premises of the sociology of knowledge. Accordingly, reality is both relative (socially, culturally, historically, and biologically) and absolute, that is, itself, true, irrespective of relativity. It follows that the appropriate approach to reality likewise is dual: both the most thorough extrinsic interpretation of phenomena (as instances of laws) and their most thorough intrinsic interpretation (in their own terms) which are possible on any given occasion at any time.

The first of these metaphysical premises (concerning reality) predicates ontological dualism; the second (concerning the interpretation of this reality) espouses naturalism, understood as continuity of analysis [46]. It should now be clear (as has been anticipated) that naturalism, in this sense, also is a metaphysical premise of the understanding which resulted as a hope from the analysis of our time and place. This analysis implied that the inquiry into the nature of man and culture and into their mutual relations and boundaries would never be completed.

## SCIENTIFIC VERSUS EXISTENTIAL TRUTH

It is important to realize that methodological problems, including those of testing methodological premises, and volitional and metaphysical problems, have different criteria of confirmation or truth. For methodological problems the criterion of truth is pragmatic in relation to a given inquiry or type of inquiry; in this sense it is a means criterion. For volitional and metaphysical problems the criterion is agreement with the result of the most rigorously imaginable intrasubjective dialectical examination of one's most important experiences: it is an end criterion [47].

The truth sought in the solution of methodological problems may be called *stipulative* in the sense that the predicate "true" is stipulated as suitable to the investigatory purpose in hand (or to the class of investigatory purposes of which the one in hand is an example). It may also be called *hypothetical* in the sense that it is contingent on the validation of a given hypothesis being examined in respect to its truth or in the more compelling sense that, even if validated, hypotheses remain hypotheses, namely propositions that can be validated only within the hypothetical methodological, pragmatic, scientific attitude—that attitude for which metaphysical propositions (concerning the nature of reality) are irrelevant. Finally, this truth may be called *propositional*, in the sense that it is predicated only (or predominantly [48]) of propositions. It is clear that this stipulative, hypothetical, propositional truth, which is the truth sought in the solution of methodological problems, is also the truth sought in the solution of scientific problems. This is widely, if not generally, recognized by philosophers of science and of value. It implies that science makes no claims about the nature of (ultimate) reality; it is not concerned with this reality. We refer to this stipulative, hypothetical, propositional truth as *scientific* truth.

The truth sought in the solution of volitional and metaphysical problems may, in accordance with the definition given above, be called experiential or *existential*. From a sociological standpoint the seeker after scientific truth who commits an error risks his technical well-being, including, if he is a scientist, his professional reputation. By contrast, the seeker after existential truth risks his life and the world. Concerning both he may die in greater error than he would if he had "surrendered" [49] more fully, consciously, and intelligently to them.

Paul Kecskemeti has illuminated the nature of Mannheim's sociology of knowledge by arguing that Mannheim in effect distinguished between two kinds of truth, which are closely related to scientific and existential truth. These are the "Aristotelian concept of truth as 'speaking the truth,' " or "the truth of propositions . . ."; and truth as "one's response to reality," "the existential concept of truth as 'being in truth.' " We should remember, Kecskemeti writes, that truth has been conceived in these two ways throughout the history of philosophy. For the first, truth is predicative of sentences; it

> has nothing to do with the things of the world as they exist in themselves. According to the other definition, 'truth' is first and foremost an attribute of *existence*, and only secondarily of *discourse*. One *is* or *is not* in the Truth; and one's posses-sion of Truth depends on being in communion with a reality which 'is' or embodies truth [50].

### SOCIAL NOMINALISM VERSUS SOCIAL REALISM

This reality, for Mannheim (for the early Mannheim, as we shall see later in this section), was history. The positing of history, or of anything else, as real is not for the scientist to do. He pursues scientific truth and in so doing ignores metaphysical questions. In other words, the scientific atti-tude "brackets"—to use the language of phenomenology—the ontological quest. To the extent, however, that a given science or scientist deviates from the type, there may be metaphysical premises that have their influ-ence on the selection and formulation of problems, on the interpretation of findings, and so on. Mannheim is by no means alone, or even an excep-tion, in such deviation. Thus it has been said of American sociology as a whole that it is characterized by "voluntaristic nominalism"; that is, by

> the assumption that the structure of all social groups is the consequence of the aggregate of its separate, component indi-viduals and that social phenomena ultimately derive from the motivations of these knowing, feeling, and willing individuals.

American sociology, therefore, is unsympathetic to any social determinism.

> A sociology of knowledge, for instance, which maintains a strict causal relationship between a specific form of social existence or class position and knowledge is unlikely to gain

many adherents among American sociologists. . . . neither
Durkheim's notion of society as an entity *sui generis* nor
Marx's interpretation of social stratification in terms of economic relations and consequent class consciousness has been
accepted in American sociology in spite of widespread familiarity with these ideas [51].

Not being pure, that is, self-conscious, self-critical, self-correcting, neither
American nor European sociology wholly rejects its own metaphysical
inclinations. As sciences, they should withhold an accent of reality,
whereas, in fact, they bestow it, although each of them bestows it on a
different sphere. American sociology places it on the individual, withdrawing it from society. We may refer to this by saying that American
sociology represents individual realism (and social nominalism, to paraphrase the term voluntaristic nominalism). European sociology places it
on society or history, withdrawing it from the individual. It represents
social realism (individual nominalism).

Social realism is related to historical realism. This relation has been
shown by Ernest Manheim in respect to Karl Mannheim's career. The
later stages of this career, Manheim observes, show increasing interest
in psychology, which "is inherent in Mannheim's adoption of the nominalist theory of groups, the view that groups have no reality of their own
beyond the existence of their individual members." (This is, of course, the
characteristically American conception of sociology.) This turning toward
social nominalism also explains Mannheim's *"abandonment of the doctrine which asserts the primacy of the historical frame of reference."* As
Ernest Manheim points out, it is only in what has been called individual
realism, that is,

> when the individual becomes the ultimate term of reference
> of sociological constructs (as is typically the case in American
> sociology) that questions of motivation can have meaning for
> the analysis of social action. Sociological concepts formed on
> the level of the group are impervious to psychology [52].

Thus we can formulate a further contrast: American sociology is characterized by psychological realism (social nominalism); European sociology,
by social realism (psychological nominalism).

It is perhaps unnecessary to point out that these are no more than
broad characterizations. For a fuller description (surely not to be undertaken here) qualifications must be entered; for instance, much recent
American work in bureaucracy and social stratification leans more toward
social realism; on the other hand, there is a strong interest in psychology,

verging on psychological realism, in European writers as different as Tarde, LeBon, and some writings by Simmel. It is also possible to make relevant distinctions on the American scene according to individual and typical sociologists, institutions, and levels (e.g., textbook versus monograph). On the whole, nevertheless, American sociology has almost from the beginning been more deeply involved with (social) psychology (interests, social forces, instincts, needs, and attitudes) than with society or history, whereas the opposite tends to describe European sociology.

Ernst Grünwald's distinction of the psychological and historical theories as the roots or forerunners of the sociology of knowledge suggests the pertinence of this discussion for the sociology of knowledge. The psychological theory, includinig its conceptions of truth and falsehood, is based on a theory of human nature; the historical theory, with the same inclusion, on a theory of history [53]. Without detailing names, tendencies, and movements, it is clear that the sociology of knowledge, although the German variant more than the French, is in the historical rather than the psychological tradition. Along with much European sociology—to add a last generalization—the sociology of knowledge operates with a concept of existential truth, sometimes at the cost of inadequate attention to the concept of scientific truth. This last contrast gives credence to the often-heard derogatory designation of European sociology in general as philosophical, metaphysical, speculative, or armchair, and to the European comments that in American sociology "reliability has been won by surrendering theoretic relevance" [54].

A summary presentation of suggested characteristics of American and European sociology may be useful (Table 1):

*Table 1. Metaphysical Tendencies of American and European Sociology*

| American Sociology | European Sociology (and Sociology of Knowledge) |
|---|---|
| Scientific Truth | Existential Truth |
| Individual-Psychological Realism | Social-Historical Realism |
| Social-Historical Nominalism | Individual-Psychological Nominalism |

## CONNECTIONS BETWEEN THE SOCIOLOGY OF KNOWLEDGE AND OUR TIME

At the beginning of our inquiry into the premises of the sociology of knowledge we spoke of the need for showing the nature of the connection between it and our time. The intervening discussion was necessary before we could hope to meet this need. Here we try to do so. It may help to recall the course of our argument. In recalling it, we rephrase it in the light of the gains we have made.

We began by asking, "What is the sociology of knowledge?"—a question raised and answered by an outsider in search of scientific knowledge. The central concern of the insider, who was then introduced, emerged as the need to recognize himself and his fellowmen in their common time and place in order to know what to do. This—our—time and place appeared to us to be characterized by the administered nature of our lives, by the world as underdeveloped, and by one-world-and-cultural-relativism, with understanding as the hope of transcending this time, and dualism—and naturalism—as the metaphysical premises of such understanding. These were also seen as the metaphysical premises, related to its methodological and volitional premises, of the sociology of knowledge. We may now make explicit those implications of the subsequent steps of our inquiry that are relevant to the task of showing that the connection between the sociology of knowledge and our time can be analyzed and can be argued to be of a determinable kind and importance.

These steps dealt with the distinction between scientific and existential truth and with the preponderant association of the former with individual-psychological realism (social nominalism) and of the latter with social-historical realism (individual nominalism). Social-historical realism and existential truth, we suggested, characterize the sociology of knowledge, and one indication is its notion of historical consciousness. We had remarked earlier on the absence of this notion from the American preoccupation with the sociology of knowledge and had illustrated this absence with Wirth's and Merton's observations on the time in which the sociology of knowledge originated.

The connection between the sociology of knowledge and our time thus appears to be the following:

1. To speak of this connection makes sense only if the concept "our time" itself makes sense, and it does this only on a historical (social-historical-realist) rather than a psychological (individual-psychological-realist) view.

2. Once such a view is adopted, the sociology of knowledge can be seen as one of several articulations [55] of the consciousness of our time, an articulation which, as it becomes conscious of being such, contributes to the transcendence of this consciousness. The sociology of knowledge thus emerges as the reaffirmation or, better, reinvention of the Socratic position, on the occasion of its insight into its own time and place.

3. In becoming conscious of its methodological, volitional, and meta-

physical premises in their historical relevance, the sociology of knowledge appears "as a revision of our way of . . . looking at ourselves and the world, . . . an elucidation of a new experience man has had and is still having" [56].

In words used earlier, the sociology of knowledge transforms a new and shattering experience into a problem.

### NINETEENTH- AND TWENTIETH-CENTURY CIVILIZATIONAL-HISTORICAL DICHOTOMIES, MODERN AMERICAN SOCIOLOGY, AND THE SOCIOLOGY OF KNOWLEDGE

In the exploration of our time and place the world as underdeveloped appeared as a correction of the notion of underdeveloped countries, that is, of the tendency to project our own underdevelopment on non-Western peoples. In that connection we commented on some civilizational-historical dichotomies as attempts at coming to terms with the emerging one world. We now wish to apply our subsequent distinction between scientific and existential truth to a reinterpretation of these dichotomies so that differences and relations between the sociology of knowledge and American sociology may be brought out further.

Henry Maine's contrast between societies based on status and societies based on contract, Herbert Spencer's military and industrial societies, Ferdinand Tönnies' *Gemeinschaft* and *Gesellschaft*, Emile Durkheim's societies characterized by mechanical and organic solidarity, Max Weber's distinction between traditionalism and rationalism, Howard Becker's sacred and secular societies, Ralph Linton's ascribed and achieved status (and universals and alternatives), Robert Redfield's folk and urban societies, and Godfrey and Monica Wilson's primitive and civilized [57], to mention only some of the dichotomies articulated during the last hundred years, are not only what they were predominantly intended by their authors to be, namely scientific hypotheses submitted for confirmation or falsification by subsequent research, they also claim existential truth:

> For decades, the pictures of primitive character brought back by anthropologists, no matter how well intended, were used by the denizens of Western industrialized civilization, either to preen themselves on their progress or to damn their cities, machines, or customs by reference to a constructed preliterate Eden—all, of course, under the guidance of such supposedly scientific terms as "folk society." "*Gemeinschaft*," "sacred society," and other such phrases [58].

In our words the existential element in these dichotomies is the mixture of faith and doubt that liberalism, increasing rationalization, reasonableness, and progress are indeed true. The faith probably is more plausible than the doubt, but we must recall that some of the dichotomists did express their worries. Thus Durkheim was disturbed by anomie, Weber by bureaucratization, Mannheim by the preponderance of functional over substantial rationality, and Durkheim looked to social reorganization through professional groups. Weber expressed his belief in prophecy, Mannheim, in ecstasy [59]. The appearance of these dichotomies and their authors' attitudes toward them thus tell the later story of liberalism (more spontaneously or, one might say, in a more clinical sense than do Nietzsche, Spengler, or Toynbee) as the doubt concerning the existential truth of the liberal historical interpretation and the scientific truth of its historical account [60]. The dichotomists (or other Westerners) have not succeeded either in writing a scientifically more accurate history or in revising liberalism toward greater historical adequacy. Instead we have been overwhelmed by totalitarianism—among other things an alternative, antiliberal interpretation of the historical moment—and have experienced and witnessed the helplessness of liberalism confronted with it [61].

Reinhard Bendix has shown that certain trends in the development of the Western image of man from Bacon through the Enlightenment to Marx, Nietzsche, and Freud represent an increasing "distrust of reason" [62]. The last four centuries, especially the last hundred years, have thrown man ever more back on himself, unmasking ideas, beliefs, customs, and traditions as unreliable and unworthy crutches, as ideologies (Marx) or sublimations (Freud).

Therefore the question, "what, then, is man?" was raised. It was being asked by the same analysts who had stripped man to the necessity of (again) asking it, as well as by many others, from Descartes through Kierkegaard to the contemporary existentialists, phenomenologists, and various theologians. This question intruded during the same period in which science and technology developed and (especially in its later phases) the standard of living rose to levels never reached before. There was a temptation, therefore, to take these developments themselves as the answer to the question, "What is man?" This question had to be asked in a whisper, in an embarrassed whisper—as a lover asks his beloved in the din of a factory, a cafeteria, a movie house, and (particularly in the twentieth century) the roar of a world war or a concentration camp. Science, technology, prosperity, and disaster seem to have kept our self-inspection in a balance between the desire for it and its postponement as long as the automobile and the screen were there as an escape, and as long as the war, which had to be fought, urged us to tell who we are by asking science and ignoring history. Witness scientism, infatuation with methodology in general, and more particularly such phenomena as formal literary criticism, philosophical analysis, structural linguistics, and the strong ritualistic element in social relations [63].

These are some historical problems to which modern sociology, specifically, might address itself. Instead, it appears to be preoccupied, in America possibly more than elsewhere, with rather ahistorical, formal structural relations and processes and with improving itself as a specialty in such preoccupation. To say this is not to suggest that sociology should not be a generalizing science. Rather it is to argue that sociology would facilitate its task of being a generalizing science if it recognized its need for a historical theory of society, no matter how crude it might be to begin with [64]. If sociology wants to be historically relevant, it cannot reject its commitment to historical realism and abide its psychological realism which no longer is historically adequate, for even a generalizing science, *if it is a social science*, starts with the historical situation. It may deny it but it cannot escape it. In this respect social science cannot be entirely true to the pure type of science which brackets the ontological quest [65].

The sociology of knowledge escapes this difficulty of modern American sociology by its historical realism and its much more openly recognized connection with the quest for existential truth. It is alien to the formalism of our time and in this sense, and by contrast, substantive [66]; it is applied theory, in the service of changing the world, whether according to Marx (specifically the *Theses on Feuerbach*) or Durkheim. Both Marx and Durkheim preceded the modern bifurcation of the world into Is and Ought, a bifurcation that has been shared and pushed by contemporary social science. Marx, much more than Durkheim, was one of the strippers of modern man, but his historical focus kept Is and Ought together. Durkheim, like Max Weber, is a figure of transition in the sense that in their actual researches both keep Is and Ought together, whereas in their explicit methodological writings they separate them (Weber more pointedly and passionately than Durkheim) [67]. In the United States the form secularization took in Marx (by way of Hegel and Feuerbach) appears to be an unmanageable alternative to American liberalism [68]. The other, the separation of Is and Ought, is intimately connected with the phenomena discussed in our exploration of the contemporary Western scene and with those mentioned above. In American sociology this separation is of recent date, probably the 1920s. It had not yet appeared in Cooley's *Social Process* (1918); Lundberg-Anderson-Bain's *Trends in American Sociology* (1929) was a milestone in its articulation and acceptance.

Already ten years later, Robert S. Lynd manifested discontent with it in *Knowledge for What?*

## MERTON'S COMPARISON BETWEEN THE SOCIOLOGY OF KNOWLEDGE AND MASS COMMUNICATIONS

Now let us consider the comparison between European and American sociology that is most pertinent here: Merton's juxtaposition of the European sociology of knowledge and the recent branch of American sociology, research into mass communications, that seems most closely related to it.

Although the sociology of knowledge and mass communications, Merton observes, have on the whole developed independently from one another, they may be regarded "as two species of that genus of research which is concerned with the interplay between social structure and communications" [69]. The numerous contrasting aspects of these two "species" may be presented in tabular form (Table 2):

*Table 2.  Merton's Comparison Between the Sociology of Knowledge and Mass Communications*

| Aspects | Sociology of Knowledge (European) | Mass Communications (American) |
|---|---|---|
| Subject matter and definition of problems | Knowledge<br>Bodies of systematically connected facts or ideas<br>Total structure of knowledge available to a few | Information<br>Isolated fragments of information available to masses of people |
| Data and facts | Historical<br>Long-range<br>Impressions of mass opinion set down by a few observers as facts<br>Chief question: "why"<br>Chief concern: problem, even if speculation is the best that can be done<br>Studies and findings are important, even if empirically questionable | Contemporary<br>Short-range<br>Collection of facts<br><br>Chief question: "what"<br>Chief concern: securing adequate empirical data, even if the problem gets lost<br>Studies and findings may be trivial but are empirically rigorous |

Table 2. *Merton's Comparison Between the Sociology of Knowledge and Mass Communications* (contd.)

| Aspects | Sociology of Knowledge (European) | Mass Communications (American) |
|---|---|---|
| Research techniques and procedures | Limited to the authentication of documents<br>Reliability is no problem<br>A tradition in and from the history of different interpretations of the same data; a humanities background<br>Cumulative nature of findings not stressed<br>No audience research because the chief question is the "why" or "how come" of the intellectual phenomena investigated<br>Impetus behind the studies is academic | A considerable array of various techniques<br>Reliability is an important problem<br>No such tradition and background<br><br>Cumulative nature of findings is stressed<br>Emphasis on audience research because the chief question is the "what" or "what impact" of the intellectual phenomena investigated<br>Impetus behind the studies is practical (market and military research, propaganda, etc.) [70] |
| Social organization of research | Lone wolf<br>No organizational pressure toward reliability | Team<br>Organizational pressure toward reliability |
| Social origins of investigators (tentative) | Investigators are marginal to different social systems and perceive diverse intellectual perspectives of different groups | Investigators are mobile within an economic or social system and get data needed by those who operate organizations, seek markets, and control many people |

It is hardly necessary to insist that Merton's comparison of the sociology of knowledge and the study of mass communications largely agrees with that of the sociology of knowledge and American sociology, presented in this chapter. (It is true, of course, that each of the two efforts has commented on aspects ignored by the other; most obviously, the present essay has left out of consideration the last two of Merton's five categories, the social organization of research and the social origins of investigators.) Translating Merton's characterizations which touch most closely on our enterprise into the language of the latter, we obtain the following propositions:

1. According to subject matter and definition of problems, the sociology of knowledge examines intellectual life as a whole, whereas mass communications takes it for granted as it finds it and explores features that unexamined traditions have made problematical (cf. the last entry under "Research techniques and procedures" in the "Mass Communications" column of Table 2); the former is practiced in a philosophical-anthropological and historical sense, the latter is unsystematically contemporary.

2. For its data and facts the sociology of knowledge is guided by history, existential truth, causality, the nature of knowledge and of intersubjectivity itself, whereas mass communications strives to register the pulse of opinion with scientifically unimpeachable methods.

3. Research techniques and procedures for the sociology of knowledge are secondary, whereas for mass communications they tend to be primary, self-consummatory, and self-proliferating; the former is in the service of culture, the latter, of civilization [71].

Aside from these all too abbreviated comments on the content of these and Merton's characterizations, a word must be said about the difference between their volitional premises and criteria of truth. Merton wishes to establish true propositions concerning similarities and differences between the sociology of knowledge and communications research. He operates with the scientific conception of truth in line with the scientific approach and, more specifically, with his effort to codify extant theory and research. By contrast, what has been said in the preceding pages has affirmed the historical perspective in which it was stated as well as the effort to arrive at existential truth. To put it differently, Merton's chief concern is "what" (a characteristic of the right-hand column in Table 2); mine is "why" or "how come" (a characteristic of the left-hand column). Merton's analysis, and the translation of some of his own hopes stated in the text on which Table 2 is based, shows us gaps in the attention to scientific problems to be filled by scientific propositions, whereas the European column shows gaps in the attention to existential problems to be filled by existentially true propositions.

It should be noted, however, that what has just been said claims to be true in the scientific sense of the term. Its attitude is the same as that of Merton's analysis. What it talks about, however, is different, namely existential truth, on which Merton is silent. To discuss the nature of truth, as is widely recognized, is not the scientist's but the philosopher's concern. It is also widely recognized that it is important to distinguish between talking about one's own views of truth, which is considered a philosophical enterprise, and about somebody else's, which is accepted as a legitimate scientific enterprise. In expounding my own views of truth in this chapter, I have sometimes talked as a philosopher (in the philosophical attitude); in commenting on Merton's, I have talked as a scientist. Social science, in contrast to natural science, is concerned, no matter how indirectly, with human beings, that is, fellow men. At least *at this time* (which I have tried to characterize)—and we have no other—social science has to start, I have argued, with this time, with the historical situation. To grasp the historical situation and communicate the process of grasping it, as this process has been going on in the making of this chapter, I had to suspend (bracket) the safety that comes from limitation to scientific truth and open myself (surrender) to existential truth. On the occasion of commenting on Merton's paradigm I have returned to the scientific attitude.

## THE SOCIOLOGY OF KNOWLEDGE AND SOCIOLOGICAL THEORY

By now the reader may have long forgotten the title of this chapter. Actually, however, this entire chapter has dealt with the relation between the sociology of knowledge and sociological theory, as a concluding summary of what it has to say about this shows.

First, let us list some of the things it has nothing to say about.

1. It has nothing to say about the relation between the sociology of knowledge and sociological theory that might be disclosed by an analysis of the work of sociologists of knowledge and sociological theorists.

2. It has no recommendation to make concerning the way in which a scientific study is carried out.

3. It offers no list of scientific problems to be investigated under the program of a sociology of knowledge it conceives of; in the present context this is too large a topic [72].

4. It urges no particular definition of sociological theory.

At this point we must make an observation about sociological theory that will lead us to the more positive statements we have to submit. It is that, with only one exception that I know of [73], the relatively few extant definitions of the term sociological theory—to the extent that they go beyond elevating a casual collection of colloquial referents to definitional status—are much more specific about its formal features [74]—what its structure is like or how it is constructed—than about its content or what it is *about*. It is almost as if sociology, in relation to which they try to define theory, had no specific content. This suggests that these conceptions of theory do not regard human beings, the subject matter of sociology, of sufficient theoretical dignity to incorporate them into a definition of sociological theory. It is a further indication of their corresponding concepts of sociology.

This observation concerning sociological theory is the major reason why this chapter has proceeded as it has. Thus it has had to say much more about modern American sociology in general than about sociological theory or particular theories. Modern sociology and sociological theory are so intimately connected that a historical analysis has appeared to be a more adequate tool for identifying them than a systematic analysis would have been. A systematic analysis could easily fall prey to the temptation to take sociology and sociological theory at their face value. It is hoped, however, that this chapter may help clear the ground for such an analysis.

If we put positively what the last three paragraphs have said in the negative, we can formulate what this chapter has to say about the relations between the sociology of knowledge and sociological theory.

1. The analysis of the sociology of knowledge in the context of our time appears to make it incumbent on sociological theory to define itself, either in a way that is adequate to the subject matter of sociology and to the historical occasion of the definition, or to disprove the relevance of this double requirement of adequacy.

2. The existing, overwhelmingly social-historically nominalistic sociological theory appears to make it incumbent on the sociology of knowledge (reinspect the unfavorable items in the left-hand column of Table 2) to clarify its status in reference to scientific versus existential truth, science versus history, and science versus philosophy. As it is, the sociology of knowledge is two things. One, particularly in America, is dead. The other is not yet—it is a heap of fragments and shoots waiting to be given form and life. Dead is the excitement attendant on the appearance of Mannheim's *Ideology and Utopia*. It would be good if this chapter had managed to show that the excitement had a greater claim than that of a fad, and that there is hope of recalling its origin in a confrontation of sociology with history, existential truth, and philosophy. Not yet alive are two potentialities of the sociology of knowledge. The first is the codification

of the great mass of relevant research into a more viable sociology of intellectual life. The other, different, even though causally related, is the injection of more self-conscious humanness and historicity, and thus greater scientific relevance, into contemporary sociology.

*Acknowledgment.* I am deeply indebted to John W. Bennett and Llewellyn Gross, and also to Aron Gurwitsch, Paul Kecskemeti, Anthony Nemetz, Talcott Parsons, Alfred Schutz, and Melvin Seeman for critical readings of earlier drafts of this paper and for their pertinent comments. Unfortunately I have not been able to act on all of them.

## NOTES

1. Jacques J. Maquet (*Sociologie de la connaissance: sa structure et ses rapports avec la philosophie de la connaissance; étude critique des systèmes de Karl Mannheim et de Pitirim A. Sorokin* [Louvain: Institut de Recherches Economiques et Sociales; E. Nauwalaerts, Ed., 1949], p. 19; *The Sociology of Knowledge: Its Structure and Its Relation to the Philosophy of Knowledge: A Critical Analysis of the Systems of Karl Mannheim and Pitirim A. Sorokin,* translated by John F. Locke [Boston: Beacon, 1951], p. 3) claims that "knowledge" in "sociology of knowledge" has greater denotations than *wissen,* which, "taken as a whole, means science, whereas 'knowledge' includes at the same time the simple act of presenting an object to the mind . . . and the act of thinking which reaches a complete understanding of this object." This greater denotation means that the German term connotes a higher claim to certainty than the French and English terms (to the latter of which corresponds the German *kennen,* not *erkennen,* as Maquet writes). By the criterion of the relation of knower to known, however, *wissen* is broader than knowledge, inasmuch as it refers not only to the scientist and his scientific knowledge but also to philosopher, artist, mystic, and religious person and their respective kinds of knowledge. For common-sense questions concerning the meanings of these terms this is the more expected criterion. It thus appears to be less misleading to say that *wissen* has a broader meaning than knowledge.

2. Along with historicism [cf. T. B. Bottomore, "Some Reflections on the Sociology of Knowledge," *British Journal of Sociology,* 7 (March 1956), 52–58, especially 52] and Nietzsche, leading to Freud and Pareto and the related current of positivism (Ratzenhofer, Gumplowicz, Oppenheimer, and Jerusalem: cf.

Karl Mannheim, "The Sociology of Knowledge" (1931), *Ideology and Utopia, op. cit.,* pp. 278–279). For the history of the sociology of knowledge and a critique of the major ideas advanced by its various factions, see Ernst Grünwald, *Das Problem der Soziologie des Wissens* (Wien-Leipzig: Braumüller, 1934). For the significance of Marxism see Robert K. Merton, "The Sociology of Knowledge," in Georges Gurvitch and Wilbert E. Moore, Eds., *Twentieth Century Sociology* (New York: Philosophical Library, 1945), Chapter XIII, *passim* [reprinted in Merton, *Social Theory and Social Structure: Toward the Codification of Theory and Research* (Glencoe, Ill.: Free Press, 1949), Chapter VIII; revised and enlarged edition *(ibid.,* 1957), Chapter XII]. For a collection of relevant texts by Marx himself, some of them previously untranslated, see Karl Marx, *Selected Writings in Sociology and Social Philosophy,* edited and with an introduction and notes by T. B. Bottomore and Maximilien Rubel (London: Watts, 1956), including the editors' introduction.

3.   This term was coined in the early 1920s. It was subsequently taken over in translation. For French, Dutch, and Italian versions see Maquet, *The Sociology of Knowledge, op. cit.,* p. 261, n. 1.

4.   Hans-Joachim Lieber, *Wissen und Gesellschaft: Die Probleme der Wissenssoziologie* (Tübingen: Max Niemeyer, 1952): Mannheim, *Ideologie und Utopie,* 3rd ed. (Frankfurt/Main: G. Schulte-Bulmke, 1952).

5.   Max Scheler, "Probleme einer Soziologie des Wissens," in Scheler, Ed., *Versuche zu einer Soziologie des Wissens* (München: Duncker und Humblot, 1924), pp. 5–146; enlarged under the same title in Scheler, *Die Wissensformen und die Gesellschaft* (Leipzig: Der neue Geist Verlag, 1926), pp. 1–229; Mannheim, *Ideologie und Utopie* (Bonn: Friedrich Cohen, 1929).

6.   Mannheim, *Ideology and Utopia, loc. cit.*

7.   Louis Wirth, Preface to Mannheim, *op. cit.,* pp. xvii–xxiii [reprinted in Wirth, *Community Life and Social Policy,* Elizabeth Wirth Marvick and Albert J. Reiss, Jr., Eds. (Chicago: University of Chicago Press, 1956), especially pp. 40–45].

8.   On the other hand, there probably is an affinity between the sociology of knowledge and a European outlook. A good deal of what I have to say later in this chapter bears on this affinity, although I do not analyze it explicitly.

9.   [See Chapter 28, n. 14.]

10.   Merton, "The Sociology of Knowledge," *loc. cit.*

11.   Wirth, *op. cit.* See also Franz Adler, "The Sociology of Knowledge Since 1918," *Midwest Sociologist,* **17** (Spring 1955), 3 ff.

12.   Kurt H. Wolff, "A Preliminary Inquiry into the Sociology of Knowledge from the Standpoint of the Study of Man," *op. cit.* p. 586 (henceforth *Inquiry*). [Chapter 28].

13.   Louis Wirth, quoted in Howard W. Odum, *American Sociology: The Story of Sociology in the United States through 1950* (New York: Longmans, Green, 1951), p. 231.

14. In his "Paradigm for the Sociology of Knowledge," Merton (*op. cit.*, p. 372, reprinted, *op. cit.*, pp. 221–222; rev. ed., pp. 460–461) uses "mental productions" without, however, advocating their sociology as a substitute for sociology of knowledge.

15. Karl Mannheim, *Essays on the Sociology of Culture*, edited by Ernest Manheim in cooperation with Paul Kecskemeti (New York: Oxford University Press, 1956), Part 1, "Towards the Sociology of the Mind: an Introduction."

16. Gerard DeGré, "The Sociology of Knowledge and the Problem of Truth," *Journal of the History of Ideas*, 2 (January 1941), 110.

17. Wolff, *Inquiry*, p. 587 [Chapter 28]. See also Franz Adler, "The Range of Sociology of Knowledge," in Howard Becker and Alvin Boskoff, Eds., *Modern Sociological Theory in Continuity and Change* (New York: Dryden Press, 1957), Chapter 13. An attempt at assembling relevant materials, though in a rather haphazard and exceedingly incomplete manner, is my *The Sociology of Knowledge: A Preliminary Bibliography* [Columbus: Ohio State University, Department of Sociology and Anthropology, 1945 (mimeographed); "Additions," 1951]. Despite its serious shortcomings and its preliminary character, it is more comprehensive than others, among which Mannheim's (*Ideology and Utopia, op. cit.*, pp. 281–304, augmented in the 1952 German edition of *Ideologie und Utopie, op. cit.*, pp. 269–291) is the most important. For a comprehensive, indispensable, and only slightly overlapping bibliography on the sociology of literature see Hugh Dalziel Duncan, *Language and Literature in Society: A Sociological Essay on Theory and Method in the Interpretation of Linguistic Symbols, with a Bibliographical Guide to the Sociology of Literature* (Chicago: University of Chicago Press, 1953), pp. 143–214.

18. [Chapter 28, ns. 5–8.]

19. [Chapter 28, n. 3.]

20. [Chapter 28, n. 4.]

21. Leo P. Chall, "The Sociology of Knowledge," in Joseph S. Roucek, Ed., *Contemporary Sociology* (New York: Philosophical Library, 1958), p. 284.

22. For Robert K. Merton see his chronological bibliography in *Social Theory and Social Structure, op. cit.*, pp. 409–412. In regard to C. Wright Mills, compare his early work in the sociology of knowledge [e.g., "Methodological Consequences of the Sociology of Knowledge" *American Journal of Sociology*, 46 (November 1940), 316–330] with his later books on labor leaders, white-collar workers, and the power elite. Gerard DeGré [*op. cit.*, and *Society and Ideology: An Inquiry into the Sociology of Science* (Garden City, N.Y.: Doubleday, 1955); this study, however, shows that DeGré has not abandoned his interest in the sociology of knowledge proper; see especially pp. 34–37]. Frank E. Hartung, on the other hnd, has continued to publish from time to time in the field since 1944 [e.g., "The Sociology of Positivism," *Science and Society*, 8 (Fall 1944), 328–341; "Problems of the Sociology of Knowledge," *Philosophy of Science*, 19 (January 1952), 17–32]. For Howard Becker and Pitirim A. Sorokin the sociology of knowledge has never been central; cf. Becker and Helmut Otto Dahlke,

"Max Scheler's Sociology of Knowledge," *Philosophy and Phenomenological Research*, 2 (March 1942), 309–322; Sorokin, *Social and Cultural Dynamics*, Vol. II, *Fluctuation of Systems of Truth, Ethics, and Law* (New York: American Book, 1937), "a treatise in *Wissenssoziologie*, considered in its basic forms and principles" (*ibid.*, p. vii); Sorokin has been treated as a sociologist of knowledge by Merton, "The Sociology and Knowledge," *op. cit.*, and Maquet, *op. cit.*

23. Arthur Child, following his extended work in the sociology of knowledge, has turned to problems of philosophy of history; his "Moral Judgment in History," *Ethics*, 51 (July 1951), 297–308, is a connecting link. Virgil G. Hinshaw, Jr., has moved from the sociology of knowledge, especially the critique of Mannheim's epistemological claims ["The Epistemological Relevance of Mannheim's Sociology of Knowledge," *Journal of Philosophy*, 40 (February 4, 1943), 57–72 *(Relevance)*], to epistemology ["Basic Propositions in Lewis's Analysis of Knowledge," *ibid.*, 46 (March 31, 1949), 176–184] and philosophy of science ["Levels of Analysis," *Philosophy and Phenomenological Research*, 11 (December 1950), 213–220]. Thelma Z. Lavine ["Sociological Analysis of Cognitive Norms," *Journal of Philosophy*, 39 (June 18, 1942), 342–356] has subsequently undertaken studies in the history of epistemology ["Knowledge as Interpretation: An Historical Survey," *Philosophy and Phenomenological Research*, 10 (June 1950), 526–540, and 11 (September 1950), 88–103].

24. The purpose of this essay is not, of course, a critique of Mannheim's concepts. They have received abundant and incisive examination. To mention only the more painstaking analyses in English (except for the first) in chronological order, Alexander von Schelting, *Max Weber's Wissenschaftslehre; das logische Problem der historischen Kulturerkenntnis; die Grenzen der Soziologie des Wissens* (Tübingen: Mohr, 1934), pp. 94–100, 117–167, and his review of Mannheim's *Ideologie und Utopie*, *American Sociological Review*, 1 (August 1936), 664–674; Hans Speier, review of Mannheim's *Ideology and Utopia*, *American Journal of Sociology*, 43 (July 1937), 155–166; Maurice Mandelbaum, *The Problem of Historical Knowledge: An Answer to Relativism* (New York: Liveright, 1938), pp. 67–82; Child, *Imputation*, 204–207, *Possibility*, 410–411, *Truth*, 20–21; Robert K. Merton, "Karl Mannheim and the Sociology of Knowledge," *Journal of Liberal Religion*, 2 (Winter 1941), 125–147 (reprinted in *Social Theory and Social Structure*, *op. cit.*, Chapter IX; rev. ed., Chapter XIII); Hinshaw, *Relevance*; Maquet, *op. cit.*, especially Chapters 3 and 5.

25. Peter M. Blau, *Bureaucracy in Modern Society* (New York: Random House, 1956), p. 14.

26. On secularization see Max Weber, "The Protestant Sects and the Spirit of Capitalism" (1906) in *From Max Weber: Essays in Sociology*, translated, edited, and with an introduction by H. H. Gerth and C. Wright Mills (New York: Oxford University Press, 1946), p. 307; Talcott Parsons, *The Structure of Social Action* (New York: McGraw-Hill, 1937), pp. 685–686; and, one of the most searching recent analyses, Hannah Arendt, "History and Immortality," *Partisan Review*, 24 (Winter 1957), especially 16–22. On rationalization see *From Max Weber, op. cit.*, "Introduction," pp. 51–52.

27. Max Horkheimer, *Eclipse of Reason* (New York: Oxford University Press, 1947), pp. 3–4, *passim*. Here the discussion of value judgments in social science is relevant. See especially Max Weber, *On the Methodology of the Social Sciences*, translated and edited by Edward A. Shils and Henry A. Finch (Glencoe, Ill.: Free Press, 1949); Felix Kaufmann, *Methodology of the Social Sciences* (New York: Oxford University Press, 1944), Chapters IX and XV; Leo Strauss, *Natural Right and History* (Chicago: University of Chicago Press, 1953), Chapter II; Dwight Macdonald, *The Root is Man: Two Essays in Politics* (Alhambra, Calif.: Cunningham, 1953), "Scientific Method and Value Judgment," pp. 36–39; Joseph Wood Krutch, *The Measure of Man* (1953, 1954) (New York: Grosset and Dunlap, n.d.), especially Chapter 4.

28. Despite terminological appearance possibly to the contrary, subjective reason is much closer to Mannheim's functional than to his substantial rationality (the unclarity in which he left the latter concept itself shows the loss of objective rationality): Karl Mannheim, *Man and Society in an Age of Reconstruction* (1935) (New York: Harcourt, Brace, 1940), pp. 52–60.

29. This experience is probably exhibited more poignantly by Max Weber than by any other social scientist. See Weber, " 'Objectivity' in Social Science and Social Policy" (1904), *On the Methodology of the Social Sciences, op. cit.*, pp. 52–57; "The Meaning of 'Ethical Neutrality' in Sociology and Economics" (1913, 1917), *ibid.*, pp. 11–15, 18–21; "Science as a Vocation" (1918), *From Max Weber, op. cit.*, pp. 148, 152–153. Leo Strauss, *op. cit.*, has clearly described and criticized Weber's position.

30. On futile attempts at deriving Ought from Is, that is, on the naturalistic fallacy, see Eliseo Vivas, *The Moral Life and the Ethical Life* (Chicago: University of Chicago Press, 1950), Part I, "Animadversions upon Naturalistic Moral Philosophies," *passim*, especially pp. 81–82.

31. In an important if not the essential respect Erich Kahler's *The Tower and the Abyss: An Inquiry into the Transformation of the Individual* (New York: Braziller, 1957) is a history of contemporary consciousness.

32. David Riesman, in collaboration with Reuel Denney and Nathan Glazer, *The Lonely Crowd: A Study of the Changing American Character* (New Haven: Yale University Press, 1950), Part III, "Autonomy," especially pp. 287–288 (Anchor edition, 1953, p. 278); Erich Fromm, *Man for Himself: An Inquiry into the Psychology of Ethics* (New York: Rinehart, 1947), pp. 82–107.

33. Fedor Dostoevsky, *The Idiot* (1869), translated with an introduction by David Magarshack (Penguin, 1955), p. 563.

34. Cf. my "The World as Underdeveloped," *Atti del Congresso internazionale di studio sul problema delle aree arretrate* (Milan: Giuffre, 1955), Vol. III, *Communicazioni*, pp. 505–508.

35. The literary record of these social scientists is impressive and important. Cf. Edward H. Spicer, Ed., *Human Problems in Technological Change: A Case Book* (New York: Russell Sage, 1952), *Human Organization*, official journal of the Society for Applied Anthropology; the increasing attention to relevant

problems in several social-scientific periodicals, especially in anthropology and sociology, including certain issues of the *Annals of the American Academy of Political and Social Science,* such as Vol. 305, "Agrarian Societies in Transition" (May 1956). For representative statements on problems of applied anthropology see *Anthropology Today: An Encyclopedic Inventory,* prepared under the chairmanship of A. L. Kroeber (Chicago: University of Chicago Press, 1953), "Problems of Application," pp. 741–894; Sol Tax, Loren C. Eisely, Irving Rouse, and Carl F. Voeglin, Eds., *An Appraisal of Anthropology Today (ibid.),* Chapters X and XI; William L. Thomas, Jr., Ed., *Yearbook of Anthropology—1955* (New York: Wenner-Gren Foundation for Anthropological Research, 1955), Parts 4 and 5, *passim;* the symposium on applied anthropology at the 1957 meetings of the American Anthropological Association [*Human Organization,* 17 1 (Spring 1958), "Values in Action: A Symposium, 2–26]. Note also the recent collaboration of several social sciences, including history and economics, on common problems (in contrast to the more accustomed interdisciplinary work among sociologists, anthropologists, psychologists, psychiatrists, and psychoanalysts); see especially Mirra Komarovsky, Ed., *Common Frontiers of the Social Sciences* (Glencoe, Ill.: Free Press and Falcon's Wing Press, 1957), and Karl Polanyi, Conrad Arensberg, and Harry Pearson, Eds., *Trade and Market in the Early Empires (ibid.,* 1957). Here also belongs Robert Redfield's qualification of the folk-urban dichotomy by his emphasis on the distinction between great and little traditions; see especially his *Peasant Society and Culture: An Anthropological Approach to Civilization* (Chicago: University of Chicago Press, 1956). This qualification appears to be particularly significant when the folk-urban dichotomy is seen alongside other civilizational and historical dichotomies in their attempts to come to terms with the emerging one world. A more specific correction of the outlook represented in them (according to which earlier or non-Western societies are characterized by sacredness, status, and ascription) is constituted by the discovery of the significance of kinship relations in societies characterized by secularization, contract, and achievement. Cf. Talcott Parsons, "The Kinship System of the Contemporary United States" (1943), *Essays in Sociological Theory, Pure and Applied* (Glencoe, Ill.: Free Press, 1949), Chapter XI [rev. ed. *(ibid.,* 1954), Chapter IX], Michael Young and Peter Willmott, *Family and Kinship in East London (ibid.,* 1957), and Leo A. Despres, "A Function of Bilateral Kinship Patterns in a New England Industry," *Human Organization,* 17, 2 (Summer 1958), 15–22.

36.   This dialectic between subjective and objective reason parallels Herbert Marcuse's between the performance (reality) principle and the pleasure principle: *Eros and Civilization: A Philosophical Inquiry into Freud* (Boston: Beacon, 1955). Space limitations forbid an examination of Marcuse's thesis.

37.   This is a proposition more pointed to than explicitly made by some of the students of the most spontaneous, unconscious, varied part of culture, namely language. See especially the work of Dorothy D. Lee [particularly "Conceptual Implications of an Indian Language," *Philosophy of Science,* 5 (January 1938), 89–102; "A Primitive System of Values," *ibid.,* 7 (July 1940), 355–378;

"Lineal and Non-Lineal Codifications of Reality" (1950), *Explorations,* **7** (March 1957), 30–45, in which she says, "If reality itself were not absolute, then true communication of course would be impossible. My own position is that there is an absolute reality, and that communication is possible" (30)] and Benjamin Lee Whorf [particularly "A Linguistic Consideration of Thinking in Primitive Communities" (1936?), "Languages and Logic" (1941), and "Language, Mind, and Reality" (1941), all reprinted in *Language, Thought, and Reality: Selected Writings of Benjamin Lee Whorf,* edited and with an introduction by John B. Carroll (Cambridge, Mass., and New York: M.I.T. Press and Wiley, 1956)].

38. This distinction is developed by Child (*Categories*) and expounded in my "The Unique and the General: Toward a Philosophy of Sociology," *Philosophy and Science,* **15** (July 1948), 203–204 [Chapter 27], and more fully, *Inquiry,* 595–600 [Chapter 28].

39. Karl Mannheim, "The Problem of a Sociology of Knowledge (1925), Chapter IV, pp. 134–190, in *Essays on the Sociology of Knowledge, op. cit.,* pp. 136–144. [Reprinted in *From Karl Mannheim, op. cit.,* pp. 59–115.]

40. *Ibid.,* p. 136. Although the first, third, and fourth factors can be accounted for in terms of the immanent development of ideas, the second, the unmasking turn of mind, must be understood in terms of real, social developments which resulted in the rise of the oppositional science of sociology from Humanism and Enlightenment with their main task, the disintegration of the monarchy and the clergy (*ibid.,* pp. 139–140). Now that we are "increasingly aware of the fact that *all* thinking of a social group is determined by its existence, we find less and less room for the exercise of 'unmasking,' and the latter undergoes a process of sublimation which turns it into a mere operation of determining the functional role of any thought whatever" (*ibid.,* p. 144).

41. My attention to whom has been called by Professor Alfred Schutz, as I herewith gratefully acknowledge.

42. Cf. Wirth, *op. cit.,* pp. xiii, xvii, xxiii.

43. Mannheim, *op. cit.,* p. 139.

44. Merton, *Social Theory and Social Structure, op. cit.,* pp. 457, 458. See also H. Otto Dahlke, "The Sociology of Knowledge," in Harry Elmer Barnes, Howard Becker, and Frances Bennett Becker, Eds., *Contemporary Social Theory* (New York: Appleton-Century, 1940), pp. 64–65.

45. Wolff, *Inquiry* [Chapter 28—the remainder of this section is a brief repetition].

46. In John Dewey's meaning, developed by Thelma Z. Lavine ["Naturalism and the Sociological Analysis of Knowledge," in Yervant H. Krikorian, Ed., *Naturalism and the Human Spirit* (New York: Columbia University Press, 1944), p. 184].

47. Wolff, *Inquiry,* 612 [Chapter 28].

48. Predominantly if (in addition to propositions) truth is also considered predicable of definitions. It can be so considered if a cognitive function of the

operational character of definitions is emphasized: in this case definition borders on hypotheses. It cannot be if a definition is considered an analytical proposition and nothing else: in this case it has no truth dimension; of course the *use* of the definition (in methodology or research) has, namely that of stipulative (hypothetical, propositional) truth.

49.   On the concept of surrender see my "Before and After Sociology," *Transactions of the Third World Congress of Sociology*, Vol. VII, pp. 151–152 [Chapter 15], and more fully, *Loma Culture Change: An Introduction to the Study of Man* (Columbus, Ohio State University, 1952 [mimeographed]), "Introduction," pp. 22 ff. [Also see Chapter 28 (Supplement), n. 5.] It is a not irrelevant characterization of our time that one should be led to ask, in a footnote, whether the concern exhibited here with existential truth will not alienate professional colleagues or, hyperbolically, whether, in trying to save my life and the world, I am not risking the loss of my profession.

50.   Paul Kecskemeti, "Introduction," Chapter I in Mannheim, *Essays on the Sociology of Knowledge, op. cit.*, pp. 15, 31. The difference between scientific and existential truth corresponds in a way that cannot be discussed here to that between mathematical and inner time (*durée*; on the latter see Alfred Schuetz "On Multiple Realities," *Philosophy and Phenomenological Research*, 5 (June 1945), 538–542; Pitirim A. Sorokin, *Sociocultural Causality, Space, Time* (Durham, N.C.: Duke Univesrity Press, 1943), Chapter IV; Igor Stravinsky, *Poetics of Music in the Form of Six Lessons* (1939–1940) (New York: Vintage, 1956), pp. 31–34.

51.   Roscoe C. Hinkle, Jr., and Gisela J. Hinkle, *The Development of Modern Sociology: Its Nature and Growth in the United States* (Garden City, N.Y.: Doubleday, 1954), pp. vii, 73, 74.

52.   Ernest Manheim, "Introduction" to Karl Mannheim, *Essays on the Sociology of Culture, op. cit.*, p. 5 (original italics).

53.   [See the next chapter.] Cf. Grünwald, *op. cit.*, Chapter I. (This important work has not been adequately appreciated in this country. Aside from a few citations there is only, as far as I know, Child's analysis of Grünwald's own position [in several of Child's papers on the sociology of knowledge referred to in Chapter 28, n. 14] and a brief exposition of parts of it in Adler, "The Range of Sociology of Knowledge," *op. cit.*, pp. 412–413.) [Portions of Grünwald's book have since been translated by Rainer Koehne and published in James F. Curtis and John W. Petras, Eds., *The Sociology of Knowledge: A Reader* (New York: Praeger, 1970), pp. 187–243.] A more detailed presentation and critique of Grünwald's discussion of the psychological and historical theories, although relevant and highly interesting, exceeds the scope of this chapter. The central significance of his own position on the sociology of knowledge, however, must be registered. This position is what might be called "interpretational relativism": according to Grünwald, the sociology of knowledge is only one among many equally valid or invalid interpretations of intellectual phenomena. (It has also, and rightly, been designated as "postulational skepticism": Child, *Possibility*, p. 404; Wolff, *Inquiry*

[Chapter 28], 592–593, especially n. 21 [Chapter 30].) If we ask how it is possible that a number of interpretations can be entertained, that is, if we inquire into the basis of interpretational relativism, we find that interpreter and interpretandum emerge as relatively unanalyzable presuppositions or "givens." We find the dualism of reality to be relative and absolute—the same dualism we came on as a metaphysical premise of the sociology of knowledge. If this dualism is in turn posited in some sense as optional, the burden of proof rests on the exploration of this positing by which the continuity of analysis is made both possible and mandatory. This consideration vindicates the continuity of analysis (naturalism), the second metaphysical premise of the sociology of knowledge.

54. Merton, *Social Theory and Social Structure, op. cit.,* p. 449.

55. Many examples of such articulations are given and analyzed in Kahler, *op. cit.,* Chapters 4 and 5.

56. Wolff, *Inquiry,* 618 [Chapter 28].

57. Godfrey and Monica Wilson, *The Analysis of Social Change on the Basis of Observations in Central Africa* (Cambridge: University Press, 1945). For a convenient conspectus of many such dichotomies (and trichotomies) see Howard Becker, *Through Values to Social Interpretation* (Durham, N.C.: Duke University Press, 1950), pp. 258–261.

58. David Riesman, "Some Observations on the Study of American Character," *Psychiatry,* 15 (August 1952), 333.

59. Emile Durkheim, *The Division of Labor in Society* (1893), translated by George Simpson (Glencoe, Ill.: Free Press, 1947), preface to the second edition (1902), "Some Notes on Occupational Groups," and, particularly, *Professional Ethics and Civic Morals* (1890s), translated by Cornelia Brookfield (London: Routledge & Kegan Paul, 1957), Chapters I-III; Max Weber, "Science as a Vocation," *op. cit.,* p. 153; ". . . . the decisive state of affairs: the prophet . . . simply does not exist"; Karl Mannheim, *Essays on the Sociology of Culture, loc. cit.,* "The Problem of Ecstasy" [in "The Democratization of Culture" (1933)], the argument of which the translator, Paul Kecskemeti, characterizes (*ibid.,* p. 239, n. 1) as the "necessity to transcend the purely pragmatist and positivist approach"; Mannheim himself writes: "We inherited from our past another need: that of severing from time to time *all* connection with life and with the contingencies of our existence. We shall designate this ideal by the term 'ecstasy' " (*ibid.,* p. 240).

60. Related to these civilizational-historical dichotomies is that between culture and civilization, independently formulated by Alfred Weber and Robert M. MacIver [cf. Alfred Weber, "Der soziologische Kulturbegriff" (1912), *Ideen zur Staats- und Kultursoziologie* (Karlsruhe: Braun, 1927), pp. 31–47; *Kulturgeschichte als Kultursoziologie* (Leiden: Sijthoff, 1935), pp. 9–10, 421. MacIver has discussed the distinction in numerous places, from *Community* (London: Macmillan, 1917), pp. 179–180, to MacIver and Charles H. Page, *Society* (New York: Rinehart, 1949), pp. 446, 486–487, 498–506]. See also Robert

K. Merton, "Civilization and Culture," *Sociology and Social Research*, **21** (November-December, 1936), 103–113, and Howard Becker, *op. cit.*, pp. 165–168. In reference to the recent chapter this distinction has a twofold significance: (1) It is a formulation of a dualism that parallels, within culture itself, that between what has been called here transcultural human nature and human culture. (2) It is an attempt at preserving historical continuity (through culture) and at the same time independence from it (civilization)—that is, at preserving both the absolute and the relative in man.

61. Its most dramatic expression is probably the confusion of Soviet communism with a historically more adequate version of liberalism and the shock, if not despair, on the realization of this confusion. See such works as Arthur Koestler, Ignazio Silone, Richard Wright, André Gide, Louis Fischer, and Stephen Spender, *The God That Failed* (New York: Bantam, 1952).

62. Reinhard Bendix, *Social Science and the Distrust of Reason* (Berkeley; University of California Press, 1951). See also Institut für Sozialforschung, *Soziologische Exurse, nach Vorträgen und Diskussionen* (Frankfurt am Main: Europäische Verlagsanstalt, 1956), Chapter XII, "Ideologie." Both this chapter and Bendix, *loc. cit.*, draw heavily on Hans Barth, *Wahrheit and Ideologie* (Zurich: Manesse, 1945). Chapter I of the Frankfurt volume ("Begriff der Soziologie") is an impressive description of the fate of social thought, beginning with Plato, in its shift toward sociology (Comte) and of the development of sociology itself to the present time. Among the various but rare critiques of modern sociology this and Bendix's are important. In this context special attention should also be called to C. Wright Mills, " 'The Power Elite': Comment on Criticism," *Dissent,* **4** (Winter 1957), 22–34.

63. Portrayed more in fiction than in social science, but see C. Wright Mills, *White Collar: The American Middle Classes* (New York: Oxford University Press, 1951), Part 3, and William H. Whyte, Jr., *The Organization Man* (New York: Simon and Schuster, 1956), Parts VI and VII.

64. See my "Before and After Sociology," *op. cit,* p. 153 [Chapter 15], "Sociology and History; Theory and Practice" [Chapter 17], and John W. Bennett and Kurt H. Wolff, "Toward Communication between Sociology and Anthropology," William L. Thomas, Jr., Ed., *Yearbook of Anthropology—1955, op. cit.*, p. 330 [reprinted in William L. Thomas, Jr., Ed., *Current Anthropology: A Supplement to Anthropology Today* (Chicago: University of Chicago Press, 1956) same pagination].

65. This, on the surface of it, would appear to contradict Alfred Schuetz's characterization of the world of scientific theory (in his "On Multiple Realities," *op. cit.*, 563–575) but actually seems to be a consequence of affirming his proposition "that sociality and communication can be realized only within . . . the world of everyday life which is the paramount reality" (*ibid.,* 575). Space limitations make it impossible to enter into discussion of this important, if not crucial, question of the philosophy of science.

66. This meaning of substantive, in contrast to formalistic, is obviously different from H. Otto Dahlke's (*op. cit., passim, e.g.,* p. 86) or from Mannheim's

"empirical" (*Ideology and Utopia, op. cit.*, pp. 239 ff.), both of which contrast with epistemological.

67. Compare Durkheim's *Rules of Sociological Method* (1895) or "The Determination of Moral Facts" (1906), Chapter II in *Sociology and Philosophy*, translated by D. F. Pocock, with an introduction by J. G. Peristiany (Glencoe, Ill.: Free Press, 1953), with his concern about anomie (cf. n. 59), or *Weber's Methodology of the Social Sciences, loc. cit.*, with his *Protestant Ethic*, and, on the discrepancy between Weber's methodological prescriptions for practice and his practice itself: Leo Strauss, *loc. cit.* [I am not acquainted with a corresponding analysis of Durkheim's work; see, however, some relevant observations in my "The Challenge of Durkheim and Simmel," *American Journal of Sociology*, **63** (May 1958), 590–596] (Chapter 2).

68. In respect to American sociology, cf. the Hinkles' remark quoted above. On the unrivaled position of liberalism in American political and social thought, cf. Louis Hartz, *The Liberal Tradition in America: An Interpretation of American Political Thought Since the Revolution* (New York: Harcourt, Brace, 1955).

69. Merton, *Social Theory and Social Structure*, Part III, "The Sociology of Knowledge and Mass Communications," *op. cit.*, pp. 439–455. The quotation is from p. 439.

70. "Such dynamic categories, with little direct bearing on commercial interests, as 'false consciousness' . . . have as yet played little part in the description of audiences" (*ibid.*, pp. 451–452). Merton asks whether communications research may one day become "independent of its social origins," which question "is itself a problem of interest for the sociology of science," and whether the development of social science might not parallel that of the physical sciences in the seventeenth century, when the impetus came not so much from the universities as from the new scientific societies (*ibid.*, pp. 452–453).

71. See n. 60.

72. For divers items from such a list, see my "The Sociology of Knowledge: Emphasis on an Empirical Attitude," *Philosophy of Science*, **10** (April 1943), 122–123. [Chapter 26.] See also ns. 17–18.

73. Alfred Schutz, "Concept and Theory Formation in the Social Sciences," *Journal of Philosophy*, **51** (April 29, 1954), 257–273, especially 271–272, and "Common-Sense and Scientific Interpretation of Human Action," *Philosophy and Phenomenological Research*, **14** (September 1953), 1–38, especially 26–37 [reprinted (abridged) in Lewis A. Coser and Bernard Rosenberg, Eds., *Sociological Theory: A Book of Readings* (New York: Macmillan, 1957), pp. 233–246, especially 240–246]. From Schutz's conception of social-scientific theory it is illuminating to go to scientific theory in general; see Morris R. Cohen and Ernest Nagel, *An Introduction to Logic and Scientific Method* (New York: Harcourt, Brace, 1934), pp. 397–399, and Philipp Frank, *Foundations of Physics* [Chicago: University of Chicago Press, 1946 (International Encyclopedia of Unified Science, Vol. 1, No. 7)], pp. 3–11.

74.   Talcott Parsons, *The Structure of Social Action, op. cit.,* p. 24; Nicholas
S. Timasheff, *Sociological Theory: Its Nature and Growth* (Garden City, N.Y.:
Doubleday, 1955), pp. 9–10; Merton, *op. cit.,* rev. ed., pp. 96–97.

---

# 30

## ERNST GRÜNWALD
## AND THE SOCIOLOGY
## OF KNOWLEDGE:
A Collective Venture in Interpretation. 1965

The *title* of this chapter suggests two themes. The first is Grünwald's own work in the sociology of knowledge; the second, an interpretation of it. This interpretation, in turn, proceeds in two steps, intrinsic and extrinsic. (The chapter thus falls into three parts.) The intrinsic refers, roughly, to an interpretation that is based only on the text to be interpreted; the extrinsic interprets this text from some "outside."

The *subtitle* tries to convey something not so much about the content of the paper as about the reader's hoped-for attitude toward it, about his relation to the writer. This relation is meant to be one between two parties to a common venture—precisely, that of interpreting Grünwald's sociology of knowledge. If successful, the reader will be drawn into it toward a perhaps unexpected climax.

### GRÜNWALD'S SOCIOLOGY OF KNOWLEDGE

Ernst Grünwald, born in Vienna in 1912, had already given great promise as a contributor to the humanities and social sciences when, at the age of 21, he died in a mountain accident. A year before, he had completed a study posthumously edited as "The Problem of the Sociology of Knowledge: An Attempt at a Critical Exposition of the Theories of the Sociology of Knowledge" [1].

This book contains four chapters. The first and third, predominantly historical, deal, respectively, with the prehistory of the sociology of knowledge and its development. Chapters 2 and 4, predominantly systematic, present systematic analyses and discuss the relation between the sociology of knowledge and epistemology.

The two historical chapters justify Merton's calling Grünwald the first historian of the sociology of knowledge [2]. As far, at least, as the German contributions of the 1920s are concerned [3] (except for Scheler's and Mannheim's), he has hitherto remained the only one.

I limit myself to the two systematic chapters, which contain Grünwald's own conception, one, however, that flows from his understanding of the prehistory of the sociology of knowledge, that is, its roots and its problematics. Hence we began with a brief sketch of this prehistory.

*The Prehistory of the Sociology of Knowledge.* Grünwald discusses two roots, the psychologically oriented (literally, psychological) and the historically oriented (literally, historical). The psychologically oriented tradition claims to be empirical, grounded in actual experience. It is based on a theory of human nature, and its views of truth and error must be understood in reference to this theory. The historically oriented tradition, on the other hand, is based on a theory of history, in reference to which *its* views of truth and error must be understood. These two traditions delimit the whole possible field of themes of the sociology of knowledge; their relevance thus is not only historical but also "logico-systematic" (p. 49). In concluding his discussion, Grünwald writes:

The contrast between the psychological and the historical theory may be circumscribed schematically under the following heads:

1. Naturalism—objective idealism [4].
2. Empiricism: the criterion of truth is experience—antiempiricism: truth must be guaranteed metaphysically.
3. Epistemological optimism—counting on the possibility of an "impenetrable" "fraud."
4. Man's essence is found in nature—historicity is man's essence.
5. The world is meaningless—the world is meaning.
6. Psychological constants are the sphere of the absolute—history is the sphere of the absolute.
7. History in the proper sense, as understood by the historical theory, does not exist—nothing exists but history.

8. The aim of study is the formulation of general laws—[it is] the understanding of the unique, unrepeatable process.

9. "History" (as the psychological theory interprets it) is a chaotic pell-mell of blind forces of nature, the object of a *"logificatio post festum"*—history is the sphere of the realization of the spirit.

10. Man in his thinking and acting is caused by the totality of nature; he is a point of intersection of natural forces —man is the organ of the absolute.

11. The determination of thought occurs indirectly by way of the interests—determination occurs directly by the absolute.

12. The determination of thought proceeds across individual consciousness—determination is unconscious, *"a tergo."*

13. All cultural phenomena are a superstructure above the interests—all cultural phenomena are the manifestations of an all-pervasive principle.

14. Interests are the causes of error: [this assumes] causal relations—the thinking of the individual is the emanation of the absolute.

15. Only error, materially false consciousness, is linked to existence [*seinsverbunden*]—all consciousness is linked to existence.

16. The subject of imputation (as in naive [spontaneous, everyday] interpretation) is the thinking individual—the subject of imputation is a concretization of the absolute, such as class, nation, etc.

17. In principle, existentiality (*Seinsverbundenheit* [5]) can be eliminated; failure to remove the "personal equation" is an offense against intellectual honesty—in principle, existentiality [of one's thought] is unrecognizable.

18. Error is my [the individual's] fault—I cannot be held responsible for my false consciousness.

19. Experience is the Archimedean point which guarantees the truth of my thought and from which I can demonstrate the falsity of the thinking of others—the absolute itself must guarantee me the Archimedean point (pp. 50–51).

Grünwald's own conception of the field is presented in seven brief sections.

*Sociology of Knowledge and Sociology.* The sociology of knowledge is the theory of "the connectedness of knowledge with social existence"

(p. 59). It can no more be considered part of *Gesellschaftssoziologie* ("sociology of society"—"(Vierkandt), a linguistically unbearable term, to be sure" [p. 60]) than can the sociology of religion, law, art, or music. These phenomena are rather the subject matter of *Kultursoziologie*, that is, of "the totality of the 'sociologies' of the various cultural phenomena, of the various 'manifestations of historical-societal reality' (Dilthey) . . . that have as their theme the connectedness of the various objectifications of culture with social existence" (p. 59).

The reasoning that leads Grünwald to this conclusion derives from his desire to find out in what sense the sociology of knowledge can be considered part of sociology at all. Among extant definitions of sociology, he examines Wilhelm Jerusalem's ("the science of the human group as a unit and its relations to the individual" [p. 56]) and Max Weber's well-known one ("a science that would understand social acting interpretively and thus explain it causally in its course and effects" [p. 57]). Both definitions leave no room for knowledge as the subject matter of sociology. Grünwald thus comes to the solution indicated.

*Understanding in the Sociology of Knowledge.*    The sociology of knowledge is a *Geisteswissenschaft*, that is, one of the human studies [6]. Its method, therefore, is that of understanding. There are three kinds of understanding: first, the understanding of motives (psychological, motivational understanding); second, the immanent or intrinsic understanding of intellectual products, which aims at grasping their intended meaning; and third, and most characteristic of the sociology of knowledge, what Grünwald calls manifestational understanding or transcendent or extrinsic interpretation [7]; that is, knowledge (ideas, beliefs, and ideologies) is understood as the manifestation of society. It may, however, also be understood as the manifestation of other things and, indeed, has sometimes been. It is this plurality of transcendent interpretations, Grünwald insists, that invalidates each, for none can be scientifically demonstrated as true:

> Any other part of human existence—race, character type, national character, some depth strata of the soul, etc.—may be considered, with as much right as the social, to be the most real sphere allegedly manifesting itself in all others. . . . By means of manifestational understanding, knowledge, law, art, in brief, culture, may be interpreted as emanating from different strata that each time are posited as absolute (p. 64).

Being only one among other transcendent interpretations, the sociology of knowledge "is not a science whose propositions are unconditionally valid for every thinking individual, but only a possible scheme of interpretation" (p. 66). [Cf. Chapter 28.]

*Validity versus Manifestational Meaning.* Every judgment, or proposition ("This is a chair," "The U. S. has a democratic government") has two aspects, communication and validity. It communicates something and it claims to be valid. We have seen that in Grünwald's view transcendent interpretation is interested in a proposition only as the manifestation of something else, namely, of the sphere posited as real. By themselves propositions have no manifestational meaning; they are endowed with it when interpreted as manifesting this sphere. Nor can such interpretation demonstrate the validity or invalidity of propositions.

*The Selective versus Constitutive Character of the Existentiality of Knowledge.* Every object of knowledge, Grünwald maintains ("a chair," "beauty," "this house," "Smith's idea of God"), is the product of two factors. The first is the object itself; the second is the social position of the individual, or the standpoint, from which he experiences the object; that is, the individual's standpoint *selects* aspects of the object. At the same time the individual imparts some of his experience to the object and thus coconstitutes it as an object of knowledge. In other words, the existentiality of knowledge is both selective and constitutive. It is selective in that it singles out aspects of the object that the individual experiences—it is selective in respect to the object of experience; it is constitutive in respect to the object of knowledge, being coconstitutive of it.

*Elements of Knowledge Not Linked and Elements Linked to Its Existentiality.* Drawing on Alfred Weber, Grünwald claims that the categories of thought and the laws of formal logic are oriented exclusively toward the object of knowledge. This means that they are *not* linked to the existence of the thinker. In contrast to the categories of thought and the laws of logic, however, metaphysical postulates and ultimate value decisions *are* so linked. A "glance at the history of metaphysical convictions shows," Grünwald writes, "that these meta-empirical postulates are variable to the very greatest extent" (p. 87); and they vary, indeed, with the thinker's existence, not with the object of knowledge, which presumably is constant. Here, in other words, Grünwald appears to affirm, even if indirectly, an actual impact of social existence on thought rather than discussing thought as the manifestation of society. He continues:

> Atheoretical forces cannot without further proof be identified
> with influences of some existential sphere, even if there is a

high probability that some sphere of human existence is at
work here—and yet, there appears to be no way in which
these influences could be ascertained scientifically (p. 88).

*Imputation.*   Because not all proletarians think alike (this is Grünwald's
example) and some nonproletarians think like proletarians, the question
is what do we mean by the proletariat to which a given thought is to be
imputed. The answer is that class, as used in this instance and in the
sociology of knowledge generally, does not mean what it means in general
sociology—a number of people sharing certain characteristics. Rather
class is a metaphysical entity, comparable to Hegel's world mind. As in
Hegel's system the various folk minds are emanations of the world mind,
the various classes are emanations of the social sphere. As to the process
of imputation itself (the object of which is the class as a metaphysical
entity), Grünwald follows Mannheim [8] in holding that a thought must
be imputed to a world view, which in turn is to be imputed to a class
(pp. 95–96). [Cf. Chapter 28.]

*Sociologism, or Sociology of Knowledge and Epistemology.*   Whatever its
variant, Grünwald argues, sociologism is based on two theses: (1) all
knowledge is linked to existence and (2) the validity of knowledge is
affected by this existentiality. Still, we can distinguish two types of
sociologism: absolute and moderate. Absolute sociologism holds that
existentiality destroys validity, but this is self-defeating for it also applies
to itself and thus invalidates itself. Moderate sociologism, or (Mannheim's) relationism, holds that truth is relative to times and groups and
that all knowledge is "perspectivistic." This is equally untenable, for the
very thesis "that all that is given can be grasped only perspectivistically
is meant to be valid not for one perspective only but absolutely" (p. 230).
The self-contradictory nature of sociologism of both types, Grünwald
observes, becomes understandable when we realize that it overlooks two
facts. The first is, as we have seen, that the sociology of knowledge, like
all transcendent interpretations, is concerned only with the manifestational meaning of propositions, not with their validity, about which it
has nothing to say. The second is that the sociology of knowledge can
establish only hypothetical, not real, relations between knowledge and
the social sphere. Hence, because the sociology of knowledge cannot deal
adequately with epistemological questions, Grünwald pleads that it not
be concerned with them. "Sociologism," he writes in concluding his book,

is such an exaggeration of what the sociology of knowledge
can reasonably be expected to accomplish that it can only end

in complete failure and thus in the discrediting of the sociology of knowledge. The sociology of knowledge can become a science only if it abandons its pretension to be sociologism (p. 234).

## AN INTRINSIC INTERPRETATION OF
## GRÜNWALD'S SOCIOLOGY OF KNOWLEDGE

*The Prehistory of the Sociology of Knowledge.* Many American sociologists will recognize at least some of the 19 points under which Grünwald summarizes his extended discussion of the two traditions drawn on by the sociology of knowledge. They will recognize them as characteristics of familiar concepts, not only of the sociology of knowledge but of sociology and social science generally. Such concepts are distinguished from one another by the point of view, attitude, or perspective from which subject matter is viewed, hence the approach to it taken. Grünwald argues that basically there have been two such points of view and attendant approaches: human nature understood psychologically and analyzed natural-scientifically and history understood culturally or processually. He claims that to adopt these points of view entails ontological commitments. This means that the student who takes either of them posits the nature of reality, or at least of the reality that comes under his purview as his subject matter, to be such as he can adequately grasp only by taking the psychological or the historical approach.

The nature of Grünwald's undertaking is that of a systematic, not of a sociological or historical, analysis; that is to say, he does not inquire into the social or historical circumstances that might throw light on the fact that the views he summarizes have been held, defended, and fought. The execution of his assignment suggests that, between the two traditions he expounds, he himself more nearly belongs in the psychological, with its natural-science approach, than in the historical.

*The Sociology of Knowledge and Sociology.* Just as he raises no social or historical questions about the prehistory of the sociology of knowledge, so Grünwald does not ask why there should have been a controversy over the nature of *Gesellschaftssoziologie* and *Kultursoziologie*.

*Understanding in the Sociology of Knowledge.* To hold, as Grünwald does, that the sociology of knowledge is "not a science . . . but only a possible scheme of interpretation" means that science cannot choose among the various realities that are claimed to determine intellectual life. In another formulation, which from the point of view of science makes little difference, it means that there is one determining reality, which, however, cannot be scientifically known. It can only be posited by metaphysical fiat, which science cannot validate or invalidate. This view of Grünwald concerning the existentiality of knowledge is well designated as postulational skepticism (Arthur Child [9]); that is, Grünwald has not shown why a given thought may not be determined in a scientifically demonstrable sense by social circumstance, climate, or childhood experience; another, by body type, teaching, genetic structure; still another, by several of these or additional factors.

If under the first two heads—the prehistory of the sociology of knowledge and sociology of knowledge and sociology—Grünwald falls short on attention to history, here he falls short on science. He introduces his discussion of the scientific status of the sociology of knowledge by posing an ontological question and points out that if the sociology of knowledge makes ontological claims it ceases to be a science. He does not seriously consider the possibility that it need not make these claims and thus, on this score at least, can be a science.

*Validity Versus Manifestational Meaning.* This distinction is consistent with Grünwald's concept of manifestational understanding and so should our comments be. Hence we must ask why a given proposition cannot be the result of one or more particular factors rather than their ontologically grounded manifestation. Indeed, to interpret a proposition as manifesting the real sphere has no bearing on the question of the validity of the proposition, but this observation, in turn, has no more than a remote bearing on the scientific question of the sociology of knowledge concerning the difference, and the relation, between the empirical genesis of a proposition and its validity.

*The Selective versus Constitutive Character of the Existentiality of Knowledge.* Grünwald's concept of this problem may be put briefly: the individual's selection of an object *for* knowledge coconstitutes it as an object *of* knowledge. He argues persuasively (p. 250, n. 59) that this concept [at which he arrives on analyzing the concept of "material of judgment" (pp. 82–83), here omitted] "actually grasps the intentions of the existing systems of the sociology of knowledge," notably Mannheim's but also Scheler's (as well as historicism). To have formulated it and to have identified it as the pervasive view of the existing sociology of knowledge is the result of an epistemological analysis, as he points out (pp. 83–84). Once more, however, as in respect to the prehistory of the sociology of knowledge and the relation of the latter to sociology, he does not ask whether and how the society and time in which this epistemological position is found may help to account for it.

*Elements of Knowledge Not Linked and Elements Linked to Its Existentiality.* We have seen that elements of knowledge discussed by Grünwald fall into two groups. The first, categories of thought and laws of formal logic, are not characterized by existentiality; the second, metaphysical postulates and ultimate value decisions, that is, the "subcategorial, meta-empirical sphere" (p. 87), are—as a look at the history of metaphysics shows. We also saw, however, that as soon as he had said this he insisted that the atheoretical forces he admitted to be at work in thought "cannot without further proof be identified with influences of some existential sphere" and that "there appears no way in which these influences could be ascertained scientifically." He thus falls back on his postulational skepticism. As in regard to his analyses of understanding and of validity versus manifestational meaning, here, too he stops short of investigating the possibility of scientific proof—this time of the existence of connections between social setting and thought. He merely proclaims his skepticism. He does not seem to see the relevance of Max Weber's discussion of this problem (to mention only the probably best known), whether in *The Protestant Ethic* or in several papers on methodology, especially his analysis of understanding and causal explanation. Once more Grünwald is short on scientific procedure [10].

*Imputation.* If class is indeed a metaphysical entity, imputation to it is a nonempirical, taxonomic, or logical process (which it is not, incidentally, in Mannheim, to whom Grünwald approvingly refers). Grünwald fails to face the scientific problem of imputation. He does not mention the possibility that class may be employed neither as a metaphysical unit nor in the sense of a collection of individuals with similar relevant social traits but instead as a self-conscious heuristic construct proof to the verificatory claims of both ontologist and census taker. Thus Grünwald is not scientific beyond showing that imputation to a class as a metaphysical entity is not scientific. Nor does he consider any social unity other than class, however conceived, to which thought may be imputed. In this sense he is caught in the Marxist frame of reference of his time [11].

*Sociologism or Sociology of Knowledge and Epistemology.* This section, we saw, consists of a critique of the two varieties of sociologism and a plea that the sociology of knowledge give it up and thus become a science. Grünwald does show that it can become one merely by renouncing sociologism, which is not identical with the fundamental thesis of the sociology of knowledge, namely, "the connectedness of knowledge with social existence" or, more briefly, the existentiality of knowledge. We know Grünwald's conviction that this thesis is not scientifically demonstrable. He thus appears as apodictic (existentiality is undemonstrable) as is the sociology of knowledge or the sociologism (existentiality needs no demonstration) that he opposes, although substantively his position is different. As class is the only unit to which he considers thought imputable, validity is the only aspect of thought he considers in connection with existentiality. He does not fully face the problem whether existentiality might not be relevant to other aspects or elements of thought, such as empirical adequacy or objectivity, world view, attitudinal structure, and many more. Not "fully face": although Grünwald does discuss closely related matters (see, in particular, his analysis of elements of knowledge linked and not linked to existentiality), he suggests the possibility neither of a tentative conceptual scheme that might guide research designed to illuminate them nor of research itself (such as, among a few others, Mannheim engaged in [12]).

## AN EXTRINSIC INTERPRETATION OF
## GRÜNWALD'S SOCIOLOGY OF KNOWLEDGE

What we have done so far is to read Grünwald carefully and to raise some questions that have come out of the reading. We have proceeded as have some other commentators on sociologists of knowledge—for instance, Child or Stark on Grünwald (and others) or Hinshaw on Mannheim [13]. Now, in an attempt to account for the characteristics we have found, we go outside his work into history. What this means will become clearer as we proceed.

Like other students of the sociology of knowledge, Grünwald thought of it as a "young discipline" (p. 1). One of the tasks he set himself was to survey it in order to clarify its place among the human studies. To judge from the tenor of his introductory pages he expected it to extend human inquiry to new areas and to enrich it by new points of view, but he hardly succeeded in defining these areas and in vindicating these points of view. He appears to have proceeded on the assumption that the sociology of knowledge is an addition to man's intellectual heritage and to have been guided by an image of orderly, cumulative progress characteristic of science, or its ideal, rather than by any image of history. Indeed, as we noted earlier, even his presentation of the prehistory of the sociology of knowledge is not historical but systematic, at least in intent: he presents ideas and their filiations, but the circumstance that these were formulated at particular times and places is irrelevant to his enterprise.

A historical, rather than a systematic or natural-scientific or scientific, approach characterizes the work of most sociologists of knowledge, notably Scheler and Mannheim. It may be asked, then, why Grünwald, who was so critical of it, should have taken its approach and *not* a systematic-scientific one. If he was short on history in his analysis of the prehistory of the sociology of knowledge, the place of the sociology of knowledge in respect to sociology, and his own epistemological position, we also saw that in his treatment of understanding, validity, existentiality, imputation, and sociologism he was short on science. Thus, if he failed in one way or the other on actually all eight counts of his presentation, why bother with him?

There may be readers of his work who will feel that he was a talented young man, confused by the authors he analyzed, yet capable one day of good social science, had it only been possible for him to receive training in scientific method. He might have learned it from the Vienna Circle or from American sociology, but he did not live long enough. Readers may find that he was ready for it to the extent of dissatisfaction with the sociology of knowledge of his time but that he was not yet sufficiently in command of it to transcend it. Had he been—and perhaps only his early death prevented him from developing toward this goal—he might have added his share to cumulative social science.

According to Grünwald's own scheme for the prehistory of the sociology of knowledge, such readers clearly stand in what he called the psychological tradition. For them the sociology of knowledge Grünwald examined, as well as his own, largely are deviations from scientific procedure or at best approximations of it—but perhaps their accounting for the characteristics and shortcomings of Grünwald's work is not exhaustive.

It is not exhaustive if, instead of taking a writer and his work literally, we take him as symptomatic, as I now propose to do. Rather than engaging in a theoretical analysis of the concept, I use "symptomatic" in the familiar practical, everyday way in which it is said that fever is symptomatic of pneumonia, upper-class juvenile delinquency of ennui, an editorial placing states' rights above civil rights of a decision for a restricted and against an expanded society. I wish to explore the symptomaticity of Grünwald's sociology of knowledge [14]. I submit that it is symptomatic of the meaninglessness of the human world that Grünwald, though not explicitly, proclaimed. I try to show this by reviewing some of the foci of his conception.

To introduce this review I call attention to one of the heads under which he summarized his discussion of the prehistory of the sociology of knowledge. For the psychologically oriented tradition, he says, "the world is meaningless," whereas for the historically oriented tradition, "the world is meaning" [15]. In this contrast there is, on one side, nature, with no place for history, "a chaotic pell-mell of blind forces of nature," and on the other, history, "the sphere of the realization of the spirit." Meaning being an exclusively human phenomenon is outside nature; in Grünwald's view and the historical tradition it is located in history. This contrast is at the base of the German division between the natural sciences and the human studies. It is reflected in Max Weber's distinction between what can be explained but is "devoid of subjective meaning" (Parsons' translation of *sinnfremd*) and what, because it is meaningful, can be understood—notably human acting [16]. Although for both the psychological and historical traditions and for Weber it is nonhuman nature that is meaningless, I now try to show that for Grünwald the human world is (or possibly is) too. I argue that his views on understanding, validity versus manifestational meaning, the selective versus the constitutive character of the existentiality of knowledge, elements of knowledge linked, and not, to existentiality, imputation, and sociologism (the last six of his eight foci) are facets of a view of the human world as meaningless.

*Understanding.*   Grünwald does not question the possibility of understanding other people's motives and intended meanings (however difficult it may be), but the possibility of the third kind of understanding, manifestational, cannot be demonstrated. For Grünwald manifestational understanding is inseparable from the idea of an ultimate reality; but all we can know about such reality, the *ens realissimum* (*passim*), is what we posit as such; nor is there any way of deciding *what* we should posit.

In other words, Grünwald is convinced that it is impossible to know reality. This conviction is more than the optimistic and expectant contentment of the scientist with hypothetical truth; it rather recalls Max Weber's passionate conviction that it is impossible to know justice and values generally [17]. Both attest not so much to gaps accepted as to needs unfulfilled: Grünwald, to the need for a cosmology, Weber, to that for a normative order [18].

*Validity Versus Manifestational Meaning.*   This distinction is the phrasing of the scientific distinction between validity and origin in ontological terms. What has been said about manifestational understanding, therefore, also applies here; that is, on the occasion of his analysis of the validity and meaning of propositions Grünwald indicates his lack of, but need for, knowledge of "reality" or a cosmology.

*The Selective versus Constitutive Character of the Existentiality of Knowledge.* The object of cognition is the product of the object itself and the experiencing subject. Like other writers on the sociology of knowledge [19], Grünwald does not raise the question of the theoretical possibility of a truth more objectively based than on a sharing of standpoints, in fact, of the theoretical possibility of standpoints being shared at all. If his analyses of manifestational understanding and validity versus manifestational meaning attest to his lack of a cosmology, his discussion of the selective and constitutive character of the existentiality of knowledge shows his lack of a truth that is independent of the knower's standpoint—universal truth.

*Elements of Knowledge Not Linked and Elements Linked to Its Existentiality.* Saying nothing to the contrary, Grünwald leaves the standpoints referred to under the preceding heading disconnected, discontinuous in time, and without order during the same time—once more like Weber's values. In the present context he seems to qualify his view of the object of cognition presented, for he now declares that certain objects of cognition are unaffected by the fact that all knowledge is knowledge from a standpoint, namely, those objects toward which the categories of thought and the laws of formal logic are oriented. If there are such objects, their existence guarantees the possibility of universal truth—a conclusion that Grünwald does not draw, nor does he draw the related conclusion that there are cognitive elements common to all men, as he could have from the possibility of understanding people's motives and intended meanings. He implied this possibility in his discussion of the first two kinds of understanding as well as in his observation that it is possible to understand the great variety of metaphysical convictions that a glance at their history displays. By failing to draw the first conclusion he denies the identity of objects or evinces an objectless world. By failing to draw the second he once more reveals his conviction that there is no common truth, nor does his remark about the history of metaphysical positions elicit in him any affirmation of history, hence a denial of the arbitrariness or disconnectedness of standpoints (metaphysical or other).

*Imputation.* This concept, too, is discussed in ontological terms: class, to which a thought is imputed, is a metaphysical entity. Grünwald does not consider the scientific treatment of imputation, the scientific investigability of social classes, the suitability of other social units for imputation, but although he considers manifestational understanding an act of arbitrary preference he does not similarly qualify imputation (we saw that he accepts Mannheim's method of it, without, however, granting its scientific status). Thus he must stand accused of arbitrarily subscribing to a scheme he considers ontologically grounded.

*Sociologism or Sociology of Knowledge and Epistemology.* Having shown his uneasy relation to science and to the sociology of knowledge as a science, his admonition that the sociology of knowledge can become a science only by abandoning epistemological claims sounds hollow. As suggested before, the discussion of the present topic is another occasion on which Grünwald shows his diffidence in regard to science.

*Grünwald's Human World and We.* Inspecting our results, we find that Grünwald wants—in the twofold sense of this term—a cosmology, universal truth, cognitive features common to all men, identical objects, points of view that could be understood with reference to an order of culture and history, and a science that can make testable claims about the origin of a given thought, about the relations between thought and social class, and about the existentiality of knowledge. His world is a world that exhibits these wants.

These wants are interdependent. Thus, if I cannot believe in the world as orderly (if I *want* an orderly world), I am bound to doubt such truth as I can even imagine all men to converge on; or, if I cannot believe in the universality of truth, I tend altogether to discard the notion of an orderly world—and similarly for relations among the other wants. This is not a world that turns meaningless by a subtraction, piecemeal or progressive, of items—cosmology, truth, objects, and so on—but rather the world of a man who has lost his continuity with history and with his fellow men with whom he is involved in a common history [20]. This man was not alone in this, nor is he (cf., among many other indications, the contemporary literature on alienation, and the mass society, etc.). Yet, being an individual, his particular meaningless world differs, of course, in some of its features and their configuration from that of others. It also differs in respect to the occasion on which he exhibited it, his inquiry into the sociology of knowledge, the "young discipline" whose promise he did not succeed in conveying.

Is there any validity in what I have said in the more explicitly interpretive parts of this paper, especially the last? How can I assert that Grünwald proclaimed a meaningless human world if we do not have his own word for it—which indeed, we have not? If we find grounds for assertion, what grounds can there possibly be for proof?

Let us go back to the imaginary but almost certainly existing reader of Grünwald's work who, we said, true to the psychological-natural-scientific tradition, would account for its characteristics in the way suggested [21]. We can characterize his procedure in a slightly different fashion by saying that this reader is interested only in the scientific or theoretical aspects of the work. He applies to it his generally characteristic interest in scientific or theoretical knowledge and truth; he examines writings that claim scientific status only with respect to that claim, that truth, that knowledge, but neither he nor Grünwald can refute the proposition that

> the type of knowledge conveyed by natural science differs fundamentally from historical knowledge—we should try to grasp the meaning and structure of historical understanding in its specificity, rather than reject it merely because it is not in conformity with the positivist truth-criteria sanctioned by natural science [22].

For present purposes historical knowledge may be grouped with practical or existential knowledge [23] and these varieties of one kind of knowledge contrasted with the scientific-theoretical. Knowledge concerning symptoms is a further variety of existential knowledge. The following passage from Mannheim's discussion of documentary interpretation also comes close to describing the procedure for arriving at truth concerning symptoms:

> This "documentary" interpretation of an *Ars poetica* or of an aesthetic theory put forward by the artist [or of any intellectual product whatever, such as Grünwald's book] does not consist, however, in merely treating these utterances as authentic reflections of the author's artistic personality. . . . *What we have to ask is not whether the theory is correct— nor what his proponent meant by it* [my italics]. Rather, we must go beyond this "immanent" interpretation [24] and treat the theoretical confession as confession: as documentary evidence of something extra-psychic, . . . just as a doctor will take the self-diagnosis of one of his patients as a symptom rather than as a correct identification of the latter's illness [25].

Why should one be interested in symptoms? The physician is, as a source of knowledge he needs the better to cure the patient. I suggested, however, that symptomatological knowledge is a variety of practical knowledge, the aim of which is broader than to cure, namely, to know how to act right. This, indeed, is the meaning of practical knowledge in everyday usage. In the extrinsic or historical interpretation of Grünwald's book (to the point we have gone with it) we have examined his concept of the sociology of knowledge with this meaning in mind. We have read his book to prepare ourselves for gaining knowledge on how to act right. To enable us to do so, our reading has been historical: we have asked who Grünwald (the "documentary Grünwald") was to learn better who *we* are as we compare ourselves with him. Is his world indeed as meaningless as we have come to hold it? Is ours? Practical knowledge or truth, unlike theoretical, is not "out there," but in ourselves: whoever wants to ask these questions seriously must ask them himself of himself.

*Acknowledgment.* This is a thorough revision of a paper presented at the 55th annual meeting of the American Sociological Association, New York, 30 August 1960. For criticisms and suggestions concerning the earlier draft I am deeply grateful to Arthur Child, to an anonymous, penetrating and critical reader, and to Michael Haber, Charles Levy, Young Ick Lew, Susan Sandler, and Dusky Lee Smith, students in a seminar on the sociology of knowledge at Brandeis University, Spring 1962.

### NOTES

1. Ernst Grünwald, *Das Problem der Soziologie des Wissens, op. cit.* The information contained in this paragraph is taken from Walther Eckstein's "Vorwort." Eckstein also reports that at the time of his death Grünwald was engaged in a major work on the phenomenology of language. Page references in parentheses are to Grünwald's book. (For parts of Grünwald's book that have been made available in English since Chapter 30 was written see Chapter 29, n. 53.)

2. Robert K. Merton. "The Sociology of Knowledge," in Georges Gurvitch and Wilbert E. Moore, Eds., *Twentieth Century Sociology* (New York: Philosophical Library 1945), p. 367.

3. The only summary treatment of the latter in English [Franz Adler, "The Range of Sociology of Knowledge," in Howard Becker and Alvin Boskoff, Eds., *Modern Sociological Theory in Continuity and Change* (New York: Dryden, 1957), pp. 399–402], is based mainly on the study by Ernst Grünwald.

4. That is, the "historical theory" postulates an objectively existing ideal realizing itself in the course of history.

5. *Seinsverbundenheit* is an untranslatable term, a key word in Mannheim's writings on the sociology of knowledge, perhaps coined by him; its use abounds in Grünwald and other writers on the subject as well. See Karl Mannheim, *Ideology and Utopia, op. cit.*, p. 239n, in which the English translation of the term as "social determination" is qualified as leaving the meaning of determi-

nation open; "existentiality" seems better (although not usable in adjectival form).

6. H. A. Hodges's rendition of the German term. See his *Wilhelm Dilthey: An Introduction* (New York: Oxford University Press, 1944), p. 157.

7. The articulation of the first kind of understanding, is, of course, Max Weber's. The distinction between the second and third, though not in Grünwald's specific sense, was made by Mannheim in his "Ideologische and soziologische Interpretation der geistigen Gebilde," *Jahrbuch für Soziologie*, **2** (1926), pp. 424–440, anticipated in his review of Georg Lukács' *Die Theorie des Romans* in *Logos*, 9 (1920–1921), 298–302 (both translated, with an introduction, by Kurt H. Wolff, *Studies on the Left*, 3 (Summer 1963), 45–66 [in *From Karl Mannheim*, pp. 116–131]. So far it has been most thoroughly dealt with by Arthur Child, *The Problems of the Sociology of Knowledge: A Critical and Philosophical Study*, University of California (unpublished Ph.D. dissertation), 1938, Chapter VII, "Immanent and Transcendent Interpretation"; Kurt H. Wolff, "A Preliminary Inquiry into the Sociology of Knowledge from the Standpoint of the Study of Man," *loc. cit.* [Chapter 28].

8. "On the Interpretation of *Weltanschauung*" (1921–1922), in *Essays on the Sociology of Knowledge*, Paul Kecskemeti, Ed. (London: Routledge and Kegan Paul, 1952), pp. 33-83 (henceforth *Weltanschauuang*). *(From Karl Mannheim,* pp. 8–58.)

9. Arthur Child, "The Theoretical Possibility of the Sociology of Knowledge," *Ethics*, **51** (July 1941), 404 (henceforth *Possibility*); see Wolff, *Inquiry*, pp. 592–593, n. 21 [Chapter 28].

10. The most cogent demonstration of the existentiality of thought I know is found in Child, *Possibility*, 413–415; cf. Wolff, *Inquiry*, 591–593 [Chapter 28].

11. On imputation cf. Arthur Child, "The Problem of Imputation in the Sociology of Knowledge," *Ethics*, **51** (January 1941), 200–219, "The Problem of Imputation Resolved," *Ethics*, **54** (January 1944), 96–109; Kurt H. Wolff, "On the Scientific Relevance of 'Imputation,' " *Ethics*, **61** (October 1950), 69–73 [Chapter 28]; Svend Ranulf, *Methods of Sociology* (Copenhagen: Ejnar Munksgaard, 1955), pp. 95–96.

12. Cf. notably "Historicism" (1924), in *Essays on the Sociology of Knowledge, op. cit.,* pp. 84–133, and "Conservative Thought" (1927), in *Essays on Sociology and Social Psychology*, Paul Kecskemeti, Ed. (New York: Oxford University Press, 1953), pp. 74–164 [the latter also in *From Karl Mannheim*, pp. 132–222].

13. Arthur Child, "The Problem of Imputation in the Sociology of Knowledge," 207–213; *Possibility*, 404–407; "The Existential Determination of Thought," *Ethics*, **52** (January 1942), 167–175; "The Problem of Truth in the Sociology of Knowledge," *Ethics*, **58** (October 1947), 21–22 (henceforth *Truth*); W. Stark, *The Sociology of Knowledge: An Essay in Aid of a Deeper Understanding of the History of Ideas* (Glencoe, Ill.: Free Press, 1958), pp. 194–196; Virgil G. Hinshaw, Jr., "The Epistemological Relevance of Mannheim's

Sociology of Knowledge," *loc. cit.*, "Epistemological Relativism and the Sociology of Knowledge," *loc. cit.*

14. Symptomaticity is related to documentary meaning as discussed by Mannheim, *Weltanschauung*, pp. 55–63.

15. *Welt ist sinnlos—Welt ist Sinn* (p. 50).

16. Max Weber, *The Theory of Social and Economic Organization*, translated by A. M. Henderson and Talcott Parsons, edited, with an introduction, by Talcott Parsons, *op. cit.*, pp. 88–93, including Parsons' footnotes on relevant German terms, and p. 93. On the problems of Weber's conception of sociology in the light of the *Gesellschafts-Kultursoziologie* dichotomy see Grünwald, p. 247, end of n. 28.

17. Max Weber, "The Meaning of 'Ethical Neutrality' in Sociology and Economics" (1913–1917), in *On the Methodology of the Social Sciences, op. cit.*, pp. 15–16; "Science as a Vocation," *op. cit.*, pp. 148, 150. For the outline of a sociohistorical analysis of "value" see Hannah Arendt, *The Human Condition, op. cit.*, pp. 163–166; cf. [Chapter 14] (henceforth *Arendt*).

18. There still remains the question why Grünwald conceived of the understanding characteristic of the sociology of knowledge in ontological terms in the first place. The answer is perhaps quite simple: he found it conceived thus by the authors he examined and was caught by them.

19. See Child, *Truth*.

20. Cf. Kurt H. Wolff, "Surrender as a Response to Our Crisis," *Journal of Humanistic Psychology*, **2** (Fall 1962), 16–17, 27–29.

21. See the fourth and fifth paragraphs of this chapter.

22. Mannheim, *Weltschauung*, p. 61.

23. The question of the relation between practical, existential, and historical knowledge and truth may be left open; cf. Kurt H. Wolff, "The Sociology of Knowledge and Sociological Theory, in Llewellyn Gross, Ed., *Symposium on Sociological Theory* (Evanston, Ill.: Row, Peterson, 1959), "V. Scientific vs. Existential Truth," pp. 579–580 [Chapter 29]; "Sociology and History; Theory and Practice," *American Journal of Sociology*, **65** (July 1958), 36–37 [Chapter 17]; *Arendt*, 77–106 [Chapter 14].

24. Cf. n. 7 and the passage to which it refers.

25. Mannheim, *Weltanschauung*, p. 58. On "Symptoms of a Time and Reactions to It," illustrated by a brief discussion of action anthropology, the sociology of knowledge itself, and Max Weber's "ethics of principle" and of "responsibility"; cf. Kurt H. Wolff, *The Means-End Scheme in Contemporary Sociology and Its Relation to an Analysis of Nonviolence* (Oslo: Institute for Social Research, August 1959) (mimeographed), pp. 109–117.

---

This chapter is reprinted in modified form from *Journal of the History of the Behavioral Sciences*, **1** (1965), 152–164, by permission of the publisher. The essay has been edited and partially revised by the author.

# 31

# THE SOCIOLOGY
# OF KNOWLEDGE IN THE
# UNITED STATES OF AMERICA.
# 1967

## *I. PURPOSE, LIMITATIONS, ORGANIZATIONS*
## *OF THIS REPORT*

This report deals with the presentation and the conception of the sociology of knowledge in the United States, that is, with (the few) American surveys whose major concern is to acquaint the reader and with statements whose major concern is to present the authors' own views. The distinction is not clear-cut: a survey presupposes a concept, which in turn is likely to be preceded by a survey. Major concern as the criterion for distinguishing the two admittedly involves imputation and for this reason alone, if for no other, has its difficulties. There may be more that speaks for than against the procedure adopted: to begin the presentation with surveys allows the ascertainment of some of the tendencies that recur in the concepts.

The limitation to statements about the sociology of knowledge (Bibliography, Part I) obviously entails the exclusion of substantive contributions [1], both those that are meant to be and those far more numerous that may be found in many places, although they have not been written with this intent. If one were to collect and classify the latter,

> one would have to assemble the knowledge that has been gathered by a great many students in a great many fields, all

of which bear upon the central problem-complex of the sociology of knowledge, the relations between society and intellectual life. Obviously, this applies to much work in the social sciences other than sociology, and in the humanities, but also in certain biological sciences . . . some of the most important areas of research and theory seem to be these: in the *social sciences,* in addition to general sociological findings and to more specialized findings (such as those in communication, public opinion, and propaganda), above all, social psychology [Blum (203), Penny (212)], in a very broad sense, . . . cultural anthropology, particularly linguistics [Hymes (216), Stoller (217)] with its various subdivisions, . . . ; in the *humanities,* social and cultural history, literary criticism, historical linguistics, and the methodological and empirical aspects of philosophy . . . ; and, finally, in the *biological sciences,* whatever throws light upon the biological dimensions of intellectual behavior (that is, especially . . . human genetics [animal sociology, and "human behavioral biology" or "ethology"] [e.g. (17); Wolff (94, pp. 586–587)] [Chapter 28].

## II. THE EMERGENCE OF THE SOCIOLOGY OF KNOWLEDGE IN THE UNITED STATES

Few suggestions concerning the rise in the interest in the sociology of knowledge that has found expression in its surveys and concepts can be gleaned from the literature. Merton (61) considers but rejects as inadequate the explanation of this interest by the influx of European refugee scholars who imported the sociology of knowledge, for they merely made it available: it was the situation in the United States itself that changed availability into acceptance. This situation was characterized by conflict, by emphasis on group differences, rather than similarities, by distrust, by the psychological, economic, social, racial functionalization of thought, and by preoccupation with the origins, rather than the validity of ideas (61, pp. 367–369) [1]. A similar atmosphere marked the Germany of the early 1920s, which saw the rise of *Wissenssoziologie* [Dahlke (35, p. 64)] but since then has spread elsewhere, including the United States [Wirth (89, p. xiii)]. We might also remember that the Marxist tradition which formed much of the thinking about the relation between thought and society—a relation that in such a situation may tend to become subject to reflection—was diffused by political movements. It may thus appear more plausible that the sociology of knowledge should have developed in post-World-War-I Germany and that it should have ended with Hitler: nazism, among other things a new settlement of the questions that provoked the sociology of knowledge and that it, in turn, raised, superseded it (along with many other things) not only because nazism warred against Marxism but, more generally, because it could not permit research into the interaction between intellectual life and its social setting—no matter whether such research followed Marxian, Paretan, Durkheimian, or other lines.

In the 1930s interest in the sociology of knowledge spread and was cultivated despite nazism and indirectly, through the refugee scholars who exported it, in consequence of nazism. In the English-speaking world it was stimulated probably more than by anything else by the appearance of the English translation of Mannheim's *Ideologie und Utopie* (1929) (57).

### III. AMERICAN "SURVEYS" OF THE SOCIOLOGY OF KNOWLEDGE

Despite Wirth's enthusiastic introduction to his and Shils's translation of this book, the first survey, only four years later [Dahlke (35)], was anything but friendly to Mannheim because of his Marxist orientation and his concern with epistemology. It thus manifested two tendencies that have characterized most, though not all, American writings in the field: *impatience with epistemology* and rejection of the idea that the sociology of knowledge occupy itself with it and, perhaps more than animosity, *indifference toward Marxism and ignorance of it* [2]. In addition, Dahlke, quite unlike Mannheim, but again like most American sociologists of knowledge, takes *an ahistorical-systematic rather than a historical approach*. As in the essay he wrote jointly with Becker [3] [Becker and Dahlke (18)], he insists on a substantive approach to the sociology of knowledge (35, p. 65); he believes that the field is developing in the direction not of Mannheim but of Scheler, whom he considers its real founder and who, he writes, has provided it with its sphere of substantive research: the interrelations of the "real factors, the theoretical-contemplative, and the ideal-normative spheres" (35, p. 86). The subsequent development of the sociology of knowledge in the United States shows the influence of Scheler in the work of Stark (82) and Parsons (69), though, so far, hardly elsewhere.

In his brief contribution to a UNESCO-sponsored trend report on sociology in the United States Barber (5) suggests that during the period 1945–1955 the sociology of knowledge and science shows among important trends, "(a) the integration of the sociology of knowledge into more systematic and inclusive sociological theory" [cf. Parsons (119), Chapter 8, and Barber (131)], "(b) the increase of empirical research," though much of it is often not labeled sociology of knowledge [e.g., Schatzman and Strauss (200)], "and (c) continuing contributions from other than professional sociologists, for example, from historians, from natural scientists, from other social scientists, and from government reports" [(5, p. 69); cf. Knapp and Goodrich (140), Gillispie (134), and President's Scientific Research Board (146)].

The survey by Coser and Rosenberg (34) is more unambiguously a survey—the last chapter of a reader in sociological theory—than Dahlke's, and, along with Wirth's Introduction (89), is one of the few presentations of the history of the field that mention some related, though independent American thinkers [Dewey (99; 98), Wolfe (129), Veblen (126, 125)] beyond those named by Wirth (Sumner, James Harvey Robinson, Charles A. Beard, William James, Mead, Cooley, Robert M. MacIver). In particular, they introduce Mead (113) [cf. McKinney (109)] as providing "a much needed social psychological basis for some of the assertions of previous researchers and theorists in the sociology of knowledge" (34, p. 568). Among recent American contributions they single out, among others, works by Merton (143; 62, Part III), Sorokin (75, 79), and Znaniecki (151), mention Child (26–29, 32), Speier (123), DeGré (37), Wolff (91), and Mills (65–68), observe that as

> the sociology of knowledge has been incorporated into American theory, it has often merged with other areas of research, and in such cases is no longer explicitly referred to as sociology of knowledge (34, p. 569).

but may be found in work in the sociology of science [Merton (143, 62), Barber (131)], the professions [Hughes (138), Hall (135, 136), Parsons (118, Chapter 8)], and elsewhere and wonder whether the "deflection of the original aims of the European sociology of knowledge" (34, p. 570), chiefly in the direction of preoccupation with public opinion and mass communication [Merton (62, pp. 200–216); Wolff (95, pp. 587–590), might not be accounted for by reference to the greater American stability and homogeneity, compared with Europe. Although somewhat more historically oriented than Dahlke, Coser and Rosenberg, like Dahlke and Barber, take a more systematic than historical approach and also reflect a further tendency of the prevailing American concept of the sociology of knowledge: attention to social psychology and to G. H. Mead in particular.

Adler [(2); cf. also (1, 3, 4) and (83, 84)] surveys many additional works and areas: ethnological contributions of the Durkheim school [with which he connects Kelsen (139)] and those combining anthropology with Freudian psychology [Kardiner (209), Kardiner and others (210), and

Linton (211)]. He praises American social psychology [Merton and Lazarsfeld (193)] as much more experimental than the Durkheim school, considers Marxist antecedents of the sociology of knowledge, discusses analyses of the power of class ideas [M. Lerner (189)], "some experimental studies of Marxian clues" [Centers (187)], Williams and Mosteller's (202) and Nettler's (199) research into the relations between opinion, education, and economic status, the Lynds' (190, 191), Mills's (194), and Andrzejewski's (181), even Schutz's (147) and Park's (116) "stratification studies" (2, p. 404), and suggests that in these and other areas of sociology and social psychology [Bossard (204), Warner and others (213), Hollingshead (208), Davis and Havighurst (206), and Davis (205)] materials are available that answer certain questions of the sociology of knowledge. As "Anti-Marxians" Adler presents Scheler, Honigsheim, and Sorokin; as "Synthesizers and Eclectics," Mannheim [with predominantly critical comments by Kecskemeti (105, 106), Wagner (127, 128), Dahlke (35), Merton (62), Mandelbaum (110)] and other Europeans, as well as the American DeGré (37), Speier (123), and Child. Under major issues he discusses Merton's paradigm (61) and some problems of empirical research and imputation, as exemplified by DeGré (37) and Wolff (91). He concludes with several tangential studies: "the sociology of the university and learned men" [Veblen (124, 125), Wilson (149), Znaniecki (151), and others], "typologies of intellectuals and their functions" [Honigsheim, Helmuth Plessner, Theodor Geiger, to which can be added, among others, Coser (133)], the sociology of science [Piel (145), Hart (137), Merton (143), Meadows (142)], particularly of sociology [Hartung (40), Wolff (179), Nisbet (177), Hayek (169), Boran (162), with reply by Lundberg (175), House (170), Bowman (165, 163, 164), and Mills (68)]. He expresses his hope, indeed his expectation, that the sociology of knowledge is on its way to becoming "an empirical branch of scientific sociology" (2, p. 423). Adler's survey shares the ahistorical character and emphasis on social psychology that we have seen before; the stress of the empirical nature of the sociology of knowledge is probably greater here than in most other writings on the subject.

The last survey, by Chall (24), suggests, more flatly than Coser and Rosenberg, that the sociology of knowledge "has lost its original language and has become a latent part of the entire range of the behavioral sciences" (24, p. 300). It has not flourished in the United States in the decade 1945–1955, the period surveyed, because (1), although this country has during this time been "full of 'conflicting perspectives and interpretations'" [quoting Merton (61, p. 368)], it has been active economically, which suggests a modification of Merton's hypothesis to read: "The sociology of knowledge flowers when conflicting perspectives and interpretations occur in a society and when such a society is economically inactive"

[(24, p. 287); cf. pp. 301–302, n. 6]; (2) sociologists of knowledge and social researchers have not come together, to attack, for example, the problem of imputation, which, "in the empirical sense, is the unraveling of 'causes' by manipulating the variables defined in the research problem" (24, p. 287); and (3), as Merton (62, p. 201) suggests, "communication and public opinion research is the American variant if not the equivalent of the sociology of knowledge" [(24, p. 288); cf. (34, p. 570)]. In particular, Chall finds "the sociology of knowledge hypothesis incorporated as a frame of reference" (24, p. 291) in Adelson's (96) and Murphy's (115) efforts to account for the wide acceptance of Freudian psychology in the United States, in Pastore's (144) investigation "of the ideological concomitants of the nature-nurture controversy" (24, p. 292), in analyses by of the Whorfian hypothesis ["Languages differ not only in how they build their sentences, but in how they break down nature to secure the elements to put in those sentences" (218, p. 21)] and in their attempts to "make it researchable" (24, p. 293) [e.g., in studies of translatability: Hockett (214), Wright (219)], and he suggests the study of "the recent penetration of economic and physical terminology into non-economic disciplines" (24, p. 294), giving examples that could undoubtedly be multiplied. Among sociological critiques of sociological research, he mentions those of *The American Soldier* (173) and the *Kinsey Report* (167) [see also on *The Polish Peasant* (161), *The Authoritarian Personality* (168), and *The Lonely Crowd* (174)]. The ahistorical, systematizing nature of this survey is also apparent.

We shall encounter the characteristics of these surveys—distance from epistemology, history, the Marxist tradition, and the effort to gather and order materials relevant to the sociology of knowledge, notably from social psychology, particularly Mead—in the conceptions too, but also others. These conceptions are presented by major issues and only secondarily by authors or chronologically.

### IV. ISSUES OF THE SOCIOLOGY OF KNOWLEDGE IN THE UNITED STATES

*Epistemology.* We have seen Dahlke's (35), Becker and Dahlke's (18), and Adler's (2) rejection of the idea that the sociology of knowledge concern itself with epistemological questions. This rejection is shared by DeGré (36, pp. 111, 114; 37, pp. 86–87) in explicit agreement with Znaniecki (151, p. 5), who expresses it by claiming that the sociology of knowledge deals only with truths as subjectively held, not with their objective aspects; and by Hinshaw (43, p. 59), who denies any epistemological branch of the sociology of knowledge, whose epistemological consequences, if any, must be investigated by the epistemologist, not by the sociologist of knowledge, who is a scientist. Hinshaw takes this position in an effort to resolve Mannheim's relativism—more particularly by making use of Morris' (114) distinction between sign-sign relations (syntactics), sign-denotatum relations (semantics), and sign-interpreter relations (pragmatics), of which pragmatics alone is the "legitimate discipline of *Wissenssoziologie*" (43, p. 67). He does advocate cooperation between the epistemologists and the sociologists of knowledge, for "it would be presumptuous on the part of the epistemologist to criticize dogmatically the sociologist for dabbling in theory of knowledge as he inquires into the relation between ideas and social conditions" (45, p. 10) [cf. also Hinshaw and Spuhler (46, especially pp. 12–13), and Hinshaw (44)]. Berger and Luckman (22), in a frame of reference quite different from Hinshaw's, similarly do not consider epistemological questions part of the sociology of knowledge, which will, however [cf. Hinshaw (45)], "along with the other epistemological troublemakers among the empirical sciences, . . . 'feed' problems to this methodological inquiry" (22, p. 12).

Lavine (50, 51) holds an almost opposite position. Indeed, she speaks (51, p. 191) of a coalition of thinkers who would exempt the logical element in cognition from sociological analysis, naming Schelting (122), Mandelbaum (110), Lovejoy (108), C. I. Lewis (107), DeGré (36), Speier (123), Sabine (120), Parsons (117), Merton (59) [though not, for some reason, Dahlke (35) or Hinshaw (43)]. She opposes this exemption by her interpretation, based on Dewey (100, p. 535), of naturalism as continuity of analysis [adapted by Wolff (94, pp. 615–617; 95, p. 579)], that is, as the principle according to which the scientific method must be used in *all* areas of investigation, including the validity of thought (51, pp. 185–186). Validity has three elements: the norm that guides validation, the validating act, and the validity of a proposition; Lavine claims—thus apparently restricting her unrestricted continuity of analysis—that the sociologist of knowledge is not interested in the last of these but in validity norms in their relation to social demands with which these norms vary. This raises the problem of relativism, which cannot be met by a probability statement, as Mills (66, p. 323), who counters a logical argument by sociohistorical considerations, does, but by the concept of the absolute function of the norm. In this way a logical absolute is rendered compatible "with a thoroughgoing, unrestricted sociological relativization" (51, p. 198), and the criterion of the cognitive value of cognitive norms emerges as their adequacy in regard to the demands for structuring experience, for responsiveness to empirical reality, and for responsiveness to the social state of affairs (51, p. 199). The antiepistemological coalition itself must be investigated for the advantages that accrue to it from the restriction it insists on:

> First, the preservation from challenge or disruption of those cognitive norms which are responsive to the social demands of the group to which the opposition belong or with which they choose to affiliate themselves. Second, the preclusion of the occupational disadvantages deriving from a revision of many phases of their line of endeavor . . . In turn, the desire of the naturalist that the special sciences be advanced without compromise in any connection indicates a dominating devotion to development and progress which may, upon analysis, be revealed as responsive to the social demands of the groups in greatest need of social change (51, pp. 208–209). [See also Lavine (52–56).]

Lavine thus goes far beyond Merton's comments on the historical situation of the sociology of knowledge toward a sociological, Marxian interpretation of its antiepistemological and its naturalistic variants. [See also Hartung (40, 41) and Horowitz (47), especially p. 135.]

The passage from Mills to which Lavine refers occurs in Mills's defense of relativism, whose critics argue that the relativist's claims are either themselves relative, "in which case he has no grounds for denying or imputing truth to the thought of others," or "unconditionally true, and hence relativism is self-contradictory" (66, pp. 322–323). Mills's reply to these critics is that the relativist's assertions can be tested legitimately only with reference to a given verificatory model and that the sociologist of knowledge is using the model generalized by Peirce and Dewey. "Granted," Mills continues, and this is the argument that Lavine considers invalid, "that this model is no *absolute* guaranty, it seems the most probable we have at present" (66, p. 323).

I, too, claim that the sociology of knowledge must commit itself epistemologically:

> a discipline which understands something other than itself—which is, in other words, not (culturally) solipsistic— . . . must accept as a hypothesis the epistemological postulate that human intellectual-affective behavior exhibits both cultural variability and biologically founded identity (92, p. 203),

as Child's analysis of the categories [Child (31); see below] indeed makes plausible. I also attempt to ascertain the methodological, volitional, and metaphysical premises of the sociology of knowledge (94: pp. 612–614).

*Relations between Knowledge and Society.* These conceptions of the relation between epistemology and sociology of knowledge are central foci within their authors' conceptions of the relations between knowledge and society. For other writers the former is of less or no interest in connection with the latter. Some thinkers already touched on have more to say on the relations between knowledge and society than has been presented so far. Thus Mills derives his view of these relations from Mead, whose "concept of mind which incorporates social processes as intrinsic to mental operations" (65, p. 672) suggests to Mills that logic be conceived as the rules that must be followed in a given society and historical epoch if thought is to be socialized and "the meaning of language" as "the common social behavior evoked by it" (65, p. 677), from which it follows that a thinker can be located politically and socially by means of an analysis of his words and their meanings [see also Mills (67, 68)].

Others whose concepts of the relation between knowledge or thought and society are strongly influenced by Mead are Child and Berger and Luckmann who are discussed after Taylor, Stark, and Parsons. According to Child, the "objectivity of social determination" (27, p. 415; cf. 25, p. 78) can be demonstrated only if it can be shown that mind itself is social, which Mead (cf. 113, especially pp. 6–8, 46–47, 90, 133–134, 155–158, 191–192) has done, although Mead's theory justifies the social interpretation of thought, not, however, the sociology of knowledge (27, pp. 392–393, 417), any more than it illuminates the meaning and the extent of social determination or the interaction between the latter, "the inherent logic of thought itself, and the spontaneous activity of the organically individualized mind" (27, p. 417). Nevertheless, it is the categories of knowledge that are socially determined (31). Kant has indeed not established their inherence in the mind, hence their universality and necessity, but Mead's claim, on the other hand, that they rise from experience presupposes experience itself to be structured or categorized. To escape the dilemma Child distinguishes two kinds of category, primal or biotic, not socially derived, not changing, and supervenient or sociotic, socially derived and changing. In act, categories are formalizing intentions; in potency, predispositions, that is, organizations "of organic processes with reference to a type of stimulus" (31, p. 321). Primal categories possess both Kantian marks of apriority—universality and necessity—supervenient categories, only the latter. In discussing what in society determines thought, Child (28) replaces class with the more general social context, and interests, again following Mead, by "group attitudes as incorporated into the structure of the individual mind" (28, p. 182). Child's position on the relation between epistemology and sociology of knowledge appears most clearly in his analysis of truth (32), particularly of two problems

attendant on it—those of the relation between the origin and the validity
of an idea and of the possibility of a common and objective truth. On
the former he holds that the origin "of an idea proves nothing whatsoever, one way or another, about its factual validity" (32, p. 24), on the
latter, following his analysis of the categories, that the supervenient categories are the sources of error but also of truth other than that yielded by
the primal categories. By virtue of the "independent directive power of
mind" [cf. Stark (82, Chapter 7)] the individual "can and does criticize
certain of his predispositions through the medium of others" (32, p. 32).
From this conception, as well as from the fact that "elements not merely
from the thought of the past, but also from the contemporaneous thought
of other and even very antagonistic groups, become inextricably incorporated in the thought" of any thinker, it follows that the "possibility of
truth . . . is not confined to any one class even at a particular period in
the development of society" (25, pp. 288–289). [See also Child (30, 33) and
Wolff (92, pp. 203–204); (93); (94, pp. 590–610).]

For Taylor (87) categories are the basic concepts or "structural beams"
of a conceptual system. Like all concepts they are socially derived. The
same process that logically yields conceptual systems, existentially yields
institutions (87, p. 129). Taylor distinguishes four situational types with
their corresponding "conceptions of institutions" (87, pp. 25, 118): one,
unlabeled, in which the institution is the basis of the individual's thinking (87, pp. 25–26); a second, individualism (exemplified by Protagoras,
Kant, and Bentham) for which the individual has ontological ultimacy,
whereas the social, including institutions, is nominalistically derived
from it; a third, positivism (Comte, Durkheim, pointing toward Mead),
which separates institution and individual and grounds objectivity in
the latter's rational thought; and a fourth, historical relativism (Mannheim), which shows a "sociological reconstruction of the significance of
the institution" (87, p. 26). Taylor leaves it to the reader to judge
whether his "own view of institutions and knowledge"—which, as he
claims in a later paper (88), combines Mead with Durkheim and Mannheim—has overcome "the bias and limitation" stemming from the necessity "to make use of tools which were themselves products of institutions"
(87, p. 12).

Stark [4] [(82); cf. also (85, 86)] presents his concept of the relation between knowledge and society—whose major single source is Scheler—by
analyzing the four fundamental questions of the sociology of knowledge.
The first concerns the basis of the social determination of ideas and is answered (82, pp. 222–223) by the coenonic-holistic theory, according to
which social determination is constituted by social interaction as a total
system rather than by any one factor. The second question concerns the
nature of social determination: it is not causal but, depending on the type

of society, one of mutual adjustment or mutual selection (82, pp. 245–273). The third concerns the extent and the intensity of social determination; the answer is that all contents of thought depend on social circumstances but that there is freedom of exploration within socially predetermined limits (82, pp. 274–306). Finally there is the problem of relativity, to which Stark responds with the metectic view, according to which every society sees part of the truth; he agrees with Scheler, that to "penetrate into the transcendent secrets of . . . [the] *logos* . . . is not given to *one* nation, . . . but only to all together, including the future ones, in collective co-operation" [82, p. 330), quoting Scheler (121, p. 27)].

Parsons, whose "position is relatively close to that taken by Werner Stark" (69, p. 25), argues that the sociology of knowledge has been chiefly concerned with the relation "between institutionalized value systems and empirical conceptions of societies and their subsystems," but that it should also address itself to "the relations between the cultural motivations of individuals and religious grounds of meaning" [(69, p. 31); cf. Berger and Luckmann (22, p. 169)]. Nevertheless it is narrower than the sociology of culture, which analyzes "the interdependence and interpenetration of social and cultural systems or their subsystems" (70, p. 991) and is indeed more specifically concerned with "empirical science and the grounds of meaning" (69, p. 31), both of which are confusingly connoted by *Wissen* [(70, pp. 990, 993); cf. Merton (61, pp. 366, 379–380), Wolff (95, p. 568)]. The analysis of the relation of "values to empirical knowledge" requires the distinction between the "value-science integrate" [(69, pp. 36–39); cf. (70, p. 978, n. 11, p. 992)], "an ideal type of objective scientific knowledge about a society . . . relative to the values of that society at a given time" (69, p. 36), which is a concept closely akin to Mannheim's general ideology [Mannheim (57, especially p. 68, n. 2)], and "ideology" (Mannheim's particular ideology), which is characterized by selection from available social-scientific knowledge and by distortion [cf. Stark's distinction between social determination and ideological distortion (82, Chapter 2)]. The source of ideology is "strain" (69, p. 41); its consequence, "to protect the stability of the institutionalized values, or conversely, . . . to undermine" it (69, p. 46).

Berger and Luckmann's book (22), based more than on anything else on Schutz (71–73), deals with everyday knowledge, with society as objective reality (institutionalization and legitimation), and with society as subjective reality (socialization and identity). To quote Berger (20, pp. 6–7):

> We have followed Schutz in his re-definition of the field of the sociology of knowledge . . . we have felt that only by under-standing society as a comprehensive dialectic between human

activity (social praxis) and its products (here, specifically, the meaningful worlds that constitute everyday reality) is it possible to resolve the seeming antinomy of the Durkheimian view of society as a world of things (*choses*) and the Weberian view of it as the ongoing expression of subjectively meaningful activity (*Handeln*). . . . The crucial theoretical question then becomes how it is possible that subjective meanings become embodied in the thing-like facticities of the institutional order, in other words, the question of *objectivation*. Insofar as both subjective meanings and social facticities are, in the final analysis, nothing but "representations" (to use the Durkheimian term), the question of objectivation becomes the obviously crucial question for any sociology of knowledge.

In our theory of society as objective reality we have been influenced by Durkheim as well as by other figures of the Durkheim school. . . . In our theory of society as subjective reality, on the other hand, we have tried to integrate some fundamental insights of American social psychology, particularly as derived from George Herbert Mead, with the perspective of the sociology of knowledge [5].

Like Berger and Luckmann, Parsons, and some others, Sorokin explicitly places his concept of the sociology of knowledge within his concept of sociology and of history. This is grounded in the discovery rather than construction (76, pp. 4–7; 77, p. 139) of the Ideational, Idealistic, and Sensate supersystems [the relation between the concept of supersystem and Taylor's "totality of the conceptual system" (87, p. 129) in its broad sense and close connection with institutions would bear analysis]. Each supersystem is "an *empirical* sociocultural system," consisting of "(1) the system of meanings, (2) the causal system of vehicles, and (3) its human agents" [(77, p. 45); cf. (79, Chapter 1)]. Subject matter and validation of knowledge vary with each: supersensory subject matter and validation by reference to sacred scriptures characterize the Ideational supersystem; partly supersensory, partly sensory-empirical subject matter and chiefly the method of reasoning characterize the Idealistic; sensory subject matter and the testimony of the senses, supplemented by logical reasoning, characterize the Sensate (76, pp. 8–9). These supersystems change immanently; the "principle of limits" (77, p. 706) accounts both for there being no fewer nor more than three and for their fluctuation. "Perhaps the deepest reason for such a fluctuation is that none of these three systems contain the whole truth, the truth of a really omniscient mind" [(76, p. 122); cf. Stark (82, p. 330)]. For empirical proof Sorokin studied the leading thinkers of the Graeco-Roman and European cultures from 580 B.C. to A.D. 1920, quantifying his data by assigning a value of 1 to 12 to each thinker, who was chosen by eight criteria (76, pp. 17–18). The result of his study was that the Ideational system of truth dominated Greek culture before the fifth century B.C., to be replaced in the fifth and fourth by the Idealistic system, then by the Sensate, which reigned until the fifth century A.D. but was followed once more by the Ideational system, dominating from the fifth to the eleventh, by the Idealistic, from the twelfth to the fourteenth, and by the Sensate, which has held sway since then. Sorokin refers to his work (76) as "a treatise in *Wissenssoziologie*" (76, p. vii); it has so been discussed by at least Merton (61) and Maquet (58) [see also Becker (10, p. 537)]. It is perhaps more justly assessed as philosophy of history, comparable to Spengler or Toynbee, and Sorokin has applied much of it to diagnoses of our time (78, 80).

According to DeGré (36), stimulated by Lovejoy (108, especially pp. 17–18), the sociology of knowledge, like sociology in general, engages in explanation, thereby operating with three elements: (1) social facts, that is, people, agencies, groups, political structures, and institutions (personal communication from DeGré, March 23, 1946), (2) their meaningful aspects, which it relates to world views (an element which is concerned only with subjective meaning, not with truth-value, as we have already seen), and (3) "the socio-historical conditions within which such 'meaningful complexes' occur and to which it relates the latter" [(36, p. 111]; DeGré's sociological explanation thus comes close to Mannheim's (57, pp. 276–278) three-phased imputation]. The sociology of knowledge, in particular, has among its specific problems the investigation of social factors that explain why a given subject matter is selected at a given time and place [cf. Child (25, Chapter 7; 28, 32)], of the "social roots of the manner in which experience is interpreted" (36, p. 112), of the societal factors influencing categories and other general concepts, and of the "reciprocal influence of socio-historical conditions and the most general structure of thinking on the logical and formal level" (36, pp. 112–113). A later version of DeGré's views places the sociology of knowledge within the sociology of communication [(37, p. 86), whereas for Parsons, as we have seen, it is part of the sociology of culture]. The sociology of communication deals with all three types of communication—rational, which is intended to inform, normative, which is intended to motivate action, and affective, which is intended to influence an emotional condition (personal communication from DeGré, 10 April 1946)—whereas the sociology of knowledge deals only with the first of these.

Merton (61) conveys his concept of the relations between knowledge and society more exclusively than Stark and DeGré in terms of an outline of the problem areas of the sociology of knowledge, even though the avowed purpose of his paradigm is to "provide a basis for taking an inventory of extant findings" (61, p. 371). These problem areas concern the existential basis (which may be social or cultural) of mental productions (cf. Stark's first question of the sociology of knowledge), their specification (spheres and aspects—cf. Stark's third), the relation between mental productions and the existential basis (causal or functional, symbolic or organismic or meaningful, or couched in ambiguous terms—cf. Stark's second), the manifest and latent functions imputed to these relations, and the extent to which they hold (historicist versus general analytical theories) [61, p. 372]. Merton discusses five approaches to these problem areas: Marx's, Scheler's, Mannheim's, Durkheim's, and Sorokin's—these, because current work in the sociology of knowledge "is largely oriented toward one or another of these theorists" (61, p. 373), modifying them or arguing against them.

Much more politically or activistically oriented than Merton's paradigm is Horowitz's (47, pp. 37–38) content of the sociology of knowledge [cf. also (47, Chapters 7 and 8) on ideology and utopia], which consists of

> a) the empirical study of the ways ideas are used to galvanize action; b) the social basis of ideas, irrespective of their truth or falsity; c) the ideational conditions for the survival of social motivation; d) the use of ideas and values to promote new forms of social relations, and the use of counter-ideas and counter-values to frustrate new forms; e) the respective functions of science, religion, myth and logic in the creation of ideological conceptions of the universe; f) the treatment of knowledge as an independent variable with its unique dynamics of change.

The central task of the sociology of knowledge is "the discovery of the social sources of truth, error, and opinion" (47, p. 68); its function, "to describe the role of social-political interests in the determination of moral choices; and thus make decision making itself more conscious and rational" (47, p. 78). [For occasions on which Horowitz shows a less activistic attitude toward the sociology of knowledge, cf. (48, 49).]

*Problems for the Sociology of Knowledge.* Various writers present more particular projects, research problems, and the like, for the sociology of knowledge. Wirth (89, pp. xxix–xxxi) believes that it would be premature to define the exact scope of this discipline but that Scheler's and Mannheim's work permits a tentative statement of its leading issues: (1) The "social-psychological elaboration of the theory of knowledge" or of the "problem of the interconnection between being and knowing"; (2) the "reworking of the data of intellectual history with a view to the discovery of the styles and methods of thought that are dominant in certain types of historical-social situations"; (3) the study "of the factors that are responsible for the acceptance or the rejection of certain ideas by certain groups in society"; (4) the determination "how the interests and purposes of certain social groups come to find expression in certain theories, doctrines, and intellectual movements"; (5) an analysis of "the agencies or devices through which ideas are diffused and the degree of freedom of inquiry and expression that prevails." This, more generally, leads to "one of the primary obligations of the sociology of knowledge," namely, an "adequate theoretical treatment of the social organization of intellectual life," "a systematic analysis of the institutional organization within the framework of which intellectual activity is carried on." Finally, (6), the concern "with the persons who are the bearers of intellectual activity, namely the intellectuals."

Merton (61, pp. 397–404) concludes his paper with a glance at "Further Problems and Recent Studies." He comments favorably on research in five areas that he suggests are fruitful fields for further investigation: (1) the thinker's public [audience, social circle: Znaniecki (151)]; (2) intellectuals (intelligentsia; cf. Wirth's sixth leading issue); (3) the inuflence of society or culture on conceptual phrasing; (4) the influence of (political and social) interests on the thinker's perspective (cf. Wirth's fourth leading issue); and (5) the sociology of science. [For a direct reference to Wirth in a similar context see Merton (59, p. 503). See also Lavine's "directional principles for the sociology of knowledge" (51, 201–202)]. I (91, pp. 122–123) mention "at random some projects . . . that may help to show the width of the field of research in the sociology of knowledge," among them studies in reading, film viewing, and spelling habits, propaganda, book reviewing, poetry, musical forms, and translation.

*Assessments of the Sociology of Knowledge.* The few explicit assessments of the sociology of knowledge lend themselves perhaps more readily than other themes to an understanding of American concepts. "The distinctive contribution of the present volume" [Mannheim (57)], and thus presumably of the sociology of knowledge in general, writes Wirth (89, p. xxvii), "may turn out to be the explicit recognition that thought, besides being a proper subject matter for logic and psychology, becomes fully comprehensible only if it is viewed sociologically." The most important thing "that we can know about a man is what he takes for granted, and the most elemental and important facts about a society are those that are seldom debated and generally regarded as settled" [(89, p. xxiv); on "taken for granted," cf. Wirth (90, p. 477), Wolff (91, pp. 119–121), Schutz (72, 73:

consult Indexes)]. Wirth hopes that the sociology of knowledge will "become a specialized effort to deal in an integrated fashion, from a unifying point of view and by means of appropriate techniques, with a series of subject matters which hitherto have been only cursorily and discretely touched upon" (89, pp. xxviii–xxix).

On the basis of his analysis of interpretation Child (25, Chapter 7) comes—or at one time did come—to a wholly different assessment. This analysis entails the necessity of undertaking for the optimal understanding of an intellectual phenomenon, both its "immanent" and its "transcendent" interpretation. Since the sociology of knowledge is concerned only with the latter, more particularly with sociological interpretation, it follows that the proper understanding of this dual interpretation "leads, when that understanding is carried to its limits, to the abolition of the sociology of knowledge itself and to its reconciliation with the historical school in opposition to which it arose" (25 p. 292) [6].

Lavine, quite to the contrary, mentions numerous scientific interests that can be reframed in accordance with the "directional principles" (51: pp. 201–202) of the sociology of knowledge, among them the social responsiveness of language types, speech itself as the response to evolutionary social demands, and the Gestalt approach to the phenomenon of perception. In fact, Lavine writes (51, p. 202):

> The sociology of knowledge will one day systematize all cognitive elements in relation to their social responsiveness. When this occurs, large areas of literary criticism, philosophy, history, psychology, sociology, economics, mathematics, physics, astronomy, and biology will need to be rewritten. For a knowledge of the social responsiveness of the cognitive elements involved cannot fail to revise the conception of their concrete sequence, correlation, and causation, as well as to bring new understanding of the significance of individual norms.

Obviously this is related to some of Wirth's leading issues, particularly to the second.

For Merton the sociology of knowledge "focusses on those problems which are at the very center of contemporary intellectual interest" (61, p. 404); some other diagnostic statements concerning the increasing empirical rigor of the sociology of knowledge, found in the same paragraph, resemble those made by Coser and Rosenberg and Adler. In the light of a diagnosis of our time I call the sociology of knowledge

> an elucidation of a new experience man has had and is still having. Through it, man adapts himself to living in one

world, and through it he transcends cultural relativism toward the view of himself as dual and inexhaustibly challenging his own exploration [94, p. 618]; the sociology of knowledge transforms a new and shattering experience into a problem (95, p. 584).


## V. INTERPRETIVE REMARKS

In conclusion, some observations and tentative interpretations may be offered, starting from the assessments just reviewed. All, it should be noted, relate to Mannheim and are hardly imaginable without him; thus they show his extraordinary impact, comparable to Marx's on the original *Wissenssoziologie* in the Germany of the 1920s. In both cases impact may mean acceptance and development or rejection after a struggle. Child's is the extreme case of such rejection: the painful realization that, on analysis, the sociology of knowledge altogether must be abandoned. We have already seen what in hindsight looks like preparing for this abandonment: Child's dissolution of two essential features of a sociology of knowledge in the Marxist tradition: class into social context and interests into group attitudes; both in these substitutions and in the analysis leading to the abolition of the sociology of knowledge, historical-practical relevance is abandoned for the sake of a theoretically more comprehensive and systematic scheme. Merton seems midway between turning away from Mannheim and developing him: he examines Mannheim systematically (60) and, along with others, according to his paradigm (61), but he also locates the sociology of knowledge "at the very center of contemporary intellectual interest." The other three authors whose assessments we have noted clearly side with Mannheim, though in different ways. Wirth in effect diagnoses a change of consciousness introduced by (Mannheim's version of) the sociology of knowledge when he calls it the source of the recognition that thought must be interpreted sociologically. Lavine goes further, listing many intellectual concerns and disciplines that she expects need rewriting as a result of the existence of (Mannheim's version of) the sociology of knowledge. I connect the latter directly with a diagnosis of the time in which it originated, which suggests its historical social-psychological function. On the other hand, it is noteworthy that critiques of Mannheim from a more radical position than his own, for example, among the German responses to him [Horkheimer (104), Adorno (97)] are absent from the American scene.

If there is something to these observations, they need to be interpreted. As to the radical position just mentioned, Veblen did not live long enough to examine Mannheim and perhaps would not have done so anyway. By the time Mills developed his sociology [about 1948 on—cf. (195–197, 176)] he was no longer interested in the sociology of knowledge with which he had started. For Hartung, Horowitz, Lavine, and some others Mannheim seems adequate as expressing a critical view (which does not mean, of course, that these authors do not develop him further or apply him to problems to which he himself did not turn).

We may also ask how the sociology of knowledge might have developed it if, instead of Mannheim [(57) and later (111) and other collections of his essays] or in addition to him, Scheler (especially 121) or Grünwald [(102); cf. Wolff (130)] had been available in translation rather than, as in Scheler's case, indirectly through the reception by Stark, Parsons, and others. The effect might well have been a strengthening of ahistorical, systematizing tendencies. At the same time we should remember that one of Durkheim's most important works (101) has been translated since 1915 but that Durkheim has nevertheless had much less influence on the sociology of knowledge in the United States than Mannheim. The comment by the Hinkles, referred to in connection with the attitude of general American sociology toward Marx, deserves quotation and renewed attention. "A sociology of knowledge," they write [it may be recalled from Chapter 29],

> which maintains a strict causal relationship between a specific form of social existence or class position and knowledge is unlikely to gain many adherents among American sociologists . . . *neither Durkheim's notion of society as an entity* sui generis *nor Marx's interpretation of social stratification in terms of economic relations and consequent class consciousness* has been accepted in American sociology in spite of widespread familiarity with these ideas [(42, pp. 73, 74); italics added, quoted in Wolff (95, pp. 580–581)].

They explain this as a consequence of "voluntaristic nominalism," that is, of

> the assumption that the structure of all social groups is the consequence of the aggregate of its separate, component individuals and that social phenomena ultimately derive from the motivations of these knowing, feeling, and willing individuals [(42, p. vii), quoted in (95, p. 580)].

In other words, they explain this as a consequence of "social-historical nominalism" or "individual-psychological realism" [Wolff (95; pp. 580–582)]. On this interpretation it becomes plausible that both Durkheim and Marx, and with Marx, Mannheim, should not have been incorporated into the American sociology of knowledge, but it obviously raises the question why Mannheim should have been, or be, so, say, tempting—stimulating, exciting, excruciating.

In an effort to answer this question a sociological interpretation must be ventured of a kind that is so uncharacteristic of American statements on the sociology of knowledge. It begins with the observation that the critical impulse, whether native or imported, appears to get channeled in American social science, and perhaps elsewhere in American culture as well, into application to the individual, even if this impulse also, or chiefly, has a social thrust—the extreme case probably is the reception of Freud and some of its consequences [Marcuse (112)]. In regard to the sociology of knowledge itself Coser and Rosenberg (34, p. 570), it may be remembered speak, of the "deflection of" its "original aims"; as Merton (62, pp. 200–216) they write, remarks [cf. Chall (24, p. 288) and Wolff (95, pp. 587–590)], "the sociology of public opinion and mass communication, a specifically American field, has to some extent taken" its place. It is as if the individual alone were real, but such a traditional liberal view, which has been argued convincingly to have no alternative in the United States [Hartz (103), Bramson (166, especially p. 49)], is likely to have become increasingly unbelievable, at least since the Great Depression, the Soviet purges, the Spanish Civil War, World War II, Nazi genocides, and the atom and hydrogen bombs, not to mention more recent events and developments, which have dealt it ever harder blows. Mannheim's work arrived on the American scene between the Depression and the war (and the war and postwar booms) and may have tempted its American readers to envisage the reality of society and to be bewildered about that of the individual; thus it may be understandable that his reception should have been as we have seen. Instead of asking, as we did, what the American sociology of knowledge might be like had Scheler or Grünwald been available, we now ask what the impact of *Ideology and Utopia* might have been had this book arrived earlier or later than 1936. If it had appeared sooner after its original publication (1929), its effect might well have been greater; if later, say at the time of Fromm [1941 (220)] or Riesman [1950 (223)], it would possibly have been less distinctly identified with the sociology of knowledge and more with the literature on alienation, apathy, anomie, and loneliness that had begun to emerge.

The picture of the sociology of knowledge in the United States that results from the preceding report would probably look somewhat different if in addition to statements *about*, studies *in* the sociology of knowledge had been taken into consideration. It would presumably not change, but both defensive [e.g., Adler (1)] and affirmative, developing features [e.g.,

Mills (68)] of the response we have observed would be more explicit and palpable and at the same time attenuated by the presentation of substantive work.

Perhaps American sociology on the whole is becoming readier to recognize the reality of society, without necessarily losing its emphasis on the individual. Social circumstances, including those that have been mentioned in an effort to throw light on the doubt concerning individual-psychological realism and liberalism, would again go a long way toward accounting for this change. In the social sciences such a change seems to have started, among other sources, from linguistics [cf. Hymes (216) and (215, including references to preceding literature)], phenomenology [Schutz (72, 73), Berger and Luckmann (22), and Garfinkel (38)], and various developments in cultural anthropology [Lee (172)], including action anthropology [Tumin (178), Bennett (160), and Wolff (180)]—not from the sociology of knowledge, although it might well make the latter a more relevant undertaking if the thrust coming from these other sources influenced it in turn. This thrust comes from studies more of social than of historical phenomena such as inspire Mannheim's sociology of knowledge with its Hegelian-Marxian background, which is still missing from American social science as a series alternative to liberalism, even though we have seen it manifest itself in some of the American sociologists of knowledge.

*Acknowledgment.* The research here reported was assisted by a grant awarded by the Committee on Faculty Research Grants of the Social Science Research Council. This is gratefully acknowledged herewith.

### BIBLIOGRAPHY

The following bibliography is divided into two very different parts. Part 1 lists all works discussed or cited in the foregoing report; it claims to contain, in addition to a few other writings, a fairly complete list of explicit statements on the sociology of knowledge, including surveys and conceptions, formulated in the United States.

Part 2 lists a large number of works cited in the writings in Part 1 as well as in Parts I and V of the report itself. Unlike the entries in Part 1, however, which are listed simply in alphabetical order by authors, the entries in Part 2 are grouped by approximate subject matter. Their grouping reflects the interests of the sociologists of knowledge discussed in the report and cited in Part 1; at the same time it suggests a few entries in several areas of sociological research whose systematic culling for materials relevant from the point of view of the sociology of knowledge (cf. the quotation at the end of Part I of the report) would yield, of course, incomparably more. Given the origin and rationale of the classification of Part 2 of the bibliography, no reader should be misled into assuming that he finds, in any sense, representative bibliographies of its subparts.

The structure of the report and of the bibliography makes annotation superfluous. Nevertheless, all titles making up the second part of the bibliography have been supplied with a general description of the nature of the work concerned (except in cases in which this clearly results from their titles).

## 1. WORKS DISCUSSED OR CITED IN THE REPORT

1. Adler, Franz, "A Quantitative Study in Sociology of Knowledge," *Amer. Sociol. R.*, 19, 1 (February 1954), 42–48.

2. _____,"The Range of Sociology of Knowledge," in Howard Becker and Alvin Boskoff, Eds., *Modern Sociological Theory in Continuity and Change* (New York: Dryden Press, 1957), pp. 396–423.

3. _____, "Werner Stark's Sociology of Knowledge," *Kyklos* (Basel), 12, 2 (1959), 216–221.

4. _____, "Werner Stark's Sociology of Knowledge: A Further Comment," *Kyklos*, 12, 3 (1959), 500–506.

5. Barber, Bernard. "Sociology of Knowledge and Science, 1945–1955," in Hans L. Zetterberg, *Sociology in the United States of America: A Trend Report* (Paris: UNESCO, 1956), pp. 68–70.

6. Becker, Howard, *Ionia and Athens: Studies in Secularization* (Chicago, University of Chicago, 1930) (unpublished Ph.D. dissertation).

7. _____, "Processes of Secularisation: An Ideal-Typical Analysis with Special Reference to Personality Change as Affected by Population Movement," *Sociol. R.*, 24, 2 (April–July 1932), 138–154; 24, 3 (October 1932), 266–286.

8. _____, "The Mobile Background of the Greco-Roman Roman World and Its Effects on Social Thought," in Harry Elmer Barnes and Howard Becker, *Social Thought from Lore to Science*, (Boston: Heath, 1938), pp. 135–176.

9. _____, "Constructive Typology in the Social Sciences," in Harry Elmer Barnes, Howard Becker, and Frances Bennett Becker, Eds., *Contemporary Social Theory* (New York; Appleton-Century, 1940), pp 17–46.

10. _____, "Historical Sociology," *ibid.*, pp. 491–542.

11. _____, "Befuddled Germany: A Glimpse of Max Scheler." *Amer. Sociol. R.*, 8, 2 (April 1943), 207–211.

12. _____, "Interpretive Sociology and Constructive Typology," in Georges Gurvitch, and Wilbert E. Moore, Eds., *Twentieth Century Sociology* (New York: Philosophical Library, 1945), pp. 70–95.

13. _____, "Max Scheler," in *Encyclopaedia Britannica*, 14th rev. ed., 1948 ff.

14. _____, "Max Scheler," in *Collier's Encyclopedia*, rev. ed., 1948 ff.

15. _____, "In Defense of Morgan's 'Grecian Gens': Ancient Kinship and Stratification," *Southwest. J. Anthropol.*, 6, 3 (Autumn 1950), 309–339.

16. _____, *From Values to Social Interpretation* (Durham, N.C.: Duke University Press, 1950).

17. _____, "Current Sacred-Secular Theory and Its Development," in Howard Becker, and Alvin Boskoff, Eds., *Modern Sociological Theory in Continuity and Change* (New York: Drydan Press, 1957), pp. 133–185.

18. _____, and Helmut Otto Dahlke, "Max Scheler's Sociology of Knowledge." *Philos. Phenomenol. Res.*, 2, 3 (March 1942), 309–332.

19. Berger, Peter L., "Towards a Sociological Understanding of Psychoanalysis," *Soc. Res.*, 32, 1 (Spring 1965), 27–41.

20. _____, *Phenomenological Influence on the Sociology of Knowledge in America*, Evian, Sixth World Congress of Sociology, 1966 (mimeographed).

21. _____, and Hansfried Kellner, "Marriage and the Construction of Reality," *Diogenes*, 46 (1964), 1–24.

22. _____, and Thomas Luckmann, *The Social Construction of Reality: A Treatise in the Sociology of Knowledge* (Garden City, N.Y.: Doubleday, 1966).

23. _____, Stanley Pullberg, "Reification and the Sociological Critique of Consciousness," *History and Theory*, 4, 2 (1965), 196–211.

24. Chall, Leo P. "The Sociology of Knowledge," Joseph S. Roucek, Ed., *Contemporary Sociology* (New York: Philosophical Library, 1958), pp. 286–303.

25. Child, Arthur. *The Problems of the Sociology of Knowledge. A Critical and Philosophical Study* (Berkeley, University of California, 1938) (unpublished Ph.D. dissertation).

26. _____, "The Problem of Imputation in the Sociology of Knowledge," *Ethics*, 51, 2 (January 1941), 200–219.

27. _____, "The Theoretical Possibility of the Sociology of Knowledge," *Ethics*, 51, 4 (July 1941), 392–418.

28. _____, "The Existential Determination of Thought," *Ethics*, 52, 2 (January 1942), 153–185.

29. _____, "The Problem of Imputation Resolved," *Ethics*, 54, 2 (January 1944), 96–109.

30. _____, "Toward a Functional Definition of the 'A Priori,'" *J. Philos.* 41, 5 (March 16, 1944), 155–160.

31. _____, "On the Theory of the Categories," *Philos. Phenomenol. Res.*, 7, 2 (December 1946), 316–335.

32. _____, "The Problem of Truth in the Sociology of Knowledge," *Ethics* 58, 1 (October 1947), 18–34.

33. _____, *Interpretation: A General Theory.* (Berkeley: University of California Press, 1965).

34. Coser, Lewis A., and Bernard Rosenberg, "Sociology of Knowledge," in

Lewis A. Coser and Bernard Rosenberg, Eds., *Sociological Theory: A Book of Readings* (New York, Macmillan, 1957), pp. 557–574 (pp. 667–684, unchanged, in 2nd ed. 1964).

35. Dahlke, H. Otto, "The Sociology of Knowledge," in Harry Elmer Barnes, Howard Becker, and Frances Bennett Becker, Eds., *Contemporary Social Theory* (New York: Appleton-Century, 1940) pp. 64–89.

36. Degré Gerard, "The Sociology of Knowledge and the Problem of Truth," *Journal of the History of Ideas*, 2, 1 (January 1941), 110–115.

37. _____, *Society and Ideology. An Inquiry into the Sociology of Knowledge* (New York: Columbia University Bookstore, 1943).

38. Garfinkel, Harold, "Aspects of the Problem of Common-Sense Knowledge of Social Structure," in Kurt H. Wolff, Ed., *The Sociology of Knowledge*, Transactions of the Fourth World Congress of Sociology, Vol. IV (Louvain: International Sociological Association, 1959), pp. 51–66.

39. _____, "Common-Sense Knowledge of Social Structures," in Jordan Scher, Ed., *Theories of the Mind* (New York, The Free Press of Glencoe, 1962) pp. 689–712.

40. Hartung, Frank, "The Sociology of Positivism," *Sci. and Soc.*, 8, 4 (Fall 1944), 328–341.

41. _____, "Problems of the Sociology of Knowledge," *Philos. Sci.*, 19, 1 (January 1952), 17–32.

42. Hinkle, Roscoe C., Jr., and Gisela J. Hinkle, *The Development of Modern Sociology: Its Nature and Growth in the United States* (Garden City, N.Y.: Random House, 1954).

43. Hinshaw, Virgil G., Jr., "The Epistemological Relevance of Mannheim's Sociology of Knowledge," *J. Philos.*, 40 3 (February 4, 1943), 57–72.

44. _____, "The Pragmatist Theory of Truth," *Philos. Sci.*, 11, 2 (April 1944), 82–92.

45. _____, "Epistemological Relativism and the Sociology of Knowledge," *Philos. Sci.*, 15, 1 (January 1948), 4–10.

46. _____ and James N. Spuhler, "On Some Fallacies Derived in David Bidney's Philosophy of Culture," *Central States Bulletin* (American Anthropological Association), 2 (1948), 12–18.

47. Horowitz, Irving Louis, *Philosophy, Science and the Sociology of Knowledge* (Springfield, Ill.: Thomas, 1961).

48. _____, "A Formalization of the Sociology of Knowledge," *Behav. Sci.*, 9, 1 (January 1964), 45–55.

49. _____, Ed., *Historia y elemenots de la sociología del conocimiento* [History and Elements of the Sociology of Knowledge] (Buenos Aires: Editorial universitaria de Buenos Aires, 1964), 2 vols.

50. Lavine, Thelma Z., "Sociological Analysis of Cognitive Norms," *J. Philos.*, 39, 13 (June 18, 1942), 342–356.

51. _____, "Naturalism and the Sociological Analysis of Knowledge," in Yervant H. Krikorian, Ed., *Naturalism and the Human Spirit* (New York: Columbia University Press, 1944), pp. 183–209.

52. _____, "Knowledge as Interpretation: An Historical Survey," *Philos.*

*Phenomenol. Res.*, 10, 4 (June 1950), 526–540; 11, 1 (September 1950), 88–103.

53. ————, "Note to Naturalists on the Human Spirit." *J. Philos.*, 50, 5 (February 26, 1953), 145–154; reprinted in Maurice Natanson, Ed., *Philosophy of the Social Sciences: A Reader* (New York, Random House, 1963), pp. 250–261.

54. ————, "What is the Method of Naturalism?", *J. Philos.*, 50, 5 (February 26, 1953), 157–161; reprinted *ibid.*, pp. 266–270.

55. ————, "Reflections on the Genetic Fallacy," *Soc. Res.*, 29, 3 (Autumn 1962), 321–336.

56. ————, "Karl Mannheim and Contemporary Functionalism," *Philos. Phenomenol. Res.*, 25, 4 (June 1965), 560–571.

57. Mannheim, Karl, *Ideology and Utopia: An Introduction to the Sociology of Knowledge* [originally published in German in 1929], translated by Louis Wirth and Edward Shils (New York: Harcourt, Brace, 1936).

58. Maquet, Jacques J., *The Sociology of Knowledge: Its Structure and Its Relation to the Philosophy of Knowledge. A Critical Analysis of the Systems of Karl Mannheim and Pitirim A. Sorokin* [1949], translated by John F. Locke (Boston: Beacon Press, 1951).

59. Merton, Robert K. "The Sociology of Knowledge," *Isis*, 27, 75 (November 1937), 493–503.

60. ————, "Karl Mannheim and the Sociology of Knowledge," *Journal of Liberal Religion*, 2 (Winter 1941), 125–147; reprinted in [62] pp. 247–264, 391–395; in [63], pp. 489–508.

61. ————, "Sociology of Knowledge," in Georges Gurvitch and Wilbert E. Moore, Eds., *Twentieth Century Sociology* (New York: Philosophical Library, 1945), pp. 266–405; reprinted in [62], pp. 217–245, 386–391; in [63], pp. 456–488.

62. ————, *Social Theory and Social Structure* (Glencoe, Ill.: The Free Press, 1949).

63. ————, *Social Theory and Social Structure*, rev. ed. (Glencoe, Ill.: The Free Press, 1957).

64. ————, Introduction to Part III, "The Sociology of Knowledge and Mass Communications," *ibid.*, pp. 439–455.

65. Mills, C. Wright, "Language, Logic and Culture." *Amer. Sociol. R.*, 4, 5 (October 1939), 670–680; reprinted in C. Wright Mills, *Power, Politics and People. The Collected Essays of C. Wright Mills*, edited and with an introduction by Irving Louis Horowitz (New York: Oxford University Press, 1963) pp. 423–438.

66. ————, "Methodological Consequences of the Sociology of Knowledge." *Amer. J..Sociol.*, 46, 3 (November 1940), 316–330; reprinted in [65], pp. 453–468.

67. ————, "Situated Actions and Vocabularies of Motive." *Amer. Sociol. R.*, 5, 6 (December 1940) 904–913; reprinted in [65], pp. 439–452.

68. ————, "The Professional Ideology of Social Pathologists." *Amer. J. Sociol.*, 49, 2 (September 1943), 165–180; reprinted in [65], pp. 525–552.

69. Parsons, Talcott, "An Approach to the Sociology of Knowledge," in Kurt H. Wolff, Ed., *The Sociology of Knowledge,* Transactions of the Fourth World Congress of Sociology, Vol. IV (Louvain: International Sociological Association, 1959), pp. 25–49.

70. _____, "Introduction" [to Part Four, Culture and the Social System], in Talcott Parsons, Edward Shils, Kaspar D. Naegele, and Jesse R. Pitts, Eds., *Theories of Society: Foundations of Modern Sociological Theory* (New York: The Free Press of Glencoe, 1961), pp. 963–998.

71. Schutz, Alfred, *Der sinnhafte Aufbau der sozialen Welt* [The Meaning Structure of the Social World]. (Vienna: Springer, 1932) (republished unchanged, 1960).

72. _____, *Collected Papers. I. The Problem of Social Reality,* edited and with an introduction by Maurice Natanson (The Hague: Nijhoff, 1962).

73. _____, *Collected Papers. II. Studies in Social Theory,* edited and with an introduction by Arvid Brodersen (The Hague: Nijhoff, 1964).

74. Shibutani, Tamotsu, "Reference Groups and Social Control," in Arnold Rose, Ed., *Human Behavior and Social Processes* (London: Routledge and Kegan Paul, 1962), pp. 128–147.

75. Sorokin, Pitirim A., *Social and Cultural Dynamics* (New York: American Book, 1937–1941), revised and abridged in one volume by the author (Boston: Sargent, 1957).

76. _____, *Social and Cultural Dynamics,* Vol. 2, *Fluctuation of Systems of Truth, Ethics, and Law* (New York: American Book, 1937).

77. _____, *The Crisis of Our Age: The Social and Cultural Outlook* (New York: Dutton, 1941).

78. _____, *Social and Cultural Dynamics, Vol. 4, Basic Problems, Principles, and Methods* (New York: American Book, 1941).

79. _____, *Sociocultural Causality, Space, Time: A Study of Referential Principles of Sociology and Social Science* (Durham: N.C., Duke University Press, 1943).

80. _____, *The Basic Trends of Our Times* (New Haven, Conn.: College and University Press, 1964).

81. Speier, Hans, "Review of Mannheim, *Ideology and Utopia,*" *Amer. J. Sociol.,* 43, 1 (July 1937), 155–166.

82. Stark, Werner, *The Sociology of Knowledge. An Essay in Aid of a Deeper Understanding of the History of Ideas* (Glencoe,, Ill.: The Free Press, 1958).

83. _____, "Reply" (to Adler [3]), *Kyklos,* 12, 2 (1959), 221–226.

84. _____, "A Second Reply" (to Adler [4]), *Kyklos,* 12, 3 (1959), 506–509.

85. _____, *Montesquieu: Pioneer of the Sociology of Knowledge,* (London: Routledge and Kegan Paul, 1960).

86. _____,*The Fundamental Forms of Social Thought* (London, Routledge and Kegan Paul, 1962).

87. Taylor, Stanley, *Conceptions of Institutions and the Theory of Knowledge* (New York: Bookman Associates, 1956).

88.  ————, "Social Factors and the Validation of Thought," *Soc. Forces*, 41, 1 (October 1962), 76–82.

89.  Wirth, Louis. "Preface," in [57], pp. xiii–xxxi.

90.  ————, "Ideological Aspects of Social Disorganization," *Amer. Sociol. R.*, 5, 4 (August 1940), 472–482; reprinted in Elizabeth Wirth Marvick, and Albert J. Reiss, Jr., Eds., *Community Life and Social Policy: Selected Papers by Louis Wirth* (Chicago: University of Chicago Press, 1956), pp. 192–205.

91.  Wolff, Kurt H., "The Sociology of Knowledge: Emphasis on an Empirical Attitude," *Philos. Sci.*, 10, 2 (April 1943), 104–123 [Chapter 26].

92.  ————, "The Unique and the General: Toward a Philosophy of Sociology," *Philos. Sci.*, 15, 3 (July 1948), 192–210 [Chapter 27].

93.  ————, "On the Scientific Relevance of 'Imputation,'" *Ethics*, 61, 1 (October 1950), 69–73 [Chapter 28].

94.  ————, "A Preliminary Inquiry into the Sociology of Knowledge from the Standpoint of the Study of Man," in *Scritti di Sociologia e politica in onore di Luigi Sturzo*, Vol. III (Bologna: Zanichelli, 1953), pp. 583–618 [Chapter 28].

95.  ————, "The Sociology of Knowledge and Sociological Theory," in Llewellyn Gross, Ed., *Symposium on Sociological Theory* (Evanston, Ill.: Row, Peterson, 1959), pp. 567–602 [Chapter 29].

## 2. WORKS CITED IN THE WORKS LISTED IN PART I OR DISCUSSED OR CITED IN PARTS I OR V OF THE REPORT

*The Sociology of Knowledge in the United States: Sources, Contemporary Influences, Related Thinkers*

96.  Adelson, Joseph, "Freud in America: Some Observations," *Amer. Psychol.*, 11, 9 (September 1956), 467–470. An effort to account for the wide acceptance of Freudian psychology in the United States; cf. [115].

97.  Adorno, Theodor W., "Was Bewusstsein der Wissenssoziologie" [The Consciousness of the Sociology of Knowledge] (1935), in Kurt Lenk, Ed., *Ideologie. Ideologiekritik und Wissenssoziologie* (Neuwied: Hermann Luchterhand, 1961), pp. 266–278 (Soziologische Texte, Band 4), rev. ed., 1964. Critique of Mannheim's sociology of knowledge on the basis of his *Mensch und Gesellschaft im Zeitalter des Umbaus* (Leiden, 1935; Darmstadt, 1958): *Man and Society in an Age of Reconstruction* [translated by Edward Shils (London: Routledge and Kegan Paul, 1940], as "harmlose Skepsis" (an innocuously skeptical stance); cf. [104].

98.  Dewey, John, "The Interpretation of the Savage Mind," *Psychological Review*, 9, 3 (May 1902), 217–230. An early effort to interpret "the savage mind" from a social point of view or in a sociological frame of reference.

99.  ————, *The Quest for Certainty* (New York: Minton, Balch, 1929). A

social-psychological interpretation of the human desire to know; advocacy of the principle that what is most probable or likely under the circumstances is a more realistic aim to pursue than the "certain."

100. ———, *Logic: The Theory of Inquiry* (New York: Holt, 1938). Dewey's most systematic and mature analysis of logic and epistemology.

101. Durkheim, Emile, *The Elementary Forms of the Religious Life* (1912), Translated by Joseph W. Swain (London: Allen and Unwin; New York: Macmillan, 1915). The single most important source of Durkheim's, if not of French thought on the sociology of knowledge. Emphasis is on the social origins not only of the sacred, in contrast to the profane, but also of the categories of thought, such as space and class.

102. Grünwald, Ernst, *Das Problem der Soziologie des Wissens. Versuch einer kritischen Darstellung der wissenssoziologischen Theorien* [The Problem of the Sociology of Knowledge. Toward a Critical Presentation of the Theories of the Sociology of Knowledge], edited by Walther Eckstein (Vienna: Braumüller, 1934). The only history of the sociology of knowledge in the Germany of the 1920s; an effort to develop a systematic conception of his own, of which Child, especially [27], and Wolff [130] give some idea.

103. Hartz, Louis, *The Liberal Tradition in America* (New York: Harcourt, Brace, 1955). A plausibly argued thesis that much in American thought and culture more generally can be understood in that in the absence of a feudalist tradition liberalism has never had a serious alternative in American history.

104. Horkheimer, Max. "Ein neuer Ideologiebegriff?" [A new concept of ideology?], in Kurt Lenk, Ed. *Ideologie*, pp. 235–255 (see [97]). A review of Mannheim's *Ideologie und Utopie* (Bonn, 1929), in which his concept of ideology is criticized as depoliticizing, spiritualizing, or idealizing its Marxist tradition.

105. Kecskemeti, Paul, "Introduction," in Karl Mannheim, *Essays on the Sociology of Knowledge*, translated by Paul Kecskemeti (London: Routledge and Kegan Paul, 1952), pp. 1–32. A general assessment of Mannheim's sociology of knowledge.

106. ———, "Introduction," in Karl Mannheim, *Essays on Sociology and Social Psychology*, edited by Paul Kecskemeti (London: Routledge and Kegan Paul, 1953), pp. 1–14. A general assessment of Mannheim's sociology of knowledge and of his conceptions of sociology and social psychology.

107. Lewis, Clarence Irving. *Mind and the World Order* (1929) (New York: Dover, 1956). A treatise in epistemology, tending toward a social perspective.

108. Lovejoy, Arthur O. "Reflections on the History of Ideas," *Journal of the History of Ideas*, I. 1 (January 1940), 3–23. The programmatic statement by the editor of the rationale of the *Journal of the History of Ideas*.

109. McKinney, John C., "The Contribution of George H. Mead to the Sociology of Knowledge," *Soc. Forces*, 34, 2 (August 1955), 144–149. The relevance of Mead's "social behaviorism" for the sociology of knowledge.

110. Mandelbaum, Maurice. *The Problem of Historical Knowledge. An Answer to Relativism* (New York: Liveright, 1938). An analysis of a number of philosophers of history and related thinkers, among them Scheler and Mannheim, in regard to the problem of the possibility of objective historical knowledge.

111. Mannheim, Karl, *Essays on the Sociology of Knowledge* (see [105].) Collection of many of Mannheim's papers on the sociology of knowledge, originally published in German (although some others are also contained in other collections of Mannheim's essays, notably in the volume referred to in [106]).

112. Marcuse, Herbert, *Eros and Civilization* (Boston: Beacon Press, 1955). An analysis of the metapsychology, that is, the sociological critique, contained in Freud's work.

113. Mead, George Herbert. *Mind, Self and Society from the Standpoint of a Social Behaviorist*, edited and with an introduction by Charles W. Morris (Chicago: University of Chicago Press, 1934). Analysis of mind, self, and society in their mutual relations; the basic work of social behaviorism and the pre-eminent source of Mead's influence on American social science, including the sociology of knowledge.

114. Morris, Charles W., *Foundations of the Theory of Signs* (Chicago: University of Chicago Press, 1938) [International Encyclopedia of Unified Science 1, 2]. An outline of semiotics, consisting of syntactics, semantics, and pragmatics.

115. Murphy, Gardner, "The Current Impact of Freud upon Psychology," *Amer. Psychol.*, 11, 12 (December 1956), 663–672. Analysis of the widespread acceptance of Freudian psychology in the United States and of the background of this acceptance; cf. [96].

116. Park, Robert E. "News as a Form of Knowledge: A Chapter in the Sociology of Knowledge." *Amer. J. Sociol.*, 45, 5 (March 1940), 669–686; reprinted in Robert E. Park, *Society. Collective Behavior, News and Opinions, Sociology and Modern Society*, edited by Everett C. Hughes (Glencoe, Ill.: The Free Press, 1955) pp. 71–88. An attempt at determining the particular form of knowledge that is represented by news. One of the few efforts among American sociologists to make an explicit contribution to the sociology of knowledge.

117. Parsons, Talcott, *The Structure of Social Action* (New York: McGraw-Hill, 1937). Parsons' first major work, in which he endeavors to show the convergence toward a unified conceptual system of Pareto's, Durkheim's, and Max Weber's theoretical efforts.

118. _____, *Essays in Sociological Theory, Pure and Applied.* (Glencoe, Ill.: The Free Press, 1949); rev. ed., 1954. Among the essays are theoretical papers going beyond [117] and pointing toward [119].

119. _____, *The Social System* (Glencoe, Ill.: The Free Press, 1951). The systematic treatment of one of the three systems (social, cultural, personality) that constitute the subject matter of social science; the work is

based above all on the three thinkers analyzed in [117] but also shows the impact of studies in cultural anthropology and psychoanalysis.

120. Sabine, George H., "Logical and Social Studies." *Philos. R.*, 48, 2 (March 1939), 155–176.

121. Scheler, Max, "Probleme einer Soziologie des Wissens" [Problems of a Sociology of Knowledge], in Max Scheler, *Die Wissensformen und die Gesellschaft* [Forms of Knowledge, and Society] (Leipzig: Neue-Geist, 1926), pp. 1–229. Scheler's most important single contribution to the sociology of knowledge.

122. Schelting, Alexander von, "Review of Mannheim, *Ideologie und Utopie*," *Amer. Sociol. R.*, 1, 4 (August 1936), 664–674. A review of Mannheim's book [57], in which the author summarizes his view of the sociology of knowledge and its limits worked out in much more detail in his *Max Webers Wissenschaftslehre* [philosophy of science], Tübingen: Mohr, 1934; not available in English translation.

123. Speier, Hans, "The Social Determination of Ideas," *Soc. Res.*, 5, 2 (May 1938), 182–205; reprinted in Hans Speier, *Social Order and the Risks of War* (New York: Stewart, 1952) pp. 85–111. An attempt at a systematic statement concerning the topic indicated in the title.

124. Veblen, Thorstein, *The Theory of the Leisure Class* (New York: Macmillan, 1899).

125. ————, *The Higher Learning in America: A Memorandum on the Conduct of Universities by Business Men* (New York: Huebsch, 1918).

126. ————, *The Place of Science in Modern Civilization* (New York: Huebsch, 1919). This and the two preceding works are probably the most influential of Veblen's critical, often satirical analyses of various aspects of the society and culture of the United States.

127. Wagner, Helmut R., "Mannheim's Historicism." *Soc. Res.*, 19, 3 (September 1952), 300–321.

128. ————, "The Scope of Mannheim's Thinking," *Soc. Res.*, 20, 1 (March 1953), 100–109.

129. Wolfe, Albert B., *Conservatism, Radicalism and Scientific Method.* (New York: Macmillan, 1923). A strongly sociological treatment of the three phenomena mentioned in the title, with advocacy of the third; an independent American "relative" of the sociology of knowledge.

130. Wolff, Kurt H., "Ernst Grünwald and the Sociology of Knowledge: A Collective Venture in Interpretation," *Journal of the History of the Behavioral Sciences*, 1, 2 (April 1965), 152–164. An attempt to present the reader with the existential significance of Grünwald's concept of the sociology of knowledge; cf. [102] and [27].

*Science, Intellectuals, Professions, Distribution of Knowledge*

131. Barber, Bernard, *Science and the Social Order* (Glencoe, Ill.: The Free Press, 1952). A treatise on the sociology of science.

132. _____, and Walter Hirsch, Eds., *The Sociology of Science* (New York: The Free Press of Glencoe, 1962). A reader in the sociology of science.

133. Coser, Lewis A., *Men of Ideas* (New York: The Free Press of Glencoe, 1965). Types of intellectual in historical perspective, culminating in an assessment of intellectuals in contemporary United States.

134. Gillispie, Charles C., *Genesis and Geology: A Study in the Relations of Scientific Thought, Natural Theology and Social Opinion in Great Britain, 1790–1850* (Cambridge, Mass.: Harvard University Press, 1951).

135. Hall, Oswald, "The Stages of a Medical Career," *Amer. J. Sociol.*, 53, 5 (March 1948), 327–336.

136. _____, "Types of Medical Careers," *Amer. J. Sociol.*, 55, 3 (November 1949), 243–253.

137. Hart, Clyde W., "Some Factors Affecting the Organization and Prosecution of Given Research Projects," *Amer. Sociol. R.*, 12, 5 (October 1947), 514–519. Emphasis on extrascientific factors in science; cf. [145].

138. Hughes, Everett C., "Institutional Office and the Person." *Amer. J. Sociol.*, 43, 3 (November 1937), 404–413. A "classical," highly influential study of the topic indicated by the title.

139. Kelsen, Hans, *Society and Nature* (Chicago: University of Chicago Press, 1943). An effort to show the origin of the modern concept of causality in ancient Greece, according to which non-Greek, including nonliterate peoples, operate instead with the concept of retribution.

140. Knapp, Robert H., and Hubert B. Goodrich, *Origins of American Scientists* (Chicago: University of Chicago Press, 1952).

141. Machlup, Fritz. *The Production and Distribution of Knowledge in the United States* (Princeton: Princeton University Press, 1962). An attempt at the quantitative determination of the sources and the mechanisms and channels of the distribution of knowledge in the United States.

142. Meadows, Paul, "Science as Experience: A Genetic and Comparative Review," *Amer. Sociol. R.*, 14, 5 (October 1949), 592–599. An essay in the social psychology of science as a social enterprise and type of human experience.

143. Merton, Robert K. "Science, Technology and Society in Seventeenth Century England," in George Sarton, Ed., *Osiris, Studies on the History and Philosophy of Science and on the History of Learning and Culture.* Vol. 4, pp. 360–632 (Bruges: St. Catherine Press, 1938). One of Merton's earliest but most important studies; an essay in the sociology of science.

144. Pastore, Nicholas, *The Nature-Nurture Controversy* (New York: King's Crown Press, 1949). A sociological analysis of the "nature-nurture controversy," with special attention to its ideological elements.

145. Piel, Gerard, "Scientists and Other Citizens," *Scientific Monthly*, 78, 3 (March 1954), 129–133. A contribution to the sociology of science, stressing extra-scientific factors in science; cf. [137].

146. [UNITED STATES] President's Scientific Research Board, *Science and Public Policy*, Washington, Government Printing Office, various dates. Exemplifies the relations between government and scientific activity and organi-

zation; a source of knowledge concerning the impact of government on science.

147. Schutz, Alfred, "The Well-Informed Citizen: An Essay on the Social Distribution of Knowledge," *Soc. Res.*, 13, 4 (December 1946), 463–478; reprinted in Alfred Schutz, *Collected Papers, II. Studies in Social Theory*, Edited and with an introduction by Arvid Brodersen (The Hague: Nijhoff, 1964), pp. 120–134. The "well-informed citizen" contrasted as an ideal type with the ideal types of the "expert" and the "man on the street."

148. Sweeney, Francis, Ed., *The Knowledge Explosion* (New York: Farrar, Straus and Giroux, 1966). Papers by representatives of various disciplines (on the occasion of the 100th anniversary of Boston College).

149. Wilson, Logan, *The Academic Man* (New York: Oxford University Press, 1942). A typological study, buttressed by empirical material, of the "academic man."

150. Zilsel, Edgar, "The Sociological Roots of Science," *Amer. J. Sociol.*, 47, 5 (March 1942) 544–562. An attempt to answer the question why there has been science only in the West and from the sixteenth century on; the conclusion generalized from several earlier detailed monographic studies by the author.

151. Znaniecki, Florian, *The Social Role of the Man of Knowledge* (New York: Columbia University Press, 1940). A typology of "men of knowledge" and their "social circles."

## Art, Literature, and Religion

152. Barnett, James H., "The Sociology of Art," in Robert K. Merton, Leonard Broom, and Leonard S. Cottrell, Eds., *Sociology Today: Problems and Prospects* (New York: Basic Books, 1959), pp. 197–214. A brief inventory of the sociology of art in recent years.

153. Duncan, Hugh Dalziel, *Language and Literature in Society* (Chicago: University of Chicago Press, 1953). An original treatise on the topic, containing an extensive bibliography.

154. _____, *Communication and Social Order* (New York: Bedminster, 1962). An effort at a systematic presentation of the relations between kinds of communication, social relations, and social orders; strongly oriented toward Kenneth Burke.

155. Lowenthal, Leo, *Literature and the Image of Man* (Boston: Beacon, 1957). A collection of essays on various writers and their works in a sociological perspective.

156. _____, *Literature, Popular Culture and Society* (Englewood Cliffs, N.J.: Prentice-Hall, 1961). A collection of essays on various literary works and on works of popular culture.

157. Nottingham, Elizabeth K., *Religion and Society* (Garden City, N.Y.: Doubleday, 1954). An introduction to the sociology of religion.

158. Rosenberg, Harold, *The Tradition of the New* (New York: Horizon

Press, 1959). Essays on recent literature from a strongly sociological and political point of view.

159.　Yinger, J. Milton, *Religion in the Struggle for Power* (Durham, N.C.: Duke University Press, 1946). Sociological analysis of responses of religious bodies to social changes, drawn from the history of Christianity in Europe and America.

## Sociology; Recent Developments in Anthropology

160.　Bennett, John W., Ed., "Planned Change: A Symposium," *Hum. Org.*, 18, 1 (Spring 1959). Reports on attempts at planning social change by cultural anthropologists involved in these attempts; with commentaries.

161.　Blumer, Herbert, Ed., *An Appraisal of Thomas and Zhaniecki's "The Polish Peasant in Europe and America"* (New York: Social Science Research Council, 1939). Attempts by various authors to assess the significance of this work, some 20 years after its publication.

162.　Boran, Behice, "Sociology in Retrospect," *Amer. J. Sociol.*, 52, 3 (November 1947), 312–320. Impressions of sociology in the United States by a foreign visitor; cf. [175].

163.　Bowman, Claude C., "Hidden Valuations in the Interpretation of Sexual and Family Relationship." *Amer. Sociol. R.*, 11, 5 (October 1946), 536–544. An analysis of ideological components.

164.　————, "Cultural Ideology and Heterosexual Reality: A Preface to Sociological Research," *Amer. Sociol. R.*, 14, 5 (October 1949), 624–633.

165.　————, "Polarities and the Impairment of Science," *Amer. Sociol. R.*, 15, 4 (August 1950), 480–485. An exploration of ideological elements implicit in sociology.

166.　Bramson, Leon, *The Political Context of Sociology* (Princeton: Princeton University Press, 1961). The influence of social and political theories on the practice of sociology, comparing Europe and the United States in historical perspective.

167.　Chall, Leo P., "The Reception of the Kinsey Report in the Periodicals of the United States: 1947–1949," in Jerome Himelhoch and Sylvia Fleis Fava, Eds., *Sexual Behavior in American Society* (New York: Norton, 1955), pp. 364–378.

168.　Christie, Richard, and Marie Jahoda, Eds., *Continuities in Social Research: Studies in the Scope and Method of "The Authoritarian Personality,"* (Glencoe, Ill.: The Free Press, 1954). An assessment by a number of authors of various aspects of this work.

169.　Hayek, Friedrich A., *The Counterrevolution of Science* (Glencoe, Ill.: The Free Press, 1952). Essays criticizing the natural-science model of the social sciences and presenting a history of scientism.

170.　House, Floyd N. "Social Change and Social Science," *Soc. Forces*, 7, 1 (September 1928), 11–17. An investigation of ideological biases in sociology.

171. Keiter, Friedrich, "Human Behavioral Biology (Ethnology): A Modern Aspect of Cultural Anthropology," *Soc. Res.*, 32, 4 (Winter 1965), 357–374.

172. Lee, Dorothy, *Freedom and Culture* (Englewood Cliffs, N.J.: Prentice-Hall, 1959). Essays in cultural anthropology, many of them based on the author's experience in the field, portraying what may be called an existentialist concept and practice of cultural anthropology.

173. Lerner, Daniel, "The American Soldier and the Public," in Robert K. Merton and Paul Lazarsfeld, Eds., *Continuities in Social Research: Studies in the Scope and Method of "The American Soldier"* (Glencoe, Ill.: The Free Press, 1950) pp. 212–251. The public reception of this work.

174. Lipset, Seymour Martin, and Leo Lowenthal, Eds., *Culture and Social Character: The Work of David Riesman Reviewed* (New York: The Free Press of Glencoe, 1961). An assessment by a number of authors of various aspects of Riesman's work up to that time; cf. [223].

175. Lundberg, George A., "Sociology versus Dialectical Immaterialism," *Amer. J. Sociol.*, 53, 1 (July 1948), 89–95. A sharp rejoinder to [162].

176. Mills, C. Wright. *The Sociological Imagination* (New York: Oxford University Press, 1959). A critique of dominant trends in recent American sociology, particularly of abstract empiricism and grand theory.

177. Nisbet, Robert A., "The French Revolution and the Rise of Sociology in France," *Amer. J. Sociol.*, 49, 2 (September 1943), 156–164.

178. Tumin, Melvin, Eds., "Values in Action: A Symposium," *Hum. Org.*, 17, 1 (Spring 1958), 1–26. Reports on field work by various cultural anthropologists, with commentaries.

179. Wolff, Kurt H., "Notes Toward a Sociocultural Interpretation of American Sociology," *Amer. Sociol. R.*, 11, 5 (October 1946), 545–553 [Chapter 12]. A critical analysis of certain features of American sociology.

180. ―――――, "Note sul profilarsi di una nuova scienza sociale" [Notes on the Emergence of a New Social Science], *Centro sociale* (Rome), 55, 56 (1964), 30–40 [cf. Chapter 24]. Generalizations drawn mainly from [160] and [178].

*Social Stratification, Communication, Bureaucracy, and Power*

181. Andrzejewski, Stanislaw, "Are Ideas Social Forces?" *Amer. Sociol. R.*, 14, 6 (December 1949), 758–764. The "sociological study of ideas must avoid both the one-sided 'interestial' interpretation and their treatment . . . as if they existed in a social vacuum."

182. Barber, Bernard, *Social Stratification: A Comparative Analysis of Structure and Process* (New York: Harcourt, Brace, 1957). A treatise on social stratification.

183. Bendix, Reinhard, and Seymour M. Lipset, Eds., *Class, Status and Power* (Glencoe, Ill.: The Free Press, 1953); 2nd ed. (New York: The Free Press of Glencoe, 1966). A reader.

184. Berelson, Bernard, and Morris Janowitz, Eds., *Reader in Public Opinion and Communication* (Glencoe, Ill.: The Free Press, 1953); 2nd ed. (New York: The Free Press of Glencoe, 1966).

185. Blau, Peter M., *The Dynamics of Bureaucracy* (Chicago: University of Chicago Press, 1955). An introduction to bureaucracy.

186. ————, *Bureaucracy in Modern Society* (New York: Random House, 1956). A treatise on bureaucracy.

187. Centers, Richard, *The Psychology of Social Classes* (Princeton, N.J.: Princeton University Press, 1949). A treatise on stratification, with emphasis on its psychological aspects.

188. Hunter, Floyd, *Community Power Structure: A Study of Decision Makers* (Chapel Hill, N.C.: University of North Carolina Press, 1953). One of the first studies in this field, which has since developed strongly.

189. Lerner, Max, *Ideas Are Weapons* (New York: Viking, 1939). An exploration of the influence of social class on ideas.

190. Lynd, Robert S., and Helen M. Lynd, *Middletown* (New York: Harcourt, Brace, 1929). The classical study of Muncie, Indiana.

191. ————, and ————, *Middletown in Transition* (New York: Harcourt, Brace, 1937). A restudy of Muncie after the Great Depression.

192. Merton, Robert K., Ailsa P. Gray, Barbara Hockey, and Hanan C. Selvin, Eds., *Reader in Bureaucracy* (New York: Basic Books, 1965).

193. ————, and Paul F. Lazarsfeld, "Studies in Radio and Film Propaganda" (1943), in [62], pp. 265–285; in [64], pp. 509–528. A fairly early contribution to the sociology of mass communications.

194. Mills, C. Wright, "The Middle Classes in Middle-Sized Cities; The Stratification and Political Position of Small Business and White-Collar Strata," *Amer. Sociol. R.*, 11, 5 (October 1946), 520–529; reprinted in C. Wright Mills, *Power, Politics and People*, pp. 274–291 (see [65]).

195. ————, *The New Men of Power* (New York: Harcourt, Brace, 1948). A study of labor leaders.

196. ————, *White Collar* (New York: Oxford University Press, 1951). A study of white-collar workers.

197. ————, *The Power Elite* (New York: Oxford University Press, 1956). A study of the interconnections among the governmental, military, and business-industrial elites in the United States, who together constitute the power elite.

198. Moore, Barrington, Jr., *Political Power and Social Theory* (Cambridge, Mass.: Harvard University Press, 1958). A collection of essays, ranging from social and political aspects of social science to the future of the family, written in a critical spirit.

199. Nettler, Gwynne, "A Test of the Sociology of Knowledge," *Amer. Sociol. R.*, 10, 3 (June 1945), 393–399. A study of the relation between opinion, education, and economic status.

200. Schatzman, Leo, and Anselm Strauss, "Social Class and Modes of Communication," *Amer. J. Sociol.*, 60, 4 (January 1955), 329–338.

201. Schermerhorn, Richard A., *Society and Power* (New York: Random House, 1961). An introduction to the study of power in its social relations.

202. Williams, Frederick, and Frederick Mosteller, "Education and Economic Status as Determinants of Opinion," in Hadley Cantril et al., *Gauging Public Opinion* (Princeton, N.J.: Princeton University Press, 1944), pp. 195–208.


*Social Psychology and Social-Psychological Studies*


203. Blum, Fred H. "Some Contributions of Dynamic Psychology to the Sociology of Knowledge," in Kurt H. Wolff, Ed, *The Sociology of Knowledge* (see [69]). An attempt to bring together aspects of social psychology and of the sociology of knowledge.

204. Bossard, James H., *The Sociology of Child Development* (New York: Harper, 1948). A treatise.

205. Davis, Allison, *Social Class Influences upon Learning* (Cambridge, Mass.: Harvard University Press, 1948).

206. ———— and Robert J. Havighurst, *Father of the Man* (Boston: Houghton Mifflin, 1947). A study of White and Negro families of middle- and lower-class cultures.

207. Erikson, Erik H., *Childhood and Society* (New York: Norton, 1950). A combination of psychoanalytic and cultural-anthropological theory characterizes this highly influential treatment of the theme.

208. Hollingshead, A. B., *Elmtown's Youth* (New York: Wiley, 1949). The reality of class in an Illinois town in its impact on adolescents, contrasted with the popular belief that class does not matter in the United States.

209. Kardiner, Abram, *The Individual and His Society* (New York: Columbia University Press, 1939). Coordinating cultural anthropology and psychoanalysis in the study of personality, with case studies of several cultures (including the Marquesans and Tanalans by Ralph Linton).

210. ————, et al., *The Psychological Frontiers of Society*. (New York: Columbia University Press, 1945). An attempt at integrating anthropological, sociological, and psychoanalytical data in a conception of personality.

211. Linton, Ralph, *The Cultural Background of Personality* (New York: Appleton-Century, 1945). The importance of culture in establishing both basic personality types in several societies and status personalities within the same society.

212. Penny, Robert T., *Toward Connecting Social Psychology and the Sociology of Knowledge*, Brandeis University, 1965 (unpublished manuscript).

213. Warner, W. Lloyd, et al., *Who Shall be Educated?* (New York: Harper, 1944). A sociological analysis of education in the United States, in the perspective of Warner's six-class stratification.

*Linguistics*

214. Hockett, Charles F., "Chinese versus English: An Exploration of the Whorfian Thesis," in Harry Hoijer, Ed., *Language and Culture* (Chicago: University of Chicago Press, 1954), pp. 106–123.

215. Hymes, Dell, Ed., *Language in Culture and Society* (New York: Harper and Row, 1964). A reader.

216. ————, *Sociolinguistic Determination of Knowledge: Notes on the History of Its Treatment in American Anthropology*, Evian, Sixth World Congress of Sociology, 1966 (mimeographed).

217. Stoller, Nancy, *New Orientations for the Sociology of Knowledge.* Brandeis University, 1966 (unpublished manuscript). Advocates that the sociology of knowledge incorporate linguistic theories and findings into its conception.

218. Whorf, Benjamin L. *Collected Papers in Metalinguistics*, Washington, Department of State, Foreign Service Institute, 1952. Whorf was one of the most influential American linguists to inject a sociological perspective into the study of language.

219. Wright, Arthur F., "The Chinese Language and Foreign Ideas," in Arthur F. Wright, Ed., *Studies in Chinese Thought* (Chicago: University of Chicago Press, 1953), pp. 286–303.

*Diagnoses of Our Time*

220. Fromm, Erich, *Escape from Freedom* (New York: Farrar and Rinehart, 1941). The fear of freedom examined mainly during the Reformation and under nazism; authoritarianism, destructiveness, and conformism as responses to this fear.

221. ————, *The Sane Society* (New York: Rinehart, 1955) A critique of contemporary Western society by the criterion of man's objective needs.

222. Marcuse, Herbert, *One-Dimensional Man: Studies in the Ideology of Advanced Industrial Society* (Boston: Beacon 1964). The disappearance of alternatives or dimensions in advanced industrial society, shown in analyses of numerous aspects of this society.

223. Riesman, David, in collaboration with Reuel Denny, and Nathan Glazer, *The Lonely Crowd: A Study of the Changing American Character* (New Haven, Conn.: Yale University Press, 1950). From tradition-directed through inner-directed to other-directed man during the history of the United States; relation of these changes in character structure to demographic changes (cf. [174]).

224. Stein, Maurice R. *The Eclipse of Community: An Interpretation of American Studies* (Princeton: Princeton University Press, 1960). The fate of the community in the United States reflected in major American community studies.

NOTES

1. Except for citing them when they are cited in the writings considered (Bibliography, Part 2). This chapter thus disregards such influential figures—to mention social scientists only—as William Graham Sumner, Charles Horton Cooley, William I. Thomas, George Herbert Mead, and Thorstein Veblen, and such works—to give a bare minimum of examples to which an indeterminately large number could be added—as may be found in social psychology [e.g., Erikson (207)], in the sociology of literature [e.g., Duncan (153, 154), Lowenthal (155, 156)], in the sociology of science [e.g., Merton (143), Zilsel (150), Barber and Hirsch (132)], in the sociology of religion [e.g., Yinger (159), Nottingham (157)], in the sociology of art [e.g., Barnett (152), Rosenberg (158)], in studies of stratification [e.g., Bendix and Lipset (183), Barber (182)], of power [e.g., Hunter (188), Moore (198), Schermerhorn (201)], of bureaucracy [e.g., Blau (185, 186), Merton, Gray, Hockey, and Selvin (192)], of communication [e.g., Berelson and Janowitz (184), Park (116), Merton (64)], in social-historical diagnoses [e.g., Riesman (223), Fromm (221), Mills (197), Stein (224), and Marcuse (222)], or in works so relevant to the sociology of knowledge as Machlup (141) or Sweeney (148). See also Mannheim (57, pp. 1–48) ("Preliminary Approach to the Problem," especially pp. 5–11, 45), referred to by Merton (61, p. 368, n. 2); Mannheim (57, p. 45): "The sociology of knowledge is . . . the *systematization* of the doubt which is to be found in social life as a vague insecurity and uncertainty"; cf. Speier (81, especially pp. 155–156).

2. On the second tendency, as it applies to American sociology in general, cf. Hinkle and Hinkle (42, pp. 73, 74).

3. Howard Becker's significance for the sociology of knowledge in the United States is comparable to Louis Wirth's; both taught for many years and directed research in this area. Mills and Dahlke were among Becker's students. Dahlke's concept (35) is representative of Becker's own (personal communication from Becker, January 11, 1946). The only two writings [but see also Becker (11, 13, 14)] in which this concept is explicated are Dahlke (35) and Becker and Dahlke (18). Becker's programmatic view of the sociology of knowledge is supplemented by research into the connections between types of society and mentality and their changes (6, 7, 8, and 15), which is related to his methodological and theoretical statements on historical sociology and constructive typology, particularly the sacred-secular continuum [see especially (9, 10, 12, 16, 17)].

4. Stark's work in the sociology of knowledge, though written and published in England, is included here because Stark has since moved to the United States, where he has been teaching for some years, and because—perhaps a more important reason—of his influence on the sociology of knowledge in the United States. The more general question raised by this case is the assignment of certain scholars, like Stark but also, to stay within the sociology of knowledge, Theodor Geiger or Georg Lukács, to single countries. A general answer need not be attempted here; the disposal of the only example that concerns this essay is being argued in this note.

5. For other expressions of this concept see Berger and Kellner (21), Berger (19), and Berger and Pullberg (23). For a related concept see Garfinkel (38, 39), and Shibutani (74).

6. Child's later theory of interpretation (33) is much more comprehensive than the dissertation chapter (which, like Chapter 1, on ideology, he did not publish in revised form) but is in essence epistemology rather than sociology of knowledge.

This chapter is reprinted in modified form from *Current Sociology,* 15, 1 (1967), 1–56 (entire issue), by permission of the editor and the publishers, *Morton, The Hague.* It has been edited and partially revised by the author.

# EPILOGUE:
## Education

Ten days ago (the everyday world with its clocktime is intruding) I jotted this down:

Probably the main thrust of the epilogue
"Trying" (for epilogue). It turns out that trying may not succeed. Refer back to trying as surrender to (part of the third meaning of trying in the Introduction). To my surprise (as I have said several times), surrender has been my *leitmotiv* for more years than I had realized. In Chapter 29 its *risk* aspect has come up. Now, in looking at the newborn, it is much greater and overwhelms me sometimes.

I also wrote another memo to myself in which I asked why I had introduced the parts of the book, instead of making comments at the end, especially since this was what I had planned to do for the book as a whole. This epilogue I would call "Education," a pun; "leading out of" and "learning from what precedes." Thus the title of the epilogue, the book's "so what" section—its "catch"—would be a pun fit to mirror that of the title of the book as a whole. "Catch" is the language of surrender. I thus find myself talking as if making this book (preparing the materials to form its chapters and writing the introductions to the six parts in which the chapters are arranged) had been surrender to what the book contains. Now (past the *tristitia post partum*) this must be inspected to discern its structure for it to shine through.

I am looking for the elements of this structure in notes taken when I reread and somewhat revised the introductions. I realize that I am proceeding as I did with my Loma field notes (Chapter 23 and introduction to Part V), when I searched for their structure in the topics under which I had subsumed them and for the structure of the topics in the categories under which I had entered the topics.

I find that the reason why I had written introductions (rather than "postductions") was to make possible the procedure I am now following; that is to say, the introductions contain the material I am to learn from in the "Educ(a)tion" of the whole book. They allow me to put together an inventory of notions that sometime in the future will have to be suspended so that a truth might emerge that is more compelling than that which results from other procedures.

I realized none of this when I considered writing the introductions. I thought that I would explain only when and on what occasion I had done the various chapters, what my attitude toward them was now, what ideas were not followed up, but above all, what continuities I had found.

Now I should like to examine the notes I took (after the two jottings I just discussed) while once again going through the introductions, curious to see what I should find. [Roman numerals refer to the introductions to parts (thus I to the introduction to Part I); Arabic numerals, to chapters as discussed in the introductions (thus III, 10 identifies discussion of Chapter 10 in the introduction to Part III)].

### SURRENDER

The truth criterion of knowledge attained in surrender is agreement with the result of the most rigorously imaginable intrasubjective examination of the student's most important experiences (II, 5). Surrender, which dawned on me in Loma (V), means testing what is offered against the least doubtful truth one has managed to hold on to (III, 9); it also means identification (V, 19, 20), honesty (V, 23), risk (VI, 29), the advocacy of the maximum suspension of received notions, of bracketing (III, 11; IV, 16; V, 20, 24; VI, 27, 28 [Supplement]). Its catch cannot exhaust it (VI, 27). Radicalisms and their types can be identified by received notions *not* suspended in them (V, 25). But the theory of surrender is not yet a politically and sociologically adequate sociology (IV, 15). It is close to the sociology of knowledge: both aim at maximum understanding (VI, 27). Indeed, an occasion for this understanding means an occasion for surrender to it (IV, 12). Surrender is a reminder of objective reason, whose cunning has shown that at this time in our history the highest exercise of reason (VI, 29), the experience of the rational at its purest (IV, 13; VI, 27), the solitary thinking in which the individual's uniqueness-universality comes to the fore occur in surrender. When falling back on himself, when he *is* rather than "leading a life" (VI, 27), the individual falls back on what he shares with mankind (II, 8; IV, 14; V, 20). Seeking surrender, however, like seeking understanding, perpetually challenges him to keep to the fine line between the belief of being in grace and the sin of pride (VI, 29).

So much on the characteristics of surrender, the theme that figures in my notes most conspicuously. I was greatly surprised by this (IV, 15; V, 25), as I was more particularly by recognizing one of the historical sources of surrender in art (VI, 26). There were other surprises and tasks, the two sometimes connected.

### SURPRISES AND TASKS

One surprise was the realization that maximum understanding or interpretation links the sociology of knowledge and surrender (VI, 28) and that I have presented both as historically new experiences (VI, 28). The task is to work out these two freshly discovered connections. Another surprise was the evidence in the recurring theme of intrinsic-extrinsic interpretation (IV, 12) of the pervasiveness of Karl Mannheim's influence. Thus both intrinsic and extrinsic interpretation are required for maximum understanding (IV, 12); it is man's dualism (IV, 14; VI, 28), man as a mixed phenomenon (V, 25), methodologically reflected in the notion of background materials (V, 20), that accounts for the need for both interpretations (VI, 26). The former (immanent) concerns the methodology (intellectual structure) of what is to be interpreted, the latter (transcendent), its approach (presuppositions) (VI, 27). This last point, based on the distinction between methodology and approach itself, may, along with this distinction, be worth re-examining, especially in regard to the phenomenon of understanding and its optimal conception. This may also apply to the concept of central (and typical central) attitude (and possibly to other holistic concepts) (VI, 26).

The conceptualization of the unique (VI, 27) developed out of the necessity to specify a term whenever there is doubt of its unambiguousness (VI, 26). The advocacy of greater scientific concern with the unique was radicalized into the idea of surrender-and-catch (VI, 27), and the contrast between the unique and routine, into that between "being" and "leading a life" (VI, 27). I had not understood these developments.

I was surprised also by questions that came up and that still required answering. There was—there is!—the relation between the atemporality of everyday and extreme situations, including surrender (IV, 17). There is the question of the correctness of the claim that the problem of the two viewpoints—of the student's and his subjects'—(like that of evil) has been treated in philosophy but not in social science (V; VI, 26, 28 [Supplement]). There is the comparison between the study of social change and history (V, 24). There are the justification and the consequences of coordinating practical knowledge with the area of the taken-for-granted and theoretical knowledge with that of distance (VI, 26). There is the founding of the categories in the biological organism or in the transcendental subject (provided that the three key terms—categories, biological organism, and transcendental subject—stand up under the bracketing that seems called for; at the very least, then, there is this bracketing) (VI, 28, 29). There also is the relation between the problem of the selective or constitutive character of existentiality and that of the relation between subject and object (VI, 30).

Further tasks include juxtaposing, codifying, and settling the passages that deal with distinctions between scientific-theoretical and existential-practical truth (IV, 16; VI, 28, 29; in this last reference the former is suggested as interobjective and only the latter as intersubjective) and between the theoretical and practical (theory and practice) (III, 10; IV, 14, 17; V, 25; VI, 26), with "values" (IV, 13, 15), with cultural relativism (VI, 27, 28), and with the movement from liberalism to radicalism to surrender (III, 10, 11).

Here they must remain as tasks for those, myself included, who might want to examine or solve them.

Verscio (Ticino [Switzerland])
1.ix.72, 0745

In one fell swoop—right?—things are becoming more transparently unique-universal. Things are both inseparably: the place and time named above are unique; whatever happens happens somewhere sometime; to make such an entry here is unique; things happening is universal. Thus yesterday at just this time two persons stood in front of our door, unexpected, unexpectedly transforming me, us—my wife inseparably from me—into who we were in the thirties; they—he to be 80 next year, she soon 60—had been on the train from Liguria all night to come to see us. Life and reality were exploding; two lives, two realities, theirs and ours, became one. All day long words said nothing, they were only charmers, always so accepted: face and voice, far more competent, did quite well, and it was beautiful.

Thus I end up with a journal entry pointing to life in Italy, before America, when I wrote the dissertation on the sociology of knowledge only among other things, let's say more like this. Thus I find myself looking over my shoulder, but this is forward: today's entry is typical of *Loma: A Hill*, the title of the version (alluded to in VI (28, n. 3) on which I have settled for presenting Loma: its form is the palimpsest. (Last year, anticipating that book, I wrote the history of surrender in a similar form: *Surrender and Catch: A Palimpsest Story* [Chapter 28 (Supplement), n. 5].)

I compare the first "intrusion of the everyday world" with this entry and find it spells both the story's and its teller's being on the way out, for although the first recognizes the world outside this book the second ruthlessly shoves in from there reckless places, times, and people: the outside thus announces its claim on the teller, calling him. Hence there is a new meaning of "leading out," and of Education as the title of this epilogue. In entertaining it, I had thought of inspecting results and taking off to act on lessons learned, but I had not realized that I had thought of it as anybody's inspecting, taking off, acting (I had forgotten my own lesson [Chapters 28, Supplement, and 29]). The new meaning is my own "e-duc(a)tion" experience as the increasing claim on *me* of the world outside *Trying Sociology*. By now I feel justified in calling this epilogue what I have.

But, again, who am I who am on my way? Ever more distinctly: I, the person, who in writing *Trying Sociology* have discovered having thereby written the prelude to *Surrender and Catch*, my next task which is to be followed by *Loma: A Hill*, a palimpsest whose first layers, if only in recollection, must go back to the sources of surrender-and-catch, and whose most recent layers must be the catch that by then shows itself, the whole being surrender (to "Loma") as wholehearted as possible then.

As if anticipating this "education," I have (in the introductions and here) commented little on sociology but much on trying. Approximately, this means that I have commented little on the *statements* the chapters of this book contain but much on their *history*, which hardly anybody but the voyager could have done. By contrast, the extrahistorical reading of statements is far more widely accessible. The voyager hopes that such reading will be of interest to some, but, even more, that their interest will be provoked by statement-within-story, which *is* more interesting. Hopes!

(Verscio, 13.vii.–1.ix.72)

# INDEX*

*Footnotes have not been indexed.

653